Praise for
The Best of Quest

There are some books that you want to keep. You don't want to read them at a gallop. You don't want to give them away after a hurried read. Instead, you want them on your bookshelf so that you can pluck them out and dip into their contents at your leisure, sometimes even again and again. *The Best of Quest* is one of those books.

– Rakshanda Jalil, *The Hindu*

Erudite & witty, *Quest's* best is a glimpse of our intellectual past.

– Trisha Gupta, *The Sunday Guardian*

Like an hourglass, this wonderful compilation inverts that golden past back to the present, and celebrates the yearning.

– Biswadip Mitra, *Sakaal Times*

It's a lively collection, and illuminates a certain period in post-Independence cultural and political history.

– Eunice de Souza, *Mumbai Mirror*

Anyone interested in the intellectual and cultural discourse of an earlier time should be thrilled by *The Best of Quest*, a collection of essays and fiction from the quarterly magazine dedicated to "inquiry, criticism and ideas".

– Jai Arjun Singh, *The Telegraph*

Some of the finest minds of the 60s and 70s, contributed to *Quest*, the journal for liberal ideas...The *Best of Quest* allows us to make connections between our vivid past and our vivid present.

– Shanta Gokhale, *Mumbai Mirror*

The story of *Quest's* illustrious life and infamous death is a story about idealism and global realpolitik... *The Best of Quest* makes the value of that archive palpable – not just because it documents a crucial piece of modern literary history, but because it reveals its breadth and range of concerns.

– Supriya Nair, *Mint Lounge*

The Best of Quest

Edited by
Laeeq Futehally
Achal Prabhal
Arshia Sattar

TRANQUEBAR

Tranquebar Press
Venkat Towers, 165, P.H. Road, Maduravoyal, Chennai 600 095
No. 38/10 (New No.5), Raghava Nagar, New Timber Yard Layout, Bangalore 560 026
Survey No. A - 9, II Floor, Moula Ali Industrial Area, Moula Ali, Hyderabad 500 040
23/181, Anand Nagar, Nehru Road, Santacruz East, Mumbai 400 055
4322/3, Ansari Road, Daryaganj, New Delhi 110 002

Published by Tranquebar Press 2011

Copyright © Indian Committee for Cultural Freedom, 2011

All rights reserved

10 9 8 7 6 5 4 3 2

ISBN: 978-93-80658-80-3

Cover Design by Gunjan Ahlawat

Inside book formatting and typesetting by Ram Das Lal

Printed at Manipal Technologies Ltd., Manipal

Contents

Section I: Foreword

Section II: In Memoriam

Section III: Essays and Opinion

Section IV: Poetry

Section V: Fiction

Section VI: Endnotes

Section VII: Postscript

SECTION I

Foreword

Stop donating your blood to bugs

Bugs are greedy blood-suckers and often double their weight after a meal of you.

Don't overlook the little bug you see around the house. It may be one of thousands.

Spray Tik-20. Ordinary sprays that kill flies and mosquitoes cannot rid your home of bugs as Tik-20 can. Because Tik-20 has been specially designed to kill bugs. Quickly and surely. Use the *new* handy Tik-20 pump for spraying.

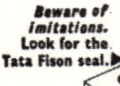

Beware of imitations. Look for the Tata Fison seal.▶

tik-20

A TATA FISON PRODUCT

'Tik-Twenty' kills bugs a-plenty!

ASP/TFIT-1/67

QUEST

Foreword

The Quest for Quest: Two Journeys

Achal Prabhala & Arshia Sattar

Like every major archaeological discovery, *The Best of Quest* is the result of a rearrangement of space. The space in question was my parents' home, and the rearrangement was a polite way of describing their efforts to save a mouldy hundred-year-old structure from collapsing. This was no tectonic shift, but secret treasures emerged anyway: useless mechanical gadgets from pre-liberalised India, suitcases of scarlet letters from my youth, and trunk upon trunk of magazines – packed with neem-leaves, folded for ever, and despatched to eternity in black metal coffins with the imprint of my father's then employer, the Indian Navy. Forced to reassess their long-standing love-affair with storage, my parents reluctantly parted with their collection. They asked me to give the magazines away to a public library.

For months, they sat in a pile by my bed. I knew of them, of course; I had even read books about some of the more celebrated magazines among them. But we were essentially strangers. To me, *Encounter*, *Imprint* and *Quest* meant little more than a footnote in history. One night, in a desperate attempt to prolong procrastination, after having tried to watch *Karate Dog* – a film whose protagonist is fox-terrier capable of human speech and martial arts – and failed, I turned to *Quest*. The issue I picked up was *Quest* 65, from April 1970, and the essay I encountered was *The Coffee-Brown Boy looks at the Black Boy* by

J.S. Saxena. The planets were aligned. I was hooked. Here was a man writing four decades ago about Browns and Blacks, jazz and World War II, smoky bars in Lucknow and James Baldwin in Paris – and with such style and such verve that I was almost afraid to go on. After the first sentence, I wanted to hug him; by the end of essay, I wanted to be him.

And that is how I came to *Quest*.

We will perhaps never know enough about the other cold war, the cultural cold war – the battle for the hearts and minds of people in the outer suburbs of utopia, which is to say, Kampala and Sydney and Bombay. In the pages of this book, you will be reminded that *Quest* was an ideologically free-wheeling enterprise; in certain quarters of the Internet, you will be told that the magazine was a CIA plot. (To be fair, the Indian journal that leads this charge also dismisses the entire canon of modern art as CIA strategy to deflect the masses from "social concerns." To be fair to the publisher of that journal, the Research Unit for Political Economy or RUPE, there is a wonderful logic to both these charges.) The truth is that *Quest* was all this and more: it lived and thrived in a milieu constituted by *Encounter* in the USA and UK, *Quadrant* in Australia, *Transition* in Africa, even *Imprint* in India. Those interested in this milieu will enjoy Peter Coleman's excellent book, *The Liberal Conspiracy – The Congress for Cultural Freedom and the Struggle for the Mind of Post-War Europe*, by far the most authoritative account of the cultural cold war.

As for me, I'm holding out for a book that might never, in fact, be written. I have a friend called Michael Vazquez, who, for a long time, edited the revived version of *Transition*. All he has so far is a title: *The Literary Agency – How the CIA created World Literature*. Since this is the kind of joke that could get me into trouble, I should reiterate that there is no evidence that editors of publications supported by the Congress for Cultural Freedom knew of the CIA connection, and also that the imbroglio is frankly and fully discussed within the pages of this book. Michael's title is merely playing with the distance between intention and consequence. Two decades on from the end of the big bad chill, who could have imagined that one effect of imperialism would be the idiosyncrasy and iconoclasm you now hold in your hands?

Achal Prabhala

My own journey with *Quest* is rather different. I remember the magazine in our house when I was a child, along with *Onlooker* and *Imprint* and *The Illustrated Weekly of India*. But it was more than these other magazines – it was special because my mother, Nazura, had worked there as a young woman in the 1950s. I was told that she had been the assistant to a great man, a man named Nissim Ezekiel. All this added immeasurably to my mother's glamour but it also gave a certain sheen to the magazine – I felt as if I was entitled to some part of it, that some part of it belonged exclusively to me, 8-year-old Arshia.

Thirty years later, I met another great man who edited *Quest*. His name was Dilip Chitre and although *Quest* was now a shadow of its former sparkling self, Dilip continued to work at it doggedly – sourcing material, pushing circulation, checking proofs, dreaming about creating an online edition. Dilip asked me to join the Editorial Board, which basically meant that I did a lot of proofing and copy-editing. My mother was thrilled at this little twist of fate that had brought us full circle – her daughter to the same job that she had held fifty years ago. She had worked in the legendary Army and Navy Building at Kala Ghoda in Bombay. I worked at home on my computer, occasionally meeting Dilip at his apartment in Pune over delicious lunches that his wife, Viju, would produce at the drop of a hat, which, often enough, was Dilip's characteristic beret.

When we knew that this book was possible, Dilip was already unwell and hugely diminished in terms of energy and verve. You will notice his declining spirit in his last essay, which closes this volume. Even as Achal and I asked him to write the concluding essay, we ourselves were captivated by a *Quest* contributor mysteriously called 'D.' 'D' was witty, acerbic, irreverent, bright, insightful – he wrote about movies and art and books and life. It was no surprise, actually, when Dilip confessed to being 'D' – for he was all those things; witty, acerbic, irreverent, bright, oh so very bright, and insightful.

Here is what Dilip says as he reveals himself in that last essay: "Now the column is dead and my pseudonym will hardly ring a bell. Few readers of the current age would care to dig through the archived coffins in the expired journal's graveyard to find 'D'. But I know it's me – of another time and season – grinning back at my present self, an older wiser and infinitely more boring self."

Dilip passed away during the time it took to put this book together. Fortunately for us, he was wrong in what has essentially become his own epitaph. Thanks to this volume, his column lives on, his pseudonym will ring another set of bells, and more than a few readers of the current age will be presented with the treasures of archived coffins in this expired journal's graveyard. You might have been older and wiser, Dilip, but you were never boring. Rest in Peace, bright star in *Quest's* firmament.

Arshia Sattar

SECTION II

In Memoriam

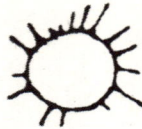

When **Sol has** done his worst

　　And really got you down

Turn on a **RALLIFAN** and be

The coolest man in town

81-RFM-76

Someone Like Nissim

Laeeq Futehally

When World War II finally came to an end in 1945, the overwhelming reaction throughout the world was *Never Again*. Never again should there be carnage on such a scale, never again should there be such destruction of civilised values and, above all, never again should the minds of men be enslaved by evil ideologies and rigid "isms." For every man – we now said – the only "ism" must be a personal brand of idealism.

A group of intellectuals set up the Congress for Cultural Freedom, and addressed themselves to the task of creating a worldwide ambience of respect for free thought and speech. In England, the Congress started a journal and called it *Encounter*. At home, the Indian Committee for Cultural Freedom, led by Minoo Masani, launched the journal *Quest*. These two journals were to counter every shade of fascism, and to encourage clear, honest and balanced discussion on issues of public concern. This hopeful activity got off to a good start when the poet Stephen Spender agreed to edit *Encounter* and Nissim Ezekiel agreed to edit *Quest*.

The principles which Nissim laid down for himself have shaped the character of *Quest* throughout its life. Everything about it must have some relevance to India. It was to be written by Indians for Indians – for in those days, we still glamourised anything foreign, including writers. This was not always easy, for it was difficult to track down good Indian writers and thinkers, and even more difficult to find good Indian publishers.

I think it is true that Nissim's insistence on desi-ness helped to raise the standard of Indian publishing. I myself joined *Quest* at its inception, and worked as its literary editor, which meant I could watch the changes in our publishing world.

In the early days – that is to say, in the 1950s – there was a total unawareness of the niceties of editing and publishing, so that in reviewing any book, its editorial and production values had to be described as well as its contents. I remember a collection of speeches of the then president, Dr Rajendra Prasad, where each chapter began with the words, "Ladies and Gentlemen, I am very happy to be here." This sort of sloppiness permeated the text – the shoddy editing and proof-reading showed on every page. On our side, *Quest* took pride in being punctilious about every detail. We got much moral support from Krishnan of the Inland Printers, who had an eye – and an ear – for good writing. He did not mince words; "Why did you publish such rubbish?" he was wont to say to me when a review did not meet with his approval.

Physically, the Inland Press consisted of a collection of antique machinery, housed in an ancient building which shuddered threateningly when the machinery went into action. But its credentials were good, for it was also patronised by the Oxford University Press, whose general manager, R.E. Hawkins – in spite of having only one functioning eye – was known to be the best editor and proof-reader in South East Asia.

Although both Nissim and Spender were ideally suited to represent the ideas and ideals of the Congress for Cultural Freedom, their attitudes differed on some points. Spender believed in paying his contributors well. "People will only write seriously if they are well paid," he used to say. Nissim's attitude was different. He wanted people to write not for money, but because they had something to say which was worth saying. Some British papers like the *New Statesman* enjoyed themselves by advising their contributors to write for "Uncle Stephen" – since he, Spender, made writing so profitable. Nissim's pay cheques for contributors were so small that we sometimes got into embarrassing arguments. I remember one set to with Nirad C. Chaudhuri when he objected to our rate of payment. He also insisted that he should be paid on the day we received his contribution, and not wait until it was published.

It was part of my job to handle the Book Review section. Nissim wanted our reviewers to return their review copies. In this, I quietly disobeyed him; and I also learnt that it was wise to warn our reviewers at the outset that we only paid "a very modest honorarium."

Sometimes, there were cases where an article was not worth printing, but it contained unusual matter which we felt deserved to be made known. I remember the case of an article which described the relationship between Subhas Chandra Bose and his English college professor. It had been widely believed that this professor, whose name I cannot recall, had done some disservices to Bose, and was responsible for his failures. The author of our article rebutted this, and showed that in fact, the opposite was true; it was to his help and support that Bose owed his start in life. The article was badly written – almost unreadable – but *Quest* felt its contents were important and so it was worked on and published. As a matter of fact, we had to cope with plenty of bad writing.

Once when I had to be away for some time, I asked my college-age daughter, Shama, to take my place. Unlike me, she had a soft spot for poetry and on this occasion, she accepted a worthless poem. Nissim asked her why she had used it. She excused herself by saying that she had received a large bunch of poems, and had felt that there must be at least one among them which could be used; they couldn't *all* be bad. Nissim was thoughtful and then said, seriously, "But they *are* bad – you know, you'd be surprised at how bad they can be." Yet, in spite of his clear judgement, Nissim had the gift of never discouraging a would-be-writer. Everyone who consulted him was made to feel that he could become good.

Quest was never a bland, faceless publication. Under Nissim's hand, it soon acquired a personality which reflected the values of the Committee for Cultural Freedom. This very success was, perhaps, an irritant to some of the members of *Quest's* Advisory Board, who complained that the magazine bore "the stamp of Nissim's face." Nissim immediately offered to resign and take his face elsewhere. The ensuing discussion showed up the unrealistic attitude of the board. They were unflustered at the prospect of losing the best editor in the country. "No matter," they said, "we'll find someone else – someone like Nissim." That someone else turned out to be A.S. Ayub. He was a good editor. But he was not Nissim.

Nissim's leaving was a great loss for *Quest*. However, it was not a total loss – for he continued to function as a "consultant" who was actually consulted. Many of the poets and writers who "arrived" in that period owed much to his help – to his criticism, his advice, his introduction to publishers. To aspiring novices, Nissim gave the biggest gift of all – his time. Shama wrote about this: "As a student who was afflicted with the desire to produce verse, I have often sat behind his desk.… His literary help was an education in itself, but the most important education was to see the attitude with which he gave it. That attitude was not kind or dutiful or conscientious or any such thing. It merely assumed as a given that his time belonged to others as much as himself."

It is an indication of our times that the glamour currently attached to "Indo-Anglian" writing has bypassed a figure as crucial to it as Nissim. His influence on this writing goes far beyond his actual work because he advised and encouraged young writers by the hundred.

This book is an attempt to show that we have not forgotten.

Moments with Nissim

Arshia Sattar

I was about eight years old when Nissim came to stay with us for a few days in Calcutta. My parents told me he was a famous writer. I remember feeling a thrill, that we must be important people if a famous writer was going to stay in our house. And I know that my parents were thrilled, too; there seemed to be a crackling energy around the house that was uncommon, reserved for those they especially cared about. When we met, Nissim leaned down at me from what seemed like a great height and said, "And what do you want to be when you grow up?" I knew the answer to that question; I had always known the answer to that question. It was simple. "A writer," I said. "Good!" he replied.

The next morning, when I came to breakfast, there was a pencil and a sheaf of ruled foolscap paper by my plate. "Go and write," Nissim said from across the table.

There was a massive storm that night. My father had decided to record Nissim reading his own poems on a trusty little cassette player with buttons like piano keys. Nissim read his poems over the sound of the thunder, my father's laughter and my mother's chuckles. I remember some of the lines I heard that night: about Miss Pushpa who was "always smiling and smiling" and about a child who was told over and over again "eat, my child, eat, how thin you are!" In all of his poetry that I read later, no lines were more special than those remembered fragments.

The tape that was made that night has long since disappeared. But the thin voice that read poetry and told me to write is still in my head.

I did obey Nissim's command to write, at least for that week. I would come home from school and feel very important as I wrote on that very sheaf of paper, with its lines of pale purple, with the pencil that he gave me.

I feel less blessed by the muse these days, but then, childhood is when magic is always present in our lives and angels come to stay.

When we decided to put this book together, and when Laeeq Futehally said that she would like to dedicate the collection of writings from *Quest* to Nissim Ezekiel (its editor for so many years and the man who gave the journal its distinctive style as well as its literary emphasis), it became apparent that we needed to mine the rich vein of Nissim-lore that was around. As a teacher and a mentor (if not always as a poet) Nissim influenced at least two generations of young Indian writers – some of whom went on to become well known and create a new landscape of Indian writing. But for all of those that are still writing and teaching, there are scores of others who also felt that benevolent hand on their heads, heard that gentle voice probe and prod, saw those pale eyes search their young faces for signs of a rich inner life.

We sent out a general mail to people that we knew had known Nissim and asked them to send it to others who might contribute a stray memory or two. We hoped to create a portrait of the man who had done so much for so many writers and poets. Within a few days, a little community had formed around this section – people recalling Nissim, people regretting that they had not met him, so many of his protégés sending in obituaries that they had written after he passed away, others saying that they had lost the pieces they had written then, still others saying they would love to write but could not for various personal and professional reasons. Because I was handling the section, I re-connected with people I had known two and three decades ago when I, too, wandered around Bombay searching for the meaning of life within myself and in the world outside. We were all young then and went to the same handful of colleges. We haunted the same libraries and book stores, met at the same poetry readings, watched the same films, attended the same concerts and wrote for the same newspapers and magazines. We fell in and out of love with each other, respected, envied and scorned each other's work, argued, fought bitterly – huge dramatic fights, lurid with big words and enormous accusations – and slowly drifted away from each other. Somewhere in all of this, in the centripetal, youthful universe that we occupied,

Nissim was the still centre, perhaps the only emotional space that we consistently shared and all acknowledged.

Over memories of Nissim, we have shyly reached out to each other again, the brash confidence and broad gestures of love and hate from our youth replaced by a more tentative, circumspect idea that nostalgia is all that it is made out to be. We have recalled the last time we saw each other, places we may have seen each other, mentioned our new work. And realised, through these renewed acquaintances, that we have quietly been tracking and most often, appreciating each other's works from a distance. As Nissim held us tenuously together when he was alive, so, too, he has given us a chance to come together long after his death. Not with the sharp pain of recent loss but with a gentler and more gracious acceptance of who he was and who he made us.

Memories of Nissim

From Githa Hariharan
I was never a student of Nissim's; we were friends; but the friendship felt as if he was my adopted teacher, and I his adopted pupil.

There's the time I was seventeen, sitting in his Bombay University room, waiting to be told what was right (or wrong) with my poetry. He said to me kindly, "This, my dear, is what is called juvenilia." I was silent, so he added, even more kindly, "Do you know what that means?"

There's the time – some years later when I could recognise juvenilia – when I was visiting his home, The Retreat, with a cactus. I tried to find a place for it on his table, but the mess of manuscripts and books made it impossible. (I found the cobwebs hanging from the ceiling doleful too.) Nissim wasn't helping. He sat there serenely, telling me about a dream of his. In the dream, something large and heavy bore down on his chest till he began to choke. He woke up at this point, he said, and found that the dream was a perfectly reasonable one. The ever-growing pile of manuscripts on his table – others' manuscripts – had toppled over and fallen on him as he slept. And in case I hadn't learnt enough about the essentials from his dream, he proceeded to write a poem for me. My cactus had almost certainly got the death penalty, but Nissim's poem was optimistically called "The Cactus Flower".

Then there's the time he visited me in Delhi. Nissim was supposed to be working in my study. But when I went in there with ice cream, one of the simple pleasures of his life, I found him lying on the divan. "I'm working," he assured me. "Poets have to think. I'm thinking."

From Molly Daniels
At the old Churchgate Station, Antoinette Diniz and I were sipping from a Coke bottle with two straws – I was reciting poems to the pigeons flapping in the cathedral arches above, and she said, "Come, let's go show Nissim your poems."

Nissim saw us as "two giggling schoolgirls." But we had big plans: life hadn't defeated us yet. Nissim accepted one poem (a reply to "When You Are Old and Grey") for the first issue of *Quest*, which also contained Dom Moraes, who later famously described Nissim's "disdainful fingers" receiving poems and novels from acolytes.

For the next half century, Nissim was a strong centre. He was no doubt disappointed that I had stopped writing. He said, "Promising young woman, do not be a promising old woman!"

Our relationship was strictly literary; yet, he turned up at my father's funeral, and he and AKR were taken by Uncle Ben's extraordinary knack of delivering an impromptu eulogy in alliterative verse. We were connected by the gold chains of English poetry.

Images from our meetings in Bombay, Delhi, London, Chicago, are chasing each other in my mind. At Breach Candy – Daisy and Nissim seemed to have sprung from the same mould… two lovely daughters, Kavita and Kalpana, little Elkana running about naked – a Jewish home, offering crushed raisin juice to visitors… On his last visit to Chicago, Nissim wept. His tears were too deep for words; he was upset about the worldly Passover Seder at the home of a Hyde Park matron. How different in spirit, he lamented, from the ritual Seders in Bombay, in Israel, in London; he was weeping over being a Jew, Exodus, spiritual deliverance, the wandering Jew… And Nissim's recitation to Saul Bellow of names of his family members that he found in Herzog. I remember Nissim's disgust at a strip-tease in London. He said, "All I want to do is go back home to Daisy."

From Shanta Gokhale
It's a story I've told a dozen times but I must tell it again. Decades ago, I was rash enough to write some poetry and rasher still to send

it to Nissim for comment. Nissim always had time for everybody and he was always completely truthful in his comments. Since I had asked for it, I got it. He said my poetry was "er… umm… yes…. well…" I read that as "Your poetry stinks." Never the one to close one door without opening another, Nissim's next line was, "Why don't you take your prose seriously?" and as a post-script he added, "Why not write in Marathi, your mother tongue?" A few months later, I had written my first short stories in Marathi. All three got published. My plays and my novels are also in Marathi.

Then sadly, there was the Nissim of incipient Alzheimer's. We were at a poetry reading in town. I offered to drop him home. I had never been to his place before, but I knew he lived near Bombay Central station. When we got there, he looked around confused. He didn't know which way to turn. A few moments of sheer panic followed, for him and for me. Then suddenly he got out of the cab and said he would walk home. Before I could pay off the cab and follow him, he had disappeared. I called his place as soon as I got back and found, to my immense relief, that he had reached. His feet must have retained a memory that his mind had not.

From Jane Bhandari
Shortly before Nissim died I reviewed his *Collected Poems*, which gave me the opportunity to become familiar with his work. I was visiting Delhi when I heard that he had died. Adil Jussawalla confirmed the sad news. We decided to organise a reading of Nissim's poems in Mumbai the following month, to be presented jointly by Loquations and Poetry Circle. Poets and friends of Nissim were asked to select and read one or two poems each.

On 3 February, 2004, the AV Room at NCPA was jam-packed. Local poets read Nissim's poems, they sang his songs, they read his prose about poetry. Others remembered him in stories and anecdotes.

I mourn Nissim's passing. I am sorry that I never met him: he must have been a fascinating man. As a woman, reading his love-poems makes me wish I had known him twenty years ago.

From Menka Shivdasani
…with my poems written out in my best schoolgirl handwriting, I went to see Nissim at Bombay University. I was convinced he would tell me this was great and profound poetry, full of pain and longing

and all the philosophy that only a sixteen-year-old can spout. He read the note, then glanced at the works of genius I had handed him, tossed them back across his vast table and said: "Type them. You can't evaluate a poem if it is hand-written."

I was shattered. Surely this was his way of telling me not to waste his time! I mumbled that I would come back again, and made my way out, vowing never to return. "Write down your name and phone number before you go," he called out just as I got to the door. I did as he asked, and left. Over the next two weeks, I struggled with a battered typewriter that was older than I was, painfully typed out my poems, and decided I would never see Nissim again.

Two weeks later, the phone rang. "You were going to come back with your poems, weren't you?" asked the voice at the other end.

When we met the next day, he read my poems (so perfect they were with all the derived rhymes and rhythms of Wordsworth and Shelley!) and said: "They're okay." This was a refrain I was to hear every week for the next six months, whenever I showed Nissim a new poem. Then one day, seeing the crushed expression on my face, he said: "Look, for your age, you are very good. But if you get it into your head that there is nothing more to learn, you will be finished." Then he told me of poets he had known who had started out well, but were still writing at age sixty exactly the way they were when they were sixteen. "No matter what level you are at," he said, "you should always go a little higher." It was a lesson that I learned for life.

Another time, when I wrote a grand poem about unrequited love, he looked at it, smiled and said, "You missed out a comma in the fourth line." Is this man nuts or what, I thought to myself, and said indifferently, "Really? That's just too bad." I put it in anyway, and wondered why I was wasting my time.

This was a frequent criticism – a comma here, a full stop there, a colon where I had put in a semi-colon instead… "What's all this got to do with the real thing?" I asked him once in frustration, and he said: "This is the age when you perfect the craft, so it becomes an automatic part of your writing. When you're 17, you have a lot of time to think about the great philosophies of poetry. First, get the grammar right."

In time, and largely thanks to his approach, I learned to look at my work just as critically as he did. In fact, I began to get so self-critical, I often tore up what I wrote. "Don't be so harsh on yourself," he said. "You have some really good work there."

Once, I told him about a poem that just wasn't happening right, no matter what I did with it. "I've reworked it four times!" I yelled. "Is that all?" he responded. "There are poems I have rewritten more than ten times and I still wasn't happy with them."

If Nissim criticised your work, he was equally open to criticism of his own. "I've written some new poems," he told me one morning, "but I don't think I should show them to you." It was the series, *Nudes*, and he was convinced I would be scandalised. At 17, and very much – at least in my own opinion – a woman of the world, I told him that nothing shocked me. So he showed me the poems and waited quietly for my reaction. Some of the more explicit lines did, indeed, shock me, but naturally I was not going to say that! "You've missed out a comma in line five of the first poem," I told him, and he laughed. "You've learned my lessons too well, you so-and-so!" he declared.

From Vijay Nambisan

I am sitting across the table from Nissim Ezekiel in the bar of the Madras Club as he talks of his experiences on LSD. Picturing the scene in my mind, as a small but distinguished cameo, I can hardly suppress a smile. This is not one of your more everyday encounters. For Ezekiel, who brought modernism to Indian poetry in English, seems to exude respectability. He looks like a minor sage – his fine pale skin, white-gold hair and simple style of dress, with long full-sleeved shirt hanging loose out of his trousers, all give him a sweetly ascetic air. And he can speak with a fervour and commitment that would sit well on a rather intellectual high priest – and Ezekiel has been called that, too, in relation to poetry and Bombay.

Sitting in the bar, as standing behind the lectern at IIT, Ezekiel is not a prepossessing figure. He lacks both the height and the aggression. Earlier I had noticed a habit of his, of fidgeting with the lowest button of his shirt, a remnant of social nervousness perhaps. Now he is perfectly at his ease. Our host asks what we'd like for dinner. There's a choice between vegetarian and non-vegetarian. Ezekiel asks for veg, please. "Oh, you don't eat meat, Nissim?" No, he tells us; once, many years ago, during one of his LSD trips, he heard a voice within which directed him to give it up. He looks blandly at us. Personally I like a little more wildness in my poets, but here is a man quite in harmony with his inner voice.

From Ranjit Hoskote

During a conversation one morning in the late 1980s, Ezekiel showed me a sunbird working industriously in the tangled bougainvillea outside the windows of his office at the PEN All-India Centre. He had just rescued its nest from the unsentimental gardener, retreating, none too graciously, shears still in hand. Bird life often supplied Ezekiel with images and models; he wrote, in that credal poem, 'Poet, Lover, Birdwatcher':

"To force the pace and never to be still/ Is not the way of those who study birds/ Or women. The best poets wait for words./ The hunt is not an exercise of will/ But patient love relaxing on a hill... In this the poet finds his moral proved,/ Who never spoke before his spirit moved."

The image that I will always carry of Ezekiel is that of a man in aquiline profile, hunched over a spot-lit desk, held in the narrow frame of a door. Immersed though he might be in writing, editing or answering correspondence, he always left his door ajar, a line of communication with the busy world of arrivals and departures, voices and sirens.

From Raj Rao

I first wrote Nissim a postcard expressing my desire to be his biographer in the summer of 1994. Those were pre-e-mail days, and Nissim was famous for painstakingly replying to every postcard that landed on his desk. I wrote the postcard with some trepidation, for a biography is a daunting task, but Nissim's return-of-post reply put me at ease. He welcomed the idea, and almost gave me a date and time to meet him for the first sitting. Before I knew it, I had plunged headlong into the project without a clue as to where it would take me.

I was then a Reader in the Department of English at the University of Pune. To meet Nissim in Bombay, I would dutifully take the Deccan Queen at 7.15 a.m. every Saturday morning, arrive in Bombay three-and-a-half hours later, hop over across the Azad Maidan to my mom's flat at Barrack Road (my birthplace!), freshen up, have a bite, and then race down to the P.E.N. at Churchgate to talk to him. Here we would spend hours chatting, as he reminisced, and I probed and took down notes.

Nissim was a model subject. He wanted to see the book out, and earnestly tried to recall every detail of his multi-faceted life that would be useful to me. The seven day gap between sessions did not confound matters. On the contrary, it worked very well, giving us both just enough time to replenish ourselves. When I met him the following week, I found he had not lost the thread, and was able to take off from where we had left with a precision and accuracy that was admirable.

Nissim made available to me all the material he thought would be of interest to a biographer. This included his uncollected poems, the reviews and columns he wrote for various Bombay-based newspapers and magazines, and most importantly, his correspondence with childhood friend Abraham Solomon, dating back to the 1940s. All this was invaluable. But Nissim did not withhold even the unsavoury bits concerning him. I must especially mention here Tara Patel's interview with him in Society magazine, where she confronts him head-on on his womanizing!

However, the one thing that he did not want to talk much about was his family. He was uncomfortable discussing his strained relationship with his wife, Daisy and son, Elkana. He knew that no biography is complete without mention of one's family. But he expected me to figure out ways of writing about his family on my own, perhaps with the help of his friends, some of whom were also my friends, and he gave me detailed lists of the people "you should and you should not talk to."

My one regret is that he wasn't "around" to see the book in print. As I signed on the dotted line in Ravi Singh's presence, I recalled with tears, both of joy and sorrow, the days when Nissim would gleefully introduce me to visitors at the P.E.N. (of which there was no dearth) with the words, "This is Raj Rao. Would you believe it, he's writing my biography!"

In the year 2000, when friends showed Nissim the book at the Susrusha Nursing Home in Bandra where he was, he couldn't make head or tail of it. He did not understand what the fuss was about. When I finally mustered the courage to go and see him in his present state, I found he had receded into babyhood again. His attendant Malti spoke to him as one does to a little child. I was startled to discover that Nissim had begun to inhabit the past. He was a Bombay University professor again, and we were his students. He had just come out of class and was informing us about a talk by a guest speaker that he had organized for our benefit, and was giving us the room number. I can swear that this was a real-life episode that actually took place in 1977, when I was an M.A. student in the English Department at Bombay University and Nissim was at the pinnacle of his glory.

From Salil Tripathi

Nissim used to eat lunch every day at Sanman, a restaurant next to the American Centre in Bombay. I knew him as a college student (I studied at Sydenham, which was nearby). And during those long summer months from March to May, when we went daily to the library to revise our coursework, some of us would go to Sanman for lunch. (Sanman used to make better sambar than Satkar, which was closer to Sydenham).

I would meet Nissim often then – he had read my early poems, and we talked about literature. My staple diet was idli sambar, and his was boiled vegetables with mayonnaise.

One day, he was at the table next to ours, and we greeted each other. I was with a bunch of classmates, and we were probably discussing the film to see that evening, instead of some calculus problem baffling us. I noticed some activity around Nissim's table. It turned out, along with boiled vegetables, that his plate housed a caterpillar. Nissim was trying to send the plate back.

He did this politely, without any fuss, without alarming other patrons, realising this was an accident – Nissim had eaten there daily for decades, and he had a long, symbiotic relationship with Sanman. When I looked at him, the plate having been taken away, Nissim winked at me and smiled. "It was a very hungry caterpillar," he said.

To see humour in something that would outrage any other patron, to be forgiving of an obvious mistake, and to not make a fuss: this was Nissim.

But he could be sarcastic as well. In the late 1980s, I went to interview him. I was a correspondent with *India Today*, and was working on a piece on the literature boom in India – Penguin had just set up shop, and new writers were emerging from everywhere. I asked him what he thought of that. And he said, "There are novelists and there are people who write novels."

He did not have to say more. Always a poet, sometimes a clown, but never a rascal. I miss Nissim.

SECTION III

Essays and Opinion

The three-year itch is legitimate!

Restless with wanderlust,
haven't left India for three whole years.
Leave now with everyone's blessings
especially ours.
With all the assistance
Air-India alone can give.
Contact us or your travel agent today.)

AIR-INDIA

AI. 1330 (A)

Direct Action: A Pattern of Political Behaviour

Rajni Kothari

(Ten Years of Quest, Manaktalas, Bombay 1966,
eds. Abu Sayeed Ayyub and Amlan Datta)

The various direct actions that have taken place and are taking place in this country seem to form a pattern of political behaviour. The general approach to the problem of direct action in this country has been merely one of approval or disapproval; there has hardly been any serious study of the subject. It is not enough to speak of the propriety or otherwise of a social phenomenon without inquiring *why* it occurs and what is the situation that gives rise to it. The direct action is objectively there. It must have causes. It is necessary to inquire into these causes.

Such an inquiry must begin with an examination of the context in which direct actions take place. In this country, they have taken place under a parliamentary democratic form of government. In the present article, we propose to examine critically the bases on which the parliamentary form of government rests, the chief aim being to investigate how far the idea of democracy can be realized in this form. We then analyse the relation between parliamentary government and direct action. This is followed by an evaluation of the direct action that took place in Kerala as a particular instance of a general phenomenon. Finally, we try to construct a causal theory of direct action based on our experience of this phenomenon.

Bases of Parliamentary Democracy

The idea of democracy has had a long pedigree from the Greek city-states to the modern times, but it is not necessary to trace its history here. The idea is simple. In the political sphere, it is the idea of participation by the whole community in the political process. It bases political authority on the will of individuals who, by a process of co-operation, make decisions that are binding on all. Our main interest here, however, is in the modern form that democracy has taken, namely, the parliamentary form. In our own country we are committed to the promotion of the idea of democracy through the institution of a particular form of democratic government. An examination into the form is more important in such a situation than in countries where a 'spirit' of democracy preceded the institution of forms and where the 'spirit' is capable of transcending the shortcomings that accompany the forms.

(a) *Philosophical Basis*: The basic assumption on which parliamentary government rests relates to the nature of the society it presupposes. It is the well-known assumption of natural harmony between man and man and between individuals and society. For, it is clear that if there is a fundamental cleavage in society, parliamentary government could not work. The belief on which the classical view of society was based assumed that there is no possibility of a permanent or basic conflict between sections of the people, the task of political organization being merely to make 'adjustments' and arrive at 'compromises' between apparently opposing points of view on relatively minor issues of policy. The 'invisible hand' would see to it that the individual, in following his enlightened self-interest, also promotes the general good of the community.

Recent developments have belied this belief. Even in England, issues like the Irish Home Rule and the position of the House of Lords in the Constitution brought the parliamentary fabric very near to breaking point, which was only saved by a determined attempt to preserve the 'spirit' of democracy that had permeated the consciousness of the British people. Elsewhere, fundamental differences both in respect of ideology and of interests have divided societies into several political splinters and rendered parliamentary government unworkable. The chief defect in this belief in 'natural' harmony, however, is not that there is no possibility of harmony among people. It is rather that by positing such a *pre-existing* harmony, the theorists of parliamentary government discounted the necessity of *true participation of the people in the political process*, which alone could have made such a harmony possible. The object of political effort was 'assumed away', and that accounts for the inadequacy of parliamentary government in many countries in the realization of the democratic ideal.

Parliamentary government found another justification in the hands of the utilitarian philosophers of the nineteenth century. For, the quantitative form that democracy has taken under parliamentary government is based on the utilitarian theory of the 'social good'. Faced by the prospect that the pleasure of one man might be opposed to the pleasure of another (for example under the capitalist mode of production), the hedonist philosophers of the nineteenth century struck upon the idea of the 'greatest good of the greatest number'. Imperceptibly the principle of the greatest good turned into the idea of a 'social good' as opposed to an 'individual good'. There was to be something like a 'total pleasure', where the pluses and the minuses were to be cancelled out. At this stage, individualism came under the shadow of a 'general will' and turned to collectivism. The idea of social good now ceased to have relevance to the individual, and democracy degenerated to a mere counting of heads. The individual who was the bearer of the head was reduced to an abstraction. It is this defect in the theoretical basis of a parliamentary government which explains the practical situation where the individual finds himself lost before the 'machine' of the state.

(b) *Institutional Basis*: The fundamental institution on which the parliamentary system of government is based is that of periodic elections. In fact, elections have become the linchpin on which the entire constitutional apparatus of parliamentary government hangs. It is also the only form of popular participation provided under this system. This gives rise to a number of problems. The enormous importance given to elections tends to equate democracy with majority rule. This is because the chief purpose of elections is to give power to that party which wins a majority of seats in the legislature. In effect, this so-called majority rule is only the rule of a minority. Under a system of franchise, as we have in India or in Great Britain, it is possible for a government to command a majority of seats in parliament on the basis of a minority of votes.

But this is both unavoidable and hardly objectionable in itself. Only the pundits of a quantitative democracy can take serious objection to it.

What is far more objectionable is the qualitative nature of the system. Elections under a parliamentary system become highly formalised. The electorate is divided among contending political parties. Political opinion gets regimented along one line or another. This gives rise to a situation where all that an elector does is to stamp his approval or disapproval on one or another consolidated programme (known as a 'manifesto') presented to him. This mechanical division of the electorate projects itself in the legislature where parties face each other as highly disciplined battalions. This means, further, that all the most important decisions are taken by the top leadership of the party in power outside the precincts of parliament. The enormous importance given to a few men in this system is also due to the fact that the parties have to rely on the 'charismatic' character of their leaders in order to appeal to the irrational instincts of the voters. All this leads to an increasing concentration of power in the hands of a few leaders. Gradually and almost imperceptibly, the institution of elections gives rise to a process whereby power is transferred from the base to the apex and concentrated there.

Finally, there is the point that elections, under the present system, fail to fulfil the very purpose for which they are devised. Even the limited mode of participation allowed to the people – namely, the casting of a vote – is highly ritualised. An election is not held when the people want it and when they are dissatisfied with the existing government, but only when it is 'due' or when the government wants it. This gives rise to a dilemma where the only type of participation allowed to the people is denied to them at crucial times. All this leads to the clear conclusion that elections provide a very inadequate basis on which a democratic system of government can base itself. The problem of democracy is, as L.T. Hobhouse said, 'how to secure any effective expression of will from the ordinary man.' This, the elections are clearly incapable of securing.

(c) *The Logic of the System*: The theoretical justification for the institutional structure of parliamentary governments is provided by the theory of representation. The theory of representation also claims two other things. It claims to base parliamentary institutions on the will of the individual and it claims to make a government by the majority of the people. The logic of these claims is as follows. Each individual in society, once he has attained maturity in age, is entitled to have his will represented through a representative in the assembly which makes laws for the people as a whole. Since the representative represents a majority of his constituency and since government represents a majority of such representatives, representative government is a government by a majority of the people.

We have already seen that such a calculus of 'a majority of a majority' is refuted by experience. But such quantitative considerations do not necessarily provide, in our view, a decisive argument against the theory, which suffers from more serious defects. Above all, there is the question of the proper function of a representative. Does he merely 'represent' opinions as he finds them in the constituency or does he, following Burke's dictum, arrive at his own synthesis of such opinions by using his judgment? The former theory of 'instructed representation' falls to the ground in a dynamic society where there is such a variety of views and where it is just not possible to 'instruct' the representative on all possible contingencies. The Burkean synthesis, on the other hand, cannot be a true synthesis. A true synthesis of various viewpoints necessitates that the constituency is itself so organized that through a free and rational discussion, an opportunity is created for a true reconciliation of all contending views. The synthesis that the representative claims to have arrived at is little more than his own viewpoint, or rather his party's viewpoint, imposed on his constituents. The upshot of all this is that a mechanical theory of representation cannot become the basis of political obligation. A democratic government must ultimately find its justification in the consciousness of the people it seeks to govern. This is not possible without true participation of the people in the political process. This, the theory of representation does not provide for. On the contrary, the political arrangement that it posits denies both the scope and the necessity for such participation.

It is an arrangement in which all representation is representation of a party. In the parliament, in the government and in the constituencies, it is his party that is represented by a representative. This means that, in effect, the representatives, instead of being the agents of the people, are truly the agents of the prime minister or of the leader of one of the opposition parties.

Conclusion: The True Relations of Power. If we now bring together the various threads of analysis that we have so far conducted, we can see that each of the bases on which parliamentary government rests suffers from serious disadvantages. We have found that the institution of elections is inadequate as a basis of democratic government, that the theory of representation is misleading and fails to base government on the will of the people, that the ethical basis of parliamentary government in hedonism renders it incapable of imbibing the true spirit of democracy, and that the assumption of natural harmony proves inimical to true participation by the people in the political process. What we find in reality is that power tends to get concentrated under parliamentary government. The participation of the people in the processes of government is kept to a minimum, the power of the people's representatives is equally minimised under the impact of political parties, and government – to speak in a language stripped of all constitutional verbiage and legal jargon – is a government by an organized minority. In a country like India, there is also the important fact that if political power is so concentrated, any attempt at diffusing economic power through the agency of the state is bound to defeat its own purpose.

Concomitant with the concentration of power in a few hands under parliamentary government is the development of a bureaucratisation of political processes. The concentration of authority at the top necessitates a vast machinery of government which spreads its tentacles throughout the state. Bureaucratic government, in fact, lies in the very logic of parliamentary government with the enormous institutional hiatus that divides the government from the governed. The result has been aptly described as apoplexy at the centre and anaemia at the periphery. Bureaucratic power becomes unwieldy and dehumanised while those that are affected by it lose all initiative and power to think for themselves.

These then, are the true relations of power under the parliamentary system of government. It can be seen that this is a far cry from the democratic ideal, and simply shows that the best ideals may be incapable of being realized if the forms evolved to express them 'become so many fetters' and thwart such realization.

The Relevance of Direct Action
We have examined so far some of the institutional and theoretical grounds on which the system of parliamentary government is based.

In the process we have tried to point out some of the weaknesses of the system. Such criticisms as have been offered above, however, touch only the surface of the problem. In order fully to appreciate it, we must now examine the ideological moorings of the system.

The Norm: Now, in our characterisation and criticism of parliamentary government, we have so far been vaguely guided by a certain norm. It is, in fact, the norm of 'democracy' itself – democracy as understood in a basic and essential sense. In this sense, the individual is the starting point of democracy. The chief tenet is that man is the maker of his destiny and the task of the political institutions is to enable him to be so. This stress on the freedom and self-development of the individual should not, of course, be taken to mean that society is to be in a state of anarchy or that there should be no law binding on man. In fact, democracy is a form of social organization where everything would be governed by a law. It only points that *man* must be the creator of his own law, in association with his fellow-beings. Freedom here is considered not as absence of law but as a right to shape law. An entity is free in so far as it creates its own laws. The degree of freedom associated with a social system is measured by the actual scope it offers to individuals towards their self-fulfilment. It is freedom to change one necessity into another. Under such a system, all laws and institutions are no more than the creation of men seeking and shaping their destiny. All government is 'self-government' in a democracy.

The Form: If this is a proper understanding of democracy, the next step in the argument follows. It is that parliamentary government is a system of political institutions designed by men who seek to realize the idea of democracy and that its success or failure can be measured according to the degree in which it enables men to realize the chief tenets of democracy as outlined here.

We have tried to show that, by and large, parliamentary government has failed to embody the idea of democracy, and this failure principally stems from the fact that under it there is little scope for popular participation. Our experience proves that there is a growing hiatus between the government and the people and a consequent electoral apathy to governmental processes. People do not feel the government as their own but view it as something 'there' and 'beyond them', initiating and executing activities of which they are the docile spectators. This has resulted in the phenomenon of non-voting, i.e. a large number of possible voters remain away from the polls. Compulsory voting laws are made in some countries to check this tendency but such compulsion is a superficial way of tackling the problem. The need is to understand the phenomenon a little more deeply. It is a phenomenon where the individual thinks of himself as a non-entity whose opinion and vote does not make any difference to the political process which seems to him to go on in an inexplicable and mysterious manner.

This lack of participation leads to a sense of insignificance in the people, especially in those sections which are more politically conscious. Faced with a situation in which political power is concentrated, they groan under a sense of powerlessness. In them, there is an inward feeling of unrelatedness to anything significant. There is therefore a complete lack of creativity and initiative. And all this is in sharp contradiction to the ideology of democracy on which the individual has been brought up from his school-days onward. For, the fact is that the maxims uttered from time to time by the apologists of parliamentary government are essentially democratic maxims. It is the large gulf that divides this ideology from the actuality that leads to a sense of impotency and frustration in the people.

The Context of Direct Action: At this stage of the discussion, and from what has already been said, certain conclusions emerge regarding the nature of the relation between direct action and parliamentary democracy. It is easy to dismiss direct action as unpermissible under parliamentary democracy; it is difficult to obtain conditions under which the need for direct action is wholly removed. This is not because the people are not mature. Nor would it suffice to say that parliamentary institutions have not taken root in our country. It is really because it follows from the very nature of parliamentary government. It is democracy which gives rise to certain deep-rooted expectations; but the fact that the democracy is parliamentary frustrates these very expectations. Frustration, more than anything else, characterises the political picture under parliamentary democracy. The conflict between promise and possibility is latent all the time. In times of strain it comes out in the open. The result is direct action.

The underlying reason for this is that in parliamentary democracy the individual is just a constitutional fiction. He has, of course, the right of casting his ballot every four or five years. On that right, indeed, hangs the whole system. But apart from that functional link in the mechanism, the individual as such has no role to play. For, under the institutional set-up of parliamentary government, power gets centralized. This leads to insensitivity at the centre to what is happening at the circumference. The gulf between the electors and the elected cannot easily be bridged, and centralized power tends to move according to its own momentum. Decisions taken at the seat of power and enforced by its agents come as *fait accompli* to the people. Grievances accumulate. A psychological case is slowly built up in the minds of the people who are affected by such decisions. The normal channels provided for removing the accumulated grievances prove to be impotent when serious disagreement is the issue. The stage is set for direct action.

Government and the governed, into which the people are divided in a parliamentary set-up, tend to become rigid categories. These categories can pull on together only under two conditions. Either the issues which divide them should be issues of only secondary importance, in which case some compromise is always possible, or the governed must reconcile themselves to the fact that it is not possible to influence the government in any significant manner. Where none of these conditions obtain, divergent interests assume the form of a permanent conflict. The result is a showdown sooner or later.

The Usual Arguments against Direct Action: It is so often argued that if direct action is allowed in a parliamentary democracy, the result would be chaos and anarchy. Fear of anarchy in the body politic, however, is the symptom of a deep-lying malady. It is no use dismissing direct action without giving due thought to the conditions in which it takes place. The helplessness of the people and the inefficacy of the prevailing machinery to relieve men from their 'sense' of helplessness might give rise to a situation where men are no longer prepared to tolerate things.

Another argument advanced against direct action is that though it is justified against an alien government, it is highly inappropriate under a government which is 'our own government'. It is, after all, we are told, 'self-government'. The snag, however, is that though self-government is indeed the ideal of democracy, it is largely unrealizable in a parliamentary matrix. We have seen the hollowness of the theory of representation which serves as the only basis for the identification between 'self' and 'government' in the parliamentary system. Not until real self-government where the 'self' in fact participates in the process of 'government' is achieved, can the people be expected to identify themselves with the government. For, until then, the state is still an *alien* 'power'; it has not established itself as an 'authority' acceptable to the people.

It is also argued that the electorate ought to give a fair chance to the government in power and that it is free to overthrow it in the next elections if found unsatisfactory. But surely the trouble is that elections, under a parliamentary system, are no more than a rubber-stamp on one party's manifesto or another's, which may be drawn up deceptively, leaving out measures which are likely to be unpalatable to the public. These manifestoes are hardly ever a true index of the parties' real intentions. Under such conditions, it is possible for power to be grabbed by a party which has no intention of upholding the values most cherished by the people. The mechanism of the 'mandate' so often proposed, also tends to become more of a tug-of-war between opposing political parties than a device for investing the people with true sovereignty.

Finally, there is the argument that direct action makes a mockery of the sovereignty of parliament. However, the fact is that while in some countries it was the parliament that fought for the liberties of the people against the arbitrary rules of the monarchy, parliament can itself, under different circumstances, become arbitrary and remote from the people. Parliamentary sovereignty in effect often turns out to be the sovereignty of an organized minority, with the majority having little participation in the political process. The curious fact, indeed, is that the only real participation possible for a majority of people under such a form of government is the participation in direct action. Kerala is a case in point.

Inevitability of Direct Action: From all these factors, it is possible to formulate one proposition. It is that *direct action may become inevitable under parliamentary democracy.* The general climate of frustration, the ineffectiveness of known channels of communication, the alienation and atomisation of the individual, the tendency towards regimentation and the continuous state of conflict (which may remain latent and suppressed for a time) between the rulers and the ruled – all these make the ideal of self-government more and more remote and render parliamentary government an unstable form of political organization. *It needs to be rejuvenated from time to time by a more general and direct impact of democracy*, and failing such rejuvenation it is likely to degenerate into a constitutional dictatorship.

There is need to guard here against two possible misunderstandings. It is not suggested that because direct action is inevitable under parliamentary government *any* direct action is necessarily desirable. We shall return to this point later. The other point is that in drawing attention to the limitations of parliamentary democracy, we do not wish to posit it as opposed to real democracy. The fact that parliamentary democracy is a great improvement on more authoritarian forms cannot be doubted. Nor can it be denied that parliamentary government, together with the institution of local self-government, has proved successful in some countries in channelling the initiative of the politically-minded. What is contended, none the less, is that in the absence of more direct participation of the populace in the process of political decision-making, parliamentary government tends to be formal. Not until the common experience of all is pooled in the political process can the arbitrary and insensitive character of such a system be removed. And so long as arbitrariness and insensitivity are parts of the system, direct action is the only method open to the people to assert themselves.

In posing the issue of direct action in this manner, we are up against a difficult problem. Without both the threat and the actuality of direct action, the limitations of parliamentary government cannot be transcended. On the other hand, to justify every type of direct action would undermine not only parliamentary government but also democracy itself. There is therefore an urgent need to reformulate the concept of 'direct action'. We may start by defining direct action in general and irrespective of the form it takes.

A Tentative Definition of Direct Action: The first thing that is clear about direct action of any type is that it is essentially a technique of political action. Secondly, it is directed against constituted authority. Thirdly, the means it follows are extra-constitutional, that is, they are not provided by the legal and constitutional machinery of the state. Its method is that of bypassing the existing parliamentary forms and evolving new categories of political behaviour. Fourthly, it takes on the character of group action. This may take the form of a spontaneous mass upsurge at the bottom or it may be engineered by a group or groups, however motivated, that either are already political or have 'become political'. Finally, it is aimed at some political change: a change of a particular policy or policies, or a change in the constitutional machinery, or a change in the government in power. In all cases a change is desired, and it is a change in the political sphere. Thus, briefly, *direct action can be defined as an extra-constitutional political technique that takes the form of a group action, is aimed at some political change and is directed against the government in power.*

Having given a tentative definition, we can proceed to formulate the concept of direct action. Now, in the formulation of any concept, the first maxim is that it should enable us to explain that part of experience to which it refers in an objective and efficient manner. In this case, the essential need is to rid our minds of a certain connotation that we are apt to attach to direct action but which does not necessarily follow from its definition. The orthodox Communist, syndicalist and other terrorist movements and theories have conditioned our minds in such a way that we have come to identify all direct action with unbridled and unscrupulous violence. We must get out of this conditioning. An action can be direct with or without inciting the baser instincts of men; it can by-pass the existing categories of political action with or without becoming, in the process, unprincipled and opportunistic. If we do not wish to exclude a large part of the experience of the civilized world, we have to admit under the category of 'direct action' activities that are admittedly directed against constituted authority but whose main aim is to strengthen the democratic character of existing forms by appealing to the 'spirit' that is supposed to be embodied in these forms.

If this is not allowed we have to dismiss all agitation from below. The result is that we have to satisfy ourselves with parliamentary government as the highest form that democracy can take at the present stage of our knowledge and inventiveness. In other words, all the disadvantages of parliamentary democracy cited above have to be accepted irrevocably as part of the system. This would be an impossible situation from the point of view of democracy. Unless our notion of direct action is rid of its existing connotations and reformulated, we would have to rule out all possibilities of strengthening and rejuvenating our democracy. Experience of some countries suggests that it is possible to rise above the parliamentary forms and participate in the democratic process by resorting to actions which are essentially direct actions.

Democratic Direct Action: In our own country, we have the example of Gandhiji, who by resorting to peaceful but nonetheless effective direct action against the government in power, forced it to change its policy on a number of issues. Gandhiji's technique of arousing the opinion of the people and thus influencing the government of the day was not confined to the British. He tried that technique even after independence on the issue of the rights of Muslims in India. Another remarkable aspect of Gandhiji's method from which we can learn an important lesson was shown in 1920 when he withdrew his movement as soon as he found that it became violent and unprincipled.

When we turn to other democratic systems, we come across instances which are a tribute to the maturity which the 'democratic sense' has reached in those countries. The British people provided such an instance during the Second World War. The wave of opinion, running across the country and at all levels of society, on the highly moral issue of whether or not to appease the Fascists, will live in the memory of all democrats as a standing testimony to the degree to which the principle of democracy has taken root in the conscience of the British people. This agitation was, for the most part, extra-parliamentary and direct, though it did find its echo in the Parliament. The Suez crisis also showed that although the government never lost its hold on its legislative majority, the way in which the people in Britain reacted to the incident and showed to what extent their moral sense had been violated had to be reckoned with. It led to a reversal of policy and ultimately to the resignation of Sir Anthony Eden. America also, very recently, gave us an example of the high degree of democratic sense that had developed there, especially among the intellectuals. We refer to the way in which the professional and academic people fought against the onslaughts of McCarthyism.

It might be objected by some that it would be a misnomer to characterize these actions of the British and American peoples as direct action and that they are in any case very tame affairs compared to the agitation that took place, for example, in Kerala. If one looks closely into the matter, however, it will be seen that each case was a case of a major difference on policy where a large part of the public could not see eye to eye with the government, and secondly that in each case what took place was an 'agitation' that by-passed the existing parliamentary forms. It is only because of the maturity of their democratic system and the high degree of sensitivity that characterizes their legislature and government that the agitation stopped short of violence. The extreme form an agitation takes in India is only the result of a situation where while lip-service is paid by all to democracy no one really acts democratically. Neither the government nor the legislature is sufficiently responsive to changes in public opinion. But that does not prove that the basic issue is any different here than in other countries.

Types of Direct Action: Assuming that the concept of direct action covers all such experiences, our next task is to distinguish between two types of direct actions – those that enable us to give to the parliamentary form a greater democratic content and those that lead to its deterioration towards authoritarianism. The characteristic of the latter type of direct action is that it uses any means to achieve its end, is unmindful of consequences and considers success as its sole justification. The former, on the other hand, is characterized by a selection of means, is careful of the democratic content of the action and judges itself not by success alone but by other considerations as well.

It is possible to define certain criteria by which to judge whether a direct action has taken a desirable form. The chief criterion is that the means used must be intended to further the principal aim of strengthening freedom and democracy. The action is desirable only if the political change desired by the group involved in direct action offers a greater scope of political freedom than is offered by the existing political arrangements. This would also mean that no section of such a group should intimidate those outside the group and thus narrow the area of freedom. Finally, the actionists should be in constant touch with informed public opinion and be sufficiently responsive to the same. The assumption here is that the conditions for a higher form of democracy exist in a rudimentary form in the system of parliamentary democracy and that these provide us with a beginning and a basis for experimentation. The great merit of parliamentary democracy is that it allows freedom of expression. That makes a direct action possible. It is clear, then, that a direct action can be justified only if it furthers, and does not impede, the cause of democracy.

Now it is true that direct action, under certain conditions, takes undesirable forms. In a situation where people's patience and forbearance have been exhausted, various forces, social and psychological, come into play. If the direct actionists act under the impulse of unconscious urges or under the direction of a wrong type of leadership and do not give due consideration to the ultimate outcome of their acts, it is quite probable that they would pull the parliamentary form of government to pieces and push the country into the hands of a dictatorship or a military junta. In order to prevent such a catastrophe, therefore, it is imperative to evolve conditions under which direct action would not take such a form. For, *if it is clear that at some point parliamentary government leads to direct action, the essential problem is to provide constructive channels to such action.* It is futile to talk of the dangers of direct action without reference to the conditions under which they take place.

Application to Kerala

So far we have tried to analyse the problem of direct action in a general manner. In the course of this analysis we referred to the Indian situation from time to time for purposes of illustration. We shall now try, in the light of this general analysis, to examine the situation in Kerala before the Union government intervened to establish Governor's rule in that state. The relevance of the recent events in Kerala to the future development of the country's internal politics is so crucial that it is necessary to analyse them in some detail here. The procedure we shall follow is to state and evaluate the social and political facts of Kerala and then to draw some general conclusions regarding the political situation in India, the place of direct action in it, and the location of the motive force behind direct action in the social structure of India.

The Background of Direct Action: The politics of Kerala on the eve of the general elections held in 1957 was in a state of confusion. In the ten years that had gone after independence, there had been as many as eight administrations in the state, including two periods of President's rule. The Congress party in Kerala had been torn by internal wrangles, and instability of government had become a characteristic of the politics of that state, with the result that urgent economic reforms were neglected and the populace suffered from mounting hardships. The general consequence was the prevalence of a deep sense of frustration among the people of Kerala.

The Political Situation: It was against this background that the Communist Party came to power in Kerala. This does not mean, however, that a search for stability led the people of Kerala to vote the Communists to power. It was believed by some at that time that the choice for the Communist Party was a conscious and calculated choice on the part of the people as a whole. The facts belie this belief. The communists came to power on a minority of votes. The communists could form a government in Kerala in 1957 as a result of (1) the acute dissatisfaction in the people of Kerala with the Congress and the PSP and (2) the disunity among the parties that opposed the Communists in the elections. On the positive side, those who voted for the Communists on the basis of their programme did so under the impression that they were the only party that could relieve unemployment and solve the problem of industrialization in Kerala.

The Communal Grouping: The communal background of Kerala politics contributed to the victory of the Communists in the 1957 elections. They drew their major support from the Ezhava community and the scheduled castes, from the split among the Nairs, a large part of whom were alarmed at the growing Christian influence over the Congress party, and from the Muslims in constituencies where the Muslim League did not put up candidates against the Communists.[1]

Economic Stratification: Such an analysis in terms of the communal and religious divisions in Kerala should not, however, be overstressed. The division into social and economic classes is also relevant and is growing more and more important in recent years. There is a constant interaction between economic class, caste and religion which must be taken into account. Thus the Christians who support the Congress are also economically and educationally more advanced than the other communities. At the other extreme, there is the Ezhava community which is economically and socially depressed and identifies the interests of its class with the Communists.

What was the class composition of the voters who supported the Communists in 1957? *Positive* support came from a large majority of landless labourers and subsistence farmers (subsistence farming is a prevalent feature of Kerala agriculture where fragmentation of land has reached ridiculous proportions) and a sizable section of industrial workers. The reasons for this support are clear. The landless labourers, who largely came from the Ezhava community and the scheduled castes, had been organized by the Communist Party. The industrial workers were also organized in trade unions, some of which were controlled by the Communists.

The Middle Class: But all this evidence of positive support from the lower classes would not have brought the Communists to power. It was the negative support they secured from the splitting of the middle class votes that did the trick. The political attitudes of the middle class, which held the balance of power in Kerala, are interesting. It is a class that has imbibed democratic values and aspirations. Although it has a keen desire for a progressive economy, it is also normally against undue encroachments by the state on the life of the individual. This has, possibly, led to a general feeling of frustration among its members in the wake of recent economic and political developments all over the country. The large majority of secondary school teachers in Kerala were unhappy over their lot. They tended to be anti-Congress though not definitely pro-Communist. The lawyers and other professionals with their ingrained belief in parliamentary government and their general sense of respectability may be said to be anti-Communist in their attitude, though not necessarily pro-Congress. Such hesitancy informed the attitude of the middle class in Kerala. It was an attitude of non-commitment. The political result of such an attitude was that during the elections the votes of this class got divided between contending parties, although there was hardly any feeling of loyalty towards any of these parties. Chance oscillation in the voting behaviour of this class, therefore, could effect the outcome of the elections decisively. It was this that made political prediction difficult in Kerala where the middle class occupied a crucial position, and it has been observed by some that the Communists were themselves surprised at their victory.

In numbers, also, this class is important. According to the 1951 Census of Travancore-Cochin, the non-agricultural classes constitute 45.2 per cent of the population, and among these the 'independent workers' and 'others' – categories constituting the usual professional and middle classes – account for 45 per cent. Thus more than 20 per cent of the total population in Travancore-Cochin belongs to the middle class. As it is also the more educated, more conscious and more influential section of the population, there is no doubt that the middle class occupied, and still occupies, a strategic position in the politics of Kerala. Thus the Communists benefited from the fact that over and above the positive support from the lower classes, the negative and politically non-committal nature of the middle classes towards the elections paved the way to tilt the balance in their favour.

And it was precisely the middle class which played a decisive role against the policies of the Communist government when it came to power. It not only brought together the traditionally rival communities of Nairs and Christians but also forced all opposition parties to unite on a common platform against the government.

Communist Conflict with the Middle Class: Had the communists in Kerala succeeded in breaking the political neutrality of the middle class and winning their support, the experiment might have fulfilled the expectations of the proponents of coexistence. But, as everywhere else, they developed a conflict with this class and succeeded only in placing it in active opposition to their rule. The conflict that developed was not based on economic reasons. For, the middle class can hardly be called a class of exploiters except on the basis of a far-fetched logic. The reasons behind the conflict were mainly psychological, although in the direct action that ensued the economic factor also played its part. As we intend to show below, with the assumption of power, the Communists in Kerala began to humiliate this class. Perhaps this is true even of the Congress party wherever it is in power. But with the Communists, it is deliberate, more organized, more direct and less subtle. Besides, with the Communists, this conflict with the middle class is part of their ideology not only in India but also wherever they have come to power. But here in Kerala their success demanded of them a greater awareness of the situation in which they were placed. They overlooked the fact that they were working under a system whose basis lay in the political consciousness and support of the middle class. They forgot that it was a system which was not of their own making. Their ideology of economic determinism prevented them from giving due consideration to a class which their theory held in contempt.

The fact is that the middle class was already finding itself politically alienated under a system of parliamentary government which made it feel powerless, and therefore indifferent, to the question of who came to power. The Communists having come to power as a result of this indifference further alienated the middle class. With the assumption of power, they found themselves placed in a peculiar situation. Their entire prestige was based on their militant opposition to the alleged exploitation of the masses by non-state agencies. Their rise to political power owed a great deal to the impression they had created in the general mind that they alone could solve the economic problems of unemployment and speedy industrialization. This impression in turn was based on the achievement in these spheres in the countries under communist rule. It was, however, largely overlooked that the basis of success in those countries lay in state-coercion of a type that is not possible to enforce in a parliamentary state which has to function under a quasi-federal democratic constitution.

Stage One: *Loss of Prestige*: The obstacles to their basic approach became clear in course of time. They could not materially affect the vested interests in the state without the cooperation of the Centre which, however, was dominated by the Congress party. One of their first declarations on the assumption of power was to nationalise foreign-owned plantations in the state. But they could not take even the preliminary steps in that direction during the whole term of their office because the Centre made its stand against any such step known to the State government. Thus the Communists in Kerala found themselves in a position where they could not 'expropriate the expropriators'. On the contrary, to further their economic goal they were led in the opposite direction. They tried to placate big business by offering liberal economic incentives of the type which even the Congress governments were reluctant to offer in their respective states. There was also considerable labour unrest in Kerala at the same time as this offer was being made. Some of this was engineered by the unions led by the Communist Party. But a sizable part of the workers in Kerala owes allegiance of trade unions led by other parties which, too, did not obviously want to lag behind in demands. However, when it came to settling these disputes, the Communist government brazen-facedly discriminated against the workers led by the non-Communist unions in all possible ways, including protection of the employers by resort to firing, as it happened in the Chandanthope factory dispute. These actions of the Communist government together amounted to a considerable loss of prestige among the progressive but 'uncommitted' sections of the middle class in Kerala.

Stage Two: *Show of Strength*: As if to compensate for this loss in prestige and for their failure to affect big business, the Communists in Kerala turned severely on the lesser among the vested interests. All such interests belonged to the middle class. The government began to enact rules against these small interests in a manner which annoyed and humiliated them. The minor incident of the ferry-boat charges in Kuttanad, after the taking over of the private ferry boats by the government-controlled Water Transport Corporation, becomes highly significant in this context. The increase in revenue could hardly have been the purpose behind the decision to quash the one-*anna* concession to students travelling by these boats. It was clearly a case of humiliating the 'petite bourgeoisie'. On the side of the middle class too, the seriousness of the protest was out of all proportion to the incident – which only shows how intense and 'pent-up' their feeling of humiliation was under the Communist government. This was the beginning of the conflict between the middle class and the government in power in Kerala. Another point to be noted here is that contrary to the communist charge that the students' movement was instigated by the opposition parties, the fact is that the initiative came from the students and their Action Council who then forced the opposition leaders to support the movement. In a sense this was a precursor to the direct action that was to follow later.

Stage Three: The Education Bill: The Education Bill could also be described as a measure directed against the small vested interests. The interests adversely affected this time were the private school managements. It is wrong to characterize the school managements as 'big' vested interests by reference to the control of the Church or of a society like the Nair Service Society. The important thing to note here is that the section which was represented by the Church or the NSS belonged to the middle class as much as the teachers who were employed by these institutions. While it is true that all was not well with the service conditions of the school teachers in Kerala and also that some statutory measure to rectify things was certainly called for, it is also true that the Communists were completely mistaken, as subsequent events proved, in treating the dispute between the managements and teachers on a class-war footing. In fact, the extreme measures of the Communists brought the two groups together against the government.

Stage Four: Deviations from the Rule of Law: When this conflict was developing, the Communists also estranged those sections of the middle class who are very sensitive to the maintenance of the rule of law. The Communists began to tamper with the administration of justice. For them it was a moral problem. How could they let down their comrades even if they perpetrated 'crimes', for the crimes were after all committed for a common 'cause' and may be at the behest of the party? This subservience of the governmental process to the interests of the Communist Party began to pervade all political relations in Kerala. The party cells in villages and towns began to function vigorously. There were allegations of intimidation and violence by the Communists. Non-communists were harassed and instances of lawlessness began to accumulate. The secretary of the local branch of the Communist Party reigned supreme in his locality. The unchallenged authority of the local secretary and his accomplices also meant that the local administration and the police force were gradually emasculated and rendered impotent. The non-communists, including the uncommitted sections of the population, naturally felt more and more insecure. It is possible that the general sense of insecurity that prevailed in Kerala under the Communist regime may have been the result of only sporadic instances engineered by some unscrupulous party-men. But the fact of the prevailing sense of insecurity was certainly there, and perhaps in a large measure.

Stage Five: Rule by the Party: All these developments and the mounting feeling of opposition to its rule made the Communist government apprehensive of the impending crisis. This made them place the faithful in positions of effective power in the administration. In all the strategic spheres, like the police, civil administration and the magistracy, the key posts were given to officers who were considered more reliable or manageable by the party. Merit became synonymous with the goodwill of the party. Naturally, therefore, an impression was created that the entire administration was passing off into the hands of the Communist Party. Not much imagination was required from this point onward to think in terms of the impending strait-jacket of communist rule one heard about in the communist countries. People who looked on with disapproval felt, therefore, that the end of freedom was close-by and that they must either give in to what seemed certain to follow or fight and get out of Communist control. Direct action became inevitable. *The urge for direct political participation, the accumulated grievances and the mounting public opinion against the government – all these factors together gave rise to a situation where the tussle between the government and the governed came out into the open.* It is futile to lay all blame for direct action in Kerala at the door of the opposition parties or a few unscrupulous individuals who might, of course, have taken advantage of the situation. The fact is that the initiative for direct action did not come from the opposition parties. Rather, the opposition parties were forced to unite on a common platform of anti-communism by the gathering temper of the people, especially of the middle class.

The Causation of Direct Action

The purpose of this paper is to make an objective study of 'direct action' so as to locate its rightful place in the sphere of political actions. Earlier, we formulated the concept of direct action and defined its meaning. Its precise character was brought out in the analysis that followed of Kerala as a particular instance of direct action. It was emphasized there that direct action was the expression of a political conflict between the aggrieved sections of the middle class and the political apparatus of a parliamentary democracy. Although Kerala had its special character, it was only one of many agitations that have taken place in India after independence. The events in Andhra, Maharashtra, Gujarat and Punjab are all instances of the same type. In each case, the movement originated in the middle class and was sustained by it, though it generally spread to other classes and thus gave direct actions the character of mass movements. A general analysis of direct action must therefore begin with an analysis of the middle class itself.

From the viewpoint of social composition, the middle class is not a homogeneous class. Various sections of this class perform diverse functions and belong to diverse social groups. In spite of this fact, however, there is a running thread of unity between all these sections. This is found in the mental trait which is necessary in the performance of these various functions. It is the capacity to represent objects on a more or less abstract level. Such capacity is common to administrators, lawyers, teachers, doctors, clerks, technical personnel, etc. The members of this class have received at least a secondary education and possess a fair knowledge of their immediate environments. *These characteristics – knowledge of environment and capacity for abstraction – single them out to constitute a social class.*

It is in their relation to the political society that we find divisions within this class. The principle of this division is the presence or absence of participation in the political process. Some are placed in positions of power and the rest are debarred from participating in the political process except in the form offered by the institution of elections. The middle class is thus divided among the rulers and the ruled. And the problem for the politically dispossessed sections of this class is now to mitigate these conditions and create new ones in their place. Direct action is one form that attempts to solve this problem.

The Hypothesis: We can now formulate our hypothesis regarding the causes of direct action. Such action is determined by four factors: (1) the division of the politically conscious middle class into the rulers and the ruled; (2) the need or desire felt by the ruled to be the rulers; (3) the rigidity of the political system in frustrating this need and (4) the ideology that this need is their birthright. Apart from these causal factors certain other conditions must be fulfilled before direct action is actually resorted to. These are (1) The feeling of dissatisfaction and the sense of injustice must have reached a high pitch (thus, to take an illustration, in the Bombay State the issue of prohibition did not lead to a flare-up but that of linguistic autonomy did) and (2) there must prevail a large consensus of opinion in favour of some drastic action and a widely felt desire for it. These six elements – four causal factors and two conditions of efficiency – provide us with a total causal scheme for any direct action. Together with the definition of direct action given above they provide us with a theory of direct action.

Prevailing Views on Direct Action: Such a formulation of the causes of direct action runs counter to the prevailing opinions, specially those held by persons in power. They trace direct action to the activity of local *apolitical* groups. Mr Nehru, for instance, had attributed the cause of direct action, when it took place in Gujarat, Maharashtra and Punjab, to the parochialism of linguistic or religious groups; while the communists in Kerala traced the direct action there to the presence of vested interests. A little analysis would, however, demonstrate the weakness of this position: (1) Following Mr Nehru's reasoning, take away parochialism and there will be an end to direct action. This stands refuted by the events in Kerala. (2) According to communist reasoning, remove vested interests and there would be no direct action. This stands refuted by almost all the direct actions that have taken place in this country. The fact is that this type of reasoning confuses cause with condition. Parochialism and the rest are merely social conditions under which direct action takes birth and develops. They play the role of giving a particular 'colour' to the action. They do not 'cause' direct action. The cause lies, as suggested above, in the urge to take part in the functioning of the political society which, being split between the rulers and the ruled, frustrates the urge for the large majority.

The difference we have drawn between the causal factors on the one hand and the particular social conditions on the other is important in understanding not only the problem of direct action but also the remedies suggested for its solution. For, the specific conditions may change but the causes remain. If a condition is identified with a cause, the remedy suggested will prove impotent. For instance, Mr Nehru, convinced of the theory that parochialism is the root-cause of direct action, tries to eliminate parochialism by generating an intense feeling of nationalism. But experience so far bears out that this does not work, not because there is no feeling of nationalism among our people but because this remedy fails to attack the root of the problem. The basic problem lies in the latent need to participate in the political process which is denied to much the greater section of society under a formalistic democracy like ours. Parochialism serves the function of merely providing moral support to this need. The need to participate is at the individual psychological level; it is an expression of the individual's need to be free. But under the peculiar cultural environments of our society the individual need is not held in esteem, with the result that the moral support is sought in parochial institutions. Our authoritarian culture tends to suppress an individual need as against an 'institutional' need, and the consequence is that direct action tends to take on an 'institutional' or parochial garb. The individual acts not for himself but for a 'cause' – language, religion, caste or class. This explains the importance of parochial groups, and also the distortion of direct action towards violence and rowdyism which are justified in the interest of the 'cause'.

The view that parochialism is not a cause of direct action is supported by the fact that practically all people have local and parochial loyalties and still are divided on the issue of direct action. Some favour direct action, others do not. The criterion by which the parochial group splits itself cannot be parochialism. There must be a criterion different from it. We suggest that such a criterion is provided by the extent to which one's 'urge to participate' is satisfied. Those who either hold power or can influence it are satisfied with the existing state of affairs; others are not. This polarization provides the political problem that India faces today and also the background against which direct action takes place.

The Need to be Free: The need to be free is basic in man. It exists at the biological as well as at the psychological level. And it is precisely this need that leads men to live in a society governed by laws. As pointed out in a previous section, freedom does not consist in the absence of laws. Even at the individual level, law is necessary. Every man has to evolve a law of his being, a law on the basis of which he orders his own behaviour. The function of such a law is to arbitrate between conflicting needs and demands of the individual self. And it is the same at the social level. In order that their freedom may be more secure, men frame laws and agree to abide by them. The function of these laws also is to arbitrate between conflicting needs and demands. Then as social institutions become more complex, this function of arbitration between conflicting needs is institutionalised in the form of a state. The state is thus no superior institution; it is merely another social form whose sole justification lies in the needs of individuals. When the needs multiply, the functions of the state increase correspondingly, and as a result the state becomes a powerful entity. It is then that the state may begin to overshadow the individual whom it was originally meant to serve. When this happens, the individual comes face to face with the state whose incursion into the individual's life increases every day. The urge to be free is now translated into the desire to participate in the political process.

The Political Need: The desire to be politically free is thus an expression of a fundamental human urge. The political need, however, may remain dormant for a long time in the process of social development. Then at a certain stage it comes to life and begins to agitate man. This activization of the need is conditioned by historical and social as well as personal circumstances. Throughout the medieval period the need was suppressed under the hoary institutions of religion. During the eighteenth century in Europe the need to be politically free was suddenly felt, at first by the rising middle classes. (The English tradition of 'freedom broadening from precedent to precedent' made the nobility also fight for political freedom.) The process culminated in the French Revolution and the Declaration of the Rights of Man, the Bill of Rights in the American Constitution and the extension of the franchise in Great Britain. The process is still continuing and spreading in Asian and African countries.

The Political Need in India: The experience of the struggle for freedom in European countries had its repercussion in India. The vehicle of this repercussion was the middle class in India, in whom the need to be free was kindled. Being trained to think at the abstract level, they alone could absorb the experience of the European people and feel the need for a similar experience of political freedom. It was the presence of a large middle class (in whom the need to be politically free had been kindled) that singled out India from other Asian countries. It also explains why today she continues to cling to the democratic ideal while other countries in the Middle and Far East are turning to dictatorship.

The Role of the Middle Class: The pioneers of freedom in India saw clearly the problem of spreading the need to be free in their fellowmen. Their understanding of this need was not limited to the idea of political independence but extended to the idea of political freedom for the individual in the ordering of his own destiny. They saw that not until the need to be free is kindled in the people, especially among the educated sections of society, could they hope to achieve their goal. They succeeded in their task. It was on the basis of such an awakening that the existing state came into being. The problem facing India today arises out of a strained relation between the need that was then kindled and is still alive and the institutions that are supposed to fulfil that need but fail to do so.

During pre-independence days, it was thought that the establishment of parliamentary institutions would solve the problem of political freedom. As it turned out, however, the problem continued. The rigidity of the holders of power in the working of these institutions created conditions where direct action took place from time to time in one form or another. It was the only way left to large sections of the middle class to express their need for political freedom.

The Other Classes: In the case of other classes like the peasantry and the working class, the need is not so keenly felt. This is partly because they are so pre-occupied with their material needs that the political need remains dormant, and partly because their conception of freedom hardly goes beyond the level of material well-being and personal security. There is also a relative absence of the knowledge of environments; the will to be a free agent requires such a knowledge. In spite of all this, however, when direct action ensues, the workers and the peasants do not remain immune from it. They are influenced in their actions by the beliefs and values of the middle class. This has been so all through in our country. The leadership of the independence movement right from the village level to the national level had been in the hands of the middle class. The historical explanation apart, in every society and more so in a semi-literate society, the educated members tend to take a lead in social and political matters. The involvement of the masses in the direct action is thus rooted in their social relation with the members of the middle class. On the whole, it can be said, then, that the middle class holds the balance of power in India, that any direct action is initiated and sustained by members of this class and that in so far as other classes join a direct action they do so by virtue of their being influenced by the middle class.

Conclusion: The above analysis is meant to be approximate and tentative. Its importance lies in assisting us in our understanding of direct action. Our approach in this paper has been to understand the phenomenon of direct action for what it basically is. The phenomenon, we are convinced, is not an accident. It forms a pattern by itself and in turn imparts a pattern to our political process. The fate of our democracy rests on an understanding of this pattern, which the conspiracy theory and the theory of parochialism do not explain. We have advanced an alternatives theory in this paper which attempts an explanation.

Endnotes

1. For a detailed discussion of this, as well as other aspects of Kerala politics, the reader is referred to a recent book by Dr Jitendra Singh, *Communist Rule in Kerala*, published by the Diwan Chand, Indian Information Centre, New Delhi.

Dichotomy in Hindu[1] Life and Its Impact on India's External Relations

Nirad C. Chaudhuri

(Ten Years of Quest, Manaktalas, Bombay 1966,
eds. Abu Sayeed Ayyub and Amlan Datta)

In one sense there is no point in speaking about dichotomy in any human being or group. All men, whether individuals or groups, are divided within themselves, pulled in opposite ways. Long before the appearance of modern psychology, Shakespeare proclaimed the dichotomy through the mouth of Hamlet, and Pascal cried out, 'what a chimera is man, what a subject of contradictions!' But the dichotomy in Hindu life about which I am going to speak is of an altogether special kind. Its expression is a permanent civil war in Hindu life, in which nobody conquers, and both sides defeat each other. The tussle is so even that it induces a stalemate, and has the worst effect possible on the life of the Hindus. Though it, the expression of each of a pair of opposed inclinations or traits is reduced to its lowest denominator. In other words, the opposed traits cut off their own noses to spite the rivals.

This kind of dichotomy is so pervasive in the Hindu existence that it influences every activity of theirs, and, today, after the attainment of political independence it is a powerful force in their political activities both in the domestic and the foreign sphere. In this article I shall describe a few of the opposites which are shaping the policies, but not all of them. The most important opposites which are operating in shaping more particularly the external relations of India today are the following: (1) A sense of Hindu solidarity going with an uncontrollable tendency towards disunity within the Hindu order; (2) Collective megalomania with self-abasement; (3) Extreme xenophobia with equally extreme xenolatry; (4) Authoritarianism with anarchic individualism; (5) Violence with non-violence; (6) Militarism with pacifism; (7) Possessiveness with indifference to property owned; (8) Courage with cowardice; (9) Stupidity with cleverness. In this enumeration the positive trait is put first, and the correlative second, but they are on a par in the power to stultify each other. I am going to deal in this place only with the first three pairs of traits. Let me set them out schematically:

Solidarity → ← Disunity
Megalomania → ← Self-Abasement
Xenophobia → ← Xenolatry

Solidarity and Disunity

It is a perfectly valid thesis to hold that India is united and disunited at the same time. The unity is derived from the original colonization of the country by an incoming and conquering people, and the creation, through that process, of a massive and self-contained culture, whereas the disunities are the natural products of the evolution of the same people which created differentiations in every field – linguistic, social, cultural, and political. In other words, the unity is an expression of Hindu solidarity, and whatever organic unity exists in India today is a survival and residue of that old solidarity. It follows from this that the unity of India cannot be maintained except through the Hindu group consciousness, supplemented by a sort of Hindu imperialism. But it is precisely this stark proposition which the present rulers of India, in spite of being Hindu, will not recognize. This utterly theoretical non-recognition is depriving the present Government of India of whatever emotional strength their campaign for the integration of the people of India might have had.

But whatever the power behind the sense of Hindu solidarity, it was always separative, not unitive. By this I mean that is made all Hindus aware of their distinctiveness from the rest of mankind, and roused their sense of unity only when, as a group of Hindu nations, they were collectively threatened by non-Hindus. So it was in the past, and so it remains at present. The sense of Hindu solidarity is still a great force, and when it is fully brought into play its coercive power becomes irresistible. All Hindus stand in a pack and bay together, *nemine contradicente et dissentiente*.

In this the Hindus present a diametrical contrast to the European peoples, and more especially, the British people. If in India there ever were a Dreyfus case, to be Dreyfusard would have been to court suicide, metaphorically in any case. Let me also give some British examples. During the Boer War there were opponents of the war who were called 'Pro-Boers'. Among these was a future British Prime Minister. Again, from the first day of the British Empire in India to the last day, there were British politicians and publicists who voiced opposition to it publicly. Had Great Britain been India, Burke and Sheridan would have found themselves in the Tower soon enough, and later John Bright would have been hanged like John Brown.

Such in expression of opposition to a national ambition or interest, or even national folly, is inconceivable among the Hindus. A modern Hindu might be anything in his politics or social philosophy – Leftist, Socialist, Communist, Liberal, Centre, Right, Ultra, Anglicized, or Orthodox, but when facing the non-Hindu world, he will be made to speak the same language and will also voluntarily speak it. Even when a man does not share a general attitude, any public dissent by him is not to be thought of. I know that many very high-placed Hindus disapproved of the occupation of Goa, but not one of them protested publicly. Such is the coercive power of the sense of Hindu solidarity that a Hindu's behaviour is controlled not only at the stage of action, but even at that of thought and feeling. This was seen all through the management of Hindu-Muslim relations before independence, as it is now being seen in the ordering of our foreign relations, particularly, the relations with China.

But the sense of Hindu solidarity, with all its emotionalism, projects itself in an outward direction, and does not bring them together for any national purpose within the country. Thus the sense of solidarity contributes virtually nothing to internal nationalism. Naturally then its internal effect is seen for the most part only in the uniformity of psychological reactions and practical conduct which tend to be similar in similar circumstances all over India. Hindus from widely separated parts of India will give the same answers to a set of questions on moral and intellectual issues, not to speak of political ones.

The Hindu *apologia pro vita sua* is absolutely stereotyped all over India, and even those who brag about their emancipation from the Hindu traditions do not show themselves as un-Hindu in self-excusing. In comparable situations they also act alike. In short the unity is obedience to a pattern of behaviour which set in its mould long ago, and it is very close to the unity of the animals belonging to the same family or genus. Everybody knows how alike is the behaviour of all the cats from the domestic one to the tiger.

But all this unity is residual, whereas the disunity produced by the historical process is both living and continuous. Therefore, that is the real evolutionary force in the development of the Indian population. It may be stated quite categorically that the natural development of the peoples of India is opposed to their social, linguistic, cultural, and political unity.

The diversities created by history have now become so hardened that the process cannot be reversed. In fact, no one recognizes this more unreservedly in practice than our present-day rulers. They have even dismembered the two great bilingual provinces taken over from the British, namely, Bombay and Madras, and created linguistic succession states. The strength of the provincial sentiment is seen not only in the provinces, but in the Government of India itself. It has a very special cast, and everybody who knows anything about its inside working also knows that it is a federation of ministries from the provinces. Almost all central ministers try to make their departments provincial by converting their personnel into provincial contingents.

The political unity of India, so far as it exists today, is a legacy of British imperialism, and till now the new Indian regime has made no contribution to it. On the other hand, the strong provincial sentiment is emerging as the true national passion in India, and its full emergence seems to be only a matter of time. Owing to the existence of this provincial sentiment as an incipient nationalism, all Hindus think of themselves primarily as Andhras, Assamese, Bengalis, Gujaratis, Hindustanis, Maharashtrians, Punjabis, Tamils, etc.

But the divisions of the Hindus do not end with the rival loyalties to the provinces on the one hand, and to India on the other. They disrupt even the allegiance to the province. Within each province there are social groupings which clash with one another in endless ways. There are classes and class interests, regions and regional interests, castes and caste interests. Below these there is not only stratification but even granulation – factions against factions families against families, persons against persons, capable of harming all corporate effort. Extreme factionalism in Hindu life is both deep-seated and stable. There is hardly any sphere of public or private activity in which this evil is not present and assertive. It is seen as much in school or hospital management as in game clubs or amateur theatricals. The unceasing and unresting groupings and regroupings of the factions under the pressure of personal rivalries are kaleidoscopic in their changes, and if one can acquire the detachment of complete non-involvement, saying – 'plague on all of you!' he can even enjoy the colourful spectacle.

In the Hindu world, all the narrower loyalties have a disastrous impact on all the larger. Modern Hindus have not heard the dictum – *publicum bonum private est praeferendum* – that is, public good is to be given preference over the private. So, in every case when the two come into conflict, the private triumphs over the public. To put it in explicit terms, a provincial interest will invariably prevail over one that is Indian, a caste interest over the provincial, the group's over the caste's, the individuals' over the group's. The alertness and energy in pursuing an interest grow as the field of its operation narrows. The play of the Hindu loyalties may therefore be compared to the spiral expansion of a force radiating outwards from a centre. Their force weakens as they spread out towards the periphery, and the self is always the vortex.

Megalomania and Self-abasement

I come now to the second pair of contrasted characters: megalomania and self-abasement. The megalomania at its origin was natural. It sprang from Aryan pride and self-confidence – from the consciousness of racial and cultural superiority over a barbarous indigenous population, and also from the pride of power of a conquering and colonising people. The Muslim and the British conquerors of India had exactly the same kind of feeling about themselves.

But the original megalomania took a negative and defensive form when the Hindus lost their vitality and strength and passed under the political domination of foreigners. They could not endure that without an illusion of greatness, which became the compensation for the humiliation. The Hindus could maintain their self-respect only by hypnotising themselves into the belief that the barbarians had won solely through brute force and that they themselves were superior to the conquerors in every human attribute.

The Muslim attacks on the Hindus before their conquest of India proper, that is, from the eighth century onwards, went on reinforcing the emotional compensation until, by the time of the invasions of Mahmud of Ghazni, the Hindu megalomania had passed beyond anything in reason. Alberuni noted this and wrote: 'According to their belief, there is no other country on earth but theirs, no other race of man but theirs, and no created beings besides themselves have any knowledge or science whatever.'

Instead of being chastened by British rule, this self-conceit became even stronger. It was refurbished in a very paradoxical manner, and I give one example. After learning English, we Bengali Hindus came really to believe that we knew the English language better than the English people, at least the English in India, whom we regarded as the butchers of grammar. This was the force behind the self-confidence of what was known as Babu English. A young nephew of mine told me after independence that he had been informed by the senior students of his school that the English people at home never used verbs, but only said 'I rice' when they really meant 'I eat rice.' Now, I cannot say that after having been taught English by my Bengali teachers in this atmosphere, I was not influenced by it, and the way I throw the weight of my English about was certainly fostered by that confident assumption.

But nothing Hindu can be anything Hindu unless set off by its opposite, and here, too, the contrast exists. The Hindu megalomania was always accompanied by the Hindu self-abasement, and even now it is. At the beginning the self-abasement was, however, a different feeling. It was a sense of the decline of worth, and it was a healthy feeling. It originated in the historical experience of the Aryans in India and did not paralyse all effort at regeneration. For one thing, like all ancient peoples, the Hindus placed their golden age in the past, and believed, without over reading Hesiod, in a sequence of retrogression of the virtues. 'What a race the golden sires have left – worse than their fathers; and your offspring will be baser still,' said the Greek, and the Roman echoed,

> "Aetas parentum, peior avis, tulit
> Nos nequiores, mox daturos
> Progeniem vitiosiorum."

And that was only a paraphrase of the Greek saying.

The Hindus placed their degeneration in the fourth age of their collective existence, and the four stages of the retrogression were Satya, Treta, Dvapara, and Kali. The last age is the age of evil, and according to the Hindu reckoning it began on February 17, 3102 BC, which shows how stupid it is to complain about our plight today. But apart from the general belief in retrogression, the Hindus were certainly aware that something regrettable was happening to them in India; they were losing their original physical and moral stature. My mother used to tell me that after being thirteen cubits (or was it eleven?) in the Satya Yuga, we Hindus had come down to a mere three-and-a-half in the Kali Yuga. Alas! It is even less by the standard cubit for me!

On the whole, the old habit of self-abasement was a good moral influence, and inspired the Hindus to a sense and also emulation of the 'antique virtues'. In the nineteenth century, more especially, the Hindus had an interlude, absolutely exceptional in their history, of rational self-criticism. The sense of self-abasement was activised into something like the Judaic notion of repentance. Nothing is more striking in the emotional power behind the movement for Hindu regeneration and reformation of the nineteenth century than the burning eagerness to get rid of the dross accumulated through the ages, and to purify the Hindu existence in an idealistic fire. Not one great Hindu leader of that epoch denied the degradation, but they also believed in redemption, and were convinced that they could purge themselves and become new men.

But this phase of self-abasement is over; Hindu society has reverted to its passive form, which is the Hindu inertia of *Klaivya* at its worst. After independence, the self-abasement is finding an expression which is incredible, and may even be called degraded. Certainly, it is opposed to every form of self-respect, and it is difficult to understand how it can co-exist with the absurd national arrogance of the same epoch. One day, I was waiting for a bus at one of the stops in Delhi, and though I knew what the bus service here was, I gave vent to some impatience at the delay. A Sikh, a very well-dressed man who spoke good English, heard me and observed, 'Why are you complaining? You are not in a foreign country.'

I give a few more instances of how our inferiority is taken for granted. Complain to any shopkeeper dealing in hardware that the nails he has supplied get bent at the first blow of the hammer, and he has his answer pat: '*Desi aisai hota*.'[2] If you take back a box of pins to your stationer after discovering that every third pin is without a point, you will get the same reply, '*Desi aisai hota*.' The electrical mechanic has fitted a plug which needs the strength of the whole body to push into the socket and is torn from the flex at every effort to take out, but if you complain, the man at once says, '*Desi aisai hota*.'

The most amusing instance of this plea that I heard was furnished by a difficulty with a water meter installed in my house. It was supplied by the municipality and showed a very high rate of consumption. The owner of the house complained to me because I have a small roof-garden. I myself went down and tested the meter, and found that it was registering 50 per cent in excess. When I drew the attention of the plumber to it, he at once replied, '*Desi aisai hota*.'

One or two additional illustrations. One day I was going in a car whose noiselessness and, more especially, absence of rattling in the body I noticed. The driver at once explained, 'Not assembled in India, Sir!' That accounts for the prices people are ready to give for a car sold by a diplomat, and also why people take such trouble to get a car from abroad paying any price. That also explains why housewives descend like locusts on anyone going abroad and request him to bring household appliances for them, especially knitting needles.

Now, I would not deny that the goods in question as made here are of bad quality. But what I object to is why our incapacity to make better things should be treated as axiomatic and no attempts should be made to remedy the shortcomings. But the answer to that is simple. The belief in our collective inferiority is so deep-seated that there is no real confidence that we can ever become efficient. Modesty, so lacking in the moral sphere, is certainly blatant in the practical and especially the industrial.

Xenophobia and Xenolatry

The last two paired traits I have to consider in this article, namely, xenophobia and xenolatry, are an extension and complement of the two I have just described. The self-regarding megalomania and abasement naturally change to xenophobia and xenolatry when the human group in question becomes other-regarding. The xenophobia is the outward projection of Hindu pride, and it developed under the impact of the foreign and, more especially, the barbarian invasions. On this Hindu attitude, too, I might cite Alberuni, to indicate the pitch to which the hatred had risen even before the Muslim conquest of the country. He wrote, '...they (the Hindus) will never stake their soul or body or their property on religious controversy. On the contrary, all their fanaticism is directed against those who do not belong to them, against all foreigners. They call them *Mlechchha*, i.e. impure.'

Alberuni went on to say that, so far as the people of the Middle East were concerned, the Hindu hatred was at first directed against the fire-worshipping Persians, and then, he added, 'came Islam; the Persian empire perished, and the repugnance of the Hindus against foreigners increased more and more when the Muslims began to make their inroads into their country.' After the invasions of Sultan Mahmud, Alberuni wrote, 'the Hindus became like atoms of dust scattered in all directions... and their scattered remains cherish, of course, the most inveterate aversion towards all Muslims.'

The xenophobia continued through the period of Muslim rule and acquired a new lease of life with the establishment of British power. I shall quote an early testimony to the substitution of the object of hatred. It comes from Abe Dubois, who wrote about the customs and manners of the Hindus in the early part of the nineteenth century. He draws attention, like Alberuni, to 'the hate and contempt which they cherish against all strangers, and especially against Europeans.'

He adds the revealing comment: 'Under the supremacy of the Brahmins, the people of India hated their government while they cherished and respected their rulers; under the supremacy of Europeans, they hate and despise their rulers from the bottom of their hearts, while they cherish and respect their government.' One may say that with independence, the Hindu mind has gone back to its pre-British norm. Nehru has been apotheosised, temples were erected to him even in his life-time, but it is hardly possible to sound the depths of the contempt and hatred for the present government in the hearts of ordinary and true Hindus.

The anti-British form of the xenophobia became part of the nationalism of modern Hindus as soon as they acquired the nationalistic sentiment. As the nationalist movement gained strength, the anti-British xenophobia also became assertive. After independence, the emergence of a low form of xenolatry has somewhat obscured the xenophobia. But it is very much alive beneath the surface, and comes out at a slight provocation. I unfortunately provided one such. I wrote a sincerely appreciative account of the English people and their culture after paying a short visit to England in 1955. The book, which was published in 1959, got uniform abuse in the Indian Press, and the malice of the personal attacks had to be seen to be believed possible. In a respectable newspaper, I was described as a dog wagging its tail, though slapped by its master. I had, of course, committed an unforgivable offence against the code of Hindu ethics in respect of foreigners – I had praised a foreign culture with sincerity, which no Hindu is allowed to do. Interested praise of foreign nations is a different matter.

But the xenolatry when voiced by the Hindus amongst themselves and privately, is perfectly sincere, and they prove their sincerity by acting on what they say. If a foreign customer, for instance, comes into a shop, say, the cottage industries emporium in Delhi, the salesmen, and more particularly the girls, will immediately desert the Indian customer even in the middle of a transaction and rush to the Mlechchha. In fact, the xenolatry is as natural as its twin brother, xenophobia. If the one was excited by a defiance of the foreigner, the other was the product of defeatism in the same situation. Even before the Muslims had conquered India the Hindus had come to feel that their new enemy was irresistible, and in the first century and a half of British rule its stability was founded on the unshaken Hindu belief in British invincibility, which did not clash with the moral contempt for the British because it operated in the amoral world of power.

I am not, however, going to deal with the xenolatry as it was during Muslim and British rule. With a set of foreigners obviously superior to their native subjects in many things, the feeling of inferiority was, partly at all events, natural. If it was created by defeatism, it also showed some moral sensibility. It gave expression to admiration for the foreigner's *virtus* as well to regret for the loss of the same *virtus* in themselves. So long as foreign rule lasted the xenolatry had a partially corrective effect. It stimulated emulation. We were piqued to do better than usual both by the foreigner's example and his contumely.

But after the coming of political independence the xenolatry is showing itself not only in a more pronounced form, but also with an inexplicably servile complexion. The new xenolatry is unashamed, blatant, rampageous. It is morally degrading and economically ruinous. That for the practical ends of government and economic reconstruction the Hindus would so completely brush aside their megalomania is a thing which no one would have found possible to believe before independence. Yet this worship of the foreigner in every field is as indisputable as it is strange. It is more assertive in the ruling class than in the ordinary Indian.

This adulation of the foreigner in the Hindu ruling order, whose self-complacence and even self-conceit hardly touch any sea-floor, is a paradox, almost a perversity. A distinguished Indian economist once told me after his return from a congress of economists in the western world that man for man no Indian economist was inferior to any foreign economist. Yet is there any country in the world which makes use of a larger number of foreign economists? In the field of technological development, our rulers will never entrust any project to an Indian if they can get a foreigner. They will not employ any Indian if they can give the job to a foreigner, and in any case they will not pay the Indian half the amount they are ready to give to any foreigner.

I give one other example of the degrading xenolatry. Soon after independence, at the instance largely of Nehru, a laboratory for research in physics was established in Delhi. In the orthodox imitative style it was called the NPL Those of us who took interest in the institution came to know soon enough that not much was being done in it. But our government obviously looked at the matter differently and went on bragging about India's eminence in physics, until suddenly they discovered that all was not well with the laboratory. So, to put it in proper shape, they at first invited Professor Blackett to become its director and when he would not accept the offer they brought him over to look into the working of the institution and report with a view to get it going.

When he was doing that I one day met him at a party. As a young man he was in the navy and was present at the battle of Jutland. He and I were talking about the course of the battle, and particularly about the squadron in which his ship, the *Barham*, was when an acquaintance of mine came along to say that he wished to introduce a high Indian official to the Professor. This official turned out to be the highest permanent civil servant in the ministry which had brought over Professor Blackett. When the Professor learned that he said, 'Then it will be you who will read my report.' The dignitary beamed with pleasure. I could not detect any embarrassment in his manner, nor any sign of a realization that the Professor's commission was in itself a disgrace to the ministry, to the government, to Indian scientists, and to the country. If I, Nirad Chaudhuri, had found that I could not work the NPL with Indians I would have blown it up with dynamite. But perhaps this bravado is due to the fact that Indians of my generation were brought up on *Self-help* by Dr Samuel Smiles, whom it has now become the fashion to deride.

Let me tell all timid Indians and all patronizing foreigners, whom I hear saying, 'But you cannot do without us,' that however uninstructed or inexperienced we might be at this stage, we really do not need the kind of help our Government is begging from every country. In my view the help is not even the spoon-feeding of babies, it is the forced feeding of geese by the dealers in *foies gras*. And the degraded begging has been made even more degraded by the importation of such English illiteracies as 'Know-how.' Have we forgotten our pride in Babu English, too?

This has been only a sampling of the dichotomy in Hindu life, offered as the canvassing of a working hypothesis. I do not think I have to expatiate on the relationship of these expressions of dichotomy in our foreign relations. That will have become obvious.

Endnotes

1. The writer does not apologize for using the word 'Hindu' in the heading instead of 'Indian'. The shyness of the Anglicized Hindus before this word is not even bashfulness of the bride, but a bizarre paradox of our intellectual behaviour, because it results in the obscuration, if not suppression, of the most massive, powerful, determinate, and active human phenomenon in India, the India of today as of the past — which is the Hindu way of life. The Anglicised Hindu does not know that the term 'Hindu' has no association of religion as distinct from secularity, and that its primary denotation is a simple definition of an ethnic group with all its outlooks and pattern of behaviour. In other words, it is just like the words 'British', 'French', or 'American'. In India there has never been an Indian pattern of life in which the different patterns of life presented by the diverse ethnic groups which constitute the Indian population, have been merged. So, to ignore the Hindu way of life is to reckon without the host, and to refuse to get introduced to the most powerful ethnic element in India. Or is it fear which keeps the Anglicised Hindus from employing the word? I think they are behaving in this matter like the common people who would not mention the dread names of 'tiger' or 'snake' at night. Neither tigers, nor snakes, nor the Hindus are going to be eliminated from our life by this subterfuge. – NCC.

2. 'Country made things are indeed such.'

On Caged Chaffinches and Polyglot Parrots

Jyotirmoy Datta

(Ten Years of Quest, Manaktalas, Bombay 1966,
eds. Abu Sayeed Ayyub and Amlan Datta)

Bird Song – experiments are being made in various parts of the country to find if birds inherit or learn their music. The method is to keep the bird, generally a chaffinch, in isolation from the time it emerges out of its egg and to make a graph of its song. These isolated chaffinches have songs without the characteristic final flourish, but they improve when tape recordings of the natural song are played to them. Groups brought up in isolation evolve slightly different songs of their own. But no captive bird has the full range of sounds of the wild songster. Dr H. Kalmus, Reader in Biology at University College, who has taken a leading part in the experiments, thinks it quite possible that there are bird dialects varying from place to place, and that nightingales may sing more beautifully in Provence than elsewhere.

That, I exclaimed as I hit upon this gem hidden in that ocean deep, Whittaker's Almanack, 1960, is true of our Indo-English writers too! Marooned in this sea of 360 million people, they are like isolated chaffinches – or, maybe, even nightingales. It is possible, I thought, these nightingales do not sing as well as those in Provence (Great Britain) but how can they help singing, and singing in their natural language? Granted, being isolated, these songsters have a stiff task and, the opportunities for learning being limited, they cannot help being repetitive. But no nightingale can, nor should, sing like chaffinches, nor chaffinches like nightingales – though by changing places, Cs could go one up in the social ladder of birds.

If English comes naturally to a person, no threat nor lure should be able to deter him from writing in English. There could be no dispute about it and yet, I was surprised to notice, there was. And, strangely, writers in English joined in the debate, writing long letters to editors of magazines in the fashion of the outraged taxpayers of Dum Dum or the members of the Society for Prevention of Cruelty to Otters.

The attempt to give reasons for their writing in English seemed strange to me because I felt that a poet or a novelist did not choose a language; if anything, it was the language that chose him. One can argue only when from among many alternatives he selects one; then his judgement, if questioned, can be defended with reasons cogent or false. I had supposed that all who wrote in India did so because they had to; it might be a misfortune for them but it was unalterable. Therefore, I thought, while those who asked them to defend what was none of their doing were being unfair, they themselves were guilty of irreverence towards English. No language is too poor for those who are born to it because it is possible to write a masterpiece in whichever language that comes naturally to one. But the Indo-English writers seemed to say that it was not enough for English to be one's own language, one had also to prove that it could do this or that which served the cause of Indian unity and world culture before one could write in it. Poor English!

If anyone asks – hybrid as our culture is, some do – why do I write in Bengali, all I can do is to stare at him. It seems to me the questioner has never written a line of verse or prose himself. My experience is that one does not first have a feeling or idea waiting to be translated into whichever language is best suited to it, but the feeling or idea takes shape as the words arise, suddenly and unbidden, in one's mind, words that seem to have been dictated to one at the unlikeliest time and place. That is the genesis; of course there is scope for planning and contrivance later. But be the genesis in Bengali, or English, or Swahili or any other language, I fail to see how one could switch on later to another language. The inner voice dictates to me in Bengali and therefore I write in that language. I admit no possibility of choice. I do not tell my tormentor that Bengali is a more musical language than most; it may be, but that is not why I write in it. I do not tell him that as most Bengali words end in vowels, it is a language so rich in rhymes that I am saved from rhyming 'blood' with 'brood' and 'freezes' with 'Jesus'; I recognize that though rhymes are of the utmost importance, great poems have been written in rhyme-short English, and anyway, Hawaiian has even more vowels than Bengali and yet I do not even dream of trying to write in Hawaiian. The market for Bengali books is bigger than for those in Oriya. True. But Chinese books should sell even better. Bengali is an international language spoken in two countries. Fact. But Hebrew is spoken throughout the world. Bengali is a more developed language than, say, Pustu? Bah! No language is more developed than another for writing good poems. There is absolutely no reason for writing in one language in preference to another except that the language of imagination is part of one's basic makeup; it precedes – not follows – choice. So, all that one can do is to accept one's fate and try to make the best of it silently and alone. There are many burning issues which need collective action, many bad choices (H-bomb, totalitarianism, the Beat cult) of which men must be warned, and good ones (free love, AID, referendum for Algeria) which people must be persuaded to accept, but the language one dreams in can hardly be the subject of controversy.

Surprised by the reaction of my fellow writers in English, I did a little bit of research. The results were startling. There were few Eurasians, very few, indeed, on the list of Indo-English writers. Some, just a few more than as many as one would call very few, though born of Indian parents, spoke no language but English. Many spoke English only just as well as one, or two, other Indian languages. But most knew an Indian language better than English. And most of them being dextrous in the use of more than one language, *Had Actually An Opportunity To Choose*! They may have chosen wrongly; their judgement may have misled them; maybe they were not good at reasoning, but we must admire them for daring to plan their destiny, to choose what their reason told them was the language best fitted for their aims.

Bastilled by 360 Million

Before going into the reasons for their choice, I would like to pay tribute to their heroism. They chose the most terrible sort of exile; the walls of their Bastille were 360 million people; like the fires of Dante's hell, these 360 million gave them no feeling of warm comradeship but intensified their sense of isolation. If only they had chosen silence too, they would all have been ideal Joycean heroes. But they could not be silent because they yearned for companionship; their attempts to persuade others to join them, their attempts to prove how Indian they were, their little booklets – miniature masterpieces of the book-marker's art – through which they communicated with one another over the heads of the separating millions, did show they were uncomfortable in their role of lonely heroes. But they were heroes all the same, and in our India ruled by the unlovely god, Demos, who can repress his admiration for them!

But Demos is a god who extracts his tithe even from unbelievers. The Indo-English writer claims he is the most Indian of us all. How? Because, says he, since English is the language of no particular Indian group (what about the Eurasians?), it is equally close (equally distant?) to all the groups and hence is the only language which is capable of expressing the spirit of all of India. English is today, claims the Indo-English writer, what Sanskrit was centuries ago: the language of the cultured elite throughout India. While Tamil poetry of the eighth century gave expression only to the Tamil spirit, Sanskrit poetry has influenced all the later vernacular writers. A similar role could be played by English, a most necessary role since India never had a greater need of unity than now.

I hope the Indo-English writer had not looked up the dates before advancing such an argument else he would be guilty of suppressing damning facts. The glorious age of Sanskrit poetry was simultaneous with the existence of Sanskrit as a living language; when the period of glittering decadence set in, Sanskrit was being gradually replaced by the vernaculars; Kalidasa is not the first of the great Sanskrit poets but the last; in the millennium between the sixth and the sixteenth century – when Sanskrit at last became the language of only the elite – no great poem was written in Sanskrit. English is today what Sanskrit was during that arid millennium. With the rise of the vernaculars, Indians became once again unilingualists – as were the contemporaries of Valmiki and Vyasa and the Upanishadic sages – and once again could create great literature which would not be mere treatises parodying the style of the ancients, mere mummies wrapped up in rules of grammar and rhetoric.

I cannot imagine writing in any language which I do not hear from living lips. Bengali is spoken in its purity by people all around me, purity which each moment is becoming impure – that is, archaic – and changed by the people and poets. It is an exciting experience for me to feel that through my efforts, and those of others, it is being continually changed. There is no use of my language which is too daring for me because what I write today need not be modelled on past usage but is likely to be a model for the future just because I have written thus. Nothing is too sacred for me to change; nothing too profane for me to use. It is my language, my very own, and no one can dispute my use of it.

Song of the Printed Page

English is not even the language of the educated few in India; it is used only to describe facts, figures and things, to give commands; not to suggest feelings but chart courses of action, not to explore new ideas but to communicate readymade ones. In schools and colleges, children are taught dead formulae for the use of certain words in set situations, but rarely do the students hear English spoken. As for English as a spoken language, there is not one but many such lingos because on the lips of Tamils it sounds like Tamil and when spoken by a Bengali, like Bengali. The Indo-English poet, even if he speaks English as it is spoken by those whose language it is, is locked up within himself, and though the inner music may sound enchanting to him, what a struggle must he put up to shut off those barbaric sounds that ceaselessly bombard his eardrums! And it is not only hard on his nerves, it deprives his imagination of the stimulus of living speech. The characters in his fiction seem wooden because the dialogue is dull and literary; the music of his verse too obvious, the lilt brazen, because his ears have been trained to listen only to the printed page, or, at best, to gramophone records of other poems. Novels feeding on past novels, poems springing from other poems – what a nightmare of sterility have our writers in English created for us!

'But our works have no relation to the language and literature of Great Britain,' protests the Indo-English writer. 'We do not wish to speak or write like Englishmen. Our language is new; only that it happens to share certain words with English but the way we use them is entirely our own. Ours is not an offshoot of English but as independent and autonomous as American literature. It is *Indian* literature. Our poems and novels should not be compared with English literary models but with the *Indian* reality, with the life of educated *Indians* living in towns, the all-*India* reality which only an all-*India* language can express.'

But is there any such thing as Indian English? Many examples of bad English, debased English, ungrammatical English, and baboo English come to mind but I have yet to come across a single specimen of Indian English. There is, of course, that magnificent example of baboo English, the autobiography of Onokool Chandra Mukherjee, and the stories by Mr Hamdi Bey with their eccentricities of grammar. But the grammatical lapses of Onokool Chandra and Mr Bey's delightful juggling with the tense are literary curiosities and have nothing in common with the way English is spoken or written in India; their style is as individual as Joyce's.

Maybe, I am misinterpreting the stand of the Indo-English writers. Though their language may not be distinctively Indian (it need not be), the content of their poems and novels may be so. If the sonnet can be used by a Bengali poet to express sentiments unknown to Petrarch, why should English be incapable of expressing Indian themes? Of course English can. Bengali too is capable of expressing feelings and ideas not yet grappled by its poets and novelists. But the question is not whether an English poet living in India could describe our tropical landscape and write good English poems about Indian problems, but whether the Indian who speaks a different language can and should do so.

The answer to this question given by the Indo-English writer seems so perverse to me that I am afraid if I give it in my own words, people will suspect me of having invented it. I have not. One who is perhaps the most talented Indo-English poet, P. Lal of *The Parrot's Death*, declares in *Writers Workshop* No.2: 'Without trying to be facetious, I should like to suggest that only in English can real Indian poetry be written; any other poetry is likely to be Bengali slanted or Gujarati biased, and so on. Only the Indian writing in English can hope to attain the Indian flavour which is a cosmopolitan flavour. I cannot imagine a Punjabi writing Bengali poetry, or a Maharashtrian writing Hindi poetry. But there are Tamilians, Bengalis, Punjabis, Gujaratis, Jews, Goans, Sikkimese – all Indians – writing in English on Indian themes for Indian readers.'

Fact. There are many such people. It is also a fact that during the nineteenth century many Bengalis wrote in Hindi on Hindi themes for Hindi readers. These facts have never been disputed. The dispute is over whether those Bengalis were able to use Hindi creatively and whether the 'Tamilians, Punjabis, Jews, Sikkimese' who write in English have created good poems and novels. Mr Lal cannot imagine 'a Punjabi writing Bengali poetry.' I can conceive of such a miracle happening. I would not say that a Punjabi can never, never, never compose good poems in English but the chances seem to me negligibly small. They should appear infinitesimal to Mr Lal who cannot even imagine 'a Punjabi writing Bengali poetry', but I am not sure whether he would be willing to apply to English the laws he has framed for mere Indian languages.

But be the chances one in a billion, or none at all, why should a Bengali or a Tamil write in English instead of his own language? 'Since Bengali literature is Bengali-slanted,' answers the IEW[1], 'and Gujarati literature Gujarati-biased, we cannot write in these "regional" languages. We want to write not about the limited reality that is Bengal or Gujarat but India – which is the bigger reality.' One cannot but sympathize with this desire to bite off as large a slice of reality as possible. That is what philosophers have been, and physicists are, trying to do, but such a desire is bound to remain unfulfilled in a poet because in literature the only way to express the universal is through the particular and the universe through the tiniest possible grain of sand. A poet writes to express neither the Bengali, nor the Indian, nor the Afro-Asian, nor the world, mind. If he wishes to realize any flavour, it is the flavour of himself. If he tries to express anything, it is himself. If he wants to be true to anybody, it is himself. If he tries to write about the *Bengali*, or *The Indian*, or about *Man*, he would be true to no man. These are so obvious as to be platitudes and yet I am forced to jingle these old (but gold) coins because the IEW does not seem to realize how true they are. The IEW's attempts to snatch the largest possible slice of experience is most likely to end in no genuine experience at all. And, anyway, if the IEW is really after universality, why must he top at the borders of India? Why not Afro-Asia? Or Afro-Eurasia? The world? Or even the solar system for how can we forget the poor Martians?

IEW and Universality

And what is this all-India 'flavour' that the IEW is after? If someone asked me what Europeanism was, I would reply that though Europeanism was difficult to define, it was a real quality. There is a group difference – what exactly I cannot say – between Chinese, Japanese, Persian and Arabic poetry and poems in Latin, English, German, French and Russian. The 'European' quality is not the monopoly of Latin literature; if at all, it is more marked in, say, modern German poems than in medieval Latin lyrics. German poetry has a German-bias, but I have yet to hear – even PhDs have not made this accusation – that its Germanic qualities take away from its Europeanism. If Goethe, with his 'world-hunger' and universal mind, had acted according to the IEW's beliefs, he would have written in French, the then pan-European language which he knew at least as well as our IEW's know English, and robbed his poetry not only of its teutonic qualities, not only of its poetic qualities, but also of its Hellenic and European 'bias'. No one was a better European because no one was a truer German. Similarly, if Pushkin had written in French, or if Turgeneyev also had – whom the Russian nationalists damned as a westerner – they would not have been better Europeans but only no artists at all – as Pushkin's school-boy effusions in French prove. And which of the IEWs, I ask, which of the IEWs are more Indian than Madhusudan Datta (who wrote his first poem in English) or a better citizen of the world than Rabindranath Tagore?

The assumption that because English is spoken by a number of people in many Indian towns and all the Indian cities, it must be more representative of India than the 'regional' languages is quite as false as it would be if someone claimed that Hebrew, which after the Dreyfus affair became the international Jewish language, is more of a 'world' language than French because it is spoken in all major commercial centres of the world. Hebrew literature, if it exists, is only the literature of the Hebrew-speaking people. The literature written by English-speaking Indians will be representative of only such people and – if it is good – indirectly also of India and the world. Many Tamils, Punjabis, Jews, etc. would, of course, be able to read IE literature, but how could the number or the geographic distribution of its readers affect its own nature? Many Britons and Germans read Valery in the original; all that this fact could indicate would be that these people might have been changed by having read Valery, but the poems themselves remain unalterable and immortal and are only as representative of the all-European reality as, say, the poems of Rilke.

Underdeveloped Languages

What other reason could there be for an Indian to write in English? One reason was suggested to me at a Writers Workshop meeting which I remember with both sorrow and pleasure. Pleasure, because the host was gracious, the beautifully furnished room a delight to (and the soft light soothing to) the eye and the Workshop members not only well-informed and intelligent but also such eager defenders of their cause and so sure of conquering the world that I felt grey and withered in face of their innocence. But why sorrow? Sorrow, because these very likeable persons were contemptuous of most of the Indian languages. One of them remarked that it was all right for me, a Bengali, to say that an Indian need not write in English but most Indian languages were not as developed as mine was, and, therefore, those who spoke the less developed languages were forced to write in English. Can anyone blame me for being shocked?

If there is one lesson to be drawn from the history of literature it is that the quality of writing does not depend upon the 'development' of the language. Rather, the early masters have an advantage over those who follow them. If the worth of works of imagination increased with the growth of a language then Homer would have been a lesser poet than Eurypides, Dante than Unagaretti, Shakespeare than Eliot, Goethe than George, and Pushkin than Akhmatova. Greatness comes easier in the infancy of a people and its language. What the Indo-English poet thinks as a disadvantage is the best bit of luck that one could wish for. If only the Anglo-Hindi, or the Anglo-Punjabi, poet realized what a tremendous opportunity he was throwing away! If, instead of staking his all on an impossible 1-to-1,000,000,000 gamble, he had accepted what a kind fate had thrust upon him, he could have been what Dante was to Italian, Pushkin to Russian and Madhusudan to Bengali. It would be a great day for themselves, for their own 'underdeveloped' languages and for English when the IEWs (who, it is obvious, are very talented people) returned to the languages they have treated so shabbily so far. Good for themselves because instead of being the darlings of their own insignificant coteries, lioncels of little literary cells, they could be true poets, initially read only in limited regions of India but later – it is not impossible – translated into all the languages of the world. Good for their own languages because no language can develop unless it has its Dante. And good for English because... well, the reasons are obvious.

There is one overwhelming reason for writing in English I have avoided mentioning so far. That supreme reason is – money. I have heard it said that an IEW got $2500 for a single novel in English. An even luckier IEW got almost as much from *The New Yorker* for writing 10,000 words of filth about India, and these 10,000 words being only a twentieth part of a book he is supposed to have written. Imagine how much he will get for his entire garbage bin! To one like me who is paid no more than 25 rupees (not dollars) even if he manages to get into *Desh* – and that is princely for a new writer – the amounts that the IEWs get are astronomical. Never before did so many tourists visit India, never before were so many Western glasses focused on this 'key-area in the battle for bread with ballots', never before did the West ask for so little in return for so much. Therefore, Indian 'material' fetches fabulous prices in the U.S. book 'market'. The right to make money through legal means is guaranteed in our Constitution, and I do not see why it should be denied to writers. Least of all can it be denied to the IEW who regards language as merely a tool – and a tool is merely a tool, valuable not for what it is but what it does.

But are there not just a few among all the IEWs who write not chiefly for money, nor recognition abroad, but because they must? Of course there are. There must be some, just a few more than as few as one would call very few, who cannot but write in English. They are the caged chaffinches who have all my sympathy in their stiff task. There is of course no way to tell the chaffinches from the parrots because the only test that one could propose is such that its results could never be known. But the IEWs themselves could carry it out in their imagination. It would convince no one except themselves, but then, the true poet has no need to prove to others why he must write in the language he writes and in that alone. The test is to imagine oneself marooned on an island far off the sea lanes. There is no hope of rescue. The poet broods gloomily for he lacks a pencil to put down the lines that rise in his mind. He totters down to the beach and writes on the sand. He does not care if the tide washes it away. He knows that even if he wrote on parchment no human eyes would be able to read his poems. Fame? The poet shrugs his shoulders as the thought – too, too familiar to him in the past – flits across his mind. Money? A faint smile crosses the face of the poet who is of course an introvert and therefore cannot climb coconut trees. 'Could money buy me those nuts in the trees, quite as far, as unattainably far, from me as the moon?' He still writes. He writes because there is a strange disturbance in him that cannot be got rid of except by writing. And whichever language he writes then is the true language of his soul.

Endnotes

1. The Indo-English writer must forgive me if, for brevity's sake, I call him IEW from now on. IEW is inelegant, I agree, but so is 'Indo-English Writer', or 'Indo-Anglican Writer', or 'Anglo-Indian Writer'.

Indian Writing in English:
A Reply to Mr Jyotirmoy Datta

P. Lal

(Ten Years of Quest, Manaktalas, Bombay 1966,
eds. Abu Sayeed Ayyub and Amlan Datta)

Before I settle down to a discussion of the points raised by Mr Jyotirmoy Datta (*Quest* 28) in his broadside against Indians writing creatively in English, I should like to record a sense of real regret at the tone of his article. Healthy discussion cannot exist in an atmosphere of innuendo and lampoon: if we must argue, let us respect each other's bona fides and discard the unpleasant (and, when you come to think of it, unnecessary) gimmicks of catchpenny journalism. Facts elevate, opinions only corrupt; and giving an ounce of sympathy does greater wonders than demanding a pound of flesh.

Mr Datta gives four reasons – he describes them as reasons – why the Indian writer in English (his codeword: IEW) 'chooses' to write in English. These are preceded by a few interesting (but not always, it seems to me, related or coherent) remarks in general about such writing. It is better that we clear up the preliminary confusion before we proceed to the hard core of Mr Datta's thesis.

1. In the first paragraph, Mr Datta draws a distinction between chaffinches and nightingales (a 'gem', he says, he discovered in 'that ocean deep, Whittaker's Almanack, 1960'). No nightingale can or should sing like chaffinches, he suggests, and vice-versa,

but 'by changing places chaffinches could go one up in the social ladder of birds.' This is surely hitting below the belt, for it implies that the Indian writes in English because he is a climber. Some, of course, are climbers; most, bless them, are just plodders. The slightly malicious imputation sets the tone of what follows – and it spoils, I think, one's case if all the time one casts doubts on the intentions of one's adversaries. This kind of googly is not cricket.

2. Mr Datta proceeds to remark: 'The Indo-English writers seemed to say that it was not enough for English to be one's own language, one had also to prove that it could be this or that which served the cause of Indian unity and world culture before one could write in it.' I cannot admire either the syntax or the sentiments of this sentence. The Workshop's principles and views must be very poorly expressed indeed if such a gross misinterpretation is possible. We have never tried to 'prove' anything about English, but we have tried to use it and later think about how we have used it, how it has affected our readers, and how best we can use it in future. The workshop is neither a factory nor a laboratory; just a group of people who do things because they have certain beliefs, and who like to examine what they (and others) have done, so that the quality of their writing might benefit from judicious doses of sympathetic criticism.

3. 'I fail to see how one could switch on later to another language,' says Mr Data in connection with what he describes as the 'choosing' of English for the purpose of creative writing. 'I admit no possibility of choice.' One wishes it were quite so easy really. Mr T.S. Eliot, to an interviewer in *Paris Review* recently, confessed that he once faced a choice. 'That was a very curious thing which I can't altogether explain.... I hadn't written anything for some time and was rather desperate. I started writing a few things in French and found *I could*, at that period.... That went on for months. The best of them have been printed. I had at that time the idea of giving up English and trying to settle down and scrape along in Paris and gradually write French. I don't think one can be a bilingual poet. And I think that the English language has more resources in some respects than the French.... I've probably done better in English.'

How one chooses is another matter. For the first time in India the possibility of such a choice being *real* and *meaningful* in terms of creative writing has concretized as a result of a fortuitous blend of historical circumstances. One might disagree with that, but to say that a choice cannot exist won't do. 'You pays your money and you takes your choice; aint freedom grand?' And if you loses your money, well…. Time's pretty ruthless anyway: look what it has done to Barrett Browning, the idol of the nineteenth century, and is doing to the *Gitanjali* translations in the West.

4. 'Bengali is a more developed language than, say, Pustu? Bah! No language is more developed than another for writing good poems.' I am tempted to say, 'Wah-wah!' and 'Shabash!' to this pretty splutter of good old-fashioned spleen, but we must not descend to the level of irrelevance (or, worse, irreverence). But humbly, very humbly, I should like to suggest that a language shows its mature quality in terms of the emotional spectrum it can successfully communicate without blurring the nuances of refined feeling. There are always over-reachers who will take up crude dialects and inject them with a range of subtleties that dazzles even a sophisticated reader. Such geniuses are rare; most of us have to make-do with what we have and, as the Workshop letter to *Quest* said, we are lucky 'to have English rich.' This is not to say that it is the *richest* – there is no such language. New dimensions are always being added, new directions constantly being given. Our belief is that English 'has proved its ability as a language to play a creative role in all-India literature.' Beliefs impel actions; and we shall continue to believe in this as long as we write in it. If Mr Datta believes that English is *not* more developed than Swahili or Pustu for the purposes of creative communication in the context of the contemporary literary milieu, that, in other words, it cannot communicate – other factors being equal – a wider range of ideas and sentiments and appeal to a more cultivated sensibility than Swahili or Pustu can, why, he is entitled to his belief as much as we are entitled to ours. But for God's sake, let's both of us hold our tongues, and get down to work – and to love – and to everything that's connected with this 'damned business of writing', as Pound called it, where one has to use one's heart all the time.

5. Mr Datta commiserates with the Indian writers in English because they are 'bastilled by 360 million people' (this needs correction: population's up by another 60 million since the last Census). They are 'Joycean heroes', he declares, 'they chose the most terrible sort of exile.' We don't think this is true: India is

still a pretty big country, and the world still bigger. But which creative writer isn't 'bastilled'? Don't Bengali publishers bring out poems in 500 copies an edition, and think themselves lucky if it sells out? *The Criterion*, under Eliot's discerning editorship, never collected more than 800 subscribers; Auden's Poems, as Julian Symons notes in *The 30s*, appeared in an edition of 1000 in 1930, and it took three years to exhaust the lot. Not very encouraging sales by any standards, but modern culture being what it is, what better can we expect? The alternative is sponsorship and dole. Give us state subsidy, and we won't be bastilled any more. But that isn't the kind of patronage one goes in for. Let Mr Datta note that the creative writer does not think of how many people are going to read him when he begins writing. He writes; and that's that.

6. Finally – so far as the preliminary confusion is concerned – Mr Datta makes certain allegations which are, to say the least, mystifying. He feels that 'a poet or a novelist did not choose a language; if anything, it was the language that chose him.' Some language, that! – but Mr Datta presumably means that a creative writer is born and nurtured in a specific linguistic milieu, or, as he puts it, 'I cannot imagine writing in any language which I do not hear from living lips.' He alleges further that most Indian writers in English 'knew an Indian language better than English', and that certain expedient, even artistically dishonest, reasons (enumerated below) made them take up English. I have met many Indian writers in English, some with established reputations, others not, and I can assure Mr Datta that only the hacks and quacks adopt English as their 'chosen' language or they know an Indian language better – they are the rejects, the sad exhibits of the profession, misfits, failed-creative-writers-turned-journalists, guilty things surprised who nibble at sour grapes. The real writer in English not only thinks, but makes love in English. English is at the tips of his senses.

These misreadings and misconceptions form the prologue to Mr Datta's enumeration of the four *real* reasons why some Indians have chosen to write in English. First, the Indian writer in English deliberately aims at what he describes as an 'all-India' audience and hopes to capture an 'all-India' flavour by virtue of writing in English, 'since Bengali literature is Bengali-slanted, and Gujarati literature Gujarati-based.' Secondly, he is 'contemptuous of most of the Indian languages' because he does not consider them 'developed' enough to be able to write creatively in. Mr Datta mentions a Workshop member telling him 'that it was all right for me, a Bengali, to say that an Indian need not write in English... but those who spoke the less developed language were forced to write in English. Can anyone blame me for being shocked?' (What is shocking is the twist given to what is really an innocuous remark, as I shall just show.) Thirdly, the 'one overwhelming reason I have avoided mentioning so far... the supreme reason,' in fact. Money. Dollars. Oodles of it. 'I have heard that an IEW got $2500 for a single novel in English. An even luckier IEW got as much from *The New Yorker* for writing 10,000 words of filth about India.... Imagine how much he will get for his entire garbage bin! To one like me who is paid no more than 25 rupees (not dollars) even if he manages to get into *Desh* – and that is princely for a new writer – the amounts that IEWs get are astronomical.' Finally, the fourth reason: the Indian writer in English is being dishonest to himself because he writes not out of inner compulsion but for utilitarian (and other sordid) reasons. Mr Datta proposes a test: maroon the writer on a desert island, and let us see what language he writes in. 'Whichever language he writes then is the true language of his soul.' The implication of course is that the Indian writer will not use English but his mother tongue. But in tests such as this, where hypothesis and fancy gallop on the backs of gay dolphins, the knife cuts both ways, and it's a fifty-fifty chance anyway. There is no answer really, unless we trust the honest voice; and Mr Datta will be 'surprised' – and 'shocked' – to find that all *creative* writers in English who matter will plump for English. I stressed in the very beginning the importance of bona fides in a controversy of this nature. Mud-slinging, muck-raking, suspicions, envies, sour grapes and bitter lemons – these will take us nowhere.

The creative writer in English in India takes his stand on certain principles. Some of these were embodied in the form of a manifesto appended to the Introduction to *Modern Indo-Anglian Poetry*, which Raghavendra Rao and I edited two years ago. It is absurd to suggest that we aim at an all-India audience and think we only can provide the 'all-India flavour'. It just so happens that English is, at present, a pan-Indian elite language. That involves certain responsibilities – and is in its own way rewarding and encouraging. But we do *not* write in English because it is a pan-Indian language of the educated; we write because we cannot write as well in any other language.

We are not 'contemptuous' of Indian languages. God forbid, even if Mr Datta doesn't. Their development is taken for granted, their contribution is mightily significant. Critical standards in these languages are, sometimes, lacking, deplorably so; but that is another matter. We are speaking of creativity. There are many plots to till; English is one. We have chosen it; or, if Mr Datta would prefer a pretty chiasmus, it has chosen us. If we are left free to cultivate this little garden, we'll be most delighted. But mockery – the hose-pipe flooding our bougainvillea, the locusts settling on our brinjals – we do not like. We care for sympathy and encouragement: and if these can't be given, just leave us alone, for heaven's sake. We can look after ourselves and our art.

We do not all get $2500 for 'a single novel'. Some do. The Sahitya Akademi has awarded prizes to various works in the Indian languages, but ignores English. Publishers outside India are more helpful: and we don't sniff at money when it comes. Besides, even in India, the English language papers and magazines have higher rates of payment than their vernacular counterparts. This is the result of a historical situation. It may well change. If it does, if English loses its position as an elite language, and we start getting the 'princely' sum of Rs. 25 for an article or story, we'll take that in our stride too. One doesn't quarrel all the time, and mope, and self-pity. One just goes ahead, doing what one values; if the money comes, good; if it doesn't, that's just too bad. We are not the first to have sat in tea-shops while the tempest hurled, and cursed our fate for what we got. And if Mr Datta is so cruelly kind as to maroon us – he has bastilled us anyway – on an island, we'll write sad lyrics on the sand, alas in English, and send out carrier pigeons and/or parrots loaded with free verse (in English), even if they get short *en route*.

About this there should be no doubt – we write in English because we feel we are 'doin' what just comes 'natcherly'. In our letter to *Quest*, which sparked off this controversy, we had said that 'the writer is not an ambidextrous man, who can switch from one language to another at will.' Many factors combine to make him write in the language he does write in. Zofia Ilinska is Polish, but writes in English; Koestler writes only in English now, though he is Hungarian; and Nabokov's decision is another on the list. What should matter is the quality of writing turned out, not the hows and whys of the choice. What I can suggest, therefore, is that we discard pettiness and petulance, and stress good faith and honest purpose.

Persistence of the Caste System: Vested Interest in Backwardness

Subhash Chandra Mehta

(Quest 36: Winter 1962-1963)

It is my aim in the present paper to study the impact of various recent trends in the political, economic, social and technological fields on the institution of caste and to see whether the caste system is on the wane and it is just a matter of time before we bury it, or whether it continues to be a dominant force.

Constitutional and Political Factors:

Formally, with the promulgation of the Constitution on January 26, 1950, the caste system lost its basis. The very preamble of the Constitution asserts that the people of India have constituted themselves into a sovereign democratic republic to secure to all its citizens justice, liberty and equality and to promote fraternity. Justice is specifically described to be of three types, not only political but economic and social as well. And equality is not only of opportunity but also of status. Justice and equality, as thus defined, between them strike at the very roots of caste.

The fundamental rights guaranteed under the Constitution are those of equality, non-exploitation, freedom of religion, culture and education, property and constitutional remedies. Of these, for the purpose of the present study, the rights of equality and freedom alone are pertinent. In 'guarantee of the right of equality', Article 15 states: (1) the State shall not discriminate against any citizen on the ground of caste; (2) no citizen shall, on the ground of caste, be subject to restriction regarding access to or use of shops, restaurants and public wells and tanks; and (3) the practice of untouchability is forbidden. The right of freedom guarantees, among other things, practice of any lawful calling without restriction. The Constitution may thus be said to have abolished caste and its lingering restrictive and coercive practices, and, on the positive side, to have proclaimed the creation of a society in which inequality of status does not exist.

But while the Constitution has abolished caste, certain factors have emerged either as a direct result of the Constitution or other political policies, influencing the caste structure. Acceptance of the democratic form of government naturally implies adult franchise. The result of adult franchise has been that many social groups have become aware of their strength and realize that they are in a position to wield power. In the traditional caste system one dominant caste alone had a corporate political existence; the other castes were ineffective. But now all castes large enough to make their strength felt are corporate political bodies. All over India, there is evidence that castes, organized to the width of the linguistic region, are politically active and courted by political parties.

Another political factor influencing caste in India has been the lack of organized special-interest groups. Only a small fraction of peasants and workers are yet organized in Indian society and, therefore, there are few outside loyalties to temper the intensity of loyalty to caste. As many potential political elements are not organized, an element of latency in politics is created. The result is that unorganized and generally inarticulate segments find ways of expressing themselves.

The gradual adoption of the system of democratic decentralisation has also fanned caste consciousness at the village level. Each caste has become conscious of the power it can wield. The members vote on various issues not from the viewpoint of the total community but of exclusive caste interests. On the positive side, however, the establishment of *panchayats* has helped to bring representatives of all castes together in one organization which ultimately may help in developing a sense of community.

A recent trend affecting caste has been the gradual acceptance of the principle of social justice in regard to those hitherto called untouchables (Harijans). The Constitution lays down as one of the Directive Principles of State Policy, that the State shall promote with special care, the educational and economic interests of the weaker sections of the people ... and shall protect them from social injustice and all forms of exploitation.

There is no doubt that untouchability is the worst feature of the caste system. If the caste system had not developed untouchability, there might have been many more who would have upheld the system. Untouchability has been abolished by law in modern India. The Untouchability Act passed by the Union government is applicable to all states. No doubt, legislation alone does not change society and social laws affecting the caste system should be viewed at best as no more than the definition of ultimate objectives to be achieved. Nevertheless they do indicate the goals towards which India is trying to move.

Effect of Economic Development:

It cannot be denied that urbanism and industrialism will ring the death-knell of the caste system. It is a fact that modern factory organization cannot be efficiently geared to the caste system. In the markets, factories, tea-shops, members of the different castes work and eat together defying the ancient restrictions of commensality and exclusive living.

Increasing efforts for the economic development of the country have also led to the development of transport and communications which tend to minimize the rigidity of the caste system. In trains and buses, in hostels, cinema halls and clubs, people are thrown together irrespective of caste. There are no untouchable travellers. The traditional caste system, with its usages of pollution and avoidance, can, as Dr Marriott says, only be conceived of as working in 'small packages'.

Another factor which is weakening the caste system is the coming into being of new types of occupations due to industrialisation. Apart from this, any individual can take up the study and practice of medicine, engineering, law etc. Recruitment to the defence services has been opened to all and no distinction is made between 'martial' and 'non-martial' races. Similarly, other public offices are open equally to all Indian citizens except for certain reservations (which conduce to the break-up of caste) for members of the Scheduled Castes and Tribes.

The extent to which there has been change of occupations can be seen from the 1951 Census which reported that of 5.13 crores of scheduled castes, only 64 lakhs were engaged in occupations that could be described as those reserved for untouchables. The 1961 census further confirms this reading.

But there is a section which feels that economic development has in some ways increased the solidarity and resilience of caste. The development of communications, together with the growth of publication has widened the range as well as the all-India solidarity of caste through the growth of caste newspapers, journals and conferences. Even the motor car drivers now form a new 'sub-caste'.[1] Srinivas also expresses a similar opinion that while, on the one hand, railways and factories have relaxed rules of pollution regarding eating and drinking and other forms of contact, on the other, the availability of cheap paper has enabled caste disputes to be recorded, and this gives permanent form to rules and precedents which were till recently dependant upon the fallible, therefore challengeable, memory of elders. He adds that several castes in Gujarat have even had their constitutions printed.[2]

Spread of Education:

Social institutions of the community are always affected by the spread of education. Professor Kuppuswamy studied the attitudes of students in South India and commented that many non-Brahmin youths assert that they look upon the caste system as intolerable and are prepared to abolish it. This opinion is reflected consistently with respect to the three important problems of marriage, dining, and the letting of house. Most of them are also non-conformists in matters of religious practice.[3]

However, the effects of education should not be exaggerated. The educated may have spent much time in activities outside the sphere of caste, but the more intimate core of their life is influenced by it. One needs only to turn to matrimonial advertisements where doctors, engineers, high government officials, people trained abroad, all indicate their caste and require brides of the same caste. Even 'highly cultured' and 'educated' brides want bridegrooms from their own caste. There are exceptions, to be sure, but they are few. Two classmates of different castes may dine together in a restaurant, but are usually not able to do so in each others' homes.

Sanskritisation and Westernisation:

To denote another trend, Professor M.N. Srinivas recently introduced the concepts of Sanskritization and Westernization in the study of caste dynamics. According to him 'the caste system is far from a rigid system in which the position of each component caste is fixed for all time. Movement has always been possible, and especially so in the middle regions of the hierarchy. A low caste was able, in a generation or two, to rise to a higher position in the hierarchy by adopting vegetarianism and teetotalism, and by Sanskritising its rituals and pantheon. In short, it took over, as far as possible, the customs, rites, and beliefs of the Brahmins, and the adoption of the Brahminic way of life by a low caste seems to have been frequent, though theoretically forbidden. This process has been called Sanskritisation.'[4] The rigid-division of Hindu society into various castes has in a sense accelerated this process because in any hierarchical system there is always a tendency to imitate the customs, habits and manners of the dominant group. 'It is possible that the very ban on the adoption of the Brahminical way of life by the lower castes had exactly the opposite effect. The forbidden fruit was the tastier one.'[5] Among the customs taken over were clothing, jewellery, cooking, vegetarianism, teetotalism; at times even the name of the caste was changed. The non-Brahmins not only adopted Brahmnical rites and customs but also institutions. Srinivas corroborates this by referring to marriage position of women, and kinship. 'Among Hindus, there is preference for virginity in brides, chastity in wives, and continence in widows. This is especially marked among the highest castes. The lower have not been very rigid in their sex code, but as the castes rise in the hierarchy, they become more and more Sanskritised and, in sex and marriage, the code of the Brahmins is taken over. Widow remarriage and divorce are restricted.'[6] By Westernisation, Professor Srinivas means the acceptance of the western cultural ethos and ideas by the caste Hindus and the attempt by them to accept, adopt or imitate British customs and habits. Westernisation resulted in increasing the social distance between the upper castes and other lower castes and brought the former closer to the British rulers, which in turn enabled them to acquire political and economic advantages. As the Brahmins were at the top of the social hierarchy, it was possible for them to adopt new practices without being subjected to ridicule.

The lower castes are trying to Sanskritise while the upper castes are Westernising themselves. When the Sanskritisation of the lower caste is complete, it tries in turn to Westernise itself. It may take, let us say, two generations for a lower caste to Sanskritise and then another two generations for it to Westernise itself; that is to say, in the course of four to six generations, a caste, if it is lucky, can go up from the bottom to the top of the caste ladder.

Shift in the criteria for aid:

In accordance with the provisions of the Constitution, the Government of India and the State governments have been giving preferential treatment in matters of recruitment, education, etc., to certain lower castes to bring them gradually on a level with other well-placed castes. The purpose of these measures was to upgrade the lower castes; instead, they sometimes seem to have down-graded the higher ones. Instead of the Harijan becoming a Brahmin, the Brahmin is becoming a Harijan. According to Srinivas, backwardness and forwardness do not go by caste in modern India – at least not any longer. The tendency to continue to think in terms of backward and forward castes is producing new tensions and difficulties which may become more intractable in the future. The country's hope lies in accepting rational criteria of backwardness and in abandoning the tendency to categorise hereditary groups as backward or forward.'[7]

He further says: 'An individual's backwardness can be determined by reference to the father's (guardian's) income, educational level and place of residence (rural or urban). When an applicant's father has a small income, a low level of education and is residing in a village, it means that the applicant is backward, be he Harijan, Rajput, Bania or a Brahmin.

'It is necessary to give weightage to one more factor. The children of manual labourers should be regarded as backward as compared to those whose parents do not do manual work. Unskilled manual work should be regarded as more backward than skilled manual work.'[8]

When these criteria are considered together, they give an index of the backwardness of an individual. No doubt, the policy pursued by the Government of India of giving preferential treatment to the low castes is in accordance with humanitarian sentiments, but it also has the effect of making the lower castes look up to the government for protection. It drives a wedge between the higher and the lower castes.

These are thus some of the important factors affecting the caste system in modern India. It is clear that regardless of the many factors which are supposed to be disrupting the system, it has withstood all onslaughts and is still a strong and tenacious force. To believe that the demon of caste is about to die is to grossly underestimate the social forces that bind a caste group together and perpetuate casteism. It is true that today there is greater mobility within the caste system than ever before, but that is quite different from having achieved an egalitarian society. While in the past caste had, by and large, tended to be negative (with its emphasis on the restrictive aspects of the social behaviour of the members), the modern trends are only making it more positive by forcing the caste-members to come together and take collective action to preserve their identity.

The Political Role of Caste:

Caste today is not merely a subject of academic research. It has become a problem for administrators, statesmen and the general public. Commenting on the Indian elections, Mr Jayaprakash Narayan said: 'Caste was the only party and ideology which fought the elections. Political ideology or economic programme as such had very little to do with the elections.'

The modern political ideas of democracy and liberty throw a challenge to the basic principles of the caste system. The problem is whether a democratic state can co-exist with a society based on caste. Dr B.R. Ambedkar once said: 'Take the Hindu social system and examine it from the point of social utility and social justice. It is a religion which is not intended to establish liberty, equality and fraternity. It is a gospel which proclaims the worship of the superman – the Brahmin – by the rest of the Hindu society.'[9] Democracy does not exist merely in its formal institutions. It lives really and truly in the life of the people; it is a way of life. It is not only through the representative assemblies that democracy works but also through the social institutions and actions of the citizens. Caste is one of those social institutions which have always exercised a predominant hold on the public and social life of the Indian society.

Barnes while analysing American culture says, 'Classical culture fell because Greek and Roman ideals and institutions – utopian philosophy and imperial politics – got ahead of the limited technology, especially in the realm of transportation. Our culture, on the other hand, is gravely threatened because our machines have moved far beyond our social thinking and institutional patterns.'[10] Indian society faces this dilemma – but in a far acuter form. Since independence, India has embarked upon huge industrialization programmes. In the fields of science and technology she is moving ahead with considerable speed. But the social institutions through which the mechanical facilities are going to be used are old and antiquated. Thinking in terms of caste is so deeply embedded in the minds of the Hindus, and, for that matter the Indian nation, that our entire outlook is coloured by it. Communalism, factionalism and groupism are only manifestations of this basic evil. 'Every one of the hundreds of sections into which this nation is divided suffers from discrimination and every group practices discrimination against others. In a homogeneous society, the innumerable acts of injustice which happen every day are regarded as individual faults. In our society they become minority grievances.'[11] Caste erects a powerful barrier against the emotional integration of the people of India. It divides them into numerous small and hierarchically arranged groups, and a man's loyalties tend to be absorbed by his immediate group.

Caste not only divides Indians into highborn and low-born, but into regional sub-caste compartments. Each of these 3,000 odd regional sub-castes can be described as an extended joint family. 'Beyond this', writes K.M. Pannikkar, 'the Hindu in practice recognizes no society or community. This is the widest social group that the Hindus evolved – the bed-rock on which the Hindu social organization is built.'[12]

It is argued that caste provides channels of communication and bases of leadership and organization which enable our rural masses to participate in democratic politics. But while, on the one hand, caste has helped in educating the masses in India politically, on the other, it also comes in the way of the growth of a healthy nationalism, which often supplies backward countries with the energy and devotion necessary for rapid development.

Stake in Political Power:

Acquisition of power has become a living reality in the new democratic set-up, and every caste and region wants to acquire as much of it as it can. Since the upper castes often refuse to recognize the achievements of individuals of low castes who may, for example, acquire education, these individuals conclude that mobility on any significant scale must be a group phenomenon. With the limited educational facilities, jobs and promotions at our disposal, every caste group tries to elbow out another for the lion's share of these. It is the economic gain, which is expected to follow the establishment of political power, that motivates caste political rivalries, especially when increasing economic opportunities coincide with increased government regulation in economic life.

There is a growing feeling that not only are elections fought on caste lines and party tickets allotted on the same basis but recruitment and promotions also are determined on caste criteria. A caste which is politically strong is able to fight successfully for schools, roads, hospitals, electric power and industries in the area in which it is dominant. Every state cabinet contains members from the main dominant castes, and the ministers are expected to be the watchdogs of the interests of their respective castes if they wish to continue in power.

Caste has been able to perform this new role by developing a new form of political activity, the caste association (Sabha). Over the last forty or fifty years, caste associations have increased in number and strength. After independence, it has become increasingly apparent that they would be a central feature of Indian politics for quite some time to come.

Vested Interest in Backwardness:

Indeed, in the southern states of India, we witness the fantastic spectacle of a competition among caste groups to be included in the list of Backward Classes. Mahatma Gandhi could never have foreseen a time when backwardness, instead of being a disability, would become a description that sections of the Indian population would choose and struggle for, yet this is what is happening, and (among others) the sociologist, Dr M.N. Srinivas, has done well to suggest that it is high time to ask whether we as a nation can afford to handicap, if not penalize, ability and character in favour of non-rational criteria? There are about 15 crores of people in India belonging to the Backward Classes. About two-fifths of the backward people belong to the Scheduled Castes, a little less than one-fifth to the Scheduled Tribes, nearly two-fifths to the other Backward Classes, and the remainder to the Denotified Tribes. The Mysore Backward Classes Committee (1961), noted: 'The general demand put forward by almost every community was that it was extremely backward and that, therefore, it should be included in the list of backward classes.' The reactions which followed the publication of this report are important indicators to the involvement of caste in politics. The committee had originally excluded the powerful Lingayat caste from the category of backward classes. This was immediately followed by intense political campaigning by the Lingayats, leading within a very short time, to them also being listed as 'Backward'.

Neither of the two communities in Mysore state, Lingayats and Okkalgas, can now truthfully claim to be politically, economically or educationally backward as a class and yet they want to cling to the privileges conferred by the label. In theory, the notification of some classes as 'backward' was supposed to serve the purpose of the Governments, Central and in the States, taking special steps to bring up underprivileged sections of the community to the economic and social levels of the more advanced. In practice, there has been a veritable competition among castes and sub-castes be listed as 'Backward'. The result is that what was intended to be a means of protection of the rights of weak minority groups has in effect become a tool of aggrandisement in the hands of politically dominant, because numerically large, caste groups in many States. Repeated efforts by the Centre to devise a workable set of criteria for drawing up an all-India list of 'Backward Classes' have so far proved unsuccessful. At present, the State lists continue to be used. These vary widely, having been drawn up over the years in response to the particular conditions and political pressures of the states concerned. In Mysore, for instance, everybody belongs to the Backward Class except the Brahmins.

The Government of India has taken note of this very undersirable development not only by deciding not to have any backward classes list of its own but also by advising State governments that if there is to be any listing of backward classes at all, it should be done in the light of economic rather than caste criteria. Economic criteria, however, are hard to define and apply and any possible formula that may be put forward is likely to bristle with potential anomalies. In any case, representation in the public services has political as well as economic significance and minority groups, whether in terms of language or political vulnerability, have as reasonable a claim to fair representation as economically weak sections of the community. Perhaps, the most practical course would be to fix an empirical limit, defined as a certain, relatively low percentage of the population, to the aggregate numerical strength of 'Backward Classes' a State government may recognize. This would reduce the opportunities open to the politically dominant castes to misuse it until such time as it can be abolished altogether.

Administrative Inefficiency:

Writing about increased railway accidents, Touchstone remarked, 'There are today ugly whispers of deteriorating morale among railwaymen as a direct result of some of the staff policies planned and pursued at the highest level. The reservation of 15 per cent of promotions to the Scheduled Castes, in particular, is held to be responsible for extensive heartburning and discontent. Although 15 per cent may seem only a fraction, it is evident that for everyone who is promoted purely on a caste basis, there may be ten or more who feel that their merit has been unjustly ignored. If a number of such cases of preferential treatment takes place, it is conceivable that the consequence will be the creation of a very considerable army of disgruntled and demoralised officials who can be a serious liability to the Administration.'[13]

Recognition is given to caste even in the matter of admission to medical and engineering colleges where seats are reserved for certain communities. In Mysore, (where Brahmins may apply for only one in five government posts) barely 30 per cent of the seats in medical and engineering colleges are allotted on the basis of merit. It may be recalled in this connection that Article 29(2) of the Constitution of India guaranteeing that 'no citizen shall be denied admission into any educational institution maintained by the State or receiving aid out of State funds, on grounds only of religion, race, caste, language or any one of them' was amended in 1951 to provide for reservation of seats in schools and colleges on the ground of caste. The Constitution (First Amendment) Act was passed in 1951 and added the following in Art. 15 of the Constitution.

'Nothing in this Article or Clause (2) of Article 29 shall prevent the State from making any special provision for the advancement of any socially or educationally backward classes of citizens or for the Scheduled Castes and Scheduled Tribes.' The Amendment Act arose out of the case of Champakan Dorairajan Vs. the State of Madras: Miss Dorairajan, a Brahmin girl, was refused admission to a college in Madras and she filed a writ petition in the Madras High Court. The Court held that Communal Government Order, under which the action was taken, was ultra vires of the Constitution. The Madras government appealed to the Supreme Court which upheld the decision of the Madras High Court. The Amendment of the Constitution was thus prompted by the decision of the Supreme Court.

The ten-year period of reservation of legislative seats and government posts came to a close in the year 1960. Yet it was given a further 10-year lease of life. The Railway Ministry, on its part, has stretched the principle of reservation even to promotions. The effect of all this is to encourage the different sections of the population to think in terms of their being separate entities.

In this context a distinction must be drawn between the Scheduled Castes and Tribes on the one hand and the 'Backward Classes' on the other. The decision to accord preferential treatment to the former was perhaps justified in the circumstances in which it was taken. These communities constituted minorities which had suffered social oppression for generations and were really at the bottom of the social and economic ladder. The motives behind their uplift were largely humanitarian. But the concessions progressively granted to a wide variety of castes by labelling them 'Backward' cannot always be explained in purely humanitarian terms. There can be little doubt that in at least a number of cases, political pressures have been equally important.

Reservation on the basis of caste is bound to result in lowering of standards. When a person is more or less assured of a position because he belongs to a particular caste, he is naturally inclined to put in less than his best. Moreover, a candidate who is abler and more efficient is often bypassed because he does not belong to the right caste. This not only leads to decline in standards but is also against the principles of social justice.

These are thus some of the new spheres of activity in social and political life into which caste has entered. We may conclude this paper with the remarks of Dr Radhakrishnan at the National Integration Conference held in September, 1961. Speaking of the danger of exploiting caste loyalties for wining elections or getting jobs, Dr Radhakrishnan said: 'Though caste is today ceasing to be a social evil, it has become a political evil; it has become an administrative evil. We are utilizing these caste loyalties for the purpose of winning our elections or getting people into jobs, exercising some kind of favouritism or nepotism.'

Endnotes

1. Healey, John: Caste and Economic Development in India – Religion & Society, Vol. V, No. 3, Sept. 1958.

2. Srinivas, M.N.: Caste in Modern India – Journal of Asian Studies, Vol. XVI, No.4, 1957.

3. Quoted by Murphy, G: In the Minds of Man, pp. 108-9.

4. Ajyappan and Balaratnam: Society in India, 1956, pp. 73.

5. *Ibid*, p. 76.

6. Barnabas, A.P.: Sanskritisation, Econ. Weekly, April 15, 1961.

7. Srinivas. M.N.: 'There is vested interest in backwardness' – Statesman, Oct. 9, 1961.

8. Srinivas, M.N.: 'Origins of Backward Classes Movement in India' – Statesman, Oct. 10, 1961.

9. Ranade, Gandhi and Jinnah, pp. 24, 25.

10. Barnes, H.E.: Social Institutions, p. 17.

11. Menon, V.P.: 'Dangerous Decades' – Hindustan Times, Independence Day Supplement, 1961

12. Indu Society at Cross Roads, 1955, p. 12.

13. The Hindustan Times, New Delhi, Nov. 16, 1961, p. 7.

Current Politics:
Reflections on the Chinese Invasion:
Anguished Awakening

Sibnarayan Ray

(Quest 36: Winter 1962-1963)

I

China's undeclared war on India is fraught with many dark possibilities, but its most immediate consequence should be the welcome disintegration of two powerful ideological myths which have exercised enormous influence on Asian intellectuals over the last few decades. The first of these myths was ably formulated as early as 1903 by Okakura in the very opening sentence of his *Ideals of the East*: 'Asia is one.' Like all myths this one too was centred round a hard grain of factual truth, namely, the ubiquitous exploitation of the stagnant communities of Asia by the more dynamic nations of Europe. This fact was used to sustain a whole framework of passionately held beliefs in a common 'oriental' culture and destiny in contradistinction to a no less legendary 'occidental' civilization. The new ideology of pan-Asianism obstinately refused to recognize that the cultural differences among India, China and the Islamic countries of the Middle East were at least as pronounced as between any one of them and Western Europe, that in the West too there were a number of conflicting traditions, and that Asian destiny in the twentieth century was to be determined by a choice which was in no sense peculiarly Asian but universal and modern. This refusal powerfully obstructed the growth of moral and intellectual maturity in Asia.

Japan's treacherous attack on China in the thirties was the first major shock to pan-Asianism. The shock was however, absorbed without a great crisis of conscience because of Asian obsession with western imperialism. During the Second World War, to the overwhelming majority of Asian nationalists the real villains were the Allied Powers, so much so that Subhash Chandra Bose was made into the archetypal Asian hero and few bothered to remember the fearful record of his friends – in China, Abyssinia or Czechoslovakia. Even after the spectacular disintegration of European empires in Asia and Africa during the forties and fifties, most of the newly emerging nations of the East refused to outgrow their pre-independence habits of thought inspite of the pressures of post-independence problems and responsibilities. The concept of an Afro-Asian bloc was an extension of the earlier pan-Asian illusion.

The second myth owes its origin and effective propagation to the ingenious leaders and publicists of the Soviet Union. Lenin, even more than Marx, is responsible for the widespread belief or make-belief among Asian intellectuals that all wars in the present age are due to Capitalism, and that Communism by its very nature means world peace. During the first two decades after the Revolution, the rulers of the Soviet Union were far too preoccupied with internal struggles for power and problems of stabilisation to consider seriously any programme of expansion through war and conquest. The Leninist thesis thereby acquired a spurious plausibility, especially among the naïve political leaders of the poor and exploited nations of Asia, many of whom had already been deeply impressed by the Communist promise of equality, social justice and material advancement. Close and critical acquaintance with Communist theory and practice would, of course, have made it evident that Communism is the very opposite of pacificism, that its aggressive ideology not only requires but would theoretically justify 'revolutionary' wars, and that through the network of communist parties in various countries of the world, the Soviet Union was actually waging a subterranean war on an international scale. But such acquaintance was and still is rather rare in Asia. In any case, the highly streamlined propaganda machine of world communism was employed to imbue the leadership of the newly awakening nations with faith in the pacificist professions of the Soviet Union. The ruthless suppression of the Hungarian revolution by the Red Army did raise some misgivings, but they were greatly weakened by the Anglo-French fiasco over Suez. Khrushchev's 'co-existence' theory also helped considerably to reinforce the illusion.

For nearly four decades the Indian political intelligentsia, by and large, has been a victim of these two insidious myths. Even Mr Nehru, essentially an internationalist and democrat, did not altogether escape their spell. Since independence, Indian neutralism under his leadership has hardly been quite neutral; most of the time it has been ever so slightly tilted in favour of the Communist powers and the so called Afro-Asian bloc. When China went communist, it profited greatly from this twofold illusion on the part of India. Against every evidence, the Indian government clung tenaciously to the thesis that Mao's China could never have aggressive intentions since it was not only Asian but also communist. Its armed intervention in Korea was glossed over by Indian public opinion. Even the rape of Tibet did not succeed in awakening the Indian political leadership to the imperial aspirations of Communist China.

With cynical deliberation, China took full advantage of this myth-fed naiveté of the Indian people and the Indian government. On the one hand, China professed Panchsheel, peace and Asian solidarity; on the other, it made large territorial claims, built up its military might and manoeuvred to isolate India from her friends and neighbours. It advocated settlement of frontier disputes by peaceful negotiation, and at the same time went on nibbling at Indian territory. Even then, India's reaction was no more positive than one of pained bewilderment. She sent long letters of friendly protest, but took hardly any measures to defend herself against Chinese aggression. Consequently, when the Chinese finally launched in October massive attacks on both the North-western and the North-eastern fronts, India found herself utterly unprepared for the showdown.

It will not stand security to argue that India's unpreparedness is due primarily to her moral scruples against the use of military means to settle disputes. India certainly did not hesitate to use her army in Kashmir when the Maharajah appealed for help, nor did she rely on Gandhian methods in liberating Goa from the Portuguese. It should also not be overlooked that India has been spending a not very negligible share of her revenue on defence. The inescapable conclusion seems to be that India's unpreparedness in the face of Chinese aggression is due far less to her general advocacy of non-violence than to her systematic refusal to confront the Chinese reality. That refusal in its turn was primarily inspired by the double illusion of Asian solidarity and communist pacifism. The extent of India's unpreparedness has been agonizingly revealed in the course of the last few weeks. On both the fronts, one post after another has fallen to the Chinese invaders. At this writing, the Chinese seem to have secured full strategic advantage; and India's main chance of halting their advance lies for the time being at least more with an early winter in the mountains than with the defensive strength of her valiant army. For this dismal situation the main share of blame should, of course, go to India's erstwhile defence minister. Mr Menon's resignation from the Cabinet, although highly belated, is a welcome step in the right direction. However, the Indian political intelligentsia would only be deceiving itself if it did not acknowledge its own share of responsibility for this state of unpreparedness. After all, Mr Menon could not have won in the last general elections with a convincing majority without the explicit support of his own party colleagues and of many liberal intellectuals in the country.

II

China's invasion of India is presumably encouraged in no small measure by the latter's obdurate unwillingness to wake up to the reality. However, it is unlikely that an overt conflict could have been postponed indefinitely. Purely geo-political considerations would indicate that in Asia today China's most formidable potential rival is India. A stable and prosperous India would be a constant threat to the Chinese bid for supremacy in South Asia. Moreover, as good communists, the leaders of Red China are firmly convinced that history is on their side, that it is both necessary and obligatory on their part to promote revolutions elsewhere, and that red Napoleonism is a perfectly legitimate method for spreading communism, especially in countries where the local communist parties are not strong or determined enough to bring off the revolution on their own. Almost from the very beginning, Red China has been opposed to the 'revisionist' theory of co-existence and peaceful revolution. Its self-imposed role as the 'liberator of Asia' has been made all the more urgent by Russia's reluctance to risk a nuclear war for the sake of world communism. China would have attacked

India sooner or later because this was indispensable to its programme of Asian liberation.

But possibly the most decisive factor in China's hostility to India is the latter's commitment to democracy. I have mentioned earlier that Asian destiny in our times will be moulded by a choice which is not specifically Asian but universal. That choice is between totalitarian dictatorship and libertarian democracy. The choice presented itself sharply to Europe after the First World War; today it confronts the newly emerging nations of Asia. Red China has unambiguously plumped for totalitarianism. India, on contrary, has chosen the alternative of democracy. Not that this commitment can be called altogether unambiguous; otherwise India would not have had to wait so long to recognize the reality of Red China. However, inspite of her pan-Asian illusion and myopic trust in communist professions, India since independence has been pursuing democratic principles and practices far more closely than possibly any other country in Asia and Africa. This does not mean that anti-democratic forces and tendencies are not strong in this country. We have, for example, to reckon with the two powerful organizations of the CPI and the RSS; our caste system is extremely well-entrenched; and political and cultural tribalism in its various manifestations continues to obstruct all efforts in the direction of democratic development. Nevertheless, it is admitted even by India's critics that during the last decade and a half, India's main endeavour has been to establish and promote conditions essential to her development as a full-fledged democracy. Not only has India forged a genuinely democratic constitution for herself; she has also made considerable headway towards social justice and material progress without violating the fundamental rights and liberties guaranteed by her constitution. The rule of law has already struck deep roots in this country; the independence and integrity of the Indian judiciary is above reproach; the three general elections on the basis of universal adult suffrage have been on the whole free and fair; and inspite of the stress of tensions and conflicts, there have been no serious attempts to interfere with the rights of free association and expression. At the same time, many significant measures have been taken to improve the national economy, to raise the general standard of living, and to reduce inequalities and social injustice. Much, of course, remains to be done, but on a balanced view the achievements are admittedly quite creditable, and in consequence,

India has acquired a degree of healthy political stability which is in sharp contrast to the record of most of the other countries of Asia.

India thus presents to Asia an alternative possibility of development from the one held out by Red China. Although India does not seem to have fully grasped the profound implications of her choice for the future of Asia, it amounts in reality to a clear repudiation of the myth of a common Asian destiny. Now a democratic system, so long as it is not directly threatened with aggression or subversion, can and does tolerate the existence of other systems which are non-democratic or even anti-democratic. Such toleration, however, goes against the grain of any regime committed to totalitarian ideas and methods. From practical considerations it may temporarily adopt peaceful co-existence as a strategy; but its very logic would impel it to seek by every means the destruction of all alternative systems. All modern totalitarianisms, but especially the communist variety, are messianic in outlook; at the same time, however, they suffer from an aggressive type of inverted inferiority complex. In the existence of other alternative systems they see a threat to their own existence.

When India began to emerge as the principal exponent of democracy in Asia, it became obligatory on Red China to bring about by fair means or foul the subversion of her government. On the one hand, under cover of friendship, it began to extend its frontiers and to prepare to attack at the most opportune moment. On the other, it tried to gain control of the Indian Communist Party so that it could be used as its effective fifth column. In this latter effort, its success has been limited, thanks to the rivalry between Moscow and Peking over the leadership of the world communist movement. In any case, the present invasion of India has been prepared for nearly a decade. But for her political short sight, this should have been obvious to India at least after the Chinese conquest of Tibet.

This ideological aspect of the Chinese invasion gives to it a dimension of significance which would not have been otherwise present in a war between two rival nations. China, presumably, hopes in the long run to subjugate the whole of India, but its objectives at the moment seem to be more limited and less unrealistic. In the first place, by inflicting a series of defeats on both the fronts and forcing India to a humiliating peace, China wants to impress on the rest of Asia the superior might of Communist totalitarianism to democracy. Secondly, by extending its frontiers into Indian territory both in the North-west and the North-east, China would keep India perpetually vulnerable to attack. Thirdly, by forcing India to divert suddenly most of her resources to defence preparations, it expects to subvert the Third Five Year Plan and immobilise all efforts towards peaceful democratic development. And finally, it may even have calculated that the stress of war and the demoralization brought about by military defeat would cause great disaffection and unrest which would then create the proper climate for its communist fifth column in this country to stage a successful *coup d'etat*.

China's unprovoked aggression, in itself, should be reason enough for all non-communist countries to extend their sympathy and support to India in repelling the attack. But more is involved in this conflict than the question of territorial aggression. If China's military adventure proves to be even partially successful, then that may be the beginning of the end of the democratic experiment in Asia. For, this will not only greatly reinforce the misgivings of the smaller Asian nations about the competence of the democratic system to defend itself against totalitarian attack. It is also bound to shake India's own confidence in the feasibility of her choice. That will be disastrous not only for Asia, but for the whole world. Consequently, it should be realized by every nation or government which cares for democracy that it has an urgent obligation to rush to India's assistance in this hour of destiny. Asia's choice between the two alternative systems of our age will be largely determined by the issue of this contest.

III

Development inside India during the last few weeks leave no doubt that although caught unawares, the country is now determined to defend itself at all costs against aggression. But determination is not enough. It is necessary at least for the leadership of this young democracy to anticipate and prepare for the many hazards and compulsions of the new situation.

In the present emergency, military requirements are bound to get top priority. But in the present stage of its economy, can India afford to prepare seriously for what threatens to become a long-drawn tussle and at the same time continue her pursuit of general economic development? In other words, will be Third Five Year Plan be the first casualty of this conflict? This is what the Chinese must have calculated. Realism dictates that India has to rely heavily on international support if she is to fight the aggressor effectively and at the same time carry on her struggle against poverty, disease and ignorance. She must appeal urgently to the United Nations, and should a decision be prevented there by the Russian veto, approach directly every member nation that can be persuaded to offer military and/or financial assistance. Very little effective help, however, can be expected from Russia or the Afro-Asian countries because the former is unlikely to back India openly against China and the latter have hardly any surplus to offer. But the United States, several West European countries and some members of the Commonwealth, being definitely committed to democratic ideals, would presumably be anxious and are certainly in a position to come to India's succour. Time is pressing and efforts in this direction cannot brook delay.

India must also make a big effort to win Pakistan's friendship and persuade it to joint defence arrangements for the entire subcontinent. This will not only permit India to concentrate more fully on her defence efforts against China but also make it easier for other nations which have friendly relations with Pakistan to assist India. For this, India may have to go more than half way to remove Pakistan's grievances and suspicions. If necessary, she should have the courage and wisdom to agree to a plebiscite in Kashmir under international supervision, provided Pakistan consents to its being held after the Chinese have been forced to evacuate all Indian territory.

Internal democracy is usually the first victim of a prolonged war. During the last few weeks Mr Nehru's government has shown remarkable responsiveness to public opinion. However, the logic of war points to increasing regimentation and centralisation of authority. This cannot be altogether avoided, but a wise leadership can try to ensure that the pressures of this temporary national emergency do not permanently injure the not-yet very securely laid foundations of this young democracy. To the extent it is possible in times of war, the government should respect and even welcome free and informed public discussion of its activities and constructive criticism from non-official sources. It is also highly desirable in the interest of both democracy and effective defence that public men of proved democratic faith and record who may not belong to the party in office should be closely associated with the government at all levels, if necessary by reconstituting the latter. Most important of all, steps must be immediately taken to ensure intelligent, organized and effective participation of the civilian population in defence efforts through homeguards and a chain-work of non-official organizations. In other words, the defence of democracy must make full use of the resources of the democratic system.

Another hazard of war is the resurgence of conservative and reactionary forces with the help of militant patriotism. War invariably breeds chauvinism, and there is a genuine danger that in the new climate militant nationalists will try to replace liberals and democratic socialists in the leadership of the country. This danger can be met if the more enlightened leadership of today tries energetically to explain to the people the basic issues involved in the conflict and to imbue them with sentiments of unshakable loyalty to the values of democracy. This is a war not merely for the defence of one's own country but also for the defence of democracy against aggressive totalitarianism. The common people must be educated in the far-reaching implications of their commitment to freedom, and this should include clear and unambiguous repudiation of all varieties of serfdom, whether of the Right or of the Left.

The threat from the communist fifth column in India is another urgent problem which must be faced squarely and without delay. The recent resolution of the CPI to support the government against China should not deceive Indian democrats into giving it the benefit of doubt. It will be suicidal not to recognize and alert the general public against the essentially anti-democratic nature of communism. This summer patriotism of Indian communists cannot and should not obscure their ultimate commitment to the most potent and insidious ideology of slavery in modern times. In particular, people must be educated to see behind their clever doubletalk and to frustrate their highly developed methods of internal subversion. This should be the occasion for developing sufficient intellectual and moral maturity so as to rid ourselves of our mythical thinking about communism and to distinguish between this pseudo-democratic ideology and the various schools of genuinely radical, libertarian and cosmopolitan thinking.

Finally, inspite of all the patriotic gestures and protestations of our businessmen, it should not be forgotten that war is an invitation to hoarders, blackmarketers and fortune-hunters. The strain of the war is bound to be felt soon in the supply of essential civilian necessities. It is not enough to enforce austerity in consumer spending; it is also essential to raise production and to ensure equitable distribution of available supplies. For this purpose, steps have to be taken to promote more effective and enlightened participation of workers in planning production, pricing and distribution. Since sooner or later rationing may have to be introduced, especially in the cities and big towns, consumers cooperatives should be formed to discharge this major responsibility in the most effective and democratic manner. Citizens' vigilance committees are also called for to check blackmarketeering and fifth column activities.

The present conflict, which is certainly not of India's seeking, has put Indian democracy to its first crucial test. We have not only to defend this country against the aggressors, we have also to protect our young democracy from internal corrosion and subversion. In fact, the strategy of defence, wisely conceived and ably pursued, should, as in England during the Second World War, considerably strengthen the democratic bases of Indian polity, economy and social institutions. It is a tremendous task and our very best is demanded.

November 9, 1962.

Reflections on the Chinese Invasion: The Silver Lining

Abu Sayeed Ayyub

(Q 36: Winter 1962-1963)

The Indian Communist Party's National Council came out on the 1st of November, 1962 with a forthright condemnation of Chinese aggression against India and gave its full support to the Prime Minister's appeal for national unity in defence of the country. The Council 'never expected a socialist country like China to settle its border dispute with India by force of arms and make astounding territorial claims against a country which is engaged in peaceful consolidation of its newly won independence.' A leading member of the party is reported to have said that 'this was the first time the CPI had taken a decision on an extremely grave issue entirely on the basis of its own reading of the situation within the country and outside.' He claimed that this was clear proof of the fact that the 'CPI had come of age.' (*The Statesman*, 2-11-62)

Coming of age is a happy event and deserves congratulations. Candour and modesty are also commendable qualities and these were shown in the confession implied by the above claim, viz., that all these years the Communist party was so immature as to find it necessary to let other people living thousands of miles away (in Moscow, Peking or London) guide its decisions on grave national issues on the basis of *their* reading of the Indian situation. How one wishes that the coming of age of the leading opposition party in this country had not been so exasperatingly delayed!

Unfortunately, I do not feel so sure that this is precisely and exclusively what the resolution does prove. In my opinion it points more directly to several other things. It might even be taken as 'proof that the Indian communists have grown out of communism. But that is only an outside possibility which we may ignore for the moment. The resolution, however, does prove that the CPI, after mature deliberation, has come to believe in one or other of the two alternatives presented by the following disjunctive proposition: either the Chinese party has ceased to be communist, or communism is just as compatible with expansionism and military aggression as capitalism and fascism. It would be interesting to enquire which of these two horns of the dilemma the CPI – its majority group, that is to say – is more anxious to embrace, or avoid.

The resolution expresses surprise that a 'socialist country like China' should be guilty of conduct which the sponsors of the resolution have been accustomed to regard as inseparable from capitalism. Critics of communism are often tempted to point out that communism can no more help being expansionist than capitalism, in its initial phases – witness the military expansion of Soviet Communism in Finland before and in Eastern Europe after the Second World War, and of Chinese communism in North Korea and Tibet, and now over the Himalayas into India. Jawaharlal Nehru went further and said on the floor of the Lok Sabha on November 8, 1962, that 'the major issue between India and China was not one of communism or anti-communism but one of an expansionist and imperialist minded country like China deliberately invading another country... Today we are facing naked aggression, just of the type which the world saw in the 18th and 19th nineteenth centuries when there was no communism in the world' (*The Statesman*, 9-11-62). I do not subscribe to this reading of the situation. I think it wrong and harmful to believe that Mao's government wants to conquer India or large parts of it, send a Chinese governor-general to rule over the conquered territory, and use that territory as a source of raw material and cheap labour and as a field for the investment of excess home capital. It is very much the issue, if not between communism as such and democracy as such, then between Chinese communism and Indian democracy. The stakes are high for both sides. For China, it is less vital but more grandiose: acceptance by the countries of South and Southeast Asia of Chinese communism and Chinese tutelage. For India, it is a question of survival as a free and democratic nation.

The immediate motives behind the Chinese invasion of India were succinctly stated by the *New Statesman* editorial of November 2: 'China may be attempting to undermine India's emergent system of economic planning, and so remove her as an alternative, democratic magnet to the peoples of Asia. Or her object may be to drive India into the western camp – which would in the long run have the same effect. Mr Nehru is fully aware of these dangers. Non-alignment remains the keystone of his policy – and rightly so.' Adherence to the five year plans, with only minor modifications, also remains the keystone of Mr Nehru's policy, and one is again tempted to say – rightly so. Simultaneous and strict adherence to both these right courses may, however, stand in the way of that quick massive build-up of our defences without which the large scale and long prepared Chinese attack cannot be thwarted. Knowing how allergic the Nehru government has always been to receiving any big military aid from western powers and how passionately devoted it is to its economic plans, the Chinese government must have reckoned that it is quite within their military capacity to make good their 'astounding' claims in the NEFA and Ladakh regions. These mountainous tracts are not obviously being coveted for their own sake. They are only a first step, a foothold. Once the Chinese have got a firm foothold on this side of the Himalayas, it will be only a question of time, and not a long time, before the pincer movement constituted by communist China's military forces on the border and the indigenous communists' party-forces inside the country succeed in turning it over to communism of the Chinese brand and owing allegiance to Peking. After that, China will not need to resort to military force in order to pull the smaller countries along the Himalayas and further east into the Sino-Communist orbit.

One is, therefore, surprised to see that the National Council of the Communist Party of India has thought fit to condemn the crossing of the McMahon line by the Communist army of China – so obviously but so nicely calculated to further the interests of world communism in general and of Asian communism in particular. Our anti-communist press and platform loudly explain this self-denying communist pronouncement as a purely hypocritical and skin-saving device, also as a move which will enable the communists to infiltrate for their own purposes into civil defence committees, home guards and other war-time organizations. It may be true of some communists, but many whom I know personally are not made of such stuff. They are honest and earnest men. Perhaps they sincerely believe that even without the strains of a war our economic plans were bound to collapse anyway, and in the chaos that could well be expected to follow Nehru's retirement from politics in the not too distant future (he is 73 now), the CPI would be able to chalk out an easy path to power. The brother Communist Party of China, therefore, need not have unleashed a wholly superfluous war, one of whose inevitable consequences would be the temporary fade-out of the Indian Communists from our political scene. Was this the point of difference between the majority and minority groups in the National Council meeting – the majority contending that they could go it alone and do the job within a reasonable time, the minority being of the opinion that it was necessary for the Chinese to give them a leg up?

That is not of course what the minority Communist group says. What it, or some of its spokesmen, have said is that it is axiomatically true that no socialist State (for some mysterious reason communists insist on calling themselves and their regimes 'socialist' in spite of their unbounded hatred for all socialist parties, Asian or European) can ever commit aggression, ergo the Chinese army has not committed aggression against India; the McMahon line is only an imperialist imposition, the proper boundary between India and China has yet to be fixed by negotiation, et al. The majority group led by Mr Dange has, as we began by saying, accepted the fact of Chinese aggression and condemned it. It follows, or else logic has no meaning, that Mr Dange's group has (we assume that it has not ceased to be communist) either renounced the communist axiom that 'no socialist state can commit aggression', or denounced the Chinese regime as having ceased to be communist. Vinoba Bhave with his Gandhian innocence of communist politics accepts the above axiom, but with his sound petit bourgeois fidelity to logic rejects the Chinese government's claim to be communist. What is the position of the Dange group?

This group has not so far been reported to have denounced the Chinese government or party as non-communist. The front page article in the *New Age* (the CPI weekly) of November 11, 1962 (claiming to based on notes taken from Chairman Dange's utterances) says, 'The genuine questioners think that perhaps we as communist, knowing communist policies and the communist mind, must be able to fathom the depths of a Communist mind everywhere. It is not so.... We admit our failure to understand China.' No hint here of any doubts being entertained as to the communism of the Chinese government. To the insistent question: 'Could you tell us why China is behaving like this', the likeliest answer is that her political understanding of India has gone wrong – not, according to Mr Dange, her understanding of communism. If the Chinese are accepted as sound communists (in spite of their comradely but unresolved differences with Khrushchev and now with Mr Dange himself) then the Dange group has publicly announced its rejection of the thesis that no communist state can ever commit aggression. This is significant. It is not a very startling revelation for those of us who had received their first shock a quarter of a century ago by the Soviet government's unprovoked assault on a weak and helpless neighbour. But it is significant that the Indian Communist Party (the second biggest party of Asia after the Chinese party) has officially admitted that communism is quite compatible with military aggression by officially branding *communist* China as an aggressor. The Italian Communist Party (the second biggest party in Europe after the Soviet party) too sees no incompatibility between communism and unprovoked military aggression.

On the other hand, and article in a Delhi weekly, reportedly written by a well known communist intellectual now in the Dange group, did, in effect, maintain that the revolution in China has gone sour. Just as Napolean, 'carrying the very tricolour of the French Revolution turned the crusade into an empire, there are indications that the establishment of a powerful centralized state in China possibly could bring about Han chauvinism under a Communist leadership.' The fellow-travelling weekly *Link* in its issue dated November 11 speaks of 'the unbridgeable chasm that divides the war-mongering expansionists of Peking and the genuine Communists of the world.' If this is the position of Dange group, then how do they explain the recent *Pracda* editorial proclaiming the Chinese as their brothers (in contrast with the Indians who are only their 'friends', and its support of the territorial claims of the Chinese government which the National Council of the CPI itself described as 'astounding'?

The silence of the pro-Peking faction is understandable, but that of the Dange group (fortunately in majority of two to one in the National Council of the CPI) is mystifying. Or is it a deliberate attempt at mystification? It is hard to believe that the leaders of this group are not fully aware of the logical impossibility of holding at one and the same time that: (1) the Chinese government is communist; (2) its military forces have invaded India; (3) no communist government can commit aggression. But that is precisely what the Dange group is doing – asseverating all the three propositions in the same breath.

Prof. Hiren Mukherjee, the deputy leader of the Communist group in the Lok Sabha, said, in the course of his speech on the floor of the Parliament on November 8, that he had been trying hard to find out what possibly could be the motive behind the madness that had seized the Chinese government in their armed invasion of India (The *New Age*, 11-11-62). Looking for motives in the actions of a man or group 'seized by madness' is a futile task. We are reminded, however, of the famous speech delivered by Khrushchev before the 20th party Congress of the CPSU (B) in 1956 in which he also attributed, in effect the absolutely unaccountable and bizarre conduct of Stalin from 1936 to the time of his death in 1953 to a more serious kind of mental derangement. One wonders if there is anything in the theory and practice of communism which leads to the development of these terrible forms of madness in the top leadership of the Party after it has been in possession of absolute dictatorial power for a decade or more. We used to be told by good old liberals that absolute power corrupts absolutely. Good communists now inform us that absolute power has far worse effects: it produces serious forms of mental derangement. Stalin's diseased mind caused immeasurable suffering to millions of Soviet citizens. Mao's and Chou En-lai's 'madness' is bound to spell disaster for untold millions of Indians who were not even remotely responsible for these leaders' assumption of dictatorial power. When a physically strong man becomes suddenly and violently insane, not the members of his household alone but his neighbours too have to suffer much until the man is safely put in a straight jacket. Stalin was too powerful to be straight-jacketed by any human agency. Who is going to cure or curb the mad men of Peking? Some people are hoping that the mighty man of peace and sanity at the Kremlin will do the job. There is no harm in hoping or praying, but we must in the meanwhile keep our powder dry, and make or procure more powder.

One of the many things which the Chinese government wants to achieve by their military adventure is to bring to dust the prestige that Nehru's India enjoys in Asia and in the world. That is yet to be seen. But what they have immediately and unquestionably achieved is to blow to bits whatever prestige the Indian Communists enjoyed in their country. However, there is another angle to it. The Chinese calculation is that their supporters in the CPI have only to lie low for the time being; as their armies advance, the time will soon come when these Indian comrades will be able to rise and overthrow the Nehru government after first having overthrown 'self-styled Marxists-Leninists' like Dange from the leadership of the Party. Only then will the Chinese government make peace with the new Communist government of India. How do I know the Chinese mind? I did not, until I read this on p. 5 of the Party organ, the *New Age* of 11.11.62 – '*They (the Chinese leaders) virtually call upon the Indian people to overthrow the Nehru government if a peaceful solution of the India-China border is to be achieved and peace on our Northern frontiers to be secured. At the same time they call upon the ranks of the Indian Communist Party to get rid of their present leadership.*' I don't like to use the pejorative expression 'puppet government', but that is just what the dictators of Communist China seem determined to establish, first in the border areas and ultimately at New Delhi. With such a government alone are they prepared to live in peace. We guessed that this is what they were saying with their guns in Ladakh and NEFA. We are obliged to the *New Age* for confirming the guess with authentic quotations. The guns were equally authentic but not equally explicit.

'Non-alignment remains the key-stone of Mr Nehru's policy and rightly so' – observed the *New Statesman*. We are all very fond of the sound of this word non-alignment, but not equally clear about its meaning. If it means that India is not going to join either of the two power blocs, that she is not going to enter into any military pacts, that she will not let military bases be constructed on her soil – then that should indeed rightly remain the key-stone of our policy. But military non-alignment is often coupled and not seldom confused with political and ethical neutrality. Now neutrality is not a good thing to swear by under all circumstances. It will be immoral to proclaim our neutrality in a situation in which a weak State has been invaded by a militarily more powerful State, and we have no reason to doubt that it is a clear case of aggression. We must boldly extend our sympathy and moral support to the aggressee and such material help as we can. We may not declare war on the aggressor, for, apart from our own military weakness, there may well be other sound reasons against that step. But stopping short of it does not mean that we are neutral. When Egypt was the victim of aggression, we were not neutral and our voice did not falter in declaring our sympathy and our condemnation. Rightly so. If Cuba were to become the victim of aggression, I dare say we would not hesitate to let the world know which way our sympathies and antipathies lie. But when Hungary was the victim of aggression by a bigger and more ruthless military power than France, Britain or the USA, we faltered and equivocated. That was not morally right; I doubt if it was even politically prudent. When Tibet fell and its ruler sought asylum with us, we gave him asylum but condoned the aggression. That again was wrong and, as it transpires now, highly imprudent. Jayprakash Narayan has drawn the attention of 'the persons concerned' to their myopic vision produced by 'mental and emotional alignment that went about in the garb of non-alignment.' A war cannot be fought with uncorrected eyesight, still less a war with an enemy whom our short-sightedness had led us to regard all these years as a friend. No nation can hope to survive whose political vision is not good enough to distinguish friend from foe. We needed the ophthalmic surgery of a treacherous war to reveal to us the face of our enemy; it will also show us who our real friends are.

Now that we ourselves are the victim of a foul attack by the Chinese, the voices of Indonesia, Burma, Ghana and Ceylon and several other countries are silent on the pretext of neutrality. Such neutrality looks mean to our eyes. We should remember that look next time when some other country falls victim to an aggression like this. There will be another thing to remember. The United Kingdom and the United States of America have answered our desperate cry for help generously and without the least possible delay. The Soviet Union consoled us by calling us their friends but did not omit to inform us that those who have committed this dastardly aggression against us are their brothers; they went out of their way to support[1] the Chinese claims on our territories this side of the Himalayan ridge, fraught with more sinister possibilities but even less justifiable than Nazi Germany's claim on the Sudetenland. They are gentlemen enough to assure us that they would fulfil their commitments made prior to the date of large scale Chinese aggression. Their political and military alignment, however, prevents them from promising *now* any kind of aid which we badly need to defend ourselves against the Chinese. We know, of course, that our aggressors owe much the greater part of their military strength to the Soviet Union. I hope I am not being politically naïve if I predict that our neutrality will tremble in the balance ever so slightly when in future we compare these two attitudes displayed towards us in the hour of our misfortune.

Nehru had told Taya Zinkin in 1954: 'They (the Chinese) have a sense of urgency and dedication which our people and the Congress totally lack. We got our independence far too easily. How I envy Mao the Long March! What a test for man it was. We did not have the Long March, we had it easy. I cannot blame the British for this but I must recognize that what we gained in continuity, we have lost in spring cleaning, if you know what I mean. Progress is slowed down because we have not had a "revolution, only evolution' (Taya Zinkin – *Reporting India* p. 209). The Chinese have given us what the British were too genteel to give, a long march and a revolution rolled into one – a long and hard war. Every one of us will have to be in this war one way or another. Only some may have to die, but all must pass through years of toil and suffering. It is possible that a cease-fire may be arranged and a truce offered – only to be broken by the Chinese as soon as their own military consolidation or the international situation suits them. Peace will come only when we succeed in making the Chinese government respect our defensive strength, when we make our Himalayan frontiers fool and knave proof.

We are too soft in brain and brawn. We will have to be steeled in the furnace of this war brought on us as a result of our poetically unreal politics having to confront the diabolical *Realpolitik* of Communist China. The Chinese treachery, instead of taking the ground away from under our feet has put our feet firmly on solid ground. We have got rid of Mr Krishna Menon, and this signifies a turning point in our political thinking. But one or two remnants of unreality still cling to our thoughts. Are we mentally and practically geared to the fact that we are up against the worst kind of twentieth century totalitarianism? Nineteenth century imperialism fought with small professional armies for limited economic gains and maybe a little military glory thrown into the bargain; twentieth century totalitarianism fights with its entire population regimented, and for the total subjugation of the entire populations of other countries to its own way of life and thought. A totalitarian power not only mobilizes its army, it regiments its art and literature, its science and philosophy. We are amazed by the way the Chinese leaders and spokesmen lie, but they are not lying; they are speaking the truth. Only, truth for them is what serves the cause of the proletariat – which is Asia is identical with the cause of the communist government to China. This is their honest conception of truth. The Chinese leaders are not dishonest; they are communist. They have sacrificed much for communism, including of course bourgeois notions of truth and honesty. Nehru thought in 1954 that communism in China would become Sinified. He was right. He thought it would become Confucianised, de-Stalinised. He was wrong there. It has become over-Stalinised.

Such a totally regimented country, fully and ceaselessly prepared for war, blind in its mighty arrogance, determined to spread Sinified communism in Asia and probably Africa through war and insurrection (Mao has scornfully rejected Khrushchev's thesis of peaceful coexistence and competition between capitalism and communism), has hurled its armies across our Himalayan frontiers. Several times in the past we failed to protect these frontiers, not because the invading armies were strong, but because we were neither united nor properly organized for defence. This time the invaders are terribly strong, but we are united as never before (except for the dissident communist group). The emotional integration of India's many religious communities, linguistic groups and innumerable sects and castes – which our leadership and government have been trying hard to achieve for over a decade – has been achieved at one stroke. It is a precious gift from the Chinese invaders which we must not squander away. Although we were taken not unawares but unprepared – thanks to Mr Krishna Menon – our military build-up is going on satisfactorily. 'And the morale of our people is as high as any government could wish. But it is going to be a terribly hard war. What makes it harder is that we are not only at war with China, we are also in economic competition against them. This war on two fronts, military and economic, is going to need every ounce of our energy, every kind of privation and sacrifice. We must not fail on either front. Defeat in war will of course mean the total destruction of all that we stand for and hold dear. But even if we succeeded in driving out the invaders only at the cost of our economic disruption, or at the cost of surrendering our democratic way of life (so painstakingly nurtured by Nehru[2]) to indigenous militarist or communal-fascist dictatorship, that would be a disaster of almost equal magnitude – not only for India, but for the greater part of Asia. The whole world is watching with deep anxiety the outcome of a frontier war which is bound to change the course of world history.

November 15, 1962

Endnotes

1. This is nothing new. The Geographical Atlas published by the Soviet Ministry of Geology and Protection of Minerals (proscribed and forfeited by the Indian Government on Nov. 14, 1962) and some other Soviet atlases had all along been lending their support to these expansionist ambitions of Communist China.

2. If we all love (admire is too pale a word) Jawaharlal Nehru in spite of his many human frailties, it is because he symbolises for us the democratic spirit and secular temper of life. Gandhi was the symbol of much that is best in our traditional culture; Nehru of much that we mean by the new, the resurgent India.

Arts: Konarak

Marie Seton

(Quest 36: Winter 1962-1963)

I

Some years ago I saw a few reproductions of sculptures at the Sun Temple at Konarak. The humanism of the imagery deeply impressed me. I wanted to go to Konarak more than to any other temple in India. These few pictures did not convey the actuality that Konarak is a Song of Songs in stone depicting every conceivable posture in which men and women can make love to one another, and revealing the range of feeling which can be evoked through the act of physical intercourse.

It was not until I was shown a large collection of unpublished photographs that I gained a comparatively accurate impression of the Sun Temple. These photographs seemed to me to be perhaps the most beautiful I had ever seen. But still it was several years before I finally visited Konarak and found the Black Pagoda still more of a marvel than the photographs suggested.

My desire to go to Konarak and form my own impression interested me for one particular reason – my ingrained aversion to the pornographic. It was evident to me that to a lot of people, the pictures I saw of Konarak would seem to be pornography. But to me these pictures of the erotic appeared to be the furthest point away from anything I understand as pornography. For me, lewdness and suggestiveness are an essential part of the pornographic. Pornography makes me feel uncomfortable not because it shocks me but because of what it reveals about the deep-seated Puritanism of the people to whom it appeals; I mean, of course, the puritan in matters of sex, for it is such puritans who have scourged humanity under many different guises and only too often have slaughtered the innocent.

I don't really think that the person who gains some vicarious thrill from the sight of semi-nude chorus girls with made-up breasts is likely to be responsive to the beauty and spirit of sincerity that inspires the sculptures on the walls of Konarak. I've never been to the temple at Khajuraho but the pictures I have seen make me feel that there is too much seductive artifice in the concept and that there is a teeter-tottering at Khajuraho between the vital and passionate and decadence. It is decadence that produces pornography as a general rule.

The consciously seductive in life can be a prologue to the realization of a great passion in love. But great passion itself consumes the impulse to be artificially seductive. Many of the ladies at Khajuraho are in love with *Love*. But at Konarak, the women are in love with men, or divinity, and they have abandoned artifice.

I have vivid recollections of the salacious attitude of many people when D.H. Lawrence's novel. *Lady Chatterley's Lover* first appeared. People tried to get hold of copies. Although the book was banned; a married woman gave it to me to read as a 'naughty' book. I don't know if she thought I was a virgin and this would educate me, but I remember her attitude impressed me and I thought this woman has been sexually frustrated. I was eighteen or at the most nineteen.

Lady Chatterley's Lover instantly struck me as the most remarkable novel I had ever read. I liked it because it lacked all suggestiveness. I could not understand how anyone, unless they were puritanical, could think the book indecent. When I read it again many years later I found it a far greater book, the only novel which has depicted for me sexual attraction and the results of sexual intercourse in a manner which I know to be true to the actual experience of a certain number of people. Lawrence realized a dynamic reality about men and women who are highly suited to each other sexually: that no matter how promiscuous either may have been before, the highest ecstasy in sexual union produces the psychological state of monogamy and may very well ignite a sense of spirituality. No other modern writer has expressed this in terms of such realistic insight. This is also expressed in certain figures high up on the walls of Konârak.

About a year ago I decided I would read *Lolita* because, while *Lady Chatterley's Lover* is banned in India, or at any rate in Bombay, *Lolita* can be bought everywhere. I waded through it from the first to the last page but it took me weeks to do so. Perhaps it has great literary merit. But I found it the most unpleasant book because it is cluttered up with paragraphs which deliberately go 'sailing near the wind'. It stops just short of any description of sexual intercourse. The perversion in *Lolita* has nothing to do with *Lolita* being twelve years old, or Humbert being old enough to be her father. It lies in the basic self-loathing of both characters and their abhorrence of their own sexuality. *Lolita* is the condensation of all frigid women. Sexuality in *Lolita* is nothing but a torturous misery to both and the most joyless of all human experience. For me, at any rate, it is the most morbid book I've ever read.

Despite my aversion for pornography because I had not been brought up to regard sex as sin, I could hardly escape having seen occasional examples of pictorial pornography. What strikes me about Western erotic art – pornographic or otherwise – is the strange absence of delight, of any real sensual pleasure, or even profoundly of passion. This 'frank' expression is not really true at all to life for in actuality there is as much pleasurable sex experience as frustrated and miserable experience. If this were not so there would be a veritable rush to espouse the celibate life. But for the most part celibacy is only enforced upon the unmarried by moral conventions, or else it is achieved through religious dedication. In the whole of my life I have only met one woman who really at bottom appeared to have no interest whatever in men and yet did not seem to be a lesbian by inclination. However deeply it may be suppressed, there is a natural sexuality in people and a desire for love – to love and be loved. There are people in all cultures who are more passionate by nature and less passionate. Having been rather far around the world, I definitely have the impression that the most highly sexed people are in the area where they are not generally supposed to be – in Northern Europe and in North America. Wherever there is Puritanism, there is a corresponding concentration on sexuality. Among the people who have been deeply influenced by the puritan approach, there is also a tremendous drive in men towards a rapist approach and an impulse to seduce women.

Most people the world over may not experience the heights of satisfaction in their sexual lives, but neither is sex for the majority of people an orgy of seduction, rape, or the involvement in a grossly unpleasant joke. Yet this is the portrayal of the erotic in almost all of Western art, even the Greek and Roman. With Christian art, so-called sacred and profane love are juxtaposed and, oh my god, the number of rakes' progresses and the amount of sexual sadism that has been recorded over twenty-five hundred years! It's simply amazing.

I don't know why this miasma of violence in sex should have appeared in the West before the rise of Christianity which, alas, has been excessively hard on its followers in that it tabbed sex as 'carnal' and of the 'lower nature' of man. But it did, and the consequences in their extremist form have been the perversity of the Black Mass, black magic, and a markedly pornographic steak in art, the peculiarity of which is the dominance of the theme of rape, on the one hand, and sex as a dirty joke on the other.

The underlying differences between the erotic art of the West, including the pre-Christian Greek and Roman, and that of Konarak are truly astonishing.

Greek and Roman myths in which deities have intercourse with human beings are very common. But the element of seduction and rape are already much in evidence. If these myths are compared for instance with the Krishna Lila or the Ram Lila there are glaring difference. The sharpest contrast lies in the aspect of conquest in sex which appears in the Old Testament of the Bible as well as in the classical mythology. The question of mutuality between men and women hardly ever enters in, whereas the element of mutual passion and consent plays a very central role in Hindu myth. It is most evident in the Krishna Lila while the character of Ravana is extremely provocative of thought to anyone who is at all familiar with the corresponding Western figures. It can almost categorically be stated that Sita, in any Western myth, would have been taken against her will.

The most astounding thing about almost all Western erotic art is the excess of idealism on the one hand (or what can be called 'sacred love'), and the amazing lack of mutuality in what is thought of as pornographic art. Hardly anyone enjoys themselves.

By contrast, it is the mutuality of enjoyment which makes so great an impact at Konarak.

II

Allowing that Konarak is a microcosm of life, certain details emerge with very great individual force. At the apex of the purely artistic aspect of the Sun Temple stand the figures of Surya, the Sun God, on the various horses symbolizing his riding of the sky from dawn to sunset. (It is interesting here to mention that the sun is also conceived of as a horseman riding the sky in the pictorial art of the Pueblo American Indians. I possess a most fascinating painting done by a seventeen-year-old Pueblo Indian which depicts the Sun riding a white horse along a rainbow). I have seen no images that excel those of Konarak's Surya in nobility of spirit and beauty of form.

It makes me feel content that such indescribably beautiful figures should be given the background of no less exquisitely beautiful men and women entwined as lovers. That man born of woman can evolve so far as to conceive the images of Surya is very adequate proof, if proof is required, that to attempt to confine the idea of sex to man's 'lower nature' is to show a two-dimensional understanding. It is simply impossible if man is born out of 'sin', or only out of humanity's 'animal' nature, that he should be so well equipped to conceive and fashion images of divinity.

The thing which is the most appealing to me at Konarak is the depiction of the profound truth which is that of all human acts that of sexual intercourse is the most intimate. It is precisely because it is the most intimate that it is the most fitting symbol for portraying the idea of man's relationship to God or the Creative Power in life.

When I see Konarak I know, and I refuse to pretend I don't know, that what is depicted on the walls reflects in the most truthful manner the range of physical and psychological experiences of which men and women are capable through the act of intercourse. This is what I see and, at least for me, there is no need to seek any explanation as to why these scenes should appear on the walls of a temple. I can see no reason whatever why a temple dedicated to the Sun – the giver of life – should not be decorated with a Song of Life, or the Song of Songs, in stone.

If high on the walls, as if reaching upwards, the lovers are symbols of the seeking of the human soul to adore divinity (as the expression on the faces suggest), I am prepared to look at and accept the sexual experience furthest away from the intercourse of man and god. There has never been a period, or a country, when some men did not in actuality derive a release from tension through copulating with animals. A vast number of people have known this eons of time before the famous and much read Kinsey Report denied it was a fact. This is perhaps the least human expression of the sexual aspect of man. Because it is, at Konarak the small plaque which depicts this act is not at all conspicuous and it is on the base of the walls. Many people may never even notice it at all. But it is there. What one could object to is if this was the image that was stressed. To stress it would certainly be to put forward a pornographic idea.

There is no doubt a certain ambivalence in the feelings of many people in regard to Konarak. Some go in search of the pornographic; others from a genuine interest in art; still others from a mixed desire. But there are also those who go with no complex feelings at all because being simple people they have never thought much about Konarak as something unique. I saw such people there, people who had obviously come to see what was for them a local, or not-so-distant temple built in the form of the temple chariot which they had seen many times in wood perhaps at Puri, or somewhere else.

I doubt if these people were concerned about the history of Konarak, or the flowery explanations and speculations that surround it. It mattered not to them that this surviving building serves as the apex of Orissa's tradition of temple building. They may not have known that it was built in the 13th century as the culmination of a long process. They probably knew from tradition that its builder was Narasimha Deva (1238-1261) and that he had been the ruling monarch who had ordered the construction of the Temple of the Sun after he had defeated would-be Muslim invaders. But beyond that, Konarak is just Konarak for them, a place that had once been a flourishing port on the Bay of Bengal.

Despite the appalling ravages of time, and the great violence vented on Surya's temple by iconoclastic hands, enough of the main temple, plus the exquisite Natmandir, or Dancing Hall, survives to suggest what the original was like. The Natmandir is a pillared delight carved with the most adorable galaxy of dancers and musicians – heavenly females – all of who look so extremely happy that their accumulated happiness tends to obliterate the fact that each individual figure is a work of superb sculptural art.

It is the gigantic Jagamohan which, though badly battered, records the evolution of human love from its most bestial aspect to its most sublime; but the Mandapa tower which once rose higher

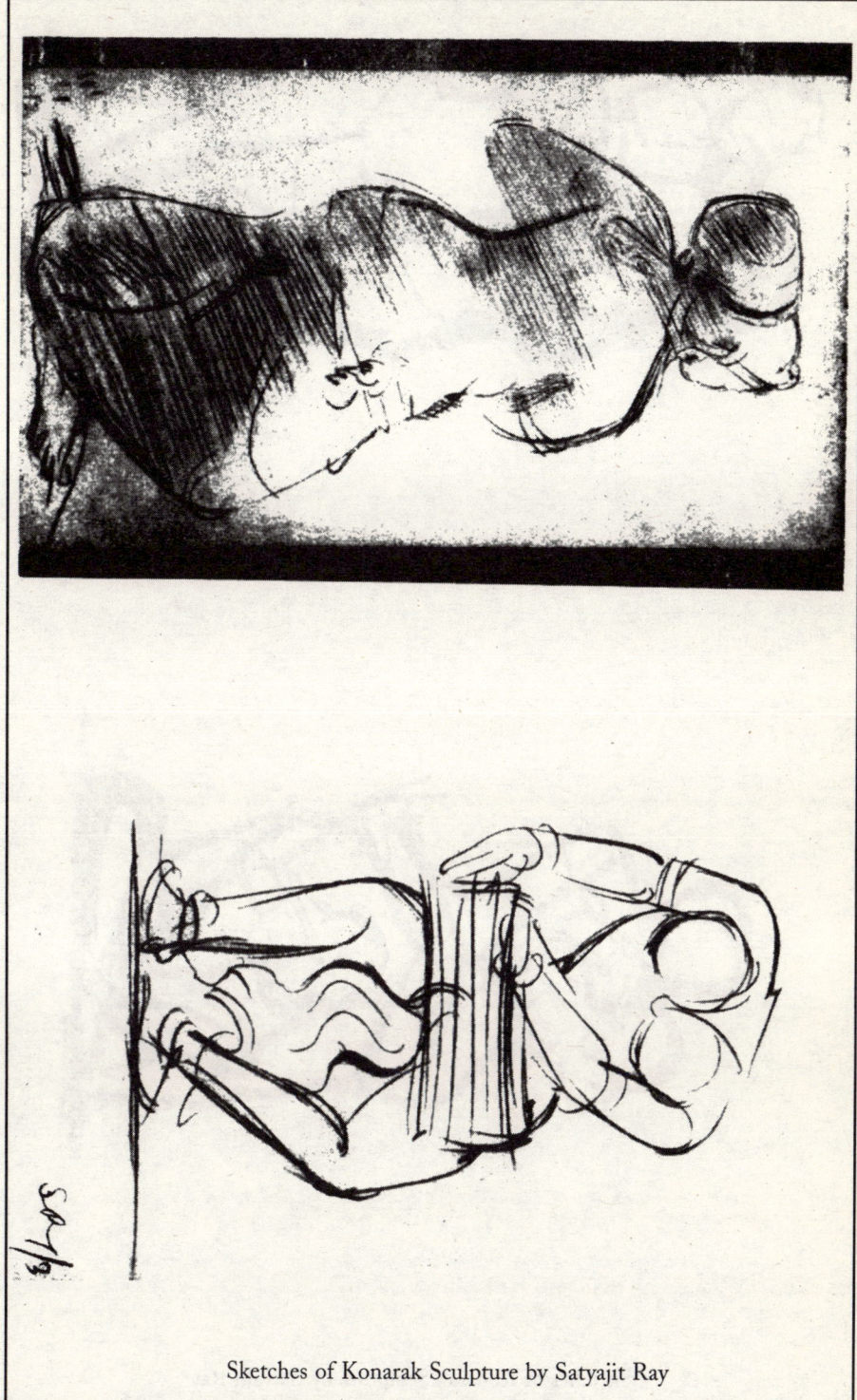

Sketches of Konarak Sculpture by Satyajit Ray

Sketches of Konarak Sculpture by Satyajit Ray

than the Jagamohan is a tragic wreck despite its setting for three surviving images of Surya. Many of the twenty-four wheels at the base of the chariot-shaped form have been horribly mutilated by infuriated hands. The seven small houses which are so beautifully fashioned at the giant feet of Surya's statues, are repeated again in huge dimensions as drawers of the temple itself. Many people have claimed to have felt that the wheels give the illusion of turning and that the whole immense structure is about to be lifted into the sky. This may be rather poetic fancy. I did not have this impression, perhaps because I want Konarak to stand forever and ever as the greatest of all testaments that it is the most excellent thing to have been born a man or a woman and for each to come together with the other.

Looking at the handwork of the artists and craftsmen who recorded their vision of the pleasure of being man and woman, I would assume that the creators can only have created from their own experience. Perhaps they were a fraternity of artists who had first learned the art of love and then, being devotees of the search for the spirit through the flesh, carved their personal sexual biographies in stone images. Many different levels of artists came together to create the whole. Some were far in advance of others both in concept and execution. This may be fancy. But it is certain that the carvers had an adoration of life and none had ever heard that there was sin in man's love for woman, or woman's adoration of man.

If every mother taught her daughter that the inner nature of woman is realised through the *quality* of the physical union with the man that is here, and every father taught his son that manhood is realized in its most civilized form in terms of the effect of intercourse upon him, the world would be a vastly more contented place. The marvel of Konarak is that the symbol of the highest humanism I have ever seen expressed is that of man making the offering of his penis to the woman, and woman accepting it with such ineffable and passionate dignity. Is it not extraordinary that this is perhaps the only place in the world where this act has been depicted with absolute simplicity and total frankness? It is the qualitative aspect of Konarak – the spirit – which is unique.

III

None of the monographs, nor either of the two films made of Konarak, give the least impression of the diversity in size of the sculpture. It is the most difficult building to describe and this is not because of the extent of the damage done by time, or by the hands of men who felt compelled to mutilate many of the figures. It is because life itself is so rich, exuberant and contradictory that no single sentence, paragraph or book can sum it up.

The basic form of the surviving Jagamohan is a pyramid and this form has signified to many mystics the union of God. Man and the Universe. It would seem to me that this idea is embodied in the structure and that the sculpture as a whole illustrates it. In life there is at one end destruction by war, and it is shown, and at the other love and procreation, which at Konarak is far more in evidence. But everything is under the jurisdiction of the Sun God.

The chariot wheels unite in each spoke the beauty of nature. And the actions of human beings, the human actions, frequently but not exclusively those of amorous couples joined in physical union, are contained within a circle. Behind the wheels on the wall are larger figures who may or may not be engaged in some action of love. From the base to the top of Jagamohan, and what survives of the Mandapa, the motif of man and woman in union is repeated. But as the motif reaches upwards as the unifying force in life – one that cuts across such activities as war shown in friezes – the size of the figures increases and the expression of emotion becomes ever more refined. There is the suggestion that the spirit ascends towards the divine as the sexual intercourse of loving couples becomes ever more human and tender.

There is something very extraordinary about the erotic art of Konarak and that is that though there never could be greater realism, there is not a single scene where a man touches a woman against her will. Not one scene remotely suggests the idea of rape. Even the scenes which can be called orgiastic are by mutual consent. In consequence there is an expression of intense joy, unbroken by violence between men and women. This joy, so intensely human in its depiction at the base and on the lower levels of the main buildings, becomes the serene ecstasy of union of the flesh and the spirit as it reaches towards the parapet where the very large figures of the heavenly musicians stand. There are no more spiritualised faces in all of art than those of the lovers high up on the walls of the Jagamohan. Konarak makes all the other erotic art of the world appear grotesquely lewd and pornographic.

Konarak is a book of life in stone where the human and the divine are united in a state of joy. And Konarak presents an unbelievable freedom from rigidity for there is absolutely no rule maintained.

Figures larger than life-size are set like jewels amidst small plaques no more than 12 or 18 inches high. Among the individual marvels are the delicately carved doorways which in execution are curiously suggestive of the most beautiful carving of Europe's Gothic period. There is even a very sedate man and wife on the base of the *Mandapa* who look most singularly like a medieval European couple.

There are innumerable stories handed down, or invented in succeeding centuries, to explain the Sun God's temple at Konarak. But it seems to me that so loving an appreciation of life needs no explanation except, perhaps, the acceptance that her sculptors must have been men who had themselves been lovers, and were lovers of all life. Konarak cannot be judged by academic standards, even though sculpturally there has never been created more marvellous plasticity of form. I am a lover of sculpture, but I have never seen anywhere a sculpture that is as appealing to the senses, the heart and the mind as that of Konarak.

The content – life itself and every aspect of love, human and divine – cannot be forced to conform to any philosophic or religious doctrine, orthodox or unorthodox though here is a building and a style which did evolve over a period of five centuries in Orissa and which is an evolution of the very earliest temple in Bhubaneshwar, the Parasurameswara. But I think Konarak has an individuality – a psychological and spiritual individuality – that makes it a thing unto itself. It seems to me that Konarak must always have spoken to each individual who came to it according to that person's own attitude to life and in the light of their own experience.

To those who see the physical union of man and woman as only 'carnal', the main thread of experience depicted on the walls can only be a disturbing seductive love song in stone images and, perhaps, 'sinful' or 'obscene'. To the true ascetic, the whole world is *Maya* – illusion – and an unreality to be transcended and escaped through the discipline of the spirit. But for those who are neither puritans nor ascetics, and seek, consciously or unconsciously, the union of their own flesh and spirit for reasons of living in this world harmoniously with themselves and others, the Sun Temple can only speak of the happiness and dignity of being human and of being possessed in various degrees of the capacity to reach spiritual heights through the personal act of love.

There are many mysteries as to the meaning of Konarak. In folk lore, the Sun's chariot is the symbol for triumph over one's sins. But sin brings suffering and marks both the body and the face. I could find but one face at Konarak which some have deigned as lustful. The only sign of cruelty is conveyed by the giant figures of horses trampling down enemies and, perhaps, the huge elephants hoisting human victims with their trunks. There are small-scale battle scenes of great force among the friezes.

Though there is not a shred of evidence for my speculation, it seems to me possible that the king, Narasimha Deva, who was inspired to order the creation of Suryas's temple, might have done so not in a spirit of triumph because he had defeated the Muslim invaders, but in honour of life in contrast to the horrors of war. It was in this land of Kalinga that the great Emperor Asoka, a thousand years before Narasimha Deva, turned away in horror of his victory and became a convert to the Path of Goutama, the Buddha, and thereafter pursued 'conquest by piety'. In the time of Narasimha Deva, Buddhism had become sterile and Brahminical Hinduism petrified. Surely it is possible that Narasimha Deva, the last great ruler of Orissa, was a man whose triumph in war may have been transcended by a prolonged moment of passionate love for a woman, even the wife so sweetly depicted among a bevy of women? Or, the sight of death in battle may have caused him to turn to life under the glowing sun with a sense of adoration?

The legends of the son of Lord Krishna being cured of leprosy, or of Narasimha Deva becoming a leper, all seem too torturous to have inspired the building of a temple dedicated to the joy of living. No faces on the walls are those of sinners. The sensitivity of the creators is vividly illustrated by one small group. There is a very realistic fat man, rather gross, but he is *not* shown in amatory play with the two women in the group. Realism stops at the depiction of the gross or the comic as an aspect of the art of love. Those who built Konarak had an attitude of mind which had transcended the ribald.

If the Taj Mahal is a poem in stone designed to commemorate the love of the Mughal Emperor Shahjahan for his wife, then may not Konarak be another earlier and more realistic song of love by a royal master of the ancient *Kamasutra*? It is psychologically true that the greatest personal experience of love, and physical love at that, can expand the consciousness towards an attitude of embracing the world with impersonal love. From this 'love thy neighbour as thyself' there can spring an adoration for the Creator.

In all our universe there is no force for life giving, its preservation, or regeneration, comparable to the power of the sun. Without the sun there is no life. At Konarak this force is personified in the three figures of horsemen (the fourth deity figure once standing inside the *Mandapa* is now in Delhi) gazing outward from the *Mandapa* walls. There is the rising sun, the midday sun and the setting sun. The rising sun is mounted on a horse that seems to rise from the darkness of a niche. The midday sun stands and below his feet are seven small horses, the central horse standing on its hindlegs. The setting sun god, Surya, also stands, but now the seven horses are symmetrically arranged.

Never was there a face, except perhaps that of the Sphinx, embodying so completely the spirit of serene beneficence as Surya's three faces. Here is the dispassionate lover of all living things, the Creator of the primeval life force. In Hindu thought, primal energy is feminine – Shakti. This is conveyed philosophically by all the women on the temple waiting to give their energy, or giving their energy, to their masculine counterparts; or waiting to give in adoration of the sun itself.

The full sculptural miracle of Konarak is revealed twice a day – at dawn and at sunset – for it is at these times that all the figures become most intensely alive as a result of the shadows cast upon them. The wall facing the setting sun begins to glow a tone between pink and gold for the main structure is of a subtle toned sandstone. High up on the second and third parapet of the Jagamohan there are set (and they are placed at intervals along all four sides of the parapets) massive, but gloriously graceful, and free standing figures of women dancers and musicians – perhaps the most famed figures of Konarak. Behind them on the temple wall are smaller figures, also of divine women. But as the sun sinks, these figures seem to fade into the wall, allowing the dominant motif of the free standing women, divine yet in the likeness of their earthly sisters, to appear to step forward when looked at from the ground below. This extraordinary effect is because these figures are in a darker, greyish-toned stone.

The vast and intricate picture of life sinks into the walls with the descent of the sun leaving the grey figure of Surya in all his peaceful nobility, and the figures of the heavenly women on the two parapets above. Each figure stands out in isolated splendour. This marvellous effect was not the original intention, for centuries back the tall tower, long demolished, that rose above the *Mandapa* obscured the women. But rain has created a new synthesis which seems to image the music of the spheres played by the celestial women who now attend, as it were, on the figure of the sun god against the disappearing scene of life, human and divine.

This is not the only transformation that takes place at sundown. Centrally placed, and almost at the very top of the Jagamohan, there is the curious visage of a huge liongryps, the fabulous embodiment of the power of nature which appears on the Rajrani temple at Bhubaneshwar and as guardian of the stages of Jagannath's temple at Puri. The setting sun changes the demeanour of this ferocious face so that it appears to become contemplative and spiritualized, tender in place of terrifying. Perhaps it is all my imagination, but I seemed to detect at dusk a kinship in inner feeling between the beautiful face of Surya and the liongryph. Since dualism is part of Hindu thought and feeling, this is not so fantastic an impression to suddenly receive.

It would be absurd for me to pretend I have grasped more than a general impression of Konarak and delighted in certain scenes here and there. Konarak is an edifice that needs to be lived alongside for a considerable time. The whole effect can only too easily escape the consciousness because of the allure of the intimate and domesticated detail. It is not the grandeur of Konarak that has captured me but the intense humanism I see in its details. For me, it is the most loving building, or most lovingly constructed building I have ever seen.

There are two friezes on a huge piece of unidentified masonry resting under a tree which I will remember for the rest of my life. The upper frieze depicts some mythological figure in human form as if swimming through the ocean with a smaller human figure on its back. The sense of limbs moving in water is breathtaking. The frieze immediately below is a line of women, some playing instruments, others just sitting cross-legged with their heads turned this way and that. I have never seen a photograph of this absolutely undamaged piece of carving and, unfortunately, I had forgotten my camera. But this fragment is at least for me the distillation of all the intimate beauty and the goodness of heart that is embedded in the walls of the happiest building that I think the creative genius of man ever achieved.

The creation or appreciation of art, like the art of love at its most harmonious, is a sensual experience uniting the flesh and the spirit, or the mind and the body according to what words you want to use. Art is the transubstantiation of life. The art of Orissa, which has very ancient roots and which finally flowered so humanistically at Bhubaneshwar and Puri, reaching its apex at Konarak, is above all else the revelation of man's human potential through love of that which is within the world of reality. It reverences woman and it honours man and it is an exuberantly healthy expression of observation and imagination. The greatest lesson that Konarak might teach to the confused and frequently brutalised and tormented people of the modern world is that passion and tenderness are not antithetical but can exist at the same moment.

Instead of an Editorial

Abu Sayeed Ayyub

(Quest 54: Monsoon 1967)

Recently I had the experience of being repeatedly assailed by the question: Stephen Spender has resigned from *Encounter*, when are you going to resign from *Quest*? I felt like replying: Spender is a good poet, but doesn't happen to be my guru. But presumably the question was based on a more plausible assumption, namely, that the reasons which impelled the editor of *Encounter* to resign should also suffice to bring about the resignation of the editor of *Quest*. Unfortunately, Mr Spender's statement on his resignation, as reported in the press here, was very brief – too brief for his resignation to be accepted as a precedent. It may be pointed out that not one of the other editors of more than a dozen CCF-sponsored magazines in the different languages of Europe and Asia (some of them as good as *Encounter*) is reported to have resigned.

The situation as it presented itself to me was like this. In April last year, the *New York Times* reported that part of the funds supporting the Congress for Cultural Freedom and its various sponsored programmes and magazines was derived indirectly from the CIA. There was no need to wait a whole year to get confirmation of this fact, for though knowledge of it was denied, the fact itself was never categorically denied. What was categorically affirmed on behalf of the CCF was that 'at no point in the history of the Congress has any donor sought to interfere with or shape its actions, policies or programmes.' And soon afterwards, it was announced that the CCF had taken steps to re-organize its financial resources and would henceforward be independent of all other assistance except from the Ford Foundation which had underwritten its entire budget for the next six years. No one has yet given any reason to doubt either of these statements; Mr Spender certainly did not. On the contrary, he asserted in the strongest possible language the complete independence of *Encounter* of all outside interference. I can say the same of *Quest* and in equally strong language.

Does it follow that if, even after the revelations, the CIA had agreed to continue to support *Quest* on the explicit condition that it would in no way interfere in my editorial work, I should be willing to be its editor? Decidedly not; though an affirmative answer has been proposed by some intelligently sympathetic correspondents in the *Statesman* of June 4. Mr A. Das Gupta wrote: 'The issue of financial relation between the CCF and CIA involves the deeper issue whether any public organization with a social, cultural, or political mission that depends on public donations should scrutinise the intentions of the donor so long as the latter does not propose to alter or influence the declared aims and activities of the former.' Another correspondent, Mr Ranabir Roy Choudhury, suggested a reason why the American Intelligence Agency should have thought it worthwhile to give liberal aid to a purely cultural organization like the CCF without seeking in any way to interfere in the activities of that body. 'There can hardly be any doubt about the fact that the CCF, as its name itself suggests, is an organ propagating the principle of cultural and intellectual freedom. One must also admit that this principle is totally alien to the communist creed. It may, therefore, be asserted with some degree of confidence that the CCF is fighting Communism, albeit indirectly. Granted this, it is in the direct interest of the free world that the CIA should promote the strength and viability of the Congress. No need arises at all for the Agency to dabble in the affairs of the CCF. Consequently, no need arises too for the current spate of condemnation and disgust.'

I see the point which those correspondents were trying to make, but I disagree with it. The idea of being associated with a journal or an institution supported by the CIA is wholly repellent to me. That I was so associated over a number of years in complete ignorance of the ultimate source of part of their finances is another matter. Moral questions arise only with knowledge. After the revelations by the *New*

York Times and the non-denial by the CCF there would have been no *Quest*, or at least no *Quest* under my editorship, if the Ford Foundation had not stepped in and assumed the entire financial burden of the Congress. The Communist allegation about the Ford Foundation itself being a mere conduit for the CIA is fantastic. Prof. Kenneth Galbraith is a Congress trustee on behalf of the Ford Foundation. A quarterly journal which does not entirely please any particular party or provide popular entertainment, but aims at maintaining a certain intellectual level in the encounter of ideas, cannot unfortunately pay its way and must accept aid. Nothing could have pleased us better than to obtain such aid from purely indigenous sources. It is a pity that philanthropic foundations of the American or any other pattern do not exist in India.

If I were a US citizen, I might gratefully look upon the CIA as an organization which was performing highly important and dangerous patriotic tasks, though distinguished Americans themselves have been greatly perturbed by the way it bungled quite a few times and at least once brought the USA and the world to the brink of utter disaster. But the CIA is primarily an organization for intelligence, espionage and subversion outside the USA. As such, it cannot but be looked upon with deep suspicion and horror by the rest of the world. Through its ill-conceived underhand financial support over a number of years (happily ended now) the CIA has brought the Congress into disrepute and raised a dust storm of suspicion and mistrust. Mud-slinging is a common enough practice in political warfare between rival parties, but workers in the cultural field feel helpless and bewildered by this kind of experience. They can meet argument with argument, but with what will they answer calumny? What doubtful service the CIA did to the CCF has been far outweighed by the unquestionable and immeasurable service it has done to the militant Communist propagandists all over the world, particularly in India. They can hardly contain their joy. Nor do they want to control their words in their smear campaign against *Quest*, its editor and some members of the editorial board. It would have been naïve to expect that Communists would not extract full value out of this wonderful gift parcel which the CIA sent them.

Their personal attacks have a two-fold purpose: (1) opportune revenge against those who committed in the past the mortal sin of occasionally expressing views critical of some aspect or other of Communist theory and practice – though this past extends well beyond the birth of *Quest* or even of the Congress for Cultural Freedom; and

(2) planned character-slaughter so that if in future these critics ever dare to commit a similar offence, they may not got a hearing, or at least a respectful hearing. But above all, the Communists want to slaughter a principle – the principle for which *Quest* and those associated with it stand. Taking advantage of the wide-spread anti-American feeling in this country, day after day they are dinning into everybody's ears that all this tall talk about freedom of art and thought is only CIA cant. For, they know that Communism implies dictatorship by the Communist party, and that the edifice of this total dictatorship can be built only on the broken chips of the principle of individual liberty.

Communism, in so far as it stands for the upliftment of the toiling masses, for social responsibility and justice, for a non-exploitative and egalitarian society, is indeed a noble ideal. But it negates the essence of humanism when it proclaims its ruthless determination to crush every form of non-conformism and silence every dissident voice, however small that dissidence may be and from whatever quarter the voice may come – political, economic, intellectual, aesthetic or religions. The real issue behind this hullabaloo about the CIA is the radical conflict between those who stand for cultural freedom and those who insist on strict cultural conformism. The thinker must think along lines laid down by the party; the artist must create according to norms set by the party. This is precisely what they demand; this is what we absolutely cannot accept.

Before the flood-tide of abuse subsides (one hopes it will subside before it succeeds in totally submerging all liberal values) it may be as well to ponder for a while some basic questions. What are the standards by which a journal ought to be judged? 'The only ultimate safeguard,' wrote the *Guardian* recently, 'is the integrity of the editor and his staff, but with this the safeguard is complete.' But integrity, it may be argued, is an inward thing: how is the reader to judge? The only way the reader can honestly judge a magazine is by reading it. A journal is as good as what it publishes. *Quest* has tried to maintain a standard of quality. We should be grateful for criticisms on that score. And we welcome contributions embodying all possible points of view which might help raise further our standards of both discursive and creative writing.

Quest's editorial policy has always been free of outside control. Since the Communists have brought in suspicion of CIA influence, we wish to point out more specifically that we have published in the past and intend to publish in future, as and when the occasion arises, articles critical of American policy. To cite only a couple of instances: on the question of American intervention in the Dominican Republic, in which the CIA was reputedly involved, *Quest* came out with a highly critical article against that intervention (July-Sept. 1965). On Vietnam we have published two articles – one very critical of American policy in that country (April-June 1965), and the other which without being strident was still at variance with American foreign policy (January-March 1967).

Marxist writers, it must be admitted, have generally been reluctant to write for us, although we acknowledge gratefully contributions from a few (including the two most distinguished Marxist poets of Bengal). Why is it that more of them did not come forward? We can only try to guess the reason. Communists want people to believe that the real combat is between Marxist ideas and capitalist vested interests. They would not risk a debate in full public view in which their ideas can be challenged with logic, for they are unsure of the outcome of such a battle of ideas. In any case, it is they who have fought shy of controversy[1] in the pages of *Quest*, not we who have decided to avoid them. The disclosure about CIA money came to them as a godsend, for they saw in it a chance to win by slander what they never hoped to gain by reason.

We welcome a dialogue not because we are sure of victory (any desire to gain merely a debating point would of course be childish), but because we believe that it is only through unfettered inquiry, criticism and discussion that truth can be approached. If truth is on their side, we would still like it to prevail; if on our side, we are nonetheless conscious that it is fragmentary and incomplete. We must move from our fixed positions and confront each other if we are to make any progress. We are often uncertain whether we are moving forward or backward, or merely in a circle. Nevertheless, the internal and external dialogue must go on. There are no resting places; the quest is eternal.

Endnotes

1. We may remind our readers that Marxist writers did participate in some controversies, e.g., on Historical Materialism (cf. *Quest* 17 & 19), and on Marx's prediction about the course of capitalist development (cf. *Quest* 20 & 23).

Delhi: Eternal Capital of Hindustan

Khushwant Singh

(Quest 54: Monsoon 1967)

Arrival:

The plane touches down at Palam airport at 19.00 hours. 'On the dot,' announces our pretty air-hostess. 'Air India planes were always on the dot,' repeats the Parsi gentleman sitting next to me. 'Always on the dot till the Babu bureaucrats started meddling in business they know nothing about.' We sit in entombed silence for an eternity. 'We have to get a health clearance before anyone can disembark,' explains the Goan steward baring his pearly dentures. India, the mother of most diseases known to mankind, does not want to add any more to her list. After much banging and shouting the door is opened. A doctor and assistant enter the plane. They walk down the aisle, looking into our faces for signs of disease. They scrutinize forms we've filled: 'Where did you spend the last ten days? Nine days? Eight days? Yesterday?' They do not trust our declarations; they do not trust the healthy look on our faces. One man takes a bomb out of his pocket and strides up and down the aisle squirting a spray of insecticide. We survive the drop out. We are allowed to leave. We troop out and down on to the tarmac. We are herded towards the customs shed. An array of powerful lights blinds us. All we can see are showers of moths with night jars and bats darting in and out, long shouted bandicoots skating on their bellies from the light into the dark, and a host of arms waving in greeting.

The policeman herds us into the shack. We are again in a queue. Our health forms are re-scrutinised. Then our passports. We face the customs man. We fill in declaration forms (in triplicate). Then foreign currency forms (in triplicate). While we await our baggage, Inspectors eye us to see if our expressions reveal guilt. After half an hour, trollies are hauled in and coolies slam cases on the ramp. I gather mine in a heap and beg the Inspector to finish with me. I know the technique. Declare a few undutiables. Avoid cameras, transistors, tape-recorders. Above all, be polite and look bored. Foreigners who think they are doing a favour by coming to India lose their tempers. They wag angry fingers at a large poster depicting a smiling Shri Nehru bidding all foreigners welcome.

At Palam airport the rule is 'no tipping of porters'. Nevertheless custom sanctions the cross of an expectant, extended palm with a rupee. A taxi. All are driven by the ubiquitous Sikh. Now two in every cab. I don't hear the meter flag being put down and know that I have started with what somebody paid to get to Palam. So it is. At my destination the driver flashes his torch on the meter. Rs. 9.50 – twice as much as I paid last month for the same journey. What is the point of arguing with two Sikhs!

The *chaukidar* hands me the key of my apartment and assures me that it has been swept, the Frigidaire and air-conditioner switched on. I enter. I press the switch – *click*. No light. *Click, clock, click, clock*. No result. '*Bullub Phooze*,' explains the *chaukidar*. He presses another switch which produces a light. I tell him to go and *chaukidari karo*.

I peel away my clothes and go into the bathroom. I turn the tap. A muddy ooze oozes down into the bucket. It is followed by a khaki liquid, a trickle of water and then a belch.

I must ring up and complain; I lift the receiver. I am on somebody's line – two girls chatting away about their *Uncleji* and *Daddyji*. I put down the receiver, slap a few mosquitoes against my naked paunch and try again. They are now discussing *Mummyji* and *Auntyji*. I put back the receiver for two full minutes. They are now discussing the comparative merits of *chaats* at the Bengali market and the new *chaatwala* at Sunder Nagar. Then *Mummyji* and *Auntyji's* expedition to eat *chholabhatoora* at Lajpat Rai Market. I lose my temper and tell them what I will do to their *Mummyji* and *Auntyji* if they don't shut up. They do. I dial my number. Engaged. Three minutes later I dial again. Engaged, I dial complaints. He tells me dial 'assistance'. I dial assistance, he tells me 'number out of order, dial complaints'. I give up.

I go to my bed-room to let the air-conditioner cool my naked flesh and raw temper. It welcomes me with a distinct lowering of its hum. In a few minutes its drone lulls me to sleep. It resents my indifference and goes off in a sulk. The bed-room becomes like the black-hole of Calcutta. Will it come on again? Yes – the fan whirs once or twice – and then no more. I give up. A sleepless night. This is Delhi, my home town, the Delhi that I miss when I am away. This is the Delhi that I love.

Next Morning:

I switch on the table lamp. 4.45 a.m. I drag my feet into the sitting room. I draw the curtains and throw open the windows: pitch-black nothingness. I open the door at the other end. The curtains flutter. A cool breeze fragrant with *madhumalati* which grows about the window drives away the dank fuzz of yesterday's dead air. I sink into my armchair and gaze out of the window. The street lights go off with a bang. The sudden dark reveals a lighter sky. I can see it through the foliage of the mulberry tree across the road. Large bats wring their way back to their perches: how much more majestic in flight than birds! A few ghostly figures pass by. A little more light. Now I can recognize the passers-by. The old woman who lives in the block opposite slish-sloshes along. She stops by the hibiscus hedge which fences the square plot of green in the middle of our block of apartments. She looks around to see if any one is watching. She plucks some flowers, thrusts them in her *dupatta* and relieved at being undetected slish-sloshes her way to the temple. An old man in loose shirt and *dhoti* follows her. He also stops by the hedge and looks around to see if anyone is listening. He puts pressure on his paunch, and lets out a long, painful fart. He walks on with a lighter step and a 'who did that?' look on his face. A light goes up in the opposite block. A woman draws the curtain, ties her untidy hair into a bun and decides there is no need for a light. More lights are switched on and off. The morning star is barely visible. Crows fly out in lines cawing to each other. The muezzin's call comes over from the mosque. The *goojar* milk seller comes round with his cans clashing noisily on his bicycle. He is followed by the tinkle of another cyclist's bell and a heavy voice going round the block 'paperwallah – Hindustan Taim, Ishtaitmayn, Indian Express-*paper wallah*'. A little later I hear the shush of papers pushed under my door. I stay in my armchair and let the morning breeze waft the light of dawn into my musty apartment. It is cool, fragrant, pregnant with sorrow and longing. It is the *bad-i-sabah* – the morning breeze sacred to lovers. This is the Delhi that I love.

Why Delhi?

Why did the many dynasties that ruled India choose Delhi to be the seat of their empire? That's easy. If you were King of India and wanted to find the most suitable place from which to survey your domains you could do no better than take a map of the country and put your finger on a spot near the centre and then find out if it has a plentiful supply of drinking water, good agricultural hinterland to feed the populace, a peace-loving citizenry and a healthy climate. Delhi has all these – and more. The Jumna has enough water to slake the thirst of the people and also protect the city's eastern flank. Some years when the summer monsoon has been good and the thaw of snow on the Himalayas (a bare 100 miles as the crow flies) coincides with the torrential downpour in July and August, the Jumna can swell to marine proportions. Those years the scene from the Jasmine Tower of the Red Fort can be truly awe-inspiring: it is a fearful expanse of muddy turbulence as far as the eye can see. During winter, the river is reduced to modest proportions: people wade across it without wetting their knees. But even in winter the Jumna gives all that a river is expected to give: water to drink; water to wash; water to drown the dead and alligators to dispose of them. It is a fruitful river full of fat carp and cat fish; its turtles lay eggs by the hundred (consumed by the hundred by Delhi's unsuspecting restaurant-goers). Its extensive sandbanks produce succulent watermelons. From the Jasmine Tower the riverside appears strewn with green marbles. The river attracts a large variety of water fowl: geese, mallard, pintail, pochard, darters, egrets, cranes spoonbills, cormorants etc.

All around Delhi is rich agricultural land growing wheat, rice, pulses and sugarcane. There are plenty of cattle to supply milk and meat. The countryside is peaceful enough. The rural population consists of Hindu agricultural and pastoral tribes: Jat, Ahir and Brahmin cultivators with Goojar cattle-breeders (often cattle-lifters). For centuries they have lived in friendly exclusiveness with the Muslim Meos.

Before 1917, the population of the city was half-Muslim half-Hindu. Hindus were merchants and shopkeepers. Muslims were divided in their occupations. The poor were craftsmen. The rich were just rich descendants of the Omarah. (Delhi has been the seat of Muslim empires for over 500 years). It was the Muslim aristocrat who gave Delhi its cultural life. He patronized the crafts: ivory, gold, silver and brass, tiles and textiles. He patronised the courtesans (at one time resident in Chawri and neighbouring bazars) and kept alive the muses of song and dance. Mohammad Shah Rangeela was the paradigm of princely patronage. They gave stipends to poets like Khusrau, Meer, Zoq, Ghalib and Dard. Some like Bahadur Shah Zafar wrote excellent verse.

Delhi has an honoured place on the map of Islam. For those who cannot go on *haj* it is (next perhaps to Ajmer) the most sacred of all cities. In Mehrauli near the Kutub Minar is the famous Shamsi Talab and the Auliya Masjid where many Sufi saints came to meditate. At Mehrauli too is the mausoleum of Kutubuddin Bakhtiyar Kaki. Then there is the tomb of Khwaja Nizamuddin Chishti – revered by hundreds of thousands of pilgrims from all over India and Pakistan.

There is little doubt that Delhi was and is destined to be the eternal capital of Hindustan. If you have any doubt, climb the Kutub Minar and count the number of Delhis lying beneath you – Lal Kot, Siri, Chiragh, Tughlaqabad, Kotla Ferozeshah, Shahjahanabad, New Delhi. There were many more whose identity remains to be established.

It took the English twenty years to discover the merits of Delhi: the Sahibs are slow in matters like these. But once the decision was made, they built a new city on a scale grander than that envisaged by Shah Jahan. What Lutyens and Baker could not do in terms of beauty, they did in terms of massiveness.

Spring:

On the day of Basant we usher in the spring. *Basant Pal Udant* – when Basant is come, winter's cold has fled. But winter's cold is not fled. Mornings are sharp. Mustard in whose honour we wear yellow is often under a shroud of mist. Dew drops that grace the rose glitter like icicles. *Simul* buds are pregnant but despite the pecking of crows refuse to open out. The grape vine is like twisted rope without a sign of life. The cock sparrow fluffs his wings and struts randily around his hen but she pecks him off in no uncertain manner. The nights are as chilly as ever. The Queen-of-the-Night wastes her fragrance in the frosty moonlight. Only tom cats have begun to caterwaul and copulate on the roof tops. But toms are as sexy as human males who bestride their females in and out of season.

Then comes spring. The *simul* bursts its fiery red or pale yellow. The *bauhinia* is also in flower-papery white and mauve. Pale green leaves sprout on the vine. Now the hen fluffs her wings, flattens her cola and cheeps at the cock to mount her – and cheeps for more. On tree-tops and balconies kites and vultures copulate with agonizing screams. The dawn is early; the twilight lengthens and after the sunset glow is gone, the sky is a luminescent grey like a sheet of emery paper. The nights are warm.

Connaught Circus:

If a city can be likened to the human body with its head, trunk and limbs then most can also be said to have a heart. Different cities of Delhi had, undoubtedly, such hearts of their own. Thus Shah Jahanabad, the city of the Mughals had its Chandni Chowk – the silver square (it is in fact a street) where all the important emporia were located. The heart of New Delhi is in its main shopping centre which consists of a large circular lawn around which are three concentric circles of double-stories, colonnaded verandahs with shops on the ground floor and residential apartments on the top. A series of roads ring these circles and over a dozen others branch out of this circle like antennae. This heart of the new city is known after the Duke of Connaught, uncle of King George V, who happened to visit the city at the time of its erection as Connaught Circus.

Over the years, Connaught Circus has developed a personality of its own. Though its cinemas, stores and restaurants have undoubtedly contributed towards the making of that personality, the more important factors are its unique style of architecture (including its ornamental trees and the birds that roost on them) and the humans who have become 'characters' and by their mere existence lent some of their personality to Connaught Circus. In one circumambulation the pilgrim will encounter most of them.

Start from the southern end along Janpath. As soon as you pass Hotel Imperial a Sikh fortune-teller will sidle alongside and start mumbling in your ear. Among the amusing sights of Connaught Circus are foreign visitors being trailed by Sikh soothsayers. Equally characteristic are the Tibetan 'antique' dealers who line the footpath outside Hotel Imperial. They have no use for the Indians, but soon get on intimate terms of 'Hey Joe!' with the Americans. 'No buy nice present for your girl friend today?'

After the Janpath stalls one encounters the real 'characters' of

Connaught Circus: the *chooran wallah* clanging the copper bell on his bicycle and his explosive yell: '*Lakkar hazam pathar hazam*' – assuring buyers that a pinch of the aperients will dissolve wood and stone; the *rangoli-makers* stamping intricate patterns on the pavement; the flute-seller flaunting soulful tunes to a three foot china figure of Sri Krishna. Connaught Circus has its own brand of beggars and pseudo-beggars; a dapper young lad on crutches with a Yankee accent saying, 'Evening Paper, Sirr'. There is the 'Blindwallah' with a pathetically prophetic 'look' on his upward turned face and his hands turned upwards like Prophet Moses. He walks silently around the colonnade displaying a soulful placard with the hymn 'Lead Kindly Light'. The pseudo beggars are little boys (and girls) who stick paper tri-colour flags into your shirts demanding charity, or insist on a tip for guarding your car. Of the same genre are some tradesmen: grape-fruit, strawberry and apple-sellers whose insistence on off-loading their little baskets (bottoms full of paper or sawdust) is an accepted irritant. Only a little better are the book-stall owners and tradesmen with booths in the verandahs of the colonnade. There is no browsing at books without an insistent 'Yes mister, what you want? Latest *Philimphare*, Playboy? More private?... Yes?' Stopping at other booths becomes a little suspect since one of the items most prominently displayed in mountainous heaps are all brands of contraceptives.

Connaught Circus bustles with tea and coffee houses. Most have regular patrons of their own who know each other well. Practically everyone is on hand-waving terms with everyone else. There is little consumption of beverage: a cup is made to last a couple of hours while reputations of politicians, film stars, artists and litterateurs are meticulously torn up spoon by spoon. From the throng of the cognoscenti one can get a fair notion of the magnitude of educated unemployment in the capital.

Connaught Circus has different aspects in different season. Some prefer it in May when the gulmohur trees in the inner circle are at their fiery best; some like it during the monsoon when the jamun trees are loaded with fruit and jamun-sellers spread themselves out on the muddy pavements. But more prefer the autumn and winter months when jay walking and basking in the sunshine is pleasanter. The evenings are cold and the trees alive with parakeets and mynahs whose screaming drowns the roar of traffic and the hawkers' cries.

Connaught Circus goes to bed early. Shops close at 7 p.m. Few owners leave their windows lit for the night. A few neon signs glimmer away, a few *panwalas* sit patiently outside the restaurants dabbing pan leaves with lime and catechu paste. A few stragglers sit round his hurricane lantern, light their *bidis* from the smoking end of a rope and ogle at passers-by. They say Connaught Circus has a night life. A local paper publishes a serial entitled 'Confessions of a Connaught Circus girl'. It assures us every week that educated girls can be bought in the Circus after dark. One hears of pimps and ponces and homosexuals. Many a time have I gone in search of them but only heard the tramp of my feet echoing in the silent corridors.

Delhi has its Delhi-wallahs; New Delhi has no one who really belongs. Its oldest inhabitants are the Sikh contractors who built most of it. Of the original dozen or more only one remains, Sir Sobha Singh. The rest of New Delhi consists of itinerant civil servants and that even less stable element, the diplomatic corps. It will take a hundred years or more before people begin to be boast of being New-Delhi-wallahs. (It would have been earlier if the city had been given a different name. Why did not anyone think of calling it by the name of one of the many villages it has swallowed up? Yogininagar, Raisina, Paharganj or Nizamuddin would have aroused more emotion than the bastardised New-Delhi.)

The Diplomatic Corps has given New Delhi a curious social pattern. Most diplomats have little to do. And they get their scotch whisky at about Rs. 10/- per bottle. New Delhi's bureaucrats spend long hours in their offices and are extremely thirsty by the time they come out of the Secretariat. For them a bottle of Scotch costs over Rs. 100/-. The diplomats are eager to make contacts; the bureaucrats equally eager to slake their thirst. The equation works out well. There's never a day when some embassy or the other does not celebrate its national day or has not an important visitor who desires to meet a few natives. If you move in the right circles in the Capital, you need not cook any food in your house. It can be one continuous round of lunch, cocktail and dinner parties. You meet the same people. Senior members of the ICS are usually the first to arrive and last to stagger out. One who fancies himself as a wit is always telling you that he has only drunk two liquids in his life: mother's milk and Scotch whisky. Another cannot resist pawing women. A Sardarji who has literary pretensions invariably quotes a version of Plomer's lines on life in Bloomsbury:

It's a succession of parties for sponges and bores

With traffic jams outside, they turn up in their scores

With first rate sherry flowing into second rate whores

And third class conversation without a single pause.

The Sardarji who is the life of every cocktail party is an acknowledged toper, whoremonger and ceaseless talker.

This too is Delhi; the Delhi that I detest.

Tughlaqabad:

May. The lid is taken off the fires of *Jehennum*. Searing loo and spiraling dust devils. The eye-scorching glare and the quick-silver shimmering on the tarmac. Not a breath of life. No mad dogs, no Englishmen. Nothing, only the noon-day sun.

The car seat burns. 'Ouch,' screams my lady companion in *pucca* strip-cartoon style. She raises her middle to let her bottom recover from the shock! 'My! How hot it is!' 'Ouch,' I reply. 'Just touch the steering wheel!' I grab her hand and put it on the steering wheel. 'Don't,' she screams again.

'Shouldn't have left the car in the sun. Tyres must be bursting with the heat.'

We take the Qutb Road – past the mausoleum of Safdarjang, through the rash of *nouveau riche* houses which have eaten up Yusaf Sarai and obliterated monuments – many centuries old, many times more durable and many times more beautiful. At the Qutb Minar we turn sharp left through village Lado Serai. There is much activity at the well. The afternoon is reserved for women – three draw wheels in action with *jat* women vigorously pulling up buckets of water and pouring them into the pitchers which line the parapet. Two women bathing. Not a stitch on them. They put their hands between their thighs and turn their backs to the road. An old woman growls angrily at them. A young one pretends to pick up a stone and hurl it at our car. There is a burst of laughter. These *jat* women of Haryana – tall, erect, full-bosomed, full-blooded with a stride that would be the envy of an Amazonian queen.

We go through Lado Serai. And once more it is the hot, shimmering tarmac and the expanse of burning *khaki* earth. The shadow of the car speeds ahead of us as the sun goes lower down. A tumulus on the left slowly becomes a stone wall, the stone wall became a massive battlement of grey and red rock rising over sixty feet. The barren road becomes an avenue lined with ancient banyan trees. I pull up under the shade. The arched gateway leading into the citadel of Tughlaqabad a few feet above us on the left; and the viaduct leading to the tomb of the builder to Tughlaqabad, Ghiasuddin, on our right.

'What's happened to all the urchins who hang around to look after visitors' cars?' I ask.

'Mid-week summer. No visitors. No urchins,' she replies. 'Calls for a celebration.'

We celebrate.

'What's that?' she demands as she pulls herself away.

I look back in alarm. A furry claw clutching the rim of the windscreen. Then the face a rhesus monkey. *'Khokhokho,'* it begs for food. Then menaces us. The girl screams and clings to me. The monkey scampers away and joins a herd which seems to have dropped from the banyan tree.

'Who said we were alone?' I say giving her a reassuring hug. 'You're never alone in India,'

'What a fright that gave me,' she says nestling against my bosom.

'Sahib, I'll look after your car.'

We break apart quickly. She smooths back her hair. 'Really! What a country!'

'Sahib, it's my turn. This boy looked after the last one. Didn't you?'

They begin to quarrel. 'I got here first... no Sahib, I asked you first, didn't I? You decide.'

A few more urchins come along and clamour for the right to guard my car. We step out, take one by the scruff of his neck and order him – 'You will look after my car.' To settle the dispute finally. 'He's the only one I will pay.'

They come on me like hornets – 'ajee vah... is this justice? I've been here all day....'

I just lock the car and walk away towards the gate of the fort. Four boys follow us. 'Sahib, I will show you the fort.'

'No... I know the fort well.'

The old Meena Bazaar, the women's market and...

'I know them all, I belong here.'

Nothing deters their determination to inform us. They trail behind.

'This is the main gate of the fort,' one informs me. 'And this – and this on the left is the big tank. It used to supply drinking water for the entire city of Tughlaqabad.'

So it goes on as we go up the paved pathway through the spread of ruins: gun placements, mosques, the Meena Bazaar, the watch-tower – all a mess of rubble with just enough of a wall or a heap of stones to give rise to conjecture. We are right on top of the ruined city. We take a footpath – I always take this footpath when I come to Tughlaqabad – and thread our way through the debris and goats nibbling at *vasicka* bushes till we are at the edge of the battlement. And the world lies beneath – a sheer drop of hundreds of feet, a large pool of water (all that remains of the once impassable moat), beyond the pool, the village of Tughlaqabad and just the dusty treeless plain on one side and the stretch of ruins on the other. My companion is stricken dumb at the vastness of the spectacle. She takes my hand and gives it a squeeze of appreciation.

'Arey, she has taken the Sardar's hand,' comments one of the urchins. She does not understand what he is saying but the sniggers that follow make her aware that we do not have the world to ourselves. 'For God's sake, get rid of these bastards. I am sick of having them trailing behind us all the time.'

I give in. I take out all the change I have in my pocket and hand it to them to be divided equally. I tell them that a party of American tourists was following us from the Qutab Minar and if they don't hurry back to the road, they will miss all the *baksheesh*. That works like magic. They scamper back over the bushes causing a stampede among the goats. Now we do have the world to ourselves. All we survey from the lofty ramparts of the city of the Tughlaqs is ours.

She sinks on the ground and pulls me down besides her. We have a boulder to rest our backs. She nestles her head on my chest and asks: 'Tell me about this place? Who was Sri Tughlaq after whom these ruins are named?'

'Sri Tughlaq! Really! His Imperial Majesty Mohammed Ghiasuddin. Tughlaq, shadow of God on Earth, King of Kings, Defender of the Faith, Monarch of the Universe, Emperor of Hindustan. He was warden of the marches when he was invited to become emperor. Ruled Hindustan for four years 1321-1325 – during which he built this citadel. He mulcted his Hindu subjects leaving them just enough to survive. He made so much money that he filled one of the reservoirs of this city with molten gold. 'He never did anything that was not replete with wisdom and sense,' said a contemporary poet Amir Khusru. Nothing except trust his favourite son, Prince Juna, who was so impatient to become King that he had his doting sire crushed under an arch'.

She laughed. 'Did this Prince Juna also destroy this city?'

'In a way. He was a genius as well as a crackpot. A cruel reformer, a generous tyrant – a schizophrenic. He transferred his capital from here 700 miles south to Daulatabad, forcing even lame beggars to move. And then ordered them back to Delhi. He introduced paper currency till all his gold and silver reserves were acquired by counterfeiters. He mounted an invasion on China losing everyone of his army of invasion. Then after 26 years of this crazy rule (in 1351) as Barani, a contemporary historian, wrote – 'the King was freed of his people and they of the King'. He had no son. His nephew Firoze who succeeded him, built a new capital, six miles north of here along the Jumna. It's called Firoze Shah Kotla.'

The sun's rays have lost their sting. It's become a large orange balloon. A line of crows flies over head towards the city. Parakeets fly across in flocks of green streaks. From Tughlaqabad village thousands of sparrows fly up, wheel about in the sky merging with other flocks of thousands and then settle down on acacia trees for their sunset twitters.

The orange sun goes down in a haze of dust. I can hear the village lads urging their buffaloes out of the pond. Their shouts mingle with chirruping of sparrows and the forlorn barking of dogs. An eerie silence descends on everything.

The evening star shines alone in the grey sky. A soft breeze begins to blow. After the intense heat of the afternoon, it is like a balm – and soporific. My eyes are heavy with sleep. I ruffle my companion's tousled hair. She has fallen asleep. I shut my eyes and within a few moments I too am lost to the world.

I wake with a sensation of someone looking at me. The moon is shining full in my face. A grey bird comes like a ghost out of the grey sky and settles on a crag a few feet away. It raises its head to the moon and a full-throated *'pecooh, pecooh'* – bursts out of its throat filling the moonlit landscape with its plaintive cries. 'Listen Eugenia.' Her name is not Eugenia. And the bird is not a nightingale but hawk cuckoo (*papeeha*). Nevertheless its bursts come crowding through the moonlight.

Eternal passion!

Eternal pain!

Monsoons and Mussulmans:

The first monsoon showers have washed the dust and sweat off the city. People whose spirits had withered under months of exposure to the scorching heat of the sun are refreshed and in buoyant mood. How can you work on a day like this? It is sinful. The dark clouds and the cool damp breeze beckon you to the open: to the parks and playgrounds, to the ancient monuments – or just the open country. The roads to Hauz Khas and the Qutub Minar are crowded with cycles, scooters, *tongas* and cars.

Parties of boys, singing and yelling as they go along. The rich have their cars. The fat Lalaji has his phaeton. He wears his gossamer thin muslin *kurta* with wide sleeves to let the breeze run up his armpits. His fatter wife and daughter are clad in colourful *dopattas* and wear their jewellery. A servant sits at their feet with a basket full of sucking mangoes and cooking utensils. The Lalaji's notion of a picnic is to first eat the air (*hava khori*) then eat fried *pooris* and highly spiced new potatoes – then get rid of the air. Each one to his own picnic. There is the brave new India of boys with side-curls, bell-bottom trousers with transistors slung across their shoulders, with pig-tailed in tight fitting bosom-enlarging shirts and bumclinging *shalwars* on the pillions behind them. The transistors pour out their ersatz hotch-potch of shamelessly purloined western tunes sung (oh so soulfully) by Mohammed Rafi or Lata Mangeshkar. New India adds its anglicized version of the same tune – *tra la la la its savan bhadon*. Each one to his own music.

In Delhi, only the Mussulman can have a sense of belonging. Delhi is Muslim. The rest, Hindus, Sikhs, Christians, are aliens to the ethos of the city. The mosque and its minarets, the marble palaces with their audience halls, seraglios, dream chambers, *hamam* baths, bead-telling apartment, the pleasure gardens, the domed mausoleum – all are Muslim. The Mussalman harmonises with the landscape: his speech is Delhi, his food is Delhi, his way of life is Delhi. The clouds take his gaily-coloured kites to their fleecy bosoms: they welcome the Mussalman's flocks of pigeons wheeling to their master's whistle and waving scarf.

All that is nice in Delhi's vice – the courtesan with the nightingale voice and sophisticated coquetry, the *hijra* with his refined bawdiness and raucous voice singing at births and weddings down to the soft-bottomed catamite – have imbibed Muslim traditions. And all that has now been vulgarised.

To see Delhi at its monsoon best (*Phool Valon Ki Sair* is good occasion) join a poor Delhi Muslim family. The man gets out his two wheeled *ekka*. He packs his mother, wife, aunts, cousins, children in its four-foot square top. The women wear their white *burqas* but have their faces uncovered. He and the men folk honour the monsoon by wearing perfumed oil on their bodies and bright red loin cloths to cover their privates. His chestnut brown horse is the best-dressed member of the family: bells on his harness, blue and golden yellow plumes on its head. And then they are out on the Qutub Road. He flourishes his cane in the air without ever insulting his horse by hitting it. The horse responds to the pat on its glossy flanks, the exultant *cry hurrr… chal merey betey sarpat chal* – come my son, the speed of the wind! He puts his whip in the spokes of the *ekka* wheel: the rattle is louder than the car bulb horn. The *ekka* flies past the fat Lalaji's Fiat Millicento. It scatters the crowd of cycling Sardarjis in their multi-coloured turbans fastened by paper pins. The Sardarji, yells: *'Oi, oi, oi, Sooer.* 'Are you out to murder us?' These Punjabis have no finesse. For finesse, the Delhi Mussalman.

Out of the huddle of *burqas* on the *ekka* stands up a little boy not yet six-years-old. He loosens his little jock strap and whips out his tiny circumcised penis. He flourishes it at the Sardarji as David must have flourished his sling at Goliath.

'Abey Sikhrey Sardar!' He retorts pointing to his instrument, 'you want to sit on *Qutub Sahib ki laat*'. But the Qutub is only 238 feet high!

These are the people of Delhi – my people – the people that I love.

The Co-ordinates of the
Indian Spring

Hamdi Bey

(Quest 54: Monsoon 1967)

In the twenties a book with a rather provocative title, *The Scientific Study of Scenery,* was published in Britain, where for the preceding 140 years, roughly since the time of Wordsworth, mountains, brooks and lakes had been the subject of aesthetic contemplation. The present essay could have been a scientific study of the elusive Indian spring had there been enough data to attempt one. While the detailed information, which alone can justify a scientific study, are being collected, some of the co-ordinates can be sketched out.

Four common trees, which grow all over India, provide preliminary evidence that spring begins as early as December at Cape Commorin and only in March at Amritsar. Between these two points it travels from south to north at a rate of four days for each degree of latitude, which is roughly the same as that of spring travelling northwards in the USA and the sun's passage from the Equator to the Tropic of Cancer.

These trees are the mango, the neem, the tamarind and the babul, which most people can recognize at sight though they might not be able to notice the flowers at a glance except in the first and the fourth. The mango flowers in Kerala in the first week of December, at Hyderabad a month later, in Gujarat two months later and in the

Punjab in the first week of March. Roughly at the same intervals occurs the first flowering of the neem in Malabar (first week of January), Mysore (the first week of February), Central India (the first week of March) and Punjab (first week of April).

Approximately the same 90 days elapse between the respective first flowerings of the tamarind and the babul at 8° N and 30° N latitudes. Though the rate at which spring travels northward is the same as that of the sun, the two phenomena are not synchronous. For example when the mango first flowers near Trivandrum, the sun is still travelling southwards to the Tropic of Capricorn. It does turn northwards but is still in the southern hemisphere when the neem first flowers. When the sun starts being overhead at Cape Commorin (in other words anywhere on the Indian mainland) in the third week of March, spring is more than a fortnight old in the Punjab. The sun is never overhead at any place north of Bhopal, and even there it is so only late in June when as far north as Srinagar spring has been succeeded by summer.

Atmospheric and soil heat, rather than insolation, might be the contributory factors, but we cannot be certain. Soil temperatures are not known but a metre above their surface, in meteorological screens which look like bee-hives, the mean temperature in Kerala in both December and January is 25°C, which amount of warmth the Punjab has only as late as April. That seems to be the spring temperature. The decisive factor may be, in all probability, an internal periodicity within a tree, which may be merely coincidental with solar and atmospheric periodicity but as little related as periodicity in women is to the phases of the moon.

That spring should travel northwards at the same rate in both India and North America, when in the one the transverse Himalayas keep out the northern cold while in the other the longitudinal Rockies let in Arctic winds, indicates that atmospheric temperatures are not to any great extent determinants of spring.

There are two growing periods for our plants – one when water is abundant, i.e., the monsoon, and the other when water starts becoming scarce, i.e., spring. And there are trees, even common ones, which flower at both these growing periods. The jarul, bottle brush, copperpod and pagoda are the more important among these.

The portia puts out one or two flowers throughout the year but many more in the cold season. The agastya and two bauhinias, the mountain ebony and the pink, flower after the rains into early winter.

The wish and the teak hibernate during spring, shedding leaves and remaining bare till June when new foliage appears to be followed by flowers in the rains. The evergreen elephant apple and the deciduous kadam also flower during the monsoon.

The true summer flowering trees, barring exotics like the gulmohur, are few, the most striking being the golden shower, the pink sweep and the ironwood.

The last named has two innings of splendour of beautiful red and pink new leaves against the background of older bluish leaves in spring and flowers in the monsoon. Being conical in form it is one of our better looking trees. The pakur has a new copper foliage in spring, but the peepul has many more colours and its transformation from a bare to a multi-colour silky rustle is another wonderful sight in spring which is as much symbolic of the season as the flowering of the mango. The handsomest spring foliage is of the deciduous kusum, whose entire tree turns successively light red, bright red and dark maroon. The flowers, which come much later in the year, of none of these are showy.

In spite of these exceptions we have a large number of trees which flower in the earlier part of the year, the flowering period varying from place to place as does spring's incidence itself. These include both evergreens and deciduous species, though leaflessness makes flowers more conspicuous among the latter. The mast, arjun, asoka, tamarind, neem, jamun, shisham, garuga and anjan do not have a striking fall and therefore the more famed are the palas, simul, gulgul, coral, bidul, bakain, drumstick, caper and mahua.

The south to north sequence of blossoming for most of these or the local succession of flowers anywhere have not yet been worked out, for the duration of the Indian spring remains undefined. Because of awareness of or panic at the increasing heat there has been confusion and the Indian spring has been presumed to be brief, but even in the extreme south a month elapses between the first flowering of the mango and the first flowering of the neem. As EHA put it 'in our spring-tide vivifying heat is divorced from refreshing moisture, so that half nature, instead of being warmed to life, is scorched to death'.

Kipling had a different view of the Indian spring which he thought to be 'the most wonderful, because she has not to cover a clear, bare field with new leaves and flowers, but to drive before her and to put away the hanging-on, over-surviving raffle of half-green things which the gentle winter has suffered to live, and to make the partly-dressed stale earth feel new and young once more.... There is one day when all things are tired, and the very smells, as they drift on the heavy air, are old and used. One cannot explain this, but it feels so. Then there is another day – to the eye nothing whatever has changed – when all the smells are new and delightful.... All the trees and the bushes and the bamboos and the mosses and the juicy-leaved plants wake with a noise of growing that you can almost hear'.

Wynter-Blyth noted that 'in the arid parts of North and Northwest India, spring is delayed until the onset of the monsoon'. According to his graph of butterfly activity, which because of its dependence on young green leaves, shoots and flowers is an index of spring, the season at Calcutta develops slowly after the first week of January, covers both February and March and continues to the end of April. Butterflies are most numerous and active in the last week of February and first week of March.

Jim Corbett thought spring at Kaladhungi, in the National Park named after him, began with the flowering of the simul in late February and ended with the hot April winds blowing about its kapok. And during spring, mingled with the many shades of green – for each tree (species) has its own individual (leaf) colour – are vivid splashes of orange, gold, lilac, pink and red of the massively flowering trees. We still do not understand variations in leaf colour, or in other words of chlorophyll, despite the researches of toothpaste manufacturers.

At Patna, spring is believed to be the period intervening between Basant Panchami (in whose rituals the first sprays of mango flower have an important role) and Holi, but even there many hold that Chaitra is an integral part of the season and that summer begins with Vaisakha. At Ranchi, spring is believed to start with the Adivasi harvest thanksgiving festival of the Magh full moon and the spring festival of the Sarhul, which celebrates the flowering of the sal, and to end when the first suspicion of yellow and green comes on the bare branches of the wish.

Spring is also the period of the rabi harvest. Vernal festivals vary with agricultural practices. The single-cropping Adivasis, whose paddy is harvested late in December, have their spring festival in January, while the double-cropping communities prefer to wait till March. The rabi harvest has to be gathered before the people can let themselves go, however intoxicating the seasonal air. Such groups have their period of abandon after the first day of Vaisakh for there are no pressing engagements in the fields and if the air is not as intoxicating as it was in spring the palm toddy can make up for diminished natural excitement.

The northern boundary of the proper Indian spring (for those in Kashmir and Hills are more temperate than tropical) is the Frostline, which runs along the foot of the Himalayas, because monsoon vegetation cannot bear fast. The western limit is the line dividing areas which get respectively more or less than 60 centimetres of rain in the year, or the boundary between the desert and the dry, hot deciduous forest. Similarly in the northeast and the southwest, the line which marks out the areas with more than 200 centimetres of rain in a year from those which get less, is the outer perimeter.

A large area, roughly most of India, from Amritsar to Cape Commorin and from Calcutta to Ahmedabad gets an annual precipitation between 60 and 200 centimetres and provides the best playground for spring, the bias being northeastern. Within this big landmass are mountains, plateaus and hills, and plains, peneplains and valleys. There are sal forests northeast of a line that we may draw on the map to connect Dehra Dun and Vizag; teak forests south of a similar line running from Bombay to Jabalpur, and shisham plantations to the northwest, as well as much mixed scrub everywhere. Mixed scrub is as truly the jungle as the high canopied woodland and both are glorious in spring. As Kipling said 'there is no spring in the world like the jungle spring'.

Outside the jungle the alluvium – the white calcareous, the reddish lateritic and the grey undifferentiated – the black regur and the tropical red soils have been everywhere converted into fields which lie either weeded under rabi crops or grazed fallows waiting for the kharif ploughing and sowing. Meadow and field flowers have little chance. So spring is more visible in the village trees or in the towns and principal cities – Delhi, Calcutta, Bombay, Madras and Hyderabad – where roadside trees, gardens and parks are as much touched by the magic wand of spring as the jungle.

Nowhere is winter severe enough to freeze the soil and deny plants sustenance. The more reasonable cause for leaf-shedding should have been a safeguard from transpiration during the hot and rainless summer, further desiccated by the looh which succeeds but does not precede spring and reaches as far east as Patna. The wish and teak respond to this immediate logic, but the equally characteristic peepul has a tapering wing-tip to facilitate drip suggestive of inertia from a wetter past. The ritual of new leaf and flowers, after a mild brief winter, on the massive scale as it is in the sal forests, too looks back to a colder, if not in parts glacial, environment over 12,000 years ago.

The Indian spring is a fine balance between plant life's commitments to the past and adjustment to present realities. The balance is fine enough to be precarious – free grazing by unpenned livestock has already driven it to the treetops for the flowers of the field and wayside shrubbery are largely extinct outside the jungle, and soil erosion may bring about changes difficult to foresee.

Neither contemporaneously climatic nor physiological, it is rather in the nature of what Jungian psychology describes as memories of the racial unconscious. The memories vary from one race or species to another, but the net result is that fall and spring are telescoped into each other, the rabi harvest and preparations for the karif sowing nearly synchronise. A gust of wind may blow dying leaves around new leaf buds. This duality finds its musical equivalent in the Basant Baga, which has both melancholy and joy blended into each other – the crackle of old leaves and the lisps of the new in chorus.

Identity of the trees mentioned in the above article in scientific terminology and regional languages:

Mango (*Mangifera indica*): Am, manga or mangga.

Neem (*Azadirachta indica*): Margosa, limba, nimbay, vera or yepa.

Tamarind (*Tamarindus indica*): Imli, tetul, puli or chinta.

Babul (*Acacia Arabica*).

Jarul (*Lagerstroemia flosreginae*): Azar, atampu, hadali, varagogu.

Bottle brush (*Callistemon lanceolatus*).

Copperpod (*Peltophorum incrme*): Rusty Shield-Bearer, ivalvagai, kondachinta.

Pagoda (*Plumeria alba*): Frangipani, gulchin, perungalli or veyyivarahalu.

Portia (*Thespesia populuca*): *Bhendi* or tulip tree, dumbla gajashundi, chandamaram, kallal, glagaiavi or parash-pipal.

Agastya (*Sesbania grandiflora*): Sesban.

Mountain Ebony (*Bauhinia purpurea*): Purple bauhinia, geranium tree, kachnar, koiral, karalla, mandarin, kanchanam.

Pink Bauhinia (*B. triandra*): Lal kachnar.

Bidul (*B variegate*): Variegated Bauhinia, Camel's Foot, baisakhi, kovidara, kanchan, mandarai, boroda, bodanta.

Wish (*Adina cordifolia*): karma, hedu, haldu.

Teak (*Tectonia grandis*): segun, sagwan, tekku.

Elephant apple (*Dillenia indica*):Chalta, kalinga.

Kadam (*Antocephalous cadamba*): Kadawal, aattutek or vellai.

Golden Shower *(Cassia fistula)*: Indian laburnum, sonalu, sonali, amaltas.

Pink Sweep (*Cassia nodosa*).

Ironwood (*Mesua ferrea*): Nagkesar, Nahor.

Pakur (*Ficus infectoria*): Pilkhan.

Peepul (*Ficus religiosa*).

Kusum (*Schleichera trijuga*): Kusim.

Mast (*Polyalthia longifolia*): Ashok, debdaru, choruna.

Arjun (*Terminalia arjuna*): Kulamaruthu, yermaddi.

Asoka (*Saraca indica*): Sita asoka, jasundi, hemapushpam.

Jamun (*Eugenia jambolana*): Java plum, Indian allspice, jambhool, blackberry, kalajam, naval, neredu.

Shisham (*Dalbergia sisoo*): Sissu.

Garuga (*Garuga pinnata*): Kaikar, kudark, karvambu.

Palas (*Butea frondosa*) Flame of the forest, dhak.

Simul (*Bombas malabaricum*): Red Silk Cotton.

Gulgul (*Cochlospermum gossypium*): kumbi tannaku, Yellow Silk Cotton.

Coral (*Erythrina indica*): Pangli, Maruka, Madar.

Bakain (*Melia azadcrachta*): Persian Lilac ghora nim.

Drumstick (*Moringa oleifera*): Horse, Radish, sajna, morunga, munga.

Caper (*Crataeca religiosa*); Sacred Barna, bilasi, barun, maralingam, ulimari.

Mahua (*Madhuca latifolia*) Butter, Mupa,mupai, ippa.

Books

EHA: *The Naturalist on Prowl*
Kipling: *The Second Jungle Book*
Corbett: *Jungle Lore*
Wynter-Blyth: *Butterflies of the Indian Region*

The National School of Drama

Gieve Patel

(Quest 54: Monsoon 1967)

When in 1962 E. Alkazi took over directorship of the National School of Drama at Delhi, the institution was mouldering and defunct. Today, in a matter of five years, it is one of the most efficiently organized and progressive of government institutions. The gearing of this change is the work of a single dedicated man. Its effect has been and will be felt by many.

The students being the *raison-d' etre* of the School, it is proper that this article look closely at them, and on how the School functions for and through them.

Considering that the students are drawn from all over the country and from varied backgrounds, it may seem unfair to try and characterize them by a few qualities, except that, after formal and informal interviews, common trends do begin to strike one's attention: the junior students appear in the main unsophisticated, even naïve, regarding their conception of theatre and its implications. Also, they are not dissimilar to a group of first-year art or science students whereas one expects the young theatre enthusiast to carry an extra depth of perception. Jumping three years, to speak now with a batch of final-year students is one test of the training. The change one sees is not just the result of the passage of time, or of the acquisition of a certain amount of knowledge. It is a deeper change in outlook and attitude.

How this is brought about I will discuss later when I deal with the working environment of the School. I would like first to dilate upon the lack of 'sophistication' I have mentioned earlier, and use it to analyse the students in more detail. I mean by this seemingly snobbish word, the attitudes, prejudices and reflexes of people living in an urban environment and in touch with the most forward ideas in art and living. Most of the students have never been part of such an environment and this leads to diverse results when they meet with the shock of living and training at the School. Some, in spite of a surface polish and know-how, fail to emancipate themselves from the influence of such a pathetic thing as Hindi cinema. On the other hand, it is surely the very stolidity of their origin which prevents the large majority from falling prey to the chatty glitter of college-club theatre. The graduates emerge serious and hard-working men and women. Delhi may have a role to play in all this. Being in fact an overgrown town it preserves many of the characteristics of provincial India, and does not, as a metropolis might, sever the link these students have with their own home-states and towns.

We would now have a look at the programme the students go through in their three years of training: important plays from various literatures are analysed in detail, including the Sanskrit and the Greek. There is special study of Modern Indian Drama. Every year a large number of new plays from all over the country are added to the School library, one of the best of its kind in India. A large number of plays have been translated into Hindi and Urdu by the students themselves since it is in these languages that they are eventually performed. The babel of Indian languages which at every other level has made for parochialism and faction is consciously set up by the NSD as a spring of richness and diversity. As defence against an impossible situation, this attitude may be as good as any other, and within the few years of its existence the NSD has translated forty to fifty plays from various Indian and foreign languages. The quality of these translations would naturally be uneven, and complaints are heard about the obtuseness of Sanskritised versions and the clumsiness, theatrically speaking, of the speech. Creative activity of this kind, however, is self-perfecting, and leads eventually to profitable results.

The problem of English-speaking students may be highlighted at this point. A number of them feel excluded by their inability to cope with the language of production and their talent also is thereby wasted. A move to introduce full-scale English productions is under study.

Students take part in five to six major productions a year. These plays cover a wide ground in style, and actors learn to adapt themselves to all these – from classical comedy and tragedy and the harmonies of Sanskrit drama to naturalism and the various styles of contemporary theatre.

More important, each student, whether he ultimately specializes in acting or production, studies every aspect of theatre – music, lighting, stage-design, costume and make-up – each of these in relation to the needs of individual plays. The development of a comprehensive vision is thereby aimed at.

To widen the student's intellectual horizon, an interest in the other arts is encouraged. There are special music appreciation classes. Production notes indicate the painters whose style and colour are closest to the spirit of the play under study. Prominent artists are occasionally invited to lecture. A forthcoming production of Lorca's *Yerma* would find the notice-boards up with authentic photographs of Spanish life; Venetian painting would be mounted for *Othello*, and so on. Further, no opportunity is lost to insist always upon aesthetic training: these photographs and reproductions are mounted on the boards by the students themselves, so that their sense of design is repeatedly challenged.

The new administration took a bold step when it decided to present School productions of a certain standard to the general public. This has exposed students to a direct experience of their future problems and rewards and has given Delhi some interesting encounters with theatre. The quality of these plays is subject to controversy. The sense of design they exhibit, the impeccable taste in costume and music, are universally praised. The rawness of student acting, and the variously accented Hindi speech come in for disapproval. The criticism, however, one hears most often is that the productions are frozen in their perfection, that a certain 'coldness' mars the immediacy of the theatre experience. There is here, perhaps, the need to understand what one means by this immediacy, and whether formal beauty of the kind the School excels in isn't a vastly neglected aspect on our stages today. These plays taken on a tour of other Indian cities and towns have been known to engender excitement and change among local theatre groups.

I had obtained interesting reports of the School's own brand of 'discipline'. I found that, in fact, it covers more ground than is usually allowed the word: not an artificial and isolated item that is vaguely desirable, but something consciously directed to accompany every part of the training, extending into the individual trainee's thinking, dress and social behaviour. For instance, a newspaper report of a horse lying injured on the streets of Delhi for days without help will find its way to the notice boards; the environment is not allowed to drift by unquestioned. Again, a student of the NSD does not appear shabbily dressed at public functions. He is not a nobody. His is a great and dignified profession and his person must reflect this. One can sense behind this the makings of a paternal authoritarianism. It comes out in other aspects of the School also, and students are quick to sense it. Since this authority is ultimately benevolent, sheltering, its more formidable aspect is readily accepted by the students and is endorsed by a reciprocal father-worship on their side. This arrangement, it has been argued, may have an atrophic influence on the students' minds, in which case, one might almost hope for a natural reaction of rebellion, at some later stage, which might release the mature student from dependence.

I may now deal with points of controversy that have been cropping up in any discussion on the School. Some of these are myths that are thoughtlessly repeated. Others are serious and need to be considered. The question of how these trained graduates are to earn a living and how to give back to the country the best in theatre is a problem of the second kind. A repeated complaint against the School has been the dearth of possible outlets for the students after they have completed their course. The variety of opinions on this subject is witness to the fact that a genuine problem does exist. There are those who believe that, in the first place, it is not really the business of the School to find employment for its students who should use their own ingenuity and initiative to create situations for themselves; that theatre is inherently a 'risky business', and that this has clearly to be seen by the students before they start training, that their situation is not in any way exceptional – of all students training at major schools of drama all over the world, very few do manage to hold on to their original vocation, and then only through years of effort and trial; and that this is as it should be since the creative excitement of good theatre usually dies with easy and static theatre 'jobs'.

Some suggest that students who are so inclined could continue at whatever employment they were engaged in before joining the School, and start amateur groups in their spare time. Theatre could also be served in this fashion. Of the students who have completed training, one hears of some success stories, but a good number see themselves drift away from the life in theatre they would have liked for themselves. Those who join professional regional groups encounter a barrier in the established professionals. The best of these groups are naïve in their outlook. Anger and passion continue to be stimulated on stage by red lights and shivering drums. Stage discipline among actors and technicians is unheard of, and they are shy of raw and bossy youngsters. However, if approached diplomatically, they have been found eager to learn fresh techniques and absorb new ideas from them. This new partnership could give to the Indian audience a fresh dimension of sensibility.

There is no doubt, however, that the country would profit greatly from the NSD if much more of the talent that emerges from it were well utilised. And this is where the state governments should move. The Rabindra theatres built already, and several more to be built all over the country are at present used but perfunctorily and some of them have been known to offer wrestling matches on their stages. I am told that the Centre is willing to bear half the expense of resident repertory companies in these theatres which could be the ideal outlet for the NSD students who, together with the local talent, could staff the repertory companies. The languages of performance would be those of the particular region. The Director of the NSD envisages tremendous possibilities in this kind of activity. The best in foreign and Indian drama – ancient and modern – could be performed in original, translation or adaptation. Repertory groups could travel through different states and give exchange performances. Directors from one state could be invited occasionally to work with a group from another state. In this way the walls of parochialism would be challenged, fertile communication established and all over the country the awareness would spread of work in theatre that could complement and enrich local movements.

And now the myths: The 'Indianness' of the NSD is challenged from time to time. It is true the School does not deal with Indian drama only, but objection to the acquisition of knowledge of all that has been and is being done in theatre the world over could come only from the most chauvinistic, particularly as our own heritage and potential is far from being neglected. The translation, study and production of Sanskrit and modern plays, I have referred to already. The work of several talented young playwrights hitherto ignored except, perhaps, for a local production, has been discovered by the School and their plays been given the dignified and accomplished production they would not have obtained elsewhere. The School hopes also to invite exponents of folk styles, like the *Bhawai* and others, to give lessons over a length of time, and plans then to produce plays in these styles.

Then there is the incantation that the School productions are created for 'intellectuals' only and fail to reach the 'people'. The audiences and reviews the School obtains on its tours around the country should calm these fears, but one might also refer, at this point, to the *Natya Shastras* – to that long chapter which describes the outlook and qualities a man needs to acquire before he is fit audience for serious theatre. And if it will be some years before we can hope for a mass audience for theatre of this kind, the School, by its integrity, has earned the right to have its work considered also in terms of the years to come.

Finally, there is an anxiety in some quarters that the powerful personality of E. Alkazi casts a shadow from which few of his students escape. That he influences his students strongly, I have hinted before. I may ask at this stage if this is not also for the best. As I have shown before, the students who come fresh into the School are untutored. At this stage, an encounter with a dynamic influence can do much to iron out undesirable notions and suggest fertile directions. The first steps are imitative but when these students leave the School, the variety of experience they will encounter, and the different personalities they will meet is bound to modify the more sensitive and creative of them. At the same time, they will have profited from this intimate contact with a man of vision in their formative years. At the present moment, few could doubt the fate of the National School of Drama deprived of the presence of its director. A certain aloneness leaves his work, strong as it is, vulnerable. Theatre, being inherently a group activity, can rarely be carried very far by a single individual. When Alkazi is surrounded finally by a staff of men and women with as much dedication and vision as himself (and these may well emerge from among his own students), the National School of Drama will have become an institution more challenging than the stimulating training school it is today.

Aspects of Pornophobia

Dilip Chitre

(Quest 59: Autumn 1968)

At long last, in 1967, a Select Committee of the Rajya Sabha produced from a mountain of contradictory evidence the mouse of a report on obscenity and the law. The Indian Penal Code (Amendment) Bill, 1963, is now going to be discussed by the Lok Sabha. Thus the famous Section 292 of the IPC, under which the Supreme Court has placed a ban on D.H. Lawrence's *Lady Chatterley's Lover*, comes up for debate for the first time since India became independent.

Diwan Chaman Lall, who has been the motive force behind these seemingly noble operations, appears to have been conducting a crusade based on the sublime slogan 'art for art's sake'.

The climate of the debate is strangely Victorian. Both the protagonists and the antagonists of the proposed amendment have displayed, in a high falutin' language, the spirit of moralistic elephants preparing for a head-on clash. That obscenity, despite its great popularity as an after-dinner subject of debate, is one of the most confusing issues ever discussed by culture-policemen is quite evident. Indeed if these well-meaning ladies and gentlemen, belonging to either camp, did not regard *all* pornography as a terrible crime certain confusions in their thinking would be very easily eliminated. But they all seem to agree that pornography is a terrible crime against society and therefore the present amendment, while seeking to exempt legally obscenity 'for the public good on the ground that (it)... is in the interest of science, literature, art or learning', proposes to increase the punishment for obscenity offences from six months of imprisonment or fine or both to three years of imprisonment *and* fine up to rupees two thousand for the first conviction and on a second or subsequent conviction seven years of imprisonment *and* up to five thousand rupees in fine. Thus, the increased punishment clearly indicates the size of the fear of pornography in official circles. The exemption of 'art', 'science', and 'literature' is much less impressive not only because it has been overdue in any case but also because all relevant definitions have been left as vague as they have always been. The concrete effect of the Amendment will thus be only an increased punishment to obscenity convicts who may include 'borderline cases' of creative writers – particularly, unknown, young, experimental writers whose work is controversial. The consequence of this is quite clear: the serious Indian creative writer will from now on be working in a far more oppressive climate than earlier. One 'mistake' in a novel, short story, or poem and he is likely to spend three years in jail. If at all he has the courage to write again in the same way, he spends seven years behind bars. In a country where 'obscenity' is not tested by the criteria of contemporary secular ethics and not in an empirical manner, nor in the real socio-cultural context, the new law strikes the writer's freedom in a most crushing manner. Considering the upswing of puritan revivalism in contemporary India, I think this Amendment is a near-fatal blow to all experimental, creative and imaginative activity which is always necessarily controversial and therefore suspicious in the eyes of ignorant and conservative people.

That most of our experts and leaders are ignorant and conservative is clearly established by the evidence published by the Parliament for a review of the proposed Bill. The chief sponsor of the Bill, Diwan Chaman Lall, considers Dorian Gray to be an author.[1] Mr A.D. Mani refers to Venus de Milan (sic)! Dr Narayana Menon, who refers to Joyce's *Ulysses*, does not know whether the book is still banned in the United States.[2] This does not prevent these gentlemen, many of whom have not cared to do their homework before giving evidence, from indulging in pompous and meaningless discourses on the subject of obscenity.

It is painful to read the 204 pages of sustained nonsense for several reasons. The most brilliantly absurd observations naturally come from Mr K.K. Shah, Minister for Information and Broadcasting. Mr Shah says in one place: 'By making art naked art ceases to be art'. Mr A.D.

Mani: 'Who says that?' Mr K.K. Shah replies: 'It is said by the second well-known person, next to Kalidasa.' I do not know who this 'second well-known person' is, but Mr K.K. Shah sounds as if he has been quoting, in free paraphrase, some of Lewis Carroll's famous characters as authorities.

Some people such as the film-maker, B.R. Chopra, have expressed views which will be readily applauded by Ministers and other edict-addicts. Says Mr Chopra in one place: 'We should try to preserve our culture and customs as much as possible. Otherwise it is not an Indian film.' Mr Chopra's contributions to Indian culture, which made the Select Committee invite him to give his views, are known to millions of illiterate Hindi moviegoers throughout India. But, like many other witnesses before and after him, and indeed like most of the interviewers themselves, Mr. Chopra goes blank with selective amnesia when it comes to sex. He forgets that 'our tradition' contains Vatsyayana, Kokkoka, Konark and Khajuraho. For sheer comic effect however, we have Miss Snehaprabha Pradhan's fantastic anecdote: 'One of my female dogs was lying on the sofa. You know when dogs are bothered with heat they usually lie in such a way as to have the minimum part of their body touch the floor because that cools them on all sides. One young boy came to visit me once. He is almost like a brother to me. He said, 'Oh, put that dog down.' I said: 'What is the matter?' He said: 'Look at the pose she has taken.' The obvious effect of the dog's posture on the young man's mind was erotic. Well, here is the average mind. How are we going to convince this young man and his like that the erotic carvings in temples are not meant for erotic pleasures?'[3] Ergo, Miss Pradhan wants stricter censorship in India to prevent seductive female dogs and erotic sculptures from ruining young minds, 'average' minds, such as the mind of her young guest. One wonders what precisely it is that qualifies Miss Pradhan, an ex-matinee idol who acted in popular Indian films, to give evidence before the Select Committee. The whole joke becomes excruciatingly painful only when we remember that it is such people who are going to influence legislation on this vital issue.

Fear of pornography, or 'pornophobia' as I choose to call it, is a terribly unbalancing mental condition. It would be much better if we followed the example of Denmark and declared ourselves a sophisticated, adult nation. For indeed, if 'our cultural tradition' were really as powerful and pervasive as it is made out to be, social responses rather than legal censorship would take care of aberrant writing and artistic expression. (One of the witnesses suggests that he considers 'sixty' to be adult age: this failure to distinguish between the beginning of senility and adulthood in any serious sense of the term has led to this comic but horrifying operation).

In what way is pornography really harmful? After Kinsey, several researchers have pointed out that there is no reason to imagine a relationship between pornography and juvenile delinquency. As for adult 'delinquency', it has been observed that chronic pornography addicts are usually well-educated, middle-class, middle-aged bachelors who lead extremely respectable lives. Healthy, normal eroticism by contemporary standards does include the display of erotically appealing elements not only in language but also in dress and voice. Here, Miss Pradhan's 'female dog test' would fail as miserably as the late Justice Cockburn's Hicklin test.

In the West, the entire censorship controversy today centres on sadistic pornography which combines violence with titillation. This is the only sane way of looking at the problem: the combination of titillating verbal descriptions with verbal instigation to violence could lead to socially dangerous consequences. But in India, sadistic pornography is remarkably absent. The harmless kind of cheap pornography would merely entertain some of the less cultivated members of our notoriously infinitesimal literate population, including Miss Pradhan's dog-fearing young guest. Who then is really going to be affected by the amended law? The answer is obvious: as usual, the victims will be young, creative writers engaged in imaginative experimentation. In short the new legislation will directly hamper the growth of modern Indian literature by killing the sense of imaginative freedom on which all avant grade creativity thrives.

Endnotes

1. '....and a hundred and one other works of art by Oscar Wilde, Dorian Gray and others could be banned.' p.6; Parliament of India; Rajya Sabha; The Indian Penal Code (Amendment) Bill, 1963: Evidence; New Delhi, May 1967.

2. *Ibid.*, p. 16.

3. *Ibid.*, p. 126.

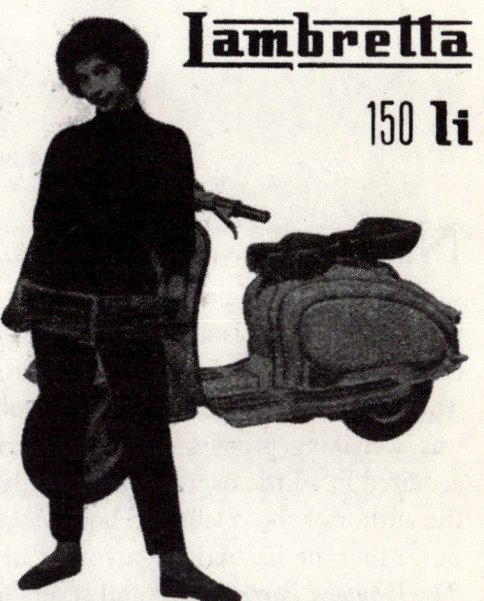

The Thought of Kissinger

A.G. Noorani

(Quest 61: April-June 1969)

No appointment made by President Richard M. Nixon has been so universally acclaimed as was that of Dr Henry A. Kissinger as the President's assistant for National Security Affairs. The academic community was delighted, the Europeans were relived, the press wholeheartedly approved and the politicians voiced no objection. It was a striking proof of the respect and authority the professor had acquired in a little over a decade. Only in 1957 did he acquire fame as the author of the celebrated book *Nuclear Weapons and Foreign Policy*[1]. Since then he has written a couple of books *The Necessity for Choice*[2], *The Troubled Partnerships*[3] and several essays. In a country which does not suffer from any dearth of literary output by the academics there must, indeed, be something unusual in the quality of Dr Kissinger's contributions to have won him the fame and respect that they did.

Yet, students of his writings cannot help feeling that with all the respect and authority he enjoys, he is barely understood. If *The New York Times*[4] could write 'Prof. Henry A. Kissinger of Harvard is distinguished among the country's defence intellectuals for his awareness of the effect of military decisions on international politics' its understanding of Dr Kissinger could hardly be as great as its regard for him. The truth is that Dr Kissinger is one of the most original and profound thinkers on the nature and dynamics of international society. The military aspects of its problems being of the utmost importance in the nuclear age, he has grappled with them and related them to the larger problem of the establishment of a durable international order. But he is no mere 'defence intellectual.' He is, if one can categorise him, *essentially* a political philosopher steeped in history and alive to its lessons. In his own words, 'National security policy is not primarily a technical problem, but a challenge to political understanding and, ultimately, to philosophical insight.'[5] The least known of Dr Kissinger's books is his first work, *A World Restored*.[6] It is a work of history – the problem of restoring order in Europe after Napoleon's defeat in Russia. But it is history with a purpose. The work is remarkable for its understanding of the times, for its literary felicity, and, above all, for the philosophy of the world orders which it propounds and which in essential is his, still.

History, he believes, can teach only if the pupil asks the right questions. 'A physical law is an explanation and not a description, and history teaches by analogy, not identity. This means that the lessons of history are never automatic. That can be apprehended only by a standard which admits the significance of a range of experiences, that the answers we have obtained will never be better than the questions we pose'.[7]

It is clear that Dr Kissinger embarked on an inquiry into those times because of their relevance to the present, namely, the problem of establishing a world order by agreement in revolutionary times. Whenever peace conceived as the avoidance of war has been the primary objective of a power or a group of powers, the international system has been at the mercy of the most ruthless member of the international community. Wherever the international order has acknowledged that certain principles could not be compromised even for the sake of peace, stability based on an equilibrium of forces was at least conceivable. Stability, then, has commonly resulted not from a quest for peace but from a generally accepted legitimacy. 'Legitimacy' as here used should not be confused with justice. It means no more than an international agreement about the nature of workable arrangements and about the permissible aims and methods of foreign policy. It implies the acceptance of the framework of the international order by all major powers, at least to the extent that no state is to dissatisfied that, like Germany after the Treaty of Versailles, it expresses its dissatisfaction in a revolutionary foreign policy. A legitimate order does not make conflicts impossible, but it limits their scope. Wars may occur, but they will be fought in the name of the existing structure and the peace which follows will be justified as a better expression of the 'legitimate', general consensus. Diplomacy in the classic sense, the adjustment of differences through negotiation, is possible only in 'legitimate' international orders.'[8] The distinguishing feature of a revolutionary power is that it seeks not the redress of specific grievances, but a fundamental change in the order. 'Only absolute security – the neutralisation of the opponent – is considered a sufficient guarantee, and thus the desire of one power for absolute security means absolute insecurity for all the others.'

This theme of the establishment of an order by agreement with the major powers, but with the full recognition that it will not secure any of them absolutely, runs right through Dr Kissinger's writings. Thus in his latest contributions[9] he writes: 'The greatest need of a contemporary international system is an agreed concept of order. In its absence the awesome available power is unrestrained by any consensus as to legitimacy; ideology and nationalism in their different ways deepen international schisms. Many of the elements of stability which characterised the international system in the nineteenth century cannot be re-created in the modern age. The stable technology, the multiplicity of major powers, the limited domestic claims and the frontiers which permitted adjustments are gone for ever. A new concept of international order is essential; without it stability will prove elusive.'

A World Restored is an incisive analysis of the challenges a statesman forces in his striving for such an order. Its *piece de resistance* is the last chapter on 'The Nature of Statesmanship'. It explains why the period was selected and the work undertakes. 'Few periods present such a dramatic contrast of personalities or illustrate so well the problems of organizing a legitimate order as the interval between the defeat of Napoleon in Russia and the Congress of Vienna. While Napoleon dominated Europe, policy based on a conception of national strategy was impossible. The fate of states depended on the will of the conqueror, and safety could be found only in adaptation to the French system. But Napoleon's defeat in Russia made clear that Europe could no longer be governed by force, that the man of will would have to find safety in a recognition of limits. And the disintegration of the Grande Armee obliged the European nations to define anew their place in the international order, to create a balance of forces to discourage future aggression, and to wrest out of the chaos of the disintegrated structure of the eighteenth century some principle of organization which would ensure stability.

'It is fortunate for the lessons posterity may draw from this period that its chief protagonists were men of marked individuality, each in his way symbolizing an answer to the problem of order: Napoleon of the claims of power; Alexander of the indeterminacy of a policy of absolute moral claims; Castlereagh of the conception of an equilibrium maintained by the recognition of the self-evident advantages of peace; Metternich of an equilibrium maintained by an agreement on a legitimising principle. Napoleon and Alexander were revolutionaries, because both strove to identify the organization of Europe with their will. To be sure, Napoleon sought order in universal dominion and Alexander in a reconciled humanity. But the claims of the prophet are sometimes as dissolving as those of the conqueror. For the claims of the prophet are a counsel of perfection, and perfection implies uniformity. Utopias are not achieved except by a process of leveling and dislocation which must erode all patterns of obligation. 'These are the two great symbols of the attacks on the legitimate order: the Conqueror and the Prophet, the quest for universality and for eternity, for the peace of impotence and the peace of bliss.'[10]

One finds here a strong emphasis on creativity of purpose and a deep and lasting distrust of bureaucracy. 'It is the inextricable element of history, this conflict between inspiration and organization. Inspiration implies the identification of the self with the meaning of events. Organization requires discipline, the submission to the will of the group. Inspiration is timeless; its validity is inherent in its conception. Organization is historical, depending on the material available at a given period. Inspiration is a call for greatness; organization a recognition that mediocrity is the usual pattern of leadership. To be effective, politically, one requires organization, and for this reason the translation into political terms of prophetic visions always falsifies the intentions of their proponents. It is no accident that the greatest spiritual achievements of religious or prophetic movements tend to occur when they are still in opposition, when their conception is their only reality. Nor is it strange that established religions or prophetic movements should exhibit a longing for their vanished period of "true" inwardness. It is the origin of mass frenzy, of crusades, of "reformations", of purges, this realization that the spontaneity of individual reflection cannot be institutionalized.'[11] Again, in the same work, he writes 'For the spirit of policy and that of bureaucracy are diametrically opposed. The essence of policy is its contingency; its success depends on the correctness of an estimate which is in part conjectural. The essence of bureaucracy is its quest for safety; its success is calculability. Profound policy thrives on perpetual creation, on a constant re-definition of goals. Good administration thrives on routine, the definition of relationships which can survive mediocrity. Policy involves an adjustment of risks; administration an avoidance of deviation. Policy justifies itself by the relationship of its measures and its sense of proportion; administration by the rationality of each action in terms of a given goal. The attempt to conduct policy bureaucratically leads to a quest for calculability which tends to become a prisoner of events. The effort to administer politically leads to total irresponsibility because bureaucracies are designed to execute, not to conceive'.[12]

It is this ability to conceive, to recognize and to act purposefully and creatively despite circumstances which marks a statesman. A scholarship of social determinism has reduced the statesman to a lever on a machine called 'history', to the agent of a fate which he may dimly discern but which he accomplishes regardless of his will. And this belief in the perseverance of circumstance and the impotence of the individual extends to the notion of policy-making. The test of a statesman is to perceive accurately the forces at work and to use that knowledge to choose from among the policy alternatives. In sum, to mould events. To do that he needs domestic support, which is as difficult as securing acceptance abroad. To interpret the international order he seeks in terms of the values of his own domestic society and to make it real and meaningful to his people, has bedeviled the efforts of many a statesman. A nation decides in the light of its own experience which hardly helps it to understand the experience of other nations. Foreign affairs, more often than not, remain very foreign affairs. For the impetus of domestic policy is a direct social experience; but that of foreign policy is not actual, but potential experience – the threat of war – which statesmanship attempts to avoid being made explicit. The statesman is therefore like one of the heroes in classical drama who has had a vision of the future but who cannot transmit it directly to his fellow-men and who cannot validate its 'truth'. Nations learn only by experience; they 'know' only when it is too late to act. But statesmen must act as if their intuition were already experience, as if their aspiration were truth. It is for this reason that statesmen often share the fate of prophets, that they are without honour in their own country, that they always have a difficult task in legitimising their programmes domestically, and that their greatness is usually apparent only in retrospect when their intuition has become experience. The statesman must therefore be an educator; he must bridge the gap between a people's experience and his vision, between a nation's tradition and its future. In this task his possibilities are limited. A statesman who too far outruns the experience of his people will fail in achieving a domestic consensus, however wise his policies; witness Castlereagh. A statesman who limits his policy to the experience of his people will doom himself to sterility; witness Metternich.

In striving to attain popular support the statesman must at no time allow his own goals to be obscured or be deflected from their pursuit. Metternich is admired because 'he knew what he wanted' and he dared to work for its achievement. 'Only a shallow historicism would maintain that successful policies are always possible.' The strongest criticism of Metternich which occurs in the work is his lack of daring at the sight of failure, 'the ability to contemplate an abyss, not with the detachment of a scientist but as a challenge to overcome – or to perish in the process.'

It would be natural to ask whether Dr Kissinger would offer the same prescription to a president of the United States, presiding over his country's destinies in this fearful age. In *Nuclear Weapons and Foreign Policy*, he has given the answer. Dr Kissinger was 34 when the book was published in 1957 and immediately became a celebrity. The book grew out of the deliberations of a study group set up by the Council on Foreign Relations, New York, but the analysis and the conclusions were the author's own. If a book can be summed up in a sentence, one would say of it that it advocated the need for a strategic doctrine which would meet the challenge of the times. Ability to wage a limited nuclear war was only an aspect of the doctrine which he propounded, but it was not the whole doctrine.

The dilemma of the nuclear age, simply stated, is that the enormity of modern weapons rules out their use except in extremity while the Soviet challenge expresses itself by means short of total war but which are hardly less consequential. The problem therefore is, first, a recognition of the ambiguous character of the Soviet moves and the need for appropriate responses. 'It is the task of strategic doctrine to translate power into policy' and its crucial test is what it defines as a threat. Mere courage will not avail the statesman. He must be armed with a sound doctrine as well. 'Because we have won two world wars by out-producing our opponent, we have tended to equate military superiority with superiority in resources and technology. Yet history demonstrates that superiority in strategic doctrine has been the source of victory at least as often as superiority in resources… Thus the key to a proper doctrine is the correct understanding of the elements of one's superiority, and the ability to apply them more rapidly than the opponent, whether through the choice of an advantageous battlefield or through the superior utilization of available weapons systems. This theme has been developed in later works with remarkable consistency. Every advanced country has more technical choices than it can afford. Its choice will depend therefore more on its strategic doctrine than on the technology available. 'But strategic doctrine must not become something theoretical or dogmatic. Its role is to define the likely dangers and how to deal with them, to project feasible goals and how to obtain them. It must furnish a mode of action for the circumstances it defines as 'ordinary'. Its adequacy will be tested according to whether these ordinary events do in fact occur and whether the forces developed in their anticipation are adequate to deal with the real challenges.'[13]

This emphasis on the practicable, however, is totally at variance with the outlook of those 'practical' men who shun doctrine and prefer *ad hoc* decisions. 'But if there is no doctrine at all and a society operates pragmatically, solving problems "on their merits" as the saying goes, every event becomes a special case. More energy is spent deciding where one is than where one is going. Each event is compartmentalised and dealt with by experts in the special difficulties it involves without an adequate understanding of its relation to other occurrences. This is the risk United States policy has been running since it undertook the stewardship of the free world.'[14]

In *Nuclear Weapons and Foreign Policy*, as in his previous work, Kissinger rejected the ideal of absolute security. 'But since absolute security for one power is unattainable except by the annihilation or neutralisation of all the others, it can be achieved only by a cycle of violence culminating in the destruction of the multi-stage system and its replacement by single-power domination. The quest for absolute security inevitably produces a revolutionary situation. A legitimate order is distinguished by not pressing the quest for security to its limits, by its willingness to find safety in a combination of physical safeguards and mutual trust. It is legitimate not because each power is perfectly satisfied, but because it will not be so dissatisfied that it will seek its remedy in overthrowing the existing system. The confidence required for the operation of a legitimate order does not presuppose the absence of all tensions, but the conviction on the part of all major powers that the disputed issues do not threaten their national survival. To the extent that this measure of mutual trust is not present, the quest for absolute security will reappear and relations will tend to be based on force and the threat of force, either on war or on an armaments race.'[15]

It is strange how very few strategists are familiar with Communist theory and how few students of Communist affairs bother with matters strategic. In a chapter entitled 'The Strategy of Ambiguity', which testifies to his immense labours, Kissinger appraises the nature of the communist challenge. 'It uses the "legitimate" language of its opponents in fashion which distorts its meaning and increases the hesitations of the other side. The belief in an inevitable historical progress leads the Soviet leaders to maintain a constant pressure just short of the challenge which they believe would produce a final showdown. To be sure, the Soviet leadership may miscalculate and thus bring on a holocaust despite its most rational calculations. But to the extent they do not miscalculate, the non-Soviet world faces the dilemma that all dividing lines between war and peace, aggression and the status quo, are gradually eroded and in a manner which never presents a clear-cut issue.' He goes on to advocate that 'the Soviet strategy of ambiguity can ultimately' be countered only by a policy of precaution, by attempting to nip Soviet moves in the bud before Soviet prestige becomes so deeply engaged that any countermeasures increase the risk of war. Yet a policy of precaution is the most difficult of all for status quo powers to implement. All their preconceptions tempt them to wait until the Soviet threat has become unambiguous and the danger has grown overt, by which time it may well be too late. The Soviet leadership, therefore, presents to the West a challenge which may be moral even more than physical. It resolves itself ultimately into questions of how much the free world will risk to back up its assessment of a situation without being 'certain', or whether the Soviet leaders can use the free world's quest for certainty to paralyse its ability to act. Many of the Soviet gains have been due in large part to a greater moral toughness, to a greater readiness to run risks, both physical and moral, than their opponents. And despite the moral bankruptcy of

Soviet theory, which with every passing year is demonstrated anew, the Soviet power centre has made gains which were not justified by the relation of forces but were largely due to the inward uncertainty of their declared victims.

It should not surprise anyone that Dr Kissinger has characterised the Johnson administration's reaction to the invasion of Czechoslovakia as 'pallid'.

But it is not a simplistic 'hard-liner's position' that he takes, either. Dean Acheson's formulation of 'negotiations from strength' does not satisfy him. 'Secretary Acheson's definition of containment implied that strength was self-evident, that power would supply its own rationale. It did not deal with the question of how the position of strength was to be demonstrated in the absence of a direct attack on us or on our allies. It did not supply a doctrine for translating our power into policy except as a response to Soviet initiative. Nor did it make clear what would happen if the Soviet leaders refused to negotiate after we had achieved a "position of strength" and instead concerned their efforts on eroding it or turning its flank.'[16]

The entire book was a forceful plea for the need for a doctrine backed up by the enunciation of one. 'The key problem of present-day strategy is to devise a spectrum of capabilities with which to resist Soviet challenges. These capabilities should enable us to confront the opponent with contingencies from which he can extricate himself only by all-out war, while deterring him from this step by a superior retaliatory capacity. Since the most difficult decision for a statesman is whether to risk the national substance by unleashing an all-out war, the psychological advantage will always be on the side of the power which can shift to its opponent the decision to initiate all-out war. All Soviet moves in the postwar period have had this character. They have faced us with problems which by themselves did not seem worth an all-out war, but with which we could not deal by an alternative capability. We refused to defeat the Chinese in Korea because we were unwilling to risk an all-out conflict. We saw no military solution to the Indo-Chinese crisis without accepting risks which we were reluctant to confront. We recoiled before the suggestion of intervening in Hungary lest it unleash a thermo-nuclear holocaust. A strategy of limited war might reverse or at least arrest this trend. Limited war is thus not an alternative to massive retaliation, but its complement. It is the capability for massive retaliation which provides the sanction against expanding the war.' In other words, the United

States, while retaining 'the capability for waging all-out war' should also develop its ability to fight limited wars, more specifically, limited nuclear wars. The strategic deterrent should ever be kept in readiness. Not only militarily but diplomatically, no less, the possibilities of a limited nuclear war should not be neglected lest the United States be confronted with an agonising choice between all-out war and abject surrender. As happens all so often, the major part of the work got obscured and Dr Kissinger's views on limited nuclear wars received greater attention and aroused much criticism.

As a matter of fact, well before him, Mr Denis Healey, now Britain's Defence Secretary, had in the July 1955 issue of *Encounter*, in an article entitled 'The Bomb That Did Not Go Off', pointed to precisely the same possibility – limited wars breaking out because of the nuclear deadlock between the super-powers. Dr Kissinger's views were open to the criticism that it was hardly possible to keep a nuclear war limited. As we shall see, he revised them in a later work.

It speaks enormously for his insight into the Soviet motivations, however, that as far back as 1957 he should have written, 'To the Soviet leaders a settlement reflects a temporary relationship of force, inherently unstable and to be maintained only until the power balance shifts'. A year later, Walter Lippmann wrote after prolonged discussions with Mr Khrushchev, 'Whereas we think of status quo as the situation as it exists at the moment, he thinks of it as a process of revolutionary change which is in progress. He wants us to recognize the revolution not only as it is, but as it is going to be. There is another very important component in his conception of the status quo. This has to do with the balance of military power.'[17]

Limited nuclear war was re-appraised and modified in *The Necessity for Choice* but it was not discarded. The author realized that given the conditions – the disagreements within the American military establishment not least among them – it would be impossible to establish and maintain the limitations essential to the conduct of a limited nuclear war. Public opinion in allied countries was also fearful of the use of nuclear weapons for tactical purposes. 'Even with the best intentions on both sides, a nuclear war will be more difficult to limit than a conventional one. Since no country has had any experience with the tactical use of nuclear weapons, the possibility of miscalculation is considerable.'[18]

The importance of avoiding miscalculation is paramount. 'However deterrence is above all a psychological problem. The assessment of risks on which it depends becomes less and less precise in the face of weapons of unprecedented novelty and destructiveness. A bluff taken seriously is more useful than a serious threat interpreted as bluff. Strategy henceforth cannot confine itself to expertise in designing weapons systems but must involve a close understanding of the opponent's calculations. Moreover, deterrence proves its mettle negatively, so long as things do not happen. Unfortunately, it is never easy to show why something has not occurred. Success may seem to have been won by the best strategic theories or by barely tolerable ones. It is also possible to maintain that the country against which defensive preparations are taken never had any intention of attacking in the first place. Thus successful deterrence can furnish arguments to sustain obsolescent theories and designs, or it can encourage neutralism.'[19]

Few American writers on foreign policy have shown as much understanding of and sympathy for Europe as has Dr Kissinger. He is far better versed in European affairs than in the affairs of Asia and *The New York Times* was not wide off the mark when it wrote that though he has advised the government in such fields as arms control, military policy and Vietnam, 'Dr Kissinger is essentially a Europeanist.' Some of his most constructive suggestions are the ones relating to America's European policy. While urging his countrymen not to be self-righteous or even self-centered in their alliance policy, he is careful also to point out that American patronage indiscriminately granted can only serve to enfeeble the alliances. In this he has been most consistent. In 1957 he delineated the dilemmas of alliances: 'Our coalition policy must strike a balance between identifying an alliance with the consensus of its members and the desire for freedom of action in situations where our views and those of our allies diverge. To conduct an alliance on the principle of unanimity will cause the alliance to be geared either to the willingness to run risks of the ally with least interest in a given dispute, or it will enable the most irresponsible partner to force all other allies to underwrite its actions. But to insist on complete freedom of action in case of disagreement with our allies will wreck our system of alliances'.[20]

In *The Necessity For Choice* Dr Kissinger was even more specific. He advocated 'structural changes within the Western alliance. It seems time to examine carefully the possibility of creating federal institutions comprising the entire North Atlantic Community, however attenuated these may be at first.' A noteworthy suggestion he made was the creation of a steering committee for the Atlantic alliance empowered to act for the alliance as a whole on defence policy, arms control, East-West relations, and a common programme for economic assistance to emerging areas. Four years later, in his major work on the problems of the Atlantic Alliance, he was less specific, but left no room for doubt whatever as to the direction in which he wanted American policy to move. 'The United States should use its ingenuity to forge a variety of Atlantic institutions not only in the political realm, but also in the spheres of economics, scholarship and the arts. But institutions based on present concepts of national sovereignty are not enough. The West requires a larger goal: the constitution of an Atlantic Commonwealth in which all the peoples bordering the North Atlantic can fulfil their aspirations. Clearly, it will not come quickly; many intermediate stages must be traversed before it can be reached. It is not too early, however, to prepare ourselves for the steps beyond the nation-State.'[21]

Within Europe itself he favoured a Confederal Europe which would 'enable the United States to maintain an influence at many centres of decision rather than be forced to stake everything on affecting the views of a single, supra national body'.[22] It needs to be mentioned that the author strongly favoured coming to terms with de Gaulle. Above all, the book was an earnest plea to lift America's European policy from out of the morass by a re-statement of the purpose of the alliances and a re-awakening to the challenges that confronted it. 'It has become fashionable to compare the disagreements of the West with the shifts in the communist world. But this comparison fails to do justice to the possibilities of the Atlantic area. In the communist world schisms are inevitable and unbridgeable. Western societies have been more fortunate. Their revolutions have been richer because at their best they have managed to relate diversity to community. Free from the shackles of the doctrine of historical inevitability, the nations of the West can render great service by demonstrating that whatever meaning history has is derived from the convictions and purpose of the generation which shapes it.'[23]

When he turns to the problems of the emerging nations, Dr Kissinger combines perception with impatience. He sees their failings, their problems and their aspirations. He does not idolize them as many American liberals did. But perhaps as a reaction to their idealization, he visits their policies with a censure which is greater than is due. The views that he has expressed from time to time on their problems are best discussed in a chronological order. In *Nuclear Weapons and*

Foreign Policy, he writes, 'Neutralism and anti-colonialism are not so much a policy as a spiritual necessity. The constant reiteration of non-alignment may be the means by which the leaders of newly independent nations reassure themselves. They can be certain of their independence only by acting it out every day and on every issue.' Few will disagree with this. If anything, events since have borne out the truth of this appraisal. He proceeded also to urge the United States not to extend too ardent an embrace to the newly independent states. 'If, then, we are prepared to exercise leadership, we may be able to induce many of the newly independent nations to travel in a direction to which they incline, if always a few steps behind us. They will not surrender their non-alignment, but they may be willing to act in pursuance of common interests provided we are prepared to chart the road and provided we tolerate a measure of dissociation. In the uncommitted nations, popularity may be less important than respect.'[24]

However this understanding deserts him when he would have the United States moralise in terms such as these: 'Condescending as it may seem to say so, the United States has for this reason an important educational task to perform in the uncommitted third of the world. By word and deed we must demonstrate that the inexorable element of international relations resides in the necessity to combine principle with power, that an exclusive reliance on moral pronouncements may be as irresponsible as the attempt to conduct policy on the basis of considerations of power alone. To be sure we should, wherever possible, seek to identify ourselves with the aspirations of the newly independent states. But we must also be prepared to protect the framework in which these aspirations can be accomplished. We should never give up our principles, nor ask other nations to surrender theirs. But we must also realize that neither we nor our allies nor the uncommitted can realize any principles unless they survive. We cannot permit the balance of power to be overturned for the sake of allied unity or the approbation of the uncommitted, for the condition of any future cooperation with them is the maintenance of a strategic balance between us and the Soviet bloc.' It is hard to imagine any of the uncommitted countries seeking or being able to overturn the balance of power between the United States and the Soviet bloc. The remarks suggest that in 1957. Dr Kissinger himself was no little confused about the best posture for the US to adopt. On the one hand we find him urging the United States to understand the aftermath of the anti-colonial revolt; and on the other, he would have had the United States play the role of a policeman in the uncommitted areas. The United States, therefore, requires a twentieth-century equivalent of 'showing the flag', an ability and a readiness to made our power felt quickly and decisively, not only to deter Soviet aggression but *'also to impress the uncommitted with our capacity for decisive actions.'*[25] (emphasis added). Such a policy could not have failed to earn for the United States the lasting distrust and hostility of the uncommitted world. However, in fairness, it may be mentioned that the prescription has not since been repeated.

We also find him as early as 1957 deploring the United States' association with the SEATO and CENTO Pacts: 'The military contribution of SEATO and the Baghdad Pact (to which we belong in all but in name) does not compensate for the decision of India and Egypt to stand apart and for the domestic pressures these instruments generated in some of the signatory countries.'

Three years later came *The Necessity For Choice* where his views on the new countries, as he called them, were expressed at greater length.[26] The most arresting part of Dr Kissinger's appraisal of the policies which the West should adopt towards these countries was his stern rejection of the theory that economic development ushers in democracy. As he pointed out, economic development might serve to buttress the very regime that has brought it about. He urged the US to give 'preferential assistance to countries which meet certain criteria for democratic institutions.' Instead of scattering aid all round, he suggested 'the best method of having a major impact on many countries will be to make a going concern of one country.' In Asia, India was his choice. As before, much that he said about non-alignment needed saying and was said well. 'We thus face two contradictory dangers: we can demoralise new nations by drawing them into the political relationship of the Cold War. But we can demoralise them also by making a cult of their non-commitment and acting as if only incorrect United States policies kept them from taking sides.'

However, resentment manifested itself, once again, in his essay on 'Power and Diplomacy' published in 1964.[27] He pointed out, perceptively, that in contrast to classic neutrality, the non-committed nations sought, not withdrawal, but involvement in world affairs and, also, that they lacked the means to defend themselves. 'When a neutral, either because of insufficient resources or deliberate policy has made itself dependent on the assistance of other countries, it has in the past often combined the disadvantages of alliance policy with those of neutrality. By itself the neutral was rarely strong enough to deter aggression, while at the same time in neutrality prevented it from making joint defensive preparations with a would be protector.' The advent of nuclear power made two important changes. It made it impossible for any non-nuclear country to defend itself against a nuclear opponent without foreign assistance. At the same time, the polarisation of power ensured him greater protection. 'In contemporary international affairs, a country suffers fewer disadvantages from being neutral and may even gain some international stature through the competition of the major powers for its allegiance. The nuclear age has unmistakably eroded the distinction between allies and neutrals. Though neutral, India was assured of much the same protection in the face of the Chinese attack as would have been extended in comparable circumstances to Pakistan, a member of two alliances'.

In such a situation, very naturally, these states were not slow to take advantage of great power rivalry. This evokes from Dr Kissinger an angry denunciation: 'This type of diplomacy is demoralising for the stability of the international system and has adverse effects on both the great powers and the uncommitted themselves. By setting up a contest *which by its own ground rules can be won by neither of the two nuclear giants*, the uncommitted nation of this new type tempts de-stabilising adventures and encourages political chaos. In the long run, the new nations will find it difficult to combine neutrality with incessant intervention. To the degree that the uncommitted nations can convince the major powers that their support is consequential, they are either courted or pressured. Neutrality then becomes an invitation to be wooed.' (emphasis added.)

It is interesting to note that the De Gaulle who plays the same game in a far most sensitive region does not arouse Dr Kissinger's indignation and, indeed, inspires him merely to greater effort at reconciliation. The contrast is too glaring to be explained away. This emotional attitude is unfortunate, for, to repeat, much of what Dr Kissinger says about the non-aligned needs saying and has been said only by a very few. Thus, in the very next paragraph alter the homily, he rightly deplores, 'With no apparent feeling of contradiction, the so-called uncommitted nations have felt free to practice vis-à-vis their own neighbours the kind of power politics which they urge the great powers to abjure. Exhortations for peace, reasonableness, and compromise seem to have no logical connection with the actions undertaken by the United Arab Republic in Yemen or Indonesia in Borneo.' Dr Kissinger, however, makes a wholly unjustified accusation that the neutrals 'also see advantages in perpetuating the competition of the super-power.' It is true that, but for this competition, they would not get the aid that they do. But it is only fair to add that the competition is not the result of the neutrals' efforts; rather, their efforts are made possible by the competition in the Cold War.

Dr Kissinger commits the same basic fallacy as the ideologues of non-alignment, in regarding non-alignment as the sum of a country's foreign policy. In truth, however, the foreign policy of a newly independent country is shaped mainly by its immediate environment and by its own concept of the national interest. Non-alignment no more explains how a country pursues that interest than a person's non-marriage explains how he pursues his happiness. When all is said and done, non-alignment is a non. No wonder that non-alignment has, as Dr Norman D. Palmer has remarked, as many varieties as Heinz pickles.

The foreign policies of the UAR, Cambodia and India, for example, have been shaped in the main by their disputes with their neighbours rather than by the concept of non-alignment. Non-alignment has only provided a convenient label which has embraced such diverse postures as India's largely pro-West policy in the late forties to its largely pro-Soviet policies in the sixties. The accusation of shortsightedness which Dr Kissinger makes against the non-aligned is perfectly justified, but not the one of opportunism. Not because the non-aligned are not opportunistic; that they are. But only it is fair to point out that the failing is not theirs alone. The super-powers have it in plenty.

Interestingly, the essay on 'Central Issues of American Foreign Policy' was written as part of the effort of the Brookings Institution 'to apply the energies of the Institution to an analysis of the substantive problems with which the new President and the new Congress would have to grapple.' Dr Kissinger is now one of the President's closest advisers. The essay, published only last December, therefore acquires added interest. 'The age of super powers is now drawing to an end,' he warns. 'Military bi-polarity has not only failed to prevent, it has actually encouraged, political multi-polarity. Weaker allies have good reason to believe that their defence is in the overwhelming interest of their senior partner. Hence they see no need to purchase its support by acquiescence in its policies. The new nations feel protected by the rivalry of the super-powers, and their nationalism leads to ever bolder assertions of self will.'[28]

After delineating the structure of the present order, Dr Kissinger expresses his views on some specific issues of American foreign policy today. SEATO and CENTO, he writes, have grown moribund as instruments of collective action. Instead, he advocates 'coalitions of shared purposes. Regional groupings supported by the United States will have to take over major responsibility for their immediate areas with the United States being concerned more with the overall framework of the order than with the management of every regional enterprise.'

He returns to his theme of European unity. 'There is no alternative to European unity either for the United States or for Europe.' It is futile to expect the United States and its European allies to seek a global partnership. 'Even within the Atlantic area a more equitable distribution of responsibilities has two pre-requisites. There must be some consensus in the analysis of the international situation, at least as it affects Europe; there must be a conviction that the United States cannot or will carry all the burdens alone. Neither condition is met today.' In sum, he would at once have the Europeans play a more active role in NATO and also assume a greater burden than they have done hitherto. We have noted his stress on the need for an agreed concept of world order. We may be sure that he will exert all his efforts as presidential assistant to see that the United States, in partnership with its European allies, seeks such an order by a dialogue with the Soviet Union.

Dr Kissinger has not expressed himself much on the problem of China and it is hard to say what his approach will be from the remark that a strong China has historically tended to establish dominance over its neighbours. He makes the striking comment that China has had no experience in conducting foreign policy with equals. China has been either 'dominant or subjected'. What policies he recommends on Asia, and, indeed, on the non-committed world at large remains to be seen.

Although there is a remarkable continuity in his basic views about the nonaligned, only the more significant aspects of which I have outlined above, Dr Kissinger's emphases have shifted. He is a man of enormous self-confidence who feels free to revise his notions. His superb equipment and the keen analytical intellect lend him an assurance which has been mistaken for intellectual arrogance. But he has shown in the past a willingness to revise opinions which smaller men do not and cannot possess.[29]

He is in the White House primarily as an intellectual. One of the finest chapters in *The Necessity For Choice* is the one on 'The Policymaker and the Intellectual'. He writes: 'The intellectual should therefore not refuse to participate in policymaking, for to do so confirms the stagnation of societies whose leadership groups have little substantive knowledge. But in cooperating the intellectual has two loyalties; to the organization that employs him and to value which transcend the bureaucratic framework and provide his basic motivation. It is important for him to remember that one of his contributions to the administrative process is his independence, and that one of his tasks is to seek to prevent routine from becoming an end in itself. The intellectual must therefore decide not only whether to participate in the administrative process but also in what capacity; whether as an intellectual or as an administrator. If he assumes the former role, it is essential for him to retain the freedom to deal with the policymaker from a position of independence, and to reserve the right to assess the policymaker's demands in terms of his own standards. However, while doing so, the intellectual must also define his role modestly. 'He must not pretend that he has panaceas which the shortsighted men in office have failed to discover, for the easy solutions have all been found. Our remaining problems are obdurate because they are complex. The intellectual can forewarn against the fragmentation of policy by calling attention to the inner relationship of events. He can supply perspective to government leaders who are overwhelmed by day-to-day details and are unable to give their full attention to the deeper pattern. Above all, he can insist constantly that no answer will be better than the question which invites it.'[30]

This last test which he propounds with almost wearying constancy may well be applied to his own work as Presidential Assistant. Addressing an international seminar held under the auspices of the International Association for Cultural Freedom at Princeton, on December 4, 1968 he refrained from expressing any opinion on the substantive issues of foreign policy and instead, posed these questions to the Seminar: 'What can the new Administration do to win the confidence of other countries abroad, and secondly what would you consider success at the end of four years? What should be the purposes and what should be some initial steps to indicate where we are going?'

If such be the questions he tends to ask, his success cannot be much in doubt particularly if he retains also his gift of readiness to listen.

Endnotes

1. Oxford University Press, 1957.

2. Chatto & Windus, London, 1960.

3. Doubleday & Co. Inc. New York, Anchor Book Edition, 1966. Published originally by McGraw-Hill 1965.

4. December 4, 1968.

5. *Problems of National Strategy:* a book of readings edited by Henry A. Kissinger, Fredrick A. Praeger, New York. 1965.

6. The Universal Library, Grosser & Dunlop, New York.

7. *A World Restored*, p. 331.

8. *A World Restored*, p.1.

9. An essay entitled 'Central Issues of American Foreign Policy' in *Agenda for the Nation* edited by Mr Kermit Gordon, the Brookings Institution, Washington D.C. pp. 585-614, December 1968.

10. *A World Restored*, p. 316.

11. *Ibid*, p. 317.

12. *A World Restored*, pp. 326-7. See also *'Nuclear Weapons and Foreign Policy*, p. 431-2. It is no accident that most great statesmen were opposed by the 'experts' in their foreign offices, for the very greatness of the statesmen's conception tends to make it inaccessible to those whose primary concern is with safety and minimum risk.

13. The essay on 'Power and Diplomacy' in the volume *The Dimensions of Diplomacy*, p. 22, edited by E.A.J. Johnson, The John Hopkins Press Baltimore, 1964.

14. *Ibid*, p. 24.

15. *Nuclear Weapons and Foreign Policy*. p. 318-19.

16. *Ibid*, p. 41.

17. *The Hindu*, November 19, 1958, reprinted from the *New York Herald Tribune*.

18. *The Necessity For Choice*, p. 82.

19. *The Dimensions of Diplomacy*, pp. 21-22.

20. *Nuclear Weapons and Foreign Policy*, p. 254.

21. *The Troubled Partnership*, pp. 245-46.

22. *Ibid*, p. 242.

23. *Ibid*, p. 249.

24. *Nuclear Weapons and Foreign Policy*, pp. 260-61.

25. *Ibid*, p. 264.

26. Chapter VII, sub-chapters 3 and 4, 'Evolution of New Countries' and 'The New Countries and International Relations.'

27. Published in *The Dimensions of Diplomacy*.

28. *Agenda of the Nation*, p. 588.

29. Freedom from dogmatism and also a due measure of intellectual humility are evident in his ready recognition of 'the element of conjecture in foreign policy'. In a brilliant and recent essay 'Reflections on Bismarck' published in *Dacdalus* Summer 1968, Dr Kissinger remarks, 'He always understood the requirements of success, but was less clear about whether to approach his task with a certain sense of reverence for the finiteness of the human scale. A statesman who leaves no room for the unforeseeable in history may, however, mortgage the future of his country'.

30. *The Dimensions of Diplomacy*, p. 39.

India's Security: Policy Options

K. Subrahmanyam

(Quest 61: April-June 1969)

It is proposed to analyse here what threats India is likely to face in the next decade or two and what policy options are available to her in this time span. The bane of our decision-making in that it is not sufficiently future-oriented. There is a tendency to take into account only the present and possibly the next two or three years at the most and then plan our course of action. In the field of National security and defence preparedness, the time spans involved in decisions are considerably longer than that. Between the decision to go ahead and deployment of a weapon system, the time interval is about eight years for the advanced industrial countries and much longer for countries at our level of technological development. In other words the decisions taken today will determine our defence posture in 1977-78, and conversely, unless the threat potential of 1977-78 can be assessed, it is not possible to have rational choices in weapons development today.

This is what our decision makers overlooked in the late fifties. If the debacle of 1962 were to have been averted certain decisions should have been taken in 1958. The roads programme should have been started earlier, and acclimatisation of our men should have begun in the fifties. The expansion of our forces and defence production facilities should have started at a time when some of our senior leaders were calling for cuts in defence expenditure and ridiculing the efforts to expand and diversify the defence production base. This happened because we were not used to a system of long range intelligence estimation and planning. From the almost complete absence of the mention of this aspect in our debates on 1962 it is evident that the nature of defence management, especially the effect of long time spans involved on planning and the consequent need for long range intelligence estimation, were concepts with which the top decision makers of this country were not familiar. And even today there is no evidence that the situation has significantly changed for the better.

Secondly the debate on national security issues should be better informed and become more professional. The tendency to leave national security to the military men and the ministry of defence should be consciously rectified, and scientists, scholars, journalists etc. should aim at equipping themselves adequately to debate such issues. Except in the matter of tactical considerations and deployment of forces, the service men have no superior knowledge or competence over others who make it their business to specialise in defence. Just as today the scientist is able to assist the professional agriculturist with generations of experience behind him, to produce better crops, so also natural scientists and social scientists are in a position to assist the professional service men and civilians in the defence ministry to arrive at better decisions in national security matters. I am emphasising this aspect because in certain aspects these tendencies of the fifties are noticed again. The debates on nuclear war and threat, revolutionary wars and their feasibility in the Indian context and the nature of limited conventional wars of the future, are not being carried out with adequate knowledge and professionalism. Very much the statements and valuations of the western world are repeated with or without relevance. An undue fetish is made of security, not because security is really involved but because it provides a convenient screen for complacency, lack of knowledge, competence and high standards of professionalism.

India is faced with three different kinds of threats and from two directions. These are of limited conventional war, insurgencies and the threat of nuclear war, and the threats are for the foreseeable future from China and Pakistan. The likely threat will have to be analysed in terms of different international strategic environments, political alignments, economic and technological capabilities of our potential adversaries. If it is not possible to reach a definite conclusion as to the potential threat then it will not be intelligence estimation but astrology. Decisions will have to be taken against a range of likely threats against a set of contingent possibilities. Here it is not possible to do more than indicate in an elementary way how this is to be done. I shall not venture any predictions but only analyse the problem of threat estimation itself and the decision-making involved on our part.

Both our neighbours China and Pakistan have irredentist claims against our country. Both of them, one in the name of religion and the other in the name of combating Indian reactionaries in alliance with Soviet revisionists and American imperialists, have also attempted to interfere in our internal affairs. China is quite capable of interfering on similar grounds in the affairs of Nepal and Burma too. Both the countries – China and Pakistan – have problems in succession to leadership and at present both are in a state of unrest. Both of them have derived benefits out of alliance systems and both of them have also had their disillusionments. Both countries have exhibited a great degree of opportunism and flexibility in their policies. India's relationships with these two countries will have to move from almost one end of the spectrum – namely active armed confrontation – to the other end, namely friendship and trust, through a number of stages such as passive confrontation, passive coexistence, active coexistence, collaboration in limited spheres and then on to friendship. Given the present degree of hostility it is going to take a long period to reach that stage. Meanwhile India can have dialogues on specific issues, even reach settlements on such issues. All these will contribute to the movement towards friendship and trust which will create what an eminent political scientist calls 'security community'. But it is naïve to think that before we have travelled substantially towards that goal there can be significant reductions in our defence effort. I emphasise this point because certain good people appear to think that if India reaches a settlement on Kashmir or on the northern border question, her defence expenditure will come down drastically. This is not to say that another clash with China or Pakistan is inevitable or specific measures for reduction of tension are not possible. On the other hand, initiation of dialogues with our likely adversaries is likely to reduce the time span involved in moving from near hostility to friendship. The present analysis is to put in proper perspective such attempts and their likely impact on defence effort.

I do not mean that we should resort to the posture of negotiating from strength in which an element of saber rattling is involved. The rational course of action is that of patient negotiation and attempt at conflict resolution while not letting the guard down. There will be indications in the external and internal behaviour of these countries which would call for further initiatives on our part. It is somewhat doubtful whether the present, when the two countries are still to settle their leadership problems and their world views, is an appropriate one to take initiatives. The probability appears to be that in the next ten years, though there may be reduction in tension or moves in the direction of conflict resolution, the relationship of India with either of her neighbours would hardly have undergone such qualitative change as to warrant a significant reduction in our defence effort or the pace of its build up.

On this premise we would proceed further to analyse what threat each country can pose at three levels of conflict – conventional war, revolutionary war and nuclear war. In respect of Pakistan her resources to wage a war against India all by herself is limited. She attempted to pose a threat to India either on the basis of support she derived from the United States or China. She has to depend for heavier equipment on foreign assistance or imports. Given her balance of payments position she is not in a position to spend large sums on imports. This explains her frantic search for suppliers of armaments on a credit basis – from France or the Soviet Union, for instance. Even this has its limitations. Further, her capability will be related to the size of force she can maintain and operate. She is already estimated to be spending about six per cent of her GNP on defence. Making certain reasonable assumptions on her economic growth rate and the burden of defence she will be willing to bear, a range of threat potential from Pakistan can be arrived at. By the middle of the seventies she may be able to support a force of 17-18 divisions and 20 squadrons of sophisticated aircraft. The threat may turn out to be less, but India should be prepared for a threat of this size.

In planning to counter a conventional war threat, an important aspect to be considered is the duration of operation. There is still in the minds of most people the image of the Second World War when industrial countries fought a total war with unlimited objectives. The probability of such a war happening today is very limited. Conventional wars, especially by industrialising countries like Pakistan, can only be of a very short duration. Her aim will be a short and swift operation which will give her a negotiating advantage. The point here is that between two alternatives of a larger force with reserves of *materiel* for a short-duration war and a smaller force with reserves of *materiel* for a long-duration war, the former is to the preferred in the present circumstances. Conventional war in the present age will in all probability have to be fought with a force in being, and the so-called mobilisation potential, unless it is of an instantly mobilisable type as in Israel, is not of much value.

The Chinese potential to wage a conventional war against India across the Himalayas will be limited by the logistic constraints of Tibet. But the picture could change significantly if the Chinese complete the rail road to Lhasa – one of their long term projects. Even then there will be major limitations imposed by altitude, terrain and the type of equipment that could be employed on the India-Tibet border.

On the other hand, if the Chinese decide to violate Burmese neutrality, they could pose a very serious threat indeed. No doubt in that case it should be possible to internationalise that war and enlist the assistance of other powers. Our diplomacy must therefore be directed to preparing the ground for this purpose.

Another threat the Chinese could pose is a sudden attack or coup-cum-intervention in Nepal. For reasons that we need not go into here now. Nepal has permitted a certain degree of Chinese presence and allowed the Kathmandu-Kodari highway to be built by the Chinese. While it may not be prudent to express disapproval of the Nepalese-Chinese relationship, it is necessary to develop our capability to go to the assistance of Nepal. Here it is necessary to recall Prime Minister Nehru's guarantee to Nepal. Further, the Sino-Indian confrontation has to be viewed in perspective. It is not for a few square miles of territory here and there but to determine whether a Chinese presence will be permitted to be established south of the Himalayan crest.

In considering the conventional war threat from China it is necessary to take into account the situation on the rest of her borders. Very few in this country will still categorise the Soviet Union and China as socialist brothers. China has the longest border – which is also under dispute – with the Soviet Union. In 1963-64, accusations were exchanged between the two countries about 5,000 border incidents. There has been unrest in the border populations of China whose ethnic brethren live across the border within the Soviet Union. There have been recent reports of tension on the Sino-Soviet border in the Uighur region of Sinkiang. Soviet military assistance to India is based on a cognition of mutual security interest. So long as Sino-Soviet relations remain in their present state, Soviet support for India will be unwavering.

Will Pakistan and China pose a concerted threat to India? There is no point in asking this question. Pakistan dare not act against India by itself. There does not seem to be any likelihood of US support for any Pakistani adventure against India. The Soviet Union's interest in India – notwithstanding the understanding on arms sale to Pakistan – will far outweigh Soviet interest in Pakistan. Consequently, Pakistan is left with only China to support her in her hostility towards India. Therefore the reasonable presumption for our planning will have to be that they would act together. This concerted action has certain limits and we should try to understand those limits.

Many consider the above picture somewhat pessimistic and alarming and may wonder whether India will be able to look after her security under these circumstances. Their thoughts may turn to grand alliances to ring round China or there may be a tendency to seek comfort in numbers and forge an alliance with a number of smaller nations in South East Asia. Some of these solutions are based on historical analogies or the outcome of the public relations exercises regarding the benefits of alliances like NATO and the containment policy. A little analysis will show that these courses of action are unrealistic and have no relevance to our security situation.

Japan is the number one trading partner of China. The latter does not regard the former as an adversary. While India is a reactionary figure in the Chinese demonology along with the Soviet revisionists and US imperialists, Japan is regarded along with France and other industrial countries as intermediate zones which can be won over. China needs the technology of Japan and Western Europe for her own development after having spurned Soviet assistance. The Soviets, having realised this are trying to win over Japan by offering the bait of joint Siberian development and trade. It suits Japan to expand her trade with China as well as the Soviet Union and make appropriate noises to keep everyone guessing. That suits their national interest and we should not grudge it. But we would be very naïve indeed if we presume that Japan is going to give up all these advantages for the doubtful benefit of a security understanding with India.

As for Australia, her role in South East Asia has been to insure herself with US protection by paying the regular premium of a token participation in the various operations in which US interests herself. In the defence industry qualitatively, she is only slightly ahead of India. She produces most of her requirements under license production and she has produced one or two of her own designs of sophisticated weaponry. India cannot and should not expect assistance by way of troops to defend her borders. Australia's capability to intervene is only a token one. It is therefore difficult to see how a security arrangement between these two nations will add to the security of either.

Let us also look at the periphery of China. In the south, Vietnam, Laos and Burma are on her borders. Burma's interest and ours are identical and there is no need for any formal pact to underline this. Vietnam has Soviet support and if US is imaginative she will also contribute to strengthening Vietnam. Laos is at present under three spheres of influence – the Chinese, the Vietnamese and the US. Given her geographical location, the US influence may not last long. If Vietnam is strengthened she may dominate Laos. Vietnamese dominance is preferable to Chinese dominance. Our interest is in bringing this about. The Chinese threat to South East Asia is stated to be in spreading and supporting the 'National Liberation Wars' which should next be considered.

The national liberation war was not invented by China, though Mao has contributed significantly to the subject. In retrospect, Garibaldi, Bolivar and George Washington fought national liberation wars. Lenin, Tito, Sukarno, Grivas, Boumedience and Castro all fought successful national liberation wars in this century. The call to use violence against an oppressive governing elite which stands in the way of orderly and rapid social change is nothing new and it is as old as Marxism, if not even older. If vested Interests will not permit the governments to be changed by ballot at regular intervals, there is no alternative except to change them by bullets. Supporting the view that unrepresentative governments who are indifferent to social change and modernisation should be supported at all costs, is only playing into Mao's hands. Those who oppose rapid modernisation, social change and representative government, are as effective implementers of Mao's thesis as those who follow it. National liberation wars and insurgencies are only symptoms of a deeper social and political malaise and should be treated as such.

Let us review the developments in the last twenty years. No national liberation war except two which happen to be exceptional cases, namely Malaya and Greece has been successfully tackled by the industrial powers. They lost it in Indonesia, Vietnam, Algeria, Cyprus and Aden. On the other hand, the newly emergent nationalist governments were able to tackle them successfully in most of the cases. India put down the Telengana insurgency of 1918, the Naga insurgency of 1956 and the Mizo insurgency of 1966. Indonesia put down the first Communist insurgency of 1949 and the second of 1965 in addition to periodical insurgencies of non-communist origin. Magsaysay of the Philippines tackled the Huks successfully, and Burma has been able to reach settlements with Karens and certain other insurgent groups. In other cases she has been able to limit their dimensions. Just because the US operation in Vietnam was a failure, there is a tendency in the West to exaggerate the scope of insurgencies and to indulge in pessimistic hand-wringing. Nobody has noticed that in this country the ex-insurgents not only came to terms with the government but are also taking part in government under the framework of the Indian Constitution. India's contribution to counter-insurgency deserves to be studied in greater depth both within the country and elsewhere in the world.

The ballot box and adult suffrage are the most potent counter-insurgency techniques. Barring the exception of Czechoslovakia, no legal communist party has ever been able to carry out a violent revolution or a coup. Maoists recognize this and that is the reason why their bitterest attacks are on the left and right communist parties, who according to them have succumbed to parliamentary criticism. Some in this country and elsewhere are not able to follow the ideological evolution in the international Communist movement. The memories of the communism, Stalinism and the unscrupulous exploitation of the communist parties of the world by Stalin to serve his purpose still haunt them. They are still unable to perceive that no communist who came to power as a result of his own struggle has ever served the purpose of Moscow or Peking except to the extent it suited him. This is what happened in the case of Mao himself, and he was preceded by Tito and followed by Ho Chi Minh, Hoxha, Castro and Kim Li Sung. Even where communist power was established by the Red Army, nationalism has asserted itself. Gomulka, Ceausescu and Dubcek are examples. The black and white type of perception is not helpful to anyone except Mao Tse Tung.

Recently a lot has been written about the Chinese and Pakistani attempts to support the insurgent elements among the Mizos and Nagas and there is some fear that they may extend such support to other tribals too. But while these activities do cost India avoidable expenditure and therefore need to be countered by action at different levels, one aspect needs to be emphasised. These activities cannot affect significantly the viability and security of India. These tribes are much too small in population and disparate to serve as the water for the insurgent fish to operate. These cannot become Vietnams, however fondly Maoists may hope for such an eventuality. One may recall the violence that followed the attempted communist insurgency in Indonesia. The carnage completely wiped out the communist party. If small tribes attempt insurgencies, deriving inspiration and arms aid from China, they may pay a very heavy price. Perhaps following the Soviet and Chinese examples under similar circumstances, such tribes may completely lose their identity thereafter and be forcibly absorbed in the major communities. It is therefore essential to study the insurgency and counter insurgency in these areas dispassionately and not feel alarmed unduly.

There is also no basis to assume that all vested interests and anti-communist elements will resist Chinese pressure and dominance. We have seen that collaborationist elements are present in all societies and they are to be found predominantly among the propertied elite. They would be willing to collaborate to save their privileged position. There are elites in South East Asia who collaborated with the British and French, then with the Japanese and collaborate now with the Americans. In spite of all the anti-communist noises they make, they are likely to be the first to collaborate with the Chinese if they come to the conclusion that the future is with them. The Chinese may prefer pliant satellites though anti-communist to strong, self reliant states even if they were communist. Hence perhaps their preference for kings and dictators irrespective of their ideologies. It is therefore essential not to be misled by ideological professions.

Next we come to the nuclear threat. Here I am afraid the pre-1962 history in regard to the Chinese threat is repeating itself. Those who warn us about the threat are contenting themselves with general statements just as there was a general recognition about the Chinese threat in the 1950's. The so-called professionals are also indulging in general statements as they did before 1962. I pointed out that before 1962 there was no professional debate nor professional writing on high altitude warfare and consequently the vague general threat perception was not translated into specific threat estimation which could form the basis for planned action. The situation now in regard to the nuclear threat is identical. Our decision-making structure is just as helpless to cope with this problem as it was then to cope with the threat estimation.

General statements are made from time to time in Parliament and elsewhere that the Chinese nuclear threat and developments are under constant review of the chiefs of staff. It is permissible to ask what the special competence of the chiefs of staff in this field is. In India, are there any professionals in the field of nuclear war and threats? Have there been specialized studies in depth? It is even more dangerous than it was in the case of high altitude war to presume that our professionals are to study this, for the plain truth is we have none. The literature in the field is mostly journalistic and a few studies, so far published, mostly repeat the views contained in the writings of the fifties and early sixties in the Western world. Neither the AEC nor the defence science organization, neither the Joint Intelligence Committee nor the Chiefs of Staff Committee are known to have set up cells to study this threat in depth and to spread professional knowledge on the subject. None of our public men, neither those who are in favour of nuclear weapons nor those who are against it, have demanded specific action by the government to study the subject and enlighten both our public and the armed forces on the subject. The nation, faced with a nuclear adversary, must first study the implications of the nuclear threat before deciding on a course of action. The debate in the country today is superficial and consists of uninformed dogmatic assertions of one kind or another.

I cannot claim to know enough about the subject to recommend a specific policy but perhaps I have devoted enough thought to the subject to pose the problem. The first issue is the situational imperative. China is ahead of India in weapon technology by perhaps seven or eight years. This is easily deducible. They had their uranium bomb explosion in 1964 – about four years ago. India is perhaps eighteen months behind an explosion of a plutonium device. If to this, one adds the development period for uranium separation technology the above time lag is arrived at. Therefore to catch up with China it is going to take not less than twelve to fifteen years provided our development can generally be 50 per cent faster than theirs. Those who contribute to the equalization theory will retort that with a few kilo-ton plutonium weapons Indian will be able to deter China with its megaton nuclear weapons and MRBMs. Is this true? A pistol can kill a person and so also a machine gun. If a man armed with a pistol faces a man with the machine gun with 300 yards between them, will the man with the pistol deter the man with the machine gun? In this game of chicken, where the will counts for a lot, deterrence works not only on the basis of one's perception of what one can do, but the other's perception of one's own capability and one's perception of the other's perception. I am not going to be assertive about this; however it appears to me that a lot more research is needed before I shall be convinced that a few kilo-ton bombs and a few Canberra delivery systems can deter a China with megaton war-heads and MRBMs.

Then how do we get our plutonium bombs? From our Canada-India, Tarapore, Pratap Sagar, Kalpakkam and other reactors presumably. I have read somewhere that while PU 239 is the material needed for the weapon, PU 240 is not useful for weapon fabrication and the way in which the reactor has to be operated for power production and PU 239 production are different. Have there been any studies in this country on this issue? Our literature treats all PU alike; 239 or 240 do no make any difference to our amateur strategists.

There is a school which is of the view that if India has tactical nuclear weapons, then that will be a sufficient deterrent because with those, India will be able to catalyse a major nuclear exchange when it becomes necessary. According to Sir Solly Zuckermann and others, the command and control problems of a tactical nuclear war and its escalation to strategic level have not been solved even by the US. Could one have some detailed scenarios about such catalytic action?

This survivability of the Government is crucial to the posture of deterrence. There is only one paper in India which has discussed this and that has come from our Institute of Defence Analysis. But even that paper did not evoke any reaction among the public men and decision-makers.

What is the nature of the Chinese threat? Will it be strategic or tactical? What will be the impact of uncertainty caused by the existence of two other superior weapon systems on that threat? What is the degree of usability of nuclear force in different contexts? Warning about the Chinese nuclear threat and issuing general statements about the need to counter it is no more help than being against sin and preaching that people should not commit it.

How about the cost and technological aspects? Lots of people have swallowed the biased estimates of costs given by alarmists. The estimates of Alastair Buchan, Leonard Beaton and Teeple and Hoagland have generally been quoted. None of these could be considered authoritative. Someone reviewing a paper of mine was annoyed that I did not quote an Indian estimate and but relied on French costs and UN estimates.

I could not have done otherwise, because there is no Indian estimate and the UN estimate was subscribed to by Dr Sarabhai. Here again, could not there be an Indian study on the subject? Where is the demand for it in our Press and Parliament?

Those who are against the weapon programme are equally superficial. An eminent person in authority has talked about the non-useability of nuclear weapons. As a student of the subject I share this view to a considerable extent; but is this pronouncement based on a deep study or just the hunch of a humane individual? If we in India are convinced about this non-usability, then why should we express our concern about the credibility of the guarantee declaration by the nuclear weapon powers? The cost aspect is often cited to oppose the weapon development. Of course, India cannot afford to divert Rs. 100 crores next year to this programme. But can India do it even if she wants to? It will take at least three to four years for the AEC to reach the level of expenditure of Rs. 100 crores and a further number of years to reach higher levels. It is, therefore, not a question of whether India can afford such an order of expenditure in the next two or three years, but beyond that period.

One has to regretfully conclude that the attitude in regard to this vital question is marked by superficiality in this country. This is the reason why it is necessary to focus attention on decision making in the country and in the government. This is not true only of the question of nuclear threat but the entire field of security. The biggest threat to our security is not that from China or Pakistan, or conventional war, nuclear war or revolutionary war, but this superficial approach to our major problems. Experience is equated with expertise, age with knowledge, hierarchical status with competence, and lack of confidence and defeatism with realism and pragmatism. Till we get rid of this traditionalist burden, that will constitute the biggest of our security problems.

Nirad's Nightmare

Dilip Chitre

(Quest 62: July–September 1969)

I

The blurb of the paperback edition of Nirad C. Chaudhuri's *The Continent of Circe*, published by Jaico Books, projects the author in a significant manner. For instance, it tells us: '*Though he fell in love with England early by reading the great Romantic poets of the nineteenth century, he never visited England until after he wrote his autobiography in 1951.*' Mr Chaudhuri's love-affair had to be mentioned even in the short space of a blurb because it has had voluminous verbal consequences. Nirad C. Chaudhuri began as an unknown Indian and, after years of striving, has virtually become perhaps one of the most authentic Englishmen of all times. Or so at least he himself imagines. In the epilogue to *The Continent of Circe*, Mr Chaudhuri says with a triumphant sense of fulfillment: '*But why should I concern myself with them? I have rescued my European soul from Circe, to whom it was a kind of happiness to be in thrall. I have accomplished another feat which was more difficult. I have recovered my Ariel's body from Sycorax, the terrible and malevolent hag who stands behind Circe in India.*' (*The Continent of Circe;* Jaico Books; Bombay, 1967; p. 376). So much, for the moment, for love and the ecstasy of self-recovery. But Mr Chaudhuri's hate-affair with India has had equally spectacular effects. In immediate continuation of the above, we read: '*So I can and should ignore the*

Yahoos. But I would save the fellow-beasts. They do not, however, listen to me. They honk, neigh, bellow, bleat, or grunt, and scamper away to their scrub, stable, byre, pen and sty.' The choice of his allusion becomes dramatically significant. The Indian reader blushes, thinking of his own poor English vocabulary, and is almost hypnotised into believing that Mr Chaudhuri's finely orchestrated English prose is the equivalent of his being spiritually liberated from *desi*, beast-like dumbness. This is a belief which the author heartily shares with him and it has also been the impression made by Mr Chaudhuri on his Western readers. One has learnt elsewhere of Mr Chaudhuri's epicurean tastes which mostly concentrate on European food and wines and his rejection of local culinary creations. We know that this most remarkable Indian, despite a handicap of nativity, dresses and speaks like an Englishman. Street-urchins in the locality of Delhi where he lives have nicknamed him 'Johnny Walker' which, apart from being the brand-name of a famous Scotch whisky is also the name of a locally more famous comedian who acts in *desi* films. There is considerable wit and acumen in the street-urchins' description of Mr Chaudhuri. When he is worked up to a climactic frenzy in expressing his love for England and things English, Mr Chaudhuri gives one a sense of parody by extreme perfection – a comic ability to run rapidly and unhindered on a track strewn with banana peels. Even an Englishman would find the strains of being so precisely and religiously English all the time quite unbearable, at least on occasion. Nor is it possible to hate India and things Indian with such dogged consistency as if the hatred served a vital aim of one's life. Even archetypal colonial Englishmen were mellower in their hate of India and less ardent in their love of England. After all, to be an Englishman naturally and unwittingly is vastly different from being an Englishman by choice. More perceptive colonial Englishmen, like Mountstuart Elphinstone for instance, retained their power of empathy in a *desi* setting. Mr Chaudhuri is extremely exclusive: to him race, geography, climate and history are crucial factors. He talks of 'recovering one's European soul' and not of recognizing one's human potential and individual identity. In short, Mr Chaudhuri's choice is not merely a choice of cultural identity but a complex choice which involves, among other factors, a racist doctrine based on the concept of ethnic hierarchy. The novelty of Mr Chaudhuri's subtle brand of racism is that he believes climate and geographical location to be crucial factors in determining the content and quality of a culture. It would be very interesting to know just how and why Mr Chaudhuri, who began as 'an unknown Indian', born and bred in British India, chose to view his personal destiny as an individual in this way and gradually objectified it in the grand form of the destiny of a people, a culture and a nation.

It is possible to view Mr Chaudhuri's monumental attempt to articulate these basic theses in two different ways. It can be seen as a theory of history and culture since Mr Chaudhuri's philosophical prejudices are both meta-historical and meta-anthropological. But this is impossible because Mr Chaudhuri's data and methods are non-comparative, non-empirical and non-scientific. The other alternative is to view Mr Chaudhuri's views as the consequence of implicit and explicit choices of belief. This is quite possible. In such a view, one would be speculating on the psychological compulsions that are responsible for Mr Chaudhuri's peculiar views. One would concede in advance that Mr Chaudhuri's views will not be prejudicially refuted in such a speculative interpretation. He may have offered as many insights and illuminating observations as distortions of fact and elements of fantasy.

There is also a third way in which Mr Chaudhuri's attempt can be viewed. The most impressive aspect of Mr Chaudhuri's writing is his style, his use of literary devices and the effects produced by them. In places, it almost attains the quality of creative writing. Mr Chaudhuri's impassioned rhetoric, whether he is writing eloquent praise or launching a bitter invective against something, reminds one of writers like Nietzsche. But the resemblance is deceptive although the pathological origin of the kind of prose does appear identical. Nietzsche used literary and stylistic devices as heuristic tools: Mr Chaudhuri uses them primarily for their aesthetic effect. Is Mr Chaudhuri, then, closer to romantic historians and religious prophets? I think so. And Nietzsche did have the same kind of prophetism, a sense of self-styled *charisma*. It reminds one of the central character in Sartre's play, *The Condemned of Altona*, who is confined to a cell and his own delusions, and addresses the twenty-second century and crowds of crabs. It also reminds one of Freud's description of Michaelangelo's Moses gazing beyond civilization and mankind, which was Freud's subconscious description of himself as a prophet.

Mr Chaudhuri's prophetism is not very subtle, covert and self-concealing. His epilogue to the book shows its shrill pitch and aggressiveness. The intimidating posture of superiority, the condescending attitude towards readers, the constant and often pointless exhibition of verbal prowess that Mr Chaudhuri offers – all have a crude obviousness in them. When one takes a deeper view of these and tries to connect them with the nature of Mr Chaudhuri's vision, thoughts and ideas, they appear to be the aggressive gestures of a deeply insecure man. In fact, they appear to be features of an unmistakably paranoid, albeit gifted, personality. Mr Chaudhuri, in this and other books, makes references to his personal experiences as data supporting his conclusions about India and Indians. These are nearly always associated with a sense of persecution. These feelings of being persecuted alternate with Mr Chaudhuri's very superior and exclusive individual qualities as he himself sees them. Such an acute persecution mania and delusions of grandeur, and such feelings of superiority and martyrdom, suggest a paranoid mind. It might be useful to speculate on the relationship between a grand literary style and a paranoid personality. And it might also be interesting to find out whether some kinds of fallacious reasoning or intuitive claims to correctness stem from psychological maladjustments.

When a person who cannot cope with his environment distorts its image to suit himself, psychologists call it a case of cognitive dissonance. Most human individuals and all cultures provide examples of such cognitive dissonance. Creative writers, artists, religious and social prophets, even some philosophers have been victims of cognitive dissonance. Their emotional involvement is often intense and inseparable from their social or moral passion and their aesthetic delight in their own vision and nightmares. Their objectivity varies but it is never total. Without interfering with the order of the world they propose to deal with, they mould its image according to their own designs. But they seldom stop at this; very often they seek to confer an ontological status on the image, thus equating it with the objective situation. A similar thing, one suspects, has happened with 'the facts' Mr Chaudhuri tells his readers. It appears that an acute sense of insecurity in his own society, a craving for status and acceptance, and a desire to identify himself with the ruling elite culturally and emotionally, have all been decisive factors in Mr Chaudhuri's formulation of his views. This might seem a harsh and prejudiced comment; but one can cite several passages from Mr Chaudhuri's writings which show that he is obsessed by the idea of becoming a full-fledged Englishman. *A Passage to England* has all the qualities of a devout and faithful pilgrim's joy in walking over sacred land: the topography of this land is highlighted by emotional involvement. There is a revealing example of this acute Englishness in *The Continent of Circe*. Mr Chaudhuri is narrating the episode of an insult to him by an 'anglicized' and 'class conscious' lady at a concert in Delhi in post-Independence India, in 1962. He observes after narrating the somewhat ludicrously emphasised details of an irritating but significant experience: *'Never in my life in British days had any such incident happened to me. I had written that from hearsay. But that evening I was made to feel the truth of my one-time observation. Only the day before I had met Sir Malcolm Sargeant, and discussed the programme with such assurance that an English lady who was near whispered to my wife, 'What a bold man he is!' But after being put in my place by the (i) Anglicised, (ii) Bengali, (iii) Hindu lady, I could hardly bear to recall that conversation: it became a cankering reminiscence of my humiliation at the hands of one of the Epigoni.'* (p. 352). It is in such personal grievance that, one suspects, Mr Chaudhuri's theses have their origin.

A little later he generalises his observation and further comments that *'all these men combine the Hindu pride of caste with the English pride of class, and they* can be *very* unpleasant': While this is true of the snobbish, status-conscious upper-crust of any society, one views seriously Mr Chaudhuri's own status-consciousness which is of a different order but is as unconcealed as it is crude. In the passage quoted above, he drops the name of Sir Malcolm Sargeant with remarkable aplomb and cannot resist mentioning an *English lady's* awe of his ability to discuss the programme with the conductor himself. What Mr Chaudhuri finds glorious and specially mentionable, however, may not impress a minority of his readers who might be more mature and less stupid and snobbish than the particular English lady. Even the sprinkles of Latin and French, the bristling classical Greek allusions, the ornamental use of little-known books and historical incidents – all of which give his museum like literary arrangements their peculiarly impressive quality – are there only to impress more people of the English lady's kind. After all, Mr Chaudhuri is a gourmet, an epicure, a stylist. He parades his learning like a coquette displaying her cultivated charms. None of his Western or Indian reviewers, as far as I know, have found these charms irrelevant to his theses and arguments. Nor have they tried to find any fault with his interpretation of history and presentation of Indian culture. Serious readers may enjoy the brief holiday from seriousness provided by Mr Chaudhuri when he eloquently flogs dead horses: the horse goes unnoticed and the eloquence of the flagellant is entertaining. But they also fail to notice the sinister theory of ethnic hierarchy that underlies Mr Chaudhuri's pathological Anglophilia and sense of spiritual Europeanness.

II

If Mr Chaudhuri were consistent and not self-contradictory, he would have been much easier to dismiss. But part of his complexity is a product of self-contradictory attitudes and it is difficult to assess the value of the partially valid observations he therefore makes. In the introductory part of his book, which is entitled *The World's Knowledge of India since 1947*, he discusses Indian writing in English on India as a source of information to the outside world. This is generally a sound and succinct presentation of the situation. Writing of Indian novelists who write in English, he says that they 'have neither the knowledge nor the strength of mind' for tackling the problem such a task raises. '*The life, the mind, and the behaviour of Indians,*' Mr Chaudhuri writes, '*are so strange for the people of the West that if these are described in ordinary English the books would be unintelligible to English-speaking readers, and unacceptable to British or American publishers. Most Indian writers solve this problem, not by choosing a genuine Indian subject and creating an adequate Western idiom to express it, but by selecting wholly artificial themes which the Western world takes to be Indian, and by dealing with them in the manner of contemporary Western writers.*' (p.14) This is a partially valid observation typical of Mr Chaudhuri. While it is true that a cultural gap creates a 'translation handicap' and poses, in the case of Indian writers describing traditionally Indian life with its nuances, a problem of adequate and precise verbal devices, Mr Chaudhuri's phrase 'genuine Indian subject' conveys a naïve attitude to creative writing. What is a 'genuine Indian subject'? Does Mr Chaudhuri mean by this a *typical* Indian subject? Does he have in mind a subject which is representative of Indian life? Representative in what sense? Would a statistically significant situation, when made the subject of a novel, become 'genuinely Indian'? Again, what is meant by 'artificial themes' which the Western world takes to be Indian? Can Mr Chaudhuri give examples? For instance, with his knowledge of Bengali, can he not compare Bengali and English novels and illustrate his point by contrast? And who are the '*contemporary* Western writers' whose manner is imitated by Indian novelists in English? It is fairly clear to literary critics who have a comparative knowledge of Indian and Western literatures that it is the *avant garde* creative writer in Indian languages who is closer in manner to contemporary Western writers than his Indo-Anglian counterpart. The Indo-Anglian writer lags behind simply because the best creative talent in modern Indian writing is expressed today in Indian languages. Leaving aside second-rate or worse Indo-Anglian writers from Narayan to Khushwant Singh and Mulk Raj Anand to Kamala Markandeya, however, the best Indo-Anglian writing does reflect both thematic authenticity and technical excellence. Any critic anywhere would take G.V. Desani and Raja Rao, for example, very seriously. The question of *their* Indianness is not so easy to settle. They have expressed complex individual preoccupations with their themes, which is what makes such sweeping observations sound rather foolhardy. *All About H. Hatterr*, for instance, is possibly hundred per cent Indian and also a literary masterpiece in English. Raja Rao is a little inferior to Desani, but he too has written novels which are authentically Indian and also genuine literature. Mr Chaudhuri's fallacy lies in assuming that the Indian writer in English has to bear, necessarily, the difficult double-burden of creating an adequate Western idiom and writing on 'genuine Indian themes'. It is not picture post-card Indianness he objects to: he only wants *better picture post-cards*. He will perhaps accuse any modern, self-conscious and highly individualistic Indian creative writer of being un-Indian. He seems to expect all Indian novelists in English to write in a naturalistic, realistic or documentary vein. That amounts to forcibly pushing them backward into to nineteenth century.

But these are matters of opinion; and value-judgements are bound to vary. What offends one here is simply the sweep and the unqualified cocksureness of the statement. Mr Chaudhuri does not cite a single writer: he wants us to accept his own view without our sacrilegious pause for illustration or substantiation. This is infuriating. Even a village schoolmaster should do better; and Mr Chaudhuri is telling the whole world the ultimate truths about contemporary as well as 'timeless' India. No wonder that he thinks that Kipling alone has captured the latter in writing, whatever Mr Chaudhuri means by saying so.

Mr Chaudhuri falls in the traps he warns others against. He claims to be extremely averse to hasty theorising about India and Indians; but this is precisely what he often does himself. Having chosen a certain fatal determinism as the basis of his view, he can turn out tirelessly remarks which have an air of studied resignation.

'*I declare every day that a man who cannot endure dirt, dust, stench, noise, ugliness, disorder, heat, and cold has no right to live in India.*' (p. 22) Apart from questions of rights, this is a realistic observation of the conditions that prevail in India. But part of these impressively repulsive attributes are the property of every overpopulated, poor and illiterate quarter of the world. Most of Europe was equally dirty until a couple of centuries ago. And *ghettos* in big cities, the poor quarters in most affluent metropolises of the world, have noise, ugliness, disorder, heat or cold. Part of these depressing features are related to the lack of modern concepts of privacy, hygiene, sanitation and individualistic living which are absent in India owing to the absence of widespread modernisation largely rooted in a lack of a this-worldly orientation. A person who has been condemned to live in India, or who lives there by conscious choice, but resents this terrible onslaught of unsavoury sensations, would try to understand and change the situation. Mr Chaudhuri's resignation amounts to a refusal of seeking any change. He may be being ironical, but he has forgotten to draw the line.

A page later he vividly describes (again!) the terrible personal problem arising out of such unhealthy environment which he would not escape since he wants to be a fit citizen and also to seek knowledge even from this almost lethal stink. He writes, heroically as well as pathetically, '*I live just inside the old wall built originally by the Mogul Emperor Shah Jehan, overlooking a fine park and commanding a magnificent view of the famous Ridge, the Jamuna, and the Jami Masjid. It is probably the finest aspect to be seen anywhere in Delhi. My Western friends say that it reminds them of the view of the Borghese Gardens from the Pincio.*' Then, for sudden dramatic (and traumatic) contrast, he writes, '*But after independence, for four years, I saw people easing themselves in this park in the morning, sitting in rows. During this time the stench was so foul that after inhaling it for a year I fell very ill and came very near to death... I have never objected to or minded all this, and I will say that if I have any living knowledge of my country it is a reward for this unflinching realism. So, when Anglicised Indians come to argue with me I expect them to possess at least a fragment of my knowledge and toleration of these conditions.*' (pp. 22-23). This knowledge, which as far as the passage explicitly imparts it, is a knowledge of the fact that the Indian landscape is extensively and regularly punctuated with human excreta. It is not a very rate piece of information even if all of us do not have views from our windows which remind our Western friends of the view of the Borghese Gardens from the Pincio. Nor is the romantic and exotic image of India about which Mr Chaudhuri wishes to disillusion his readers so widely prevalent any more. What is significant is Mr Chaudhuri's relentless intensity and vivid pondering on this commonplace phenomenon. He takes pains to establish the delicateness of his own sensibility and his great sacrifice in watching and suffering the situation for the sake of knowledge.

Mr Chaudhuri has a knack of producing, from a mountain of cultivated style, the mouse of such ordinary knowledge. The effect is always anti-climatic considering the gross disproportion between his verbal pyrotechnics and the intelligible core of factual or theoretical propositions he makes. Extreme ego-centricity – and I use this as a euphemism for pomposity and vanity – has considerably enhanced the obesity of his book, but it has also damaged its more serious content. Typical Chaudhuri anecdotes and reminiscences crop up suddenly anywhere in the book; and they have a most disconcerting effect. Here is where grand style, pomposity, the insistence on creating one's own legend, prophetism, and finally grand theorising, become the suspicious symptoms of paranoia. Elias Canetti, in his brilliant dissertation on the phenomenon of crowding and paranoid tendencies signifying the craving for power, has exempted creative writers and scholars from the collection-mania of the rest of the human herd. But symbolically a grand style and a compulsive display of not very relevant details of one's own learning are perhaps another form of collection-mania, of the craving for power motivated by a deep anxiety and insecurity. At least Mr Chaudhuri's writings lead one to suspect so. As a sheer stylistic exercise, one occasionally enjoys Mr Chaudhuri's writing. But the pursuit of style mars the content of his theses by repetitiveness, clustering of diverse elements in single sentences or paragraphs, sudden losses of continuity in argument for the sake of stylistic self-celebration or anecdote-riding.

It is evident to the reader that Mr Chaudhuri is a much tortured man. But the reasons for this torture are unconvincing. It is the self-torture of a status-seeking man who is bitterly frustrated and has become latently hostile to the common sub-stratum of humanity in whose presence an enlightened humanist becomes humble in spite of his acute critical faculties. He sees, by choice, the rest of the Indian elite as fatally degenerate; what is more frightening is that he writes off the populous anonymity of the Indian masses as an incurably infrahuman species. To imagine this to be an irreversible situation is terrible not so much because it is doom-spelling as because it is an articulate rejection of human concern.

I have named this syndrome Nirad's Nightmare. There are many Indians today who fashionably suffer from it. They mourn the loss of the British Empire, whose spoils they could not share, more than the British. They also mourn the gain of independence whose spoils they cannot share. This is typical of the Indo-Anglican who was born and brought up during the heyday of the *Raj*. Does not Mr Chaudhuri himself suffer from a combination of the Hindu pride of caste and the English pride of class? He fears pollution. He has a contempt for the non-Indian as well as for the newly rich or the newly powerful. Other Indo-Anglicans are vulgar, cultural bastards in his view because they are not as purely culturally English as himself. How many of them have studied classics and can sanctify arguments by sprinkling Latin, Greek and French quotations as he does? No wonder he is an isolated man basking in his own uniqueness and grumbling about the grossness of a vulgar world enveloping him against his wishes. Maybe others are under Circe's spell: Mr Chaudhuri has chosen to be spellbound by himself – he is Narcissus, not Ulysses. India remains a mythically eternal inferno; and Mr Chaudhuri remains a self-liberated demigod secure in the warmth of his own legend created by himself.

This is the impression Mr Chaudhuri's style and his pathological preoccupation with himself create. People of my generation, who are in their twenties and thirties, have to protect themselves from Mr Chaudhuri's own Circe-like spell. His cynicism and his extreme narcissism, his paranoid self glorification and his contempt for India, would inhibit their sense of a necessary engagement. Having too many prophets of doom has one plain consequence: it leads dissident, activist, radical members of the very infinitesimal intellectual elite in India away from their problem. I am no chauvinist. But if I were Mr Chaudhuri I would rather say good-bye to my 'fellow-beasts' and be an expatriate by choice than write off India. I would rather not expose myself resignedly to dust, dirt, stench, ugliness, disorder etc. for the sake of mere knowledge. For it is not much knowledge. It is mere sensation. Since it is disagreeable and since I am condemned to live as an Indian, I would rather endlessly seek to change the situation. Which might be a Sisyphian task; but its burden must be borne, as a matter of moral duty to oneself, by everyone who presumes himself to be an Indian intellectual.

III

The merit of Mr Chaudhuri's monumental essay lies largely in his interpretative account of the Hindu mind in the entire gamut of its expression. Although he draws his evidence from history. Mr Chaudhuri is centrally concerned in the 'timeless' aspects of the Hindu mind juxtaposed against or set within a 'timeless' India. The argument follows the pre-modern altruism that culture is historically determined and history culturally determined so that no rational and free-willed interference really helps us to get out of the vicious circle.

It is obvious that 'the Hindu psyche' is not a biological, genetic, and ethnic endowment. What is typically Hindu is a set of Hindu cultural norms, mores, and patterns of social operation. The Hindu tradition has been polymorphous and heterodox in spite of the formidable and abiding presence of the Hindu orthodoxy. There seems to be a pact of non-confrontation and non-interaction between the Hindu orthodoxy and the heterodox cultural drop-outs in India. This is a special feature of the Hindu view of society: parallel, stratified, and mutually non-intersecting communities co-exist within Hindu society without cross-pollination or mutual confrontation. Thus the caste-system operates at all levels. One imagines that even the classical erotologist Vatsyayana, in classifying men and women into four types according to the size of their genitalia, used caste overtones. For instance, a *Raja's* or a *brahmin's* lingam is small and his build is medium-to-small and his complexion fine; in contrast to these hare-men, at the other extreme we have horse-men with fearfully outsized members whose physical appearance suggests both non-Aryan and lower-caste people. This is only a half-humorous suggestion; its serious half invites comparison with the popular white-Western description of negro 'horse men' at the root of rape and pollution fantasies. The Hindu concept of human destiny is linked up with one's congenital caste and thus it runs counter to a secular, individualistic conception of destiny which allows individuation and encourages competition as well as the pursuit of life-goals of one's own choice. Along with *varna*, which determines social and material destiny, the Hindus have a conception of the four ashramas or life-phases. Initially, it must have been a sensible system for phasing the libido in and out of life. But as understood today and for many centuries, they are exclusively *alternative* pursuits of *moksha*. Nobody seems to have noticed the disastrous consequences of this: one can be a social drop-out and become a *sanyasi* even in one's early twenties when one's biological capacities and life-energy are at a white-heat and can be channeled into socially and culturally creative engagement. The dissident, heterodox, radical and creative elements in Hindu society have thus been shown a permanent emergency exit from their social moorings. Thus senile or middle-aged and orthodox men have contained a dynamic conflict of generations in society and precluded social change. The modern apolitical and asocial intellectual in India, who professes Mr Chaudhuri's kind of disengagement, is a new type of *sanyasi* modeled on the same prototype. Uncreative alienation is not new to India; it is an established safety-valve for the protection of a clock-work society which has a belief in the immortality of the soul as an alternative to a this-worldly, secular orientation.

There is no secular Hindu tradition and Mr Chaudhuri is brilliant when he illustrates the Hindu motivation in accommodating contradiction as a means to nullifying the effects of heterodoxy. Thus Islam and Christianity transplanted on the Hindu cultural soil have become hypertrophied, functioning only in their non secular aspect. Its *apaurusheya* revealed element reigns supreme over the minds of its subjects when any outside religion is Indianised. In spite of their obvious bloodthirstiness in the defence of their dogmas, both Hindus and Muslims in India are culturally passive and fatalistic because they already live in a timeless, non-secular world where the protection of one's beliefs is more important, material, and therefore infinitely valuable individual existence. Such a society has rejected the conception of dialectical socio-cultural change. But then, its fate is not historically determined. A consciousness of history involves an extension of oneself into the past in order to seek identity with one's ancestors and a sense of continuity. It is a form of self-consciousness even if it nearly always inhibits a multi-polar conception of the future. Hindus lack even the pre-modern sense of historical determinism which is implicit in Mr Chaudhuri's view. Most of the time, all Indian peacefully co-nonexist. They know that to be immortal, they have to nihilate their own existence.

Most of them, however, do so only dishonestly. Existence is *maya*, there is no relationship between the soul and its physical container. Greed, prurience, despotism are mere appearances. Squalor and conditions of abject dehumanisation too are appearances. Withdrawal of the libido is one conventional Hindu solution to the agony of existence: the other is a callous, negative permissiveness which is mistakenly known as the absorptive, flexible, liberal and resilient feature of Hindu culture. Mr Chaudhuri, who is always at his best when he finds an object for his vituperative urges, assails these features of Hindu culture with evident delight. It makes very good reading, too.

If it were an attempt to shock 'fellow-beasts' out of their self-complacency, Mr Chaudhuri has done an excellent thing. But the book attempts an interpretation of India to the West and so the vindictive nature of the invective seems a little out of place. Not only that: Mr Chaudhuri, in his attempt to shatter the myth of Hindu non-violence, tolerance, and charity goes to the other extreme of portraying the Hindu as essentially a savage, uncouth and blood-thirsty being – I wonder if this is a uniquely specific feature of the Hindu: bloodthirstiness is universal and is a property of even the materially most advanced mass-civilization of the West. His basic proposition therefore assumes the dangerous form of statements like 'The Chinese are cruel', 'Americans are delinquent', 'Arabs are filthy', 'Sikhs are stupid', 'Keralites are cut-throats', 'Bengalis are pompous', 'Maharashtrians are uncouth' and so on. It sounds too much like a description of one of the twelve astrological types.

Again, Mr Chaudhuri's dangerous and unsubstantiable assumption that culture is ethnically determined, leads to further distortion. Aryans were corrupted, in his view, by their settling down in India. At one point, he suggests that a break in race-memory is responsible for their degeneration; at another, he claims that the English Aryans also degenerated when they entered the 'Continent of Circe'. The Indian Aryans were corrupted by the climate and the aboriginal patterns of life, according to Mr Chaudhuri. And the English Aryans were corrupted by the climate as well as the corrupt patterns of the Hindu Aryans' life. Thus India, in his view, is infested by a virus against which there is neither immunity nor therapy. The prognosis is nil and the fatality certain. If this were really so, how is it possible for even Mr Chaudhuri to recover his 'European soul'? By writing a book in a major European language?

Mr Chaudhuri's latent racism, as reflected in his writings, will require a special study. Essentially, it is not very far removed from the Nazi concept of ethnic hierarchy and racial superiority. First, Mr Chaudhuri is a peculiar kind of atavist who believes in the innate superiority of the Aryans. Then he concludes that since the Aryans who settled down in the Indo-Gangetic plain and later spread further out into the sub-continent are basically made of the same racial substance as the European Aryans, the dynamism of the latter and the degeneration of the former must be largely due to their choice of habitation and the former's mixing up with the aborigines. This may be an interesting theory in itself and I would reserve any comment on it. But it can be proven neither true nor false: it is unverifiable. A temperate climate, similarly, may have been once more suitable for man's all-round cultural progress than an extreme climate in which the struggle for survival sucked in all man's creative potential. But even then, Mr Chaudhuri, writing in the twentieth century, could have placed a greater faith in science and rational endeavour. However slow it may be in coming, such a faith is dawning even upon those enslaved to a fatalistic world-view and living in abject conditions. Modernisation of human attitudes in backward societies is indeed a complex and a difficult task; but it is not obligatory to hold a belief in a religiously necessary recovery of one's original 'European soul' to achieve this. Why stain one's physical existence with the conception of any soul at all? But Mr Chaudhuri's deep Europeanness has also, alas, given him a Christian original sin complex. The Aryans' stepping into India is the equivalent to Adam's fall; yet they must strive to return to the European spiritual Eden. And so, the Christ-like suffering of Mr Chaudhuri on the cross of India, and his last testament offered to his fellow-beasts, heralds a new religion. What prophetism!

IV

One must allow oneself a necessary digression at this point.

Mr Chaudhuri, whatever his defects, is a product of the Enlightenment euphemistically known as the Indian renaissance and traced back to Raja Rammohun Roy. That this enlightenment could not transform itself into a full-fledged renaissance is too obvious a fact. Almost up to 1947, the most talented products of the enlightenment placed politics and mass-movements above the need for a deeper and more comprehensive social transformation. This had led to India's having neither political maturity nor cultural modernity. A Vivekananda who spoke fluent English and captivated Western audiences was the Indian's conception of a spiritual hero; a Gandhi going back on his Western education and speaking of a highly religious *Ram Rajya* with his idea of a mass-leader; a Subhas Bose flirting with second-hand military power was his dream of a political redeemer. At best, the Enlightenment produced minor social reformists still largely pre-modern in their views. Conflicts between tradition and modernity were thus usually avoided or minimised. This isolated the exceptional authentic moderns and minimised their impact even on the intelligentsia and the literate minority. For example, a great modern Indian like R.D. Karve could not have any effect on the Maharashtrian elite because the more glamourised social leadership either ignored his efforts or scoffed at them.

M.N. Roy's earlier, romanticized and revolutionary career became so inalienable from his social image that his later cultural radicalism and depoliticisation of his movement had little impact and, worse, was misinterpreted as a suspiciously motivated betrayal of communism which had hypnotised the adventurist intellectuals of the thirties and the early forties. Politics still remains a superior preoccupation to culture. The renaissance has been shelved as a goal by all but a few members of the Indian elite.

This is hardly a problem of complete Anglicization or Europeanisation. The West has her own anomalies and evils. No concept of national or continental cultural identity is really relevant. It is not a question of accepting this or that cultural model; it is a question of choosing a set of fundamental values and criteria, a metacultural structure which will keep man open to continual self-transformation without having to face a perpetual identity crisis. In this light expositions like Mr Chaudhuri's, despite the valuable insights they offer, appear basically anti-modern and anti-humanistic. They perpetuate the myths and nightmares of historically determined doom. They are rather like horror comics which plunge us into orgies of imaginary violence which some time become real to us and distort our objective understanding. History gives images which mar our future more than help us to freely create it. It creates a profound psychosis which can permanently jaundice our vision or make us withdraw from our involvement with our environment. That is why one ultimately rejects the kind of 'knowledge' Mr Chaudhuri offers and, even more vehemently, the perspective in which it is presented. Accounts of India by writers like Segal, Naipaul, and Koestler are more relevant. Interpretations of 'the Hindu mind' by writers like Agehananda Bharati are more stimulating. It is sad to witness Mr Chaudhuri's wealth of information and verbal facility falling a victim to a crude, biased, irrational and irrelevant hypothesis. And his Herculean exercises in self-aggrandisement raise altogether sinister doubts about the origins of his views, which one is inclined to locate in a gifted but cracked up personality trying to create its own legend.

Sadhus and Hippies

Roderick Neill

(Quest 65: April-June 1970)

Anything written under the present heading, particularly a brief note such as this one, is bound to be full of shortcomings owing to the complex nature of the subject. Furthermore, the subject is one which arouses strong passions, people regarding sadhus and hippies as either the salt of the earth or its scum; some people would regard the two groups of men as identical, some people would regard them as diametrically opposed types; thus it is controversial even to deal with the two groups under one heading.

It is the experience of this writer that the two groups have a great deal in common, not only in their avowed beliefs, but also in their origin and life-style. Large numbers of sadhus have always tended to appear in ages of confusion; the ages into which Buddha and Sankaracharya were born were characterized by religious chaos, and a cursory glance at the present era is enough to see that we are living in just such an age of anguish. Both groups are avowedly motivated by a longing for salvation, even if this means no more than the wish to escape from a humdrum human existence. Both groups are characterized by a certain fearlessness, unconventionality, otherworldliness, quietism and a *laissez-faire* attitude to the issues that empassion human society generally, such as social reform and welfare. The main differences between sadhus and hippies are in their mores; sadhus tend to be much more rigid and inflexible in their daily rituals, eating and drinking, sleeping, travelling, and in their use of intoxicants and relations with women, but it is quite evident that since both sadhus and hippies tend to deny the reality of phenomena, these differences cannot be considered very significant.

The meaning of the word 'sadhu' is derived from the same Sanskrit root as 'sadhana' which means the path to enlightenment; a sadhu is one on this path. The present writer is using the name to denote the bearded wanderer with matted locks and few or no clothes and possessions, who is such a common sight in Northern India. These sadhus rarely have a high level of education, even in Sanskrit, very, very few can speak English and many indeed are totally illiterate. There are mendicants in India who have a considerable knowledge of the Vedas and Puranas, but they would normally be referred to as 'Swamins' and very rarely belong to the ranks of the bearded and long-haired sadhus.

'Hippy' has a less easily verifiable meaning and derivation; the word is obviously related to 'hip' and 'hipster'. 'Hipsters' were originally certain denizens of the northern American cities with a large negro population, particularly New York, Chicago and Detroit, either negro, or what Norman Mailer called. 'The White Negro' in his essay of that name describing the psychopathology of this novel outsider in post-war America. To be 'hip' in common parlance means to know, not just to know a lot of facts, but to know life and human nature as it is. 'Hippy' is a diminutive formed from this root, and coined only in the early sixties to describe the sudden wave of longhaired, cannabis-smoking 'drop-outs' (largely white Anglo-Saxon Protestants) in bourgeois America. Until this wave, the word 'beatnik' (derived from the same Latin root as 'beatitude') was used to describe what was essentially the same phenomenon, but the massive scale of the dropping out in the past decade called for a new name.

There is no single factor responsible for this wave; the heightening pressures and tensions on all sides in an increasingly competitive and aggressive world and the threat to the age-old values of liberal individualism posed by the population explosion and by recent advances in electronics have all had their impact. However, in looking for factors that led to the manifestation of the hippy phenomenon one thing stands out, and that is the discovery and distribution of LSD. Enough has been written elsewhere and by more competent authors not to need repetition here. LSD has become the sacrament of the hippies; their holiest *prasad;* many users regard 'acid' (as it is commonly-known) to be their guru, some hippies familiar with Sanskrit terminology refer to it as the 'avtar'. But there is one point about Lysergic acid diethylamide that should be made; since organic LSD can only be prepared from ergot, a rare fungus of the rye grain, which is now more or less unavailable because of government action (and Sandoz Pharmaceutical Company who originally developed the drug no longer supply it), most of the so-called 'LSD' that is supplied to hippies is manufactured by the 'underground' (as hippy society is often called) and being synthetic, is usually impure and unsatisfactory. Thus many hippies who are wholly committed to their path of 'dropping out' of society and who believe steadfastly in the initiating power of LSD have not themselves had that 'annihilating illumination' that characterizes the LSD experience. In this respect they are no different from those people who claim membership of some religion without understanding its theology or practicing its tenets.

Some readers will feel that this digression on LSD has deflated the thesis that sadhus and hippies have much in common, maintaining that Indian sadhus are the epitome of self-restraint and temperance. Not so the sadhu babas whom the writer has lived with for many years. The use of psychedelic drugs is common not only to Indian sadhus and western hippies but also to Moslem fakirs, African 'witch-doctors', Mexican and Guatamalan *curanderos* and Amazonian and Andean tribal sages and doctors. The intoxicant used daily by the majority of hippies, sadhus and the others mentioned above is *ganja* or cannabis sativa known as Indian hemp, marijuana, *bhang* and *charas* are also prepared from the same plant. There is evidence that the association of cannabis with Siva Mahadeva, the ascetic God of the great Trinity of Hinduism, symbolising the changes in the evolution and dissolution of the universe, the centrifugal inertia of the cosmos, goes back a very long way in Hindu mythology. One of the names of Siva is 'Nilakantha' or blue-throated; in the story of the creation, the churning of the ocean of milk, two heavenly substances are produced, the sweet, nectarine, ambrosial *amrit* and the bitter, intoxicating poisonous *halahal.* The nectar was taken by the *devas,* the many bright ones or Gods, who had secured it before the *asuras,* the dark ones or demons, could do so. But four drops fell on earth, at Hardwar, Prayag, Ujjain and Nasik; these sites are the sites of the Kumbh

Melas, in twelve year cycles. Siva Mahadeva, unaided, drank the *halahal* and his throat turned blue from its venom.

There are numerous allusions to Siva's fondness for *ganja*, *bhang* and *datura*, (the latter is a very powerful depersonaliser and hallucinogen that grows wild almost everywhere in India) and he is offered their flowers and fruit in temples, often by matrons who have no idea of the effect upon human consciousness of these plants, having been reared in the belief that they are deadly poisonous. Most Saiva sadhus even believe *datura* to be deadly poisonous, so strong is its effect, which is somewhat akin to LSD. Correctly prepared, even cobra venom, scorpion poison and arsenic, are used to intoxicate: cobras and scorpions are Siva's constant companions, indeed they are his necklaces and ear-rings, according to some hymns and votive portraits. There are of course the Vaishnava sadhus such as the Ram worshipping Vairagis from Ayodhya who do not use much cannabis but they tend to resemble Brahman householders, often to the extent of having farms and families. The general Vairagis are much less ascetic and hard-living than the Saivas, and consequently more soft or mild-natured and therefore often more respected, especially by Brahmans and Vaishyas, whereas the orthodox Saiva Nagas are largely derived from and maintained by the *kshatriya* (warrior) caste, and the Saiva Naths and Udasins the favourite of the lower castes. Nagas are forbidden not only meat and alcohol but also opium, garlic, onions and several other things, turnips for example, whereas Udasins sometimes, and Naths often, take alcohol, opium and meat and have none of the restrictions on certain foods.

This article is concerned with Saivas because of the great resemblance that hippies bear to these sadhus. The three main orders of Saiva Sadhus are the Nagas, Naths and Nirvans who are largely confined to the northern half of India. Besides these there are Agori sadhus who are usually free-lance and quite unconventional, however they are worshippers of Shakti or the female energy of nature in conjunction with Siva the predominant male energy. This approach comes close to Tantric Buddhism and the polarity of yin and yang in Confucianism. Agoris are most commonly found in Bengal.

By far the largest most orthodox and entrenched sect of Saivite Sadhus are the Nagas, the 'force' of the Dasanami Sanyasia sect founded by Sankaracharya. Of the ten 'families' names of Sankaracharya's order, which are Giri, Puri, Bharati, Saraswati, Parbhat, Sagar, Ashram, Tirtha, Van and Ram, nearly all called

Giri are Nagas from Northern India speaking Hindi-Hindustani-Urdu. There are also Nagas called Puri, particularly in Gujarat, Maharashtra and S. India, and some called Bharati and Saraswati. The remaining names are largely used by the Swamis and 'dandi' swamis who inhabit Sankaracharya naths, principally in Puri, Dwarka, Sringeri and Joshi nath in the Himalayas and are headed by the Jagadgurus Sankaracharya of which there are always four. To these Jagadgurus the Nagas pay nominal allegiance as lineal disciples of Adi Sankaracharya who organised the order. Besides Sankaracharya, the great histo-mythological God/guru of the Nagas is Dattatreya, Girnari Baba depicted in the iconography as three-headed, bearing trident, conch, necklace and water-pot, surrounded by cows and dogs. (Nagas are among the few born caste Hindus who keep dogs). Although Sankaracharya and Dattatreya are not normally considered to have been contemporaries (indeed Dattatreya is a shadowy, almost pre-historical figure) there are stories among the Nagas telling how these two great Rishis got together to form the Dasanami sect – a stroke of genius uniting all the disputing sects in existence at that time! There is some evidence that this is what Sankaracharya actually did at the time of the collapse of Buddhist monasteries.

The Dandi swamis are purely Brahmin and all to some extent educated in Sanskrit, at least to literacy and in some cases to excellence comparable to that attained by scholarly theologians anywhere in the world. The Nagas loosely regard themselves as the bodyguard of the Swamis, which indeed they must have been from time to time, with *trisul* (trident) and *chimta* (fire-tongs) and *lath* (staff) they are well able to defend themselves and others. In the processions at the great *melas* it is not uncommon even today to see Nagas (often stark naked) armed with firearms, swords and spears and once, many say, they had cannon. This is credible since several Naga *akharas* are forts (e.g. Dattatreya Akharain both Girnar in Gujarat and Ujjain in Madhya Pradesh and many other *akharas* elsewhere.) The term 'Senapati' (chief of force) and 'Kotwal' (keeper of fort) are used for Naga officials. In the past they used also to maintain the 'purity' of the ochre robe by defrocking and chastising uninitiated sadhus – a good thing in many ways, but fraught with dangers. To this day they maintain a high standard of discipline among themselves in many respects; Nagas suspected of transgressions such as those involving wine, women, flesh or opium are severely dealt with; it is indecorous for Nagas to beg in bazaars, stay in private homes, eat onions and garlic. However, Nagas, as well as all bodies of Sande Sadhus permit ganja-smoking, indeed, since Dattatreya is accredited with the invention of the clay hand-pipe or *chilam* used by all sadhus, *ganja*-smoking is almost sacramental. Swamis do not smoke *ganja* and their main criticism and reason for despising Nagas, who at best they regard as servant, road-guide or audience for their dissertations; (he needn't understand) is the Nagas use of ganja.

Many Nagas are quite illiterate. They are usually either Brahmins with a yen for the wayward life, or Kshatriyas with a yearning to be priests, hence the composite devotional and military character of the sect. However, since nearly all Nagas are 'dropouts', they tend to drift widely in life, sometimes living alone in the jungle or with one or two like-kindred souls, but very few seem to have done that for any length of time. Most Nagas have usually lived several years with their gurus as 'mahapurush' at the beck and call of all Nagas, but living a life both numinous and slightly adventurous. Only at the Kumbh Melas are Nagas initiated, as they say, if their 'sanstragas' are in order, and to these great sadhu get-togethers they are taken by their gurus and initiated into a particular akhara. Nagas have seven *akharas* (of which today the largest Panchayati Jan Akhara, having some 15,000 able bodied Nagas, and the smallest the Panchayati Anand Akhara having a mere 150) and thenceforth they are full sadhus in their own right and able to go on pilgrimage to the great Siva shrines. There are several hundred such shrines in all India where they will find at least survival-rations provided by local caste-Hindus to the akhara or to individual Naga Baba and disciples and their *stan* which is invariably found at such shrines. In a few cases the shrines themselves and the income from pilgrims is in the hands of Naga Babas, but more often than not where this was the case a committee of lawyers and politicians, usually Brahmins, has taken over. An example of a temple held by Naga Babas is Alakhanath outside Bareilly, and of one they lost to a committee, an example is Tarakeshwar outside Calcutta.

In days gone by the Naga *panch* (panchayat-governing body) used to travel all the year with dozens of elephants, hundreds of horses and bullock carts of cooking equipment and tents for the thousands of Nagas in train. Nowadays with no Kajas and Zamindars to support thousands of unexpected guests, this colourful, rather spectacular scene has vanished, like the Rajas themselves. There are many 'Nagas still living who recall the 'good old days' of Raja Panchem George.

Until recently the Girnar Hills of Gujarat lay within a *jagir* (gifted land) held by the Naga Mahant of the Dattatreya Akhara of Girnar – in this large area of jungle the Mahant more or less 'ruled' like a petty king. The land still held by the seven *akharas* must amount to about one lakh hectares; the Jun Akhara alone has 28,000 hectares, a lot of which is highly productive, producing mostly grains and fruit for the sadhus' own consumption, although surpluses are often marketed.

Nagas are identifiable by their matted locks and beards and either their ash-smeared or ochre-clad bodies; they carry *trisul* or *chimta* or a staff (not wrapped in ochre-cloth as by the Dandi Swamis) and usually a waisted, gourd-shaped brass post with three knobs on the handle (these water pots, like the Nagfani snake-horns that they also sometimes carry come from Girnar, the real Naga headquarters in India). Nagas also have a characteristic range of armlets, such as the *rudraksha* necklace and arm-bands, crystal and coral stones, copper, steel, rhino-horn and ivory bracelets, all having special symbolism and accompanying mantra. Old Nagas often quiz the younger ones on the mantras for their necklaces or bracelets, bathing, ash-smearing and eating. Young Nagas in the first years after initiation are generally exceedingly ascetic and kept that way by group pressure; rising at 4 a.m. they take cold baths, even at great heights in the Himalayas, and smear on ashes, which besides a loin cloth deerskin, water-pot, and rough shawl is usually their only property. As they become older (many die young because of the rigorous regimen and traveling) they tend to abandon not only the ashes and loin cloth but also the austerity, living mostly in one place where if there isn't already a Siva temple they may build one, may be on their guru's *samadhi* or tomb. They are served by disciples to whom they teach the traditions, *pujas* and mantras of the sect. Upon death a Naga's disciple may build a temple upon his *samadhi*. Nagas are buried, often in salt, and never burned – most Siva temples in India are tombs of sadhus, less commonly of kings; all other Hindus are burned so that they may re-incarnate.

In the temples and ashrams, which today are usually near centres of population capable of supporting them, the sadhus are the *pujaris*, but they also provide a service akin to the Catholic Father's hearing of confessions; sometimes their prescription for atonement makes the sale of indulgences which so enraged Martin Luther look like a very mild form of priestly extortion. Usually, however, people receive genuine solace from a visit to a Naga Baba in a Siva temple. The Babas sit most of the day by their *dhunis* or sacred fires, hearing the world's complaints, chiding severely and characteristically, sometimes most coarsely in a manner that only a Baba could do and not provoke anger. At dawn and dusk and from time to time in between they will reverently prepare and smoke ganja, shouting out the appropriate mantras.

Because of the lack of 'sewa' – hospitality on the road, now that there are so many *mowali* (riff-raff) going in the guise of sadhus – Naga Babas mostly live in temples instead of in the open and on the road. When they travel by train they usually have tickets, are going on a specific pilgrimage and returning after a fixed number of days. The younger Nagas always spend a few years wandering, but if they survive this, which may take them to every corner of India in the footsteps of Sankaracharya, they invariably settle somewhere in middle age. There are always exceptions, some of whom embrace complete austerity and even silence at initiation and never relax it. However, the highest virtue to Nagas *jnan* – wisdom – and this they have in common with the Dandi swamis. Their practice of a synthetic Raja Yoga is a sort of middle path – indeed Indian sadhus in general seem to differ from Buddhist monks, both of the Northern and Southern schools only slightly in respect of mores and theology. One difference between the Nagas and the Southern Buddhists (and all Christian monastic orders) is that *sewa* – service – means service rendered by the public, not done for the sick and suffering, and perhaps it is largely this which is the cause of the unpopularity which they share with almost all sects except the Swami Vivekananda's Ramakrishna Mission.

In earlier days, before the soil of India was raped, the jungles cut, cities established and the population began to grow unchecked it was possible for an other-worldly brotherhood of men who, rejecting the realm of matter travelled the countryside regaling the public with myths, history and news, to conspicuously consume vast quantities of fine food, drink seers of cane juice and milk and smoke great ritual chillums of ganja, to be called 'Maharaj' by all the world and bless their benefactors with the promise of a hundred sons. Today the Nagas and all their fellow sadhus are reduced to the economic level of poor Brahmin-farmer-beggars. Some westerners say that the akharas are not monastic orders but male secret societies. The Nagas are the only orthodox Saiva sadhus in the sense that they have always enjoyed the favour of the higher castes. Nonetheless they do represent a break with the rigid social taboos of Hindustan, primarily by renouncing the householder's life. Many Brahmins and Kshatriyas still rigidly regard sannyas as the fourth stage of the life of a 'twice born' man, and anyone who embraces the sadhu life in their youth to be a deviant. But Sankaracharya, who took *sannyas* at the age of eleven, is the indisputable precedent of all Nagas. The Adi Guru wrote that one must have fully discharged one's duties as a householder in one lifetime or other to embrace *sannyas* in youth in this life.

The other groups of Saiva sadhus are unorthodox in the sense that their origins are recent and are the result of schismatic movements in Hindustan. Philosophically the most interesting is the Nath Samprataya founded by the disciples of Guru Gorakhnath, a great Guru who probably lived in the twelfth century AD in the area between the Ganges at Varanasi and the high Himalayas of Nepal. Gorakhnath, concerning whom there is not much sound historical information, is associated with the Eighty Four *siddhas*, revered by Hindus and Mahayana Buddhists alike. The Tibetans commonly associate Nagarjuna with the Eighty-Four but Nagarjuna lived in the fourth century AD. However, since one of the traditions concerning the *siddhas* is that they continually re-incarnate there always being eighty-four on earth at one time, there is no inconsistency with the Hindu association of Guru Gorakhnath and the Eighty Four *siddhas*.

The Naths might even be described as a tantric sect. Nagas regard *tantra mantra yantra* as either dangerous – their mantras have more in common with Vedic mantra. There novices are called Agori who must not be confused with the completely 'free-lance' Agoris mentioned above; the name implies complete abandonment. Both kinds of Agori are commonly found in burning grounds, often take meat and liquor as well as ganja (if they take liquor habitually they often stop taking ganja) wear black cloth and have a rather fierce demeanour. Agornaths however always wear black cords carrying minute ivory whistles around their neck, in addition to the Saiva *rudraksha* necklace and various stones and charms. There are seemingly many Agornaths but few Darsani (i.e. fully initiated Naths). A fully initiated Nath may be identified by the large wooden or ivory rings in the body of his ears, where a gaping hole has been cut. At the Kumbh Mela at Ujjain in May 1969 three Agornaths died in the course of initiation at Pir Goofa temple, apparently of some kind of shock when their ears were cut. Of course no anaesthetic is used in what must be a painful operation, but Naths maintain the cutting has some effect on the nervous system that induces a state of *samadhi*, hence the title 'darsani', meaning one who has been in the presence, presumably of the Lord. Those who died had karma. The philosophy of Gorakhnath (of which most Naths are ignorant) is eclectic and synthetic, attempting to reconcile Hinduism and Buddhism by formulating a system which largely ignores metaphysics and the eternal self/non-self controversy that is thought to divide Vedantins and Buddhists, which concentrates on the human condition and the human form; the meditation prescribed by Guru Gorakhnath is the popular and supposedly tantric meditation on the three channels and *seyen plexi* or centres of the spinal column (which Western physiologists have not traced in their dissections, apparently because the system is not a gross physical phenomenon.).

The headquarters of the Naths are at Gorakhnath's temple in Gorakhpur in Uttar Pradesh. The late Mahant of Gorakhnath, Digvijaya Nath was also a politician; at the time of his death he was President of the Hindu Mahasabha, a Member of Parliament as well as head of the Nath Samprataya. Membership of the Samprataya is open to all Hindus and therefore Naths receive more donations from tradesmen and working people than the Nagas. Naths tend to be less fussy than Nagas about where they will go with whom, about where they will sleep and what they will eat. They are more 'dropped out' than Nagas: some even marry and raise families but these seem to be few. If a family is what a man wants why be a sadhu? A sadhu's sect replaces his family in every sense – caters to his need to belong – innate in all humans, cares for him when he is sick and aged.

The only other large group of Saiva sadhus, the Udasin, nearly all come from Punjab or Haryana. In fact the Udasi is a link between the Sikhs and non-Sikhs of that area. The order, which is now divided into two *akharas*, the Prachin (ancient) and Barra (large), was founded by Sri Chand Avdhoot, the youngest son of Guru Nanak, and regarded by his followers as an incarnation of Siva.

Apparently Sri Chand was a prodigal son finding his father too austere, so he flew to the jungle and realized his Self there. His sect provides an escape for Sikhs who find the rule of the Granth Sahib too austere and yearn to worship the old Gods, and an escape for Hindus who admire the monotheism of the Sikhs but cannot break with the rituals of their forefathers. The same symbolism of the *chakra* occurs in the meditational texts of the Udasi (there even is a text attributed to Sankaracharya called the Sundaryalahiri or ('wave of bliss' which elucidates this system though recently its attribution to the Jagadguru has been questioned). This system of meditation, which involves concentration on the chakras combined with the mental repetition of the appropriate *mantra* is also the most popular meditation among hippies who practice these things. Today few Naths and Udasin (and fewer hippies) have any real understanding of the system and its total cosmological as well as psycho-physical scope and significance. The goal of the system is the arousing of the *kundalini* (or coiled serpent) power that unites all the *chakras*, bringing Man's fragmented and separate planes of existence and awareness together. Raising the *kundalini* is the object of our embodied existences, may be equated with enlightenment, *samadhi*, *nirvana*, God realisation. Although tantric to the extent of worshipping Siva and his consort, Sakti (*kundalini*), Udasin are more conventional than Naths, enjoying the generosity of the wealthy Sikhs.

In as much as they all represent channels for social deviants and adventurous individualists (religious monomaniacs would not be happy either with the sadhus or hippies but then neither would rationalists) the sadhu sects of India are bodies of 'drop outs'. The fact that Nagas, and to a lesser extent Naths and Udasin have many taboos, merely reflects their background of Hindu conventionality.

It is the hippies' lack of taboos that distinguishes them, but they have so much in common with Saiva sadhus in their psycho-philosophical being that they can be regarded as varieties of the same type. Their outlook is other-worldly, if not self-denying, as often as not improvident; they feel strongly that the world owes them what they need to survive and if they accumulate more than they need they will not be too attached to the excess. They believe in the tenets of astrology, chiromancy, in signs and portents, in karma, or concordant action and reaction as the fundamental law of the cosmos. Both hippies and sadhus nearly always know the phase of the moon, but rarely the 'English' date; they may sleep all day but often sit all night and watch the moon perhaps against the mountains or among the clouds. They love to travel and to meet their own kind on the road; they are more disarmingly frank than most people can afford to be. They both regard themselves as superior types of human beings. They both prefer life on special planes, they take ganja or other drugs or stand on their heads and do breathing exercise. If Indian sadhus are conventional it is because in this day and age they have to conform to the narrow minded Puritanism of the people upon whose charity they depend, but once they obviously enjoyed greater liberties, as their traditions indicate. Hippies have greater freedom of action and as yet no traditions. They are amply provided for by their wealthy families or by the industries they have invaded or stimulated (pop-music, acting, design, and even shop keeping of 'Hip' requisites like necklaces and Ramnami shawls from Varanasi). However the complete lack of any special formula resulted in prescriptions for enlightenment combining Buddha and Christ, the Beatles (and Maharishi) space-fiction, the writings of Marcus Aurelius and William Burroughs, astrology, Ravi Sankar, etc., etc., with no discrimination or coherence.

The first dramatic fruition of the undisciplined pursuit of the absolute was the sensationally gory murder of the film-star Sharon Tate and some friends in Hollywood last year. At first the murder baffled detectives but finally clues led to a Hippy 'commune', the equivalent of a sadhu ashram, where the long haired and bearded 'guru' was training his disciples in a peculiarly twisted version of the gospel of love. The makings of a movement reminiscent of the notorious thugs of India was nipped in the bud.

Both sadhus and hippies are regarded as a menace, as charlatans of the first water by respectable, responsible, bureaucratic men in every part of the world. However, they represent a very real protest against the mundane condition of most men, constantly aware of and reminding their brothers of the existence of ideals that transcend all misery. Many sadhus and some hippies are 'mad' beyond the reach of most men's powers of communication and if it were not for the protection provided by their fellow sadhus and hippies, would suffer greatly at the hands of pragmatic and unsympathetic men.

The Coffee-Brown Boy Looks
At the Black Boy

J.S. Saxena

(Quest 65: April-June 1970)

The coffee-brown boy, like Abe Snopes, is 'without depth – a shape flat and bloodless, as though cut from tin… harsh like tin and without heat like tin.' He is not an existence but a scatter or a spectrum of attributes and qualities. The Black and the coffee-brown in cold entablature reflect a society which has little warmth, much terror and much more arrogance. Between them there is a moat with a drawbridge to which the White Boy has the keys. Most of the things which the Black and the coffee-brown claim for themselves are really historic products which the disenfranchised, disinherited White Boy created out of his agony. Free speech, religious toleration, equal rights for women, rights of assembly and expression, individual freedom from arbitrary arrest and the far more abstract concepts of individualism, solidarity, toleration, democracy, freedom, co-operation, even romantic love and individual personality, were won by disenfranchised White groups through a gruesome struggle. Of course, the White Boy has now forgotten all about them. The Black and the coffee-brown have to put the old questions, the questions about the quality and the content of human relationships in society, back into circulation again.

The racing pulse of the coffee-brown boy's liberal fever will always reduce his anger to a matter of tactics. *Indignatio ergo sum.* I rage, therefore I exist. The raging 'I' is an evasive foxy retreat in the face of the choice between violent death and a zoo. Why not, argues the coffee-brown intelligence, go in with the wolf? Why not get all the life's honey without ever being stung? Why not pant and slaver after the hounds or yap derisively at the cheated hunters rather than nip the fat paws of the killers with your blunted teeth as you die? The attempt to reconcile, or hold together, the dilemmas throws up by the pretence of intimacy with the two worlds, Blacks and White, is an act in which rage breeds more rage almost in geometrical progression. The coffee-brown boy gropes about and around this rage, translating it from pain into yet another form of pain, in his quest to return where he never came from. The result is an entirely passive, contemplative world where despair results in triviality, boredom, isolation – a refuge for the privileged, insulated from every jibe where the coffee-brown try to tell the truth about their lies. My rage is a kind of a joke. Because my rage is a kind of joke and I exist through my rage, I am a man because I joke and rage. Through my anger, through the joke, I assert that the joker exists. Doesn't the proof of the existence of the joker confirm, at least for the joker, that the pack of cards of which he is a part must also exist?

The Black Boy will always have an edge over the coffee-brown boy's politics and aesthetics of self-pity. He has to articulate or else suffocate in the stink of his own memories. Even though the American Negro is condemned to be in a perpetual minority in a colour-bar society, he would still remain a fluent improviser. His lack of consciousness whether in dress, speech or music or in the mocking arrogance of that rolling gait of his in that cat-like walk from the hip are a form of integrity which I shall never know. Between that 'cat like walk from the hip' and that 'bear-like from the shoulders', is the coffee-brown slouched wriggle from the thighs – the wriggle which, I am told, is the symbol of our virginity, a virginity that we claim is indubitably ours. Once upon a time, this virginity might have been the whole of our personality. Without it, my ancient predecessors believed, life was no longer possible in the world. It has to be preserved even by death in acts like *johar* or mass-burning of women. The point about our virginity now is that it has no point except perhaps as a stubborn, antiquated remnant of a beautiful quality which we imagine we once had. The American Negro had a life of his own, a life that matters, even when he didn't know what it is or who he was. He always had something to measure it by: mine has been a permanent mental inflammation of the fragmentary abstract existence. The experience of colour, I have come to believe, is not specifically transferable from the black to the White or to the coffee-brown.

The Black boy has an advantage which I will never have. For me, the experience of 'colour' will always remain a mental plaything, a fashionable dummy to try attitudes on, another phase in the intellectual fun and games which the coffee-brown boy has with himself. The infinite irreverence which should have gone into the direct response to an almost visceral experience, in the case of the coffee-brown boy degenerates into the callous pleasure a sober man takes at egging on a drunk. More often than not, all those acid-bulbs and screams shooting off inside me will turn into funny talk, even a romp, but never to frenzy and hysteria. I will always remain a poker-faced spoilsport, a glum-teetotaler, who plonks himself with a glass of fizzy pop in the hope that the alcoholic spirit will somehow enter into him by proxy. I do not even have the advantage of the American Negro's lack of self-consciousness. The colour, the subtleties, the mocking arrogance, the defensive qualities in the life of a people who have tried to survive through a painful touching irony without fawning on their oppressors will never be mine. 'Blues' and 'Jazz', as I see them, used to be the mode of appropriating the experience of a people who were condemned to be a perpetual minority, a minority which could never be integrated with the core of White power, money and dominance. They were created by a people expressing themselves, their entire self in all its macabre, baroque, tortured subtlety: and the Self this kind of music tried to express was not only the Self that made music but also the part which protested and revolted against the American Way of Life, against what Du Bois described as 'the American Assumption'. Blues and Jazz, I should think, are the most un-American music. I wonder why McCarthy or Daughters of the American Revolution did not take them to be unpatriotic. Before Jazz became the complex, involved, intellectual, modish thing it now is, in other words before the entertainment industry turned it into a gimmick it was, at least when played by the American Negro, an attempt of an embattled minority forever moving further out, way out, to evade definition and thus protest and survive. Lester Young did not capitulate to White culture and he was not a primitive but a sophisticated man who was not White and certainly not imitation white. But when the coffee-brown take up jazz, they are neither protesting nor revolting but only trying to be American, Blues, to the coffee-brown I suppose, means only a preoccupation with sexual themes. 'People should hear the pure blues,' said Muddy Waters as far back as 1959.... 'the blues we used to have when we had no money. I'm talking about when you couldn't buy even moonshines, a hotdog even, when you were making thirty-five cents a day. But how can I have that kind of blues with this in my pocket'. The Negro too has capitulated to Muddy Waters', 'this' fat wad of dollars in an accidental sort of 'modernism' but he still has the whole shape of his historic experience buried deep down inside him and ready for being retrieved.

I wonder whether the Black Boy can retrieve his experience of personal and historical vulnerability through the current modes of literature and art. He cannot afford to turn away from a reality too complex, too ugly, too brutal to contend with; there is no nicely got up little 'coloured' island in the Past or the Future. Unfortunately all the contemporary assumptions about art treat experience as pure texture, isolated, refined, dense, baroque. Abstracted from the concrete contexts, the social hinterland, integrity, identity, personality burn with a pure gem-like flame. The twentieth century novel, as Iris Murdoch put it, in its 'crystalline' form is 'a small, quasi-allegorical object' portraying the human condition: in its 'journalistic' form, it is 'a large quasi-documentary object'. Neither form can cope with the crisis of the Black or the coffee-brown boy's identity, for, by their very nature, they can only see identity if it exists in its pure, rarefied, autonomous form. Without the whole historical and personal shape of the Black or the coffee brown boy's existence, there would simply be no texture but a gaping hole.

For instance, *Notes of a Native Son* unifies the harrowing experience of the desire to murder a White waitress round an existential core in the manner of a Modern Jazz Quartet. Within the fragmentary beat of Baldwin's basic theme, the death and the burial of his father, the wild, tormented, anguish of being an astral Negro archetype, he improvises solos of melodic memory fragments in a 'spread rhythm' to gather up the mounting tension of ideas and feelings in the mood and the state of the Harlem of his time. He plays across or behind the beat of his theme with passages of intense, direct swing. The oblique childhood memories which seem to spring right out of one another as Baldwin subtly manipulates the 'pitch', the contrast of tonal qualities of the higher and the lower registers, the counterpoint of shrewd observation and those microtonal intervals, 'the intervals that carry that human quality' (Ornette Coleman) have a sophisticated complexity worthy of a Monk, a Coltrane or a Solly Rollins. There is a searing, terrifying structure in the experience of being oppressed which a Baldwin has, but which I will never have. But, even I can see that Baldwin, elegant, willowy, with a voice training after him like the shreds of his own life which has curdled into lusts and agonies, strives his alto saxophonist's best to prevent the paradoxes from catching up and rupturing the imagination. Baldwin's shape is based upon the toy-replica of a rather truncated, over sophisticated reality. The route is the route of a sensitive aesthete handicapped by his colour rather than that of those 'pure' blues, that uncontaminated jazz which made the American Negro live through the hot reality of his un-American self-assertion and all its tortures, agonies and ecstasies.

I was a chaste bouncing fourteen when I first saw this crevice open up in me. The mechanical, unromantic act of filling one's self with a bottle of beer had then a magic and a charisma of its own: the ice-cold sensation of a forked white fire which burnt and froze its way down the throat and lit the insides up while one gulped, choked, gasped, coughed, grimaced luminously, moronically. There was a War on and in the provincial town where I was receiving what my elders euphemistically called my education, there were American troops. Negro as well as White, on a mission or in transit, the mission being to save me from the Japanese devils and the transit, I should guess, to wherever dead soldiers go. In this provincial burg, there was hardly any public transport, all the bars and movies were in the Civil Lines. One April afternoon, the day I received my money for the month from home, I decided to have a fling: have a beer and do a movie. I remember I had cycled down a good six miles or so in the stinging sun. I felt a little more than usually thirsty and bearish. I shuffled uneasily into a bar, a rather respectable joint, almost as if I was entering a brothel. I hoped I would have a quick bottle or two and leave unseen. For next to fornication, my educators, my American teachers included, placed drinking – it made you unfit for a college course. Education, in the good old days, was the special preserve of the chaste who slaked their thirst on tap-water, bottled milk, lemon squash or an occasional ice-cream. Any deviations from the norm led either to expulsion or confinement to your hostel room in the evenings for a week. Of course, the sinner had the compensations of a Byronic hero but, at that time, I thought heroics to be rather boring. Heroism very often is. Therefore, I could not afford a scene and least of all in a public place like a bar. I slunk into, what I now think, was a rather chintzy, grimy cabin, shouted for the 'boy', and began to nurse my worst fears. Could I be spotted by the milk-swilling, ice-cream guzzling set of the College? I was hot, I was tired, I was afraid, that stinging April sun brings out the worst even in Indians. And yet somehow the thought of a tankard of ice-cold beer as the culmination was too good to let go. Started that long wait for the 'boy'. Ten minutes, fifteen minutes twenty minutes... my own nervous, febrile guilt, the fear of being caught up in a café brawl which in my coffee-brown case would have meant being beaten up by a British Tommy or an American GI and an Indian police-inspector, the prospect of being turned out of college, of becoming the butt-end of ridicule, the recipient of that pathetic, bovine snigger which relatives in such cases reserve for the victim unnerved me almost completely. I could hear people's chatter and laughter about five feet away from my cabin in the hall. On the table next to the cabin, there were three Negro GIs. They had come in after I had. They had finished half their beer and about a plateful of snacks. The waiter was fluttering round them, hovering, cringing, unctuously playing with the wrinkles on the new table-cloth he had especially laid for them. 'Gee, that zany dame was good. Got any more?' said one of the GIs to the waiter who benignly smiled and mumbled something. Something inside me broke then. I have had enough, enough of my own chastity, enough of my class, enough of my past, enough of my nation, enough of those hoary, musty, moth-eaten Vedic predecessors, in fact enough of everything. And I could burst. The April heat, the prickliness in the throat, the fatigue, the guilt, the nervousness, the humiliating transparency of all the deception which I carried in my bones, surged up till I could vomit. And I could not even vomit: I was alone with three hulking descendants of Joe Louis and all the weight of the US Army, the British Administration, my own academic Gestapos, my friends and even my relatives on their side. I could have murdered them for their crinkly hair, their elegant, willowy, rippling muscles, but coffee-brown boys, who did not have even segregated bars and movies to go to, were not permitted this Baldwinesque luxury of that near traumatic experience of the desire to kill another human being – they had to let their blood scream and howl in the void. I must have shouted for the waiter in a more than matter-of-fact though cold-blooded and spine-chilling way, for the soldiers looked up. And that did it. The tongue that Shakespeare and Milton spake contains a few very effective, dehumanising words precisely for such occasions. I was a tiny smug little racist of fourteen, cursing my own marginal, defenceless, hopelessness while shouting blue murder. I had looked into the pit: what stared back at me, in all its frightening dimensions, was my own crude, unsubtle vulnerability.

What is an Indian? Who is he? Of course, he has a past history, personal as well as cultural, but, at the same time, when he needs it most, when he is facing a crisis of identity, it just shrivels up and crumbles in his hands. He is at the mercy of waiters of his own colour or, for that matter, anyone else of any colour. With a frightening lucidity, you see that a life, like the child's famous definition of a net, is a lot of holes tied with a string. You try to slip, weightless as the dark, through your particular hole unless you want to have the string round your neck and go on tugging at it, tightening it, till the wind-pipe snaps and the hole that has swallowed you up like the wisp of air you are is meshed in with another string or another hole. And what is one hole less in a net of millions and millions of swarming, seething, bubbling. Self-perpetuating and self-strangulating holes? With the Hellhound on your trail, you have got to keep moving and leave the running to those who can. The black boy will 'always move with an authority which I shall never have', regarding me 'as a latecomer, bearing no credentials, to everything' he has, 'however unconsciously inherited'. The world never was, neither is, nor will ever be coffee-brown. The coffee-brown boy is led to believe that he is in Western Civilisation as well as of it. He runs the impious risks implied in catching up with Europe, takes the blood-money and blesses when he should be cursing his guts out in the cold. The black boy, though not yet in Western Civilisation, is still of it even when he is 'always in the position of having to decide between amputation and gangrene.' The coffee-brown boy's relation to the West is that of a lecher in a cosmopolitan brothel, the black boy's that of the lover to his love-object even when it 'don't mean a thing', even when he feels 'like jumping through the key-hole in your door.' The black boy's is a lover's quarrel which leads to the crime of passion: the coffee-brown boy's pimping turns him into an accomplice bartering his lust for small change.

For the coffee-brown boy, the faceless images of Black and White are no more than mirrors endlessly reflecting his own image, calm and tamed. Distances are only distances, defined and measured, and not heart-breaking schisms or crevasses. Imprisoned in other people's metaphors, he cannot even experience his prison. His life, bloody-minded, self-pitying, a cross between a yawn of boredom and a yell of outrage, explodes round in him in wave upon wave of fury and violence. But he is hooked to his private, self-elected no-man's land, and he does not even know that he is hooked. In his dance of the prophetic signs, the much vaunted Western privations and liberties only confirm or endorse his inalienable right to scorn the present and despise the future. Gangrene he has learnt to live with, about amputation he couldn't care less. All he wants is that others should see that he is trying to catch up and affirm his rather lone hope that some time he will. The coffee-brown boy's ambiguity is a part of the world-system which generates the fear of itself and a still more massive fear of this fear. He thinks that people need, in fact can do better, if they have his confidence, his respect, his sympathy. It is incredibly and terribly clear that the damned of the earth have nothing but their damnation to hold them up. But this minor slur on obscure Vedic myths, this enormity with Oxbridge and Ivy League manners produced by grafting European deceit upon Oriental despotism, this ragingly besotted pinhead with the imaginative daring a squashed fly, still thinks that people need his flexed intellectual muscles, or value his mental *pirouettes*.

People, black or coffee-brown, could very well do without some of the celebrated liberal humanist virtues. Human beings are not a dust-bin for any and every culture's rubbish. They are not a flexible, cosmopolitan museum ('with walls' or without walls) which can accommodate any and every picture. They are ice, fire, the withered leaf; blood, lymph, instinct; history, purpose, rage; pain, love and mania; humiliation, absurdity, vulnerability as well as policy, history or purpose. Put them in a frame, sometime they will break out of it and begin to live. Caress them and they will snarl. Tickle them and they might weep. Their head-pieces could be stuffed with liberal humanist glitter but their asses will be full of their own self-made shit. Nobody keeps power for ever: the ideas come and go but the shit remains, the shit remains and kills.

Those who get all het up and worked over the frightening depersonalisation of the American Negro should, for a change, turn their feelings inwards towards their own self-made shit in their own God-made asses. Here is an eminently flattering write-up about the First Lady of a sovereign, independent, democratic African state in a Free World magazine with a circulation of millions among the coffee-brown: "No caged bird, but a delicious, capricious worldling, the X's sensuous, luxury-loving Madame B, 31, delights Parisians even more than Jacqueline Kennedy or the Empress Farah... The First Lady... is coifed by one of the most exclusive Parisian hair-dressers (Carita), and dressed by Dior whose salon is strategically located across the street from the B's apartment... The affluent B's also have a villa in the stylish Swiss resort of Gastaad (her six-year old adopted daughter, H, is attending school in Switzerland), an X beach-house, an ultramodern five-storey tower in the fashionable C sector of A... (Madame B) loves orchids and sables, pilots a fast Lancia... Frenchmen who call her X one and see her, the forerunner of a new Europe-influenced African woman delight in her exuberant, ultra-feminine wit. It did not go unappreciated at a recent luncheon-party at Bobby Kennedy's house, at which, latching on fast to New Frontiersmanship, she switched tables after every course. Murmured Madame B raising made expectations: 'I suppose I'll be in the swimming-pool for dessert.'"

The gallant New Frontiersmen like the writer of the 'human interest' story saw nothing sordid or morally horrifying in the antics of this uncaged 'forerunner of the Europe-influenced African woman'. Perhaps they thought that their much-vaunted Western values in the American liberal tradition were being dramatically enacted for the edification of the blacks and the coffee-browns by the wife of the President of an African State whose per capita income is less than two rupees a day. Neither the New Frontiersmen nor the celebrated Free World magazine which champions the cause of Europe almost all the time, seem to have any use for a poor country blues singer like blind Lemon Jefferson. Before jazz became the craze it now is and hit the commercial jackpot, Lemon Jefferson made many records but he was never paid well. One morning during the winter of 1930, he was found dead and frozen on the streets of Chicago and it was announced later that he had died of a heart attack. Lemon Jefferson is neither Europe nor values nor liberalism for the New Frontier: Madame B is. I envy Madame B, but I also wish that when such gracious embodiments of French culture as the B's ring their hymns or requiems on Christian love and democratic liberty, somebody stripped them and scrawled 'Shit' in capital letters on their bums. 'You're a fine looking girl but you ain't never learned no rule (Jefferson: Chock House Blues)', Madame B. If every American Negro wants to be like the B's, I wish him joy of it but I wouldn't trust him when he shouts hell and Day of Judgements next time: whether he ends up in the swimming-pool or in the Atlantic Ocean for dessert is his own Free World 'free' business though it would be wise of him if he remembered Leon Bloy's parable of the Prodigal

Son. When Bloy began to elaborate on how the son lived among the swine, a society lady piped up to say, 'We all know the end of the story; the son came back to his father.' 'No, madame,' retorted Bloy, 'it was the swine who came.' The swine have the shrewdness, the dry sardonic wit, the 'cool' to hedge their bets, split the difference, legitimize compromise and defeats even if they have to clown the role imposed upon them by what they call their values. And they always come back, whatever be the period of history, for their share in the fatted calf.

Not that the coffee-brown boy's ambiguity, is without its ambiance charlatanism and deceit. If that black cat can be White, why can't I? If that black or coffee-brown 'primitive' does not have to be segregated and is treated with courtesy by the Whites, can I put up with it as an American citizen? As long as this desire to be White ceaselessly, remorselessly, haunts and ravishes the being of the black and the coffee-brown boy, there cannot be even a unity of resentment between the two except on the level of lies. The coffee-brown boy's hate turns outwards, becomes sympathy and a protest against injustice, or turns inwards upon itself till he is forced to accept other people's fictions which pour in upon him from every side.

Suppose four out of every five American Negroes were persuaded to go and drown themselves in the Pacific Ocean, and the papers and the mass-media mounted a campaign to prove that the Negro problem had been solved, would you know what happened? Suppose your clairvoyance, your second sight, told you the truth, apart from making sympathetic or indignant noises, what would you do? Suppose the one out of every five who escaped was given a million dollars and made you a free gift of a Cadillac, a TV set, a washing machine, a dozen suits and shirts, a tape-recorder, a type-writer, would you in your guilt, hate and shame, tear the flesh off the accursed man's bones? Or would you not sheer off into those personal and hyper-personal transparencies of ignorance and connive at the genocide by that 'change of heart' or 'we didn't know' kind of moral rhetoric? The moral *mala fides* of the coffee-brown boy compel him to repudiate and the searing opaqueness, the stab of white fire in the guts, that Bigger Thomas streak in his original nature of which he is so afraid and ashamed. Not that he is more holy or Christian or non-violent but because it is so easy to roll your eyes, purse the lips, take a deep breath, fart the words and assume that you have hit the dragon at its most vulnerable spot: he will go away and die of shame.

The Bigger Thomas nerve makes living with the gangrene painful and amputation a lived outrage rather than an elaborate charade of concepts or second hand feelings.

The coffee-brown boy looks for meanings in other people's acts, figures, gestures without connecting them with enthusiasms and agonies. He can hardly make any meanings for himself. He can change his car every year and swill champagne till he bursts but he can never feel through or make sense of the labyrinth within the symbols, the conditions which produced them. The fun or the thrill is not in the champagne or in the car but in the man who drinks, the man who drives, not in the mimed functional rationalities or habits but in the substantives of experience, the fine meshing within the turbines of one's life. The zest with which the status symbols of Europe and America are imbibed and assimilated, honed up, refurbished, renovated in the race for catching up cannot, and do not, cover up the nullity and the boredom of the coffee-brown boy's existence. Miming is not living for it cuts out the substantives in its quest for the functional. The car and the champagne minus the attitudes and the instincts within the structure of work and leisure are a part of that never-never land of pathetic manoeuvres where nothing happens, nothing will ever happen, on any level of intensity. The traumatic confrontation with humiliating vulnerability in Baldwin's face-to-face encounter with the White Waitress as well as the English language which modulates in the cubist panorama of a wasteland that was war-time Harlem, that is Harlem even now, crumbles up into a nicely got-up, tame little coffee-brown desert of parish-pump dissertations and home-made Indian lies. Does the American Negro need my sympathy, confidence, or good faith? I doubt it. He would be a fool if he did. In any case, I wish I had some of it to spare. At the moment, I have nothing to give except my gangrene which, I suppose, he can do without and a sense of the 'Hell-hound on my trail' which he doesn't need because he doesn't feel even half so damned as I do, and certainly not the way I do.

Left to himself, the American Negro would like to be, perhaps already is, as much of an American trying to keep up with the Jones's as the Jones's themselves. Sammy boy ran and ran till he outstripped Joe Smith at his own game and he is infuriated because, now that he has almost won the race in terms of the American Constitution, he sees that the prize that never was and the race that was already rigged have turned into ashes in his mouth. Endowed by their Creator with the inalienable rights of life, liberty and the pursuit of unhappiness, both White and Black are trapped in an ambiguous Freedom whose walls have been closing in upon them slowly, remorselessly. From the beginning, it should have been clear that no matter what the Negro did or does, he would still remain in the 'frame' devised for him. He would still remain a mélange of ideas, feelings, paradoxes in the White mind. He began as the Black Man's image in the mirror of the White Man's thought and experience, miming feelings and gestures appropriate to him, rather than a flesh-and-blood identity. After being detribalized, he internalized the White man's stereotypes, including those of himself, to placate, survive and become human. The image hoped that some time it would step out of the mirror and begin to live. The Negro put on a mask and he had to do it so well that the mask turned into his face. The face was a face because it would and did fit any possible mask that could be devised for it. Jim floats through Twain's book as if he was the dream-memory of Huck's humanity, the focus of white 'good' feeling, rather than a dense, opaque, 'otherness' of authentic existence. The process of being an 'image' in a mirror which could always tell you *what* but never know *why* turned him into a zany dance of prophetic rage and ominous signs.

In this game of 'play fool to catch the wise,' the Negro thought he was cunningly clowning a role to outsmart those who, through their power, imposed roles and stereotypes upon the weak. By not being himself at present, he thought he would, at some later stage, become himself: so this not-being-one's-self appeared to be the only authentic way of being one's self when the chance came. The miming of the White Man's version of the Black Man's role and nature, the keenness with which the Negro stepped into the shoes the white man made for him, was a part of the put-on act. The 'good nigger' became 'good', inferior, childlike, zany, stupid, spiritual, the interiorisation of *all* the White fantasies about himself, and blared back at the white man. The roles the White Man invented for him were turned into a profound psychological advantage with its overtones of power for the Negro's 'inverted' weakness or goodness could outmaster the master. But the white man who knew what the Black Man was doing to evade the definitions and identities meant for him by conforming to them while moving far out, way out, into unknown realms of being incorporated this element of 'pretence' too into his stereotype of the Negro; and the element of 'pretence' was again internalised as a part of the put-on act by the black man. What began as a put-on act intended to deceive turned into a life which became more and more of a put-on act. The process of acquiring an 'identity', of becoming human, by living out the role appropriate for human beings of his kind was, for the Negro, a kind of 'playing'. But by playing too long and too often, black life acquired a parodic zaniness of its own. By the time he himself had arrived at definition, the real 'he' had moved for away in its quest to evade all those contours of thinking and feeling which could be ascribed to, or inferred from, 'him'. Sammy boy ran and ran through all the subtle and unsubtle hurdles on his gashed and bleeding feet. He had begun as a commodity: the buying and selling which has made America began with him. But the ogre who knew this tendency of human commodities to turn into focal points of rebellion altered his stance. No matter what Sammy boy thought or did, he would still be chasing his own image in the White mind. Stretched between arson and the miracle of cold grace, one part of the image rapes and kills as it shouts in anguish 'how I yearn to burn, baby, burn' the other part of the image deliberately, delicately, applies the scalpel and 'probes the White Liberal conscience at its tenderest spots.'

The White Man who in spite of go-slow, sabotage, Nat Turners etc. had efficiently managed a slave-economy and made it pay fairly high dividends in the competitive conditions of a free market, prepared to deal himself with the various versions of Bigger Thomas and others who smile, go to church or write brilliantly. The Negro too cannot help generating Bigger Thomases and James Baldwins. His tragedy is not that he cannot live by his dreams: his dreams ruthlessly expose a life which falls short of all that it set out to promise so much so that whatever he dreams and whatever the life he lives, cannot be connected by the imagination. The barrier between realities and dreams has come crashing down round him. He too is learning to put up with the malevolence behind his skin which condemns him to be a Bigger Thomas even when he is a James Baldwin. 'Alas, Poor Richard' with its overtones of 'Oh, the futility of being a Bigger Thomas' is echoed back as 'Alas, poor James' and 'Oh, the futility of being a James Baldwin'. Dollars, prestige, respectability, publicity build-ups, welfare programmes; desegregation, and on the other hand, a private life which detonates with malevolence and explodes in fury till the fire is not next time but this time.' And yet the discipline of the social structure, the sharp concrete realities in which it expresses itself remains intact and we, the coffee-brown, condemned to our brand of the catastrophic, urge the Negro to accept a more universally valid form of despair – 'Anywhere, anywhere out of this world' – as the way out of the dilemmas we have contrived for ourselves. Somewhere in the universe, there must be somebody really nice, really real and, in any case, what people do doesn't change their nature. The only snag is that what people do *is* their nature.

The coffee-brown boy's smugness about the ambiguity of his nature or his status is the symptom of a deep seated insecurity. His ambiguity is the ambiguity of confusion and deception; the black boy's, on the other hand, is that of a contradiction which cannot be resolved and is, therefore, frozen. Both exist in a static frame of anguish which turns real lives into silhouettes and shadows. Both do somebody else's dirty work by delegation and not by letting the left hand know what the right hand was doing. The White criterion of knowledge and feeling may fit a ghost but it will never reveal the substantives in our experience because it was neither devised nor meant to deal with the facts of *our* lives. Clamped within this static frame, we, the black and the coffee-brown, are illusions which tremble on the verge of going over the line, shake themselves free from the discipline of an alien structure. Our lives are detached, morose, abstract meditations on the experience of discontinuity and loss as the European consciousness would have experienced it if it had lived like us. We see the pain but it is no longer ours; we live through the searing tension, the high harsh notes of utter anguish, pitched with perfect counterpoint against a melodic line which is calm, remote, tame, austere, European. Even our agony is the agony of the European living out our lives for us, re-experiencing the coloured man's condition through feelings or ideas which are neither black nor coffee-brown but White. How do we stop being somebody else's image, an image that drags the coffee-brown and the black 'towards mutilation, imposes upon the brain rhythms which very quickly obliterate it, wreck it' (Franz Fanon)?

Even when we talk of Indianisation and negritude, we are White Liberals draped in black or coffee-brown skin, trying to cope with the uniqueness of the black or coffee-brown experience by imposing upon it the White Liberal's structure. How can this structure contain the collective and individual terror behind its hegemony over us, a hegemony we did not invent but which invented? The black and the coffee-brown are neither heroes nor victims: they are like the child's version of the net, a lot of gaping holes tied with the White man's string. The Black boy tries to fight his way of the contradiction while the coffee-brown boy dreams of extracting some kind of a bonus out of it.

Even in my childhood the challenge of catching up used to make me feel a trifle uncomfortable. Those avuncular voices of resurgent India which used to blare at me then through public-address systems, news-media, and particularly through Pt. Nehru, made my gorge rise. Now I know that there is something outrageously vulgar, frighteningly stupid, about catching up. I refuse to be put in a frame for the convenience of nation-builders, culture-heroes, politicians and spend my life miming other people's ideas, feelings and gestures. I do not want to be an image, even the most luminous image, in somebody else's mind. I do not want to waste my life catching up with somebody else's dream of me in the hope that the dream will, sometime, somewhere, shake itself free from the dreamer, become flesh-and-blood and turn into a better me. Dreams do not concretise into dreamers though dreamers do, sometimes, dissolve into dreams.

Freedom does not lie in searching for meanings in the debris of your own life which someone else has hidden for you to find. It consists in *making* meanings for yourself, in improvising out of the flimsy materials of thoughts, feelings and sensations which are the concrete YOU, a set of resonances you can really call your own. In the beginning, I had to be dug out by archaeologists, resuscitated by scholars and pundits, dunned into stupidities by parents and teachers to conform to the image of some remote Vedic predecessor, before I could begin to live. There was a real coffee-brown boy in a small town of Uttar Pradesh in the early thirties but he wasn't really real: he was only real when he went back to the Mahabharata. But the coffee-brown boy's present is not a quantitative complication or simplification of his Past. His present agony, his present hunger, his present poverty, his awareness of waste, violence, parasitism and injustice cannot be a mere deprivation of proto-historic ecstasies or Vedic profundities. When I am reminded of my past and what my predecessors made of it in terms of sensibility, conscience, and intelligence, the only feelings I can have are guilt and shame. They really trampled all over what I would call human with great hob-nailed boots. Four thousand years of Indian history should be enough to detribalise the coffee-brown boy almost as completely as two hundred years of Negro slavery. Even my spirituality, my intense mystic heritage, is so riddled with socio-economic deprivation and insecurity that, instead of being something unique, appears to be a part of the world-wide culture of enforced poverty with its fatalism, its resignation, its sublimation of futilities and defeats.

Why the coffee-brown boy should split himself into a Yogic-Vedantic profundity, a luminous Tantric scroll, and a stinking, hunted animal who cannot even yap derisively at his hunters and must crawl like a thirsty dog to the meanest of streams, is not quite clear to me though it seems rather obvious to all the 'flower people', the men with the new needs? Why should I let the sick ghosts of my Vedic predecessors strangle whatever chance there is of growing out of this state of arrested rusticity in which I live? Perhaps in the sleek, clean desert of Marcusian 'One-Dimensionality', the poor and the filthy stand out, gleaming like silver, safe and proud and innocent, a standing joke or a permanent refuge from the horrors of being rich and bitchy. Perhaps like Mellors they love coffee-brown chastity 'because it is the peace that comes out of fucking': perhaps they love it as the 'snow-drops love the love', 'a snow-drop of forked white fire', which they want to carry away with them to their wearisome philandering. Between the repelling parasitism, the arrogant superficiality, the cheap commercialism of the Past as it appears in the life of the coffee-brown boy and the pure shield of chaste light it really was or could have, there is an abyss. The trauma of intense socio-economic deprivation within the religious sensibility makes me more of a foreigner to my Past. It appears as if my Past existed solely for the Department of Tourism. Would the tourist who crawls up dusty holes and smelly streets into a temple take half as much trouble or get one-tenth as excited about a beggar's hovel? I can re-experience my Past only in an anonymous a-social world which guarantees primal innocence and eternal bliss. But such an innocence would be the worst kind of treason.

No, I do not want to catch up with Europe either, neither with Jacobin France nor with Victorian England, Roosevelt's America or Stalinist Russia. Failure to catch up with Europe, I know, would be a disaster. But success may turn out to be a catastrophe which the world might not be able to survive. Two centuries ago, as Franz Fanon put it, a former colony of Europe and, if I might add, a rather backward Euro-Asian country decided to catch up with what was known as the West. They succeeded so well that the United States and its mirror-image, the Soviet Union, have become the most frightening monsters Man has ever known not only in his history but even in the most macabre, spine-chilling fairy-tale. In the greasy dawn light in which

I live, there are neither sanctuaries nor islands and monasteries but tortured negatives and tortured individuals. Can the black and the coffee-brown transcend that deep, depressive core, the core which is never acknowledged? Can they put together and make an abiding sense of the world and their place in it by fusing all their abstractions about themselves and their needs with the sheer, concrete thinginess of things? Their problems, the problems of the world, cannot be solved by catching up or reaching down; that would only tend to stabilise them. A catastrophic outcome is always possible and in order to avoid it, the existing society must produce out of its own guts, the 'material' and the basis of the 'alternative'. The black boy and the coffee-brown boy, I dare say, feel the need for an alternative which will revolutionise instead of stabilising the crises of identity and human relationship but neither of them is willing to accept the risks of an adventure, the pure logic of a refusal, the kind of refusal, which produced 'pure' blues and real jazz, not the present White stereotype of 'What Jazz ought to be.'

Neither of us is in a position to turn over a clean sheet and choose a mode of life rationally and dispassionately. It is easy to be a victim, easier to be a hero, but much more difficult to be a part of that permanent reserve of misfits and rejects who can be profitably squeezed, expended and replaced. Mr Baldwin does not know it. I do. Neither strategy nor tactics, neither pure guts nor pure intelligence matter in the Long March through the texture of the skin one is born with, except a faith in the fact that though twice two is not five, twice three is six. The Negro does not know it. I do.

The City as Antagonist:
Three Recent Films

Saleem Peeradina

(Quest 70: May –June 1971)

In terms of content, Satyajit Ray's new film is utterly satisfying, because its subject is entirely new and relevant to the pattern of contemporary living. In style *Pratidwandi* is comparable to Ray's best films; camerawork as usual is of the highest order. Its psychological appeal to the young is immediate because its hero is an intelligent, sensitive, responsible young man from a middle class background, just out of college and looking for a job. The film (based on Sunil Ganguly's story) is meaningful not only because identification with characters and situations is instantly established, but also because it attempts objectively to relate the city's life with that of the individual and the individual's effort, through conflicts, frustrations, aspirations to come to terms with the outer world.

Although the film is set in Calcutta it does not exist wholly in its milieu. There is a Bengali objection which finds fault with the film because its reality does not correspond to the social and cultural detail that the Bengali has known. For example, for a boy with his economic and social background Siddharta has too sophisticated a mind and is too reflective; that the kind of English he speaks would be a factor decidedly in his favour as far as jobs went; that Tunu, his brother, reflects the general mood of Bengal more than he does. This kind of argument even if correct, is not legitimate. In fact, by using a particular milieu as setting, the film can project an objective world-view that in its essentials would be true about any other metropolitan area in India. It is not meant to be a portrait of Calcutta. It is a portrait of a city which in this film happens to be Calcutta. Even if one talks of a Bengali boy in a middle class set-up, I think the categories can be and are meant to be extended and universalized.

In *Pather Panchali*, the train, not yet a threat as a symbol of the city civilization, is on the fringe of the undisturbed pace of village life. In *Pratidwandi* there is an inversion of images – the bird is trapped in the bewildering chaos of an urban area. One of the most evocative flashbacks is the scene where Topu rebukes her brother Siddharta and her cry of "Dada" echoes in an open outdoor waterside place which was part of their childhood: she asks, 'Did you hear that bird?' And the children's sense of wonder awakens to the magical note which comes through sharp and clear. The bird, which signifies a striving after some quality of the self, a quality that one was in touch with in one's childhood or in certain relations with people and nature, is what Siddharta is trying to retrieve and preserve. The search progresses through situations that are absurd, comic, pathetic, delicate and violent like hoping to find the actual bird by attempting to define its particular verbal music, in a bird-house that is collectively agog with an unrecognizable chatter.

Topu places her hand on her brother's head but there is no continuing communication. Siddharta suffers in the knowledge that his sister means to use her physical assets to advance in her career. For her, survival is not enough; she must remain ahead of the competition. Krishna Ghosh who plays Topu has a limited range of facial expression but Ray has used this to advantage. The wistful smile, with the hint of resolve, is not only a necessary mask in the world she moves in but, sadly, has come to be a permanent part of her. As soon as she enters the house she appears not to belong to the shabby domestic scene. The camera, rightly, takes her at body-level.

The realization that Topu has surrendered to the pressures of her environment is part of the larger realization on Siddharta's part (I will speak later of his meeting with Topu's boss) of the futility of attempting to overcome the forces that the socio-political organism generates. One compromises or adjusts, or one joins the establishment. One silences the bird; or one fights the evil, or alienates oneself from it.

Siddharta's two friends are typical in their behaviour, attitudes and pursuits, and his brother is realistically sketched although his activities are kept a mystery or dealt with in a hurry. To the extent that he too is elusive and inaccessible to his brother who fails to establish contact with him, this would be reasonable. Ironically, the single instance when Ray makes an attempt to turn the camera on him for a probe, he brings forth the unconvincing memory of the chicken being slaughtered and the boy steadily watching its spasmodic end. The connections of this image with the boy's development and with a wider social reality are evident. But this is too facile a way of explaining the prevalence of violence in general and its existence in the boy in particular. Siddharta, with his restraint and his awareness of human suffering, is representative in a deeper, more lasting way than the other characters although the 'solution' when it comes is a strictly personal one. That he ultimately dissociates himself from a monstrous reality is seen by same as a defeatist and pessimistic statement. At the same time, Ray does not exclude the possibility of other kinds of change brought about by revolution and resistance hinted at through the portrayal of Tunu.

There are Ray's usual witty asides. Siddharta waiting to cross the zebra lines sees a girl coming from the opposite direction and there is a cut-back to the anatomy lecture illustrated by a muscle-and-fibre diagram, on the physiology of the female breast! When Keya's aunt, who for some unknown reason is made to look like a tart and whom Keya's father is going to marry, swallows an aspirin after due *nakhra*, Siddharta's mind goes back to the talk on the versatility of the human throat. The wishful 'I am (botanical) master of all I survey' while sitting trouserless in the tailor's shop, the image of the revolutionary projected in the mirror, the romantic shooting down of his sister's boss are good touches. The unbridgeable gap between the world of the privileged typified by Sanyal who exploits all the advantages his wealth, position and easy morality give him and that of the struggling individual majority is suggested skillfully through scene (the spacious house, the car), attitude (the physical distance between boss and visitor, the gold buttons, the trunk call), and facial study (the expression of steady business-like assurance that Sanyal wears and the look of defeat on Siddharta's face).

The crowded bus, the accident and the beating up of the car-owner, the aerial view of the city teeming with people and noise, the unreal hippies; Adinath's 'The whole country is going down, brother. If I didn't go down I'd be suspended in the void' capture the city's characteristic complexity although the documenting is arbitrary and insufficient.

To consider an unsatisfactory scene: the visit to the prostitute and the meeting with Keya. A boy of Siddharta's middle-class upbringing would be mortally afraid if he were facing a prostitute for the first time and would wish he had not come. With Siddharta it is more, a moral revulsion than a physical disgust which, for a city boy, is not an authentic emotion. Immediately following this episode, he encounters a girl waving out to him from the shadow of a house and in spite of all his rational and psychological impulses, which at that moment would have told him to look straight ahead or look straight down and continue walking, he moves in her direction after a slight hesitation. Of course, from the point of view of the development of the story, the director is deliberately preparing to spring a surprise but the whole scene appears contrived. The girl herself, instead of going to the neighbours for help, waits at the edge of the road to try her luck with a stranger.

The use of the negative; purely in terms of effect and response I think the idea comes off. The second time also when the proximity of the prostitute is going to become much too unsettling for Siddharta, the frame turns negative and it does carry an unpleasant emotional charge in its inversion of tones. The negative is repeated in part of the dream sequence and as I have argued, in terms of effect it succeeds. But it comes close to being a technical novelty and, as was suggested by a friend who had seen the opening scene in the positive and found it colourless, Ray likes to make the introduction striking and different and this was an approach he had not used before. The second example was probably devised to get the scene past the censors!

The powerful climax, I felt, was spoilt by a crude use of the skeleton-image of human existence. Clearly the sense of an accumulating crisis leading to an outburst comes at the appropriate time but the *bare* skeletons should have been avoided. The freeze and the emerging inner reality imposed on statuesque figures conveys the sub-human desolation and desperation forcefully. Needlessly the bodies dissolve and reappear again. This misjudgment makes it a slight overstatement. Perhaps this is a niggardly objection because the film is really brilliant and sweeps you bodily into its experience. Of its total richness only an element can be verbalised.

The end is a very firm affirmation of Siddharta's sense of individuality. After accepting that part of the social role which is necessary for survival, it is a withdrawal to that area of himself which he must nurture and combine with an outer belief that would corroborate his own inner sense of right. The belief begins with Keya because she has awakened his feeling of kinship for her. The physical place restores him, if only temporarily, to that early memory where communication comes naturally. The bird after all is alive and kicking. Ray is not unduly romantic here: the poverty and the want is equally emphasised and faced. Death seen in perspective is now seen casually as part of the total equation of individual and daily realities. In the final freeze, the bird, Keya and the suburban scene merge in an assertion that is a declaration of abiding faith and striving which Siddharta has found in himself in his journey to and from the city.

Marianne Faithfull opens her eyes, makes sure she has a husband, closes them again, reflects on electronically created effect of coloured images of early morning birds, girl, husband, lover, speed, wind, circus act with lover holding the whip... returns to the bedroom, gives the husband a considered shake (he sleeps on), gets up, escapes for some reason from the camera's immodest eye, is caught getting into a leather outfit (note: no under things) which zips up to the neck which lover Alain Delon is going to zip right down and the policeman at the checkpoint is going to attempt to feel her hips through its half-inch thickness. Boots are as sparkling as the motorcycle is in showroom condition and wedding-gift from none other than Alain Delon ('I don't ask you to come'; but you gave me the motorbike') who is intellectual-bikerider-turned-lover. After helmet is lidded on, Marianne Faithfull becomes *The Girl On A Motorcycle*. The petrol-pump attendant, not in the know, naturally mutters 'Lucky Bastard', meaning the husband, as Faithfull starts her journey to Alain Delon who entered her life just in time to give her a little variety before marriage day, and from sheer force of habit continued to depend on the complication.

The rest of the film moves with her moving through a beautifully photographed territory of trees, fields, water, houses, mist (all beautifully pointless): memories, very profound reflections on identity, individuality, meaninglessness, sexual love of the ultra-modern girl caught between an adequate husband and an adequate lover. ('The point is', she begins to write to the former, 'I am leaving you I mean I am never coming back' and to the latter, 'I am returning the bike; I am going far away....' then tears up the note.) If only she had listened to the father who had once told her from the doorstep, 'Don't go too far', meaning of course the ride that Alain Delon was about to take her on after he had told her father, 'I can't wait to get my hands on that', meaning of course the book that her father had fetched for him from his library.

She never makes it finally. Which is a bit of a let-down. At full throttle through bend of road and curve of thought, she managed to keep a beatific smile on her face. Indeed, whenever the camera caught the upper half of her frame, she almost seemed to believe she was standing under a shower! (Director Jack Cardill). The accident was as realistic as it could be made. She will be remembered for the impulsive Bastard! Bastard! she screamed at no one in particular in the busy metropolis, but took one unwary passer-by by surprise.

About Merchant-Ivory's latest production, all one can say is that it takes guts to make a film as bad as *Bombay Talkie*.

A cool idea on gracious living

Live with an elegant table Rallifan.
Chic, streamlined. With the famous
Rallifan quality built into every
feature: whisper-silent operation,
greater cooling power, excellent
after-sales service. And a 2-year
guarantee.

You're cooler with a

Rallifan

A product of the Ralli Group

Am I a Muslim?
Islam and Bangladesh

Mahbubul Hok

(Quest 72: September–October 1971)

Author's Introduction: This article was written in Dacca in October 1968, shortly after a Law Commission for improvement of the Pakistani legal system was set up by President Ayub Khan. In 1958 Ayub Khan abrogated Pakistan's Constitution of 1956 but in 1962 he gave the state a new Constitution. Both these Constitutions were committed to not allowing the passage of legislation repugnant to the laws and principles of the Quran or Sunnah. The Constitutions had to adopt this provision because Pakistan was meant to be an Islamic state. The Law Commission invited suggestions which might help their work. As a student of law I tried in this article to expose the fundamental contradictions between the ideology and the legal system of Pakistan.

The article could not be sent to the Law Commission as I was sent to prison shortly after its completion and the Government of Ayub Khan was about to fall when I was released.

The main emphasis of the article is not on the failure of the modern Muslims to follow their religion but on the fact that the implementation of many of the Quranic laws will be harmful to any society of our time; and that a state cannot be called Islamic unless all the Quranic laws are implemented by its authorities. The Quran demands such implementation of its laws.

On 28 July 1969 President Yahya Khan said in a radio broadcast: 'Any individual, any group or any party which propagates against the basic principles of Islam and the ideology and integrity of Pakistan or works towards rifts in the solidarity of our people will incur the wrath of the people and their armed forces.' As a reply to this I wrote a letter to him on 23 August 1969 giving a fairly exhaustive statistical account, taken mainly from Pakistan Government sources, of the exploitation of East Bengal by the West Pakistani imperialists. It was entitled 'West Pakistani Imperialism in East Bengal'.[1] To help him attain a proper understanding of Islam I sent also a copy of this article with the letter. But the Legal Framework Order (1970) of Yahya Khan under which the general elections were held, demanded that the proposed Constitution of Pakistan would have to be an Islamic constitution. This proves that either he ignored this article or it failed to impress him.

Under Pakistani rule the cry for Islam was so loud even in East Bengal that Maulana Bhashani, an avowed Maoist, had to talk in the name of Islamic socialism. He was about to start an Islamic University before the Bangladesh War of Independence began. Even Sheikh Mujibur Rahman found it advisable to declare, in a public meeting in Dacca on 11 January 1970, that the Awami League government would not pass any law repugnant to the Quran or Sunnah. This declaration was incorporated in the Awami League Election Manifesto adopted in June 1970.

It may be said that I have been severe in criticizing Islam and those who use the name of Islam to serve their personal or group interests I was born in a Muslim family. I am grateful to the family and society in which I was brought up and educated. I pursue truth and should feel happy of the outcome of my pursuit would in any way help the improvement of those who call themselves Muslims. If I am proved wrong, I shall welcome the light of truth to lead me to the right path.

Do the people and intellectuals of present-day Pakistan enjoy the freedom of expression which is essential for a legal or any other true reformation? And is the government tolerant to the truths which may question the very basis of its existence and its violation of the constitutional and other laws of the state?

What is the outlook of the vast majority of the population of Pakistan today? Are they tolerant? Why did Dr Fazlur Rahman, Director of the Islamic Research Institute, Pakistan, have to resign? Why were there posters at Dacca demanding his execution by hanging? Why was the US Consulate at Lahore attacked by the students when an imaginary picture of the Prophet of Islam was published in a New York magazine?[2] Why was Dr A.N.M. Mahmood, Head of the Department of Economics, University of Dacca, ruthlessly beaten by the students of the same university? And why was he compelled to leave the university?[3] Why were there communal riots in East Pakistan when the preserved hair of the Prophet of Islam was lost in Hazratbal (Kashmir)? Why were the Kadianis massacred in Lahore in March 1953? Maulana Maudoodi was sentenced to death for his complicity in the Kadiani disturbances; how is he today the head of an all-Pakistan religio-political party? Is his party liberal?

However, it may be a little unjust to put all blame for fanaticism, orthodoxy and intolerance upon the present Muslim society and government of Pakistan alone. One should also study the character of Muslim society and the Muslim rulers from history.

The teachings of the prophets and of other great men have often been the slogans of their unscrupulous followers, but in practice they only mocked their teachers. The Quran says, *lakum deenukum walia deen* (to you be your way, and to me, mine). It also says, *la ik raha fideen* (let there be no compulsion in religion). These verses testify that God taught Muhammad to be tolerant. But what happened with his followers?

1. Of the first four Caliphs three were assassinated – the third, Osman (644-656) and the fourth, Ali (656-661) by the Muslims themselves.

2. When Alexandria was occupied by the Army of Omar (634-644), the second Caliph, it is said that he ordered the library of Alexandria to be set on fire. He said, 'If these hundreds of thousands of books of the library of Alexandria do not teach more than the Quran, then they are superfluous. But if they teach men any knowledge beyond the knowledge of the Quran then they are *haram* (forbidden). Therefore, under no circumstances can these books be saved.'[4] Barmatullah remarks: 'Even if the dilemma is taken as totally false, its inner satire hints only to the blind orthodoxy of the ancient Muslim'.[5] But the 'dilemma' may not be false at all. Omar's Phraseological art in his other speeches shows great similarity with that of the 'dilemma' quoted above Iqbal quoted Omar as having said: 'The Book of God is sufficient for us.'[6]

3. The episode of Karbala shows how cruel Muslim religious fanaticism could be.

4. The Kharijis upheld the principle of popular vote instead of hereditary succession to the institution of Caliphate. But they themselves were fanatics. 'The tense fanaticism of the Khariji at once manifested in a series of extremist proclamations and terrorist actions…. They went further and began to brand everyone infidel and outside the law who did not accept their point of view…. They then committed many murders, not even sparing women.'[7] But they too had their turn. 'Abu Muslim, newly appointed Governor of Khurasan, led his army against them (Kharijis) and is said to have slaughtered fifty thousand before pacifying the province.'[8]

5. The Arab Muslims were intolerant to the newly converted non-Arab Muslims (*Mawali*). 'They occupied a position half-way between the Arab lords and the non-Arab subjects…. Their revolt under Mukhtar showed the danger they threatened to be to the Arab realm and indeed the suppression of it cost them many lives.'[9]

6. Imam Abu Hanifa (699-767) had been flogged for eleven days, ten stripes a day, by the order of the Governor of Kufa. The Caliph later put the Imam in prison and he died in prison. 'Abu Hanifa's offence was his speaking the truth fearlessly and in a straightforward manner.'[10]

7. Imam Ahmed Ibn Hambl (780-855) too was cruelly flogged at a very old age by the order of the Caliph. The offence of the Imam was that he could not accept the Mutazila doctrine which the Caliph upheld.

8. The Mutazila – 'In Damascus. Ghaila al-Dimoshki, who figures among the fathers of the Mutazila was put to death by the Caliph Hisham for holding the doctrine of free will.'[11] 'But it is a fact of great concern that at the instigation of this free-thinking community the Caliph al-Mamun instituted an inquisition in 833 to deprive the learned (*ulama*), experts on Hadis (*muhaddes*), moralists (*fukuha*), judges (*kazis*) and the God-fearing Muslims of their civic rights and to convert others to the Mutaliza sect even under the threat of capital punishment.'[12] But the Caliph al-Mufawakkil (817-861) gained the support of the people and the orthodox learned (*ulama*) by persecuting the Mutazilites. And that was the beginning of the end of the Mutazila movement.

9. Imamd Ibn Hajm (994-1064): 'The cultured and educated sections of the country (Spain) were attracted to his message and teaching. But the reactionary traders of religion, the *ulama*, declared his teachings and opinions as quite contrary to Islam and they aroused the people against him. Ibn Hajm was so much irritated by their torture that he felt compelled to quit his country.'[13]

10. Ibn Rushd (1126-1198) 'was exiled to Morocco and many of his books were burned by the order of the Monarch when his new book on philosophy, supporting' the Mutazila doctrine, was published. Ibn Rushd died in exile like the Italian philosopher Dante.'[14]

11. Imam Ibn Taimia (1263-1328) was sent to prison for a divorce fatwa in 1318. He was sent to prison again in 1326. This time his enemies snatched away all his books, papers and pen from him. He was much shocked by this and died in the prison only after twenty days of this incident.

12. Jamaluddin Afghani (1839-1897) was expelled by the Sultan of Turkey when the Sheikhul-Islam was enraged by one of his lectures at the Turkish University. He had to die in the lap of a faithful Christian servant, without any facilities for medical treatment being available to him.

This sort of religious fanaticism and intolerance was not unique with the Muslims. In fact, every great religion, particularly Christianity, had similar or even more shameful phases in its history. 'The intolerance that spread over the world with the advent of Christianity is one of the most curious features, due, I think, to the Jewish belief in righteousness and in the exclusive reality of the Jewish God.'[15] Buddhist priesthood – as it exists, for example, in Tibet – has been obscurantist, tyrannous and cruel in the highest degree.'[16] The tyranny, cruelty and oppression of the Hindu caste system is well-known to the people of this sub-continent and needs no comment.

What is the reason for this religious intolerance? Most of the followers are hopelessly inferior in character to their prophets. Prophets preach lofty ideals and practice them in their lives. But the selfish and hypocritical ones among the followers of a prophet utilize his saying as slogans to achieve their personal ends. Leaders and politicians hypocritically utter the names of the great prophets, their religion and the Holy Books to acquire and maintain state power, and nowhere in the twentieth century have they been more successful in this than in

Pakistan. But the Muslim society in the past produced many honest and courageous thinkers. 'They knew that their opinions were not adjustable with the preached religion; they also knew that for that offence they could be beheaded any moment; yet they neither feared nor shrank from the propagation of their views.'[17] The cruel, orthodox and ignorant among the Muslims harassed, tortured, killed or exiled them. But their philosophy and scientific knowledge awakened the European spirit, suppressed by a more ignorant, authoritarian and hypocritical Christian Church.

Muslim philosophers and scientists not only inspired the fore runners of the Italian Renaissance, but also its torch-bearer. Francis Bacon (1561-1626), says Bertrand Russell, 'has permanent importance as the founder of modern inductive method and the pioneer in the attempt at logical systematization of scientific procedure'. But 'he (Francis Bacon) was...an advocate of the doctrine of "double truth", that of reason and of revelation. This doctrine had been preached by a certain Averroist (follower of Ibn Rushd) in the thirteenth century but had been condemned by the Church'.[18] The religion of a people is the totality of those laws and principles which uphold or seek to uphold their society. When a prophet preaches a religion he gives the basic ethical principles as a guide to the formulation of laws. He also gives some model laws relevant to contemporary society. The prophet is enlightened with the highest spiritual knowledge, understandable to the people of his time. Thus he gets a proper understanding of his time, while other lawmakers, without spiritual experience, take only a partial view of life. In my opinion, in a modern state payment of income-tax and avoidance of ticketless travel are part of the religion of all citizens. To violate these laws are 'sins', for such violations are crimes.

Law is necessary for the administration of society. The essence of law is to live and let others live. With time and human advancement, the structure and character of societies change, and it is necessary that with the changing needs of society its laws and principles should also change. In other words, religion should be transformed with the progress of time. Otherwise culture, civilization and life itself would become stagnant. Do any of the existing Holy Books say anything about such a transformation of religion? Does Islam visualize such a transformation of itself?

The four sources of Muslim Law are the Quran, the *Hadis*, *Ijma* and *Qiyas*. The Quran is the highest authority in Islam.

Though a number of *hadis* (sayings of the Prophet of Islam) are recognized by Muslims as *sahi* (true), controversy over the genuineness of many has gone on since the death of the Prophet. Osman stopped the controversy about the Quran but not about the *hadis*. About a century later, Wasil bin Ata, founder of the Mutazila school, had to separate from Hasan al-Basri, the leader of the Hadis movement. In the opinion of Dr Fazhur Rahman, 'the character of the *hadis* is mainly artificial.' 'In fact, in the name of the Prophet, but not totally rejecting the historical relation with him, messages containing the gist of truth, which the Muslims themselves formulated and presented make the body of *hadis*?'[19]

The concept of *Ijma* is based on *hadis,* though sometimes it is claimed that it can be traced in the following *ayat* of the Quran:

And hold fast

All together, by the Rope

Which God (stretches out for you), and be not divided

Among yourselves. (3.103)[20]

However, 'the theory of *Ijma* was that the learned men of the community had the authority delegated to them to lay down the rules of conduct by the exercise of their Ijtihad'.[21] *Qiyas* is judgement based on analogical reasoning. There is a *hadis* attributed to the Prophet which encourages *Qiyas*: 'When Ma'ad was appointed ruler of Yemen, the Prophet is reported to have asked him as to how he would decide matters coming up before him. 'I will judge matters according to the Book of God,' said Ma'ad. 'But if the Book of God contains nothing to guide you?' 'Then I will act on the precedent of the Prophet of God.' 'But if the precedent fail?' 'Then I will exert to form my own judgment.'[22]

Now the question naturally arises, can *Ijma* and *Qiyas* repeal the Quranic Laws? It is said that 'according to some Hanafi and Mutazila writers *Ijma* can repeal the Quran'. But Iqbal emphatically says: There is not the slightest justification for such a statement in the legal literature of Islam. Not even a tradition (*hadis*) of the Prophet can have such effect.... *Ijma*... meant only the power to extend or limit the application the Quranic rule of Law, and not the power to repeal or supersede it by another rule of law.'[23] However, Iqbal contradicts himself. If the Quran is 'dynamic' and 'not inimical to the idea of evolution', why can the Quranic laws not be repealed or superseded? Throughout the world modern Muslims have been suffering from such self-contradictions. The contradictions may have their root in the Quran itself, for the Quran says:

None of Our revelations

Do We abrogate

Or cause to be forgotten

But we substitute

Something better or similar:

Knowest thou not that God

Hath power over all things? (2.106)

This was said with reference to Judaism and Christianity. Those too were religions from God. Muhammad did not come to abrogate them, but to 'substitute something better or similar' according to the needs of the time. God makes this substitution only through a prophet. The religion was improved through a long line of prophets. But why did prophethood stop with Muhammad? The Quran says:

Muhammad is not

The father of any

Of your men, but (he is)

The Apostle of God,

And the seal of the prophets:

And God has full knowledge

Of all things. (33.40)

Why was it supposed that the religion preached by Muhammad would not require, with the progress of time, 'something better or similar' to replace its outdated laws and principles? The Quran says:

This day have I

Perfected your religion

For you, completed

My favour upon you,

And have chosen for you

Islam as your religion. (54)

The Quranic laws which completed the religion of Islam are fixed, static or immobile – they are neither dynamic nor evolutionary. There is no law in the Quran, nor a *hadis* of the Prophet, by which a law written in the Quran could be amended or repealed. The Quran says:

And when the Quran

Is read to them, they

Fall not prostrate

But on the contrary

The unbelievers reject. (84.21-22)

Only 'the unbelievers' can reject, repeal, amend or supersede the laws and principles of the Quran. *Ijma* was encouraged for a situation for which there was no Quranic law or the precedent of the Prophet. But to give women equal rights with men by law and to send a person to prison (instead of cutting off his hands) as a punishment for theft are violations of the Quranic laws. The present government of Pakistan has done so (in my opinion quite rightly), but by repealing the Quranic laws the government has also violated the *Islamic* Constitution of the state, which lays down that 'no law shall be repugnant to Islam'. This is the result of the self-contradiction which I have mentioned above and about which I shall say more later.

We have already said that the religion of a community is the totality of those laws and principles which uphold or seek to uphold that community. The religion of Islam is inconceivable without the Quran. The laws of the Quran taken in their totality is the basis of Islam and without them Islam loses its identity. Some of the Quranic laws are:

1. Amputation of hands for theft. (5.41)
2. Flogging (100 stripes) for adultery or fornication. (24.2)
3. Amputation of hands and feet of those who wage war against God and the Prophet. (5.36)
4. Interest is *haram* (forbidden). (2.275)
5. Non-Muslims are to pay *Zizyah*. (9.29)
6. Killing of a believer is an offence. (4.92-93)
7. Muslims cannot fight in a war during the four sacred months of the year. (9.36-37)
8. A Muslim has the right to have four wives at a time. (4.3)
9. 2 women = 1 man in the eyes of the law. (2.284)
10. Flogging (80 stripes) for failure to produce witnesses. (24.4)
11. Women do not have equal rights with men in the law of inheritance. (4.2)
12. Adoption is prohibited. (33.4,37)

13. Wine and gambling are prohibited. (2.219)

From the above account it should be clear that Pakistan today has quite different laws (except the Muslim Marriage Law and the Muslim Inheritance Law) from many of the Quranic laws. *Ijma* or *Qiyas* does not allow a Muslim to repeal the Quranic laws. In the words of Amir-i-Shariat syed Ataullah Shah Bokhari, 'Our *deen* (religion) is complete and perfect and it amounts to *kufr* to make more laws.'[24] Maulana Syed Abul Ala Maudoodi has proposed nine basic principles for an 'Islamic state' of which two are: (a) 'That there shall be no such legislation as would contravene any of the dictates or principles of the Shariah (Muslim Law)', and (b) 'That all such laws as are in conflict with the dictates of the principles of the Shariah shall be abrogated'.[25] One can easily under stand that the Maulana did not exclude the Quran from the Shariah. In their Report of the Court of Enquiry (constituted under the Punjab Act II of 1954) Mr Justice Munir, then Chief Justice of the Supreme Court of Pakistan, and Mr Justice Kayani observed that the constitution of an Islamic state must contain the following provisions:

1. That all laws to be found in the Quran and Sunnah shall be deemed to be a part of the law of the land for Muslims and shall be enforced accordingly;

2. That, unless the Constitution is formed by Ijma-i-Ummat, namely, by the agreement of the Ulema and Mujtahids of acknowledged status, any provision in the Constitution which is repugnant to the Quran and Sunnah shall, to the extent of repugnancy, be void;

3. That, unless the existing laws of Pakistan are adopted by Ijma-i-Ummat of the kind mentioned above, any provision in the existing law which is contrary to the Quran and Sunnah shall, to the extent of repugnancy, be void;

4. That any provision in any future law which shall be repugnant to the Quran or Sunnah shall be void; and,

5. That no rule of international law and no provision in any convention or treaty to which Pakistan is a party which is contrary to the Quran and Sunnah shall be binding on any Muslim in Pakistan.[26]

Mr A.K. Brohi quotes Dr Zaki's definition of Islam and accepts it as valid. Dr Zaki's definition is: 'It is of course a religion, a body of doctrines and beliefs clustered around the principle of *Tawhid* (asserting oneness) which teaches that God is the ultimate spiritual basis of life. It is universal and not a national religion. Its message is addressed to mankind in its entirety and not to any one nation, even though the prophetic Revelation is through the instrumentality of Arabic language.'[27] Mr Brohi himself enumerates the essentials of Islam as follows: 'Islam thus is the natural religion of man and enjoins three basic principles to be freely accepted and adopted by him.' These principles are:

(a) Unity and all-comprehensive authority of one sovereign power who as creator reflects himself in creation and yet is independent of it; and further that the entire creation endures in the law and its continued existence is made possible by the sustenance it derives from the law.

(b) The universality of divine revelation of the pre-Islamic period of human history, belief in Muhammad's Mission and the acceptances of the entire pre-Islamic development of Religion; and,

(c) Man's direct responsibility and accountability for all actions that he may do or omit doing.[28]

Both Dr Zaki and Mr Brohi put stress on belief or faith. According to Iqbal, 'religious life appears as a form of discipline which the individual or a whole people must accept as an unconditional command without any rational understanding of the ultimate meaning and purpose of that command'.[29] But is mere belief in (1) the unity of God (*Tawhid*), (2) Muhammad's mission and acceptance of the entire pre-Islamic development of Religion, and (3) man's direct responsibility and accountability for all actions sufficient to be a Muslim? Many people throughout the world have faith in the unity of God. The Upanishadic philosophy of 'Ekamevadvitiyam' (One without a second) was preached more than a thousand years before Muhammad was born. Millions of Hindus, Buddhists, Jews and Christians today recognize Muhammad's mission and the entire pre-Islamic development of religion and millions of them have faith in 'man's direct responsibility and accountability for all actions'. What then is the difference between Islam and Hinduism or Buddhism or Judaism or Christianity? Metaphysical and ethical concepts are almost similar in all great religions. Every religion speaks of the transcendence and omnipotence of God, every religion asks its followers to be truthful, honest, just and kind. But if the Hindus disown the authority of the Vedas, the Upanishads and the Bhagavadgita, there remains no Hinduism; if the Buddhists disown the Tripitika, there remains no Buddhism; if the Jews disown the Torah, there remains no Judaism and if the Christians disown the Bible, there remains no Christianity. And similar is the case with Islam. If the Muslims repeal the Quranic laws or disown the Quran, there remains no Islam. But if some people repeal the Quranic laws and still call themselves Muslims and become the patron-protectors of Islamic culture, how are we to judge their character? Well, let the Quran itself speak about such people:

Hast thou not turned

Thou vision to those

Who declared that they believe

In the revelations

That have come to thee

And to those before thee?...

When it is said to them:

'Come to what God hath revealed

And to the Apostle'

Thou seest the hypocrites avert

Their face from thee in disgust

(4.60.61)

The idea of implementing the Quranic laws in a modern state is simply an absurdity. It is either foolishness or hypocrisy to conceive an Islamic state or Islamic culture today as Islam is adumbrated in the Quran. Neither the Quran nor the Sunnah permits a Muslim to repeal any law or principle of the Quran. But no man of common sense in the modern age will propose (1) to ampute the hands and feet either of the thief or of fighting unbeliever, (2) to whip hundred times for adultery or fornication and eighty times for failure to produce witnesses, (3) to impose *Zizyah* on the non-Muslims. (4) to ban killing the believers in a war against a Muslim or any other country, (5) to refrain from fighting during the four sacred months in the case of a war against a foreign country, (6) to consider two women equal to one man in the eyes of the law, (7) to deprive women of equality with men in the law of inheritance, and (8) to prohibit adoption of children. Yet these are all Quranic laws. And without the Quranic laws an Islamic state exists nowhere except in the minds of the fools or on the lips of the hypocrites.

Now the people of Pakistan may ask Maulana Maudoodi (claimed to be 'the greatest leader and thinker of the Islamic movement of the twentieth century'), Amir-i-Shariat Syed Ataullah Shah Bokhari and all those who want either to implement the Quranic laws or not to pass any law which is repugnant to them whether the above-mentioned Quranic laws shall be implemented in Pakistan, and whether the annulment of any of those laws is Islamic.

Most educated people in a modern society understand that they can no more live their life or administer a state according to the laws of the Quran. Yet why do they call themselves Muslims or want to found an Islamic state where no laws shall be repugnant to the Quran? The answer lies in unreasonable sentiment, ignorance and hypocrisy.

Many of the modern Muslims are 'Muslims' only because they have Arabic names. They are born of 'Muslim' parents who too bore Arabic names. They are 'Muslims' because some of their forefathers used, and some of them use, to observe the two I'd days in the year, once a year organize lamentation in the month of Muharram, offer Namaj (in most of the cases without understanding the words uttered in the prayer) a few times everyday, go to Arabia to perform the *hap*, kill animals 'In the name of Allah, the Most Beneficent and Most Merciful' and eat their meat, and bury their dead with the head in the north. These are the distinctive formalities which make up Islam today. One need not even observe all these formalities. One is a Muslim even if one only has an Arabic name and supports these formalities.

They do not know, or try to ignore, the fact that the Muslims as a creative people ceased to function about five hundred years ago. During these five hundred years they contributed practically nothing in the field of science, arts, economics or jurisprudence. The President of Pakistan and the ex-Chief Justice of the East Pakistan High Court talk about the separation of powers. This conception was formulated by the French political philosopher Montesquieu. Almost all the contributions to modern civilization have been made by the non-Muslims. The wealthy Muslims today are totally dependent on the amenities originally conceived or supplied by the non-Muslims. The architecture, decoration and furniture of their homes, their dress, toilet, kitchens, cooking utensils and meals, their walking, resting and even sleeping styles – everything is non-Muslim. They can only procreate in the old style (if one chooses one may call it

Muslim or Islamic style), but if they think about birth-control, there too they are dependent on non-Muslim ideas. Muslims of all the classes today are dependent on the means of industrial production, of travel and communication which were originally discovered by the non-Muslims. The 'Muslims' seem not to realize, or they do not like to acknowledge, how much they have been 'de-Muslimised' with the passage of time. The President of Pakistan says: '…We are in a hurry, we have got to fight against time, we have to catch up the rest of the world.' 'The rest of the world' means here the modern non-Muslim Europe and America. But why should one run after a non-Muslim civilization with a declaration of 'Islamic culture' on one's lips? Why should the Constitution which President Ayub Khan gave in 1962 profess not to enact laws repugnant to Islam? And why should the National Assembly of Pakistan enact at the same time, laws repealing the Quranic laws and violating the constitution of the state?

Many of the politicians of Pakistan use the words 'Islam' and 'Muslim' (a) to create and nourish an anti-Indian and anti-Hindu feeling among the vast majority of the illiterate masses, (b) to exploit the economic resources of East Pakistan to enrich a group of West Pakistanis and West Pakistan, and (c) to earn the support of the illiterate and fanatic classes of the population. These politicians know that even the power of the military will topple down in the face of a violent opposition from those classes. So in order to keep the illiterate people quiet and to maintain their own power, they use the names of Islam and Muslim, while many of their acts and activities are grossly anti-Quranic and therefore anti-Islamic.

In his message to the annual magazine of the Pakistan Inter-Wing Students' Association, the President of Pakistan says that Islamic concepts make Pakistanis 'one people, one country and one culture'. Let us see the nature of this 'Islamic culture'.

1. Every year East Pakistanis are being cheated of their earnings by the West Pakistan-dominated Central Government of Pakistan. Is it Islamic?

The Quran says:

Woe to those
That deal in fraud and to

Those who, when they
Have to receive by measure
From men, exact full measure
But when they have
To give by measure
Or weight to men
Give less than due
Do they not think
That they will be called
To account?
On a Mighty Day,
A Day when (all) Mankind
Will stand before
The Lord of the work!? (83.1-6)

2. There are hundreds of political and non-political prisoners in Pakistan who are wrongly kept in prison for years without any trail. Is it Islamic?

The Quran says:

How many towns have We
Destroyed (for their sin).
Our punishment took them
On a sudden by night
Or while they slept
For their afternoon rest.
When (thus) Our punishment
Took them, no cry
Did they utter but this:
Indeed we did wrong. (7.4-5)

3. The whole economy of Pakistan is based on the interest system. Is it Islamic?

The Quran says:

> Those who devour usury
> Will not stand except
> As stands one whom
> The evil one by his touch
> Hath driven to madness. (2.275)

4. Gambling has become a part of Pakistani life. Government premium bonds, various types of 'word-making' or 'filling-the-gap', competitions in the newspapers, horse races, etc. are gambling. There may be other sorts too. Is it Islamic?

The Quran says:

> They ask thee
> Concerning wine and gambling
> Say: in them is great sin. (2.219)

5. Wine drinking has become essential, with many a habit, in the 'top circles' or 'upper classes' in Pakistan. Perhaps, no state banquet is conceivable without wine-drinking. Many of the ordinary people also drink freely, for it is legal in Pakistan. Is it Islamic?

The Quran says:

> O ye who believe!
> Intoxicant and gambling
> (Dedication of) stones,
> And (divination by) arrows,
> Are an abomination,
> Of Satan's handiwork;
> Eschew such (abominations)
> That ye may prosper. (5.93).

6. Any woman in Pakistan can become a prostitute with a licence from the Government of Pakistan. Is it Islamic?

The Quran says:

> The woman and the man
> Guilty of adultery or fornication
> Flog each of them
> With hundred stripes. (24.2)

Adultery and fornication are criminal offences according to the Quran. Does it follow that the Quran upholds prostitution?

If the President of Pakistan takes these characteristics of 'Islamic culture' as the basis upon which the unity of Pakistan rests then one can only wish him and his concepts immortality in the history of the human race. The President has not said what the other factual aspects of 'Islamic culture' in Pakistan are. In the opinion of the Grand Mufti of Palestine, the *Unani* system of medicine should be called 'Islamic medicine', for it was originally developed by the Arab Muslims.[30] If a system of medicine developed by the Muslims be called 'Islamic medicine' then why should not the wine brewed and the gambling organized by the Muslims be called 'Islamic wine' and 'Islamic gambling? In that case, at least logically, we could take the 'Islamic wine' and 'Islamic gambling' as parts of 'Islamic culture' in Pakistan. But whatever one says about Islamic culture must be compatible with the Quranic laws and principles. Big airy and hypothetical talks on culture are either bluff or meaningless nonsense. The culture of a man or woman, of a community or society bears the testimony of what he or she, the community or the society does in practice. One must practice what one preaches. Otherwise, one's culture is the culture of the hypocrites. And whatever may be the position of the religion of Islam today, the Quran has made strong pronouncements against the hypocrites.

Iqbal quotes a Muslim sufi, who says: 'No' understanding of the Holy Book is possible until it is actually revealed to the believer just as it was revealed to the Prophet.'[31] Iqbal defines revelation in the following words: 'The world life intuitively sees its own needs, and at critical moments defines its own direction. This is what, in the language of religion, we call revelation.'[32] I try to understand myself, life. God and the Universe. I know God exists and acts. I know God reveals truth and knowledge to the properly attuned human mind. Every prophet, indeed every man, understands

God's truth and knowledge according to the capacity of his own intelligence. In understanding the truth revealed by God sometimes we may be right, sometimes we may be wrong. What, however, is most important is our honesty. I have no doubt as regards the honesty of any prophet, though it is my conviction – based upon my experience about God – that every prophet understands God's revelation according to the capacity of his own intelligence. Prophets are men. Not every man is born with the same degree of intelligence and so the understanding or realization of the truth differs from man to man. It is not a crime if one's understanding of self, life, God and the Universe differs from that of others. My understanding is that:

1. Many of the Quranic laws are harmful to human society in our time and they should be repealed. But there is no provision in the Quran for the annulment of such laws.

2. *Salat* (Namaj) is unnecessary in our time as a mode of prayer. Kowtowing before anybody or the image or idea of anybody is humiliating to human beings. Even the noble among men do not want – in fact, they hate – flattery or self-abasement from others. God is the Noblest and the Greatest. How can God want flattery from men? Effort to acquire more knowledge, to understand self, life, God and the Universe should replace all the earlier modes of prayers. And one should practice what one learns or preaches.

3. Worship of graves is bad. *Kabar Jiarat* is tantamount to worshipping the grave. So it is useless to perform *jiarat* (pilgrimage) to the Prophet Muhammad's grave in Madina at the time of *haji* or at any other time. Of course, I support international gatherings to promote mutual understanding and friendship or to solve some international dispute. But, in my opinion, to worship any grave is bad.

4. Fasting is a good training for self-restraint. But it is quite unscientific, unhygienic and inconvenient to fast as the Muslims have been doing through centuries in the month of Ramzan. There should be fixed hours according to the clock for *iftar* (breaking the fast) and the last meal before going to bed in the night. *Sehri* (meal before dawn) and the lunar calendar should be abolished.

5. I'd-ul-Azha should be forbidden. Only an underdeveloped soul can sacrifice other's life in the hope of spiritual salvation

or benefit. It is extreme cruelty to kill an animal and call it *I'd* (merry-making).

6. There is no Devil or Satan who is ever active against man and God. God controls both good and evil. So when we are fighting evil we are fighting only against the evil forces of God. In other words, we are fighting against God for God.

7. The prophet Muhammad is not the last prophet. This world is no prophet's world. God has to take care of its administration. In the past, whenever human society became degenerate, there came a prophet to enlighten the people. Nowhere is it said that a human society will not be in the grip of decadence after Muhammad preached the religion of Islam; one has only to look at the Muslim society of today. There had been prophets in the past and there shall be prophets in the future. It is God's responsibility to enlighten the dark souls.

God Himself guides and helps me to attain or improve my realization about self, life, God and the universe. Am I a Muslim?

Endnotes

1. The letter is now published in the form of an article in the *Journal* of the Institute of Defence Studies and Analyses, New Delhi, Vol.. 3, No. 4, April 1971.

2. *Science Digest*, November 1967. The BBC (Overseas Service) broadcast the news of the Lahore disturbance on 16 February 1968. *The Morning News*, Dacca 18 February 1968 published the statement of Mr Benjamin Oehlert, US Ambassador to Pakistan. '…I am however, bringing the seriousness with which this matter is viewed in Pakistan to the attention of my Government.'

3. *The Pakistan Observer*, Dacca, 16-19 February 1966. Dr Mahmood was manhandled at about 1.15 p.m. on 15 February 1966, a few minutes after the Vice-Chancellor (Dr M.O. Gani, who holds his post till now) was convicted by the High Court of East Pakistan in a suit brought by the former against the university authorities misuse of power. Though the verdict of the High Court was the immediate cause of the assault, it was well known that Dr Mahmood was bitterly disliked by the people in power and by some students for his opinions as an economist.

4. Barkatullah, *Parashsha Prativa* (in Bengali), Great East Library, Dacca 1960, vol. 1, p.33.

5. *Ibid.*, p.33.

6. Muhammad Iqbal, *The Reconstruction of Religious Thought in Islam*, (1934), S.M. Ashraf, Lahore 1954, p. 162.

7. H.A.R. Gibb and J.H. Kramers (eds), *Shorter Encyclopedia of Islam*, E.J. Brilli, Leiden 1953, p. 246.

8. Anthony Nutting. *The Arabs*(1964), Mentor Books 1965, p. 101.

9. J. Wellhausen, *Arab Kingdom and Its Fall*, Khayat, Beirut 1963, pp. 278-79.

10. Abdul Moudud. *Muslim Manisha* (in Bengali), Nabajung Prakashani, Calcutta 1955, p.2.

11. H.A.R. Gibb and J.H. Kramers (eds.), *op. cit.*, p. 423.

12. Abdul Moudud, *op. cit.*, pp. 35-36.

13. *Ibid.*, p. 85.

14. Barkatullah, *op. cit.*, vol. I, p. 31.

15. Bertrand Russell, *Why I Am Not a Christian*, Unwin Books, London 1967, p.36.

16. *Ibid.*, p. 29.

17. Barkatullah, *op. cit.*, vol. 1, p.28.

18. Bertrand Russell, *History of Western Philosophy*, Simon & Schuster, New York 1965, pp.352-53.

19. 'Sunna o Hadis' in *Islamic Academic Patrika* (in Bengali), April-June 1963, Dacca, p.577. Cf. also Dr Fazlur Rehman, 'Prathamic Jugay Sunna, Ijtihad o Ijmar Dharma' in *Islamic Academic Patrika*, October-December 1962, pp. 271-85.

20. All quotations from the Quran are from A. Yusuf Ali's translation.

21. A.K. Brohi, *The Fundamental Law of Pakistan*, Din Mohammad Press, Karachi 1958, p.774.

22. Quoted in Iqbal, *op. cit.*, p.148.

23. *Ibid.*, p.174.

24. Quoted in A.K. Brohi, *op. cit.*, p.775.

25. Abdul Ala Maudoodi, *Islamic Law and Constitution*, quoted in A.K. Brohi, *op. cit.*, p.749.

26. *Report of the Court of Enquiry Constituted under Punjab Act II of 1954 to Enquire into the Punjab Disturbances of 1953*, Superintendent, Government Printing, Punjab, Lahore 1954, pp.209-10.

27.   Quoted in A.K. Brohi, *op. cit.*, p.735.

28.   *Ibid.*, p.735.

29.   Muhammad Iqbal, *op. cit.*, p. 181.

30.   *The Morning News*, Dacca, 18 February 1967.

31.   Muhammad Iqbal, *op. cit.*, p.181.

32.   *Ibid.*, p.147.

Every Home a Fortress/ Proclamation of Independence

Mujibur Rehman

(Quest 72: September–October 1971

This struggle of ours is for the complete liberation of seventy
million people of Bangladesh. Our struggle will go on until our rights

are secured. The people of Bangladesh will no longer be cowed down by bullets, guns and bayonets, for today the people are united.

We must be ready for any sacrifice in order to achieve our goal. Every home must be turned into a fortress of resistance. Ours is a just demand. So we are sure to win.

Joi Bangla

Sheikh Mujibur Rahman
19.3.71

Autobiography of Violence

Mihir Sinha

(Quest 72: September–October 1971)

The Illusion.

I am told that I was born in 1930, in a dark ramshackle house which still stands next door to the prayer hall of the community of Brahmos, in a shabby middle-class locality of north Calcutta. We were not Brahmos, though my father was almost one by inclination and associations. At any rate, our struggling family must have absorbed some of their genteel ways. For I distinctly remember that when I was a child of seven or eight and had shifted to another (and shabbier) neighbourhood, my playmates would be instinctively aware of a streak of 'artificiality' or 'effeminacy' in my make-up. Perhaps it was nothing more than my aversion to violence – a typically Brahmo affectation in their eyes. I also recollect to have valiantly tried to play up to their normal standards, in speech if not in action. It would, however, be wrong to give the impression that I did not have my share of childish cruelty, particularly in dealing with insects and small animals. It was only that I grew out of it rather sooner than my contemporaries did. And I could never stomach the astonishing kind of brutality that it was customary to show to an unlucky burglar or a careless pickpocket.

Apart from such episodes of burglars and pick pockets, collective violence did not have much place in those slow stagnating times, although many of us knew individual acts of violence (sometimes reaching very cruel proportions) in our respective family life or in the more miserable lives lived in the nearby slums. The adults as well as the children not only shrank from physical danger but were also quite scared of the police and the penal code. I suppose that many acts of (private) violence could be committed only on the presumption that, because of the particular circumstances, the process of law would not be put into motion by the aggrieved party. Still, in a few cases, a brother would be hauled up for fratricide, or a father would try to avenge the murder of his daughter by her husband and mother-in-law. The ghoulish press reports of such exceptional proceedings, while lapped up by sensation-hungry readers of the daily newspapers, would at the same time reinforce the popular conviction that crime, if detected, did not pay. On the whole, violence was associated with criminality and, therefore, it was usual either to avoid it or to keep it private and individual. Only the professional criminals indulged in acts of violence which were public, often collective, and by nature impersonal. The criminals, motivated by a perverse sense of economic gain, would rarely have anything personally against the unfortunate victim of their violence.

There was but one major exception to this pattern: the sporadic violence of a communal nature, usually restricted to certain particular parts of the city. Tension between the two largest religious communities was, of course, the biggest factor. But there were other factors as well. Occasional fights between Bengalees and non-Bengalees, annual free-for-alls on the days of important fixtures between community-oriented football teams, almost ritualistic engagements between men of different localities on the night of the immersion ceremony of the Goddess – all were part of the city life. The recurring riots between the Hindus and the Muslims, or the skirmishes between the Bengalees and the Eurasians, could be ascribed to provocations or acts of aggression on the part of the 'other side'. But even that plea was not available in the other cases. Anyway, the results were more important than the motives. For one thing, the general taboo on public violence seemed to be suspended on such occasions. While the timid and the prudent concentrated upon how to stay out of its range, the ambitious and the unscrupulous often tried to increase their hold over the community by encouraging or even participating in the raising curve of violence. Such violence, started generally by proud professionals and occasionally by talented amateurs, could hardly be sustained on personal animosities. Many non-combatants would eventually be drawn into it, thereby widening the circle of bitterness and distrust and providing a post facto rationale for the whole thing.

Every time the pattern was almost the same. The twilight of ugly rumours, the night of frenzy, and then the morning of bewilderment and pain – neither of the two sides had, on the whole, gained anything. Only, the professionals in violence would have gained some respectability, made new recruits, and also won some material prizes. Since no challenge was thrown against the civil authority as such, and since the police would eventually make their appearance and 'bring the situation under control', it was really a wonder that such eruptions of violence were at all permitted to take place, and with such regularity too. Most probably, the authorities wanted some steam to be let off or actually required the residual elements of disillusionment and communal hatred for administrative purposes. That might also explain the unmistakable bonds of understanding between the toughs and the local police. They must have been genuinely useful to one another. As for my neighbours, they displayed a curious ambivalence. In spite of their general lack of physical courage, they were not only very tolerant of the atrocities committed during these spells of violence, they actually seemed to relish the excesses and to admire their perpetration, even as the prudish elders would smile on the acts of gross immodesty on the part of the usually demure womenfolk on the licenced occasion of a marriage. However, in spite of my best efforts to be a conformist, it was obvious that I was too something or other to be a full member of the community in which I lived. In retrospect, my aversion to violence seems to have been due, in part at least, to the crescendo of unseemly violence in which the parental incompatibility came to be expressed in the course of time. I grew up to be deeply ashamed of violence, particularly physical violence, public or private.

I was nine years old when one of the bloodiest chapters opened in the history of human civilization: the Second World War; the Abyssinian prelude had taken place earlier. But the press photographs and the field dispatches were as much anesthetized by the intervening distances as were the fairy tales and mythologies lavish with their rolling heads and dripping swords. Our minds were not touched. Even the nearer violence in Manchuria and the rest of China, then being perpetrated by Japan, was hardly more real. The net reaction in my own immature mind was a rather vague kind of horror. Horror at so much violence, and so utterly illogical too – like the communal riots of Calcutta. However, many of my older friends and relatives gleefully speculated on the possibility of the mighty British being humbled by the apparently mightier Germans. It was, I believe, the typical wishful thinking of the physically weak, a vicarious indulgence in violence which I have witnessed often since then.

In 1941 my family shifted to another locality. Here the roads were winder and we lived on the upper floor of a double-storeyed house. The slums too were out of the range of sight, sound and smell, all this meant one thing above all – the violence of the city impinged less on our daily lives. As if to compensate, the truant younger son of the landlord brought in an element of violence during his periodic visits to his family who occupied the ground floor. He was a drunkard and was reputed to be the boyfriend-cum-bodyguard of a rich prostitute. Violence was obviously a part of his life, and the clash between him and his family (Brahman priests by profession) was horrible and fascinating at the same time. The local community did censure the unmentionable ways of the scapegrace fellow and was particularly loud in its condemnation of his unabashed flaunting of brute physical strength. Yet I could clearly discern in the eyes of my neighbours the glint of an instinctive admiration, an unmistakable yearning for the unknown frontiers of personal freedom which could supposedly be gained upon the steed of unscrupulous violence. His way of life was, of course, all wrong, but nonetheless appeared to be more interesting than, the 'right' kind of life lived by the nondescript multitude. On looking back to those distant times, I cannot honestly say that notwithstanding my distaste for violence, I too did not entertain a lurking fancy for the exotic criminality of that young roughneck. No, not quite that, violence was undesirable, but its fruits were very desirable. And, what was more important, these were definitely out of reach otherwise.

The year 1941 was destined to be important. Rabindranath Tagore died on the seventh of August. He had been ailing for a long time and had been brought over from his Ashram at Santiniketan to Calcutta for treatment. After his death, it would have been natural to take the dead body back to Santiniketan for cremation. That was believed to be his own clearly expressed wish too. But as soon as the news broke, a great crowd collected in front of his ancestral place, turned riotous, literally broke into the house, and even before the mourners from outside the town could arrive to pay their last respects, rushed the dead body to a nearby burning ground. My elder sister, who had gone to see the funeral procession, tearfully gave an eye-witness account of the damaged bed-stead (used as a bier) with the body awry and the head fallen down from the pillow. A little child of the family, who is now my wife, still remembers the frenzied mob milling all over the place and shouting obscenities at the inmates. The next morning, the newspapers reported how the poet's son had not been able to come through the hysteric crowd to do the last rites. My father's intimates gossiped among themselves how some popular leaders had played upon the parochial sentiments of Calcuttans, particularly the students. On the other hand, the majority of my class-fellows and neighbours boasted that Calcutta had 'got the better of Santiniketan'. To them it was only rather funny that even the beard had been torn off the dead poet's face by his supposed admirers. I have no doubt that if the poet had lived to be one hundred and ten and had died in 1971, bombs would have been used by his exuberant admirers and the police would have had to fire a few shots and burst some tear gas shells. Nor do I doubt that the exercise must have been quite useful to the leaders in strengthening the mass base of their popularity.

That memorable incident set a pattern which was to become the standard. It had a few easily distinguishable features: a vague background of something idealistic. In this particular case it was the hazy admiration for a great man. The second element was an emotion shared by a large number of people, specially the younger people, representing some kind of transformation of the original element of idealism by the catalytic action of frustration. Since the frustration could not be identified as due to failure in achieving some definite objective, the edges of the accumulated frustration too were not sharply etched. The third factor was the eagerness (and, of course, the ability) of the leaders to capitalise on this widely shared sense of frustration, which was quickly given a concrete shape. The shape was deadly, it was that of anger. Some comparatively easy objective was set before the people, by whipping up collective hatred against some real or imaginary enemy. The multitude would turn into a mob, vent its anger against the enemy and gain the proximate objective by the sheer weight of numbers and actual or potential violence. In the final analysis, however, it was all as meaningless as were the communal riots. As in the communal riots, the only net gain was that made by the leaders of the agitation. And, in the year of 1941, the nemesis was still a long way off.

In 1941 we made yet another change of residence. This was certainly a promotion. The flat was in one of the cleanest and quietest blocks of the whole neighbourhood, favoured by Brahmos and university professors, on the second floor, and faced toward the south which is always the desired thing in Calcutta because of the south breeze in the summer. But the covered balcony on the south which was practically my living room would always by associated with the memory of much violence. As the Japanese attacked Pearl Harbour, the worldwide violence of the Second World War suddenly loomed nearer home. Daily newspapers acquired a new urgency in that the Japanese army arrogantly strode through the Southeast Asian countries intervening between India and an unfamiliarly violent Japan. There was great panic in the sprawling city and, along with thousands of other people, we fled to a village some forty miles away from Calcutta in a frantic effort to escape from the imagined horrors of aerial bombing.

Some six months later, we rather sheepishly returned to the still unbombed city, to experience not only the violence of Japanese bombs later in the year, but also the unprecedented violence on the streets of Calcutta, touched off by the Quit India movement of 1942. This was my first taste of mass violence for a political cause. There were no pipe guns or bombs or knives – not much of them anyway – but the other things were all there. Throwing of brickbats, setting fire to street cars, barricading the roads, shooting by the police, the burning smell of tear gas – with all this we became familiar in the course of a few memorable days. Naturally, it was a very unequal fight. The police quickly mastered the situation, leaving the people only the more bewildered for the exercise which had been quite expensive in terms of lost lives and damaged careers, if not anything else. For a brief spell, however, the people did seem to have displayed a rare degree of physical courage and the will to use it in serving a definite idealistic cause. This was also the first of the many violent battles to be fought between the masses and the police on the streets of Calcutta.

But the spell was broken the most cruelly within about a year; 1943 was the year of the famine. I was thirteen, smarting under the memory of the movement that had either been crushed or had just fizzled out. The famine was, therefore, sad and humiliating.

Hundreds of thousands were starved to death, thousands among them having trudged their way from the villages, vainly looking for succour in the city. Hundreds of them roamed through our locality, rending the air with their plaintive cries – not for rice, but for the excess water which is usually thrown away after boiling the rice. So emaciated that there was no telling between when they were still living and when they were finally dead – even after their bodies had been lying on the road for a number of days. There was no riot; nor much resentment, except against an inscrutable Providence. A number of literary and artistic reputations were made with these sordid ingredients. Fiery journalism ascribed the famine to machinations of the British Raj and complicity of Indian merchants. Yet there was hardly any political programme either to ensure effective redress or to build up a movement of protest. The sickening sentimentality of the general reaction made me ponder whether violence was not cleaner and more natural than hypocrisy and opportunism. The millions of half dead behaved in correct Gandhian fashion, unfortunately with no change of heart on the other side.

The crisis of the famine passed. But life became increasingly difficult. Inflation, scarcity of food and other essentials, senseless high-handedness of the billeted soldiers of the Allied army, a thriving black market, typical war-time graft and easy money, erosion of morals – all these became a regular feature of our life in the city. Crime became big business and the circle of associated crime widened. The atmosphere was gradually charged with bitter resentment against the order of things. Then came, in a trickle, the rumours about Netaji. Since there was little love for the Japanese in our circle, our reception of the news was rather skeptical at first. Soon, however, the trickle became a torrent. His political theories were of little interest, but his Indian National Army provided us with the first example of organized counter-violence, quite in accord with the usual pattern of freedom movements in other lands, and refreshingly different from the near-theological niceties of Gandhism. In the meantime, the war was coming to an end. The vast armies gradually withdrew, leaving the host society in a stinking mess. The general elections in England sent up a new tenant for 10 Downing Street. Our leaders came out of their internment. The tenuous talks for Indian independence got under way. But we were not interested in talks.

I was fifteen when the war ended, coinciding with my passing out of school into college and getting involved in the student movement 1945, for Calcutta, was the year of student movements. Or to be more accurate, it was the year of youth movements. The street urchins and youthful toughs joined in the fray with an astonishing abandon. There was no preplanning, little organization, and no big leader. Against the stirring back-drop of the Indian National Army and the mutiny by the naval ratings, physical violence gave us intense emotional satisfaction, specially due to the close integration between the broad ideological objective, which was national independence, and the proximate target of attack, namely the Government. All of a sudden, the inhibitions about the police and the Penal Code came to be shed on the blood-stained streets of Calcutta. As for myself, I did no longer have to make a painful compromise with any precious value in order to rejoice when the forces of law and order would suffer even a minor defeat at the hands of my violent fellow citizens. Another great attraction of this phase was the unprecedented unity cutting across communal and social barriers; this could be achieved only during a true Gandhian revolution or under conditions of a typical war of liberation. On the whole, this was the cleanest type of mass violence that I have so far witnessed personally. However, the subliminal image still influencing our thoughts was not that of a ruthlessly victorious captain of violence, but that of a patriot who was essentially a man of peace, compelled to take to the cruel ways of violence, possibly getting the better of his more resourceful opponent in one or two rounds, but ultimately dying a martyr's death.

This idyllic phase had to end within a few months when violence, ironically enough, became the instrument again to drive asunder the two principal religious communities. 1946 and 1947 were the year of communal riots, engineered in the perspective of the great political haggling for the elusive shares of the cake of national independence. In the process, we were all cheated of our shares. Calcutta finally started to become what it is now, originally at the initiative of the Muslim League but immensely facilitated by the responding beastliness of my own and other communities. It was altogether a new dimension of violence. The consequences too were far reaching: people learned to live with violence. The traditional distance of brickbats was replaced by the growing intimacy of knives. We graduated to more sophisticated weapons of killing, like bottles of acid or petrol, pipe guns, homemade stenguns, and even the modern small arms purchased from army sources. Large chunks of the law enforcement machinery itself became partisan and were recognized as such by the lawbreakers. The practitioners of violence made permanent entry into the mainstream of social life and secured positions in the political hierarchy. Leaders learned how to use them in the game of power. Very soon, the enlarged system of violence came to be accepted and justified by ordinary people as a means of self-defence.

Somehow or other, I was never convinced by the spoken and unspoken arguments in favour of communal violence. Through the year-long riots I saw houses burn, smelt the stench of putrefying corpses, sat through the night atop the roof watching for surprise attacks, but nevertheless went beyond our block to a sort of no-man's land so that I could meet a Muslim friend of mine and would risk sure death by taking him along on foolhardy visits to other localities. On the evening of 14 August 1947, I was one of the thousands who literally danced through the streets of the ravaged city in advance celebration of the transfer of power due a few hours later, and out of joy at the miraculous victory of non-violence achieved a few hours earlier under the personal leadership of Gandhiji who was then camping in a notorious slum of Calcutta. My cynical father wept when the new flag was raised at the stroke of midnight. I was seventeen, idealistic, full of hope that violence would be unnecessary in achieving economic progress and social justice, and willing to undertake any effort or make any sacrifice for the sake of the motherland.

...and the reality

The process of integration between politics and violence was reversed after 1947. The supremacy of the party in power was so overwhelming that there was no need to employ violence in meeting any political challenge. Violence certainly became endemic in the sphere of inter-community relations, including ethnic and linguistic animosities. But to control that, the party now had at its disposal the massive organization of state violence. In fact, the real struggle faced by the leaders of the party in such situations was not so much with the leaders of other parties as among themselves, representing as they did almost all shades of social and political opinions.

Society itself had, however, been impregnated with violence. Besides communal tension, entrenchment of gangsters and racketeers in positions of authority, and the creation of virtual kingdoms of crime by the local chiefs of communal defence, violence had become the way of life for a large number of people in weird new 'industries' like wagon-breaking and smuggling. Logically, one of the first tasks before the new government should have been to eradicate these factors of violence instead of talking about Satya and Ahimsa. Somehow or other, the government was strangely impotent against the vicious triumvirate of unscrupulous businessmen, corrupt public officials and the ubiquitous men of violence. It was no wonder, therefore, that the greedy politicians (not necessarily excluding those in the opposition or in the trade unions) quickly found their place in this web of perverse usefulness to one another. Under such circumstances, possibly common to many Afro-Asian countries in the post-colonial era, Gresham's Law came to operate with a vengeance in almost all the sectors of society. This, taken together with the recent diffusion of the know-how of violence, installed violence as a permanent tenant of the social structure. The men of crime and violence maintained perfect co-ordination with their formal enemy, the police, while the law-abiding citizens learned to be wary of both. Getting on the wrong side of either might quite possibly invite the wrath of the other as well.

That these developments did not attract immediate attention was due, above all, to the remarkable success in maintaining the form of parliamentary democracy. The rich, in the process of growing richer, committed many crimes and engineered many acts of violence, but generally managed to keep the form. The middle classes which had been the most vocal of the critics of the colonial order were silenced by material prizes. The elephantiasis of culture was also a powerful hypnotic for them. And on the other hand, the lower classes, potentially the most powerful because of their number, were not only weighed down by a lingering feudalism, but their predominantly middle-class leadership, even when perfectly honest, was also curiously inefficient, suffered from the age-old Bengalee addiction to theoretical hair-splitting and, in some cases, displayed a slavish internationalism. It must also be appreciated that actual physical violence did not touch the life of the upper and middle classes, provided that the rules of a stratified society were not strained overmuch. Thus Calcutta society continued to wear the looks of general nonviolence or only of routine violence, while deep violence was being done to Gandhiji's concept of Social Trusteeship and the British concept of the rule of law. Any critic of the system who, by reason of birth or social position, stood a chance of being heard, was labeled a communist or a traitor.

By the middle of the fifties, the charms of freedom had worn off. The next half decade witnessed an inexorable accentuation of all the facts of this non-violent violence, accompanied by a strangely shortsighted craze for conspicuous consumption by the rich, an alarming deterioration in the material organization of the city's life, an appreciable hardening of the attitude of those who had really made the grade towards the less lucky bulk of the middleclass brotherhood, and, above all, a growing awareness among the young. In our younger days, the great illusion was National Freedom. We had hung all our expectations on this one peg. When the peg came off, the hole remained – to serve as the centre of our heart-breaks, a sort of inverted patriotism. To the new young even this was denied. They had seen with their cruel eyes of innocence that patriotism was not practised. As the gulf between expectation (inflated by every election speech and all the media of mass communication) and fulfillment (strangulated by each move in the big swindle) increased, the instinctive path lay towards anger, irreverence and cynical selfishness of the moment. Unlike us, they were not much hampered by a sense of self-pity. Their art forms, their manner of speech and dress, their whole attitude to life indicated this fundamental shift. That son of my former landlord had thousands of emulators, not necessarily restricted to the poorer classes, who wanted the fleeting pleasures by the 'easiest' means.

Sooner or later, individual rebels were tamed by social security or economic factors. But, the cumulative effect of all these 'angry' and 'hungry' creations of art, often commercialized in themselves, and always multiplied by the new-found community feeling of the large number of young men and women thrown together on the university campuses (or by the decay of family life), gradually built up an enormous tension. The confused and divided leadership of the political opposition began to come out of their ideological shells and tried to give a direction to it. In contrast with this, the movements of protest built up among landless labour in the surrounding districts, organized labour in the industrial belt, as well as the white-collar workers and school teachers in and around Calcutta were from the beginning based on economic deprivation and had clear political orientation. Each bloody confrontation between the police and the protesters further widened the base of discontent and deepened the violence in the minds of men. In fact, large-scale violence might have erupted earlier, but for the two wars of 1962 and 1965. The middle classes and the middle-aged leaders themselves were, however, still rather protected from the direct incidence of violence.

What was really notable were the reactions of the people in power whose main objective was to protect their private nests of comfort. At first, they were only rather vexed. Then came the phase of vindictiveness, followed by a gripping sense of panic which lingers even now. But they hardly ever tried to isolate or remove the causes at the root. Where they vacillated in favour of an eventual compromise, they convinced the young and the under privileged that violence could wrest concessions which non-violence and reasonableness could not. Where they applied counter-force, they did win, but the crushed protesters did not accept it as a blow for the rule of law, because the blessed rule had already been sabotaged. The protesters only wished that they had more strength. Easy examples would be the food marches in the late fifties and early sixties. Moreover, private practitioners of violence were often used to supplement the state forces, as in the notorious assault on Calcutta journalists in 1954. This would further undermine the credibility of the machinery of the state as the upholder of the rule of law.

With the growing estrangement of the people from the government, it became necessary not only to repulse the periodic attacks on the Establishment, but also to maintain constant counter pressure. As in the typical case of Belghoria, a northern suburb of Calcutta, private practitioners of violence were given specific areas to work upon, while the law and order machinery was either neutralised or made to assist in the process. The system was eminently successful at first, as it always had been in the countryside and many industrial areas. But this very success gave rise to a storm of protests, largely alienated the intellectuals and government servants; and encouraged the formation of 'defence parties' mainly composed of East Bengal refugees and industrial workers, but under the leadership of middle class men committed to leftist policies. It is roughly to this phase that one could trace the origin of the 'private armies' of the political parties. Leaders of the opposition also took full advantage of this situation and brought about a change in the public opinion, which forgot the points in favour of the Establishment and more or less condoned the acts of political violence against it as being defensive in character.

An interesting aspect of the situation was that the constitutionally elected houses of legislature ceased to be taken by many really to represent the people. The movement of protest hardened into a wide distrust of the effectiveness of the constitutional machinery for ridding the country of corruption, inefficiency, inequality and poverty. This distrust, mainly arising out of the millions of personal frustrations, cut across the boundaries of explicitly held political beliefs. But it was obviously more acute in the minds of the young than of the middle-aged or the old, who were more resigned to social injustice and more conscious of the role of the Establishment in stabilising society against the alternative possibilities of military rule and revolutionary change.

Eventually, the change came through constitutional means. The election of 1967, perhaps unexpectedly for the opposition leaders themselves, catapulted them into legitimate power. But, the rural middle class, really fighting their private fight against the urban cliques of power, and the urban intelligentsia, academically enthusiastic over a vague concept of 'revolution', were taken aback by the character of the popular support: students completely disillusioned with the educational system and the socio-economic order, white-collar workers with their newly acquired knowledge that determined disobedience was much more rewarding than efficiency and loyalty, industrial workers convinced that trade unionism had to be fortified with politics and violence in order to serve its purpose, and the hordes of the landless and the unemployed with their aggressive lack of personal fear because they had so little to lose. Moreover, in the panic and confusion following the defeat of the Establishment, the law and order machinery was neutralised and the vast army of auxiliary violence had been dispersed. The now famous phenomenon of 'gherao', basically violent and unconstitutional in character, could be said to be a sort of organized reaction to the deliberate disruption of the rule of law over the first twenty years of political freedom.

The dethroned elites, in the perspective of their India wide shake-up, had little morale to light back. But reaction apparently arose from within the ranks of the erstwhile protesters. While one section tried to consolidate the gains by pragmatic alliances with the dominant economic interests, and another section tended to dissipate the gains through further agitations, a third section entered into some understanding with the recently defeated political interests. This section, formally committed to non-violence, was at the point of staging *a coup d'etat* when the second mentioned section, formally committed to violence, appeared to vacillate. This brought about a fiasco and eventually ushered in a short-lived revival of the pre-1967 system, including the use of state violence. But, as before, the active and the passive protesters were the more convinced of the efficacy of violence.

In the second round of elections occurring in this phase, the rout of the former Establishment was complete, mainly due to an adroit adjustment of seats among the parties in opposition. But between then and the latest round of elections, the second and the third partners of the 'anti-Establishment' front have been virtually eliminated, while the former Establishment has staged a remarkable come-back, giving the look of a political polarisation (without the benefit of stability) to this State alone in the whole of the country. Even if this be accepted as the main product of the forces of current history, the awful by-product of violence is hardly less important. The whole of the current violence may not be explicitly political in nature, but it will necessarily have an impact on current politics. In Calcutta today, politics is violent, while violence in itself is a political issue.

This critical change became clearly perceptible during the second ministry of the United Front, although it must have been started in the days of their first ministry. The uneasy partners of the Front, if they all practised what they professed, might have largely achieved without much violence what the then leaders of the bright young democracy had ostensibly set out to achieve twenty years earlier, namely, economic progress, social justice and the rule of law. Some of the partners in the Front, of course, maintained that this was impossible within the Constitution and the social framework. But did not their acceptance of the parliamentary obligations imply that, according to their own assessment, some compromise was possible and desirable? The fact that they had to operate in a small part of a large country was possibly a greater inhibiting factor. But would not even some limited success have given them immense political leverage in the other part of the country? Likewise, the more conservative partners could not have been completely uninformed about the belief and the modus operandi of the radical ones before coming to political adjustments with the latter. So, in theory, all that they had together to do was to remove the distortions which had been introduced or allowed to accumulate over the preceding two decades, and to provide impetus at a few key points. In practice, however, they chose to fight among themselves – by playing to the gallery, by adding to party funds and membership rolls, and lastly by raising and using what may very well be called their respective private militias. Each could perhaps be held guilty of unconstitutional practices, although the incidence of private aggrandizement was apparently lower than in the preceding regime.

Then came the fall, the unbelievably maladroit handling of the situation by the dethroned rulers, their complete rout – and the even cleaner state for the second ministry of the Front to write its destiny upon. That in spite of the experience of the first ministry, they chose to remain together must have been due to one basic factor: the people's desire for a change. The obvious effectiveness of the ballot should have discouraged the forces of violence. But exactly the opposite was the outcome. If the accusations and counter-accusations are accepted at their face value, which is not entirely without usefulness as a first step in resolving such a controversy, violence this time stemmed from an acute power struggle among the partners, and not between them and the cornered forces of the Establishment. Apparently, much of the law enforcement machinery and the civil administration divided themselves into partisan groups, professional criminals and the disbanded mercenaries of the former rulers were either recruited by or gravitated towards the various partners of the front, the sophistication of bombs and small arms was introduced, and whole localities were subjected to the conditions of a form of civil war.

If the violence preceding the elections of 1967 and 1969 could be likened to magnified and more purposive editions of the episode of Tagore's cremation, the violence occurring since then might be likened to the communal riots. So much cruelty and counter-cruelty have been committed that it would be futile now to judge who started the thing. Though the larger and the more powerful a party, the greater should have been its stake in not allowing things to come to such a pass, it is no secret that the largest of the parties got the biggest share of the blame and quite soon, the medley of the strifes between each pair of them was largely replaced by a grand fight between the 'big brother' on the one hand and all the rest, on the other. This team of 'the others' came to include, in the course of the next few months, the split forces of the former Establishment and also the ultra-radicals and the urban guerrillas. For all practical purposes, it is now a civil war between these two sides with deep fissures running down the length of the community, including the guardians of law and the professional men of violence. There has been a change in the basic tactics: public anger is no more worked up into mob violence, though the motive force is always there; the standard technique is to have carefully selected enemies liquidated through well planned assassinations against which the middle-aged or the middle class no longer get any protection from the social organization. The obtrusive bombs are mostly used as cover or in defending the strongholds, and not as weapons of mass violence.

Thus, after two years of intensive violence, politically motivated violence might be said to have become highly professionalised and very largely dissociated from the masses. In brief, therefore, it has almost assumed the character of an extended gang war. It is risky to make any prediction, but if the situation continues, this type of violence might cease to have any direct political significance and might either just peter out or be snuffed out by a massive expression of public anger. After all, direct violence could hardly be expected to capture power or to retain it within the existing structure of the country; the ultimate power still resides with the electorate. And that gives a clue to the real nature of this violence. In as much as it is politically motivated and is not directed against the structure itself, it is a fight over the electorate. Violence is to stop the people from voting against, compel the people to vote for, stop others from stopping the people to vote for, and if it comes to the worst, to stop the people's verdict from being given effect to.

Let us not be moralistic about, it; all these practices have long been familiar to us, just as false voting is not something newly discovered in 1971. Even the association of violence with these illegal practices was not unknown. What is really new this time is the degree of violence – its intensity, its spread, and above all, its continuation. If violence of this nature were to start from the foolish assumption that it was the monopoly of someone, one might choose to wait till the assumption was exploded through an initial acceleration (which we are now witnessing) followed by the phase of diminishing political returns, or through an overwhelming dose of violence administered by the state, or the people, or one of the parties. But in the meantime, the whole society will be infected with secondary infections. In place of the manipulators who dominated for twenty years, the criminals will dominate – a bizarre proof of Gresham's Law in human affairs.

The people who still believe in violence must be made to realize that while an ordinary man or an ordinary society should be prepared to be violent in self-defence, it is, on the whole, safer to eschew violence. It will be a pity if, in spite of so much pain, we do not live to see the emergence of a good society. We do not have the memory of having lived in any.

Since the bright dawn of 15th August 1947, I too have trodden the path of bitter disillusionment; I have earned money – which has always involved a certain amount of degradation of myself, I have fallen in love and raised a family; I have been defeated by clever people in battles of wits; I have occasionally been violent in my domestic life out of impatience, frustration and impotent anger; I have eventually learned to be resigned and 'non-violent'; and I have gradually arrived at the conclusion that it is impossible to be happy within this perverted system unless one is either a knave or an utter fool and is insensitive to injustice. The only relic of integrity to which I still cling relates to my occasional writings: I try not to write what I do not believe for instance, unlike so many of my friends, I do not first preach violence for the sake of notoriety or commercial gain and then flee from the reality of its rudeness. But I know that, primarily out of consideration for my family. I am prudent enough not to write all that I believe. For instance, I have never written anywhere that money plays a large part in today's violence. But the realization that I cannot bear is that I can hardly bring the material means of happiness either to myself or to any person dear to me without causing unhappiness to someone else. The organization of society is wrong. Is that the root of violence? Or does my personal mismanagement of my private affairs cloud my vision? Violence is, of course, wrong. It certainly creates problems even as it solves some. But, how do I preach non-violence to a person who has taken to violence either intuitively or selfishly?

Chastened by my experienced of having 'to give up living in order to make a living'; I am willing to concede that the organization of society will always be wrong. It should not, however, be so wrong as to bring about so violent a reaction. Politicians and public men will always have mixed motives, but let them not think that violence is anybody's monopoly, and let them not be so very hypocritical; the young people of today know that almost none of them is above doing violence in thought or deed. To the under-privileged and the young in age, I could not honestly say that the edifice of the present society is such as intrinsically to deserve protection from the ravages of violence. I would even tend to sympathise with their disconcerting logic of selfishness. We all are selfish. But let them be intelligent. Why should they play into the hands of dishonest leaders? They will be here for a longer time than their old or middle-aged leaders. The present system should certainly be replaced; but should it not be by a better specimen? They must also remember that no foreign power has ever been a disinterested friend to a struggling nation and, on the other hand, a young nation can never automatically expect peace and prosperity just because it has paid a heavy price in violence and anguish. I would not end this autobiographical note by talking about searching of heart; all the wrong people are mouthing the right things today. Let us rather be intelligently concerned about our self-interest. Our country has enough resources to make us all tolerably happy. Or is that the lingering illusion of a mind sick of violence?

The Charisma of Rajesh Khanna

D.

(Quest 72: September–October 1971)

It is rumoured that his disarming smile costs Rs. 1.4 million. Young women devour him with hungry eyes in the afternoon darkness of cinema halls. Mothers witness his filmic deaths with helpless pangs of frustrated protectiveness. Young adult males project themselves into his limelit presence on the screen and later yearn to recreate themselves in his image. Millions of Indians queue up for long hours to see him break into his smile, get drunk, become furious, whisper love-words or burst forth into a husky, vibrant played-back song. If there is one person in India today who surpasses the Prime Minister's charisma, he is Rajesh Khanna. The multimillion rupee Hindi film industry which prolifically produces stereotyped dreams unanimously regards him as the only authentic super-star it has so far produced. He is what makes a sure-fire box-office hit. Even films with all the essential ingredients for making a sure flop have run for weeks just because he starred in them. His success is so phenomenal that it challenges anyone who pretends to understand mass behaviour.

He is of medium height and build. He has mannerisms of his own which show through whatever character he plays – or perhaps that is unfair to him. His producers and directors want him to play no other character but his own unique self. He has a rare plasticity: that which makes a natural actor, something which James Dean had impressed upon movie-addicts during his meteoric Hollywood career. For he gives the sense that he lives his assumed role, however crudely it is scripted and directed. Yet he will not get an Elia Kazan or a George Stevens to direct him. And his hurt-youth image, which is a factor in his success, will gradually age.

The best script and director he got so far was in the film *Anand*, directed by Hrishikesh Mukherjee who is one of the better directors in the world of commercial Hindi cinema. His worst role was the one in *Haathi Mere Saathi* in which he plays a sort of elephant-boy and in which one of the three corners of the conventional love triangle is occupied, of all animals, by elephants.

Curiously, Rajesh Khanna is considered a hero worth killing – which is amazing since in Hindi films it is a taboo to kill the hero. Curiously too, he has to die of cancer. He died of cancer in *Safar* and again in *Anand*. In *Safar* he is the leukaemic lover of a would-be doctor. In *Anand*, he is a cancer patient who spends his limited spell of life to make people around him happy. In *Andaz* he dies in a motor-bike accident for a change. Is it, one wonders, the expression of a mass death-wish? Some fifteen years ago, Dilip Kumar, the matinee idol then, specialized in dying as a hero. However, Dilip Kumar's screen deaths brought no shock to the audience since he moved and spoke, from the start, as if he were his own pall-bearer. Rajesh's screen deaths have some novelty: he is a warm, ebullient, vivacious, blithe young man. Even if he is destined to die, it seems unfair and too early. One has seen teenage girls sob witnessing him die. Or heaving unmistakably erotic sighs when he sings a love song (with the inimitable Kishore Kumar play-back singing for him). For the first time in the history of the commercial Hindi cinema a single person has acquired such following.

What has Rajesh Khanna got that others haven't? He does have acting talent. But there are others who are much better. He is good-looking. But that is neither here nor there. He is certainly not very handsome. What is it then?

One hypothesis about his charisma is that Rajesh Khanna has all the quintessential characteristics of the sort of romantic hero contemporary Indian masses would like to dote on. Here, even within the hackneyed formulae of the commercial Hindi cinema, the new generation audiences had been looking for some positive new content. In the fifties, the triumvirate of Dilip Kumar, Raj Kapoor and Dev Anand dominated the scene. The first was a tragic hero who was the product of middle-class pessimism and sentimentality. The second was a comic actor appealing to the masses through his mask of a little fellow. The third one was a slick, urban westernised Indian. All three box-office draws. The sixties saw the emergence of Guru Dutt who added new values to the Saigal-Dilip Kumar image of a tragic hero by investing greater sensitivity into his existing joint-stock image. The handsome-buffoon image of which Dev Anand was a pioneer, was extended in the form of Shammi Kapoor, Joy Mukerji and a number of others who danced and leaped energetically singing duets with their assorted heroines. Then came Dharmendra, who looks like a capable, middle-aged elder son and also Shashi Kapoor, the shy boy-lover of aggressively inclined heroines. In the meantime, despite his blank face, Rajendra Kumar emerged as a substitute Dilip Kumar being to the elder hero what saccharine is to sugar. Sunil Dutt tried to introduce a little different hero-concept, but had only limited success. Trials continued. Errors went on being committed. And then came Rajesh Khanna like a deluge.

Rajesh is close to the teenager because he shares some of their norms of group behaviour and mannerisms. His actions have a suggestion of a devil-may-care anarchistic element. However, as in *Do Raaste*, he can even play successfully the younger brother in a Hindu joint family rising to rescue it at the time of crisis. He also has a very infectious warmth and a very charming smile. What is interesting about Rajesh is that unlike other leading male actors he seldom shows off his histrionic talent by exaggeration. His acting is always an understatement of emotion. This is something which he shares with the younger mass audience in India. They don't dig melodramatic acting any more (which is the reason why Sharmila Tagore and Tanuja, for instance, are liked by them according to a recent survey: and, of course. Waheeda Rehman, whom the late Guru Dutt introduced).

Next time you see Rajesh Khanna on the screen, therefore, please note that his behaviour on celluloid is going to lay down a norm for most of the male teenagers around you and a number of people even up to their middle thirties. He is a sort of boy with whom four out of five urban female college students would be thrilled to elope. In short, he is one of the top-selling *consumer products* in India today. And the packaging, here too, is the product.

Gromyko, I Love You

It has been like an international wife-swapping party, what with Kissinger embracing Chou and kissing Yahya and we finding ourselves, rather suddenly, in Andrei Gromyko's passionate arms…

The greatest consolation this big power diplomatic orgy gives this columnist is our own shedding of old-maidish virtues in matters of foreign policy.

The Indo-Soviet pact does not make us any more dependent on the Russians than we have been so far. On the contrary, it ends the era of vague speeches on peaceful co-existence – which was an obvious euphemism for troublesome non-existence on the internal level – and brings in some element of geo-political *realpolitik* in our foreign policy thinking.

This column had earlier hinted at the importance of the port of Karachi to the ambitions of the Chinese. It had also hinted at the repercussions of a Sino-American *détente* on the politics of this region. The columnist only hopes that Mrs Gandhi will use the Indo-Soviet pact with the astuteness of a de Gaulle rather than a Soviet satellite without a firm spine.

It must be stressed now that the Russians have begun to realize that Pakistan is a slippery customer and that only with India on their side can they eventually gain some operational advantages in the Indian Ocean area which will restore the balance of military power in their favour. As for India, there was no better assurance for it that only a limited war will be fought on the sub-continent, than the one it gets as a result of this pact.

If India intended to put the pact to an acid test, it should now recognize Bangla Desh without any delay and press the Soviet Union to follow suit. Only then could the problem of the refugees be solved and our impossible economic burdens made somewhat bearable. Pakistan is likely to act imprudently in any case and it should not be allowed the first strike even in a limited war, considering its distinct air-strike superiority. It should be realized that an invisible war is already on and even a proclaimed emergency would be of great advantage in turning the minds of the people to the realities of the situations. China cannot risk any involvement in the war on the eve of its entry into the UN. The USA cannot do so either when it is pulling out if Asia after so many half-hearted adventures. Who are we afraid of? Of Dear Kremlin?

East Bengal has paid a war-sized national price for having asked for a democratic rule. We will soon have a crore of extra mouths to feed, and that upsets whatever we may have achieved through an expensive family-planning drive. The influx of refugees and their continued stay will soon adversely affect the morale of the poor and troubled eastern states. Even a pacifist, if he is rational, will opt for a war in such a situation.

The minus side of the pact is that it has been signed by an Indian government which already has strong crypto-communist elements. It has come at a time when the government is already trying to push through Parliament a bill which aims at taking our fundamental rights away. While a civil war continues on our borders, while refugees continue to pour in, while the Americans seem almost as villainous to us as the Chinese, and while the democratic nations of affluent Europe seem callous towards our problems, we are in danger of being pushed towards 'socialist' totalitarianism almost beyond the point of no return. Because of Bangla Desh, one would like to see the whole nation unanimously supporting the Prime Minister who has at last taken an initiative in re-aligning our foreign policy in a modern, pragmatic manner. Yet, if she uses this feeling of solidarity to remove by unenlightened consent in a highly emotional climate, a few of the cornerstones of the Constitution, it could well be the beginning of a black chapter in India's history.

The 007 Version

There is, believe it or not, a 007 version of why Kissinger dashed to Peking and Gromyko to New Delhi.

According to this version, Mrs Gandhi's pact with the Russians was a pre-election deal, gradually negotiated with Moscow. The CIA and the Chinese and Pakistani intelligence knew what was coming. The counter move thus preceded the move. Both the Americans and the Chinese were worried by Mrs Gandhi's victory since they knew of the deal in the offing.

According to the imaginative author of this theory, how could a twenty-year pact be signed between India and the Soviet Union unless it was pre-planned? Again assuming that the CIA, the Chinese and the Pakistani intelligence know of it, was it not logical for Pakistan to force the issue with a 'pro-Indian' Mujibur Rahman, for China to support the West Pakistani regime, and for the USA to come closer to Pakistan and China in view of the emerging Indo-Soviet *power bloc?*

An alternative theory attributes the developments to earlier secret talks between the two coastal nations – the USA and China – trying to encircle the hinterland power, the Soviet Union, of which the KGB got wind. Pakistan was to be the common Sino-American military base to stem the Soviet Union's traditional attempt to seek an oceanic outlet.

Now who is more intelligent? The CIA? The Chinese intelligence? Pakistani spies? The KGB? Or an armchair hypothesis-monger in India? Or is there a supreme inventor of the planted lie hidden somewhere behind dusty files in a dingy cellar who has caused this tremendous reshuffle in the Asian balance of power?

Women's Lib in India

D.

(Quest 75: March-April 1972)

'Muslim Women oppose Change in Personal Law' reads the headline in *The Times of India*, Bombay, dated January 24. The report concerned a meeting organized by the Jamaat-e-Islami in Bombay.

In a unanimous resolution passed at the meeting, they stated that through false propaganda an impression was sought to be created that Muslim women were beginning to oppose polygamy. 'However, this public meeting states that Muslim women consider such a demand a challenge to their religious freedom which has been guaranteed to them by the Constitution of India', the resolution said.

The speakers, most of them college girls and school teachers, told the gathering that at a recent meeting organized by the Muslim Satya Shodhak Mandal and the Indian Secular Forum in Poona, a false impression was created that Muslim women wanted the law to be scrapped. The number of Muslims attending that meeting had been negligible, they added.

The 'creators of the false impression', by a curious coincidence, voiced their view in the same issue. V.K. Sinha, honorary secretary of the Indian Secular Society, wrote in a letter to the *Times*:

It is significant that as many as 170 Muslim women came to the conference not only to assert their rights as free citizens of a free country but also fully aware that their demands are resented by obscurantist groups in Muslim society. Some came despite severe pressures, abuses and threats.

Mr Sinha also gave the chilling information that 'the escort of the group which came to Poona (from Amravati), Mr Sheikh Vazir Patel has been threatened with nothing less than murder! He has to move about under police protection.'

While the Poona conference was attended by only 170 women, the Jamaat-e-Islami meeting was reported to have been attended by 2,000. Subsequently, the reported size of the audience was challenged by letter-writers in *The Times of India*. The meeting was held in the hall of the Nagpada Neighbourhood House, which can physically accommodate less than 300 persons. Even if the first floor of the building was used, the audience could not have exceeded 600. Of course, there is a possibility that each member of the audience was a Muslim married woman representing not only herself but two or three co-wives also, thus making up a Wordsworthian total of 2,000 as claimed by the Jamaat. Mrs Rashida Maddu, the only speaker to be named, is the wife of Ibrahim Maddu, CPM worker of riot-famed Bhiwandi. He was detained in the public interest in 1965 as well as in 1970. *Via* the CPM, perhaps Engels makes a compromise with the Jamaat's Prophet!

By the established logic of populism in India, therefore every political party – including the ruling Congress headed by the most achievement-conscious woman in Indian history – should ignore the 170 voices against polygamy. After all, if the people of India were to demand re-institution of slavery even the Parliament is 'free' today to amend the Constitution suitably!

It is no wonder that after the defeat of Pakistan in the recent war, reactionary Muslim organizations like the Jamaat-e-Islami turn more and more atavistic and cling to the medieval law of the *Shariat*. It is very likely that Indian Muslims, who have been conditioned to see everything in religious and communal terms, will commit a mass suicide now, viewing every modern reform as a threat to their Muslim identity. The dialogue started by the Indian Secular Society is one way out of schizophrenia that is centuries old.

However, attacking the obviously iniquitous Muslim personal law is not enough. The larger problem is the liberation of the Indian windfall who, regardless of caste or creed, is universally oppressed. Excepting the traditional upper caste Hindus, whose liberalism is accompanied by greater political and economic stakes, the rest of the

Indians generally live in conditions similar to those in which Indian Muslims live. They are all willing slaves of oppressive cultural traditions and inhuman customs. One has only to think of the neo-Buddhists. A great visionary and radical led them through mass conversion into – a religion, of all things. And today they flock to Baddha temples, worship the great Babasaheb as the Buddha's *avatara* and also continue to worship local stones, trees and political leaders. Their women are not in any better condition than before, and then men continue to exploit them. Or think of the Indian Catholic women. If Muslim women 'oppose' a uniform civil code and their husbands' right to keep a mini-harem on to give them an instant oral divorce (sometimes even on the telephone), Catholic women 'champion' their husband's stud bull like authority to compel them to produce a litter of children by opposing contraception with modern medical means, which the clergy has the check to condemn as 'artificial'!

India's Prime Minister is a woman. (Frank Moraes once described her as the only 'man' in her cabinet; a remark which is excellent meat for a Freudian mincer). In the elite classes there is a sizeable section of intelligent, socially active, economically self-supporting women. But a large section of elite women consists of the amoral, asocial, apolitical types such as the ones found in professions like advertising and in the film industry. They are also found in large numbers at cocktail parties in the capital and the metropolises. One sees their glamorous or aggressively determined faces in the mass circulation English language periodicals for women. Aren't these women concerned with women's rights and women's liberation as natural, biologically distinct interest group? Why shouldn't women's own secular institutions launch an India-wide campaign for the emancipation of women? Or even contest elections on a programme for the liberation of Indian women, a programme to better their condition?

Perhaps these elite-class women, who can divorce as easily as their *burkha*-confined Muslim counterparts, do not oppose polygamy as such. In which case, purely as a catalytic movement, they might as well launch a movement for bilateral or reciprocal polygamy, i.e. for polyandry. The reason why the real battle must be fought on the sexual level should be obvious. Sexual identity is immutable and universal. In the Post-Pill period (no gynecological pun intended), it is logical for women's leaders to see the immense political potential of such a liberation movement. After all, exploitation – political, economic and social – begins at home. The ills of any society are inherent in its family, which is only its microcosmic unit.

Alas, women's liberation does not come by *lungees* alone. Or else, the lavish fashion shows in our cities would have revolutionised more than fashions. It need not be the necessary consequence of the magic of the contraceptive pill (even ancient hetairai knew of some crude means of contraception). It need not come through education such as is given in a male-dominated society. It certainly does not come through coeducation by itself. It must pass from woman to woman, from those who suffer from the same condition but have found the way out.

One would have hoped that the dynamic Mrs Gandhi, if she so desired, would solve this problem by pushing through a uniform civil code and also by creating more opportunities for women to participate in the mainstream of Indian life. But why would she. After all, Mrs Gandhi is a politician, not a reformer. Recently she gave us the slogan of 'democracy, socialism and secularism'.

As one writes this, one is disturbed by yet another pretty news photograph of hers. This time she is accepting *teertha* from the high priest of Sri Venkatesa temple at Tirupati in Andhra Pradesh. Secularism indeed. Why should a Hindu Prime Minister of India be concerned about the plight of Indian Muslim women – even if she is herself a woman? Mr Moraes should not have called her the only 'man' in her cabinet. 'Man' cannot be a euphemism for 'politician'. Or can it?

Sex and the Hindi Heroine

Desi culture has come a long way from the sage Vatsyayana and his manual of sexual acrobatics. It has come a long way, too, from the divine lack of censorship enjoyed by the sculptors of Khajuraho and Konarak. Nobody is allowed to kiss on the Indian screen. The only kind of sexual foreplay allowed is the singing of a duet. Much energy is wasted in singing and performing it. The man chases the woman, both run like expert sprinters, leap about, hide and seek, seek and hide Both, after the song, are apparently too exhausted for a straight forward sexual act.

The tragic part of it is that the audience accepts the duet rather than healthier forms of sexual activity as the norm. Or do they really?

Why is Rehana Sultan a hit? What accounts for the popularity of Mumtaz? How could Rekha hit the headlines? Why is everybody interested in seeing Helen perform her cabaret act? Or even, what precisely are the ingredients of Sharmila Tagore's sex appeal? These questions do not seem important to intellectuals. But these are the facts of our folk taste in sex today.

All pornography is a cheap euphemism for healthier sex. Most commercial Hindi films and some even of the new wave ones are no exception to this rule. However, if one takes the view that sex is all-pervading, one becomes a Freudian voyeur seeing a symbolic sex act even in the pattern of the solar system. Fortunately, sex in Hindi film is so close to the surface that one need not be a Freudian to notice any but its Oedipal features.

Since even oscular eroticism is taboo in Hindi films, they have to use fetishes. Now, the things cannot be called a euphemism for the female genitalia nor do the breasts symbolize the ultimate human sexual ambition except for a minor age group. These, then are the most exhibited parts of the female body in a Hindi film. Female arms, forearms, parts of the female leg above the level of the ankle are also considered erotically exciting.

There must be certain class associations attached to these fetishes. For, in naked and starved India, more women are seen exposed these days than covered. However, the poor women one sees half or more naked in Indian streets are all undernourished, dirty and generally reduced to an infra-human condition. On the other hand, heroines, supporting actresses and dancers on the Hindi screen are glowingly overfed. In fact, most of them (with the slim exception of Sharmila Tagore) are full of excess fat. One therefore sometimes wonders whether the audience considers them literally devourable. This suspicion is strengthened by the observation that in most Hindi films feats are gargantuan and the principal characters obese. Raj Kapoor, who looks like a ripe red tomato, is an outgoing hero. But even Rajesh Khanna, the super star, looks pink to the point of seeming unreal. With every box office hit, he seems to be adding a few inches to his girth. Coming back to the heroines, Mumtaz and the upcoming Rekha are full of glowing fat. While Helen is trim in spite of her age, she is usually shown bare up to her panties and the expanse of bareness makes up for the lack of extra fat. The plumper ones usually are also considered the sexier ones, which goes to strengthen one's suspicion that more than one kind of starvation accounts for the female star's appeal in the Hindi cinema.

The exceptions are Sharmila Tagore and the newcomer, Jaya Bhaduri (Waheeda Rahman no more being a real box office attraction these days). The former is the super female star of the Hindi screen Sharmila has several peculiar status symbols. She was introduced to films by Satyajit Ray and she is married to the former Indian test cricket captain, the ex-Nawab of Pataudi. She has been the lucky heroine to establish Rajesh Khanna as a super star. *Aradhana* being the lucky film.

I saw Sharmila at a poetry reading some years ago. Not a reading of Urdu or Bengali poems but a playback of Andrei Voznesensky reading his poems and his English translators reading their own versions. The shock was great because it was entirely in the retrospect. (It was another member of the audience who, after the programme, confirmed that the girl was the star!) One never suspected that the charming woman among the half a dozen people present was none other than the super star. Therefore, one is inclined to believe that the popular part of Sharmila's sex appeal is largely the creation of cinematographers. It is strange but Hindi film audiences do not realize the role a cinematographer plays in creating a screen charisma. Miss Tagore is a lively person but she is perhaps more than a glamorous commodity outside films. (This could also be true of male stars like Rajesh Khanna; they are perhaps *reduced* to a specific screen image). Yet Sharmila Tagore, as depicted in the films, is a sex doll – subtle or obvious. The camera becomes a sex-starved sixty-year-old male peering or drooling at her in every Hindi film. Perhaps this is so because all the directors of Hindi films are themselves voyeurs.

Anyone who has been behind a commercial camera knows how practically every young female, beautiful or ugly, can be made sexually formidable to a sex-starved male audience. For that matter juicy meat or even a prosaic thing like boiled potatoes can be made attractive when one knows that one's audience is dying for a meal. The level at which the audience of a Hindi film appreciates the sex appeal of a heroine is not far above the level of the anxiety for food of a famished human being. In fact, hunger rather than glamour accounts for the appeal of Hindi film stars, male or female college girls devour Rajesh Khanna because in his warm exuberance there is the promise of sexual fulfillment. Sharmila Tagore's appeal is even wider. She is a female to be consumed only visually. Her appeal lies in her unapproachability. The hero is approachable, the heroine beyond approach. This is only as it should be. In India, a woman is only to be seen and admired: even her sex. If she came nearer, she would become more real, if sex came nearer the audience, it would become a real disturbance, too. It is much better to *view* things. The audience of Hindi films is involved in them only visually. Thus sex is only a visual phenomenon to them. The sex they have in real life is tactile and olfactory and ugly and riddled by the red triangle of family planning and its sinister associations.

On the Riviera

The title may evoke, in the minds of male readers, images of sunny Mediterranean beaches, blue surfing waves, bikini-clad females, occasional glimpses of suntanned breasts, international celebrities sprawled comfortably in the sand...

One will never be able to associate such images with the Riviera again. For 'Riviera' is the name of an apartment house in Bombay where the Union Finance Minister has a flat. And not bikini-clad girls but *khadi*-clad politicians crowded it recently. It was here that the lists of candidates for contesting the forthcoming state legislature elections in Maharashtra minus Bombay were to be finalised with the help of Indiraji's own personal emissaries. In the background was the big tussle for the state's Chief Ministership between Mr V.P. Naik and Mr S.B. Chavan. New Delhi's inclination was the suspense factor. It was not ticket seekers alone who comprised the milling white-capped, *khadi*-clad, Marathi speaking crowd. Each ticket-seeker had brought with him, presumably at his own expense, a number of supporters. Many long-sitting members, including the clever Education Minister of Maharashtra, pleaded for being relieved of their seats and allowed to 'work for the party' – a tune which they thought would be appreciated by Indiraji and would purify their own image. But this was only a gimmick. Their supporters backed them vociferously, in the presence of the bigwigs, to continue representing them for one more term. This was staged with a purpose, the hypocrisy of which was all too obvious to the public of Bombay silently watching the disgusting spectacle.

Behind-the-scenes canvassing of a most interesting kind was also in full swing. It is understood, for example, that Mr R.K. Khadikar, the new Congress Socialist Minister at Delhi vigorously championed before the Election Committee the cause of Mr Shankarrao Mohite of the fabulous marriage feast fame (*vide* Editorial in *Quest* 71) in the name of socialism in Maharashtra. And why not? If Dr Karan

Singh, the affluent former Maharaja of Jammu and Kashmir can be an authentic socialist, so can Mr Shankarrao Mohite. India is not the only country in the underdeveloped world where there can be a natural symbiosis of feudalism and socialism. After all, as Shakespeare would put it, a socialist by any other name stinks as bad.

Mrs Gandhi, in the meantime, had dramatically appointed Mr Rajni Patel, the suave trade unionist, wealthy practicing barrister and communist fellow-traveller as the new president of the Bombay Pradesh Congress Committee. A combination of the new rich and the old communists seems to be Mrs Gandhi's recipe for the Indian brand of socialism. Her 'radicals' do not, of course, come from rural India. They are all comfortable, urban, sophisticated socialites with Marxist 'convictions' on record. In Maharashtra, the 'intellectual radical', who is generally an upper-caste Hindu if not a Brahmin to boot, cannot get elected from a rural constituency except at a high price. In the city, on the other hand, he has just the right kind of Janus-image necessary to please both the working class and the white-collar slogger. Didn't income-tax evading, millionaire film stars campaign for Mr V.K. Krishna Menon in the same city once? Bombay has the richest Marxists in all India. And now they are all new Congressmen.

Indira Gandhi: The Gatecrasher

Dilip Chitre

(Quest 76: May-June 1972)

The late Dr Ram Manohar Lohia, a somewhat pathological hater of the Nehru charisma, once described Indira Gandhi on the floor of the Lok Sabha as a 'dumb doll'. Mrs Gandhi's family heritage was potentially is much a political hazard as it was her popular capital. It would not be entirely correct to say that she became Nehru's dynastic successor as Dr Lohia would have maliciously alleged. She is almost self-made, considering the situation in which she assumed full leadership. It should also be recalled that Nehru's last days were days of frustration and resignation. He was never a master decision-maker although he was greater in some respects than most hardened politicians who cash on the contingent. His great charisma had already developed noticeable cracks when death removed him from the Indian political scene which he had dominated for several decades without dispute. Indira Gandhi had, in fact, to overcome the lingering taste of her father's failures in his final years, still bitter in public memory when she arrived on the scene. In the brief interlude, Lal Babadur Shastri had come and gone. A tough war with Pakistan, despite the dubious Tashkent pact to follow, had helped to make him a little legend. His sudden death after signing the pact made the real evaluation of his contribution as Prime Minister, a matter of unrewarding debate.

Mrs Gandhi has now been on the scene long enough to convince anyone that she is here to stay, but not long enough to resolve the enigma around her image and the role she is likely to play in the future. Since she is in undisputed command of the situation at present, a midstream speculation about her political style and what it probably implies in the context of the present situation in India should be of interest.

Both because he was her father and also the first Prime Minister of India, Nehru provides a meaningful index to Indira Gandhi's performance. From the outset, this will be nothing except a study in contrast. Nehru's nobility lay in the unresolved conflict between his liberalism and his revolutionary romanticism; his failure lay in the gap between the patriarchal postures he assumed so easily and his legendary capacity to defer decisions, which were described as Hamlet-like by his critics who could not pin him down as a political type. Nehru's failure was also the failure of the Indian Constitution whose ethos presupposed a liberal industrial society in which socialism emerged as an evolving consciousness of the widest public interest. British rule in India may have helped to create a liberal Indian elite in a purely political sense. But there has not been a liberal culture in India for all these known centuries and the British rulers of India were hardly concerned with such a noble mission. The struggle for independence was mostly a kind of agitational crusade with nationalism – or chauvinism – acquiring, thanks to people like Gandhi, an almost religious halo. This was hardly the kind of political education conductive to democratic culture. At best it created in dubiously useful traditions of demagoguery and populism which now firmly hold the ground. Democratic elections and legislative procedures hardly suffice to create a democracy in an illiterate and obscurantist society founded on a pernicious system of apartheid since Manu's time. The elite in India continues to play the Brahmin's pontificating role; the politicians thrown up by the Indian elite succeed only in the manner of a manipulative Chanakya. Neither Nehru nor any other political leader could have coped with this patently anti-democratic factor inherent in the patriarchal and authoritarian culture of India. What made Nehru's charisma possible also made his – or anyone else's – democracy impossible.

At the same time, Indian culture is not conducive to a straightforward dictatorship because of the extremely diversified and stratified organization of Indian society. So far, the only unanimously acceptable leadership in India has been founded on regional or national chauvinistic sentiments. Like the Hindu saints of the Middle Ages, some of our national leaders have had to build up their images on quasi religious mystiques. The kind of appeal and influence, Indian leaders have exercised on the Indian people always had a messianic element such as neo-gurus and seers have. They may occasionally look upon a leader as a liberator but that is only how unconscious slaves or well-adjusted serfs look upon their lords. All this has been slowly changing and five elections have had something to do with it. The place of 'Great' leaders has been taken by small ones who are more localized and do not enjoy a vast and uncritical distance from their followers. Gradually, followers have ceased to be followers 'and have become bargainers instead, which is politically and socially much healthier. By the time Mrs Gandhi sought the popular mandate by way of a mid-term election early last year, Indian elections had become much more commonsense than ever before.

This writer was among the many forecasters who went wrong about the outcome of the last elections. Nobody had expected Mrs Gandhi to be returned to power with such a decisive majority. Her strategy was grossly underestimated and her opposition was grossly overrated. As a matter of fact, what she had achieved at Bangalore should have been a pointer to the shape of things to come. She had broken down the political situation into several issues, assessed the real interests and knew exactly where they were vested, studied all the probable responses to all her probable movers and in short, played a grandmaster's game of chess with her opponents. As for the people, her greatest plus point proved to be the failure of earlier economic policies, bureaucratic corruption and other evils. She was successful in pinning all these on her erstwhile Congress colleagues who had been identified even with her father's regime. Obviously, none of these leaders had, to put it mildly, untarnished reputations, and she made them pay for it. The split in the Congress was perhaps the most painlessly achieved massive purge in recent international politics. Its beauty lay in the fact that those who were purged were cleverly compelled by her to isolate themselves and defend themselves from an increasingly absurd and self-defeating position. To people conditioned to witnessing a different style of politics, Indira Gandhi had gatecrashed into modern Indian politics against what seemed to be insurmountable odds.

After her victory began a more crucial period in Indian politics. Mrs Gandhi had promised the people at least a minor social and political revolution. Somewhat like the proverbial bull, the fifth Lok Sabha, completely dominated by her party, entered the china shop of our Constitution and passed radical amendments. But these ritual sacrifices of some of the old-fashioned democratic fights could not be said to be steps towards greater equity or even towards a tangibly bright GNP. Mrs Gandhi's New Economic Policy still has to undergo severe tests. If it really proves to be as doctrinaire as the thinking of the old-fashioned Marxists who surround her would like it to be, then God – or alternatively, even Marx – help us. A crypto-communist new class based in comfortable shells in Delhi and elsewhere and committed only to super-bourgeois holidays behind the iron curtain will not usher in a socialist revolution any more than Mr Tata or Mr Birla would. What Mrs Gandhi needs today is not ideologues but efficient managers. Her public sector appointees are spectacular managerial failures. The colonial type of bureaucracy she has inherited from the preceding governments functions on a sinister combination of corruption and the Peter Principle. The sources of information on which she acts are of questionable value. The doctrinaire advice she receives is equally so. In fact, her likely failures will not be the failures of her intention but might prove to be the failures of the very elite, red or blue, on which she has to rely for the effective execution of any policy and, more vitally, on the very formulation of her policies. This elite has a vested interest in the status quo. One would not envy Mrs Gandhi her position. It is still difficult for her to make real history. By effectively helping the process of the balkanisation of Pakistan. Mrs Gandhi has made India a potential major power in Asia. But this will have no bearing at all on its relative industrial stagnation nor can it accelerate its overall development as a viable modern society. Mrs Gandhi has either to get together the best professionals or to become a more liberal-radical.

Nehru's failure lay, partly, in his tendency to make decisions by consensus among his colleagues who represented every political shade from the extreme left to the extreme right and represented, also a conflict of vested interests. Thus he compelled his rightist colleagues to join in a socialist chorus while he coaxed his crypto-communist colleagues into assuming liberal democratic postures. This was the character of the Indian National Congress during the pre-independence period. It had outlived its utility but stayed on even after independence. The real reason why a viable opposition failed to emerge in India is the ideologically motley nature of the ruling party.

It is to Mrs Gandhi's credit that she could trigger a process of acute polarisation within the Congress party itself and that she could isolate all those who opposed, or were likely to oppose, her own polices Mrs Gandhi's purge was conceived in very different terms as compared to the Kamraj plan, which aimed at phasing out the older generation. She was successful in forcing out en masse the entire right wing in the Congress ranks. Centrists like Y.B. Chavan have still stayed with her but their position is already precarious. In the first phase of her rule, Mrs Gandhi let the axe of her socialist policies fall on the industrial private sector while allowing a live-and-let-live policy towards the rural kulaks. In other words, she chose the agricultural capitalists as her allies. Fattened by the green revolution and the co-operatives which they controlled and managed as they pleased, and enjoying tax concessions in an obviously iniquitous proportion, these people remained the Congress party bosses in the newly affluent rural India. Today, these allies of hers pose a greater problem than her open opponents.

Mrs Gandhi can be a most unsparing step-mother. While treating the decadent public sector and the agricultural capitalists in a generous way, she has suppressed the industrial private sector in the cruellest fashion. This suppression is in the form of controls which place in the hands of the bureaucracy the power tools of permits and licences. This is perhaps the largest tributary to the swelling river of India's black money economy. Capital resources are rapidly going underground in India and they cannot but become stagnant. With about 10 million people in the employ of the Central and State governments and in semi-government bureaucratic establishments, a large proportion of the privileged and semi-privileged classes in India have a direct stake in bureaucratic controls as a vital source of income and power. Civil service is still the largest organized avenue of elite employment in India and the productivity of bureaucracy is always less tangible as compared to agriculture, industry and commerce. This bureaucracy, large in size and long in reach, continues to inhibit and defeat the kind of managerial revolution that alone can pull India out of a static rate of economic growth. Once the banks were nationalised, other controls should have been minimised so that the economy would have reorganized itself under the new conditions. After all, the nationalised banks have to justify their nationalisation by actively re-shaping economic life. Even if they played an aggressive developmental role like the Japanese banks, assuming some policy control over their creditors' ventures, it would be helpful. Taxation cannot be the largest source of revenue in an underdeveloped society. The kind of taxation we have cripples only the salaried executive class which is the backbone of economic activity in India. Unlike government servants, this class cannot hope to earn compensatory pin money by way of bribes to supplement their incomes. Like Lenin's, Mrs Gandhi's NEP has taken a kindly view of agricultural entrepreneurs. But Lenin's Russia did not have such a diversified salaried executive class in the non-government sector as we have in India. Nor did China or Cuba. Even if some sort of Marxist policy is going to be followed by Mrs Gandhi, it will have to be a native Indian innovation based on Marxist methodology. The mistaken assumptions made in India at either extreme of the politico-economic spectrum are due to the effort to base policies on the analogue of highly developed Western industrial capitalism or of one of the many established communist models. In the process, precisely the most talented, skilled, trained and capable section of the elite has been crippled by taxes and a total lack of incentives. The public sector cannot absorb them. The private sector cannot give them further incentives. In a grand attempt to strip the richest of their riches, Mrs Gandhi is only decimating the Indian middle class. The poor remain very much where they were.

The larger the middle class in any society, the more socialist it is. The rich and the poor have to converge towards the middle class. The exploding unemployment amongst educated and trained Indians indicates that it is our potential middle class that is being pushed towards poverty. This waste of national talent is even more criminal than the phenomenon of capital resources going underground. Soon this will blow up into waves of student unrest throughout India and perhaps unprecedented middle and lower management strikes against the top management and similar strikes by middle and lower level public servants. If an Indian revolution is likely, it will have to take some such course. The Marxist misinterpretation of such a phenomenon will be that a section of the middle class has assumed the leadership of a basically proletarian revolution. But this would be obviously wrong. Strike or no strike, the growing middle class Indian apathy to both productivity and politics indicates that the middle class is already dropping out. It may only cling to the status quo. Yet this is the class which is the real strength of any political party or social movement since it alone is articulate, possesses the skills to bring about systematic changes in the government, and has a sharp consciousness of privileges. It is the leadership class.

Victory in the war against Pakistan has made Mrs Gandhi the heroine not only of this class but of all other classes. But if military glory could become a permanent substitute for economic and cultural achievement. India's history will take a different turn. The role of a major power in Asia has already been thrust upon us. Whether we wear its mantle in the Chinese fashion with increasing bluff and chauvinism or, with determined pragmatism, reject all doctrines and ideologies and remain an open and developing society will largely depend on how Mrs Gandhi uses the unchallengeable political power placed in her hands. She has gatecrashed into politics in a most successful way. Will she be able to gatecrash into history with equal success? Her father searched for a liberal, modern socialism but failed to find it because his colleagues were mediocre or hypocritical. The company she keeps will determine Mrs Gandhi's contribution. She has the ability to make decisions and the capacity to execute them. But the quality of her decisions will depend entirely on the sources of ideas and information that she is able to have. In defence and foreign policy it is easier to make decisions and execute them than in the fields of social, cultural and economic policy. For in the latter, the quality of information and concepts matters. Ideological superstitious and doctrinaire soft corners can completely sabotage what seems to be her greatest opportunity yet to earn a permanent place in history.

The elections to the state legislatures, held in the wake of a decisive victory against Pakistan and the creation of Bangladesh, have invested in Mrs Gandhi, greater faith than ever before. There is a strange irony in all those sweeping victories of the new Congress. Mrs Gandhi's camp has attracted all sorts of opportunists ranging from ex-communists of ex-Swatantrites. She has had to make compromises with many of her not-so-radical colleagues who still hold power in their own regions. The situation is extremely tricky. It is quite likely that the new Congress of 1972 contains a greater variety of conflicting interest-groups than it did immediately after the historic crackup at Bangalore. Since in India, today political power is directly translatable into economic power, manipulative entrepreneurs in every sphere of activity are drawn towards the ruling party. This may not prevent Mrs Gandhi from pursuing a misadventurous economic policy. It only means that her policies will continue to benefit those corrupt entrepreneurs who regard politics as the only industry which offers the best monetary gains in India today. After all, even election funds come from the swelling reservoirs of black money. It is black money which is the grease that makes every wheel in Indian public life move. The higher the taxes, the greater will be the incentives to avoid or evade them. The greater the restrictions on private enterprise, the greater will be the use of management skills in evading them. The new class is here to stay and it will co-operate with capitalist speculators, feudal chiefs controlling the rural co-operatives, millionaire smugglers and corrupt top executives. These are the only beneficiaries of the parallel economy and they comprise, by and large, the Establishment.

The concentration of all effective power in New Delhi will only help these interests to flourish. Increasing nationalisation of major sectors of the economy will, in such a situation, hardly help the ruling party to reach its professed socialist goals. In the meantime, the slogan '*garibi hatao*', which was the pivot of Mrs Gandhi's persuasion programme, has heightened public expectations to such a degree that they are likely to create discontent on a scale unwitnessed in India so far. Economic development and economic equity are not related goals, nor are they necessarily compatible. With a massive Malthusian apocalypse looming large ahead of us, our greatest problem is the increasingly disparate ratio between the elites and the masses. A shrinking middle class can lead eventually to bloody chaos. Lethal taxation, rising prices, stagnant wages, increasing unemployment among the educated and the skilled – all these are leading to the decay of the Indian middle class. This is the decay of culture and of creative morale itself. It has already eaten deep into our educational system. It has paralysed the teachers in institutions of learning. Primary and secondary teachers already belong to the lower fringe of the middle class and professors still do not belong to the upper middle class. Thus there are no incentives in education for the educators themselves. There is a brain drain in this vital field. Similar demoralisation is spreading through clerks, lower management cadres, skilled workers and engineers, and other members of the middle class. These are fairly educated or trained people who have some potential productive talent. In a society consisting of the old and new rich and the eternally poor, this dying middle class is our only hope of coping with the enormous challenges of the coming decades. What will be the size of this middle class by 2,000 A.D. when we would be 1,000 million people? Today they are hardly fifteen per cent of the total population at a fair guess even if we consider an income of over Rs. 200 per month as the qualification.

Due to the abortion of land reforms, the growth of an agricultural middle class is also similarly inhibited. This spells due consequences.

When a revolutionary leap is taken from feudalism to socialism, an artificial middle and upper middle class are created, as in the Soviet Union. An artificial middle and upper middle class is the result of party bureaucracy. It has only political competence and competitiveness. Whereas an authentic middle class is the core of a democratically evolving society, and it necessarily moves towards a modern form of socialism as in the Scandinavian societies.

Here, perhaps, is Mrs Gandhi's most unusual chance of creating history by launching a purely Indian cultural revolution. She can initiate a number of infrastructural projects in which a kind of Indian peace corps could be involved. This way, the generation with the greatest and the longest stakes in the future will be involved in a national renaissance. Our periodic spurts of chauvinism show that while we are still immature as a democratic society, we passionately admire the armed forces and even our cricket teams when they score victories. Our achievement consciousness has risen much higher during the last two years. Mrs Gandhi's charisma as well as her style of decision making has something to do with it.

To reduce the number of our future poor, the family planning programme requires to be intensified. The young cultural army could be entrusted with this task. They could also be used as propagandists to persuade people to save, to consume less conspicuously and to use their financial resources productively; this will be a movement aimed at the upper classes as well as at the middle class. They can also man a number of 'management consultancies' operating as a public service to farmers, craftsmen, small scale industrialists, and self-employed people. They can be engaged as social and economic surveyors in backward regions. They can be used for educating adults. A special wing could work on the emancipation of women and another against casteism, communalism and obscurantism.

Such a corps could be organized like an army with standardized uniforms, food and lodging. They could be paid a fixed stipend. Enrolment could be either voluntary or by selective drafting. For example college and university scholarships could be offered to those who agree to work in the corps for two years. Travelling expenses, medical treatment and other fringe benefits could be offered to them. They could also be given leave with full stipend once a year.

By directly involving the younger generation in such a programme, Mrs Gandhi can radically alter the national cultural ethos. It is likely to be something like a peaceful and democratic alternative to a bloody cultural revolution. Members of such corps could be given preference in the administrative service and they may help to cleanse the future administration of corruption.

Similarly, since Mrs Gandhi is almost in a despot's position now, she can afford to remove her ideological blinkers and seek advice from independent experts and thinkers in every field. For instance, if she convenes a national seminar of economists openly to debate policy alternatives she will be able to get out of the ideology bound inbreeding which has been the bane of planning in India. She should similarly listen to other professionals, intellectuals and creative men.

It was all right for an Indira struggling for power to have a secret kitchen cabinet. As an almost all powerful head of the government she must either chase the sinister ambition to total power or give us a real taste of democratic community enterprise in a nation still waiting to experience both genuine democracy and authentic contemporary socialism. Does she have the courage to distribute political power as equitably as she promises to distribute economic power? Has she the bold imagination of a cultural leader enjoying the fruits of the debate of the best minds in India on the one hand, and motivating the younger Indians to lead a cultural revolution on the other? She must remember that she has made people forget her father who had cast an equally powerful spell on the average Indian. She could do this because she simply promised people what they obviously needed and are asking for. But the goods are not easy to deliver. Indian society is so heterogeneous that a Chinese revolution is not possible here. India in 1972 is unlike Russia in 1917. It is not small and purely agrarian like Cuba. It compares with no society in which a communist revolution has taken place. It compares with no other society for that matter. Economically, its problems may look like those of another society. But the diversity of interests and interest-groups, the co-existence of several phases of civilization all at once in the same nation-state, the marked differences among its sub-nationalities, the peculiar impact of a colonial but democratic and English-speaking power's culture on its ruling elite – all these make India the enigmatic and paradoxical nation it is. No single person can try to wield central authority in such a nation without risking loss of power. Mrs Gandhi is too shrewd not to know this. But power such as she holds today has been held by few leaders anywhere in the world. And none of them have wielded it well after losing sight of their opposition or of their colleagues who had the courage to oppose them.

Portrait of the Artist as a Brahmakshatriya Clown

D.

(Quest 76: May-June 1972)

Bhupen Khakhar is a very serious painter who loves making jokes. Most of Bhupen's paintings, like most of his jokes, are profoundly disturbing. They negate the viewer's painfully cultivated reverence for art and give him, instead, a shocking awareness of its unexplored possibilities in contemporary India. Bhupen mimics traditional art; he even emulates vulgar calendar art with ironic meticulousness. He blends savage sarcasm with tender lyricism, deep pathos with defiant humour, unpainterly attitudes with painterly acumen. If it is a joke, then it is a complex joke with a richness of style, a many-fanged pun. He is a metaphysical clown.

At his recent one-man show at Gallery Chemould in Bombay, Bhupen issued a catalogue which will be long remembered as a minor masterpiece in that difficult genre. Art catalogues are meant to entice potential buyers and collectors and to build up a formidably persuasive image of the artist whose work they introduce. Bhupen's catalogue looks like a fifty paisa plastic notebook cum diary such as is sold on the pavements, which in fact it is. Open it and behold the cheerful face of Bhupen – a photograph cut into a round shape – with the slogan, 'Truth is Beauty and beauty is God'! The contents of the catalogue are: 1. Biography, 2. Explanations of the

Paintings, 3. Gratitude. Inside, we see a diagrammatic Khakhar family-tree covering its last three generational branches. And the very first sentence of Bhupen's autobiographical introduction is, 'I am a young Brahmakshatriya.'

The catalogue is great fun. It is profusely illustrated with photographs in which Bhupen has had a field-day posing, often with an appropriately dressed up attractive young woman, as the archetypal analgesic-consumer, filter tipped cigarette-smoker, ex-sufferer from bad breath instantly emancipated by the right toothpaste and also as James Bond.

Coming to the paintings, Bhupen offers – in that order – a 'description of each painting', a 'symbolic interpretation', a 'formal interpretation', and even 'sources'. His tongue-in-cheek thoroughness is utterly unnerving. The sheer nonchalance of the catalogue is absolutely devastating. After reading the catalogue, I looked at the review of the same exhibition in *The Times of India* which was pinned to the Gallery's notice board. The deadly implications of Bhupen's joke cannot escape our art critics. They cannot easily wipe the egg from their painfully bewildered faces.

Bhupen's paintings are based on a very calculated strategy. He makes the assumption that his audience is familiar with traditional Indian miniatures, with vulgar calendar art, with cheap label designs and pictures and also with Henri Rousseau's symbiotic landscapes in which man and plant both appear as the detailed and blowing foliage of the same invisible tree. There is an echo of William Blake in the conception of *Tiger and Stag*. And in his portrait of Nilima Shaikh, Bhupen somehow strikes chords reminiscent of Modigliani, on the one hand, and the early Amrita Sher Gil, on the other, in capturing the strange, essential loneliness of a human face. Some of these are deliberate allusions and quotations, as in literature, made by Bhupen to ramify his own visual statements. But precisely because such disparate elements are brought into one single focus by him, his paintings acquire a very sophisticated ambivalence. The average art audience, with its fixed notions of stylistic categories and modes of expression in painting, is confused and disturbed by such an interpenetration of diverse styles and influences. At the same time, even averagely sensitive viewers can directly apprehend the directness and originality of Bhupen's paintings. I have not seen anything quite like Bhupen's paintings before.

Each of Bhupen's major paintings employs more than two different visual modes and presents their tense interpenetration. The structural norms of traditional Indian miniatures get juxtaposed against human faces painted in a very different tradition; *desi* pop *art* gets placed alongside Rousseauesque trees and foliage. Very mystical and almost mythological mountains and hills, often floating in space with their asymmetrical shape and weight, loom in the background. Bhupen integrates these usually unrelated elements with bold imagination. His paintings often give one the feeling that, among other things, they are a crazy comment on the act of seeing a painting, a learned but esoteric criticism of the art of painting itself as known to the contemporary Indian elite.

Bhupen creates a painting of multiple discord. In an otherwise static and decorative landscape in the fashion of Indian miniatures, Bhupen introduces savage irony and discord as in *Portrait of Shankerbhai V. Patel Near Red Fort*. The lonely figure standing at the right hand bottom corner of a square canvas is in total contrast with the Red Fort in the top left hand quarter of the canvas, the off-centre tree in the right half of the square and slightly above the head of the male human figure, the miniature still life of fruits laid on a table in the bottom left hand quarter of the canvas and the off-centre row of decorative palms and other trees in the left hand half of the canvas. There is a lone palm tree at the bottom, in front of the man, almost at the optical centre of the horizontal lower half of the space which also includes the fruits on the table at its extreme left. Minus the human figure and the fruits on the table, the whole painting would have been a thoroughly familiar formal cliché strongly reminiscent of traditional Indian miniatures. It would have been completely static and decorative. The fruits on the table, by themselves, would have increased the visual weight too much to the extreme left. In fact, it still does so to some extent. But the human figure at the right corner introduces a totally alien element with such a force that, although insignificant in size and mass, it becomes the powerful antithesis of the entire visual mode of the rest of the painting. The details of the man's face and his posture suggest a stern, severe, erect and disciplinarian human personality. This is in total discord with the architectural and natural elements, although the Red Fort, the trees, the well-laid table and the man have all – so to speak – 'correct positions' in their own way.

This gives a clue to most of his other paintings. In *Portraits of Mother and Father Going to Jatra*, the garlanded busts of an old Gujarati papa and mama occupy most of the foreground. In the background, at a vast distance, is a bungalow. In the verandah, we see clearly a young man stretched rigidly in an armchair. It is the son. The entire background is a flat and arid landscape with a few houses and streets and hills in the distance. A few decorative tree shapes appear in the top left hand quarter of the canvas. In *Mrs Nilima Sheikh Looking At Orange Flower,* the female face in the foreground has, for a background, two formal trees at equal distances from the woman's head, buildings and a fairly large hill in the extreme background. *In Factory Strike,* the striking workers occupy the right hand section of the foreground while the factory buildings are diametrically opposite to them in the top right hand quarter of the canvas with an empty truck placed in front. In the background, at the right hand, we see a Mercedes sedan parked near the closed gate and inside the gate are the figures of two well-dressed, proprietorish-looking men standing to attention, watching the strikers. In *Mukubahini Soldier With A Gun*, one sees the portrait of a young man wearing spectacles, and a vest, the bayonet of his gun crossing his vest. The background is an almost childlike panoramic painting of war with houses, professional soldiers in fighting postures, a tank, a mortar, a few airplanes hovering over hills in the farthest distance. At the extreme left hand is a vertical strip showing the Bangle Desh flag. At the extreme right is a similar strip showing the Indian flag. The two vertical strips 'frame' the composition.

All the paintings described so far are somewhat literary in conception. They compel the viewer to make a verbal interpretation of their content, followed by a symbolic interpretation in non-visual terms. The visual ambivalence of Bhupen's paintings is a direct result, one suspects, of his rather un-painterly preoccupation with the possible verbal implications of the pictorial elements used by him and his systematisation of them. He disturbs the viewer on two levels; one of them consists of bringing together mutually unrelated visual modes. The other is the level of quasi-literary pictorial metaphor. Bhupen's metaphorical method completely inhibits his latent powers of direct visual communication which can be felt in his *Old Men Playing Chess* or even in *Tiger and Stag*. The former was his largest canvas showing two tiny human figures of chess players on a white terrace in the right hand section of the foreground and the rest of the painting dominated by a glaring orange desert. But the powerful effect of *Old Men Playing Chess* was somewhat marred by the decorative repetition of too many trees planted in the desert. The other painting I liked, *Tiger and Stag*, was fantastic in conception. Smooth and rounded masses of mountains and trees with detailed foliage (*a la* Rousseau) fused together in a mystical symbiosis lay in the background. In the foreground was a stag being pounded upon by a ferocious tiger. Only, the tiger and the stag were crudely pictorial. The rest of the painting consisted of fluid masses, suggesting mountains and hills and even the trees with detailed foliage emerged out of these masses as if they were living extensions of the latter. The more distant mountains looked curiously as if suspended in space. The painting has the completeness of a strange and disturbing vision. One does not seek to solve its enigma in verbal terms because the visual form is immediately valid, despite its unusualness.

Back to Bhupen's catalogue and one could trace the gimmick to its root, the joke to its serious hard core. Yet, one felt that whether in verbal terms or in pictorial, Bhupen's paintings were neither primarily literary nor essentially painterly. He hasn't exactly fallen between the two stools: he seems to be suspended between them in mid-air, upsetting people on either side.

An Interview with V.S. Naipaul

Adrian Rowe-Evans

(Quest 78: September–October 1972)

'As you get older you begin to write more profoundly: you think less of the way words lie on paper, and more of the meaning.'

Q: Mr Naipaul, the most overwhelming impression I get from your books is of a pursuit of honesty above all things. Is that a fair comment?

Naipaul: I hope so. It's the impression one ought to get from serious writing. The wish to become a writer (which is how we all begin) has been brought about by our reading of other people, which gives us a vision of what a writer is. But then we have to find out what we want to do ourselves, what is our own voice; and that takes time. In my own case it took a lot of time. I had to go through a lot of writing, a lot of work, before I discovered what I really wanted, what I really felt, and how to trust my own reactions and not to prettify them in any way. So you have to discard the vision of yourself as 'a writer', and find out what you want to say, and how you want to say it. For example, when I began reviewing in the *New Statesman* about thirteen years ago, my work was appalling, because I was trying to fill the *persona*, as I conceived it, of 'the reviewer' – and I was writing rubbish. Until one day, in total despair, I tried just writing down what actually occurred in me when I read a particular book. It came out beautifully; the words seemed to write themselves and to sing – and people liked it. It was a great event, the discovery that it was myself and my own views that really mattered.

Q: That was the start. But you were saying that it takes a long time. As you went on, did you feel that you were getting nearer to this honesty, this truth; and to being able to express it?

N: Well yes; you have to. Otherwise you aren't really writing; you're falling into patterns. Even now I can often be seduced into applying a type of dramatic pattern to what I am portraying, so that I falsify the situation as I really perceive it. Or I might be seduced by the rhythm of the words themselves to say something which isn't really what I see. That's what one is fighting against all the time. On the other hand, if I react truly to a situation, I am reacting to what is true about it; I am discovering the truth about it.

Q: Then you believe there is an objective truth?

N: Yes, Provided that one takes every thing into consideration, when one reacts to it.

Q: Integrity? The whole personality reacting to the whole situation?

N: Yes; you're not keeping anything back or glossing over anything or ignoring anything; you're trying to make a whole, an integrity, of it. You have to become adept at looking for the truth of your own response. I think it's much more important for me coming from a place which is not real, a place which is imperfectly made, and a place where people are, really, quite inferior, because they demand so little of themselves. They are colonials, in a type of perpetual colonial situation. Coming from such a society, I didn't really have views of my own: I didn't know what I thought about anything, because the world was out of my hands. So this establishing of a position, and intellectual stance, has come to me quite recently. In writing my first four or five books (including books which perhaps people think of as my big books) I was simply recording my reactions to the world; I hadn't come to any conclusion about it. (It was the reviewers who came to a conclusion!) But since then, through my writing, through the effort honestly to respond, I have begun to have ideas about the world. I have begun to analyse. First of all, the deficiencies of the society from which I came; and then, through that, what goes to make this much more complex society in which I have worked so long.

Q: Is it an advantage, to begin in a simpler society?

N: Well, there are two sides to that. But on balance it is a great disadvantage. A writer floats at the level of his society; you can't have a tree growing in a desert. In Trinidad, in my childhood, there wasn't even a proper general bookshop as you'd understand it. There was nothing like Criticism, naturally. You were doing it all yourself. So there was intellectual isolation, added to the commercial and practical disadvantage of not having an audience that will buy your books or support you as a writer. In that sort of country some people may feel that writing is an aspect of their political assertion, or an aspect of the tourist trade. But that has nothing to do with the real quality of life, or with the liveliness of the culture; it is no substitute for genuine cultural activity; the writer has no living cultural world about him, and has to make his way into another world, one which is entirely alien to him. Imagine a writer like Dostoyevsky, trying to sell his work to, say, the Australians in 1865, and you'll get some idea. Well, when I began writing I believed in the Universality of Art – if one produced a work of art, then there would be universal recognition of it. Now I know that all art is local, a communication between the maker and the receiver of it. They must both have the same equipment.

Q: In The Mimic Men, *one of the characters tries to divide up the world's culture into three groups – those of long, medium and short vision.*

N: Yes, I remember. The people who are going to get things done are those of medium vision. The long-visioned ones, the people who had long vistas of eternity to play with, were so overwhelmed by all that that they weren't going to do much, whereas the short-visioned man, say the hunter in the South American bush who is going to kill an animal and eat it all at once, has no place in his thoughts for anything other than the immediate act.

Q: Does that also mean that the medium-visioned man is more likely to deceive himself? The long-visioned man may be able to escape to a large extent from immediate circumstances and not react to them; he distinguishes completely between the act and the spirit. For the short-visioned man, pursuing his animal, the spirit and the act are the same thing. The medium-visioned man in getting so much done may be bound to compromise and muddle up the spirit and the facts, each for the sake of the other. In other words, the man of action has dirty hands – often bloody hands?

N: No doubt. I often wish I could have been a doer. But then I do have a great distrust of *causes*, simply because they are cause and they have to simplify, to ignore so much. As a man of action one would be continually weakened by harking after the truth, by too-honestly reassessing the situation all the time; so that for example in Africa you can get a profound refusal to acknowledge the realities of the situation; people just push aside the real problems as if they had all been settled. As though the whole history of human deficiencies was entirely explained by an interlude of oppression and prejudice, which have now been removed; any remaining criticism being merely recurrence of prejudice and therefore to be dismissed.

Q: But need all action lead to dishonesty? For example, writers seek their own truth; they describe it, they publish and they influence other people. Is that a form of action?

N: One can only speak for oneself. I've gone through a great deal of anguish to achieve a certain kind of understanding of the world. If one could pass that on to one's readers, so that if, for example, one of them wanted to be a writer, he could start working at a much higher level than I did, or could more easily avoid the sort of nonsensical ideas that I had – then one would feel one had acted, and feel rewarded.

Q: You must surely have such a feeling. But there must be dangers in it, too; for instance, I've come across African writers who were altogether too anxious to develop 'African writing', so that those who came after them could more easily be better 'African writers'. I always felt they were mistaken.

N: Why yes, it is a mistake. Of course there are good writers who are African. Chinua Achebe is a grand writer by most people's standards, but he is not published in his own country. His work needs the blessing of the foreign market, and for a very good reason; because the local society doesn't have any body of judgement as yet; it can't trust itself yet to make its own appraisals.

Q: But surely that must come, eventually?

N: I think it will be a long process. One of the terrible things about being a Colonial, as I have said, is that you must accept so many things as coming from a great wonderful source outside yourself and outside the people you know, outside the society you've grown up in. That can only be repaired by a sense of responsibility, which is what the colonial doesn't have. Responsibility for the other man. As a colonial, you must first seek to remove yourself from what you know, and become blest personally, before you can become responsible for others.

Q: Are you laying too much stress on that? There are so many forms of dependence and dependence always breeds irresponsibility. You don't feel that a writer brought up in an 'advanced' society can be equally dependent, and equally emasculated by the dependence?

N: Perhaps. But as I said before, a writer should have a dialogue with his own society and to have writers who have got one eye on an exterior world is to use writers as a tourist trade, as a cultural or political weapon, and perhaps this is why so little of that kind of writing has made any impact. To write honestly about one's own undeveloped society would offend it; ten years ago in Trinidad, if you called an African 'black', the man was mortally offended. In those days many people were offended by writings. Now, I get letters from tourist boards asking if my work can be used, and so forth. What future can there be for a kind of writing which can be treated, or used like that?

Q: All right. But it isn't only Africans who abuse African writers. There plenty of people, literary people, in this country who say to them: 'Please do something absolutely African! Bring a stream into our culture, wake us up, make us sexually alive or something of the kind; we are short of something we think you might have; please tell us what it is!'

N: Well, yes. But I think not many people set up that cry. Intelligent people, people of refined intellect always long for writers who will help them to place themselves in the world. And they won't get that sort of help from the sort of self-conscious 'African writing' which is obsessed with tribal *mores*, for instance. Yet that is part of the trap in which Africa has found itself; a lot of this writing is being encouraged by publishers who have London bases, who are hoping to exploit a new market. They are publishing work on London presses, which wouldn't stand a chance in the regular market. Cotton goods for the natives. And I think it's being promoted by a salesman who thinks he understands the native.

Q: Neo-colonial?

N: Certainly. Because that seems to be one of Africa's fundamental functions – to keep on being a perpetual colony; a little treasure-house; a playground for people who want a play-culture, a play-industry, a play-development.

Q: I think you're right. Even the Romans, so long ago said Ex-Africa semper aliquid novi – *a new thing, not in the intellectual sense, but in the sense of a play thing, a conversation-piece, something amusing and strange?*

N: Yes, and I find that I have no desire to understand Africa in that way. I don't want to be given descriptions of exotic manners: I want writing, somehow, to light up my position as a fairly educated man who has thought a lot about the world in the twentieth century. If people think that something cruder is needed, then they are greatly mistaken. On the contrary, a greater depth and subtlety is needed, and I wonder whether it could come from the Africa of today. We want more realism, not more romanticism; the time for that is finished. When I was in East Africa recently, I was constantly hearing on every side that this was the decade of Africa, as if Africa were suddenly going to become technically, educationally, culturally advanced, and politically powerful. I was appalled to find that people who possessed a few tiny skills were so convinced that they, simple people, were carrying the seeds of all civilization, all culture, all literature, all technology. That was rubbish. If you buy a typewriter made in Germany and, using Swedish paper, type out a story in English, which you then submit to a London paper – how can you regard yourself as a local writer? The idea that all the things which have been presented to Africa have somehow been already assimilated and appropriated by Africa, is the most hideous type of conning. It may be a willing conning, voluntary on both sides, but it remains conning.

Q: But what is the alternative? What should I do, if I'm an African and I feel the urge to write?

N: It's easier to say what he shouldn't do. I do feel, very strongly, that Art is one and indivisible, and there is no point in a writer, whether he comes from Africa or anywhere else, doing today what Dickens or Tolstoy did a hundred years ago. African writers can't cover all that ground again. On the other hand, to encourage a young man merely to write nostalgically about tribal life is really slightly ridiculous. A man must write to report his whole response to the world; not because it would be nice to do something for the prestige of his country.

Q: So the dilemma is rather like the political one. You said somewhere, speaking of political action, that it is the very reason which makes the political movement possible, which also makes it futile. The fact that you can succeed along these lines, destroys the very meaning of success.

N: Yes, Revolutions can come about very easily in undeveloped societies, precisely because there is so little understanding of the society even as it is; so little intellectual base. And of course for that reason, the result of the revolution is nothing. Nothing has changed; the deficiencies remain, they remain un-analysed; and the response is the same; the march, the borrowed ideas, the refusal to understand what makes a whole society – or a whole world.

Q: What about the coming generations? You wrote once about the particular dishonesties of youth: its pathetic eagerness to embrace the apparent solution, the sham idea.

N: You mean in Universities? Yes, when they join political movements one suspects it's just part of pretending to be adult, pretending to be responsible, pretending to be grown-up.

Q: Well, there's terrible irony about student life nowadays. On the one hand, you're trying hard to develop your mind, to widen its grasp, to make understanding more complex and subtle. On the other, you must have answers now, simple answers which will give you the power, the passion, that you hope will make a grown man of you. You can't grow up, in fact, because you too desperately want to.

N: Yes, and then you get the creation of the myths, which people will cling to, however absurd they are. Take a place like Trinidad, where they talk about Black Power and appear to believe in the ridiculous idea that there is somehow a great movement in the world, for black people only. It's a kind of hysteria, which can happen easily enough in places where people feel that they are on the other side of the real world. You do, from time to time, get these movements which promise Jerusalem. In about 1836 there was an ex-slave, called Daga, who thought he would walk back across the Atlantic Ocean to Africa, and he did have a little following; there was a mutiny that was quelled. A hundred years later there was a sort of holy man who formed a movement, created a strike in the oil-fields – again Jerusalem didn't come. Then, more recently, you had Dr Eric Williams, operating at an entirely different level, introducing people to politics and the hope of political redemption. Now, fourteen years later, it's Black Power, offering salvation again. The hysteria recurs, but the situation doesn't change. Black Power is a great mirage, and I fear it will end badly.

Q: Harsh words. Yet I can't think of you as a harsh person; for me, gentleness pervades your work. You are gentle to your characters, and gentleness is one way of finding out the truth about them. On the other hand you do want the truth, and that implies a certain ruthlessness. If there a conflict between the loving approach and what one might call the surgical approach to character?

N: Interesting question. One can't be entirely sympathetic; one must have views; one must do more than merely respond emotionally; I can get angry, impatient, like anyone else; I can be irritated, bored – but you can't turn any of that into writing. So you have to make a conscious effort to render your emotions into something which is more logical, which makes more sense, but which is more, and not less, true. But, although you can't use the shallower emotions, they are of great value in getting you started. I may sit down in enormous rage to write something; I might even begin in terms of caricature and animosity; but in the course of writing, something will happen. That side of me, that comes out in the writing, is the better side, and better not because it's nicer, but because it's truer; it's the side that in one's rage one might wish to forget. I began my recent book about Africa with a great hatred of everyone, of the entire continent; and that had to be refined away, giving place to comprehension. If one wasn't angry, wasn't upset, one wouldn't want to write. On the other hand it isn't possible to get anything down until you've made sense of it, made a whole of it. To write one has to use all the senses; all the pores must be open.

Q: Then you see writing as a refining, perfecting process. Do you believe in human perfectibility – are you an optimist?

N: I'm not sure. I think I do like to look for the seeds of regeneration in a situation; I long to find what is good and hopeful and really do hope that by the most brutal sort of analysis one is possibly opening up the situation to some sort of action; an action which is not based on self-deception.

Q: Your books do, I think, show a faith in humanity. You seem to be able to approach all characters without fear, and fear is what distorts and depresses people's writing, as well as their lives. Does fear play no part in your life?

N: Well, you know, the nature of the life which I have imposed on myself has been one of physical non-involvement. I have never had to work for hire; I made a vow at an early age never to work, never to become involved with people in that way. That has given me a freedom from people, from entanglements, from rivalries, from competition. I have no enemies, no rivals, no masters; I fear no one. I used to have a sense of doom, which is not like fear; an irrational feeling of disaster about to come. But if a writer comes to fearing a principle, or a kind of person which he thinks is inimical to him, it must of course upset his writing. I think it is this fear which underlies a good deal of what is called satire, or the attempt to be contemptuous of what you fear. That can't be done; rather you will be contemptuous of what you love, and exalt what you fear. This is particularly true of a lot of American writing. But I have been spared that particular kind of distortion. I come from a small society; I was aware that I had no influence in the world; I was apart from it. And then I belonged to a minority group, I moved away, became a foreigner, became a writer; you see the degrees of removal from direct involvement, from direct fear.

Q: I wonder how far the achievement of a comprehensive world-view tends to cast out fear! Perfect knowledge; or perfect love, as the Bible puts it; casteth out fear. But that might well lead to another kind of fear – the sense of doom you mentioned; the fear of the disintegration of the familiar structure. Our worldviews, our patterns of life, get out of date, and then we look to the artist to re-compose them; to make a new pattern which is somehow continuous with the old one.

N: Yes, one must make a pattern of one's observations, one's daily distress; one's daily knowledge of homelessness, placelessness; one's lack of representation in the world; one's lack of status. These, for me, are not just ideas; when I talk about being an exile or a refugee I'm not just using a metaphor, I'm speaking literally. If daily one lives with this, then daily one has to incorporate the experience into something bigger. Because one doesn't have a side, doesn't have a country, doesn't have a community; one is entirely an individual. A person in this position risks going mad; I have seen it happen to others – it is a bizarre and frightening thing, and it is one of the great strands in my own writing. I long to be happy, I still have a great instinct towards great happiness and delight and pleasure. And the idea was that the work would absorb and obliterate all my distress, continually. At first I looked for that release in humour, but as the horizon of my writing expanded I sought to reconstruct my disintegrated society, to impose order on the world, to seek patterns, to tell myself – this is what happens when people are strong; this is what happens when people are weak. I had to find that degree of intellectual comfort, or I would have gone mad.

Q: But surely everyone has to recreate the world for himself? Even someone whose background seems very intelligible and constant?

N: Perhaps, I really cannot enter into the mind of a person for whom the world seems intelligible and constant; to whom their own situation appears normal and common. I think they too must have difficulty in understanding my work – for example many people in this country seem to think that when I am writing about, say Trinidad, I am writing about a society which is a quaint version of their own, with all its order and its regularities. Very few people in any kind of society can see anything except in terms of their own society. But it is worse in a society which is so culturally undeveloped and depressed that people can't even see things in terms of their own society, because that society is not a coherent, understandable thing. Yet someone like myself, who has developed his gift in another place and is now trying to express the problem of his own background, will be speaking in a way that the man at home simply cannot follow.

Q: I can't help being reminded of the same sentiments being expressed by writers who came from provincial backgrounds in England – say D.H. Lawrence or Wells.

N: Colonial places are less than provincial. The province, you see, implies the existence of the metropolis; access to it, a partaking of the culture, the wealth, the political life of the metropolis, in however remote a way. In the colonial situation, one has only the most fleeting of glimpses.

Q: But is it rarely different? In your own case, you had to adopt, to write from the metropolitan point of view. Yet you have built up an enormous admiration and respect, in this country, for your work. One feels that your readers must have more than a superficial knowledge of what you are talking about. Isn't it true that every human being, in the deepest psychological sense, is an exile in the world; that he is oppressed by the incoherence of the world, and the futility of trying to understand, or to be understood? And isn't that the starting-point of all great writers, wherever they come from?

N: That may be so. But in many practical ways, things are harder for the writer who comes from an undeveloped society. Apart from the sheer difficulty of getting away in order to get started at all. I can't help thinking that I might have had much greater success, been much better understood as a writer, if I had been born in England. As it is, one has no cultural attaches in a hundred countries pushing one's work. If I have a reputation in England, well, it has taken a long time. I have been writing now for more then sixteen years. I have done nothing else. It has been a life's dedication, and I think an American, even a British, French, German writer, would scoff at the rewards I have received. I don't mean only in money, either; I am concerned about the dignity of myself as a writer, and when I find people offending the status of my writing I can get very angry. I have to protect that status, because there's no one protecting it for me.

Q: Of course, you must feel entirely responsible for the protection of your work, because it is art, as well as for any other reason. And I have noticed that even people like yourself, who are of great and assured stature, can never feel in their hearts secure in that stature.

N: No, writers can never really know where they stand. How can you know? You do your work; you do it over long periods of total isolation; in the end you get your notices and your royalty statements, and apart from that, you know nothing. It's a rather horrible life, you know; you can become awfully self-centred, and you get easily perturbed. You become crankish – I used to wonder why the writers I got to know were all so crankish. I understand more and more; it's the sheer solitude and loneliness of the job! They all long for human contact; they want to see people, to be in touch with people who are reading their work. And in a writer's life that's almost impossible. I've just been talking to someone, someone young, who does a little writing, and I was trying to analyse the difference between myself and her. I think it is that my panic is always greater than hers – and all my work begins in panic. Which she, maybe, can only simulate. But with me it's entirely real and lasts for a long time. It's a feeling you can't communicate, explain to other people; you can assuage it only by starting to write, even though your mind is as blank as the next man's; you have no consciousness of anything you want to say. And then, given the panic, the next thing you need is a certain fortitude, a tenacity, to carry on through all the ups and downs. They are very painful, these downs that can hit you even when the work is quite advanced, and you have been practicing for a long time. They can last for years, literally; and the only cure is to lever yourself out of it, bodily, by sheer work. And sheer luck – you need luck all the time.

Q: So you begin with panic. Then you need guts to keep going, and even then you won't get there unless you're lucky.

N: Yes, look at the book I've just finished. Such a strange process. It came out of this great panic; it went on in this enormous pain and anguish for months and months. It took fourteens months to write, and in that time I did nothing else except two articles. And yet, now that it's over I feel, as I feel about all of my work, that in a way I was not really responsible. I feel I was just a little vessel into which the thing was gradually and painfully distilled. In the end I just feel responsible for judgement, not the gifts of imagination and language; I feel that many fortuitous things have conspired to produce those gifts; all that is out of my hands.

Q: Are you saying that the writing and the judgement of it are entirely separate processes? That they are almost being carried out by separate people?

N: Not quite. If one could feel that the judging process was completely austere and objective, that would be wonderful. But it isn't quite so. In all my work, in all my life, I will always be dependent on outside opinion and encouragement. In the early stages of any piece of work I have no idea of the value of anything

I am writing, and I need to be told: 'It's good – you must go on!' Sometimes I don't go on, because I really know it's bad. Even when it isn't, there are lots of false starts and disappointments. Within oneself, both the executant and the judge become very tired, dispirited; one longs for more help, support, encouragement. Then, towards the end, even that's no good; everything depends on working, holding on, husbanding your slender resources of energy. You're on your own, then. You feel threatened; every distraction, every single thing, can lessen your creative capacity. You have to be so very careful, over the last few months.

Q: Carrying this vessel with extreme care. You make it seem an anxious, painful, laborious life. Do you sometimes want to get away from it, or can you not imagine a life that was not writing?

N: Oh, yes! About ten years ago, when I was going through a time of really monstrous labour which extended over nearly three years; my biggest book; I used to console myself with that fantasy. I would imagine that a man would come to me and say. I'll give you a million pounds, if only you will stop writing; you must not finish this book. But I knew I would have to say, No. Well, today I wouldn't say no. I've changed. As you get older you begin to write more profoundly; you are thinking less of the way the words lie on the paper, and more of the meanings, the timing, the emphasis – not thinking of style or language at all; just the effect. That has been my concern for so long; to achieve a writing which is perfectly *transparent*.

Q: Isn't that perhaps simply the result of developing skill, of mastery?

N: No. I know now that I can always write, turn out a good paragraph. But the result is that I am more concerned with thought, meaning, philosophy. Having discovered and then overcome the great difficulty of writing, one is confronted with the intractable nature of truth, the difficulty of one's own position, the futility of expression, the absence of reward for art, and the fact that all one is now really seeking, a true communication with a society, is non-existent and impossible. Having discovered that in absolute terms there is a great hollowness in my endeavour. I might be prepared to give it up; I might even do it easily. But yet, paradoxically, I do retain a real concern for the dignity of my past work. I would like that to remain as it was done; to do nothing that would in any way belittle it. I would not like to start writing for the sake of money. If it could be done, I would like just to go silent; there have been many writers who, after a great success, have just gone silent. They are without the panic. And the early unspecific promptings to create a work of art, of wanting to be a writer, of wishing to be famous; they have all gone as well. Writing has become a much more practical business; communication of ideas; one's ambition has grown up into a simple desire to help – to serve.

Q: But in your own case there can be no question that you help, you serve. There's the work, it does influence people, it illuminates their lives, the service continues. You are almost saying that the body of your accomplished work has an independent existence now; it is something which you can look at apart from yourself. You can think of its future, apart from your own future.

N: Yes, I've lost both the arrogance and the humility that I once had. When I was young, I suppose the only people I really worshipped and adored were rich people, and writers. I no longer worship the rich, and I now respect writers, enormously respect them; but I don't worship them. I remember in those days, seeing people like Joyce Carey at Oxford. They seemed magical men, and I just stared at them. Magic, magic, magic! But now, having known the sheer labour of the work, the hours that go into it, and the years; the trials and failures that nobody sees; I am left with respect, for their work and my own.

Q: When you speak of your respect for writers, how wide is that term? Would it include people who are not novelists, who deal in smaller forms? Poets, for example?

N: Well, I began with the simple idea of the writer as the creator of the work of art. That is something I have moved away from, now. There is the other idea of the writer as the communicator, the moulder, rather than the man of imagination, and that is what interests me now. I suppose that doesn't mean that there is no place for imagination to play in literature. I used to be very humble about poetry. I felt that because my background had been deficient there was something there I didn't, couldn't, understand. Now I feel that most people called poets are tiny people, with tiny thoughts. I don't like technical virtuosity, and I am not interested in trivial. Again, I admire journalism; a strong and immediate response to the world; I admire it in principle but in practice I can't say that I have ever looked at any journalist with the kind of respect that I feel for a great magician figure, the wise man.

Q: Do you think the whole future of the novel, as well as your own future as novelist, will be tending further away from the romantic, the imaginative function?

N: Yes, I do. You might go on needlessly writing 'creative' novels, if you believe that the framework of an ordered social exists, so that after a disturbance there is calm, and all crises fall back into the great underlying calm. But that no longer exists for most people, so that kind of imaginative work is of less and less use to them. They live in a disordered and fast-changing world, and they need help in grasping understanding it, controlling it. And that is how the writer will serve them.

V.S. Naipaul's books include *The Mystic Masseur* (1957; John Llewellyn Reys Memorial Prize), *The Suffrage of Elvira* (1958), *Miguel Street* (1959; Somerset Maugham Award), *A House for Mr Biswas* (1961), *The Middle Passage* (1962), *Mr Stone and the Knights Companion* (1963; Hawthornden Prize), *An Area of Darkness* (1964), *A Flag on the Island* (1967), *The Mimic Men* (1967; W.H. Smith Award), *In a Free State* (1971; Booker Award), all originally published by Andre Deutsch and also available as Penguin paperbacks.

From Sex to Samadhi

D.

(Quest 78: September–October 1972)

Bhagwan Rajneesh is a merry old sage. He views some of the standard Hindu sins with aggressive benevolence; the simple experience of copulation, for example. This is one experience which the Hindu mind of today regards with anxiety, suspicion, prurient interest, shame, helpless search for justification and mystification. Rajneesh simplifies the task of contemporary Hindus by advising them to copulate till they reach the state of *samadhi*, provided they regulate their breathing during the action in a manner prescribed by him. This, indeed, is a great breakthrough. Vatsyayana, our own drill-master in sexual matters for centuries, permitted smoking and reading during intercourse only to promise a prosaic prolongation of the experience. It was different with the authentic *tantriks*. *Tantra* involves much more than copulation and slow breathing. True *tantriks* are required to follow precise ritual steps, recite mantras with a concentrated awareness of their significance, treat one's sexual partner as a symbol of a cosmic principle and to regard the sexual act itself as a ritual sacrifice. Ancient Hindu sexual epicureanism and traditional Hindu sexual yoga are both carefully cultivated and difficult to practice. The problem, therefore, was how to make things easy for the contemporary upper class Hindus; or rather, how to enable them to justify the embarrassing joys of making love. Bhagwan Rajneesh has solved this problem and his solution is amongst the merriest since the stethoscope was invented.

Only the most outstanding among men and women require no justification for sex except its own unique joy. The Judaeo-Christian morality of the West, inverted during this century, still seeks a justification for the sex act. It is an *act*. And therefore, perhaps, a *bill* must precede it. That explains why a combination of oriental sexual recipes and scrap-book mysticism can create best-sellers in Europe and America. In the East, the situation was different; sex was forgotten, only apologies for it remained.

Bhagwan Rajneesh has published a book (I have seen its Hindi version) which purports to be a guide to the attainment of *samadhi* through sexual intercourse. *Samadhi*, unlike sex, is hardly a popular sport. In fact, *samadhi* is respectable precisely because it seems so difficult to achieve. The concept of *samadhi* is today coated with thick lore and fuzzy descriptions. Reading Marathi newspapers in Bombay, for example, one becomes aware of the dangerous proportions which do-it-yourself mysticism has reached. Week after week, amateur mystics and ambitious neo-gurus or their chelas write enthusiastic features on these subjects. The urban, upper-class contemporary Hindu thus continues to caress his own adolescent ego. Social, political, economic and cultural issues occupy him less. During the last few months, I have come across a number of bored and well to do people who enthusiastically talk of the liberating influence of gurus like Rajneesh. His benevolent view of their hitherto repressed libidos, one suspects, contributes in no mean measure to their rabid enthusiasm for liberation.

Going through the Hindi version of Rajneesh's book on *samadhi* through coitus, I was impressed by the guru's deft technique of persuasion. He already has the advantage of having most of his audience on his side. He tells them not to repress their natural instincts but to use them as means to self-realization. This is hardly an original piece of advice. Nor is it controversial. However, the combination of such non-controversial altruism with glib spiritual terminology and attractively irrational, analogical reasoning creates a concoction which is as fascinating as it is repulsive. Sexual orgasms can be described quite accurately in precise physiological terms. They can also be described less precisely but very evocatively as a kind of aesthetic experience. But to propose that sexual intercourse is a means to *samadhi* requires, to demand the least, a precise definition of the term 'samadhi'. Otherwise, there is nothing to prevent anyone from proclaiming that *samadhi* is merely a seven-letter synonym for sex. Rajneesh proceeds to prescribe a certain breathing exercise, to be performed during coitus, which delays male ejaculation and female orgasm. Indeed, he believes that this exercise can prolong copulation for hours and in this state of prolonged coupling, the sexual partners begin to experience *samadhi*.

Even this is not an original idea. Without ever seeking *samadhi*, people all over the world have been seeking techniques of prolonging the sex act. When the American mass media, using Kinsey's findings, instilled into the American male a disquieting anxiety about female orgasm, several consequences followed. Research in the sexual syndrome became more and more microscopic since sex was a major item of consumption in affluent societies endowed with increasingly tense periods of leisure which they were not adequately trained to use creatively. People have used narcotics as aphrodisiacs psychologically to prolong intercourse. They have practised suspension of copular movement, concentration on subjects remote from erotic pleasure, smoking *hookahs* and reading, one supposes, even such abstruse works as *The Critique of Pure Reason* so as to delay the erotic climax. Why not use the idea of *samadhi*, which is suitably vague anyway?

Rajneesh's success seems to be based on two fundamental needs of his clientele. Being mostly modern Hindus, they need even their spiritualism to be vicarious. They feel guilty about pure sex. They also feel helpless vis-à-vis pure spiritualism. After the decline of the *tantrik* tradition, there remained no living branch of the Hindu tradition which did not exclude sex from its notion of virtuous life. In fact, erotically we have already become as moronic as the Judaeo-Christian West. Those Hindus who chose the path of *moksha* were all ascetics who denied sensuous values and earthly emotions and practised varieties of yoga requiring a rigorous discipline. The yogic idea of *samadhi* sounds like reward through punishment. Rajneesh tries to simplify matters and makes it rewards all the way. Contrary to popular prejudice, the role of coitus in *tantrik* practices is not as simple as Rajneesh's breathing exercise.

It is quite easy to understand why a certain class of persons provide Rajneesh the bulk of his followers. But in this context it is also painful to remember that the late Raghunath Dhondo Karve, the pioneer crusader for a more rational approach to sex, was persecuted by the same Hindus and died almost penniless. On the other hand, the finest contemporary mind engaged in research on esoteric Hindu traditions, Agehananda Bharati, had to leave India and is not allowed to return till this date. Agehananda's fault is that he is an Austrian and while we proudly export gurus to the West, our innate racism does not permit us to accept the notion that a white foreigner can be an authentic Hindu *sannyasi*. Agehananda's *tantricism* is suspected by illiterate Hindus. Commercial gurus, on the other hand, are not only tolerated but enthusiastically followed.

As for R.D. Karve, he was a rationalist who attacked the very institution of gurus. A dedicated sex educationist, Karve battled for all his life with thick-skulled but socially more powerful Maharashtrians. His ideas were so radical that some of them would still create a debate anywhere in the world. Karve was against the mystification of erotic experience and he tried to teach the Maharashtrians the importance of a scientific attitude to life. Long before the advent of Women's Lib, Karve wrote lucid and sharp editorials against the exploitation of the female by the male and raised basic questions about the structure of the family itself. At the same time, without resorting to any voodoo, he propagated rational sexology and techniques for increasing erotic efficiency and pleasure.

The question is not whether or not to have sex; the question is simply whether to wear the concept of *samadhi* like a condom while doing so.

Letters re: From Sex to Samadhi
(Quest 79: November-December 1972)

Sir,

I object strongly to the 'comment' on Bhagwan Shree Rajneesh by 'D', in your September-October 1972 issue, entitled 'From Sex to Samadhi'. The ignorance of the author about spiritual matters is appalling. Furthermore, the author was so cowardly that he did not even give his full name. For the record, I would like to set the facts straight.

Obsession with sex has long been known to be a barrier to deep meditation – the process which leads one to *Samadhi* (Cosmic Consciousness). A society which teaches suppression of the sexual instinct only creates an obsession with it. The sexually suppressed individual is constantly desiring, then fighting with his desires and suppressing them, then again desiring and again fighting. Thus his mind is constantly on sex, and yet he is often hypocrite enough to claim he is spiritual because he forces himself not to indulge in it.

Such a person can never go into deep meditation, let alone achieve a glimpse of *Samadhi*. A truly spiritual person must be mentally free of sex and relaxed enough in body and mind so that deep meditation can flow in him. This is obviously not the case with suppressed persons, and anyone can observe that inwardly they are filled with tension and a deep violence.

So how does one achieve a relaxed mind free of sex? Bhagwan Shree Rajneesh teaches that the first step towards *Samadhi* is total acceptance of oneself as one is, including total acceptance of one's sexuality, rather than an endless struggle that leads to an obsession with it. And by totally accepting it, one has taken the first step towards transcending it. Only then is one ready for meditation.

The sexual suppression enforced over many centuries in both East and West has only created a perverted, obsessed mind, says Bhagwan Rajneesh. His aim is to help individuals overcome this so they can begin their journey towards *Samadhi*. And most likely, the one who is preoccupied with sex will have to go through a stage of experiencing it fully in order to overcome it; otherwise he will remain obsessed. Experiencing it fully, says Bhagwan Rajneesh, means understanding it as the first Diviner gift given to man, living it out in a deep, loving way and seeing one's partner as a form of the Divine. One who retains antagonistic attitudes towards it cannot live it fully or know it as a Divine gift.

After passing through such a stage of experiencing it fully, one becomes unconcerned with it, and begins to feel a new door opening in him where his inner energy can travel – towards love and compassion, towards deep meditation, and finally, towards *Samadhi* which is towards the Divine.

So Bhagwan Rajneesh's plea is a sane, sensible attitude towards sex – one of acceptance, so that one can transcend it for once and all and become a true *sadhak*. And among his followers many relaxed, meditative, blissful persons can be found who have overcome sex and gone deep enough in meditation to have experienced glimpses of *Samadhi*. With proper training from a true master like Bhagwan Rajneesh, the experience of a glimpse of *Samadhi* is not so elusive as the author thinks.

Bombay

Ma Ananda Prem

For Neo-Sannyas International.

'Absolutely' First Class!

There's class about Air-India

Come and belong to the most exclusive club in the air. You could be sitting next to men who move big business, or a famous Nobel prize winner you've been reading about. You could be saying "Kanpai" (Cheers!) in sparkling Japanese style, or discussing behind the scenes with a lovely, French starlet!

Air-India's First Class

Our air hostesses speak five languages very fluently: Hindi, English, French, Foods and Wines.

You'll discover the sensual pleasures of eating when you plunge your fork into a luscious 'Poulet Chasseur' or discuss Plato over a plate of exotic caviar. And when you lift your frosted glass of champagne and look into the warm eyes of a beautiful air hostess you'll know you have really lived. (There's enough to get you high and happy!) Later when (if) you leave your super cushioned throne, you can saunter up to the suave Maharajah Lounge, our plush 747 clubroom. Play a round of bridge, make important contacts, clinch a deal.

Or do something you've always wanted to—nothing!

You haven't really flown if you haven't flown Air-India. First Class.

Be a first-class Air-Indian

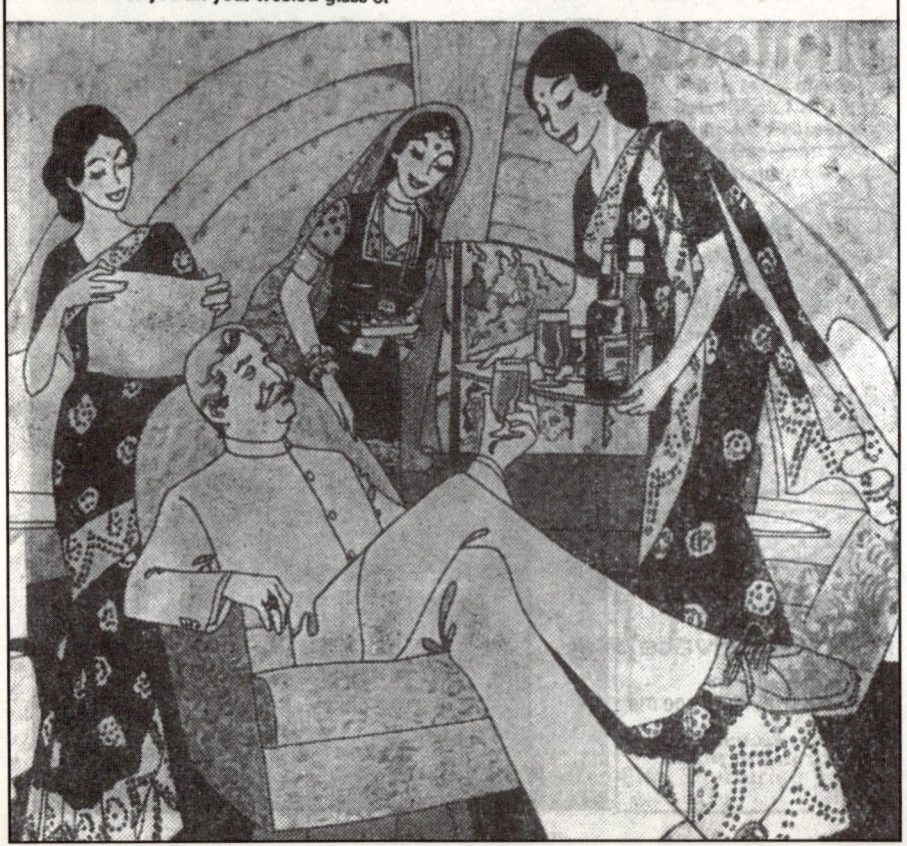

The Married Woman and Our Sex Morality

Sudhir Chandra

(Quest 81: March–April 1973)

The evolution of a morality represents the response of a community to the prevailing social forces. But these forces emerged before their prevalence is realized by men. This creates a time lag between the emergence of a force and the human responses it elicits. Still more time elapses before the community exposed to this particular force is able to react to it is the form of new mores or institutions, or adjustment in the mores and institutions already in existence. Such reactions, however, are not necessarily the result of a conscious comprehension of an external stimulant. A community may also evolve, unconsciously, mores or institutions in order to adjust itself to forces of which it is not consciously aware. In either case, the time lag does exist, though its duration may vary.

The morality of the day is thus aimed to cope with forces that are not strictly contemporary, unless these have continued unchanged for some time, a supposition ruled out by the flux of modern life. To say this is not to conceive of a situation with no time lag between morality and its sociological background. The point simply offers a constant justification for changes in a given morality.

It is desirable, at the same time, to appreciate the limited, though now increasing, role of human volition in the development of morality. On the conscious plane, different persons advance different moral ideas on the basis of different considerations. But 'society' adopts as its morality only a particular combination of these conflicting ideas. In the complex dynamics of morality, the rationality of a model occupies only a minor place. However, the rapid advance of education and individualism promises to make both human volition and rationality major factors in the formulation of social morality.

Considering the vital role of sex in the formation of human personality and relationships, three considerations seem to be specially important for discussing a sex morality for our society. These are: perpetuation of the species, development of a wholesome personality by men and women, and the creation of a harmonious relationship among members of the family, particularly between husband and wife. It will be admitted, except by a few who are easily led into conjuring up visions of sexual promiscuity, that our present sex morality fulfils only the first of the three main purposes. To the extent that the other two functions are not performed by it, this morality curbs or deforms the development of personality and creates unhealthy tensions which colour, for worse, the total outlook of people. It is arguable if a morality that has not proved conducive to the development of a healthy mind is not really, though imperceptibly, tearing the social fabric. In any case, a morality that can only perpetuate the species is not to be preferred to one that is capable of performing all the three functions.

Marriage forms the bedrock of sex morality in 'civilised' societies. In our society it has been invested with such sanctity as to make sex outside of marriage taboo. Circumstances are however changing, more so in the bigger cities, making varying degrees of pre-marital sex acceptable. But the hangover of the traditional expectation in this respect continues; and even educated, 'progressive' men will, at the bottom of their hearts, want to get a 'pure' spouse. As things are at the moment in the metropolitan cities, it is generally expected that the girl must have had, at the time of her marriage, some amount of experience stopping short of actual sexual intercourse.

But the state of affairs continues to be as of old in regard to the married woman. This is a sensitive issue on which discussion is made particularly difficult by the fact that even in the West, from where we take most of our advanced ideas, morality – at least in theory – is rigid about fidelity in marriage. It is seldom realized that to taboo all extra-marital relations is anachronistic, being inconsonant with a finer conception of love, sex and fidelity, as also with the frequency and freedom of contact between men and women.

Love knows no monogamy. Nor does sex. But social organisation needs order and discipline. Marriage represents a compromise between the instinctual urge of the individual and the demand of the group. Yet society being largely man-dominated, other channels than marriage were devised for the satisfaction of his 'polygamous instinct'. Women were confined to the *zenana*, and their extra-marital exploits were surreptitious and, perhaps, rare. In the course of time opinion gained ground that men, unlike women, were polygamous, thus relieving them of whatever tension they might suffer from as a result of being unfaithful to their wives and society.

Age-old belief apart, no person with a passing acquaintance with human psychology would hold that man alone, and not woman, is polygamous. It is only traditional brain-washing that instills into the Indian woman a certain aversion to sexual commerce with a person other than her husband. So far this sort of training has been sufficiently efficacious. But it can hardly be expected to keep on delivering the goods in the face of the lure of modern ideas and facilities.

What happens today? The married woman is not condemned to the *zenana*. She often works in an office. She moves about with her husband and meets his friends. She develops a liking for a particular person. As the opportunities of meeting are not limited, the initial liking keeps on incubating until it blossoms into love. The response from the other side has throughout been encouraging. The dilemma is complete, and excruciating. Her whole being is rent into two. On the one hand is her allegiance to her husband and children, and to her traditional ideas which loudly proclaim such names as Sita and Savitri into her ears; on the other hand is her loyalty to her new love, which her feelings and her knowledge tell her is not something to be ashamed of. After a period of terrifying uncertainty, she makes a decision. It can be either to go ahead with love without leaving her family whom she so dearly loves, or to sacrifice her love for the outsider for the sake of the family.

In either case, the dilemma continues for the married woman. She cannot, all her feelings and knowledge notwithstanding, extricate herself from a feeling of guilt as easily as man can since he has the advantage of centuries of extra-marital intimacy. Sooner or later it takes a heavy toll of the woman's peace of mind. Then starts pressing the urgency of confessing everything to her husband, an urgency that is matched only by the terror of actually doing so. But she cannot live without telling. And in nine cases out of ten, divorce follows disclosure for the simple reason that most men continue to be rooted in the traditional morality about sex. Even if they are able to grasp intellectually the naturalness of a woman loving two persons at the same time, their emotional reflexes make them recoil from the idea of living together with such a woman. Love seems badly unhinged. Even in the odd case that the husband decides to let things on as if nothing had happened, things just do not remain as they were before the disclosure. A shadow falls between the man and his wife, an invisible shadow that they always sense and rarely talk about. But much depends on their love and genuine rationality as to how little they would be bothered by the shadow.

In case the woman decides to withdraw before having gone the whole hog, the tension of a vigorous passion left unfulfilled as a result of her moral cowardice or uncertainty haunts her persistently. She tends to become easily irritable, and to that extent her love for the family diminishes. She tries to defend herself against herself by reminding herself of her venerable ideals. But this brings solace only at the conscious level. In such a case the woman does not even confide to her husband the fact of the sprouting but snapped relationship between her and the man. Something vital between the couple is lost forever which, unknown to at least one and often to both, manifests itself in a thousand apparently irrational irritations.

Let us admit as a hard reality the fact that both sexual love and sexual passion can spasmodically afflict either the married man or the married woman. The case for the married man has for long been settled. But the case for the married woman is hardly even broached though the very fact of the allowances we have started making for the unmarried girl would suggest that willy-nilly we have recognised the existence of sex outside of marriage for women also. This is not enough; nor is it consistent. As contacts between the sexes become freer and the risks of sexual union progressively disappear, and ideas of freedom and equality gain a firmer ground, extra-marital intimacy, like pre-marital contacts, would irresistibly tend to increase.

Neither prohibition nor divorce offers a solution. The one is impracticable and the other undesirable. So long as extra-marital intimacy on the part of the woman does not bring about a decrease in her love for her family, divorce would be an unwelcome imposition for her. The husband who insists on treating this temporary 'deviation' as an adequate reason for divorce must learn not to curb his own extra-marital craving, but to take those of his wife in his stride. This is undoubtedly a difficult proposition. But this is the only solution to a stable social order. This will also produce healthy human minds that are capable of enjoying life on terms of mutuality without denying to others what they themselves must have. For in the traditional morality, the health and happiness of the male population, irrespective of its real worth, is ensured at the cost of the female.

Intellectual acceptance of certain ideas does not immediately alter the emotional reactions of a person. That becomes possible only after a period of emotional gestation of this intellectual conception. In this gestation, unlike biological gestation, a few emotional shocks leading to a de-romanticisation of reality contribute to the health of the progeny. These shocks need not be contrived; the changing social scene will take care to deliver them in plenty. What we must consciously do is to analyse the problem from a rational point of view, the essence of which lies in the dictum; do unto others as you would be done by them.

Social norms, in fact, are disregarded by either the rebel or the hypocrite. In one case the disregard is open and sustained by reasons for the departure from tradition. In the other case, it is clandestine and within the framework of the traditional norms. The hypocrite swears by the very norms that he secretly defies. But even in the case of the rebel the open defiance may be, it often is, accompanied by greater or less personal inability to absorb completely and in one stroke the psycho-emotional-attitudinal implications of the break with tradition. The complex delicacy of the structure of human behaviour refuses to undergo an abrupt command adjustment. Prisoners of the unconscious as even the rebels are, there remains a gap between their principles or actions and their intimate emotional reactions.

The ideal sex morality of the future will grant to both men and women the maximum freedom compatible with the maintenance of social stability. Marriage will provide its base, and itself rest on love and trust between the contracting parties. Sex will be prohibited when backed by force or fraud. This may sound rather romantic. If so, it differs from the romantic puerility of traditional sex morality in the sense that, being based on the recognition of a universal reality, it saves men and women the torture of discovering and failing to resist something they had been taught was sinful. An attitude towards sex as embodied in such ideas may not be forthcoming in the near future. But an uninhibited discussion of the issues involved will save an increasing number of people from unnecessary tension and help them lead fuller, happier and more honest lives. In doing this, it will also facilitate the incorporation of these ideas into the sex morality of the day after, if not of tomorrow.

But can this happen? Is such a morality compatible with the possessive nature of the human male and female? Will it not, though intended to create wholesome personalities, deprive men and women of whatever little enjoyment they manage to get in spite, if not because, of the existing sex morality?

Such suspicions about the soundness of a new sex morality stem from a failing that all generations of mankind have more or less shared the tendency to treat their own behaviour patterns as manifestive of human nature. Despite spectacular advances in 'comparative' knowledge we tend to ignore, with much less justification than our forbears had, the distinction between that part of human nature which is instinctive and that which is acquired.

Most of what is called human nature represents the ossification of certain attitudes which having once been evolved, are transmitted from generation to generation within a particular community. These attitudes sustain the basic values upon which different social institutions rest. And these institutions, as we noticed at the outset, emerge in response to the needs of a community. This is the process by which 'human nature' is moulded in accordance with the socio-economic needs of a community in such a way as to ensure that the artificial sanctions employed to sustain the social order are obeyed with the minimum possible damage to the human personality. It is this malleability of the human mind that has enabled man to construct increasingly complex social artifacts without being deprived of his sanity.

Nothing instinctive in human nature demands monopoly in sex. What is instinctive should apply universally to the species. But the existence of polygamy – polygamy as well as polyandry – and of the sex values that go along with it would show that attitudes towards sex have differed in our own country from community to community and from time to time, though they appear to the members of the community in which they prevail as being rooted in human nature, Amba, Kunti, Madri and Draupadi would indicate that even in a society which had begun to frown on pre-marital sex, extra-marital sex was permitted for acquiring progeny. This was not a compulsion which, while submitted to as a bitter necessity, would undermine love between husband and wife. Even pre-marital sex was not altogether condemned. The status of Satyavati and Kunti, if we see through the literary stratagem employed to shield the latter, would suggest this. But the most remarkable, perhaps, is the fact of Pandu forcing Kunti to have sex even after she had given him a son. Equally remarkable is Kunti's gesture in sending Madri to have sex though she herself had been asked by Pandu to give him children. It would seem that Pandu, incapable of satisfying his wives, was gracious enough to let them have what he knew was essentially an enjoyment of life; though, it seems further, Kunti and Madri were considerate enough to their impotent husband not to let him feel that they were eager to have this kind of enjoyment. In fact, even in our own times, we have tribes and castes and classes among whom the 'possessive instinct' does not constitute an essential ingredient of 'human nature' and sex outside of marriage is not tabooed.

It is neither easy nor necessary to trace the process of change in the Indian attitude towards sex over the centuries. By the 19th century, however, these attitudes had frozen into the moulds acquired by us and now exposed to mounting external pressure. The widow remarriage movement typifies our middle class attitudes towards sex. May and December marriages being very common and the old groom unlikely to outlive the young bride, nineteenth century Hindu society always had thousands of virgin widows. It was only these widows, whose marriage had not been consummated, that were considered legitimate for remarriage by even the more ardent among the champions of widow remarriage. This could not be otherwise, given the middle class obsession with getting a spouse untouched and unsullied by another man. The situation is but marginally different today. Yet the fact that some of us as individuals have moved considerably away from the traditional attitudes, no matter whether impelled by a conviction or by compulsion, confirms that human nature is changeable, though the process takes time.

Because it is an acquired habit of mind and not an instinct it is possible for us, as it has been possible for others in earlier and our own times, to get rid of the tendency to own and monopolise the object of our desire. That this may not happen in our own generation offers no reason against envisaging a sex morality that would dispense with the habit of *possessing* a wife or a husband.

The choice, to begin with, is not so much for society as for individual men and women to make. They may try to react creatively, insofar as their own life and relationships are concerned, to the need for consciously restructuring on a more rational basis our sex institutions and the values underlying them. The alternative to this conscious restructuring is to be dragged along uncertainly by the force of changed circumstances. The new morality practised by these individuals may provide a model to be emulated by the others in society whose initial resistance to the shifting of attitudes from the traditional grooves would give way only after gradual acquaintance with the alternative attitudes.

The discovery of self is a terrifying business. We, each one of us, invent a world of delusions in order to be able to forget realities that are inconvenient and shameful to us. The urges we feel almost every day of our life fail to disabuse us of faith in the mythical instincts of possession and jealousy. We do desire connections that militate against monogamy. The private worlds of our private desires – often hidden from our own view – constitute, even when not one of these desires is fulfilled, a solid proof against the instinctiveness of the instinct of possession.

But there are occasions when the continuance of traditional concepts in one segment of human life may impede the adjustment of attitudes in another sphere in accordance with changing realities. Our thinking and attitudes are so powerfully influenced by values and concepts that emanate from and perpetuate the institution of property as to render extremely difficult the evolution of a sex morality that is consonant with equality between the sexes and with the situation produced by easy prevention of the biological consequences of mating.

However, the implementation of sex ethic based on the acceptance of extramarital intimacy is not necessarily dependent on the abolition of the institution of private property. It is possible, after all, to treat only things and not human beings as property. If this can happen in regard to slaves, it can also happen in regard to husband and wife; particularly because, it may be reiterated, the desire to monopolise is the result of an acquired habit and not of an instinct.

Future generations may do away with the very institution of marriage. But the stability of society at the moment needs the continuance of this institution. Since polygamy is likely to do greater violence to the existing human nature in our society, maybe the least objectionable and the most rational and practicable alternative at the moment would be to accept extra-marital sex.

Marriage and Morals: Updating the Pativrata Prostitute

Dilip Chitre

(Quest 82: May-June 1973)

The *Padmapurana* defines a *pativrata* as the wife who works like a slave, gives sexual pleasure like a prostitute, feeds her husband as his own mother would and, in times of crisis, acts as a wise counsellor to him (*Padmapurana*, 'Srstikhanda', 37-55). One finds that this is still the view of most Hindu males whatever emblems of modernity they wear and display. Hence one would argue that the Hindu male, even within his own family, needs a slave and a prostitute. He also needs, perennially, a mother to feed him and is incapable of making decisions on his own in times of crisis. This is empirically verifiable.

What kind of modern sex morality will be acceptable to such a creature? Frankly, none. Most answers to the questions raised by Sudhir Chandra (*Quest* 81) will be *bona fide* answers only to the extent the Hindu male is cured of his neurotic obscurantism. The situation has not altered with the emergence of university educated or working women in the Indian cities. A working woman, even when she works outside the home, is a neo-slave; as for her pleasure-giving in bed, judging by the obvious violence and frigidity in most marital relationships, the wife can hardly come up to the high Hindu expectations based on the courtesan norm. Hence the popularity of the para-prostitute such as the dancing school girl, the steno-typist with a lower-middle class background or even the better-off career girl. In a pseudo-modernised metropolis like Bombay, one witnesses the paradox of the pseudo-liberated woman who is only a more sophisticated slave-prostitute. High caste Hindu vocabulary always consists of euphemisms for a variety of evils that comprise their value-system.

However, even in the age of contraceptives and a little more honesty in interpersonal relationships than we have been used to, 'adultery' provokes hostile or ambivalent responses. Married men as well as married women regard marriage as the permanent sacrifice of extra-marital erotic interest. The result is repression which is violent to oneself and since the behaviour of repressed persons is often too demanding vis-à-vis others it is also violence to others.

However, unless a society as a whole evolves a cultural strategy by which natural polygamistic tendencies are accommodated within normal behaviour, neither men nor women are likely to have a more satisfactory erotic life. Such a strategy cannot be evolved in the abstract when we are dealing with a specific society, in this case, contemporary Hindu society.

The ruling sex in Hindu society (regardless of a few exceptions) has always been the male. If one is allowed to coin a scholarly-sounding word, one might call it *androcentric*. Since the family, as a microcosmic political unit, is itself androcentric the female is the exploited class which must serve the needs of the male alone. Even as a glorified slave, woman is a slave in the last analysis. Unmarried working girls from middle class urban Hindu families illustrate this slavery very well. While their incomes sustain the family, they do not enjoy to a corresponding degree decision-making powers within the family. Married working women fare even worse. In a majority of cases they work overtime, partly doing household chores in addition to working full time in an office. Thus they are under greater physical and mental stress although they tend to be taken for granted by their husbands. To this severe stress, one must add the effects of severe emotional monotony in the life of any working person who is not fully identified with her job and who is not allowed by her present situation to develop a variety of heterosexual interpersonal relationships. Therefore, young working women from Hindu middle class families have a rather drab life ahead of them. The situation becomes more painful and complicated for them since most of them have studied at co-educational institutions and have been exposed to the idea of individual freedom as a value. Girls have a greater number of heterosexual contacts and chances of forming friendships while they are adolescent or near-adult students than in their later life. One may take it that married life is an anti-climax for most of them since their high expectations are systematically frustrated in a marriage based on sexual fidelity and economic slavery.

However, the questions raised by Sudhir Chandra need to be placed in the context of erotic satisfaction and erotic relationships. And, further, we should separate erotic relationships from heterosexual interpersonal relationships which have a wider significance. If we do so, the following alternatives emerge:

(i) an erotic contact between a woman and a man which is not based on mutual erotic satisfaction but is based rather on individual pleasure of either or both of the partners;

(ii) an erotic relationship between a man and a woman based on reciprocal pleasure and erotic understanding;

(iii) an interpersonal relationship or friendship between a man and a woman who are erotically not interested in each other; and

(iv) an interpersonal relationship or friendship between a man and a woman in which mutual eroticism also plays a part.

It is easy to see that these four broad types of heterosexual involvement include both erotic and non-erotic involvement. Moreover, I have attempted here to distinguish between an involvement, which can be subjective to a great degree, and a relationship, which is reciprocal and is therefore based on a mutually acceptable code of communication and behaviour.

With the contract of marriage, several other factors enter the picture of a relationship or an involvement. In most monogamous cultures, the married couple has an identity of their own, apart from the partners in marriage. The couple is superior to both husband and wife as individuals and hence both the partners are advised to act in the supreme interest of their contractual relationship even when this tends to thwart their individual purposes. Why? The couple is a firm which produces children and propagates the family tribe in competition with other couples. The couple must therefore cease to subscribe to polygamy and the principle of continuous and spontaneous natural selection and, instead, promote family loyalty as their supreme interest. Even in modern monogamous societies which have become permissive in sex, children are identified as a product of the couple and hence, in divorce suits, the possession of children is often the main bone of contention. A certain androcentric logic is also used here; most such societies are patrilineal, i.e., woman is only the reproductive plant and man, the manufacturer of children (his brand carrying his *corporate symbol*), is the real social entrepreneur. I am using this industrial-economic metaphor deliberately. In the Prophet Muhammad's time, woman was the soil and man the tiller. Even the Hindus, from Manu till the emergence of Raja Rammohun Roy, regarded woman as an instrument for producing children and externally belonging to one man. *Sutee* was the destruction of the plant after its proprietor's death. Earlier, and even later, remarriage was condoned only on reproduction grounds.

The problems raised by Sudhir Chandra exist because of several reasons. I recognise some of them as follows:

(a) Men would like to continue to dominate and exploit women, however devious and sophisticated their methods, and hence women continue to be alienated from their true potential as individual human beings.

(b) Behind every successful marriage lies the sordid story of a woman's deprivation of her individuality unless the marriage is based on sexual equality, which is rare in modern society even outside India.

(c) Even non-productive erotic relationships between men and women are governed by the norms of marital relationships, i.e. if a woman sleeps with a man other than her husband her 'infidelity' is considered symbolic of her repudiation of marriage *in toto*. All this means that woman is an object; she shares no human identity with man.

I do not, therefore, see any perfect solution to these problems in the near future. At the same time, I expect extra-marital (and pre-marital) heterosexual relationships to become an increasingly real problem for middle class urban Indians. If I am asked why I give this class dimension to the problem, my answer, I am afraid, will be cryptic: the upper and the lower classes do not perceive the need for cultural liberation as much as the middle class does. For, it is the middle class which creates culture norms and it is both fanatically orthodox in their preservation and enthusiastically modern in changing them.

Mohammed Ali Jinnah:
A Study in Hatred

Hamid Dalwai
Translated from Marathi by Dilip Chitre

(Quest 84: September-October 1973)

The emergence of Bangladesh was the final blow to Mohamed Ali Jinnah's grand political dream. Curiously, contemporary apologists for Jinnah still refuse to accept this reality. Now that Jinnah's delusions, which were shared by his followers in the Indian sub-continent, have been shattered, Jinnah's apologists are trying to give him a new image. They now suggest that Jinnah's politics was not communal and, on the contrary, he was indeed a humanist. Some of them even go to the extent of suggesting that Jinnah combined the great qualities of Christ and the Buddha, of Asoka and Akbar. The naïveté of these interpretations should be obvious to any dispassionate student of history. But an objective approach to history is foreign to our intellectual tradition. Nor is this unique to the sub-continent; all other Asian societies share with us in varying degrees a lack of scientific approach to social, cultural and political history.

Dr Ambedkar once observed that a man should be judged by his professions when one found no evidence to the contrary in what he did; however, if his actions differed from his words, he should be judged by what he did rather than by what he said. One may go further and suggest that in judging the work of a leader, the public consequences of the policies advocated by him or the movements led by him should also be taken into account.

Coming to Jinnah and Gandhi, it is necessary to make an impartial assessment of the roles they played in shaping the politics of the sub-continent. The partition of the sub-continent has exacted a terrible cost in human terms. Worse still, pre-partition communal politics continue to pollute the mind of the average Indian Muslim and communal tensions still prevail. When an attempt is made to assess the work of the two leaders, emotional biases and prejudices often lurk beneath seemingly rational comment and interpretation.

However, once it is granted that Jinnah and Gandhi were the chief protagonists in the dramatic events that took place in the sub-continent, the two leaders' work will have to be evaluated in terms of the public consequences of their ideas and actions, as well as in terms of those events themselves and the motive forces which historically made them possible. This is hardly being attempted today. Otherwise, it would be difficult to explain why prolific nonsense is dished out under the respectable labels of analysis and comment on contemporary political events, social tensions, political leadership, foreign policy and other interrelated subjects.

Jinnah's political career can be broadly divided into three phases. In the first phase, Jinnah belonged to both the Indian National Congress and the Muslim League. In the second phase, between 1920 and 1947, he was the leader of the Muslim League and, as such, of the Muslim community in the sub-continent. The third and last phase is Jinnah's leadership of Pakistan from August 1947 to September 1948, when he died.

Jinnah's career shows contradictions, changing postures, and varying roles during these three phases. Through these emerges the graph of an evolving human personality as well as the complex pattern of a political career. If one were to assume that Jinnah was evolving towards a certain personality, then the apparent contradictions in his various postures and roles are easily resolved. For the thread of Muslim communalism can be shown to run continuously through all the three phases of Jinnah's political career. In fact, his career was founded on Muslim communalism and with this foundation it always remained consistent. This proposition, if shown to be correct, would suggest that those who see some contradictions in Jinnah's role in different periods are unable to see what a single minded and dedicated communalist he always was.

From the outset, the real bone of contention between Jinnah and the Congress leaders had been the nature of Hindu-Muslim relations. Jinnah and the Congress could find no common ground for a compromise only because their concepts of Hindu-Muslim relations different and were mutually exclusive. Till the bitter end, Jinnah consistently adhered to the view that the Muslim community should have a specially privileged position. Till 1940 he demanded such a privileged position as a price for agreeing to an undivided India. When he realized that the Congress was not prepared to pay this price, he started demanding a separate state for the Muslims. There is no real contradiction between these two stands because the specially privileged position for the Muslims demanded by Jinnah was only a characteristic expression of the separatist attitude of the Muslim elite in India. A separate homeland for the Muslims was not demanded merely because of the Congress refusal to grant a privileged position to the Muslims in undivided India; separatist politics is a permanent feature of the tradition of Islam itself and Jinnah's earlier demand for a privileged position was only a symptom of this chronic affliction. It is for this reason that Muslim demands were continuously multiplying and finally Jinnah went to the extent of demanding a fifty per cent share in power for the twenty-five per cent (Muslim) population of India. It should also be noted that these demands increased in direct proportion to the rights conceded by the British government to Indians.

There is a certain pattern underlying Jinnah's demands at various times. This pattern can be explained in terms of certain characteristics of Islam, its traditional ideology, and its characteristic expression among Indian Muslims. If between 1916 and 1947 Jinnah's demands increased so phenomenally, the reason is not to be found in Jinnah's earlier 'flexibility' and his later 'helpless desperation'. The fact was that the Hindus had nothing to gain nor did Jinnah have anything to lose in 1916 and for some time later. It was only when the Hindus made some gains that Jinnah also made his own demands in proportion to them. Similarly, the apologia that Jinnah became a separatist only because a political solution to Muslim demands was not found represents a rather shallow view of history. As a matter of fact, the Congress under Tilak had made a pact with the Muslim League in 1916. Those who blame Gandhi and Nehru for their failure to solve the communal problem invariably avoid explaining why Jinnah did not change his position after this pact. Jinnah's apologists always claim that he was eager to befriend the Hindus and wage a united struggle against the British. According to them, it was Gandhi and Nehru who refused to make the necessary compromise with Jinnah. If this were correct, after the Lucknow Pact of 1916 we should have found Jinnah right in the centre of the battlefield fighting the British. However, even after this major compromise by the Hindus, there is hardly any evidence of Jinnah's fighting the British. On the contrary, it appears that during this intervening period. Jinnah was making an assessment of what the British were likely to concede and what share of these concessions the Muslims should demand. And when it was apparent that the British were going to concede further reforms, Jinnah came out with his famous 14-point demand.

In a sense it is true that if Gandhi and Nehru had satisfied Jinnah's demands, partition would have been avoided. But then it was not the prime objective of Gandhi and Nehru to avoid partition at *any* cost. If *any* cost were to be paid for avoiding partition, every Indian could have been converted to either Islam or Hinduism to achieve such a goal. Alternatively, Muslims could have been given a fifty per cent share in political power for avoiding partition. Or partition could have been avoided by declaring the Muslim League flag as India's national flag and Urdu the national language of India. These 'simple' but high-cost solutions were hardly realistic.

The Hindus and the Muslims settled in the sub-continent in a certain chronological sequence, and for certain historical reasons the Muslims remained a minority. When a nation is formed, the relationship between the minorities and the majority is based on certain criteria. When a modern democratic nation is formed, the relationship between a minority and the majority is based on secular, democratic principles. Jinnah rejected both secularism and democracy in deciding a basis for Hindu-Muslim relations in India. One can understand this as part of politics, but when a minority claims special rights in relation to the majority as the price of unity, the unity itself is precarious and permanently in peril. Gandhi and Nehru had enough political insight to understand this. They saw that a compromise with Jinnah's separatism would not lead to a strong and united nation. Lasting unity could have been achieved only if Jinnah were to give up his separatist doctrine in favour of the modern concept of territorial nationalism on a secular and democratic basis. Jinnah did not compromise because he knew the Muslims well. Even if he had made a compromise, the Muslims would not have accepted it. It was a vicious circle. After all, leaders are only symbols of the aspirations of their followers. They cannot aspire for anything very different from what their supporters do. The price individuals have to pay in order to become leaders of the masses is that the leader can only act in a manner acceptable to his followers. Therefore, in fairness to Jinnah, one must concede that he only did what the Muslims wanted their leader to do. When Jinnah belonged to the Congress, he had very few Muslim followers. The moment he assumed a rigid anti-Hindu posture, the Muslim community started revering him as the Quaide-e-Azam. This phenomenon will have to be explained in sociological terms since one is considering Jinnah not as a person but as a leader of the Muslims.

Indian intellectuals are fond of 'Gandhi-whipping'. When some contemporary problem cannot be easily solved, they resort to this favourite ritual. Indian intellectuals have not actively contributed much to the shaping of the nation and its society; hence the false intellectual heroism that makes them blame Gandhi as the source of all the ills of India. It is no surprise that Muslim propagandists in India, who still are ardent followers of Jinnah, join the chorus of those Indian intellectuals who continue to attack Gandhi. They attack Gandhi as a Hindu revivalist and claim that Jinnah was more modern than Gandhi but was driven, in sheer desperation, to use the same revivalist methods and resort to political separatism as a reaction to Gandhi's revivalism.

Now the term 'revivalist' has a specific connotation. A revivalist tries to chain society to a traditional religious ethos. Gandhi did the opposite of this. He was the first Indian leader to launch a mass movement against untouchability which shook the very foundations of the traditional caste system. He attacked the narrow world-view of the Hindus and tried to give the Hindu religion itself a new humanistic spirit. When Gandhi said, 'I am a good Hindu and so I am a good Muslim', he did not merely imply that all religions were equal. He also meant that unless man became a good man he could not become a good Hindu or a good Muslim. It is true that Gandhi employed Hindu religious symbols in order to convert Hindu society into a more humanitarian people. However, this cannot be described as a revivalist activity by any stretch of imagination. When British socialists used Christian religious idiom in order to attract public support for the socialist movement, nobody ever described them as religious revivalists. If Gandhi were to be dismissed as a revivalist simply because he used religious symbolism in order to appeal to the latent sense of human values among the Hindus, it would be as absurd as dismissing the Red Cross and its good work on the ground that the Red Cross was founded by the Church. Simplistic logic of this kind may even lead to ridiculous conclusions such as 'Hitler was a secularist' or 'Jesus Christ was a revivalist'.

Those who argue in this manner imply that Muslim communalism has always been a reaction to Hindu communalism. This thesis can be questioned on empirical grounds. If we were to accept this contention, it would be impossible for us to explain why, after the creation of a Pakistan based on the separate religious identity of the Muslims, Gandhi and Nehru did not become rank communalists accepting a Hindu revivalist value system, instead of the secularism and humanism that they always cherished. It would also be impossible to explain why the forces of Hindu communalism are still unable to wipe out the forces of secularism in India.

Some people defend Jinnah as if he were accused of having been a champion of Muslim theocracy. However, no one has ever accused him of having tried to establish the sovereignty of the *Shariat*. Jinnah demanded a separate state not because he wanted to establish a Muslim theocracy but precisely because a Muslim theocracy would not have served his own interests. He founded Pakistan on the basis of Muslim communalism and not on the basis of Islam. It was the *ulema* who wanted to establish a Muslim theocracy in the whole of India and who, therefore, were opposed to partition. The *ulema* were prepared to wait in view of this long-term objective. They were prepared to work within the framework of equality guaranteed by Gandhi and Nehru and were confident that, working within this framework, they could gradually bring about the sovereignty of the *Shariat* in India. There could be no agreement between Jinnah and the *ulema* because Jinnah wanted power for the Muslims immediately since power was his primary goal. The goal of the *ulema*, on the other hand, was primarily religious. There was thus a conflict of interest between the two. Jinnah might have wanted the Muslims to be supreme in an undivided India. However, his political instinct told him that with seventy-five per cent of the population of the sub-continent being Hindu, it would have been extremely difficult for the Muslims to enjoy supreme power in undivided India. Hence he invented his principle of parity. He saw the possibility of the Muslim minority in India ruling the Hindu majority in the three-point plan of the Cabinet Mission. He accepted this plan because it would have not only enabled the Muslims to enjoy political power in the Muslim-majority provinces but also to get a fifty per cent representation at the Centre, thus allowing them to rule over the Hindu majority. Frank Moraes has observed that Jinnah wanted to use 'Muslim India' and 'Princely India' as counterweights against 'Hindu India'. It would be interesting if Jinnah's apologists tried to prove that Jinnah was flexible, compromising and non-communal since he accepted this formula while Nehru was communal, narrow-minded and short-sighted because he rejected it.

Jinnah's apologists always avoid explaining Jinnah's peculiar stance about the Princely States. According to the Cabinet Mission formula, the Princely States were to comprise a separate political group. Jinnah's view was that they should remain a separate entity. In fact, Jinnah persistently opposed the demands of the subjects of the Princely States for more rights for themselves. If the Cabinet Mission formula had been accepted and the people of the Princely States had then demanded democratic rule, or if the people of some Princely States were to demand a merger with the neighbouring British-ruled parts of India, insoluble problems would have been created. Would a linguistic re-organisation of the provinces have been possible after accepting the Cabinet Mission formula? Could the State of Hyderabad have been reorganized according to the wishes of the various linguistic groups there? Jinnah's apologists avoid even a consideration of such questions. It is true that once Nehru rejected the Cabinet Mission plan, partition was proposed and Jinnah accepted it reluctantly as the last resort. However, just because Jinnah rejected partition it does not logically follow that he was a secular nationalist. He preferred the Cabinet Mission plan to partition because the former would have enabled the Muslims to exercise hegemony over the Hindus. If this were not possible, then Jinnah wanted partition. It is clear from the stand that Jinnah took on various occasions that he did not wish the Muslims to remain in an India where all human beings were equal. He wanted them to be more than equal in relation to the Hindus.

On the eve of partition Jinnah made a speech in the Constituent Assembly of Pakistan which is often quoted as evidence of his secularism. Even if one assumes that this speech reflected Jinnah's honest views, it is hardly sufficient to prove that he was a secularist. All that it would mean is that after having established a state in which

Muslims were supreme, Jinnah wanted the new state to have a secular administration. Jinnah's position here can be understood in terms of the historical tradition of the Islamic world. Wherever the Muslims lack a decisive majority and cannot monopolise state power, they refuse to identify themselves with the nation. Thailand, Ethiopia and the Philippines, all of which have a sizable Muslim minority like India, face the same problem of Muslim separatism refusing to accept any national identity based on secular or non-communal principles. On the other hand, wherever Muslims come to power by virtue of a majority, they try to combine communalism with territorial nationalism. Those who try to absolve Jinnah of communalism by pointing to his pre-partition politics and his post-partition proclamation of secular administration should judge him in the light of this historic motivation, of which there are several examples in the Islamic world. Once this is done, it would be obvious that while Jinnah was not a champion of theocracy, his political separatism was based on a religious identity and falls perfectly within the collectivist religious traditions of Islam.

I stated in the beginning that the ultimate evaluation of Gandhi and Jinnah will have to be done in the context of the history of the sub-continent. These two leaders were instrumental in the creation of two different sets of principles. Muslim intellectuals say that Gandhi's India is 'revivalist.' They also take pains to point out that Jinnah was a 'secularist'. But there is an obvious paradox here, which they refuse to see. In Gandhi's 'revivalist' India the minorities can at least survive, and the country has a secular Constitution. It has launched a great experiment to build a modern nation. In spite of sixteen languages – all equal – and nearly eight hundred dialects, this multi-racial and multi-religious nation is still integrated. The women of this nation have the franchise without having had to struggle for it. Democracy has so far been a successful experiment and social transformation is attempted here with peaceful means. Inspired by Gandhi, men like Jayaprakash Narayan have been striving to promote among the people an awareness of fundamental rights and to create a liberal and humanistic ethos. This is the India described as 'revivalist' by Muslim intellectuals. On the other hand, Jinnah whom they characterise as a modern and secular leader created a Pakistan which has moved in an anti-secular and anti-democratic direction. Within barely two months of its creation, fifty per cent of the Hindu minority in that country was forced to leave it. The narrow and rigid traditions of Islam were increasingly strengthened;

the state itself became Islamic with no trace of democracy and can still not find its national identity. It is curious that this difference should be so persistently overlooked. We evaluate individuals in the context of historical events and their consequences. Therefore we blame the leaders of the French Revolution for the terrible slaughter that followed it. When we evaluate Lenin we do so in the context of the Russian experiment to transform a traditional social order and we evaluate Gandhi's leadership with reference to our successes and failures during the past twenty-five years. Why should we make an exception in Jinnah's case? If Jinnah was a modern secular democrat, why did his Pakistan become a country which could not have adult franchise and whose politics has all along been founded solely on blind hatred of the Hindus? Obviously, Jinnah's apologists lack either understanding or integrity.

I am of the view that these issues should not be discussed merely in the context of Jinnah's demand for a separate state of Pakistan. The means adopted by him to achieve this end are equally relevant. Jinnah systematically encouraged riots and mass violence. At the press conference where he gave the call for the 'direct action' of 1946, Jinnah said: 'I am not going to discuss the ethics of violence and nonviolence.' His colleagues openly threatened mass murders until the demand for Pakistan was conceded. This is not a question limited to a discussion of whether violent means were justified in view of the end. One can understand an armed struggle to reach a particular goal. But this was hardly an armed struggle. It was genocide based on blind hatred and contempt for human life itself. The victims were innocent millions and these communal riots were used as a means of political blackmail as much as of intimidation of innocent people. After the Calcutta riots, Jinnah laid the blame squarely on his political opponents and went to the length of saying that these riots were engineered by those who wanted to malign the Muslims and the Muslim League. Later, when after the riots of Noakhali the Hindus hit back in Bihar, Jinnah demanded a massive population transfer. In an interview with the British journalist, Norman Cliff, he stated that the Hindus and Muslims were not only separate communities but were also antagonistic and no amount of statesmanship would enable them to live together in peace.

It is argued that Jinnah changed this position as soon as Pakistan came into being. This is erroneous. Jinnah gave up his insistence on an exchange of population only when he found that Pakistan would not have the size and area he had hoped for. The moment he recognised that forty million Muslims would still have to live in India after the creation of Pakistan, he declared that Pakistan would be a secular state.

Jinnah's attitude towards the minorities in Pakistan also needs to be scrutinised. Jinnah led Pakistan for thirteen months after its inception. During this period, there were widespread communal riots in Pakistan and there is no evidence that Jinnah ever blamed the Muslims for their role in these riots. Thirteen months is a sufficiently long period for studying the gap between Jinnah's professed policy towards the minorities and the practice of his government and people. It was during this period that all the Hindus of West Pakistan were forced out of that country. Therefore, Jinnah's speech in the Constituent Assembly of Pakistan provides no criterion for testing his claim to have been a secularist; it would also be necessary to establish that Jinnah made some concrete efforts to protect the religious minorities of Pakistan. During the communal riots in Pakistan, not once did he step out of the Governor-General's residence. On the contrary, as soon as he learnt about Gandhi's assassination, he was so much worried about the possibility of a similar fate overtaking him that he ordered a strong wall to be built in the backyard of his mansion. These facts suggest that he was either a moral coward or a political hypocrite, if not both. In either case, it is clear that Jinnah's concern for human values was rather weak.

All that Jinnah's apologists cite as evidence of his secularism and liberalism are a few remarks he made to some Hindus who met him. It is absurd to expect Jinnah frankly to admit to them that he wanted to drive the Hindus out of Pakistan. On the other hand, it is pertinent to examine his private conversations with his colleagues on this subject. Once this is done, it may be easier to point to the yawning gap between his precept and practice. Jinnah's innermost attitude is revealed in what he said to Choudhury Khaliq-uz-Zaman, one of his close colleagues who after the partition of the sub-continent became leader of the Muslim League in India. At that time, Pakistan had alleged that India was systematically exterminating its Muslims. Khaliq-uz-Zaman pointed out that communal riots had taken place in *both* Pakistan as well as India. Later, Khaliq-uz-Zaman and Suhrawardy tried to persuade Jinnah and Gandhi to issue a joint appeal to the communities in both the countries. Gandhi agreed to sign such an appeal. Suhrawardy and Khaliq-uz-Zaman then went to

Karachi to seek Jinnah's support. Jinnah read the draft of the appeal but refused to sign it. He even chided Khaliq-uz-Zaman for having said that there were communal riots in Pakistan, for such an admission had harmed its interests. Jinnah's implied suggestion was clear: even after partition, he wanted the leaders of Indian Muslims-to regard the interests of Pakistan as supreme.

While Jinnah publicly declared that minorities needed protection, he refused to sign a joint appeal with Gandhi which would have helped to create a climate conducive to the protection of the minorities. While he publicly advised the minorities of both the nations to be loyal to their respective countries, he privately advised Indian Muslim leaders to give priority to the national interests of Pakistan even at the expense of the interests of Indian Muslims. These are blatant contradictions, which cannot be resolved by the hypothesis that while Jinnah desired a genuinely secular Pakistan he was unfortunate in having to meet conditions beyond his control. The question is: what steps did Jinnah take to bring the situation under his control? How was it that his followers, who otherwise used to follow him blindly, suddenly went out of control as soon as Pakistan was created? To pretend that the editor of *Dawn*, Altaf Hussain, and the Chief Minister of the Frontier Province, Abdul Kayyum Khan, dictated things to Jinnah is to suggest that Jinnah was a political weakling. Jinnah's leadership was never weak. He was always stubborn, headstrong and autocratic.

Even if we accept the hypothesis that Jinnah used violent means only to achieve a separate state and that once he achieved his end he began gradually to give up his rigid anti-Hindu position, several questions still remain. Jinnah's policy vis-à-vis the Princely States makes it clear that he did not change even after the creation of Pakistan. He took the view that the Princely States had become sovereign in their own right and accepted the accession of Junagadh without any regard for its people's wishes. He instigated Hyderabad to remain independent. At the same time, when Indian troops entered Kashmir he raised a great hue and cry, alleging that this amounted to cheating. If Jinnah believed that the princes were free to choose, why did he talk of the people's sovereignty in Kashmir? Was it because Kashmir had a Muslim majority? And if Jinnah believed that the Nizam of Hyderabad and the Nawab of Junagadh were, as native princes, free to choose, why did he not concede the same right to the Maharaja of Kashmir? Was it because the latter was a Hindu? Jinnah instigated the Princely States to declare themselves independent. What were his objectives in doing so? Were they consistent with his proclaimed policy of friendly relations with India?

Jinnah's apologists claim that he wanted to bury the hatchet as soon as Pakistan was accomplished. They do not, therefore, answer the above questions which are rather inconvenient. However, these questions have to be answered and the answers lead one to conclude that Jinnah did not want to bury the hatchet; on the contrary, he wanted to continue the conflict, albeit with different methods and in a different manner after partition. Pakistan came into being according to the plan of 3 June 1917. Jinnah was far from satisfied with the Pakistan he got according to this plan. There were no Muslim majority provinces left in India which he could make a new bone of contention. He had no option but to accept the Radclyffe award determining the borders in Bengal and the Punjab, since Lord Mountbatten had already made both the Governments accept the award in advance as final and binding. Therefore, if Pakistan wanted a larger share of territory, the only chance lay in exploiting the sovereignty granted by the British to the Princely States of India. This was the only way Jinnah could force the balkanisation of India and make it relatively weak. He did not lose this chance. Kashmir was the only Princely State which was inconvenient to him in this strategy but Jinnah seems to have been confident of overcoming even this obstacle. His actions amply illustrate this point.

In their eagerness to project him as a perfect leader, his apologists have, however, made some amazing discoveries to the contrary. They claim that Jinnah accepted Junagadh's accession only in order to make the point that Kashmir should rightly merge with Pakistan. The real sequence of events does not support this hypothesis. Mountbatten had earlier made efforts to ensure that both India and Pakistan adopted a common policy towards the Princely States. Vallabhbhai Patel on behalf of the Congress and Abdur Rab Nishtar on behalf of the Muslim League had agreed to this. According to the unwritten understanding arrived at, neither Dominion would accept the accession of a Princely State falling within the other's territory and, in respect of the Princely States on their common border, the question of accession would be decided in accordance with the wishes of the people. By accepting the accession of Junagadh, Pakistan violated this understanding first. Had Pakistan not done so, its case in Kashmir would have become much stronger. If Pakistan had really respected local public opinion vis-à-vis the future of the Princely States, there might not have been such bitterness later between India and Pakistan. Jinnah did not want only Kashmir to be merged with Pakistan; he also wanted Princely States like Hyderabad, Travanoore and Junagadh either to merge with Pakistan or to proclaim themselves independent. And while paying lip service to the sovereignty of Princely States, he had already sent his armed invaders into Kashmir. Before doing so, he had also merged Junagadh with Pakistan. When Mountbatten questioned the propriety of this act, Liaquat Ali Khan gave him the arrogant answer that if she wished, India could go to war to settle the issue. When the Indian government was negotiating a standstill agreement with Hyderabad, Jinnah summoned its Prime Minister, Mir Laiq Ali to Lahore and advised him to delay signing the agreement for some time. This was in the middle of September 1947. Within a month of this meeting, armed tribals from Pakistan were to enter Kashmir and Jinnah's plan was to proclaim the independence of Hyderabad as soon as Srinagar fell to the Pakistanis. If Jinnah had succeeded in this plan, India could not have invoked the legal sovereignty of the Princely States in respect of *both*, Kashmir and Hyderabad. Jinnah's plan to balkanise India failed because Nehru could see through these plans in advance. He accepted Kashmir's accession and sent Indian troops there. After this Hyderabad read the writing on the wall and signed the standstill agreement. After Indian troops had entered Kashmir. Mountbatten asked Jinnah why Pakistan had accepted the accession of Junagadh. Jinnah replied that this was done without consulting him! Only the naïve would accept Jinnah's answer as convincing.

The drama revolving round the accession of the Princely States ended in the total failure of Jinnah's machinations and his calculations regarding India's grasp of the *realpolitik* of the sub-continent. In its attempt to gain Junagadh, Hyderabad and Kashmir, Pakistan lost all three of these states. Had Jinnah's territorial greed known the limits of reality, and had he refrained from making an attempt to balkanise India, perhaps Pakistan would have peacefully gained Kashmir.

It is interesting to note that Jinnah's apologists criticize India's Kashmir policy and its refusal to keep the promise to hold a referendum there; but they do not utter a word in criticism of Jinnah's stand on the 'sovereignty' of the native princes and his instigation of Junagadh and Hyderabad to exercise this sovereignty. Nor would they blame Jinnah for violating the Patel-Nishtar agreement arrived at through Mountbatten's initiative. When they discuss the Kashmir dispute, they overlook these facts though they have a direct bearing on the issue. Nehru's tactics in Kashmir were India's response to Jinnah's attempts to balkanise India and to make it permanently weak in the sub-continent. Critics of Nehru's Kashmir policy forget this larger context because unless they ignore certain facts of history, they cannot glamourise Jinnah as a modern secularist, even as a humanist, and as a man who wanted friendly relations with India. They have no choice but to distort history in order to lend credence to their favourite myth.

Today, even the Pakistan that Jinnah created is shattered. This was inevitable. Jinnah's Pakistan was based on a medieval concept, the concept of Muslim nationalism. Sooner or later, this concept itself would have been challenged by a more modern concept of nationalism. Jinnah's medieval mind had not changed in spite of its contact with the modern world. But the product of that mind had to crack because it could not cope with contemporary realities. In fact, Jinnah's failure – the sad debacle of his grand dream – is part of the larger failure of Islam itself in the modern world. Had Muslim culture and society become more open-ended and cultivated a sense of liberal human values, there would not have been such a massive failure.

Jinnah was the only Muslim leader in the sub-continent who had a large Muslim following in spite of his being a poor practitioner of Islam. This paradox exemplifies a contradiction inherent in the Muslim mind. Under the impact of western culture and modernity, Muslim society has only changed in external appearance. What moves it most even today is the *jehad* motive. Unlike Christian society, Muslim society has been unable to elevate religious values to the level of truly universal human values. There have been no movements in that direction either. Although Hindu society has not yet attained the level of Christian ethical and humanistic attitudes, there are signs of a struggle towards a higher level in Hindu society. Gandhi's martyrdom is a symbol of this continuing struggle. Nowhere in the Islamic world do we find evidence of such struggle and sacrifice. For social and historical reasons, it was not possible to find it among the Muslims of this sub-continent. Jinnah had to lead such a society and hence it was impossible for him to have been both a secular and yet a successful leader of the Muslims.

And yet Indian liberals are at pains to place Jinnah on a high moral pedestal. This kind of concession could only be made by the Hindu mind. The Hindus are given to wishful thinking and they wish that everything in the world should be beautiful and sacred. This is closely related to Hindu asceticism. The Hindu refuses to distinguish the good from the evil because he believes in their ultimate metaphysical unity. On the basis of this attitude, he believes that Hinduism has given a great 'philosophical' legacy to the whole world. As a matter of fact, this refusal to make a clear distinction between good and evil helps him in masking the defects and evils of his own social system. He wishes to forget them. Muslims have been fighting with the Hindus for some years. But the Hindus wish to pretend that there is no real conflict between the two communities, which is equivalent to asserting that Jinnah was not Jinnah at all. After all, the Hindus do not have an intellectual tradition which calls a spade by its proper name. But this is bad semantics.

Storm Over Aligarh: An Inside View

A.H. Bilgrami

(Quest 85: November-December 1973)

Quest 82 (May-June 1973) contained a discussion on the controversy over the Aligarh Muslim University – one viewpoint presented through the extracts from the speeches of Maulana Abul Hasan Ali Nadvi and Mr Basheer Ahmad Sayeed, and the 'opposite' point of view presented by Professor A.B. Shah. Whatever I have tried to say here is rather different from these opposing views. First, I have been consciously led to take a course somewhat in between the two views and secondly, the views so far expressed are of persons who are not directly involved in the internal affairs of Aligarh. My own comment could therefore be termed as a 'view from inside'. Moreover, my viewpoint is in some respects a sort of 'silent' consensus arrived at in part or as a whole in consultation with my many friends – colleagues, administrators and students in the university and people elsewhere, not in so much as to what they actually said but how they felt about these matters. But, it is for them and others to judge the extent to which I have been able to articulate those unspoken words and feelings.

The controversy over the Aligarh Muslim University has witnessed the emergence of two antagonistic groups in the form of two 'schools of thought' concerning the nature and objectives of the university; one group favouring the maintenance of the 'Muslim minority character' of the university, while the other wanting it to become a 'modern national university'. Both the groups have taken seemingly irreconcilable positions, each emphasizing one aspect to the neglect of the other. Some of the protagonists of the 'Muslim character' of the university have gone to such an extent in asserting their point of view that they seem to have forgotten that what they are talking about is essentially a *university*. The other group, in its zeal for making Aligarh a 'modern national university', relegates the historical Muslim character of the university to a place of secondary importance.

Both the words 'university' and 'Muslim' are essential elements of the name 'Aligarh Muslim University'. The point, however, is how the two-word phrase 'Muslim University' can be meaningfully understood and explained.

As far as 'university' is concerned, it is a seat of higher learning, a community of teachers and students deemed to be engaged in the acquisition, dissemination and creation of knowledge. A university, whatever its colour and character, is devoted to the essential task of training its men and women in various academic and professional skills that would make them useful members of society.

A 'Muslim' university must doubly perform these tasks for the well-being of the Muslim community. Its alumni should excel others in the growingly competitive society of India and carve out their own place by becoming *indispensable* members of India's heterogeneous community. Prejudice and discrimination do exist against the Muslims, particularly against the products of this university. The socio-political environment in post-Independence India continues to be infected with the biases, prejudices and controversies of the pre-Independence past. Secondly, the Muslims of India are overburdened with the past, and the Muslim University has also been controversially associated with the pre-Independence past.

The maintenance today of the Muslim character, whether historical or minority, or both, needs a revaluation and re-interpretation of the values and objectives of the university in view of its controversial past (and debatable present). One thing which can be done by the university in this respect is to follow the recommendations of the Chatterji Committee, namely, 'to develop and emphasise the study of what we might describe as the contribution of [the] Muslim community to the complex pattern of our national culture.... It is this living traditions, this dynamic force, which we should like to preserve and cherish in this university. This would involve not only study and research into those patterns of the composite (Muslim Indian) culture which would help the Muslims of India to understand the vagaries of their changing role in the country today, it would also require a sensitive inculcation among its students of those aspects of the culture which make them worthy torch-bearers of the gospel that Sir Sayyid Ahmad Khan wanted them to spread to the four corners of the country – the gospel 'of free enquiry, large-hearted tolerance and pure morality'.

The 'Muslim character' and 'modern national university' should not and need not be two incompatible and irreconcilable terms at Aligarh; rather, their enlightened and healthy fusion would help in the performance of the rightful role of the university. Further, the 'Muslim character' can only be preserved if the teachers and students of the university remain engaged in their academic and educational pursuits with added dexterity and devotion, and without caring for or indulging in extraneous affairs. Such a development would be welcome from several points of view. It would be as fruitful for Aligarh students to attain excellence for making their individual careers as the emergence of a Muslim *elite* possessing the breadth of outlook and vision necessary to spearhead the regeneration of the Muslim community, and to help it in its problems of adaptation in post-partition India. An essential corollary of this would be the involving of the Muslim community in a bigger way in the development process in the country as a whole. If this happens, the controversy over the character of the university would hardly remain tenable even if all of its teachers as well as students belonged to the Muslim community. This is not to say that Aligarh has not been attempting to do so. It is simply to stress the point that enough has not been done to identify Aligarh with the overall national purpose. The controversies inside and outside Aligarh tend considerably to distort the image of the university, and prevent it from fulfilling its objectives.

Today the Aligarh Muslim University is confronted with a situation similar to that faced by the founder of the institution nearly a century age. Muslims then had completely lost even the semblance of their dominion by 1857 and British rule over the sub-continent had become an accomplished fact. Economically the Muslim community lay prostrate without jobs and professions. Their culture, intellectual tradition and belief postulates faced the challenge of western culture, rationality and science. An entirely new appraisal of the values of the Muslim community was called for, to meet the complex and difficult challenge.

Sayyid Ahmad Khan had closely watched the situation. His experience had convinced him that Indian Muslims must make terms with the West if they were not permanently to remain in a social and political backwater. The first thing in this connection was that Muslims should be prepared to take their rightful place in the public life of their country by acquiring western education. To this end Sayyid Ahmad Khan founded the MAO College in 1875. Also, he firmly believed that the Muslim intellectual tradition and belief postulates could be reconciled with those of the West. He argued, amidst vehement criticism and opposition from Muslim orthodoxy, that reason and scientific outlook were not alien to Islam but that, on the contrary, they were basic to its intellectual system and needed emphasis. For further emancipation of the Muslims, whose loyalty was suspect in the eyes of the British, the Sayyid encouraged them to join the services of the British government (to become known as 'our loyal Mohammadans of India'). It was perhaps the fear that the Muslims might not be charged with disloyalty once again that he dissuaded them from joining the Indian National Congress.

Aligarh was to be the centre of Muslim regeneration; an educational institution preparing for jobs and professions, a place for cultural identification and preservation, and a seat of intellectual development based on reason and the scientific outlook. This was Sir Sayyid's scheme for the Muslims to cope with the times. 'If the times do not make mends with you, you must make mends with the times.'

The Aligarh movement and the Aligarh Muslim University did to an extent help the Muslims in 'making mends with the times'; but the times were solely British. Without going into details, it would suffice to say that the educated Muslims, with only a few exceptions, became so much involved in keeping up with the British that they accepted it as a *sine qua non* for all times to come. The British were, however, interested only in preserving their rule. Indians got western education all right, but only of the kind necessary to subserve British imperial interests: they could not acquire that rational outlook and scientific bent of mind which would have helped Indian society to evolve on healthy modern lines. Both Hindus and Muslims fell back on their past. Historical incompatibilities between the two communities were emphasised, and revivalist movements took them further apart. The British, in accordance with their policy of divide and rule, helped to widen the breach further. The Muslim League first sought constitutional safeguards in the form of separate electorates and reservation of seats in the services and legislatures to preserve their separate minority identity, and the British government willingly obliged them. Then came the two-nation theory and the demand for Pakistan leading to the division of the country in 1947.

The basic contention of the proponents of the two-nation theory was that the Hindus and the Muslims of India were two distinct nations diametrically opposed to each other. It followed that the Muslims as a minority were unable to live in a sovereign democratic state having a Hindu majority. They demanded a separate state within the sub-continent in which the Muslims would be in a majority.

The creation of Pakistan could not prove to be a solution of the Muslim 'minority' problem. Muslims still remained in India in sizeable numbers and in a 'minority'. The fate of those Muslims who have migrated to Pakistan from the areas of India where they were in a minority – Bihari Muslims in East Pakistan (now Bangladesh) and the Urdu-speaking UP Muslims in West Pakistan – gives the lie to the solution.

The Muslims, however, found themselves in a precarious position. Pakistan had virtually pulled them up from their roots. The very basis of their existence in India was being questioned. They needed an entirely new reappraisal in terms of their values and thinking which could take them away from the overbearing shadows of the two-nation theory and help them in the difficult and complicated profess of readaptation and readjustment within the larger Indian society. This was the task ordained by Sir Sayyid for the Muslim University.

But the University carried with it the stigma of complicity in the partitioning of the country, and faced the crisis of its own legitimacy. The educated elite which it had created had taken an active part in the Pakistan movement and had left for Pakistan, leaving behind a vacuum in the Muslim community. The bulk of the teachers of the university had migrated. In order to justify its existence, the university needed a role commensurate with the changed circumstances of India.

The university could have done nothing more befitting than taking up the task of reinterpreting the role of Muslims in Indian society. It is from Aligarh that the Muslim elite could have emerged, an elite totally different from the past in thinking and capacity, and which could help the Muslim community in its complex and difficult problems of adaptation in India. There were so many extraneous factors which thwarted the Muslim community from developing a capacity for introspection, and the Muslim University from helping in that process: continued hostility between India and Pakistan and the consequent suspicion of the Muslims in India; exploitation by the politicians playing up communal feelings in elections to win votes; and the continuous insistence and impatience that Muslims should change despite the unsuitableness of the social and political climate for that purpose.

The Congress government under the leadership of Jawaharlal Nehru and Maulana Azad visualized that the Muslim University did have an important and constructive role to play in post-partition India for bringing out the Muslim community from the trauma of partition. Dr Zakir Husain was persuaded to accept its vice-chancellorship in order to give the university a nationalistic tone-up. Muslim scholars of nationalist persuasion from other Indian universities were inducted on its faculties to fill the vacuum caused by the mass migration of its teachers.

Although the induction of teachers from outside into the university apparently gave Aligarh a nationalistic look, it led to a kind of inner struggle on the campus. The teachers imported from outside enjoyed the patronage of Dr Zakir Husain and came with a missionary zeal to change Aligarh's controversial character. Naturally, they came into conflict with the old Aligarhians, who in turn wanted to preserve some of the good Aligarh traditions. In the beginning the controversy seemed to be between the Aligarhians and the non-Aligarhians – local versus outsiders. But soon it took the form of an ideological conflict. Quite a few who came from outside were 'leftists' and 'progressives' and were outspoken and assertive.

One important but unfortunate consequence of this inner fight was the development of a spoils system – each group supporting its own people in practically every affair of the university, be it admission of students, recruitment and promotions for various jobs, and even in student union elections. Students, teachers and other employees of the university joined in the fray for sharing the spoils. Academic merit and professional excellence without group support became irrelevant!

Gradually the spoils system developed its own vested interests. Each influential person in the university either developed a spoils system of his own, or found himself a member of one already developed. Community of interests, family ties and personal equations became matters of consequence in the university. Most of the members of the teaching and administrative staff owe some relationship to one or the other spoils system. The role of certain important and influential families gave added fillip to the system. Inter-group rivalry for promoting vested interests, however, continued unabated. Teachers involved the students in pulling their own chestnuts out of the fire or for settling old scores with rivals.

The controversies of the two groups have time and again rocked the university. It is significant that there are very few among those involved in the controversy who want the university to go on normally with its teaching and examinations, irrespective of the controversy over its character. Some of them like to get examinations postponed and the university closed down over trivial matters. Thus the conflict within and controversy without the university have a tinge of unreality and aimlessness. The wrangle over the character of the university seems to be a garb under which a fight to preserve one's own spoils system based on vested interests is being carried on.

This kind of wrangling over the spoils is not peculiar to Aligarh. What is peculiar to Aligarh is its special character and the special responsibilities that go with it. What has been happening at Aligarh for some years past and particularly during the past ten months or so are symptoms of an acute ailment requiring a thorough diagnosis. A comprehensive probe in the affairs of the university is long overdue. Let a commission of enquiry (judicial or other) scrutinise the affairs of the university. Besides, the teachers and students of the university should also debate among themselves what has gone wrong with the university and what should be done about it – of course, with the utmost seriousness of purpose and in a spirit of introspection.

For a person who has been involved in the struggle for democratising the administrative structure of the university and who feels a personal stake in its academic wellbeing, the Aligarh Muslim University (Amendment) Act of 1972 does need some changes so that the historical character of the university could be a little more strengthened. Some changes should also be made to provide meaningful representation to the teachers and students on the academic bodies of the university to make them more representative. And more importantly, the powers of administrative officers like the Vice-chancellor, the Deans and the Heads of departments should be further curtailed. In all this what I would like to promote is a more efficient *academic* functioning of the university, so that it could become a worthier seat of learning, a national asset rather than a place for personal and party squabbles. The Aligarh Muslim University is an academic institution, and the response on its behalf to the 1972 Act should have been academic rather than political. I feel that the academicians cannot and should not attempt to meet the politicians on a political level. They should use the academic method of discussion and persuasion by making a studied response to an Act of Parliament. What should have been done is that the teachers, students and well-wishers of the university should have got together, analysed the 1972 Act carefully and made concrete suggestions to the government and Parliament regarding the changes they desired in the Act.

It is unfortunate that the reaction towards the Act has been political and agitational rather than academic. The Act has been made by the government of a political party which has an overwhelming majority in Parliament and which has a shrewd leader in Mrs Indira Gandhi. Those agitating against the Act have involved the political parties of the opposition, thus foreclosing the chance of striking a deal with the Congress government of Mrs Gandhi and undermined the prospects of getting the Act suitably changed by the present Parliament. It is equally doubtful that the opposition parties, even if they won the election, would help in making the desired amendments. Another equally unfortunate thing is the involvement of the Muslims at large with those political parties whose record has been distinctly communal and reactionary. It means that the Aligarh Muslim University and the Muslim community are getting involved with those who are already discredited in the eyes of the country, and that too against the government of Mrs Gandhi which has a massive mandate from the people. The question they must now face is whether such politicking is likely to help resolve the problem or confuse it further.

Who is Afraid of Shivaji?

D.

(Quest 84: September-October 1973)

Dr Pandharinath Ranade is supposed to be a historian. He is also supposed to be a Marxist. I had not heard of him until, one fine morning, the Poona fortnightly *Ranangan* published an article by him which claimed to analyse Shivaji and his times from a Marxist point of view. The title of the article suggested a scathing attack on the contemporary cult of Shivaji in Maharashtra and threatened to cut down to size the myth of the first King of the Marathas.

There is no doubt that the Maharashtrian worship of Shivaji often verges on pathological fanaticism. The fascist and chauvinistic tendencies of certain Maharashtrian leaders have found in Shivaji an image amenable to insane hero-worship. But this is not Shivaji's fault. The uses and abuses of Shivaji by latter-day Maharashtrians are based on Shivaji's brilliant military and political career culminating in the foundation of the Maratha state. When Shivaji's successors later sought to colonise other parts of India or simply plundered and looted them the Maratha state threatened to become the Maratha Empire though really there was no such thing. Because the Marathas were one of the last native Indian powers to succumb to the British, their memories of their militant past are still very much alive. Shivaji-worshippers in this century include Bal Gangadhar Tilak, V.D. Savarkar and several other lesser men. Mr S.A. Dange, the leader of the Communist Party of India, and Mr Bal Thackeray, the Fuhrer of the Shiv Sena are both ardent public admirers of Shivaji. Mr Y.B. Chavan, India's present Finance Minister, was hailed as the Second Shivaji by his numerous *chamchas*. Mr Bal Thackeray, on the other hand, has tried to project the corporate image of the Shiv Sena – name onwards – entirely in pseudo-Shivajian terms. Thus there is no denying the fact that Maharashtra continues to suffer from a surfeit of Shivajis. Shivaji, the historical figure, is either obscured or grossly distorted by this fanaticism.

But it is one thing to attack the collective idiocy or spurious motives of contemporary Maharashtrians, and quite another to create another tabloid version of history in blatant defiance of the scientific method. Dr Ranade went in for cheap sensationalism. His theses are not valuable either as a Marxist interpretation of history or as a Marxist critique of contemporary Shivaji-worship.

However, the main point Dr Ranade seemed to want to make was about his own intellectual and moral courage. There were, as anticipated, irrational and angry reactions to his theses. But Dr Ranade was so eager to become a heroic martyr that he resigned his teaching post in Marathwada University in a desperate hurry claiming, according to reports, that he was democratically bowing to his students' wishes. Now, who is afraid of Shivaji?

Another Marxist, an eminent poet, similarly hurried into an apologetic posture recently. He was Vinda Karandikar. Karandikar recently published a poem on *Ganesha* entitled 'Vakratunda Mahakaya'. The poem written with secular literary convictions caused an expected reaction of protest from Hindu revivalists. Karandikar rushed into print with an apology cleverly couched in literary critical terminology. But the fact that he had to do so in desperate hurry seemed to echo Panurge's classic statement: 'I am afraid of nothing; except danger.'

It is, indeed, futile to fight for the cultural freedom of those whose dissent itself stands on an apologetic pedestal.

the successful man
knows the importance
of time

that's why he prefers a watch by FAVRE-LEUBA

FAVRE-LEUBA

FAVRE-LEUBA AND COMPANY
LIMITED

P. O. Box 845 Bombay   P. O. Box 474 Calcutta

The Concept of Justice and Personal Law in India

A.A.A. Fyzee

If the father has promulgated good laws, they should be preserved; if they are bad, they should be replaced with good ones.

The Emperor Babur

(Quoted by V.V. Bartold, Musulman Culture, English Translation by S. Suhrawardy, Calcutta University 1934. p. 133)

(Quest 86: January-February 1974)

The words 'justice' and 'law' are in common use all over the world. But to the layman it may, if he is not instructed, come as a surprise when he is told by the pundits that there is a great deal of difficulty in defining them with precision. The word 'law' has three distinct forms: (1) *The* law; (2) *a* law; and (3) law/laws. The easiest to understand is law/laws, for instance, the laws of inheritance, of income-tax, of the Constitution. International law, polite laws, etc. But when you go to the authorities, their definitions differ. The difference arises because of their deeper analysis of the nature of law as it affects human society, and of the importance a particular thinker gives to one particular aspect. For me, born in the 19th century, a working definition is that of my student days: 'The law is the body of principles recognized and applied by the state in the administration of justice.'[1]

On examining this definition, everything seems clear until we come to the end. What is justice? When we turn to Salmond, he does not discuss it, much less does he attempt a definition. This is like a paramount rule of Indian law; a fact is said to be relevant only if the Evidence Act declares it to be relevant. But what is 'relevant, relevance, relevancy'? The books are silent; we have to learn by sad experience and hard work.

So we have to scratch our heads about 'justice', a far more elusive term, relegated to the realms of philosophy rather than of law. Let us begin with a simple proposition; while an exact definition is difficult, if not impossible, a particular act can easily be identified in most cases as legal or illegal; for example, when you say that buying a banana is legal, or driving a car on the left side of the road is legal in India, but not in the USA, or making a will is legal in India. Such propositions are self-evident, even without a philosophical understanding of the term 'the law'.

Similarly, you may say that the criminal laws of India are just; or the law of civil marriage is just. A conflict however arises when you say that a *law* is *unjust*; for instance, a man may say in India, 'the Income-tax laws are unjust', or 'the divorce laws applicable to the women in community X in India are unjust', or 'that although the Constitution so provides, it is unjust to take away the property of a person without paying adequate compensation to him'. If you make such statements, the meaning may be clear to every one of your hearers, but the deeper significance of the term 'justice' or 'just' is still elusive.[2] This reminds us of G.E. Moore when he asserted that, generally, it is quite easy to agree that an action is good or bad, but no precise definition of 'the good' has yet been formulated.

One of the earliest axioms of justice goes back to Aristotle: 'Justice is thought to be equality; and so it is, but for equals, not for everybody. Inequality is also thought to be just; and so it is, but for unequals, not for everybody.'[3] A little reflection will show that this is possibly the most famous dictum relating to justice in the realms of thought. Then follow the views of Plato, Kant, Spinoza and Hegel and a host of brilliant thinkers, such as Rawls; but as the Koran says: 'The prior ones have priority'; or the homely maxim of equity: 'where the equities are equal, the first in time shall prevail'; this gives the crown to Aristotle.

Let us attempt to understand Aristotle in the simplest possible cases. We shall name his principles as (A) Equality as Justice, and (B)

Inequality as Justice. As to (A): A man, M, kills another man, S. In the modern world, whether

(i) M is a man or a woman (sex distinction), or

(ii) M is a Christian, Buddhist, Muslim or atheist (religious distinction), or

(iii) M is a Secretary to Government or a taxi driver (professional distinction), or

(iv) M is an Englishman, Scandinavian, or Nigerian (national distinction), or

(v) M is a Negro, Chinese or Eskimo (racial distinction)

would be irrelevant in a court of law. If he has committed the offence, he will be declared to be guilty according to the law of the country where the offence has been committed.

This is the Principle of Equality, as it affects the concept of justice. Now let us take (B):

(i) M is an executioner, ordered to hang a murderer, or

(ii) M is a mad man who believes that he is cutting the throat of a goat, or

(iii) M is a child of five who shoots a man with a rifle in play, or

(iv) M is a servant who kills his master by inadvertently giving him a pill of poison instead of a tablet of medicine.

In all these cases no court in the modern world would hold him guilty of murder.

This is the Principle of Inequality as it affects the concept of justice.

In some cases, the offence may be mitigated by well-known principles of law. For instance, (i) there is a grave and sudden provocation, or (ii) M is a drunk and does not know the nature of the act.

This is called mitigation of an offence in law.

Now mitigation is not permissible on the ground of religious belief, contrary to the criminal law of the land: (i) M asserts that S is a renegade or is an outlaw, according to his faith. This plea cannot be entertained, (ii) M asserts that S belongs to a lower order of human beings, or is an outcaste, and according to his faith, killing such an individual by M who is of the highest caste, is not murder. This plea cannot be taken in India at present.

Certain laws may also be termed 'unjust' or 'just'. The first point to be noted is that such laws will be administered and executed by the state; it is before the bar of private conscience that the laws may be deemed to be just or unjust. For example, a follower of Bentham may argue that his property cannot be taken away by the state without compensation being paid to him. On the other hand, a follower of Marx may well say that private property is an obnoxious thing, and that the state has every right to claim it for public purpose without paying any compensation. In both cases, the law of the land will be administered and executed, whatever may be the opinion of an individual in these matters.

Religion creates difficulties of various kinds. A man may say that his marriage was a sacrament, and cannot be dissolved. But a court of law may pass a decree of divorce in favour of his wife who would then be perfectly entitled to marry another person under civil law. Such a state of affairs is possible among Catholics in every part of the world. Similarly, the Koran forbids a Muslim woman to marry a non-Muslim; but if a civil marriage takes place between her and a non-Muslim, the marriage is valid according to civil law and the children legitimate.

Both law and justice are related to time, circumstance and provenance. A discussion of the vital issues is only significant in a given set of circumstances, at a given point of time, and in a particular country. The *Mejelle*, an Ottoman Code of Laws based on Hanafi principles in the days of the Caliph Abdul Hamid, says:

Art. 39. It is an accepted fact that the terms of law vary with the change in the times.[4]

It is now my purpose to deal with the religious personal law of Muslims in India. Whatever may have been the nature of the validity of religious laws as legal norms during Mughal times, this state of affairs clearly ended when George II granted a Charter to the East India Company in 1753. This was followed by the plan of Warren Hastings in 1772; and by Sec. 27 of the celebrated Regulation of 1780, it was laid down that:

> In all suits regarding inheritance, marriage, and caste, and other religious usages or institutions, the laws of the Koran with respect to the Mahomedans, and those of the Shaster with respect to the Gentoos, shall be invariably adhered to.

If only one of the parties were a Hindu or Muslim, the laws and usages of the defendant were to be applied.[5] Some rules were to be applied specifically; others were to be applied as matters of 'Justice, Equality and Good Conscience'; and yet others were to be abolished. The expression 'Justice Equity and Good Conscience' was interpreted by the Courts to mean the English rules of common law and equity.

It therefore stands to reason that (a) rules laid down by a non-Islamic sovereign which are tempered by (b) a non-Islamic system of jurisprudence, cannot be termed *shariat* by any stretch of imagination or by any elasticity of interpretation. To name the present system of personal law as '*shariat*' is political euphemism, not scientific nomenclature. A detailed history of the introduction of a few principles of the Islamic civil law in India is beyond the purview of this article, but the results of the fusion of English law and equity with Islamic law in India have been summarized in the introduction to my *Cases in the Muhammadan Law of India and Pakistan* (Clarendon Press, Oxford, 1965).

The concept of justice in the modern world clearly distinguishes between law and religion, between the duty of the judge and the forum of personal conscience. Sir Erskine Perry, Chief Justice of Bombay, has done this in memorable words, which ever bear repetition:

> A jurist *qua* jurist has only to deal with human laws; he recognizes the existence of divine laws, and their validity in *foro conscientiac* with those to whom it is addressed, or those who believe in the revelation containing them; but he does not recognise them as enforceable in Courts of Justice any further than the secular power has ordained. Under a government as that of England, which has established the principle of universal toleration as to religious belief, it is no doubt the duty of the secular judge to pay the utmost respect to the religious opinions of every suitor who comes before the Court.[6] But the question on every such occasion for the judge would be, what the law was which had been delivered to him for administration by his sovereign.[7]

Then we come to the Government of India Act 1935. Sec. 211 lays down that 'the law declared by the Federal Court and by any Judgment of the Privy Council shall be followed by all the Courts in India'. And, finally, by the Constitution of India, Art. 372 (1), it has been held that such parts of the English law as were in force before the Constitution, and have not been altered or replaced, remain the law of the land until they are expressly repealed.[8] Thus the Muhammadan law as received in India, is the *shariat*, modified by the principles of English law and equity, in the varying social and cultural conditions of India; and during the centuries, it has tended to become a discrete system, somewhat at variance with its original sources.[9] It is a system of law in its nature civil, and therefore capable of being amended by a human agency, the Parliament of India.

By Art. 44 of the Constitution it is laid down: 'The State shall endeavour to secure for the citizens a uniform Civil Code throughout the territory of India'. The plain meaning of this Directive Principle of State Policy is that the state in India, following the principles of 'Justice' and 'Equality', as laid down in the Preamble, will draft a code for the acceptance of Parliament and then adopt it as the law of the land. In doing so it will follow the concept of justice as understood in this century, and as far as possible, the Universal Declaration of Human Rights adopted by the United Nations in 1948,[10] and give due consideration to the prevailing systems of personal law in India, namely, English, Hindu, Islamic, Jewish, Christian and Parsee. It will also be guided by fundamental principles adopted by other states and try not to adopt norms which offend the *World Conscience* – a phrase which implies the basic principles of Equality and Justice accepted as legal norms in the civilized world. If, in such an attempt, a certain community demands that, *on the ground of religious faith*, some principles peculiar to its sacred law but offending against the World Conscience should be adopted, such special provision would be contrary to the principles of justice and equality affirmed in the Constitution.[11] It would also be contrary to the concept of justice as understood by jurists in the twentieth century. Such reservation may be good politics, or utilitarian prevarication, or party bargaining – and from anything but jurisprudence, I wish entirely to dissociate myself – but it is time to do away with the mystification which surrounds a part of the law in India, as in other parts of the world, so felicitously expressed by Professor H.L.A. Hart:

> The words 'mystification' and 'demystification' have appeared fairly recently among us in the literature of the radical New Left. The central idea that these words are used to express is that unjust, anachronistic, inefficient or otherwise harmful social institutions, including laws, are frequently protected from criticism by a veil of mystery thrown over them. This conceals their true nature and effects, perplexes and intimidates the would-be reformer and so prolongs the life of bad institutions. The forms of mystery thus used in defence of established abuses are, according to

these radical critics, various. They include not only glorification by open eulogy and pomp and ceremony; not only the use of archaic dress and diction unintelligible to the layman, but also, and more importantly, mystification consists in the propagation of a *belief*, the belief that legal and other institutions of society are infinitely complex and difficult to understand, and that this is an invincible fact of nature, so that long-standing institutions cannot be changed without risk of the collapse of society. The attitude appropriate to this belief is one of humble deference to tradition: 'we ought to understand it according to our measure and venerate where we are not able presently to understand' (Burke).[12]

Endnotes

1. Salmond, *Jurisprudence* (5th edn.), London 1916, p. 9. For a modern discussion, see H.L.A. Hart. *The Concept of Law*, Clarendon Law Series, Oxford 1961.

2. The standard work on justice is John Rawls. *A Theory of Justice*, Oxford University Paperback, 1973. A shorter, but very illuminating discussion will be found in N.M.L. Nathan, *The Concept of Justice*, Macmillan, London 1971. I have referred to them as Rawls and Nathan, respectively, in this paper.

3. Nathan, p.5, citing Aristotle's *Politics*.

4. Mejelle, Art. 39, in C. A. Hooper, *Civil Law of Palestine and Trans-Jordan*, Vol. I, Jerusalem 1933; Arabic text, ed. Najib Bek Hawawini, Damascus/Beirut 1923, p. 25.

5. Fyzee, *Outlines of Muhammadan Law* (3rd edn.), Oxford 1964, p. 54.

6. The same is the law in India, of Art. 25, *Constitution of India*.

7. Fyzee, Cases, citing *Perry's Oriental Cases*, 122.

8. *Bank of India v. Bowman* (1955) 57 Bombay Law Reporter 345, 364 cited in Fyzee, *Outlines*, p. 55.

9. Schacht, *Esquisse*, p. 86: Fyzee, *Ibid.*, p. 50.

10. I. Brownlie, *Basic Documents on Human Rights*, Clarendon Press, Oxford, 1971, pp. 106-112.

11. It may be argued that the Constitution itself recognizes a proviso of inequality

as respects the Scheduled castes – namely, Arts. 15(4), 335 and other related clauses. This would be unsound: (*a*) the reservation is not on the ground of religion; (*b*) it is in the nature of social justice to a community denied justice in India for thousands of years; (*c*) it was supported by the greatest Hindu that lived in this country for a long period; (*d*) it was agreed to by all Indians regardless of religion or a religion; and (*e*) rightly construed, it is in the nature of a transitory regulation until equality and justice have been achieved. These considerations do not apply to a community which attempts to make a distinction drawn from one of the sacred books for special privileges which the other communities do not enjoy, or for the purpose of treating certain men and women as sub-human creatures.

12. Bentham and the Demystification of the Law (1973) 36 *Modern Law Review*, 2.

What Has Dimple Got that Satyajit Hasn't?

D.

(Quest 86: January–February 1974)

Have you seen *Bobby* yet? And have you seen *Ashani Sanket?*

For, this time, I propose to make yet another absurd comparison: I want to discuss, in the same breath, the success of Dimple Kapadia and the failure of Satyajit Ray. Miss Kapadia, who is now the wife of superstar Rajesh Khanna, has swept movie audiences throughout the country. Mr Ray has flopped miserably in convincing even his art film audience that his cinematic imagination is somewhat better than the genius of the Films Division itself. *Bobby* – wherein Miss Kapadia stars – is a film made by that veteran showman, Raj Kapoor. It is a spectacular commercial success and it was meant to be one. *Ashani Sanket* is an ungainly artistic flop and such as was certainly not intended by Mr Ray.

Bobby is an unashamedly escapist adolescent love story designed to capture the imagination of sexually unstable and mentally deficient Hindi movie-goers of all ages. Miss Kapadia's legs are the chief attraction; Mr Rishi Kapoor, her lover, has the subsidiary role of looking unduly energetic, forlorn, passionate and crazy in turns. Since both these kid stars look charming and since the audience's own urge to make love is satisfied merely by watching films and humming erotic tunes in the bathroom or singing sad songs in the kitchen, the pair becomes an instant rage.

Mr Raj Kapoor – the producer-director of the film – has the knack of imposing his own limitations on his audience. His hero (and his son in real life), Rishi is the son of very rich, Anglicized Hindu parents who spend most of their time living conspicuously, i.e. attending vulgar parties such as *nouveau riche* Indians do in real life. The boy has been brought up away from this parent and is a product of a public school. He falls in instant love with 'Bobby', i.e. Miss Kapadia, the only daughter of a Roman Catholic Goan fisherman. In Hindu India, such a couple cannot marry. In Hindi film-India, however, they might be able to sing their way through to a sweet union.

The Goan Catholic's life-style is a stereotyped caricature in the film: they wear suits, drink continually, dance occasionally and wear golden crosses. They also speak bad Hindi. Note that the *boy* is Hindu and the girl Catholic. Subtle but inevitable aggression. Note also that the Shankaracharya and the Pope notwithstanding, calf-love shall ultimately win. Most of the footage is devoted to love scenes and the dialogue between the lover is an almost exhaustive and nearly computerized working out of all the possible ways of saying 'I love you' in Hindi – an outburst of verbal pimples punctuated by public sighs and songs which substitute for a healthy tumble in the haystack. All the same, the lovers are given some filmic problems to solve: they elope and their respective fathers, hitherto opposed to their union, soften in the end.

After the movie, don't forget to observe the audience and its reaction. Rishi Kapoor is a hit with all sub-teenage, teenage, neo-adult and even near-menopausal women while Dimple Kapadia affects the males much in the same way. When Dimple and Rishi are accidentally locked in a cottage they touchingly sublimate their sex urge through a duet sung by them to fool the censors and to win the audience's erotic sympathy.

Now to *Ashani Sanket*: the audience is different here. There are the snobs, the Bengali cultural chauvinists, the art people, the middle and the high-brow. They are awed by Ray's reputation and by the fact that the film has bagged an international award. The film opens with commercial calendar-type 'breath-taking' stills of landscapes, and the live action begins with an extreme close-ups of the bare arm of Babita, the Bangladesh actress bathing in a pond. The camera sensuously ponders over her. Then we learn that she is the wife of a barely educated young Brahmin and the two are just married and are trying to settle down in the village. They are the only Brahmins there and the husband is quick to cash on the caste system although he is portrayed as a conscientious, innocent and rather sissy fellow. He becomes the village priest, medicine man and school teacher, and lives off the rich and poor peasants. Then comes World War II and the great man-made famine of 1943 in Bengal. Since the Bengali's supreme value is expressed in terms of *macherazol* and rice, the scarcity of these items causes a breakdown of their entire value system. But Ray's famine is beautiful, decorative and colourful. He visualises moral degradation in terms of a woman selling her body for some rice and apparently enjoying it. A few dying and hungry humans, some stray shots of failed crops and tabletop montages of newspaper headlines about the rice price indices are the only attempt by Ray to depict the ravages of the famine.

Since we have been going through increasing periods of strife due to man-made shortages, I wonder whether we cannot equate Ray's saccharinous famine with Raj Kapoor's chocolate-box love story. Their moral and aesthetic import is on the same level of mediocrity. Except that Ray fails to entertain the masses which Raj Kapoor does, I do not find any vital difference between the kind of cinematic statements they are making. Incidentally, I have always felt that Ray is a grossly over-rated film-maker. He is certainly not in the class of Kurosawa, Buñuel, Antonioni, Fellini, Bergman, Polanski, Godard, Bresson, Resnais and half a dozen or more other top film-makers in the world. The much unluckier Ritwick Ghatak is the only Indian film-maker who has so far touched the heights that these great directors have touched in their best work. It has been said that Ray is a master of cinematic technique; I have always felt that his camera is non-functional and his sound-track and visuals are too much dominated by quasi-literary concepts.

However, to return to my barbaric comparison of Raj Kapoor with Ray, of *Bobby* with *Ashani Sanket:* Raj Kapoor produces opiates for the masses, including the educated uncultured, while giving them traces of cinematic value; Ray gives the middle class its own kind of high-brow drugs, heaps of crude cinematic values coated with the sugar of a static pre-modern imagination. Ray's best work has dealt with pre-modern, traditional, rural and urban Bengal. Even there, he shows a romantic nostalgia for a decaying environment and its values. He cannot be free, he cannot move forward. He made an effort to face his own times in *Pratidwandwi* and failed. In *Ashani Sanket* he fails even more convincingly.

I would like to suggest that Ray's failure lies in his constant effort to repeat his own patches of success and create a masterpiece out of them. His shot compositions are visually powerful but his camera movements lack functional rhythm; his visual symbols are illustrative or allegorically pictorial translations of statements which might sound better as literature; he handles the soundtrack very sensitively, often adding apt auditory suggestions through selective use of incidental sound – he can even bring off effective complex montages of auditory images or auditory-cum-visual images; yet he is too rhetorical. His cutting is also static: he cannot bridge movement with movement. On the other hand, when he uses jump cuts or a succession of freezes, his syntax is not functional but decorative. His use of close-ups and extreme close-ups is more dramatic than telling. Ray is eloquent at times, lyrical at times, witty at times: *Pather Panchali*, *Charulata* and *Paras Pathar* exemplify these strengths. As in *Jalsaghar* or in patches in *Devi*, he is a minute observer of the private tragedy of an individual human being. But Ray's attempt has been to cover more on his canvas than he can cope with: he attempts to depict a whole epoch, a whole ethos, a whole environment, an entire culture. It is here that he fails. To anyone who has seen Ghatak's *Suvarnarekha*, Ray has nothing more powerful or succinct to offer. Why Ghatak, even a Mrinal Sen occasionally surpasses Ray in this direction. Perhaps Ray's world is still Tagorean and therefore alien to our own ethos. Ray's best work reflects the best in the Tagorean tradition through the medium of film. Ray's own Bengal vanished in the early 1940s, the period *Ashani Sanket* deals with. And Ray cannot cope with the world that followed because he cannot penetrate it beyond a point. Had Ray chosen to work within his own sensibility and within his own framework of cultural, ethical, aesthetic and ideological values, he might have even now given us the masterpiece that he is assumed to be sweating towards.

Killing the Press: The Indirect Approach

C.R. Irani

(Quest 87: March-April 1974)

A free press is undoubtedly the cornerstone of all free institutions because without it no honest debate is possible. Unfortunately, however, the press is a major casualty of our time. The International Press Institute in its annual report for 1972 admits as much. It shows that of the 132 member countries of the United Nations, only about one-fifth can today claim a modicum of freedom of the press. It also shows that the trend continues to be away from freedom of the press. This trend is not only in respect of communist and fascist regimes. In many countries which are, on the face of it, blessed with a democratic government, freedom of the press is becoming a major casualty. A recent example is the Federal Republic of Germany. Chancellor Willy Brandt's Social Democratic party is even now engaged in evolving 'new rules' for the press. The government, which is developing a very thin skin, is seeking by some well-tried methods to dilute, if not to eliminate, criticism and fearless comment. The proposals include the exclusion of a publisher's own personal editorship of the paper that he may own. Where a publisher employs a chief editor, the right of editorial decision is to be transferred from the chief editor to an editorial council, a body which will determine on a collective basis the policy that the paper is to follow, and would subject the editor's plans to majority conference decisions. The excuse is that it is improper in our democratic times for one man's opinion to prevail and there must be a plurality of views in each and every newspaper. On the contrary, it is easy to see that this method will ensure not only that the possible minority view of a publisher is excluded but that, indeed, all minority views would be altogether silenced. This must be the logical consequence of majority decisions. But somehow in the public mind the impression has been assiduously created that, here, there is an equation between capitalism and an unfree press and between socialism and a free press.

Other proposals include laying down new educational qualifications for journalists. It was left to David Astor, then editor of *The Observer*, to put the case for the press in well-chosen words. Arguing against such rigid regulations, David Astor made the point that this educational straitjacket overlooks one quality of special value to journalism – a talent for writing. This talent can appear without any form of training or advanced education and should, in our view, count as a 'specialist' quality of immediate value…. A similar case can be put forward for the capacity to express a powerful political argument; to deny direct entry to a person with an exceptional talent of this kind is to limit a newspaper's freedom to say what it wants. We must go on to remind ourselves that the freedom of the press has neither been won nor defended by the standard mediocrities who would fill senior positions with such props supplied by 'rules', but by powerful publishers and gifted writers and first-rate journalists. The idea of rigid educational qualifications has been borrowed directly from Spain where, for a number of years, the government has made sure that journalists are produced out of government-sponsored schools of journalism and contributions from all others are debarred on the ground that journalism is a profession like law and medicine and that lawyers and doctors do not allow outsiders to encroach on their preserves. The situation in our immediate neighbourhood is not much better. In Pakistan the muzzle slipped over the press during martial law has never quite been removed. In Ceylon, an original application of the theory of diffusion of ownership has brought about a tame and moth-eaten press. And so the story goes on through Burma and Singapore and even Malaysia.

In our own country the following judgement has been passed by the editor of *The Statesman*. Writing on 14 August, 1973, he says: 'At present there are shortages of yarn, cement, pig iron, fertilizers, edible oil, power, chemicals, tyres, fish, food grains, butter and many other commodities and prices are rising rapidly. But the press is called upon to avoid negative criticism, abandon the sports and financial pages, reach for the masses however this is to be done and generally fall into line.'

How did this situation arise? A brief recapitulation is necessary. Suddenly in the middle of 1969 (at the time of the split in the Congress party), the press began to be attacked by politicians in power for the barely concealed objective of drumming up the maximum possible support for the survival of the ruling party. The initial attempt was to separate the more prestigious editors from their publishers, but after Frank Moraes openly snubbed the minister of state for Information & Broadcasting by describing his concern for editors 'hypocritical', this attempt seems to have been largely given up. Editors continue, however, to be called 'literary hacks' and 'stooges of monopolists', and whatever is the current favourite phrase of abuse for men of sturdy independence who do not toe the line. Then in August 1971, a small group of people led by Mr Raghunatha Reddy (now minister for labour) and Mrs Nandini Satpathy (then minister of state for information broadcasting) drafted wide-ranging amendments to the Companies Act, in consultation with a few journalists of a particular political persuasion. This would have denied owners the right of ownership, managements the right to manage and editors the right to edit. All would have been lost in a morass of equality – the proposition that all men are equal to all others. Equality of opportunity is a respected objective; equality before the law is another. Both have their roots in fundamental human values, but to deduce from them that all those who work in a newspaper organisation must collectively determine the policy of that newspaper is like saying that the country's foreign policy must be framed by all those – clerks and peons and all others – who work in the External Affairs ministry. The absurdity of the argument notwithstanding, in the current climate of populist slogan-mongering it was small wonder that these amendments were welcomed in certain quarters. However, the opposition to them was so strong that they were hastily dropped and one does not hear of them any longer, in spite of newspaper 'monopolies' continuing as before.

The next development of note was the sudden decision towards the end of 1971 to impose a 10 page ceiling on newspapers on the ground of newsprint shortage. At the same time, large dollops of additional newsprint were handed out to those newspapers who had not been able to rise to the level of ten pages. This also was justified on grounds of equality. In the pursuit of a dubious political objective it was overlooked that many newspapers who then produced well below ten pages did so because of lack of the necessary expertise and quality. Equally overlooked was the fact that the government, powerful though it is, could not suddenly decree an increase in the number of pages of the smaller newspapers. The answer was given by the Supreme Court of India which described this policy as being one of 'hostile discrimination' against the larger and the more prestigious newspapers.

Thereafter, a more low-keyed strategy was adopted. Raising aloft the slogan of holding the 'price line' an attempt was made to acquire a stranglehold on the revenues of newspaper organizations. As recently as July last year, when, thanks to our own bungling, the worldwide newsprint shortage hurt us more than many other countries, the government announced that such newspapers as wished to raise their selling prices and/or their advertisement rates must come to the government as supplicants. Newspapers have made it abundantly clear that selling prices and advertisement rates are matters for individual newspapers to determine and interference with their rights in this fashion would not be acceptable.

It would be worth pausing to see how the government has itself acted on the question of holding the price line in the context of newsprint supplies. It is well known that there is only one plant making newsprint in this country and this belongs to the state. Newsprint production is, therefore, a government monopoly. Suddenly, without warning, the Nepa Newsprint Mills announced on 1 October 1973 that the selling price would be raised from Rs. 1,362 to 1,500 per tonne. No reason was given for this increase, but it was understood on all hands that advantage was sought to be taken of the rise in prices in the world markets. Barely six weeks later a further circular was received by newspapers from Nepa, indicating that the position had been reviewed and with effect from the same date (i.e. 1 October 1973) the price would be not Rs. 1,500 but Rs. 1,800 per tonne.

Apart from the small amount of newsprint produced in the country, newsprint is still an imported item. Barely two years ago the price of this commodity in India was the equivalent of $167 per tonne. The STC (State Trading Corporation) has the monopoly for importing newsprint from abroad and newspapers warned the STC that a newsprint crisis was imminent and urged that long-term contracts be entered into – these were available at that time for an extra $7 per tonne. These pleas were brushed aside. Recent purchases in Canada have been in the neighbourhood of $300 per tonne and our Russian friends have capped it all by insisting on a price of $120 per tonne under the news trade agreements. And yet, because of its hypocritical concern for the consumer, the government seeks to use every opportunity to propagate the view that newspapers' selling prices must not be raised. At the same time, it says that advertising rates also must not be increased because some advertisers would not be able to afford the new rates!

To suggest that we are moving in the direction of four-fifths of the members of the UN is hardly a consolation. The question is broadly divided into one of principles, on the one hand, and of methods and approach, on the other. The principles are self-evident and are not negotiable. It is no part of the business of the press to pay heed to the sensitivities of governments. Its duty is to its own high professional code – to report objectively, to analyse logically and to criticize fearlessly, but always with an ear to the voice of dissent. For any democratic government, including ours, to say that they do not subscribe to these principles must indeed be difficult and hence the adoption of what Col. Liddel Hart, the military strategist, would have called 'the indirect approach'. In the Indian context the threats that are developing today are from the following directions:

(i) Organisations of newspaper employees are being cultivated and encouraged. The encouragement given is in the direction of slogans of worker participation which, to put it bluntly, means offering positions and authority to those who are unlikely to reach them on merit.

(ii) A tactic being recently adopted, is also to encourage as quietly as possible, the various schools of journalism in the country with a view to making them dependent on government support, and to bringing forward at some later date legislation which, with disarming simplicity, would provide that only those 'professionally trained' should be allowed to write in newspapers.

(iii) An attempt to control the revenues of newspapers by (a) controlling their selling prices through the medium of fact-finding committees, on the one hand, and the encouragement of newspaper hawkers to become more militant, on the other; and

(b) to try and make it difficult for newspapers to make ends meet by instigating and encouraging advertisers to insist that – in a general inflationary situation – only prices of advertising space should remain constant.

The financial health of newspapers ought not to be the concern of only those with the direct responsibility of making ends meet. A thoughtful journalist of high stature in this country has recently said that 'in spite of what the government may say about how proprietors use their newspapers for their own selfish ends, in India the first condition of a free press is that it should be financially viable'. The Sakal Papers case is still good law. It holds that anything that impinges on the capability of a newspaper to reach its desired audience is, to that extent, interference with the right of freedom of speech and expression. Not only the press but the Indian people have been warned. If they do not read the signs correctly and do not identify and resist the pressures that are now appearing on the horizon, India's free press will not be the only casualty; thereafter what the government is about will not even be known to the citizens. As Edmund Burke said long ago: 'The only thing necessary for evil to prevail is that enough good men do nothing.'

Talking of the current difficulties facing the Indian press, Shri Mulgaonkar, Editor-in-Chief of the *Indian Express*, said on 23 July 1973: 'I can see that some people will welcome the new stresses under which the press will operate as an opportunity to tame it. There is no point in naming them, but nobody by now associates them with a vibrant faith in democracy. They have been permitted to work from inside and gnaw at the foundations of democracy for too long. It may soon be too late to stop them.' We have indeed been warned.

The Significance of Bihar

A.B. Shah

(Quest 91: September-October 1974)

The people's movement in Bihar led by Jayaprakash Narayan marks a turning point in the political history of independent India. Its outcome will decide whether free institutions will survive in this country or whether they will be subverted as in most other countries of the Third World which became independent after the Second World War.

It is natural, though not quite right, that the ruling party and its allies like the Communist Party of India should look upon the Bihar movement as a direct challenge to them. If the movement succeeds in its immediate aim of bringing about the dissolution of the Bihar legislative assembly, it would mean a unique and the first ever *peaceful* assertion of the people's right to call to book their elected representatives when they betray their faith, and violate the letter as well as the spirit of the Constitution. The success of the movement is also bound to lead to the emergence of a new kind of political leadership first in Bihar and then in other states of the Union.

In spite of progressive land legislation and twenty year of planning, Bihar is economically one of the most backward states. It would sound incredible but it is a fact that even tenancy records are not available in this benighted state. Regardless of party affiliation, the old leadership has obstinately refused to implement even partially the laws it has passed. That this leadership and its communist mentors should describe

JP as a 'stooge of vested interests' and 'an agent of the CIA' should not cause surprise to those who are familiar with the jargon of the left.

What is difficult to appreciate is the reservations – sometimes even hostility – of the liberals, the academicians and the urban intellectuals. They are unhappy that JP should have given a call for a *gherao* of government offices and recalcitrant ministers and members of the legislative assembly. According to them, only constitutional opposition – which in effect means holding public meetings and submitting memorials to the government – exhausts the scope of democratic action; anything beyond this, even if completely non-violent, is incompatible with the norms of democracy. It is necessary to meet this criticism since it is motivated by a genuine concern for the survival of free institutions and a strengthening of the democratic ethos.

The core of representative democracy lies in the fact that the elections are free and fair, and that the citizens are able to exercise effective supervision over those whom they select to rule in their name for a stipulated period of time. If these representatives violate their part of the contract, misuse their position by shameless pursuit of self-interest and refuse to respond to public opinion unambiguously expressed, it would be unrealistic to expect the citizens to adhere to the obligations of constitutional politics. If in addition, the rulers exhibit calculated disregard for the canons of civilized government and unleash massive violence against peaceful protesters, the citizens right to recall their elected representatives and, if necessary, even force them to resign constitutes the essence of the sovereignty of the people.

In Bihar not only the government but also most of the members of the legislative assembly have exhibited callous indifference to the grievances of the people and the decencies of public life. For years Bihar has been known as the most corrupt and caste-ridden state in India. Elections in Bihar have always been notorious for large-scale corruption, bogus voting, capture of polling booths and forcible prevention of Scheduled Caste and Adivasi voters from casting the ballot. In such a situation, to throw up one's hands in horror over the people's demand that the legislative assembly should be dissolved is to betray a text-book conception of representative government.

The leadership of the Bihar movement was not of JP's seeking. He agreed to accept it mainly for two reasons. For the first time since the death of Mahatma Gandhi there appeared a hope that where political parties had failed, students and ordinary citizens might succeed in effecting a breakthrough from the morass into which Indian democracy had steadily sunk. The student agitation in Gujarat, which was contemptuous of all political parties, had succeeded in securing the dismissal of a corrupt ministry and an irresponsible legislature. This was the first gleam of light that JP saw in the enveloping darkness from which he was groping for a way out.

The second consideration which influenced JP's decision was the failure of the Gujarat movement to bring about a significant change in the situation after it had attained its immediate goal. The assembly was dissolved but everything else remained the same under president's rule – except, of course, the fact that corrupt ministers were no longer able to play with the prices of essential goods in order to fill their own pockets. However, this was not enough. What was necessary was a fundamental re-examination of the policies pursued by the government in the social and economic fields in order that the mistakes of the past might be rectified before it was too late. The Gujarat movement could not promote such a re-examination because it did not have a leadership which had given thought to long-term problems and their policy implications from the standpoint of growth with justice.

Jayaprakash Narayan wanted to avoid the shortcomings and destructiveness of the Gujarat movement, which could only be done if he assumed the leadership of the movement in Bihar. His insistence on nonviolence and his effort to evolve a system of continuing education for those who came out of their colleges in response to his call, provide a guarantee that so long as he is free to guide it, the movement will not have a purely negative character as in Gujarat. Besides throwing out a corrupt ministry and, by and large, an equally corrupt legislature, it would seek to undertake a programme of land redistribution and radical reform in elections, education and the public life of the state.

This is the main objective of the Bihar movement. The dissolution of the assembly is only a pre-condition without which no improvement of any kind can take place in Bihar. In an open letter to Vinoba Bhave (*Everyman's*, June 15) JP made it clear that 'the resignation of the Bihar ministry and the dissolution of the Bihar assembly did not form part of the original 12 demands of the students'. They were added to the list, and indeed given top priority, only after the deliberate and indiscriminate firing on peaceful demonstrators in Gaya on Apil 12. The Ghafoor ministry not only refused to order a judicial inquiry into these firings, but it also sought to whitewash them by sending Mr

Abraham, a member of its own revenue board, to Gaya to 'inquire' into the incidents. Mr Abraham duly visited Gaya, carried out a *one-day* 'inquiry' and submitted a 'report' which justified all the three firings. Mr Abraham's report may or may not earn him a promotion; it certainly proved the last straw on the camel's back.

Earlier, the Bihar government had already denied the right of peaceful protest to students and the people at large. On March 21, permission was refused to a silent procession of the Chhatra Sangharsha Samiti and a number of arrests were made. The Samiti was also not allowed to hold a public meeting, and at least two of the arrested students were reported to have been beaten up in custody. Even the Bihar Shanti Sena Samiti, which wanted to take out a silent procession in Patna continued to get only evasive replies which neither gave permission to take out the procession nor denied it in clear terms.

It was against this background of violent suppression of civil liberties by the government and its cynical endorsement by the legislative assembly that JP ultimately supported the students' demand for the dissolution of the assembly. As JP put it in his letter to Vinoba Bhave mentioned above, 'had the assembly censured the Bihar government for its inefficiency, corruption... and misdeeds, and established a cleaner and better government, the situation would have been very different.'

The liberal objection to the Bihar movement does not take account of the history of democracy even in the land of its birth. It would be difficult to cite a single example of democratic rights having been won by any section of the populace in a pre-modern society without offering a bloody fight for them. The *Magna Carta* was the outcome of an action which was the English equivalent of the Indian *gherao;* only, the nobles of England were not committed to non-violence in dealing with their monarch. A few hundred years later the people of England had to behead their king in order that their rights as citizens might be recognized by his successor. And as late as the present, century, women in the West had to court imprisonment before they could earn the right to vote.

It is not surprising that the history of democracy should be replete with instances of this kind. No ruling class has ever willingly given up its privileges out of concern for the under-privileged. Before the emergence of modern representative democracy and in the absence of a ruling class responsive to the pressures of constitutional politics, struggle in the streets was the only method available to those who wished to have their grievances redressed. In India while the institutional framework of full representative democracy was introduced in 1950, the ruling elite has in recent years been guilty of increasing corruption and insensitiveness to public opinion unless it was backed by violence. The Constitution itself has become like modelling clay in two hands of the 'people's representatives'. The electoral system too has been brought under the control of money power. Worse still, the Ordinance issued by the President to nullify the effect of the recent Supreme Court judgment on the election to the Lok Sabha from the Sadar Bazar constituency in Delhi shows the Union government lent official sanction to the role of money in elections to the nation's legislatures. The only question therefore which is really relevant is not whether people should resort to non-constitutional methods to fight against tyranny and injustice, but whether these methods should include or eschew the use of violence.

Principles apart, on pragmatic considerations alone, non-violence is the only method that can succeed in the present age The modern state is so powerful and has such means of destroying its opponents that violence would be a self-defeating mode of fighting corruption and injustice. The French Revolution was the last people movement which could succeed through violent means. True, the Russian Revolution succeeded through violence but success was limited; it destroyed the Tsar regime but did not make the Russian people any more free than they were under Tsar. If anything, the Soviet dictatorship is more ruthless, more thoroughgoing and more safe from violent challenge than predecessor, whose tradition it has carried over and developed to a degree of perfection which would have been inconceivable in the 19th century.

The issue in Bihar is therefore not whether it is permissible for a popular movement to demand the dissolution of an elected legislature. Nor is it one of whether the movement led by Jayaprakash Narayan would undermine the foundations of democracy in India. The question one may legitimately ask is whether the success of the Bihar movement is likely to lead to the emergence of a better political and economic order in that unfortunate State; or whether, even if the movement fails to attain its immediate aim of the dissolution of the legislative assembly, it would contribute to the strengthening of democracy in India. For anyone who has tried to understand what is happening in Bihar and the kind of consciousness that JP is attempting to develop among his followers, the answer would be 'yes' on both these counts. At the same time, it must be realized that if the government puts down the movement by launching what the Congress president has described as a counter offensive in collaboration with the CPI, it would give the movement the character of a civil war, and lead to two undesirable consequences. For the time being, the people of Bihar will become utterly demoralized and resign themselves to oppression as to a calamity from God. Those who have been brought up in the authoritarian tradition would, no doubt, prefer such a docile population to one which is conscious of its rights and is willing to fight for them. But demoralisation would be only one side of the coin. During the years since independence the Indian people have developed some awareness of their rights as citizens of a democratic state and have exercised their franchise in five general elections. Some of them, especially of the younger generation, are not likely to bend under government repression. If they find that non-violent agitation is a sterile form of protest, they will not hesitate to switch over to political terror and anarchic violence. Once this trend assumes significant proportions, a totalitarian dictatorship of the communist or Nazi type – and there is little to choose between the two – can alone keep it under check.

Mrs Indira Gandhi is not the Lenin of India. She should not, even unwittingly, play the role of Chiang Kai Shek. She can, if she is so minded, play the much nobler role of healing Bihar's wounds and in the process initiate a new phase in the nation's march towards progress in freedom. But, for this she will have to adopt a different approach and espouse different policies from those of the past twenty years. She has shown remarkable courage and flexibility of approach in conducting India's foreign policy. But she has yet to display these qualities in dealing with domestic problems, which are more complex and of a different order of importance from those of war and diplomacy. Power and cunning are not enough to solve them. Their solution will presuppose a willingness to admit mistakes and rectify them without making it an issue of prestige, to break oneself free from outdated dogmas, and shed the jargon of pseudo radicalism which has fouled the atmosphere in which the Prime Minister has lived and worked since the *coup* of July 1969. The extent to which she is able to do this will determine the shape of things to come in Bihar and later, in the rest of the country.

The Bihar movement has also posed some tasks to social scientists. It has demonstrated in an unmistakable manner that western parliamentary institutions have not yet taken root in India. Is this failure only a necessary preliminary stage in the political evolution of India, or is it a sign of their unsuitability in the Indian context? If the latter, what would be the pattern of representative democracy best suited to India? Secondly, whether the movement in Bihar succeeds or fails in its objective of restructuring the political life of the state, it is clear that the present phase will in due course have to be followed by one of comprehensive reconstruction of the state's public life. On what lines, for example, should economic development be undertaken in Bihar? How should education be reorganized so as to make it more challenging intellectually and more meaningful socially? It would be wrong to expect men engaged in a struggle also to prepare a blueprint of the future. It is for academicians and intellectuals to give thought to these and similar problems regardless of their attitude to Jayaprakash Narayan and the movement he leads. If they abdicate their responsibility, they would only justify the contempt in which men of action hold them.

Srinivasa Ramanujan: Science, Tradition and Self-Esteem[1]

Ashis Nandy

(Quest 92: November-December 1974)

Srinivasa Ramanujan (1887-1920) did not live the life of a born genius trying to reconcile science and culture, fighting the spectre of alienation, or desperately protecting a modern self against a traditional environment. His is the story of a conservative but integrated scientist, for whom ancient meanings and modern knowledge were one. I do not deny the immense psychological conflicts which dogged his steps throughout life, but these conflicts only marginally involved the content of his work. In fact, one marvels at the remarkably consistent way Ramanujan used mathematics to symbolise his inner states, without either damaging his mathematics or showing any intense preoccupation with the political or social implications of his success.[2] There were a number of reasons for this.

First, Ramanujan's psychological conflicts arose out of his attempts to cope with an alien outer world, not with an alien self within. He never internalised the modern culture of science.[3] In fact, traditions, whether expressed in rituals and customs or in 'scientific truths', were part of his innermost core and he never had to be apologetic about them. There is no evidence that he ever seriously tried to prove the modernity of his religious ideas, or to Indianise Western science,[4] or even to use his professional success to counter his feelings of inferiority.

Ramanujan was no conflicted proselytiser like his contemporary Jagadis Chandra Bose (1858-1937) who tried to replicate in science the attempts of Swami Vivekananda, Rabindra Nath Tagore and Shri Aurobindo to 'carry the message' of India to the West and that of the West to India. All these men were sensitive to the West's political and cultural dominance, and their missionary zeal was, at one level at least, a glorified version of their own sense of humiliation. Ramanujan was far truer to Hindu orthodoxy, which is its long history has rarely shown any missionary passion.

This self-confident professional style was expressed in various ways. G.H. Hardy and J.E. Littlewood, when they said that Ramanujan had no clear conception of proof and showed little interest in its methodology, had in mind not merely the mathematical limitations of their Indian friend. They were also vaguely conscious of Ramanujan's sturdy reliance on the efficacy of his own intuitive powers and insights.[5] For example, it must have become obvious to Ramanujan in Cambridge that the days of formulae were more or less over and that his style of speculative mathematics had become slightly *passé*.[6] His closest friends in the university also tried to introduce him to the newer concerns of the discipline. But in success as much as in failure he remained true to his own concept of mathematics. And though he tried half-heartedly to adapt his style to the culture of modern mathematics, it was obvious to all who knew him that he could neither be easily taught nor formally educated. At the most, he could proactively learn things he was himself interested in.

This sense of autonomy sprang from a sense of being 'chosen'. He once reportedly said – and this would have deeply hurt his agnostic benefactor Hardy – 'An equation has no meaning for me unless it expresses a thought of God'.[7] The statement, if his, was less an expression of a work value and more of a sincere belief in being in possession of God-given gifts. This serene self-assurance grew out of his faith partly in his own supernatural pre-cognitive powers and partly in the sacred origins of his mathematics. He had internalised very early his primordial group's estimate of him as a mystic genius. And his later success at convincing his immediate interpersonal world of these powers validated this estimate. His subsequent exposures to Indian and Western skeptics did not alter this self-image. It remained, in essence, the traditional image of a *yogi*. He did not perceive himself as an *acharya*, a Brahminic professor or preceptor, but as a man of superlative extra-sensory powers – a man possessed.[8]

Secondly, there was Ramanujan's peculiar love-hate relationship with the dominant scientific culture of his time. Overtly, he accepted this culture; while at a deeper level, and unknowingly, he led a one-man non-cooperation movement against it. An analysis of this ambivalence would require a brief digression on two critical differences between the Western and traditional Indian attitudes to science. I shall first discuss the more obvious of these differences.

The traditional Indian concept of science, contrary to whatever its contemporary interpreters might say, was certainly less empirical than its Western counterpart. However, in one respect the Indian scientific tradition was more empirical than the accidental: it admitted that science could be a product of man's intuitive, infantile, a-rational self, and that the questions of 'trans-science' might intrude into the very structure of scientific knowledge.[9] In fact, if one ignores the ritualistic and magical elements in this conceptualisation of science, it would be found remarkably consistent with some of the emerging strands of consciousness in the modern philosophy of science. On the other hand, in Ramanujan's time, the operational principles of Western scientific activity and the dominant Western philosophy of science had become disjunctive. While creative scientific activity went on according to hypothetico-deductive principles, and comprehended large elements of aesthetic considerations and speculative thinking – and demanded, one may add, personality capacities compatible with these principles – the dominant Western philosophy of science feared its cultural and psychological determinants and favoured a rather crude form of inductive empiricism. Towards the beginning of this century psycho-analysis and theoretical physics did challenge the basis of these values, but Ramanujan had no access to these new strands of thought.[10] That is why, when he was exposed to Western science for the first time as an adult, he was caught between two powerful sets of attitudes. One seemed congruent with what every scientist was saying and only the applied scientists were doing, while the other with what very few scientists were saying and pure mathematicians were doing. Belonging to the last group, therefore, Ramanujan had to borrow from the Sanskritic world-view to legitimate his own work values. There was nothing in the dominant culture of science in the West which could support these values. (I have shown elsewhere how Hardy, faced with the problem of explaining the 'peculiar' solution his Indian collaborator offered to this contradiction in the culture of science, chose to reduce his own cognitive dissonance by reinterpreting Ramanujan so as to look a self-consistent agnostic English don.[11])

This brings us to the second major difference between the Indian and Western concepts of science. Pure mathematics is unashamedly non-empirical, and the 'philosophy' of pure mathematics is in some ways akin to the rationalist attitude to science. With the growth of modern science, it was this rationalism which was superseded and discredited in the West. The Indian philosophy of science, fixated at the medieval period, somehow maintained some of this rationalist flavour. At least, it continued to be skeptical of the positivist emphases on application, control, prediction and testability in the 'real', phenomenological world. After all, in the greater Sanskritic culture, absolute – and abstracted – reasoning and relationships had always been the major defences of the Sanskritic culture against the onslaught of history and the sufferings of the real life, consisting of persons, events, feelings and senses. Such an orientation may have stunted the growth of other sciences, but it provided nurturance to mathematical talents all right.

Ramanujan's inner science, being a product of this orientation to the external world, was a vigorous protest against the dominant Western concept of science. His mathematics had nothing to do with either social usefulness or the control of nature and men.[12] Nor did it involve anything as non-Brahminic as experimentation, observation and proof. His was rather the clean, speculative universalism of Advaita, a school of monistic philosophy which as dominated the greater Sanskritic culture from about the thirteenth century. Two themes associated with this philosophy – a belief that contradictions represent aspects of the same indivisible truth, and a pantheistic and vitalistic belief that explorations into the nature of things will reveal them as either essentially compatible with one another, or as belonging to a unified living system – perhaps also justified – the mystical feelings of uterine oneness with the universe that is frequently associated with scientific creativity, particularly with the *satori* experience of creative moments. At least, both the philosophical themes as well as the cosmic feeling of creative moments were present in Ramanujan.

It was this which gave Ramanujan the esoteric touch that seemed so attractive to the scientific world in the inter-war years. Even his hard-headed collaborators could not remain immune to this charm. It is revealing that in his later years a slightly embarrassed Hardy had to reject as unjustified sentimentalism the following assessment of his friend previously given by himself:

> It (Ramanujan's work) has not the simplicity and the inevitableness of the very greatest work; it would be greater if it were less strange. One gift it has which no one can deny, profound and invincible originality. He would probably have been a greater mathematician if he had been caught and tamed a little in his youth; he would have discovered more that was new, and that was, no doubt, of greater importance. On the other hand, he would have been less of a Ramanujan, and more a European professor, and the loss might have been greater than the gain.[13]

But as long as Ramanujan lived, it must have been the earlier Hardy who endorsed Ramanujan's self-identity, strengthening the Indian's allegiance to world of science, giving him self-esteem within the dominant scientific culture, and making it possible for him to have the necessary personal faith as well as the sense of gestalt as a scientist.[14]

These issues of self-esteem, autonomy and creativity can be approached from another historical vantage point. This alternative approach is best defined with reference to two specific questions. First, why did Ramanujan's Brahminic orthodoxy never interfere with his creativity, while, at about the same time, the more modern idea systems such as nationalism and Brahmoism could not check the professional disintegration of another Indian scientist, Jagadis Chandra Bose?[15] Do the differences between these two men tell us something about the prototypical adaptations to the culture of modern science which individual scientists have attempted in India?

At one level, the answer to the first question is simple. Ramanujan died young and could not develop into an institutionally entrenched symbol of Indian supremacy over the West or become a displayable ornament in his country. He never got involved in any organisational activity, and always remained outside the academic bureaucracy. He also bypassed the elaborate and ornate status systems of the Indian educational world which engulfed many of his contemporaries. But this, while obviously true, is only part of the story. One must look deeper for a full answer to this question. I try to do so by analysing some elements of the identity of Jagadis Chandra Bose, who happens to be the only other Indian scientist about whom I can speak with some confidence.

One clue to the differences between the two men is the nature of pure mathematics. The discipline, as compared to the other sciences, is obviously less influenced by personal and social forces, and is less open to defensive projections. Its abstract, non-empirical structure is so formidable, and its ready-made delibidinised structure so attractive, that even when cultural or personal themes are introduced into it, they lose their particularist edge the moment they enter it. It is, after all, the purest of sciences.

Pure mathematics is pure in another sense. Both modern physics and biology share with the social sciences the problem of contamination from observation: the more detailed and intensive the study of a scientific phenomenon, the greater the likelihood of its being altered in the process of investigation.[16] Atomic physics, which, apart from psycho-analysis, has most explicitly recognized this relationship between the observer and the object observed, also suggests something else: it is possible partly to transcend this indeterminacy only in the mathematical theory of a phenomenon.[17] In this sense, perhaps, pure mathematics is the closest to an observer-free science.

As a corollary, there are certain specific demands which mathematics makes on the scientist's personality. Evidence has it that creative mathematicians and mathematical physicists have identifications that are comparatively more impersonal, and that they tend to use withdrawal as a solution to their interpersonal problems.[18] The diffuse identifications and emphases on the defences of isolation, denial and intellectualization encouraged by the modal socialization of Brahminic culture, and withdrawal from the profane world it glorifies,[19] are, consequently, especially compatible with creativity in mathematics. In this sense, the traditional Indian ideal of mastery over self, and the complete abstraction of this self from worldly goods, instinctual needs, emotions and social relationships found – and, in some cases, still finds – its supreme expression in mathematical creativity.[20]

This was one of Ramanujan's main advantages. Bose, on the other hand, was working in, what was at that time, the unsure and inchoate disciplinary context of plant physiology and biophysics. He could not sense that while his vitalistic concept of science, rooted in some aspects of the Upanishadic theory of life, could provide a valid philosophy of science, it certainly could neither furnish rounded or readymade scientific theories nor foreclose alternative explanatory models.

Ramanujan's other advantage was his self-contained Brahminic world-view. This did not make overbearing demands on the content of the imported sciences; its demands were confined to the personal life of the scientists. It had its own science and it cared little for any other confident of itself, it also permitted an individual to segmentalise his life-style and maintain a certain amoral distance from his non-traditional professional roles. Naturally, this culture left Ramanujan's science alone. Things were different in the case of the tempestuous Bengali. Semeticised Brahmoism, the Hindu reformist sect to which Bose belonged, could not permit this distance between what a person did and what he valued. It was, after all, a rebellion exactly against this role diffusion, amorality in the modern of organized sector, and segmentalisation of life. In addition, the totalist Shakto traditions, which are distinctive of the Bengali high culture, may have induced Bose to see himself in a situation where the old and the new, the indigenous and the imported, seemed more directly in opposition.[21] This self-perception could have been endorsed by the efforts which the Bengali elites were making, precisely then, to define Indian nationalism essentially as a modernist movement.[22] As a result, the Bengali version of nationalism was in direct touch with the modern sector and was more cognizant of modern science. Its demands too were personal as well as scientific, and it also insisted on greater consistency between one's personal and professional existences. All these three influences – Brahmoism, Bengali high culture, and nationalism – forced a clear-cut choice between the traditional and the modern more markedly in Bose than in his Tamilian compatriot.

Finally, the absence of any pronounced feeling of national inadequacy, and of defensive, self-assertive tendencies, allowed Ramanujan to use his fluid, unself-conscious, and projective animism for purposes of self-transcendence. Mathematics for him was a personal medium abstracted from his attitude to his country's political fate. The defensive science of Bose, on the other hand, coloured by the psychology of subjecthood, and his own deeper-lying feelings of inadequacy, did not allow him to think of the work of other scientists as merely works of science. He had to take into account their nationality and the political implications of these sciences. Unlike the Western scientists of the age of faith, the personal faith of men like Bose not merely had to provide meaning and inspiration, but also to reduce inferiority feelings and to increase self-esteem. It had to be juxtaposed against the dominant culture of science and upheld with allegiance and fidelity against alien attacks.

I wonder if this could have been avoided. In the ultimate analysis, those very sensitivities which made Bose a creative man, also made him sensitive about his colonial status. If his nationalism was strait-jacket, it was a jacket he could not help wearing, given his level of awareness and the crisis of culture which colonialism precipitated. Perhaps, one could even speculate that it is this peculiar sensitivity to issues of dominance and submission which often is the major contribution of colonialism to professional degeneration, rather than any actual interference in the processes of research. Ramanujan, less aggressively nationalistic and yet more confident in his Brahminic orthodox, escaped this sensitisation. And, if one could define autonomy as insensitivity to issues of dominance and submission, he was certainly the more autonomous of the two scientists. Bose, in his nationalism as much as in his Westernized modernity, was far more deeply bound with the West, both in admiration and in hatred.

But one could also define intellectual autonomy as a continuous search for new identity elements which help integrate borrowed structures and ideas into an indigenous frame without humiliating the recipients, and a pursuit of those universals of science which are not the particularist concerns of a dominant culture of science in the garb of scientific universalism. At that level of autonomy-seeking, Bose, in his defeat, remains a more relevant figure in the history of Indian science.

Endnotes

1. This paper forms part of a larger study, 'The Other Science of Srinivasa Ramanujan', to be included in the author's forthcoming book, *Alternative Sciences*.

2. Even Suresh Ram, in his otherwise innocent biography recognizes that the 'majesty' of Ramanujan's search for self-definition 'lay in the harmony of his

inner and outer beings'. Suresh Ram, *Srinivasa Ramanujan*, National Book Trust, New Delhi, 1972, p. 76.

3. Ramanujan never articulated, but always seemed to act according to the dichotomy between the content and the environment of modern science. The first, to him, was part of the eternal verities, the second, peripheral in his concerns.

4. He was also not wholly oblivious of the political and social changes taking place in India. But he kept his mathematics uncontaminated by his political or social beliefs – as if religion was the only load his work could carry.

5. For instance, G.H. Hardy, *Ramanujan – Twelve Lectures Suggested by His Life and Work*, Cambridge University, Cambridge, 1940, pp. 4-5. See the section on Ramanujan in J.E. Littlewood, *A Mathematician's Miscellany*, Methuen London, 1957, particularly pp. 85-88.

6. See his letter to S.M. Subramanian, 7 January 1915, quoted in P.K. Srinivasan, *Ramanujan*, Muthilpeth High School, Madras, 1967, Vol. I: *Letters and Reminiscences*, p. 21.

7. R. Srinivasan, quoted in S Ranganathan, *Ramanujan, the Man and the Mathematician*, Aziz, Bombay, 1967, *op. cit.*, p. 88, James Jeans, in another context, once said that God was a mathematician. In the world of Ramanujan, mathematics was a system which integrated God, nature and man.

8. It must have already become obvious to the psychologically minded readers that Ramanujan's ego ideal in some ways was the mystic union with the Godhead, often sought after by schizophrenic patients. This is particularly significant in the context of his early object relations (not discussed here) which also were, in many ways, consistent with the family dynamics of schizophrenics. However, the more interesting fact is the manner in which this dynamic has been integrated within the range of a particular, slightly esoteric, form of normality in the Indian society. We shall come back to this.

9. A.M. Weinberg, 'Science and Trans-science', *Minerva*, 1972, 10(2), pp. 209-222.

10. Much later, the philosophical implications of these influential disciplines led to a search for a new normative justification for the hypothetic-deductive technology of scientific discoveries. And, once again, the manifest structure of scientific values began to correspond to the latent structure of scientific behavior. Two examples of the positivist effort to build such a normative justification are Michael Polanyi, *Personal Knowledge*, University of Chicago, Chicago, 1958 and Karl Popper, *The Logic of Scientific Discovery*, Basic Books, New York: 1959. Such a rethinking of the normative basis of scientific functioning became necessary because empiricism had come to be operationally defined – due to both cultural compulsions of the Western science and the needs

of the industrial revolution – as closeness to the physical senses and as a manipulative, power-seeking orientation to the outer world of living beings and nature.

11. Ashis Nandy, 'Ramanujan's Passage to England: A Psycho-historical Note on the Public and Private Cultures of Science', forthcoming.

12. Hardy had to make the same point aggressively and, in consequence, was considered an eccentric down by many scientists.

13. G.H. Hardy, 'Notice', in G.H. Hardy, P.V. Seshu Aiyar and B.M. Wilson (eds.), *Collected Papers of Srinivasa Ramanujan*, Chelsea, New York, 1962. I think the younger Hardy was more perceptive. The later Hardy was merely trying to make Ramanujan look a fully rational man, exactly as some of his Indian admirers have been trying to make him look an occult magician.

14. On the importance of these, see Polanyi, *op. cit.*, passim, particularly pp. 17-18. See also P.A.M. Dirac, 'The Evolution of the Physicist's Picture of Nature', *Scientific American*, CCVIII, May 1936, quoted in Polanyi *op. cit.*, p.12. On the view that scientific discovery is a creative act akin to creativity in the arts, see J. Bronowski, *Science and Human Values*, Hutchinson, London, 1956; S. Toulmin, *Philosophy of Sciences*, Harper and Row, New York, 1953.

15. See my 'Defiance and Conformity in Science: The Identity of Jagadis Chandra Bose', *Science Studies*, 1971, 2(1), pp. 31-85; also 'Indianized Science: J.C. Bose's Experiment with Truth', *Quest*, 1973, (84), pp. 19-34.

16. Max Born, 'Man and the Atom', in Morton Grodzins and Eugene Rabinowitch (eds.), *The Atomic Age*, Basic Books, New York, 1963, pp. 590-601.

17. *Loc. cit.*

18. For example, Anne Roe, *The Making of a Scientist*, Dodd, Mead, New York, 1952; see also D.C. McClelland, 'The Calculated Risk: An Aspect of Scientific Performance', in C.W. Taylor and F. Barron (ed.), *Scientific Creativity: Its Recognition and Development*, Wiley, New York, 1963.

19. G. Murphy, *In the Minds of Men*, Basic Books, New York, 1955; G.M. Carstairs, *The Twice Born*, Indian, Bloomington, 1957.

20. I have in mind here not only the mathematical achievements of the ancient Indians, but also the comparative performances in contemporary India of say, the more mathematics oriented scientists, on the one hand, and the applied scientists on the other.

21. Content-wise, the Shakto cult of Bengali Hinduism is perhaps more modern: style-wise, more totalist.

22. See my 'Making and Unmaking of Political Cultures in India', *Daedalus*, Winter, 1973, *102*(1), pp. 115-137, for a brief discussion of some of the socio-political reasons of the sharper opposition.

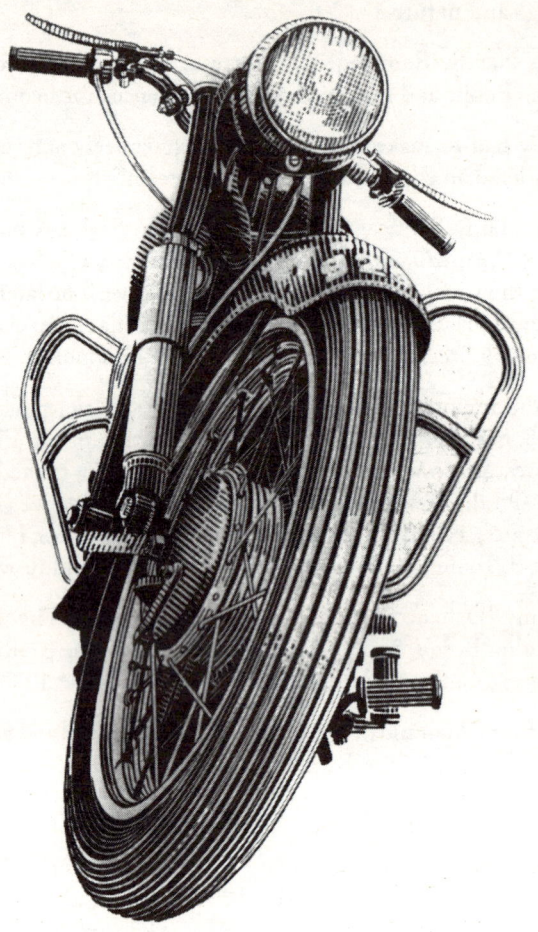

Unmatched in Safety and Comfort

The unique swinging arm suspension, both front and rear, is offered exclusively by RAJDOOT. It combines the soft riding comfort of deep shock absorbers with safe stability for fast, sure cornering. The big wheels give better grip —there's more rubber on the road—braking is easier, better, surer.

The 175 cc RAJDOOT gives you all the power for safe, fast and comfortable highway cruising, economy for city driving, and the stylish, sporty look that people admire.

Go Ahead ... Go Rajdoot

Rajdoot
MOTORCYCLES
Manufactured by :
Escorts Limited

ESCR 4310A2

Printed and published by Miss Sheela Singh *for the Indian Committee for Cultural Freedom, Army and Navy Building, 148 Mahatma Gandhi Rd., Bombay 1. at Inland Printers, Victoria Mills Buildings, 55 Gamdevi Road, Bombay 7.*

Sri Aurobindo: Superman or Supertalk?

Claude Alvares

(Quest 93: January-February 1975)

This is how he came to Pondicherry. One night, while at the office of the *Karmayogin*, the fiery nationalist paper he edited, he received secret information that the government intended to search the office and arrest him. He did not delay. In ten minutes, he was at the river *ghat*, and in a boat travelling the Ganges; in a few hours, he reached French Chandernagore; in a few days, in a boat manned by some young revolutionaries of Uttarpara, he slipped to Calcutta, where he boarded the *Dupleix* to reach French Pondicherry on 4 April 1910, finally safe from British hands.

(Later, he was to write that an 'inner voice' had prompted his decision to enter French India. This 'inner voice' however was a rationalisation of a necessity forced on him by circumstance. We must remember that aside from French India, he had *no other refuge* from the pursuing British.)

In Pondicherry, political exile was transmuted into a preoccupation with yoga, and visions began to shake his frame and expand his mind. Standing as it were on his own spiritual greatness – a distinction he accepts and discusses with ease in a volume *On Himself* – he touched the ceiling of mental existence, of Mind, where he glimpsed the next stage and consequence of nature's struggle and history: a race of supermen, gnostic beings, their minds divinised, their bodies charged with immortality through the presence of a supra-mental consciousness, constituting thus a divine life on earth, the Mystical Body of Brahman.

Here too, very much like Upton Sinclair's Jesus,[1] who realizes one day that he is not merely a country carpenter but the Messiah, the Son of God, Aurobindo and his followers were seized of a conviction that he was an *avatar*, a reincarnation of Krishna, the Samkhyan *Purusha*.

Prakriti was a French lady, Mrs Mira Richard, on board the *Kaya Muru*, en route for French India, in March 1914. And the Samkhya says, when Purusha and Prakriti come into contact, evolution begins.

The War however forced an interruption and Mrs Richard, with her husband, returned to France. But she was back in the April of 1920. Slightly later, Aurobindo announced to all his followers that she was indeed an incarnation of the divine Mother, *Mahakali*, and to be therefore regarded henceforth as his spiritual equal and partner. In 1926, he retired into almost total seclusion and Mira became the Mother of the Ashram.

The mystification of Sri Aurobindo and the Mother had begun, if only for their small band of followers. For in a country where *avatars* proliferate and *gurus* become god-men with divine facility, their claims to divinity were not very distinctly heard.

However, they continued their yoga, aiming at a 'complete organic change from one grade of evolution to another, a total divinisation not only of mentality and vitality but also of physicality, a transformed body ultimately functioning like a god immune to disease, decay and death'.[2] This would be possible when the Supermind, the creative force and aspect of *Satchidananda*, descended into the material dimension through the yogic efforts of the two pioneer avatars.

Then, all of a sudden, in 1950, Aurobindo died. Of a disease. And the Ashram reeled under the shock and the blow.

The Mother however quickly restored confidence. Aurobindo is not dead, she declared, He has merely 'withdrawn' from his physical body for it proved to be too frigid in its response to the blandishments of the Supermind. His body therefore was not ready for the transformation; it resisted all attempts at it. So he had to sacrifice himself to dissolve that resistance.

Nobody explained why Aurobindo waited for a disease to force him into 'withdrawal'.

The Mother, now the sole agent left to bring about the fruition of Aurobindo's vision, carried on her yoga.

In 1956, on the 29th of February, came the startling news that the supra-mental consciousness had descended on the earth's atmosphere. (The Supermind made an initial entry into the subtler side of the whole earth-plane and became a permanent part of the earth's future evolution; now inevitably, in the course of time, the Supermind would take organic form in the gross side of the terrestrial plane'.[3]) It was now only a matter of 'working out the consequences'.

'In 1973, on November 17, at the age of 94, the Mother died of old age.

Faith plummeted, but was raised again, this time by the pontification of the senior *sadhaks* of the Ashram.

The Mother did not die, they asserted; she is not dead; she withdrew like Sri Aurobindo.

This is what Nolini Kanta Gupta, the senior most *sadhak,* said:

The Mother's body belonged to the old creation. It was meant to be the pedestal of the New Body. It served its purpose well. The New Body will come.

The revival of her body would have meant revival of the old troubles in the body. The body troubles were eliminated as far as could be done by her while in the body – farther was not possible. For a new mutation, a new procedure was needed. 'Death' was the first stage in the process.[4]

Another explanation came from M.P. Pandit:

A new body was under formation, the supra-mental body, in which she was to take her embodiment as the end-result of the transformation of this body. She gave in *Notes on the Way* descriptions of this body, described how it looked. And about a year ago she told someone, 'I am trying to force this material body into that body but I have not been able to get the clue...'[5]

One day (continues Pandit) it flashed to me that as soon as that luminous body was ready the Mother would just walk into it without dying, 'without dying' means not necessarily keeping the body, but without the gap in consciousness; keeping up the continuity of the personality she would just cross into that luminous body.

That evening at 7.25 p.m. (November 17), the Mother withdrew from her body. They say the cause was heart failure, but let me tell you the heart failure was not the cause, the heart failure was the result of her withdrawal. . .'[6]

These tortuous defences would make Aurobindo turn in his *samadhi*, for they go against the genius, the spirit and the essence of his integral philosophy, the worth of which lay in its emphasis on the value of the previous levels of existence (matter, life and mind) because of their integration in the final essence of supra-mental beings. Apologies in the form of the body prolific of old and new creations, fall outside the logical possibilities of the Aurobindovian philosophical system.

Significantly, it was only after Aurobindo's death, and during the absolute reign of the Mother, that his philosophy underwent these mutations. It is for this reason that no serious student of Aurobindo's philosophy considers the Mother's ideas as part of the sages' system; her idiosyncrasies proliferated as her rule hardened. Morarji Desai during his visit to the Ashram during the time of Aurobindo noted already then how she dressed in costly saris and used all the modern accessories of make-up'.[7] Later these accessories only served to accentuate the image of decay. She often distributed flowers and spoke on Beauty, but when she died – this must be admitted – she was one of the ugliest women in the world. By that time however she had sedulously and discreetly provided the grounds for her eventual sanctification. Her *darshans* remained till the end a theatrical performance. Today, she outsells Aurobindo: the earnest visitor to Pondicherry will be dismayed to find that all talk centres round her dominating personality. But disciples are like children – they need mothers always.

It is for reasons such as these that the question weighing most uneasily on men's minds is whether the supramental consciousness did descend on the material plane in 1956. Evidence that is usually pedalled in favour of its occurrence, while it may seem conclusive for Auro-*bhaktas*, seems fatuous and amusing to others.

Internationally, a number of happenings have been attributed to the force and influence of the Supermind. For example during the Bangladesh War of Liberation, when news reached the Ashram that the US Seventh Fleet had passed Singapore and entered the Bay of Bengal, one of the Ashram disciples is reported to have sent in a message to the Mother asking whether the fall of Dacca could not be expedited. And of course, Dacca fell the next day. I have not been able to get Jagjit Singh Arora's opinion on this.

In 1956, to give another example, a senior statesman in Delhi from his knowledge of Mid-Eastern affairs, deduced that the Suez Canal crisis would erupt on the 9th of November of that year. The crisis actually peaked on the 2nd. Our diplomat is reported to have been perplexed at this reversal of his sagacity, until he met the Mother, on a chance visit, and she told him that he had not taken one important factor in his calculations: the supra-mental force had played the necessary havoc with his logic.

The founding of an institute for Psychical Research in the USSR is also cited as a piece of evidence, though all it may actually prove is that the Russians are getting barmier. It is also claimed that henceforth there will never be a nuclear war among nations. A very safe prediction, for if one does take place, there will be no one left alive to check this. And so on.

In most other people's minds, however, there are considerable and weightier reasons for denying altogether the Mother's claim that the divine has come down on earth. The evidence for this is woven into the very history and fabric of the Ashram, its development and growth, and its role in the life of Pondicherry.

The tiny town of Pondicherry is conveniently sliced into two residential units, a 'white' section and a 'black' section, by an 18-foot-broad canal called the *Quai de Gingy*. When the French ruled the roost, they occupied the white section, and the local Tamils the other. The white section is bounded on the East by the sea.

When the French left in 1954, the Ashram and its inmates came to monopolize this white section (the buildings are all painted white.) Economically, the situation on both sides of the *Quai* remained the same. The local people on the West of the canal lived (as they do today) in pretty gruesome conditions, not very different from those in which a number of their countrymen live; so that today an ironical situation has arisen: on one side of the *Quai* people are struggling to live human lives; on the other, a group of people are attempting to create super-men.

The Ashram at its inception in 1926 had decided to remain solely a spiritual organization. As it grew in size, however, certain anomalies arose in its functioning, chief of which centred round its attitude to Pondicherry's merger with India, around the time of the country's independence. As Aurobindo was no longer in control of the Ashram, the peculiar attitudes of the Mother came to the fore.

Not surprisingly, the Archives of the Government of India of that period confirm that the Ashram stood solidly against French decolonization. Undoubtedly, the Ashram received very favoured treatment from the French administration in the form of exemption from fees and taxes; besides, its head was a French woman.

G. Parthasarathy, then reporting for the *Hindu;* wrote in 1948:

> The wide currency given to the idea of a free and independent India, at any rate, a free Pondicherry, which will maintain close relations with both France and India, has only been possible because of the moral support given to it by the Ashram.... The French Ambassador, M. Levi, is now openly canvassing the possibilities of making the French settlements into another Monaco or Andora. M. Baron, the Governor, seeks to impress on French Indian politicians the virtues of neutrality as the means of avoiding hostility both from India and France. This propaganda done from such influential quarters... is meant to divide the nationalist forces. And it is stressed by local observers that the campaign would have had little value but for the support of the Ashram.

(Aurobindo had once said: 'First therefore become Indians.')

However, when it became increasingly clear that Pondicherry would become a part of India, the Ashram reversed its stand to jump on to the merger bandwagon. But the alien attitude remained. For example, when the whole country was plunged in gloom in 1964 on the death of Nehru, the Ashram remained untouched by grief, the Indian flag was not lowered, and the Aurobindo International Centre of Education did not close as a mark of respect to the departed leader.

Ironically, in 1956 (the very year the Mother announced the descent of the supramental presence) the workers of the Ashram struck work on grounds of low wages, insecurity of service, meagre fixed D.A., and lack of leave facilities. More than a hundred of them were dismissed. Later, the majority were taken back, except 35 who remained staunch unionists. The Ashram authorities did not give in even when two of these dismissed workers were hospitalized after a prolonged hunger strike.

Tensions were aggravated further when the people of Pondicherry found the Ashram overflowing gradually with Bengalis and Gujaratis (who could speak French but not Tamil). And in the anti-Hindi agitation that swept the South in 1965, the Ashram was attacked by riotous mobs. Arrested rioters were later identified as disgruntled employees and fishermen whose lands had been appropriated and converted into Ashram playgrounds.

The most remarkable part of this agitation came *after* it had subsided. The Mother (an avatar, touched by supramental light) issued a pamphlet condemning the acts of violence on the Ashram buildings and ended up accusing the Christians, the DMK, the Communists, the merchant community, and the students – all of whom together make up the total population of Pondicherry – of antipathy to the Ashram. The Ashram had by this time finalized plans for the Rs. 1,000 crore international city of Auroville, an experiment dedicated *to creating human unity and international fellowship.*

The agitation, however, prompted questions in Parliament, as a result of which a Joint Secretary from the Union Government was deputed to conduct an inquiry and file a report. The report was found unfavourable to the Ashram and consequently quietly suppressed.

The report spoke about the 'evolution' of Ashram activities and the erosion of its previous spiritual intentions, its entry into commerce and industry in a big way. It complained against the favoured treatment given to the Ashram by the governments of India and the Union Territory of Pondicherry in the granting of licences and the supply of raw materials, including zinc, cement and iron. The report mentioned as an example how a Pondicherry government order allotting licences for zinc sheets to local traders was later reversed by a central authority, which freshly granted a licence for the purchase of 17 lakh worth of zinc sheets to Honesty (*sic!*) Enterprises, the economic holding of the Ashram.

The report also listed the 43 industries either owned or controlled by the Ashram or by devotees who, the report suggested, were using the Ashram's position as a charitable organization to avoid taxes. It detailed the value (running into several crores of rupees) of the properties owned by the Ashram in Pondicherry itself. It also compared the wages earned by Ashram employees to those earned by others elsewhere in the area and found them lower than the mean. (The Ashram employs practically an army of workers including domestic servants, gardeners, mechanics, carpenters, moulders, electricians, masons, printing press workers, weavers, farm and dairy hands, tailors, shop assistants, cooks, cobblers, workers in soda, sugar, metal and cottage industries, and so on.)

It finally concluded that the root cause of the antipathy of the local people could be traced to these economic reasons: exploited labour, small traders driven out of business and the local merchant community forced out of competition since it could not face the huge capital behind Ashram holdings.

Today, the situation is very much the same, probably worse. The week I was in Pondicherry, the Ashram announced plans to enter the fishing industry. Local fishermen, who use oar-driven boats, predict that the mechanised vessels of the Ashram will soon knock them out of the market.

Every single Pondicherry native I talked to, spoke bitterly of the Ashramites as people who thought themselves a new and separate class and continuously behaving thus, literally living in a seclusion prompted by spiritual arrogance and smugness. It would appear that an organization pledged to transforming or aiding the transformation of human potential would not show such a callous disregard for what goes on outside its portals. Yet the local people complain of being treated 'like dogs'. They are not allowed to enter Ashram buildings, partake of Ashram sports or study at the education centre. However, foreigners and tourists are welcomed without reservation. MPs and ministers arrive and their photographs are published with pride in the Ashram journals. The Ashramites, however, are not the only people in India who believe that ministers are exemplars of the new super-consciousness.

Morarji Desai supports what we have said above. He writes of one part of his visit to Pondicherry and the Ashram:

'I also got the impression that those people who were influential in society received greater attention and care when they came to the Ashram. Shri Hukmichand came to Pondicherry while I was there and was received with great enthusiasm and cordiality. I had never heard of him having any religious philosophy.'[8]

The Ashram activities are now extending beyond Pondicherry. Recently Ashramites were found at work in the State Bank offices in Bombay, a contract being given to them by Mr R.K. Talwar, State Bank chairman, an Aurobindo devotee. The State Bank uses its funds also to advertise in Ashram journals regularly, though these have a commercially valueless circulation.

Local feeling against the Ashram flared again recently when the proposal to name the coming Pondicherry University after Aurobindo was made public. The proposal was withdrawn following a total *bandh*, the first in Pondicherry's political history.

Another place for discrimination is the Aurobindo International Centre of Education. Here 700 students are taught by 200 professors! Until the mid-sixties, the Centre, although aided heavily by the Education Ministry in Delhi, was not open to the public. After the gates were opened for all, fees (Rs 150) became a strong disincentive to the locals. The degree is not recognized by other institutions. However, no charitable institution in the country receives grants from government that does not cater to people of all classes and creeds and income groups. The Pondicherry Centre is an unintelligible phenomenon.

All the available evidence goes to prove that the Ashram is not a charitable organization at all. Its Olympic-style swimming-pool, the sports grounds, the hospitals, the education centre, are out of bounds for the people of Pondicherry though they have been constructed partly through public funds. The profits of the Ashram's commercial activities are ploughed back into its coffers; they do not go into the development of the state and its people.

Auroville, the Ashram's brainchild, situated on the borders of Pondicherry and entering into large tracts of Tamil Nadu, comes more as a shock than as a revelation of glorious visions. Most foreigners are perplexed on seeing it: Rs 1,000 crore being spent to create a new city, replete with cultural centres, industrial units, ultra-modern residential apartments and including pavilions that will *serve sixteen different types of Indian foods*, while in the villages In Auroville itself, poverty is still pervasive, total.

The fate of the 20-odd villages in the Auroville area is a question. Authorities say they will be 'incorporated' into the life of Auroville. Right now, their inhabitants do most of the manual labour in Auroville, milking the cows and tilling the fields. But since Auroville will soon automate its dairy industry, and later the others, the labour of these villagers will no longer be needed. What then? One Frenchman had a drastic answer: 'If they do not find the atmosphere congenial, they will be welcome to leave. But while they're here we'll provide them with employment' and, I might add, that at the cheapest rates going.

The manner of employment is a tourist stunt: in one village, three young boys have been dressed in clean saffron shirts and placed in a 'modern' hut, where they are working at *agarbattis*. The tourists are shown this, and think the set-up very commendable. Hardly have you left the hut, however, when you find 150 children outside, gaping at the whiteskins, hungry, unschooled.

But it would be an error to think that the Ashram and Auroville are big centres for the sole production of supertalk about superbeings and supercities. Some of the foreigners at Auroville are very sincere people – they have to spend a year there working on their own resources before they can be accepted into the community. However, one does not find the atmosphere of an Israeli *kibbutz* anywhere. All the menial jobs, like carrying cowdung around, all manual jobs, are left to the second-class citizens of Pondicherry.

All said and done, as long as the Ashram provokes hostility and anger in the rest of Pondicherry, it is nowhere near the benign glow of supra-mental existence. Some of the younger Ashramites are disillusioned with the attitude of the Ashram seniors to people with no other qualification than a claim to huge bank accounts. Dissent is not possible and the Ashram is well on its way towards becoming another Ford Corporation.

The statement of a student to the Ashram a few years ago still retains its edge and poignancy: 'You claim to be a spiritual organization. Then please tell us WHY people around you are (according to you) your enemies? Why after so many years of your existence have you not been able to win the love and esteem of the people around you?'

This souring of the dreams of Aurobindo in today's Pondicherry is to my mind not so much a consequence of the pervasiveness of human fallibility; it stems rather from a denial of the fact of such weakness and a concomitant uncritical inflation of personalities. The roots of this malady have their origin in Aurobindo himself. The day he decided to accept the adulation of his obsequious fawning disciples and glimpsed in himself elements of avatarhood saw the birth of the spiritual arrogance that hovers thickly around the high-brows of many Ashram inmates today; the same day also saw the crystallisation of Aurobindo's view that *his weltanschauung* was indubitably inspired by a final supra-mental vision of truth beyond all dogmas and creeds, beyond all conflicting ideologies.

In subscribing to this tendency, Aurobindo had obviously overlooked Hegel. We know that Hegel had once ended his lecture series with the statement that history had indeed culminated with and in his philosophy. Aurobindo had of course a similar opinion about his own philosophy by the time he died. But neither could be taught that apparent megalomania is entailed in the very philosophic quest for comprehensive truth itself. After all, whoever feels he has actually found comprehensive truth cannot perhaps be blamed for viewing all former philosophies as having been aiming somehow at what he has found. In a sense perhaps he is honouring them when he supposes this.

Such an attitude of general superiority is radically evident in Aurobindo's claim, for example, to have written *the* perfect poetry, the future poetry. The literary critic, Mr Nissim Ezekiel, has mercifully laid that claim to rest. What could *any* critic do when confronted with passages such as these?

'In poetry anything can pass – for instance, my " voice of a tilted nose"':

O voice of a tilted nose,

Speak but speak not in prose!

Nose like a blushing rose.

O Joyce of a tilted nose!

This is high poetry but put it in prose and it sounds insane.[9]

In an age that has 'metaphysically shuddered' at the discoveries of Einstein, Planck and Bohr, we have perforce to assume a skeptical attitude toward the claim of any man to final answers about the structure of the universe or the essence of its truth. We remember immediately what Judge Learned Hand said: 'The mark of a free man is that ever-gnawing inner uncertainty as to whether or not he is right.' Or the declaration of the great atomic physicist, Niels Bohr: 'Every sentence I write must be understood not as an affirmation, but as a question.'

No man owns the whole truth; if he believes that he does, his belief will inevitably produce distortions in him and in those who profess to follow him. What a man *can* lay claim to is person truth, but here again were he to universalize this, he would refuse to other men their own right and ability to reach their own truth. Gandhi's Truth, when applied to his sons, destroyed them. And the ideal city of Auroville will be ultimately constructed through the deprivation of the lands and means of livelihood of the peasants of more than 20-odd villages, which even now are resting uneasily in the area.

When I asked a tourist what he thought about the new city, he made a remarkably mature observation: 'I wonder whether Auroville is justified in a poor country like India; but should we forget the phenomenon of men so enthralled by a vision that they forget all else?'

The communists of Russia, we are told, were inspired by the Marxian utopia of a stateless, proletarian society: Aleksander Solzhenitsyn's *Gulag* tells us how they went about it. The German Nazis had a similar aim but six million Jews provided the boost. That the disciples of Aurobindo have already become insensitive to the poor around them is an indication that they are driven by similar visionary utopias, and this, not to any lesser degree.

Critics of the French jesuit Pierre Teilhard de Chardin have pointed to his praise for totalitarian regimes, which he held to be in line with the essential trend of the 'cosmic' movement. The Jewish genocide was resolved by de Chardin as a necessary backfire preceding a phylogenetic boost to newer evolutionary phases. Tomorrow Aurobindoites might make similar claims. The indications are already there: both de Chardin and the Aurobindo group betray in their ideas a general lack of serious interest in social questions. In fact, what is most significant about these visionaries is their overriding impatience with the messiness of ordinary human life – the real mark of the totalitarian.

Life, de Chardin writes, 'shows signs... of requiring us by very virtue of its movement toward a state of higher being, to sacrifice our individuality.'[10] In Aurobindo's opinion, individual consciousness will dissolve into a collective divine consciousness, which will no longer be *human* supramental consciousness. In such a situation, freedom will belong only to the supramental consciousness. We will be free only when we have repudiated our human significance. In order to save humanity then, we will first have to destroy it.

What really amazes me is that Aurobindo did not wish to accept one of the prime lessons of history, the tendency of all disciples to make use of their masters for their own selfish ends. What is taking place in Pondicherry today cannot be identified as anything other than the fabrication of a new religion. The central office of the Ashram is crowded with 'holy' pictures and objects; pictures of Aurobindo and the Mother stare at the inmate and the visitor from the walls of every room within the Ashram precincts. The personal lives of the two avatars are being carefully doctored in significant historical details. The Mother is no longer referred to (in her pre-Pondicherry phase) as Mrs Mira Richard; her maiden name, Mira Elassa is used. Paul Richard has ceased to exist. No mention is made of Mrinalini, Aurobindo's wife.

Now Aurobindo's philosophical system is a vast one and it took him 29 volumes to examine every aspect of it. The possibility of error of course increases with the scope of the undertaking. After two years of careful study, I have found myself forced to the conclusion that the Aurobindovian system is, to a sufficiently large extent, scientifically and philosophically indefensible.

An important qualification is necessary here. In the past few years a number of books have been published eulogizing the philosophy of Aurobindo and its great relevance for our times. As far as I am aware no major critical analysis of his philosophy has yet appeared. This essay is an attempt to test the credibility of Aurobindo's system and measure 'its value against an index of sound opinion.

My starting point is the philosophy of science and the implications of the great discoveries in science that have taken place during the past seven decades. Aurobindo might not have had the time or the inclination to enter into a proper study of the scientific picture of the world. Also, some of the great discoveries took place after his self-imposed seclusion. However, the theories of relativity and quanta were formulated in the first two decades of the twentieth century, early enough to merit sufficient attention. But I am willing to excuse those lapses.

However, I find it unreasonable to excuse professors of philosophy who talk quite glibly and unthinkingly today about the extraordinary brilliance of his philosophy and its relevance to our contemporary understanding of the world. I disagree sharply with any of the glorious assessments of Aurobindo's philosophy primarily because I believe them to have been made not by serious thinkers on intrinsic grounds but by men who have found it beneficial to their own interests to jump on to the Aurobindo bandwagon, to cash in on the sudden popularity that his philosophy has attained in the West, particularly among people who have always been a little soft in the head whenever it came to accepting anything 'philosophical' from India. (Philosophies from India are like Indian handicrafts: they are valuable not because they have value for life but because they come from exotic India.)

I submit that the principal reason for the attractiveness of Aurobindo's philosophy has to do with its psychological reinforcements. Peter Medawar puts it thus: 'Once again there is a feeling of despondency and incompleteness, a sense of doubt about the adequacy of man, amounting in all to what a future historian might again describe as a failure of nerve. Intelligent and learned men may again seek comfort in an elevated kind of barminess. Mystical syntheses between science and religion, like the Cambridge Neo-Platonism of the mid-seventeenth century, have their counterpart today, perhaps in the writings and cult of Teilhard de Chardin and in a revival of faith in the Wisdom of the East.'[11] In the historical evolution of consciousness, the value of such attractions is temporary, as the later denouement of Cambridge Neo-Platonism shows.

The indefensibility of Aurobindo's philosophical system is due to a built-in obsolescence. The theories of relativity and quanta, the implications of Goedel's theorem, the significance of the second law of thermodynamics, and the elucidation of evolutionary processes at the level of the micro-sphere are some of the major difficulties his philosophy must face. A philosophy or theology that does not take seriously the knowledge of the structure and development of the world and of man which the perspective of modern science affords, has no claim to any serious consideration as embodying truth. In Aurobindo's case, the absence of a critical approach to his ideas has greatly vitiated their relevance to our contemporary understanding of the world. Aurobindo, as I have already noted, formulated his opinions without being aware of the implications of the momentous discoveries in science that were taking place around him during his time and before. If its scientific innocence has been preserved till this day it is because of the presence of disciples who have suspended their critical faculties to swallow totally all he said, and because of the dominating influence of Mira Richard.

Like most Indian philosophers of yore, Aurobindo too was driven to claim that his philosophy was not only the most worthy but also the only possible interpretation of the essence of the *Prasthanatryayi* (which comprises the Upanishads, the Gita and the Brahma-Sutras). In other words, Aurobindo's meaning system remained solidly within the larger framework of the Indian tradition. He was an Indian philosopher, first and last. Scholars who do not understand the principal elements of the Indian philosophical tradition will find it difficult to make sense of a large amount of what he says.

The major premise of his argument is assumed in the form of the Absolute (*Brahman*) of Indian thought, the fundamental reality behind the manifold appearances of this world. In Aurobindo, this reality has two aspects. In itself, it retains the non-qualifying qualities of the Absolute of Shankara: it is timeless, immutable, infinite, unknowable – ultimately, *neti, neti*. In its relation to the world, it is *Satchidananda*. Perhaps this second formulation is not quite accurate, for Satchidananda is the world and its forms, progressing through an evolutionary process from the initial stage of Complete Ignorance (matter) through Life and Mind, to Supermind (Spirit, absolute consciousness). *Maya* then is the ignorance that is inherent in our ordinary mental being which creates a false identification with the limited ego and thus inhibits us from realizing the nature of our true self and its potential. Each individual, each being, is a spark of the Divine.

The conception of these truths is placed by Aurobindo in a cyclical context for a reason that is principally logical. Matter (ignorance) and Spirit (consciousness) are irrevocably opposed. There is no possibility therefore of spirit arising from matter, unless of course, it is already present in matter in a hidden state. In other words, unless we pre-suppose consciousness in matter, we cannot explain its later emergence from it to provide a basis for this view, Aurobindo introduces the process of 'involution' by which Satchidananda descends into matter, into Ignorance, then through 'evolution' progresses to a more unrestricted, unveiled and wholesome consciousness.

The terminus of such a process therefore must be its beginning; evolution will therefore continue till it reaches the stage of the Supermind or the Absolute, fully conscious of itself, manifest in the collective supra-mental consciousness of gnostic beings. In other words, these gnostic beings, constituted essentially on the supra-mental plane, would create by their very existence a blanket of divine life on earth. Thus will Brahman have consummated its 'supreme adventure' of attempting to manifest its light, truth and bliss under conditions which seemed totally antithetic to these qualities.

The logic of such a cyclical process or presupposition of a hidden consciousness is akin to the logic that took hold of men's minds after Darwin, which demanded divine intervention at the critical points of the evolutionary process. It was thought then that life's beginnings in a material base that was, phenomenologically at least, distinct and different from it, and likewise, the emergence of mind from life, could not be satisfactorily explained unless one pre-supposed the agency of the power of God.

However, scientists have been able to refine our understanding of the evolutionary process to such a remarkable degree that there is no more any necessity to think of 'critical' points of transition in the process requiring any divine agency; in fact, 'critical' points no longer exist, for what one now finds is a continuum without any sharp 'leaps'. It appears that there has been a tendency in evolution for matter to assume increasingly complex forms of organization in a hierarchy whereby the more complex are assembled out of the less so. There is therefore no more logical or empirical need for the Aurobindovian theory of cyclical evolution than there is for the theory that the Earth is flat.

As a matter of fact, every major component of Aurobindo's philosophy disintegrates when confronted with contemporary insights into our understanding of man and the universe. For example, an analysis of the law of entropy and the theory of relativity does not support, to any appreciable degree Aurobindo's ideas of time and space.[12]

The proposition that forms the basis of our critique of Aurobindo's dilations on the nature of time excellently summarises what the German physicist, Carl F. von Weizsaecker has discussed at length in *The History of Nature* and is to be found in Rushton Coulborn's *Feudalism in History*. It says: 'History is the fundamental knowledge in every world of existence and the physical scientist is at last being forced to recognize this.'

What is historical is temporal, temporary, contingent. The human consciousness that creates history is itself time-bound. Our sense of time and temporality is strictly in keeping with one of the most fundamental laws of our universe, the second law of thermodynamics or the law of entropy. If we examine carefully the history of our dominating ideas and pretensions, we notice various attempts to slip by the influence of this law. These began with Plato, who absolved his world of ideas from any allegiance to it and went over to the other extreme of asserting that if there was anything that was subject to that law, it was a valueless contamination. Indian systematic philosophy which culminated in Shankara also followed a similar pattern.

Scholars who are normally enthused over the contemporariness of Aurobindo in his attention to evolutionary theory are in for a rude shock. For whichever way the evolutionary process is defined and elucidated by scientists today, it *makes no difference* to Aurobindo at all. A philosophical system that claims to rely on evolution as a scientific fact, and then considers any further refinement or change in our thinking of it as irrelevant to its grand scheme, has something substantially erroneous in its very construction.

Aurobindo writes: 'A theory of spiritual evolution is not identical with a scientific theory of form-evolution and physical life-evolution; it must stand on its own inherent justification: it may accept the scientific account of physical evolution as a support or element, but the support is *not indispensable.*'[13]

In another place he writes again: ...the development of one form of life out of a precedent less evolved form, natural selection, the struggle for life, the survival of acquired characteristics *may or may not be accepted*, but the fact of a successive creation with a developing plan in it is the one conclusion which is of primary consequence.'[14] It is indeed ironic that the very factors Aurobindo once considered 'not indispensable' have now been mapped in such great detail by scientists like Simpson. Monod and Dobzhansky that no vestige of any 'plan' is anymore in evidence. Simpson caustically remarks: 'The extreme view that evolution is basically or overall an orthogenetic process is evidence that some scientists' minds tend to move in straight lines, not that evolution does.'[15]

The classical ontology of time was based on an attitude that had once coloured Plato's ideas. For Plato, as we know, the operations of this world were indeed a contaminated fall-out of a pristine world of Being-Ideas. The very word 'ontological' displays the interest of traditional metaphysicians in the logic of the *ontos,* the logic of being. The basis of being was timeless and so logic, if it intended to explain the relations of such a being, had also to be timeless. It is only in our own century, that we find Martin Heidegger repudiating the construction of being independent of time, and beginning his thinking along the lines of an essential relation between Being and Time.

How is a timeless logic possible? Simply, by eliminating all temporal and historical considerations from the perspective of thought. What we experience in consciousness is the fullness of time, historical time. An individual is a concrete concentration in historical time. As consciousnesses differ, time differs and no two things are therefore identical. For the circumstances differ with each individual as each one lives in his own specific time and is a combination of unique factors not available to anyone else in the unpredictable conspiracy of heredity and environment. Even twins, we must admit, are born one after the other.

Like Newton, Aurobindo understood time and space in absolute terms because he had to; he related his understanding of both phenomena to the action of his Absolute and the constitution of his Absolute. Assuredly, this notion of absolute time was not meant to be a tool of understanding as Newton's was, but this does not absolve it from facing the same difficulties, presented especially by the theory of relativity.

The very conception of an Absolute does not include time. A philosopher might make the statement that the Absolute is an ontological necessity, but the grounds for making such a statement must remain exceedingly shaky and precarious. For we do not experience the Absolute, we reach it by a process of thought, by abstraction, by elimination, by the process of *neti, neti*. Aurobindo himself notes: 'When we look at existence itself, Time and Space disappear.'[16] In another place he writes: 'If this indefinable, infinite, timeless, spaceless Existence is, it is necessarily a pure Absolute. It cannot be summed up in any quantity or quantities, it cannot be composed of any quality or combination of qualities. If all forms, quantities, qualities *were to disappear*, this would remain.'[17] He continues in another place: 'It is pure existence, eternal, infinite, indefinable, not affected by the succession of Time, not involved in the extension of space, beyond form, quantity, quality – Self only and absolute.'[17] This is a roundabout way of evading the law of entropy again. After Plato we cannot forget that permanence belongs only to the conceptual.

Eternity is the common term between Time and the Timeless Spirit; they are two-fold states of being and consciousness, one an eternity of immobile status, the other an eternity of motion in status (Time).'[18] Aurobindo then proceeds to provide the ontological basis of time and space. Here I quote passages where his stylistic gaucheries blur all his profoundly obscure insights.

He writes: 'Space would be Brahman extended for the holding together of forms and objects; Time would be Brahman self-extended for the deployment of the movement of self-power carrying forms and objects; the two would then be a dual aspect of one and the same self-extension of the cosmic Eternal.'[19]

Aurobindo therefore admits that time in real and eternal.

In another obfuscatory paragraph, he concludes: 'In its fundamental truth the original status of Time behind all its variation is nothing else than the eternity of the Eternal, just as the fundamental truth of Space, the original sense of its reality, is the infinity of the Infinite.'[20] Further,

> For Being can see the whole Time development [in what sense can a pure Absolute see?] from outside or from above the movement; it can take a stable position within the movement and see the before and after in a fixed, determined or destined succession [God has become Laplace]; or it can take instead a mobile position in the movement, itself move with it from moment to moment and see all that has happened receding back into the past and all that has to happen coming towards it from the future; or else it may concentrate on the moment it occupies and see nothing but what is in that moment and immediately around or behind it.

It can see Time from above and inside Time, exceeding it and not within it; it can see the Timeless develop the Time-movement without ceasing to be timeless, it can embrace the whole movement in a static and dynamic vision and put out at the same time something of itself into the moment-vision.[21]

After such excruciating gibberish, I prefer to stick to the fundamental insight of Heidegger's being-in-time, and relegate all non-temporal conceptions to the sphere of non-being, non-existence, non-meaning. For those however who *feel* that Aurobindo *has* something to say in passages like these, but who are never able to extract any of his ideas from his clumsy prose, Aurobindo has presented an escape hatch in the form of his Logic of the Infinite, which is actually no logic at all. A typical instance, relevant to what we have been discussing is:

Their simultaneity (the Timeless Eternal and a Time Eternity), however contradictory and difficult to reconcile it might seem *to our finite surface seeing,* would be intrinsic and normal to the Maya or eternal self-knowledge and all knowledge of Brahman...[22]

In other words, if there are a couple of things that seem irreconcilable to our limited minds, we should not be unduly perturbed, since from the point of view of an Infinite Mind, they present a perfectly harmonious picture. Of course, Aurobindo is suggesting here that irreconcilables make no difficulty for him too, and that we should be free to draw the implications about a nature that has such powers.

In general, the philosophical implications of the theory of relativity and the limitations placed on nature by the law of entropy do not support Aurobindo's explanations of the phenomenon of time. The concept of eternity has been subjected to devastating criticism. We have no direct experience of eternity in the sense in which we have direct experience of time. More commonly, the word 'eternity' has been used to denote a state of timelessness, something of a qualitatively different order from an expanse of time, however long. And it is widely agreed that everlasting time and timelessness (the eternity of time and timelessness) are such totally different conceptions that any attempt to *unite* them must be extremely hazardous.

On the other hand, we live within time: indeed, within a strictly limited period of time. Heidegger put this very well when he insisted that temporality is the meaning of the Being of that entity which we call 'Dasein'. Temporality, rather than time, is the primordial state of being or existence, for each of us exists 'toward our end', which is death. What Heidegger calls 'within-time-ness' is something given *along with existence* itself. 'Temporality is the reason for the clock'; and, 'in a certain manner Dasein itself is the clock.'[23] Time-sense is a primary fact of consciousness.

Time itself is not however a part of the external world, as Aurobindo believed. *Change is a fact of nature.* And biological change within our own organism is experienced subjectively in consciousness as time. Our human condition is firmly linked to the order of nature, throughout which there is a single direction of change. To the subjective awareness this is the direction of time.

The direction of time, or *time's arrow* as Eddington put it, we perceive from the operation of the law of entropy, which states that in any transformation of energy from one form to another in a closed system, the entropy of the system tends to increase, i.e., it may increase (and it in fact generally does so), or it may remain unchanged, but it never decreases. This law clearly expresses a fundamental limitation, imposed by nature itself, on the feasibility of transforming energy from one form to another completely. It stands for a definite trend in the natural order. And this trend points to a direction in time.

The basic biological change, which involves a continuing increase of entropy, is internal to us and is experienced subjectively in consciousness. The sense of time which each one of us undoubtedly possesses may therefore be correlated directly with entropy increase, minimal though this may be in the case of biological, open-ended thermo-dynamic systems. Of course, it is not suggested that the experiencing subject recognizes his internal change as change of entropy, but that change which is so characterized in the language of physical science is what underlies temporality as a fact of consciousness. For the trend of entropy is uni-directional.

As we noted before, all religions and a great number of absolutist philosophical systems attempt to convince their followers that a human being can evade the basic law of entropy: such, in fact, is the sum and substance of the idea and promise of immortality. The 'soul' of religious theory is not subject to the law, but the ordinary body is. Christians believe that this body will one day rise from the grave, *intacta,* and from that moment on be able to disdain for all time the jurisdiction of the second law. The Indian philosophy of rebirth, to which Aurobindo gave added impetus, is another variation on the same theme, created originally in humanity's childhood. Jacques Monod speaks of man's continual urge to deny his contingency and is quite convinced that there must be a genetic source for man's drive to compose ontogenies and other allied security corporations.[24]

Aurobindo might not have heard of entropy, but what about the theory of relativity? He had of course heard of Einstein. In a discussion on Eddington, Russell and Jeans, he noted: 'Russell ranks as a great mathematician but there too Eddington has one superiority over him; he is supposed to be the only one, so say some, one of the only five, say others, who have a complete understanding of Einstein's mathematical formulation; Russell is not counted among them and that perhaps disables him from understanding the full consequences of Relativity.'[25] Aurobindo was not one of the five who were supposed to have understood Einstein, and it is ironic that the implications of the theory do not bear out his own pontifications on time.

Newton's misleading definition of absolute time spoke of it as something which of itself flows equably without relation to anything external. We know now that there is no such thing as absolute time, any more than there is such a thing as absolute space. If Newton predicated an absolute, physical, mathematical time, in terms of which to express the equations of motions of classical mechanics, Aurobindo spoke of space and time as extensions of his Absolute. Newton's purpose in introducing absolute time was to introduce consistency into the theoretical characterization of a vast range of phenomena. And it was the discrepancies in classical mechanics that led Einstein to his theory of relativity, which formally rejected the conceptions of absolute space and time. Aurobindo, I am afraid, laid the foundations for the discrediting of his Absolute by relating space and time to it in absolute terms.

Aurobindo did talk of space-time, but not even he would be willing to admit that his formulation of the relation of these two phenomena was similar to what Einstein proposed. The theory of relativity is an epistemological theory, formulated for purposes of natural philosophy – it is the most perfect *representation* of external reality available to us, and in this sense it bears importantly upon every discipline which claims to say anything meaningful about external reality. At any rate, it destroys effectively the credibility of such a conception of time as Aurobindo proposed.

At the end of this discussion, I think it would be worthwhile to attach a few conclusions. Firstly, I do not think it profitable any more in our age, and for a long time in the future, to organize our experience in any final philosophy centred round an Absolute. This is not to deny that we shall come across a few men like Aurobindo who do not hesitate to rush in where wiser men fear to tread. What we should guard against is our perpetual tendency to universalize the validity of our experiences and to permit our imaginations to run away with the evidence. Many a time a genuine scientific theory has been manipulated and exploited to reinforce conclusions reached earlier by means other than scientific or frankly mythological.[26]

An example is provided by the talk current even today of 'cosmic evolution'. Now we can talk with some credibility of a cosmic evolution only as far as our small portion of the universe is concerned. This is because the theory of relativity effectively prohibits us from meaningfully talking about any 'simultaneous' events that are taking place in other parts of the universe. This is why it is nonsensical to talk in terms of an Absolute undergoing a cosmic process. For, an absolute, if it is to fulfill the proper definition of an Absolute, must embrace the totality of all experience, in fact, the entire universe and all the events in it. And this is something that we are barred forever from even talking about. And we cannot talk in any proper sense of an Absolute when all that we actually mean is the cosmic process that we know about, that is the evolution of our star, the evolution of life on our earth and its final consummation. In other words, we have a limited Absolute, which is of course, no Absolute at all.

It is not my intention to blame Aurobindo in any way. He was born in a tradition in which truth has always been conceived in absolute terms, and his examination of the phenomenon of evolution led him to think of it in terms of his hereditary philosophic insights.

In the end, the picture of the world as it emerges from any a-historical, a-temporal theory or conceptualisation must lead to distorted and illusory claims. For, man is a historical being; mankind and history must one day find an end, if the law of entropy follows its rigorous course. Only the gods are a-temporal, a-historical, which means, for our purposes, no different from non-being, nothing, non-meaning. In any absolutist system of reality, the world is generally looked upon as connected in every detail – any input in a part of the 'system affects the system as a whole.' We can see the distortions of absolutist thinking in the cosmic determinism of Laplace. Or in the moral determinism of Mahatma Gandhi, who often felt that all his failures in national affairs were due to his failures in his moral life to change his environment. Or in Aurobindo, who was convinced that he was in fact, through his supra-mental power, aiding the Allies in their final victory over Hitler.

Endnotes

1. Upton Sinclair, *Jesus*, Mercury Books, 1962, paperback.

2. K.D. Sethna, *Mother India*, January 1974, p. 19.

3. *Ibid*, p. 11.

4. *Ibid.*, p. 22.

5. *Ibid.*, p. 27.

6. *Ibid.*, p. 28.

7. Morarji Desai, *The Story of My Life*, Macmillan (India), 1974, p. 125.

8. *Ibid.*, pp. 127-128.

9. Sri Aurobindo, *On Himself*, Volume 26, p. 315.

10. Teilhard de Chardin. *The Future of Man*, 1964, p. 42.

11. Peter Medawar, *The Hope of Progress*, Methuen and Co., 1972, p. 115.

12. An objection could be raised here that it is unfair to apply the results of the law of entropy to Aurobindo's ideas of time. The objection is sustained if one intends to examine the system of Aurobindo in itself; it is overruled in an evaluation of the relevance of that philosophy *for our times*, which is the purpose of this essay.

13. Sri Aurobindo, *The Life Divine*, Volume 9, p. 835.

14. *Ibid.*, p. 836.

15. G.G. Simpson, *The Meaning of Evolution*, London, 1950, p. 14.

16. Sri Aurobindo, *The Life Divine*, Volume 18, p. 74.

17. *Ibid.*, p. 75.

18. *Ibid.*, pp. 77-78.

19. *Ibid.*, pp. 359-600.

20. *Ibid.*, p. 360.

21. *Ibid.*, p. 362.

22. *Ibid*, p. 363.

23. *Ibid*, p. 364.

24. Martin Heidegger, *Being and Time*, London, pp. 426-472.

25. Jacques Monod, *Chance and Necessity*, Collins.

26. Sri Aurobindo, *On Himself*, Volume 26, p. 486. Aurobindo here compounds his ignorance. Russell was not a mathematician; he was a logician and a philosopher of mathematics as well as of science. His magnum opus, *Principia Mathematics*, of which he was co-author with Whitehead, is a work on the nature of mathematics, not on mathematics proper as, for example, is the work of Newton, Gauss, Weierstrass, *et al.* Secondly, one does not have to be a creative mathematician in order to understand fully the theory of relativity – just as one does not have to be a poet in order to understand poetry. Indeed, unknown to Aurobindo, Russell has written a well-known exposition of the theory of relativity – *The ABC of Relativity* – and Whitehead had proposed an alternative theory of relativity!

27. A. Macintyre (Ed.), *Metaphysical Beliefs*, London, 1957. The point referred to is discussed by Toulmin in his essay, 'Contemporary Scientific Mythology'.

Fair and Free

Laeeq Futehally

(Quest 95: May-June 1975)

The two sexes are today at the crossroads, as they say, as never before in all the centuries. The word which has got us into trouble is, I think, *equality*. The word seems to have been invented by the French Revolution, and has confused us ever since. Men and women are not equal in every way, and *vive la différence*. The word which we should have used instead is *fairness,* a much more subtle, amorphous, advanced and civilised word. Unfortunately it is a word without an exact equivalent in most of the major languages, although the concept is beginning to have world acceptance. Luckily, since I am writing in English, I can use this important word.

We women, then, should ask for fairness, rather than equality. Placed as we are, because of certain psychological as well as biological facts – not necessarily limitations – our range of functions and potentialities will cover a larger area, swing in more directions, generally be more volatile and less predictable than those of men. As long as we were confined to the housewife's role – and, more than that, confined to the three R's, it was fair to expect us to be passively content with our role. But the man who invented higher education for women opened a Pandora's Box. We now want to do all the things that a man with the same education would do; and we want to keep a lien on our traditional business of running a home and rearing children.

We need, then, a wider space, psychologically and emotionally, than men do. In other words, what we specially need – all through the world, but especially in India – is *flexibility*. We need plenty of choices and the opportunities to choose various combinations and permutations of the roles of career/ wife/ profession/ mother/ breadwinner/ housekeeper/ part-time/ full-time. And we want the right to change gears in mid-life, to change roles, slowing down the one, pressing on with the other, to backtrack, retire, advance as and when we wish. This free-wheeling position for women will be especially difficult to accept in India. Our whole society and culture is based on immutable positions and frozen postures. And the most frozen posture of all is that assigned to women. I cannot imagine that any reason, logic, or sense of reality could induce us to change our standards of expectations. But it is likely that economic compulsions may be successful in doing what rational philosophy cannot do, and that we may tacitly allow women many choices at the same time as we continue to theorize about her ideal role.

I think we can take it for granted that every man, in order to keep the respect of society, is committed to the position of having to earn his own keep, by some not illegal means. He cannot avoid this without forfeiting the respect of his contemporaries. The same is now likely to become expected of women, especially unmarried women, although only covertly.

In a purely theoretical way, it may be said that no woman today ought to be allowed to have more than one child. And as this need not cause an unduly long interruption in her earning capacity, she too should be fixed in the position of having to earn for herself. Well, even assuming for a moment the unreal argument that each woman will have only one child, the large majority of women are emotionally unfitted for long professional lives, apart from the fact that it might be difficult to find enough jobs to supply all the males as well as the females of this country. No, for many women the business of 'pampering' a man, of softening and sweetening the non-working part of his life, is a serious vocation. And men would be fools to deprive themselves of this luxury.

Nevertheless, it is also true – and much truer than most people think – that for the educated woman, housework, housekeeping, home-making can become a deadly bore, a prison house, a slavery. Often the actual skills required in running a home are of a common or low-class variety. It is the personal quality and education of the home-maker that sets the tone and quality to the home. And the maddening fact about making a home where there are young children is that the most important requisite is time, not skill. Although she may have nothing concrete to show for it, the home-maker's greatest contribution to family and domestic life is her time – a dimension as important as anything else that can be priced more accurately. With all the merging of the sexes, it is difficult to see a man contributing this dimension to the cause of bringing up his children.

Whichever way you look at it, then, a long spell of unadulterated housework or family-minding can drive an intelligent woman round the bend, resulting in ridiculously aggressive postures. The excesses of the Women's Lib are understandable as a reaction to the frustrations of baby-minding. And the answer is, again, flexibility, not the makeshift flexibility of today, but a more methodical, deliberate flexibility of organised part-time work as well as other kinds of stop-and-go jobs. Above all, perhaps, a conscious loosening of social pressures and a liberalising of the attitudes of our people who, even now, can think only in terms of the 'traditional woman' at one end and the 'emancipated woman' or 'siren' at the other.

To someone who had only a paper knowledge of India it might seem that Indian women were the best off in the world. We have the vote, we have the right of abortion, and we have practically everything else in between. The Special Marriages Act is the most sensible and dignified marriage contract possible to imagine. In actual fact, of course, only a fraction of the women get the advantage of its liberal provisions, prominent among the exceptions being the Muslim women. Perhaps, someday, the live facts of the woman's position will catch up with the paper position. But meantime many women's organisations are hinting that in this important year, the government ought to think of giving us women a special present. What shall we ask for? Too much equality could be rather frightening. We might find ourselves having to pay alimony to our estranged husbands. Apparently the special gift planned for the women of India this year is equal pay for equal work. By all means, accepted with thanks, and may it not boomerang and hit those very people it was meant to help! But first, please make sure that the threat of clubbing incomes is withdrawn. For, to offer equal pay but at the same time to tax the joint husband and wife income is to give with one hand and take away with the other. Today a single breadwinner per family is not enough, so that, financially as well as in terms of her own self-respect a woman needs the right to earn and control her own money.

But we want the Government to give us another present, something which will reach every single woman in the country, wage-earning or not. And I have a petition ready in case the Government asks what we want. We want an era of easier housekeeping. If you think a bit, the struggles of house-keeping cause a disproportionate amount of tension and disgruntlement. As Churchill was wise enough to realize during the war, people will face real hardship with heroism; but they must not be asked to bear a lot of pin-pricks at the same time. The Indian housewife must be the most long-suffering consumer in the world. She never protests, because she cannot imagine that her protests would ever improve things for her. Without suggesting that the government should enter the consumer market – which Heaven forbid – it could certainly enforce ISI standards better, and deal in a more deterrent way with every kind of adulteration. This is not the place for a long list of the woes of the Indian housewife – we know them all. The point is that many of them can be remedied without any great outlay of funds, although I believe it would be easier to get an allocation of a few crores from the government rather than merely effective and sustained action.

The fact is that whether we are professionals or not, old or young or middle-aged, housekeeping is still likely to be the most important single facet of life for most of us. So we come back to our plea. What about making housekeeping easier for us?

My days in the RSS

Edited and slightly abridged from the original Marathi article published in the Divali (1974) number of Monj.

S.H. Deshpande
Translated by Ramesh Deshpande

(Quest 96: July-August 1975)

About thirty miles out of Poona, on the Satara road, lies the village Shirwal, where I had my early schooling. In 1938, I came to Poona to go to an 'English' school. Most of my new school mates were village boys, with one of whom I made friends. Ram lived with his mother near the school and I would often spend the mid-day recess with him at his home. It was he who introduced me to the RSS.

Before long I found myself a regular member of this organisation. My initiation into its rites was rapid. They consisted of the volunteers congregating every evening on a playground, where they would spend about an hour, playing Indian games or going through the ritual of PT and *lezim*. The evening's programme was rounded off by a community singing of the RSS prayer. I now had a number of friends. I was glad that my days of loneliness were over – those days, immediately following my arrival in Poona, when I hardly knew anyone in that city. Gradually I came to realise that there was some purpose behind all that ritual of PT and *lezim*. Eventually, I was promoted and made a group leader. I went home that evening in high spirits. I could hardly wait to tell my people the glad tidings.

Our 'branch' (*shakha* in the correct RSS parlance) would meet on an open piece of land, skirting the long winding Shivaji Road. The road virtually bisected the city into its two halves, the eastern and the western. It was no mere physical division. Sociologically speaking, it was a virtual frontier separating the 'Brahmin district' of the western half of the city from the 'non-Brahmin' one, sprawling eastwards beyond this road. I was technically a resident of the eastern half.

In the evenings as we returned home from the *shakha* we were often shouted at derisively by the boys who had their homes in the eastern part; or a man might glare at us threateningly. I remember, a boy once hit me with a stick and then disappeared in the rapidly deepening twilight.

These stray incidents brought home to me, albeit slowly, the realisation that these 'easterners' looked upon the RSS as a 'Brahmin club'. Ironically enough, the head of our branch was a non-Brahmin, a fact which I need not have been aware of since he spoke Marathi without the slightest trace of an accent. I realised that he was a non-Brahmin only when I happened to call at his house in the eastern part of the city.

There was of course no gainsaying the fact that by and large the non-Brahmins shunned the RSS. Nevertheless, those few who had thrown in their lot with it were not one whit less devoted or dedicated than the Brahmin volunteers. I had personal experience of their genuine faith in the RSS cause. In the early forties the RSS decided to expand its rural base. In the city of Poona, this meant opening branches in the eastern part. I was made the chief instructor of one such branch, with a non-Brahmin as my superior. He was one Sadashiv, who once valiantly warded off a threatened attack on our branch by the 'eastern' boys. I remember he came from a very devout Hindu home and along with his brother Sitaram, worked for the RSS with a missionary zeal.

This zeal, which was shared by many other non-Brahmin volunteers, has left a lasting impression on my mind.

Lezim had an important place in the training programme of us 'boy' volunteers, who were not yet considered old enough to handle a *lathi*. We would go through its intricate patterns, which were regulated by the shrill sound emanating at regular intervals from the Chief's whistle. The RSS *lezim* was however different from its rustic counterpart in my native Shirwal, which was danced with gay abandon. The former was more of a drill, the latter an intoxicating experience. The RSS *lezim* tended to be more mechanical and though it had vigour, there was no ecstasy in it. It is the *lezim* of my village childhood that I remember fondly and even today whenever I see the boys from the hovels dancing to the rhythm of *lezim,* I feel an irresistible urge to join them. However, I was to grow up in the tradition of the RSS *lezim* – with its measured steps. In retrospect I think the RSS *lezim* symbolised the general RSS ethos: controlled enthusiasm. This was to become apparent to me as the years passed by.

While still a novice, I was witness to an incident which to me was quite out of the ordinary. The evening's programme had concluded and the talk was about 'guts' and who was the most gritty amongst us.

A. coolly turned to his companion and said, 'I won't mind if you put a knife through my thigh.' The latter took out his pen-knife. The sun had already set and there was hardly anyone around except our group. 'Let me see, if you can really stand the pain,' he dared A. Without much ado, A. fell flat on the ground. His friend pierced the blade a good three quarters of an inch through his thigh. A. uttered not a word. When the blade was withdrawn, he got up as if nothing had happened. Someone had the presence of mind to bandage the wound. Another went to the group of senior volunteers, squatting at the far end of the ground and told them what had happened. 'Oh, how very brave of A. A splendid chap!' was their unanimous verdict.

One more incident has stuck in my memory. We had gathered one evening for a discussion and the meeting dragged on late into the night. It was getting on to midnight, and someone suggested we go to a cafe on Laxmi Road for a cup of tea. On our table stood a large glass jar full of biscuits. Having had our tea, one of us emptied the jar into a satchel he was carrying and we stalked out of the place in great jubilation. The owner (was he an 'Irani'?) simply stared at us in amazement. I too was no less amazed.

All I could do in those days was to let my mind absorb the impressions of such incidents. I had not yet learned to ask questions.

My friend Ram had a peculiar hobby. He would roam the *mohallahs* around his house with a catapult. He hardly ever missed his target, which used to be any lone fakir in search of alms. I would find myself in a quandary. 'Was it right, what Ram was doing? Of course it was. Mussalmans are after all one's enemies,' I would tell myself. But then a voice deep inside me would admonish me. I would feel uneasy, at the thought that the fakir must reel under the pain. Our own house, an old fashioned *wada*, was regularly visited by a fakir, who would stand in the quadrangle and sing his hymn. The tenants on the ground floor were all poor *hamals*, who worked as loaders in the local vegetable and fruit market. They never failed to give alms to the fakir. 'Surely this is not done. You should properly get angry!' I would tell myself. So I would try and get myself worked up but the mood never lasted very long.

The 'theory' classes (*bouddhik varga*) of the RSS were by no means all dull.

There were notable exceptions. I can still recall the names of quite a few of those young men who were skillful raconteurs. Among them were men who spoke with passion and delivered speeches full of sentimentality. There was one who would hold us children spellbound by a clever mixture of bravado, mimicry and plain tomfoolery. He was our hero. Even after so many years, I sometimes see him playing the 'pied piper' with the children in the 'tiny tots' section of the *shakha* following him, shouting, singing and dancing!

V. on the other hand was easily the dullest speaker I have ever heard. Indeed I have not come across anyone who could hold a candle to this master of empty rhetoric. His speech was like a vast barren desert, reaching right up to the horizon. His words meant nothing to us who would sit there, yawning, plucking bits of grass or gathering stones, while he went on and on in his staccato voice. What we found unbearable, however, was his insistence that we direct all our attention to what he happened to be saying! The moment he noticed that your thoughts were somewhere else, he would stop talking, fix you with a stare and say, 'I want you to be attentive!' This made the torture all the more excruciating.

It fell to the eminent litterateur Dr P.G. Sahasrabuddhe, to raise these classes to an intellectual level. In one of his books he had expounded the thesis that the Hindus were not a nation at all and had asserted that they would never become one. Apparently he had had second thoughts on seeing the RSS take such spectacular strides. He became an ardent RSS follower, if you ever reminded him of that thesis of his, he would make a clean breast of it and say, 'The RSS has made me change my stand.' P.G. was a teacher in my school. He was a brilliant orator and was held in awe by his pupils. There is no doubt that it was his untiring efforts that had won for the RSS hundreds of my schoolmates. An intellectual that he was, he would choose for his sermons such subjects as 'Capitalism', 'Socialism', 'Fascism', 'Social and Political Philosophy', and what not. He had of course no idea that he was thereby breaking fresh ground, something which ran counter to the RSS tradition. Inevitably therefore he fell foul of its leadership. On his part too, he became fed up with the rigid RSS code which demanded unswerving loyalty to the leader. Moreover he must have felt suffocated in an atmosphere which shut off all free discussion.

Once a week we had what can only be described as a parade day. On this day all the branches of the city held a common ceremonial parade. You wore either a 'half dress', or a 'full dress'. The former consisted of a white shirt and khaki shorts with a black belt. Your headgear was the black RSS cap and the footwear either chappals or *patthani*. The latter dress was more formal. Your shirt was khaki with shoulder straps. The metallic badges on them displayed the English letters 'RSS' and you wore socks and shoes. Your shoes and the buckle on your belt were polished to perfection, and your clothes were freshly laundered and starched. All this meant quite a tidy sum. But Ram had expert knowledge of the second hand bazaar in the vicinity of Shanwar Wada. He took me there and got me all the paraphernalia, save those badges, which you bought at the RSS office. The shorts had to have a particular cut. You got them tailored by Nathuram Godse.

The uniform did buck you up. Some of the boys looked really smart in it. Our battalion commander, for example, cut a truly fine figure, and he barked at you in a proper military fashion if he found you even a shade sloppy on the parade ground.

Then there were cross-country marches which were the last word in endurance tests. You marched for miles together with the sun beating down relentlessly. The only respite was a five minute break at the end of every hour, when you were given a lemon drop. The five minutes over, on you marched, not knowing when the ordeal would end.

Or a route march would be taken out for a change through the streets of Poona to the accompaniment of a band. I remember a Dasara day, when the march lasted several hours in driving rain. The annual three-day winter camp too was an unforgettable experience. You lived in a tent pitched in the wilderness of Aranyeshwar. The day started with the reveille at five a.m. The cold would be enough to freeze water. You somehow managed to lace your shoes with your numb fingers and reported for the parade, which might end around midday. You took turns as a night sentry. A notable feature of camp life was the alarm that might be sounded at the dead of night to warn you of an impending attack of the 'enemy'. You then jumped out of the bed, got into your uniform in about a couple of minutes and made a dash for the parade ground. In the court martial which was held on the last day, those found guilty of breaking the camp discipline would be mercilessly divested of their headgear and badges and a harsh sentence would be pronounced on them! You could not but thrill to the strains of the bugle that was sounded at the reveille, flag hoisting and flag lowering ceremonies. The sound of the alarm was indeed frightening. It seemed to shout in your ears, 'Get up, get up! The whole camp has caught fire!'

However, I must say that for all this soldiering, my progress in the RSS military hierarchy was nothing to shout about. Much as I would have loved to become an officer and swing a swagger stick, this dream of mine remained unfulfilled. Before I could so much as become a lowly right or left marker, the government put a stop to the RSS imparting military training.

But the other courses, designed to make you tough and brave, continued. I was now what they called an 'adolescent volunteer' (*tarun*), which meant I might wield a *lathi*. There were two kinds of 'battles' which you had to fight. In one you took on a lone opponent, while in the other you were set upon by several of them, whom you kept at bay, by swinging your *lathi* around you at a brisk pace. It was not all fun, though. I had got a fractured wrist in the bargain, which took quite some time healing. Eventually, we had an opportunity to put our mettle to test. This came when the atmosphere in the town became tense in the wake of a rumour that communal riots were likely to break out. We took out an impressive march through the various *mohallas*, particularly the Muslim ones, to make the latter realise that we meant business. And it worked!

Sometimes this battle élan was carried to a ridiculous length, in that a dagger was given to a fellow volunteer as a wedding present. It was also considered fashionable to wear a metal handglove with hidden 'tigerclaws', but the fashion was short-lived.

It must have been in 1939 that I saw Dr Hedagewar for the first time. He struck me as a rather colourless personality. Not long thereafter, he passed away. I still retain a vivid memory of that day. It was during the midday school recess that news of his death came and we boys broke into tears. That evening the last post was sounded at the *shakha* and I remember it pierced our hearts like a rapier.

We now directed all our veneration to Golwalker Guruji, who had succeeded Dr Hedagewar as the Supremo (*Sarsanghchalak*). We would muster in full strength to receive him at the Poona railway station, and later in the day call at his host's house to pay our respects to him. He would then be in a relaxed mood and joke with our seniors, who sat nearest to him. We boys would just sit there, a little overawed, for hours together staring at his serene face in a worshipful manner.

My elder brother, Vamanrao the musicologist, had a surprise in store for me. In the thirties, his job often took him to Nagpur – he is an auditor by profession – where he had come in close contact with Guruji, who was a keen student of Hindustani classical music. Seeing that I had become an enthusiastic member of the RSS, he showed me several letters Guruji had then written to him. When I read them, I felt proud and happy at the thought that so great a personality was so close to me, even if in an indirect way. I remember the letters were all written in very ornate English. Their genre clearly showed Guruji as a highly emotional young man.

The great respect and esteem I held him in may be illustrated by one more incident. It was a remark I happened to overhear in the course of a conversation between my eldest brother Pandurangshastri and Govindrao Tembe, the renowned musician and harmonium player from Kolhapur. The latter casually said to my brother, you know, K felt rather let down, because they did not make him the supremo after Dr Hedagewar. I was shocked beyond words. I could not bring myself to believe anyone should have ever aspired to the exalted position which the one and only Guruji now held!

All our teachers were staunch supporters of the RSS, some of whom regularly attended the *shakha*. In fact, the entire milieu of our school was conducive to the RSS philosophy. By early 1942, I along with several of my comrades had the impression that the RSS had transformed itself into a truly revolutionary organisation.

The war psychosis and the life histories of the revolutionaries which our teachers used to tell us had heightened our expectations about the impending struggle. Add to this the following episode which was designed as a sort of trial of strength for some of us boys.

It was a starless night when we assembled at the *shakha*. We were ordered to go to a spot on the bank of a small stream at the foot of the Parvati hill where we would find a lighted lantern. The prospect did not look too foreboding till we were told that each boy would be sent on this mission all by himself. To ensure that they did not meet *en route*, there was an interval of about half an hour between the despatch of two boys. It was a trek of more than a mile, and the dirt track to the hill went (in those days) through a rough, desolate terrain. With a thumping heart I set out, though outwardly I maintained a brave face. Avoiding pitfalls, which in the pitch darkness was almost an impossible task, and fighting a guerilla war with the unfriendly mongrel dogs from the Parvati village, who resented encroachment on their territory at that odd hour by a mere fifteen-year-old, I somehow managed to reach my destination. The sense of relief I felt at the sight of my comrades there can well be imagined!

The meeting which followed at the foot of that hill that night was a truly memorable experience. The thought that we were all going to return home together, and not singly, was a comforting one and we listened with rapt attention to the inspiring speech which J gave in the still of the night under the pallid glow of a single lantern, which seemed to accentuate the darkness around us. In the course of his speech, he announced with all the emphasis at his command, 'The RSS is an organisation of revolutionaries, and make no mistake about, it!' Those words startled me as they no doubt must have startled many others present there. True, J would often tell us about the exploits of Bhagat Singh and Rajguru, but none of us was aware that we were already members of a conspiratorial group!

However, when the Quit India movement gathered momentum the RSS remained a passive onlooker. In one of the theory classes this isolation was justified on the ground that neither the RSS nor the country was yet strong enough to overthrow the foreign yoke. The speaker told us that all the blood that was being spilled in the firings was in vain!

This argument matched my way of thinking, since I was not one of those young men whose ambition was to free the motherland through a bloody revolution. The Quit India movement therefore understandably left me unmoved. On the contrary, it made my preconceived notions about the Congress and its volunteer corps the Rashtra Seva Dal, all the more deep-rooted.

I was now in the matriculation class and held a position of some importance and authority as a leader of those of my schoolmates who were in the RSS. I could therefore see to it that not once during the days of the 1942 movement did our school remain closed, although we had often to face Congress-sponsored picketing by students from the other city schools, who would stand outside our school gate and shout slogans. Once when a batch of demonstrators threatened to stop classes, we got together a small band of RSS volunteers outside the gate, broke their cordon and forced them to beat a retreat. I must, however, add that in this I had had no directive from the RSS authorities. I was entirely acting on my own, supported by some of my RSS friends.

However, in the course of time the relentless antagonism of the Congress to the British Raj seemed to have affected the RSS too. There were a number of unmistakable signs which pointed towards the fact that the RSS was now poised to strike at the Raj.

In the May of 1942, I attended the Officers' Training Camp at Poona. The presence of hundreds of trainees there, who had come from all districts of Maharashtra, was a clear indication that the RSS was becoming a force to reckon with in Maharashtra. The address which Guruji gave at that camp was obviously inspired by the revolutionary spirit that was then evident throughout India. Though it was full of abstract allegories, it inflamed us no end. He depicted mother India as the ferocious Kali Mata, who would not be satisfied unless her sons laid their bloody heads at her feet! Surely the D Day was not very far now, we thought.

I followed the Winter Camp of that year. The accent of the training that was imparted was on battle manoeuvres – rope climbing, jumping off high rocks, erecting barricades, target practice with soda water bottles, and the like. Later in the year, the RSS launched a campaign to recruit full-timers to spread its message throughout India. There were many young men who responded to the call and left their careers, jobs and homes. It was rumoured that they were sent on secret missions to collect information about the locations of the ammunition depots, police stations, army installations, etc.

Nothing came out of this.

After passing the Matriculation in 1943, I fell ill, I left Poona and spent a whole year convalescing at my home in Shirwal.

In mid-1944, I returned to Poona and joined college. I rented a room near the college which was a stone's throw from one of the RSS *shakhas*. I had begun to toy with the idea of renewing my contact with the RSS, when a new acquaintance, T. decided the issue for me. He took me along with him one day to the *shakha* near our college.

The atmosphere here was more free, robust and uninhibited. Indeed some of the volunteers – we were all young college students now – whose homes were in the district towns of Maharashtra, had the cheek to ridicule many of the more pompous leaders of the RSS. One of the standard jokes was that in spite of so much honest *lathi*-wielding, there was no sign of the Hindu Rashtra coming off! It was all light-hearted fun, though!

T. was the moving spirit behind our *shakha*. Indeed, he was endowed with a charismatic personality which you found irresistible. He embodied the spirit of the couplet: '*sarfaroshi ki tamanna ab hamare dil men hein; dekhana hein jor kitna baaju-e-katil men hein.* (Our hearts are athirst for martyrdom; let us dare the enemy and test his strength.)

No wonder, so many of my colleagues, impetuous and by no means meek followers, felt themselves drawn to him.

A short time after joining the new *shakha* T. told me that on a certain day at five a.m. I was to attend a meeting in a secluded place on the college ground. I could see that the small group that had collected there consisted of many others in addition to my *shakha* colleagues. I could also see that they did not belong to any specific stratum of the RSS hierarchy. This was something of a mystery to me. Someone solemnly recited Savarkar's verse which meant: 'We are martyrs, not from blind passion, but from conviction derived from the study of history....' This was followed by a short speech. The programme over, I asked T., 'Who are these people?' 'They are our friends,' was all that he had to say by way of reply.

In due course I learnt that those who frequented T.'s room (which I now shared with him) were all 'friends'. They came from such far-flung places as Bombay, Nasik, Sangli, etc. I once saw a letter, written in blood, by a Bombay boy called Damle.

Once on a visit to Bombay to attend a friend's wedding, T. took me to the Bandra slaughter-house. This, I later realised, was part of the training T. had planned for me. We spent an hour there watching those huge skinned hulks, pools of blood and the glistening blades of long knives in the butcher's hands. At the end of it all, T. clearly looked pleased to see that I had taken all that horrible sight in my stride. I myself was no less surprised to find that I had neither swooned nor retched!

T. had many original ideas. He took us once on one of those nocturnal outings in the country. As usual he gave us no indication as to what he was up to till we reached our destination, a small brook. We were all shivering in the bitter cold. T. outlined his plan thus: 'Imagine that you are carrying a hand grenade in your left hand. Now each one of you will jump into this brook here and swim across to the other bank, keeping the left arm aloft, so that the hand grenade does not get wet!'

We had among us a strongly built athlete, who I knew was a great meat-eater. He flatly refused to do anything of the kind. T. was so furious with him that in a fit he cancelled the whole plan!

I am sure I would have jumped into that ice-cold water and followed T.'s instructions if the others had done so. Still, it was a great relief to me that we returned home without having to go through that ordeal. This incident was symbolic in that though technically wedded to the RSS doctrine, I somehow managed to remain no more than a passive participant till 1947, when India became free and then of course the need for staging any revolution was obviated, once for all!

There is no doubt that there did exist within the RSS a group of ardent revolutionaries, who would have gladly embraced the gallows for the sake of the motherland. It must however be said that though staunch followers of the Hindu Rashtra ideology, unlike the general run of RSS volunteers they never considered anti-Muslim activity as their sole objective. First and foremost they were freedom-lovers. The sources from which these firebrands derived their inspiration lay outside the RSS. Were they trying to use the RSS merely as a front organisation to achieve their ends? I am not sure. Once when I asked, a straight question to someone he answered, 'What else then is the RSS for?' – a very clever answer indeed!

T. was by no means the only leader of this band of revolutionaries. There was the mild-mannered N. who was totally committed to the cult of revolution. He was a strict disciplinarian and could not brook the slightest tardiness on the part of any member of the group. Once I was a little late in arriving at a secret meeting held at a Maruti temple. N. was standing at the entrance, brandishing a wicker stick. He asked me to put out my palm and struck it with the full force of his stick. I felt terribly humiliated until I saw that he meted out the same treatment to all late-comers. Nevertheless, for a long time thereafter I harboured a grudge against him. Eventually, I realised that it was unfounded, when I discovered a rupee note in my wallet. I was sure it was N. who had planted it there. He had called at my room that day and seeing that I looked worried had asked me whether I had had my meal. As it happened, I did not have a *paisa* on me that day and hence could not go out to eat. I assured him, of course, that I had eaten only a short while ago. I left him in my room, while I went out to the water tap to wash my clothes. When

I returned to my room, I found that he had left. I was now famished and started for the umpteenth time rummaging through the pockets of all my shirts and trousers, and my wallet, and lo! there was this one rupee note! Later when I asked N. since when he had started donating money on the sly, he answered blandly he had not the faintest idea what I was talking about!

In 1945, under the leadership of Dr Shyama Prasad Mukherji, the Hindu Mahasabha seemed poised to join the freedom movement. Apparently, this produced repercussions in the RSS. In the Winter Camp of that year, we were asked to be ready to sacrifice everything for the country.

Subsequently Dr Mukherji himself came to Poona to address a public meeting. In the course of his speech, he said he expected the movement to spread 'from one end of the country to the other'. I remember he uttered this phrase so gravely, with a pause after each word, that I saw flashing before my eyes the whole of India from the snow-peaks of the Himalayas to Kanyakumari.

Later in the evening, he talked to a select gathering which included some RSS volunteers. At the end of the talk he was asked, 'Are we this time going to send our representatives abroad for propaganda?' His answer was, 'Of course, we shall.' As we came out of the hall, T. explained to me what the question put to Dr Mukherji really meant. According to him, the questioner wanted to know whether the Hindu Mahasabha was going to try and get arms and ammunition from Germany and Japan!

This was another of those glimmers of expectant hope that was never to be fulfilled.

Although the RSS mystique had now come to exert an appreciable influence on my thought processes, there was also a counterbalancing force at work. This was provided by the lectures and discourses of Dr P.G. Sahasrabuddhe who by this time had been thoroughly disillusioned with the anti-intellectual atmosphere of the RSS. My own alienation from the RSS was thus mainly due to the frontal attack launched by him on everything the RSS stood for. I must however confess that my alienation was not wholly an intellectual one. The truth is, I had simply had enough of the daily ritual at the *shakha*, which I had been faithfully following for eight years. I decided not to participate in it any longer and stopped attending the *shakha*.

It is now almost thirty years since I severed all contact with the RSS. They say the RSS has now changed. Be that as it may, it would not be out of place to describe here an experience of a personal nature.

Last year I was invited to preside over the 'Guru Pujan' function at a local *shakha*. I made it plain to the organisers that I no longer held any brief for the RSS philosophy and that they would have to bear with any critical remarks I might have to pass. They said I could speak as freely as I wanted. Finally I accepted their invitation, although not without a feeling of uneasiness. At the outset, I congratulated the congregation for having consented to listen to a 'renegade' like me and then delivered a highly critical speech. Mincing no words, I told them what I thought about things like 'the Hindu Nation', 'The Holy Cow' and other pet conceptions of the RSS. I had expected my speech to infuriate them, but to my surprise they listened to me in polite silence. In the small get-together too which was arranged after the function, no one asked me any question nor contradicted any of my statements. I felt rather let down and disappointed. As I was about to take leave of my hosts, a young man approached me and asked me if I could spare some time for him. 'Certainly,' I said, elated at the thought that I had been successful in making at least one of them indignant enough to cross swords with me. He came to see me the next day at the university. All he had to say to me was: 'Sir, could you help a friend of mine get admission to the M.A. course?'

I suppose I can dispassionately analyse my RSS experience now after an interval of almost three decades. When I ask myself today if the eight years I spent in the RSS were a waste, I find it rather difficult to give a categorical answer. I think I was both a loser and a gainer. For one thing, all those evenings which I spent at the *shakha* could no doubt have been devoted to the study of painting and sketching for which I had a genuine liking. My eldest brother with whom I stayed in Poona was also a connoisseur of music and a leading exponent of the art used to give private performances at his house. I had no time for that either.

My gain was in the capacity I developed to take the rough and tumble of life in my stride. What is more, I came in contact, though by no means a close one, with ardent revolutionaries who had devoted their lives to the cause of the nation. The aura of romance that surrounded their lives fascinated me. It was the sort of experience which one finds ennobling in early youth.

All the same, I developed an analytical mind by that many years later. For eight long years I went on thinking robot-like. I was rather like a bull, who goes on running in a circular groove. My deliverance from this life was a mere chance happening. Surely it would now be idle for me to speculate on what other turn my life would have taken if I had not joined the RSS. Indeed, no man can look back upon his past and say that the lessons he learned then were wholly useless or, for that matter, wholly useful.

The RSS did leave certain imprints on my mind which have not yet been erased. The military precision, which was the hallmark of every activity of the RSS, is one of these. One has only to see how other parties and organisations conduct their business to realise the importance of its insistence on orderliness. However, the one achievement, which is by far the most significant from the point of view of national integration, is the sense of unity and brotherhood the RSS has been successful in creating in the minds of its adherents. True, this is confined to the Hindus, but the fact cannot be overlooked that in spite of its Maharashtrian parentage, the RSS is wholly devoid of any taint of chauvinistic Maharashtrianism, which is decidedly a credit to this organisation. Invitations to its functions held in Maharashtra have always been printed in Hindi, a fact which underscores its opposition to parochialism. In fact the easy camaraderie amongst its volunteers, be they Tamils, Bengalis, Maharashtrians or Punjabis, is its most heartening feature. Notwithstanding the fact that the overwhelming majority of Indians have remained beyond its pale, the RSS undoubtedly tried to create an integrated community.

Indeed, the *leit-motif* of the RSS philosophy has always been the Gandhian precept that man can be won over by love. Strengths and weaknesses of the RSS can be understood only in this light.

The RSS made a very subtle use of this technique of 'love' to win over new entrants and, I must say, in doing so it displayed a deep knowledge of human psychology. Even a fresher was addressed not just by his surname. It was always preceded by his first name. Then again, if you were married, your wife became everyone's *'bhabi'*. If anyone was ill, every one of his colleagues would visit him at his house, practically everyday, till finally he perforce became well rather than go on facing their solicitous enquiries after his health! Though this business of calling on an ailing colleague was a little overdone, you could always bank on help and guidance from your fellow volunteers in any emergency or difficulty. There were informal get-togethers when everyone present had to introduce himself to the gathering, no matter how long this took, and this practice was consistent with the personal approach the RSS always valued.

Through such devices, which were obviously implemented in good faith, the RSS sought to create a fraternal feeling in its *swayamsevaks* (volunteers). This aim was no doubt unexceptionable, since given the type of organisation that the RSS is, it could not but rely on a policy of getting its followers emotionally committed to its creed. Exclusive reliance on love, however, begot anti-intellectualism in the RSS. Naturally, it did not countenance any kind of free discussion or dissent and even suppressed intellectual curiosity. Inevitably therefore the RSS turned its followers into mere human automata.

Even a second-rate intellectualism had no place in the RSS scheme of things. No intellectual premises were ever sought when spreading its message. The sole intellectual food of the RSS volunteers has been the speeches and writings of Savarkar. How very dependent they were on Savarkar can be gauged from the fact that the day he was to address a meeting in Poona, it would be announced at the various *shakhas* of the town that the evening's proceedings stood cancelled and that the volunteers could 'go home' (i.e. to Savarkar's meeting! This was never officially mentioned). This concession was not granted on any other occasion. Even if it is conceded that all Fascist-type movements propagate their message through psychological methods, they too are known to take recourse to intellectual or semi-intellectual premises. Hence the RSS's total disregard for the need to find at least a bare intellectual rationale for its creed becomes all the more surprising!

The Sangh's anti-intellectualism must also have emanated from the fact that discussion and debate were associated with democracy and in the RSS view democratic bodies of all kinds only 'talked and did nothing'. There is, of course, the possibility that a discussion on any topic may degenerate into an empty debate, but here again it is a matter of balancing various considerations. One can always get out of a dilemma by the simple expedient of taking a negative and reactionary stand and this is precisely what the RSS did. Hence it must be said that far from facing them squarely, the RSS has not even been able to identify the challenges which arise when new institutions are sought to be established in an underdeveloped society.

The philosophy of 'love', resulting in anti-intellectualism accounts for the utter vacuousness of the speeches that were delivered at the meetings, misnamed theory classes. For one thing, the speaker was chosen not so much for his erudition as for the rank he occupied in the RSS hierarchy. So long as he merely mouthed sentimental platitudes, you found him at least bearable. But the moment he sought to give a theoretical basis to his arguments, he would stand exposed. This consisted of clichés like 'Hindustan belongs to the Hindus', 'The Saffron flag is our National flag', 'One Nation, one Leader', etc., which would be repeated *ad nauseam*. For a change, he might evoke the 'glorious' past of the Hindus, or ridicule the democratic polity, or find fault with the Indian National Congress because it was 'founded by the British'. The discipline of the Germans and Italians would be extolled and you were invited to consider the Himalayas as the flagstaff of the saffron flag which was the terrain of the Indian continent including Burma. You searched in vain for any rational or original thought in all this demagogy. Moreover, the RSS combined this intellectual poverty with intolerance of criticism. At least three Marathi authors were physically assaulted for writing articles which were critical of the RSS philosophy.

It is, however, *vis-a-vis* the Muslims that this intolerance of the RSS acquired a sharp edge. Indeed its original *raison d'etre* was to defend the Hindus from the atrocities perpetrated on them by the Muslims, and in the twenties it could not be faulted on this score. Nevertheless, the image of a Muslim in the mind of an RSS volunteer is often extremely bizarre. An intellectual friend of mine, who like me has now left the RSS, only grudgingly concedes that a Muslim too could be a well-educated, cultured and soft-spoken person. He cannot yet get rid of the equation, 'a Muslim = a dagger'!

I am not too sure that appeals to religious sentiment invariably fail in this so-called 'modern age'. One thing is certain, however: the appeal to 'Hinduism' is too weak to unite all who come under the rubric 'Hindu'. This is because of the caste stratification of Hindu society in which the 'Hindu' feeling gets more and more diluted as you go down the caste ladder. What becomes important from the point of view of each caste is its special semi-religion. There is really little as compared to other religions that holds all Hindus together.

It is all too obvious therefore that the RSS failed to unite the diverse castes of the Hindus in its fold. This is not surprising when it is seen that its entire case was based on an undiscriminating concept of love. It is not any generalised kind of love which cements society but, shall we say, love proportioned to the needs of various classes – which is what social justice means and which is what the lower orders of the

Hindus are in dire need of. The real meaning of love was thus never understood by the RSS, nor indeed by the entire Hindu tradition. Consequently, it was only a small percentage of high-caste Hindus which the RSS was able to unite. Its appeal could not evoke any response from the rest.

Having spent the most impressionable years of my early youth in the RSS, which were also decisive in the life of our country (1938-46), I sometimes look back on them with a touch of nostalgia. During this journey down memory lane, a question always exercises my mind. An attempt to seek an answer to it would be a fitting epilogue to this article.

The question is: Why didn't the RSS convert its well-knit organisation into a political force, whereby it could have almost certainly dealt a crippling blow to the British Raj in India? I think the answer should be sought in the difference in outlook and personality between its founder, K.B. Hedagewar and his successor, M.S. Golwalkar or 'Guruji' as he was known.

After a careful study of the former's biography, the reader is left in no doubt that the Doctor was a politician who believed in armed uprising. Although he had founded the RSS to counter both the rising Muslim communalism and the Congress policy of Muslim appeasement, he was also simultaneously aiming at liberating the country from foreign yoke. Indeed an independent India was a prerequisite for the creation of the Hindu Rashtra of his dreams. One cannot therefore escape the conclusion that the initial aloofness of the RSS from politics was merely a mask. His biographer says that the Doctor was in constant touch with the revolutionaries of his day. Subhash Chandra Bose too had tried to meet him twice, though the meeting never materialised. It took the Doctor long to dispose of the arms and ammunition he had collected in his revolutionary past. All this points unmistakably to the fact that he was plotting to overthrow the British Raj through an armed uprising. His biographer has described the sense of frustration he felt at the thought that the RSS was not strong enough to strike at the Raj when the Second World War broke out. He felt that the war situation presented an ideal opportunity to do so. Undaunted by his failing health, he then devoted all his energies to expanding the RSS. It was during these days that he gave his followers the target of bringing into the RSS three per cent of the urban and one per cent of the rural population. In those days I remember to have participated in 'short-notice rallies' in which all the volunteers of the Poona city mustered in full strength within scarcely more than two hours of the issue of the first order to the City Secretary. The paramilitary character of the Sangh, its secrecy, the great care it took not to infringe the law – all make sense in this light. The Doctor was thus essentially an organiser of men, with an acute political awareness. He was a down-to-earth realist.

Golwalkar Guruji, on the other hand, had a spiritual side to his personality which Dr Hedagewar used to find rather frightening. Guruji was not wholly a man of this world. Whenever the RSS work took him to Calcutta, he would find time to visit the Bellur Ashram. He was deeply versed in the Gita and the Hindu-scriptures. An episode in his life during the 1952 general elections is revealing of the man's personality. As the election tempo quickened, Guruji, the ascetic, decided to retire to a quiet spot. He chose the famous Sinhagad fort near Poona. All his reading, during the month he spent in seclusion, was confined to the *Ram Charit Manas*, the *Mahabharata* and the Upanishads. Once during an imprisonment, he hardly read the newspapers that were sent to him during the last three months of his term.

This was then the man on whom the mantle of the RSS fell when the country was passing through the most crucial phase of its modern history. I believe that with the ascension of Guruji in 1940 the RSS withdrew into a shell. What was fashioned as a political weapon by its founder became a limp, lifeless thing in the hands of his successor. In 1946 an unheard of thing happened: a group of Young Turks most of whom were my friends got together and met Guruji to voice their discontent and press for a constructive direction to RSS policies. A firm 'No' was Guruji's answer.

It is significant that a full-length biography of Dr Hedagewar was published only in 1960, twenty years after his death and four years after the publication of Guruji's own biography! Which really means that the average *swayamsevak* knew little about the founder of the organization – his background, his aspirations, his motives and methods.

In Hedagewar's time it was dangerous to reveal the true intentions of the RSS. That is how probably clichés like 'organizing for the sake of organizing', 'protection of culture', etc., came into vogue. For Guruji they became the real thing, the essence of the RSS. The RSS thus became a 'withdrawing sect' under his long reign of thirty-two years.

The language remained but he poured a different and crassly literal meaning into those words and the real content of the Sangh as the Doctor had seen it was drained out of it completely. Sporadic working up of revolutionary air, carefully controlled suggestions of imminent participation in the national struggle, ding-dong games of hope and despair – was all that he gave to his thousands of followers to keep them tied to the RSS cause such as it was.

And yet the phenomenon cannot be considered as exclusively the result of Guruji's personality. For there were, and probably even today are, hundreds of *swayamsevaks* who did believe in the empty words and rituals and were prepared to sacrifice their lives for a goal which had no realistic content. How does one explain this? Is this a reflection of the traditional Hindu philosophy of activity bereft of any aim? Does activity lose its meaning for us as soon as its aim is concretized and is attractive only so long as its purpose remains unspecified and nebulous? The answers, most probably, are in the affirmative. This attitude incapacitates us for facing reality which, as Max Weber noted long ago, we either endure or try to run away from. The RSS as I experienced it must, in that case, be considered an expression, in a modern garb, of a deeper strain of the Hindu character.

Invitation to a Beheading:
A Psychologist's Guide to
Assassinations in the Third World

Ashis Nandy

(Quest 98: November-December 1975)

The relationship between an assassin and his victim is deep and enduring. Death only openly and finally brings them together. Of course, there are tyrants who turn virtually everyone in a country into a prospective assassin and leaders who build bastions against their assassination in the minds of men, thereby reducing the circle of prospective assassins to the microscopic group of hired sociopaths and the mentally ill. Emperor Nero belonged to the first category and Martin Luther King to the second. There is also the special case of rulers who, by the consent of the majority, are tyrannical within the country and, to the extent they get the chance, in the world outside. Their pathology leads to collective suicides rather than individual assassinations. Adolf Hitler is the hackneyed but glaring example of the species.

But such leaders are hardly typical. There is a much broader range of situations where the ruler is popular and charismatic but, propelled by his inner drives, prepares the ground for his assassination. In such cases there is a close fit among the motivational imperatives of such a man, his attempts to remould the polity after his own psychological needs, and the type of invitation he extends to his potential assassins.

The first characteristic of such a ruler is an inability to trust deeply and wholly. Though his flamboyant style may hide it for a long time, he lives in an inner world peopled by untrustworthy men. Even when he trusts some, it is transient. A chain of lieutenants come in and go out of his favour in a fashion reminiscent of people getting in and out of a railway compartment The ruler suspends this suspiciousness only in the case of his family members, men recruited from outside politics to act as 'commissars', and politicians who have no independent bases and are fully dependent on him.

Now, politics is a game of modulated trust. The politician uses a mix of the basic trust and distrust in his personality – to use the well-known conceptual polarities of Erik Erikson – and operates within a system of interpersonal coalition-building, negotiations and competition. If this inner balance of trust and distrust is disturbed, he becomes either a paranoid or a 'sucker'. In either case he goes out of high politics. However, there is also the politician who retains this balance till he enters a critical power position and then begins to falter and the politician whose paranoid predispositions match the political culture and institutions of his country (such a man may perform exceedingly well in political competitions which are cut-throat and in struggles for succession which are bitter). In both cases, once in power, the distrust gradually forces these men to circumscribe the area within which policies are made, to strangle or ruthlessly contain those who generate alternative models and fundamental criticisms of the polity, and to pack the decision-making system with loyal lieutenants, whatever be their competence.

Power, thus, continues to be concentrated in the ruler's hand. Worse, he is seen as all powerful. As a result, all grievances gradually begin to be directed at him. After a while, there remain no intermediate shock-absorbers whom he can fob off as subverters or reactionaries within the ruling circle. Unlike Jawaharlal Nehru, who was simultaneously the head of the government and the leader of the opposition, such a ruler personally becomes the focus of all the anger and frustration of which a poor country is capable. And remember, in the more deprived sections of the world, the successes of a régime are invariably less obvious than its failures. To say that a Third World leader is deeply identified with his nation is to say that he is primarily identified with its failures.

Moreover, no decision-making structure is monolithic. Even in the smallest of polities, there are bound to be piques and hostilities against petty officials, against the ruler's relatives who actually may have nothing much to do with him, and against men who use his name or pretend to act under his orders but in reality are time-servers and petty tyrants operating independently. These hostilities cumulate against the ruler himself. Increasingly it seems to many that the régime can be changed by merely changing one individual. Traditional monarchies fall in this category and the American presidency, depending upon its incumbent, is sometimes not very different. The régime which Richard Nixon built must have nurtured many political assassins and those who hooted him out might have, for all we know, saved his life. Sheikh Mujib's Bangladesh, too, was an instance of such a polity.

Not merely may the ruler become too deeply identified with the régime, the régime may seem closed to internal competition to large numbers of people.

Yet no régime is psychologically closed. It could be so only normatively. Even the most rigidly closed régime is open to one whose values permit him to include in the available means of political competition revolution, rebellion, *coup* and assassination. Of these, revolutions require immense planning, massive organisation, first-rate mobilisational skills, and a developed ability to feel the pulse of a large section of the population. Naturally, in the Third World, containing some of the least organised and most apolitical societies, revolutions are at a discount. Of course, every petty rebel or tyrant may call himself a revolutionary, but Lenins and Maos can hardly be mass-produced. To some extent, the pre-conditions of revolutions apply to rebellions and *coups*, too.

On the other hand, assassination is the cheapest of the four means mentioned, requires the least planning and organisation, and does not need the assent of any section of the population. Understandably, it is at a premium in the Third World. In some parts of it, such killings have, in fact, become a standard means of deciding political succession. In Latin America, for instance, the popularity of political assassinations is exceeded at the moment only by bull-fights.

It is through this linkage that the average assassin and his average victim ultimately find each other. The few studies of assassins done elsewhere in the world show them to be unhappy marginal men, having low conformity to social norms and deep feelings of inferiority, and impotent. The portrait which Irving Horowitz draws of the terrorist applies to the assassin, too. He is likely to be young, male, middle-class, economically marginal, relatively well-educated but without high achievements, and cut off from the peasants and the working class by his origins. Such men are produced in many traditional societies by urbanisation, expanding communications, collapsing traditional hierarchies and norms, technological changes and occupational insecurities.

When living under an authoritarian régime, these marginal men sense that their society is open on one plane. A majority of their compatriots, conforming to the operant political norms, may remain convinced that it is closed. But these norms are not applicable to the sector from which the assassin comes. Having low esteem and trying to redeem themselves in their own eyes, these potential assassins are always seeking a situation in which they can do something dramatic and, in one move, counter their own poor self-esteem and passivity and, through an act of desperate violence, get a new self-image endorsed by the world at large.

The assassin is not a murderer. A murder is too personal, too mundane and has too little dramatic and exhibitionistic potentialities. As Arthur Danto points out, you and I are safe from the assassin's bullet because we are only the prospective murdered and do not enjoy the 'privilege of assassinability'. Even if we are accidentally killed in an assassination attempt, it will be only a failed assassination attempt with inadvertent lethal consequences to us. The reason for this is obvious. We can only relieve the immense tension of undischarged aggressive needs of the murderer, but cannot satisfy the assassin's search for grandiose self-validation and protection against self-abnegating oblivion. Nor can our murder provide the assassin with the ideological rationalisation which he needs to express openly his deepest aggressive feelings, directed against a symbol of parental authority.

The assassin badly needs this rationalisation. The major political philosophies of our times provide excellent justifications for political violence, but not for political assassinations. Hatred towards a particular person is difficult to rationalise in an age which prefers to speak in terms of collectivities such as classes, races and strata. Thus, like Horowitz's terrorists, most assassins have to operate on the basis of poorly defined, home-made ideologies. In this respect, too, the assassin is a lonely man.

No one can kill himself, psychologists say, unless he feels like killing somebody. Suicide always is, symbolically, an attempt to murder an unacceptable part of one's self modelled after a figure outside. Perhaps the reverse is true for the assassin. His attempt is to kill a figure in the external world who represents an alien self. If he succeeds, the result may turn out to be popular, and there may be a widely shared discharge of psychic tension, a justification of the assassin's way of handling his private problems. It may also be unpopular, arousing guilt of patricide in the onlookers to the extent they identify with the assassin. This guilt can hardly be bound by the small symbolic expiations which the assassin-turned-ruler often makes – like burying the assassinated ruler with full military honours as in the case of Mujib – or by the *post facto* rationalisation of the patricide through improved statecraft, more popular policies, and a more democratic style. Unconsciously the assassin fears this potent guilt which may turn against him. In response and as an atonement, he resorts to a behaviour pattern which invites his own assassination. He begins to protect himself through authoritarianism and blind terror. He dangles before the other little men in society the opportunity not only of self-advertisement but also the chance of transcending their alienation by assassinating the assassin and satisfying the free-floating feelings of revenge which the first assassination let loose. Psychologically, this revenge promises to undo the first patricide, in a primitive magical way, through a second. It is often thus that a culture of assassination emerges in a country.

The tragedy of the assassin is that the symbolic killing of only a part of himself never ends the story. Only his own assassination can do so. After all, he seeks to acquire through assassination the public prominence his victim has and he lacks. The ultimate validation of this acquired renown is his own assassinability.

The tragedy of the assassinated ruler is that, though he can avoid the fate towards which he often moves blindly and inexorably, he is in effect a driven man. Like his killer, he rebels against a part of himself which seeks self-preservation, rationality and contact with the real world of people.

What can such a ruler do to grapple with his own self-destructive tendencies? Danto believes that two courses are open to him. He can seek total protection which means an impregnable shield of bodyguards. But who can protect the ruler against a treacherous guard? And who will guard the guards and guard the guards who guard the guards? Total security, therefore, is a situation of infinite regression. The alternative strategy is to treat all subjects as if they were loyal. Benign policies by themselves are not enough; the modern prince must make citizens out of his subjects. Only then can he hope to abridge their alienation and marginality and exorcise the ghost of assassination.

In Defence of Pulp Literature

Murli Das Melwani

(Quest 100: March-April 1976)

As Indo-Anglian literature approaches a hundred and fifty years of its existence one finds it losing its self-consciousness. Self-consciousness is inevitable in any expression of a native sensibility in a non-native language. As a result, its practitioners had to justify their use of it against the well-reasoned attacks of their critics. This phase is now over. Two factors indicate that this literature is ceasing to be self-conscious. One is the extension of themes. The second is a paradox: the growth of what may be called a lower level of literature or 'pulp' literature.

Novelists till the seventies dealt with three major themes. Writers like Raja Rao in *Kanthapura,* Narayan in *Waiting for the Mahatma* and Malgonkar in *A Bend in the Ganges* dealt with the national movement for freedom. Narayan's *The Guide,* Anand Lal's *The Seasons of Jupiter* and Bhabani Bhattacharya's *He Who Rides a Tiger* represent the divergent approaches to the theme of faith in Indian life. Balachandra Rajan's *Too Long in the West* epitomises a genre that has been highly fruitful: the problems of adjustment which face a Westernised Indian at home. These subjects have a pan-Indian relevance and they have helped to give Indo-Anglian literature a distinct personality.

There has been, in the seventies, an extension of these themes as well as an exploration of new ones. Arun Joshi's *The Foreigner* and

Saros Cowasjee's *Goodbye to Elsa* examine the effects of alienation on sensitive Indians of mixed heritage. Four recent novels, notably Dilip Hiro's *A Triangular View*, have taken up the plight of the immigrant Indian. The subject of inter-communal marriage is attracting writers. The exploration of the individual consciousness is Anita Desai s forte, and she enriches it with deeper probing in *Where Shall We Go This Summer?* Her lead is being accepted, and the problems of the individual are receiving more attention in recent fiction.

The second factor is of equal literary and historical importance. The growth of a lower level of literature implies that books cease to be the preserve of the upper or upper middle and educated classes. It implies that other classes are reaching out for books which will provide them an escape from their humdrum lives. This literature performs the same function as the much maligned Hindi film – it provides a cathartic release. The parallels with the Hindi film do not end there. These books work out situations similar to the Hindi film. Behaviour is patterned on the stereotypes of the screen. Sentiment and sentimentality are its stock in trade. Unreality becomes the reality. Romanticism is its keynote.

K.A. Abbas's novels written after *Inquilab* (1955) fall obviously into this category. Obviously, because novels like *When Night Falls, Mera Naam Joker, Maria, Bobby, Boy Meets Girl* are based on the scripts of Hindi films which Abbas has written and 'successfully' directed.

Another writer associated with films, Bunny Reuben, has used the technique of the film in *You, I and Her*. In it a single sequence of events is narrated from three different points of view. In this novel Reuben has not been able to rise above technical virtuosity as he did so successfully in his collection of short stories, *Monkeys on the Hill of God*. The sequence of events, though retaining a hard realism on the surface, has all the qualities of a tear-jerker.

Reuben is one of our better writers who has written a poor book. Another is Sasti Brata in *She and He*. Apart from the title, there is similarity in the technique of Brata and Reuben's books. *She and He* centres round Zameer, half Arab, half French, and Sally. When their affair ends, Zameer receives a manuscript in which chapters by Sally are followed by blank ones. Zameer gets the message; he must fill in the empty pages and thus arrive at an understanding of himself. This novel has the typical Brata mark – a variety of sex and lots of it, psuedo-intellectual posturing and good writing – but it lacks the seriousness of *My God Died Young* or even the honesty of *Confessions of an Indian Lover*.

Nergis Dalal could have been a better writer had she eschewed the cliché and brought more seriousness to her writing especially since she has a facile pen. In *Minari* she introduces us to the peccadilloes of high society which includes a prince and the lecherous editor of a successful magazine. In *Two Sisters* the eternal motif of jealousy is worked out between twins, one beautiful, the other not so. The beautiful one has the good times, the other one the brains and the last laugh. In *The Inner Door* the gullible foreigners who come to India to seek solace are satirized at the same time as the fake gurus who make money at their expense. It tells the story of Rahul, a handsome young man who is being trained up to help his patrons make money in America. He foils their plans when he begins to search for answers. The satire recalls Jhabvala, the theme recalls Narayan's *The Guide* and Syed Waliullah's *Tree Without Roots*, but Nergis Dalal could not escape the snare of the cliché.

Manohar Malgonkar's *Spy in Amber* grew out of a film script. Ironically, he was one of India's best novelists who gave respectability to this branch of literature. Shyam Dave in *The Kumbh Docket* and Amarjeet Khullar in *Shadow of the Dragon* followed his example. These three novels incorporate all the elements of the internationally best-selling thriller: a diabolical plan by a power-hungry organization, person or nation to gain control of important secrets or possessions; the plan foiled by the skill and strength of a versatile hero; colourful backgrounds; a dash of sex; plenty of suspense and twists galore.

Aamir Ali's *Assignment in Kashmir* rises above the level of pulp literature although it has all the trappings of a popular adventure yarn: guerillas training in the mountains with the intention of setting up an Independent Kashmir, an Indian Army captain assigned to find out the details, gun-running by a Swede, the romantic interest provided by his pretty but unhappy wife, humanity asserting itself when the Indian and a Pakistani captain help each other to escape over a snow-swept pass. The lowbrow reader may think that the story takes time to gather momentum. But *Assignment* makes pleasant Sunday morning reading for the high-brow or serious middle-brow reader because of the author's interest in history, knowledge of Himalayan mountaineering, ornithological background, understanding of political forces and his ability to evoke the scenic beauty of Kashmir.

Mayah Balse in three novels – A *Matter of Mistresses*, *The Sensuous Saint*, and *The Singer* – introduces the complications and characters of the Hindi film. She takes long to weave the many threads of the sub-plots; the devices of the cinema help her to unravel them without difficulty. The heroine of *The Singer* belongs to the show world, and one can imagine how an enterprising producer would have to fill in the songs and dances.

The blurb describes Veena Nagpal's *Compulsion* as 'the inspiring, at times incredible story of a man's rise to a position of eminence. The story of Chandu – his poverty, love, passion, greed and wealth. The agonies and ecstasies of the unfettered and undaunted Bina… who loves Chandu but hates his ruthlessness.' It is also described as 'the most uninhibited, naked and powerful novel an Indian woman ever wrote.'

Sasti Brata's *She and He* and the novels of K.A. Abbas, Nergis Dalal and Mayah Balse have sold well. The others command fairly good sales. The demand for this literature makes one reflect. Its popularity indicates the spread of English among a larger number of people. It is clear that this branch of Indo-Anglian literature does not have any social significance. One must not overlook however that it has sociological importance. It mirrors the longings, responses and moral attitudes of a class of readers. Its value to Indian society is the same as that of any other form of escapist entertainment; it lightens the burden of a hard existence. This body of writing has made Indo-Anglian literature more broad-based. By taking literature out of the drawing room into the street, by dealing with situations which give pleasure to many instead of arousing the interest of a few, by using language as a tool for all purposes instead of preserving it as a handle-with-care object for specialized jobs, it has performed an important function. In the process it has helped Indo-Anglican literature to lose its self-consciousness, and also to strengthen the claim of English to be regarded as one of the languages of India.

George Orwell's Indian Involvement

Hamdi Bey

(Quest 101: May-June 1976)

George Orwell did not love India as much as Kipling did, nor did he respect it as much as E.M. Forster did, but he was more just to it.

Kipling and Orwell were both born in India but the thirty-eight years that elapsed between their births made a great deal of difference in their respective attitudes. Kipling grew up in a period of England's self-sufficiency. Though he was touched by both Russian and French literature, he retained the insular English attitude which he had grown up with. This insularity was punctured by England's involvement in the First World War and at the time Orwell was growing up, the English literary intelligentsia were making a rediscovery of Europe.

It was natural for Orwell, who decided early in his childhood to be a writer, that he should study Kipling who was a kind of household god in Anglo-Indian families. His four favourite boyhood authors included two born in India – Thackeray and Kipling. The difference between the outlooks of Kipling and Forster and Orwell illustrates a facet of the process of decolonisation which has so far been ignored.

Orwell thought that much of Kipling's development was traceable to his having been born in India and his having left school early. When Orwell passed this judgment on Kipling he probably thought that he himself had escaped such determinism. Surely he made an effort but one cannot be sure of the results. Orwell's childhood in

India was shorter by two years than Kipling's, he having been taken to England at four and Kipling at six, but Kipling as an infant had once been taken to England and that was before the Suez route had been opened. India seems to have made less of an impact on the child Orwell's imagination than on Kipling's – though Orwell recalled his Indian childhood years as Kipling did. One reason for this might be that Orwell, unlike Kipling, did not write an autobiography. On the other hand, Orwell expressed the wish that nobody should write his biography. We are not aware of the psychological reasons for such a wish, but can associate the wish with some facts of his life. For example, his adoption of a pseudonym – his own name was Eric Blair – and his sliding for a few years into the anonymity of the world of tramps.

By contrast, Kipling seems a simple person who had been denied entry into the closed society of native India as a child, and as an adult exiled by Anglo-India to Britain, the USA and South Africa as a punishment for re-seeking entry into the criminal fringe of that closed society. He appears a martyr, but a rather shy martyr who hid the fact of his martyrdom by covering it with literary success. The camouflage was so successful that one hardly notices the martyrdom except in the bitter self-commiseration of Mowgli *(Jungle Books)*, the 'I wish it had happened to me' dreams in *Kim* and the voiced protest: 'They won't let me live where I want to live – Bombay.'

Orwell wore his martyrdom more ostensibly for he had a strong masochist trait in his character, and it is the story of his life which becomes more prominent than his work. Kipling provides a contrast against which it is easier to understand Orwell and hence a few more details of their respective lives. Kipling returned to India at 17 to become a journalist, which enabled him to write, and he had written himself out by 1902 – three years before he won the Nobel prize at the age of 42. Nobody yet has won the award for literature at a younger age. Orwell returned to India (Burma was part of India till 1934) at 18 to become a policeman, which prevented him from writing till he was 26 and away from India. Orwell's point about Kipling's leaving school early needs to be clarified, for Orwell did think himself superior in education to Kipling, not only on the strength of a year more spent at school but also having been for four years at Eton, whose chief merit in Orwell's opinion was its 'atmosphere of literary scholarship', which was absent from the cheaper public schools like Kipling's United Services College, only four years old when Kipling joined it.

On the strength of Eton, Orwell considered himself civilized, while he accused Kipling of being 'coarse' enough to keep his mouth shut in Anglo-Indian clubs. His own situation – and Kipling's too without the name being mentioned – is examined, by Orwell in five or six pages of his first novel, *Burmese Days* (1934). The diagnostic remark is: 'It is one of the tragedies of the half-educated that they develop late, when they are already committed to some wrong way of life.' Kipling was committed to the middle class and Anglo-India; Orwell to the 'dirty work' of the Empire – 'living a lie the whole time, the lie that we're here to uplift our poor black brothers instead of to rob them', the 'ever bitterer hatred of the atmosphere of imperialism in which he lived' poisoning everything. One commitment was ideological, the other merely professional. Orwell could resign his job as he did in 1928 but the escape for Kipling was in the company of outcastes and half-castes of Lahore, through the *Gate of Hundred Sorrows*. It was the same escape which Orwell also sought by turning a tramp – the tramp of *Down and Out in Paris and London* (1933), a tramp in Europe rather than India. Yet Orwell met Indian tramps in Britain and spoke to one of them in 'bad Urdu' and was in reply addressed as *tum* – 'a thing to make one shudder, if it had been in India.' And he also met an old Etonian who 'began to quaver out the Eton boating-song' but not the '*Song of the Bower*' which Jellaludin Melutosh recited to Kipling (filed for reference in *Plain Tales from the Hills*).

I am not trying to prove Orwell was a fraud. He had a respect for truth which few have, but Kipling was very much in his sub-conscious, and Orwell had to break loose from Kipling, to defy him, and to lay his ghost in two essays on Kipling – one after Kipling's death in 1936 and another on the appearance of Eliot's *Choice of Kipling's Verse* in 1942. In the earlier essay, Orwell admitted that he 'worshipped Kipling at thirteen, loathed him at seventeen, enjoyed him at twenty, despised him at twenty-five, and now again rather admire him.' Orwell was 33 when he made the above recollection of his varying attitudes to Kipling – at 13 he was in school, at 17 he was preparing to come to India, at 20 he was policing in India, at 25 he had resigned from the Indian police and at 33 he was a Leftist author.

For an India-born there was no other author to turn to, for as Orwell noticed, Kipling's was not only the best but the only literary picture of 19th-century India and that he had 'put on record an immense amount of stuff that one could otherwise only gather from verbal tradition'. E.M. Forster's *A Passage to India* had appeared in 1924 but the earliest reference to it in Orwell's writings is in 1936 – at about the same time that he had resolved his conflicts about Kipling and had settled down to a qualified admiration. Orwell thought of the *Passage* as 'not the perfect novel about India, but it is the best we have ever had and the best we are likely to get, for it is only by some improbable accident that anyone capable of writing a decent novel can be got to stay in India long enough to absorb the atmosphere.' This chance remark introduces us to an important item in the Orwellian eschatology. He firmly believed that civilized men did not readily move away from centres of civilization and that few able men went east of Suez. He had also argued that it was an error to imagine that George Moore, or Gissing, or Thomas Hardy would have written better novels about 19th century India if they had had Kipling's opportunities. 'That is the kind of accident that cannot happen,' said Orwell.

It was not only repugnance at doing the dirty work of Empire that induced Orwell to resign from the Indian Police. It was a belief that he was civilized (while Kipling was coarse) and had to be in the centres of civilization, London and Paris, even if down and out. *In Burmese Days* two ways of life are contrasted: sitting in Paris cafés with foreign art students, drinking white wine and talking Marcel Proust or being in an Anglo-Indian club with whisky and Edgar Wallace. One was civilized and the other coarse. It would be possible to argue that their high rating for white wine and Marcel Proust was part of the contemporary rediscovery of Europe by the British literary intelligentsia. But there might be more intimate reasons. Orwell's mother came from a French family which had been in the timber trade at Mandalay. That fact had probably determined the choice of Burma as the province of India where Orwell went as a police officer, though he had been born at Motihari in Bihar and his father had served as an opium officer in the Bihar districts of what had been Bengal till 1912. Orwell did not like his father and saw little of him till he was eight. His favourite aunt was his mother's sister, Nellie Limouzin, who emphasised her French descent by staying in Paris, and the admiring nephew followed her there. It was a British dilemma, rather more prominent in our own times, whether to be part of the Commonwealth or of the European community.

Orwell chose the European community; he wanted to disown the Raj. That was the post-World War I trend with international communism providing the theoretical basis for anti-imperialism (Lenin, the prophet of anti-imperialism had died only in 1924), for pointing out that 'the Indian Empire is a despotism – benevolent, no doubt, but still a despotism with theft as its final object.' In Burma, Orwell had 'no tie with Europe, except the tie of books' and grew as lonely readers grow 'all the while knowing that somewhere within one there is a possibility of a decent human being.' These are quotations from *Burmese Days*. He had to speak out but that was not possible in Anglo-Indian society; Kipling had found that out, for he had been exiled even though he had only written and not spoken. Orwell too discovered it. In Burma, free speech was unthinkable, though all other kinds of freedom were permitted – to be an idler, a coward, a backbiter, a fornicator.

If one would not read anti-communism in Orwell's last novel, *1984*, published a year before his death in 1950, as many have done, one can see that Orwell's first novel *Burmese Days* anticipates it. There is a genetic continuity between the two: the European bureaucracy is despotic like the Party, the titled Verral is like a member of the Inner Party, the lounge suit is like the blue overall, the Chinese shop is Charrington's junk shop, Flory is unable to speak his mind out, the *pukka sahib's* code is the ideology, the sexual act successfully performed is a rebellion and Flory, like Smith, is ruined through a liaison with a woman who denounces him. The only hope in Kyauktada or Oceania's Airstrip Number 1, is a revolt by the ruled, the natives and the paroles who, like animals, are free. Even the morning jerks of Macgregor, the district magistrate of Kyauktada, and of Winston Smith of *1984*, have some resemblance.

The central issues of the two books are the same: freedom of thought under collectivisation, and hysteria. When men are different from one another and do not live alone, as in the Club at Kyauktada or in Airstrip Number 1, there is little freedom of thought. Gregariousness implies orthodoxy, for orthodoxy means not thinking, and what is worse, not needing to think. The enemy of the moment represented absolute evil and it followed that any past or future agreement with him was not possible. The native bazar and the Chestnut Tree Cafe are both out of bounds though there was no law, not even an unwritten law against frequenting them, and yet the places were somehow ill-omened.

In both the places 'it was not by making yourself heard but staying sane that you carried on the human heritage', though the secrecy of your revolt poisoned you like a 'secret disease'. Such is the consistency of Orwell's work that the first quotation is from *1984* and the second from *Burmese Days:* Flory did not stay sane, and Smith was broken by torture.

In his first novel, Orwell made a European declare that the natives were becoming as insolent as the working classes at home. Orwell believed that imperialism and class domination were related, and he thought Kipling became 'a sort of imperialist' because he looked at the working class from the viewpoint of the upper classes. Both Kipling and Orwell were unhappy at the first schools in England they went too – *vide* 'Ba, Baa Black Sheep' and 'Such, Such Were the Joys'. Kipling was looked down upon because of his Indianness, Orwell because of his parents not being rich. *The Road to Wigan Pier* (1937) tells us of how lower middle-class children used to pine for jobs in India where it was possible to play rich without being actually rich. Orwell detested his association with this make-believe, and allied himself with the working classes.

In 1937 he went to fight in the Spanish Civil War and returned hateful of Stalinism and international communism. He had already fallen out with the elitist British Left for the moral masochist in him demanded of him to be watchful of the attitudes of those with whom he identified himself. He was continually probing the psychology of the groups he worked with – the English bureaucracy in India, the British elitist Left, the Stalinists – and had to pay the price in loneliness. He could not be gregarious, for that meant surrendering his individuality.

He had an opportunity to return to India in 1938 when the *Pioneer* offered him a post as a leader-writer. It was a paper on which Kipling had worked, and Orwell this time could write instead of supervising the torture of suspects and the hanging of condemned men as he had done in his first job. Orwell accepted the offer, but ill-health prevented him from coming. L.H. Myers, chiefly remembered for his novel *The Near and the Far* set in Mughal India, made it possible for him to go and rest in Morocco. A new and different kind of Anglo-India was claiming him – of Malcolm Muggeridge who had worked on the *Statesman*, Lawrence Brander and Rushbrooke-Williams who had taught here and E.M. Forster who had written critically about India, and J.B.S. Haldane who later sought Indian citizenship. Between 1941 and 1943, Orwell was in the BBC's Indian section, and as he observed in a manuscript notebook, 'a little bit of India had been transplanted in Britain'.

The context of the observation was not complimentary to India, for a certain Indian employee of the BBC had sneaked to him about another Indian. Orwell had not much respect for the Indian character and agreed with Forster that 'maniacal suspiciousness is the besetting Indian vice as hypocrisy is the British vice'. Orwell came in touch with Mulk Raj Anand and Ahmed Ali; he was anxious to encourage the Indian intellectuals and was canvassing the *Partisan Review* to publish articles by them. It was a very active period, for he was engaged in anti-Fascist broadcast campaigning and in advocating immediate Dominion Status for India with power to secede when the war was over. As he put it in *The Lion and the Unicorn* (1944), without the right to secede there could be no equality of partnership.

> What India needs is the power to work out its own constitution without British interference…. This is unthinkable until there is a Socialist government in England…. The moment that England ceased to stand towards India in the relation of exploiter, the balance of forces would be altered. No need then for the British to flatter the ridiculous Indian princes, to prevent the growth of Indian trade unions, to play off Moslem against Hindu, to protect the worthless life of the moneylender, to prefer the half-barbarous Gurkha to the educated Bengali. Once check that stream of dividends that flows from the bodies of Indian coolies to the banking accounts of old ladies in Cheltenham, and the whole sahib-native nexus, with its haughty ignorance an one side and servility on the other, can come to an end.

When the Cripps Mission came to India in 1942, Orwell noted that the secrecy surrounding the mission destroyed the hope of full independence being offered to India. Then, on 10 August 1942, he noted: 'Nehru, Gandhi, Azad and many others in jail…. Ghastly speech of Amery speaking of Nehru and Co. as "wicked men"…. It is strange, but quite truly, the way the British government is now behaving upsets me more than a military defeat.'

August 14: 'Horrabin was broadcasting today, and as always we introduced him as the man who drew maps for Wells's *Outline of History* and Nehru's *Glimpses of World History*. Today the reference to Nehru was cut out from the announcement – Nehru being in prison and therefore having become bad.'

September 15: 'Ghastly feeling of impotence over the India business, Churchill's speeches, the evident intention of the Blimps to have one more try at being what they consider tough, and the impudent way in which the newspapers can misrepresent the whole issue, well knowing that the public will never know enough or take enough interest to verify the facts. This last is the worst symptom of all – though actually our own apathy about India is not worse than the non-interest of Indian intellectuals in the struggle against Fascism in Europe.'

When two Indians were accused early in 1947 – several months before Independence – of having collaborated with the Fascist powers by broadcasting on their radios, Orwell entered a defence for them. 'What right have we to describe the Indians who broadcast on the German radio as "collaborators"? They were citizens of an occupied country, hitting back at the occupying power in the way that seemed best to them.' That was fourteen months before he began *1984*, but much of the intervening period was wasted away in sickness. Orwell's last novel drew a great deal on his experience of loss of liberty in the Second World War, and his work with Forster and others on the Defence of Freedom League. He also foresaw the parcelling out of the world among three superpowers, and he thought it was necessary to warn the public, to drive home the moral of his own life-time, that all despotisms and all oligarchies – of bureaucracies in dependent countries, of the aristocracy in independent countries and of parties in totalitarian countries – were bad.

He however never liked what he called 'the cow and spinning wheel paradise' of Indian revivalism. In a review of Lionel Fielden's *Beggar My Neighbour* he thought the former chief of All India Radio had made a plea for 'spirituality' against 'materialism'. 'On the one hand, an uncritical preference for everything oriental', wrote Orwell, 'on the other a hatred of the West generally, and of Britain in particular, hatred of science and the machine, suspicion of Russia, contempt for the working class conception of Socialism. The whole adds up to Parlour Anarchism – a plea for the simple life, based on dividends.'

The above quotation shows Orwell as a kind of Marxist but what follows would place him as a Freudian too – and it was this combination, abhorrent to both the Marxist and Freudian orthodoxies, especially the Communist Party of Great Britain led by R. Palme Dutt, which distinguished Orwell from most other Leftists. He wrote later in the same review:

In the last twenty years, western civilization has given the intellectual security without responsibility, and in England, in particular, it has educated him in scepticism while anchoring him immovably in the privileged class. He has been in the position of a young man living on an allowance from a father whom he hates. The result is a deep feeling of guilt and resentment, not combined with any genuine desire to escape. But some psychological escape, some form of self-justification there must be, and one of the most satisfactory is transferred nationalism.... If you throw in a touch of oriental mysticism and Buchmanite raptures over Gandhi, you have everything that a disaffected intellectual needs. The life of an English gentleman and the moral attitude of a saint can be enjoyed simultaneously.... The actual facts don't matter very much. The fact that the eastern nations have shown themselves at least as war-like and blood-thirsty as the western ones, that so far from rejecting industrialism, the East is adopting it as swiftly as it can – this is irrelevant, since what is wanted is the mythos of the peaceful, religious and patriarchal East to set against the greedy and materialist West. As soon as you have 'rejected' industrialism, and hence Socialism, you are in that strange no man's land where the Fascist and the pacifist join forces. There is indeed a sort of apocalyptic truth in the statement of the German radio that the teachings of Hitler and Gandhi are the same. One realizes this when one sees Middleton Murry praising the Japanese invasion of China and Gerald Heard proposing to institute the Hindu caste system in Europe.... We shall be hearing a lot about the superiority of eastern civilization in the next few years.

Orwell was opposed to pacifism and sainthood and one of his last essays was devoted to *Reflections on Gandhi* (1949). He had read the openings of Gandhi's autobiography while in Burma and had been favourably impressed. He had not liked Gandhi but conceded that 'even Gandhi's worst enemies would admit that he was an interesting and unusual man who enriched the world simply by being alive'. Orwell's main criticism of Gandhi's teachings, was that they could not 'be squared with the belief that man is the measure of all things, and that our job is to make life worth living on this earth, which is the only earth we have. They make sense only on the assumption that

God exists and the world of solid objects is an illusion to be escaped from'. He argued:

> And finally – this is the cardinal point – for the seeker after goodness there must be no close friendships, and no exclusive loves whatever. Close friendships, Gandhi says, are dangerous, because 'friends react on one another', and through loyalty to a friend one can be led into wrong-doing. This is unquestionably true. Moreover, if one is to love God, or to love humanity as a whole, one cannot give one's preference to any individual person. This again is true, and it marks the point at which the humanistic and religious attitudes cease to be reconcilable. To an ordinary human being, love means nothing if it does not mean loving some people more than others.

Orwell continued:

> The essence of being human is that one does not seek perfection, that one is sometimes willing to commit sins for the sake of loyalty, that one does not push asceticism to the point where it makes friendly intercourse impossible, and that one is prepared in the end to be defeated and broken up by life, which is the inevitable price of fastening one's love upon other human individuals. No doubt alcohol, tobacco and so forth are things that a saint must avoid, but sainthood is also a thing that human beings must avoid.

Later he said: 'But it is not necessary here to argue whether the other-worldly or the humanistic ideal is "higher". The point is that they are incompatible. One must choose between God and Man, and all "radicals" and "progressives" from the mildest Liberal to the most extreme Anarchist, have in effect chosen Man.'

The essay on Gandhi stated very simply what Orwell stood for, both in *Burmese Days* as well as *1984* and in *Animal Farm* (1945) and his other writings, and the ideals responsible for the way he lived and lived out his social protests.

But Orwell was a writer and before we conclude this study of him we must emphasise the respect he had for truth.

He thought of *A Passage to India* as a truthful book, and was not dismayed when, during the Second World War, the Nazis broadcast a shortened version of it. 'So far as I know they didn't even have to resort to dishonest quotation. Just because the book was essentially truthful, it could be made to serve the purposes of Fascist propaganda…. Indeed, anyone who has ever written in defence of unpopular causes or been the witness of events which are likely to cause controversy, knows the fearful temptation to distort or suppress the facts, simply because any honest statement will contain revelations which can be made use of by unscrupulous opponents. But what one has to consider are long-term effects. In the long run, can the cause of progress be served by lies, or can it not?'

Orwell welcomed the emergence of an 'English-language Indian literature' which he thought 'will have its effect on the post-war world…' How much of the special atmosphere of English-language Indian literature is due to its subject matter is uncertain, but in reading Mr Mulk Raj Anand's work, or that of Ahmed Ali and several others, it is difficult not to feel that by this time another dialect, comparable to Irish-English, has grown up. He though both Anand and Ahmed Ali to be much better writers than the average run of English novelists' and in saying that he was deflating the *pukka sahib* whose code of conduct called for derision of *babu* English. In fact, a hatred of all English-educated Indians for they demanded equality which the *pukka sahib* could ill afford, for all his privileges would tumble down.

But Orwell's enthusiasm for Indo-Anglican writing was not in consonance with the view he had held, that civilized persons rarely left the centres of civilization, and that was why there was a dearth of good colonial literature in all languages. Dr Susanne Howe, author of *Novels of Empire* would agree with Orwell for at least English, French and German. Was Orwell admitting the existence of a native civilization? Probably he did for the time being, putting away his ideals of Progress which he believed fervently, only wanting that Progress should be achieved in a humane manner and that there should then be a civilized respect for literature and the arts.

Orwell believed in democratic socialism; Kipling was a sort of imperialist. Between them stood India and civilization and in regard to these they agreed and differed as any two persons who have seen much, undergone much and thought much would.

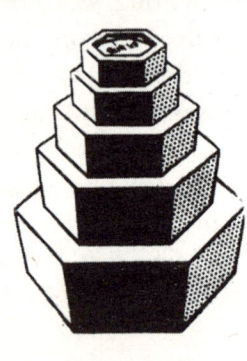

Power and Personality

Sudhir Kakar

(Quest 101: May-June 1976)

The nature of the link between a leader's personality and some of his crucial decisions which have an impact on his nation's history has always aroused great interest and speculation, both among his contemporaries and among the later generations of biographers and historians. Thus Plutarch makes a psychological character assessment when he informs us of young Alexander's reactions to the battlefield victories of his father – 'Instead of rejoicing at it altogether, he would tell his companions that his father would anticipate everything, and leave him no opportunities of performing great and illustrious actions. For being more bent upon action and glory than either upon pleasure or riches, he esteemed all that he should receive from his father as a diminution and prevention of his own future achievements' – or assesses Pericles as admirable 'not only for his equitable and mild temper... but also for the high spirit and feelings which made him regard it the noblest of all his honours that in the exercise of such immense power he never had gratified his envy or passion.'

The interest in the personality of powerful leaders not only serves theoretical and scholarly purposes but can also be dictated by eminently practical considerations. For example, consider the speech of Yasuhiro Nakasone, Japan's Minister of International Trade and Industry, as reported in the New York *Times* of 19 February 1973: 'Japan has not tried hard enough to understand President Nixon's hopes and pattern of behaviour…. Mr Nixon is an energetic, ambitious, and practical man who believes in experience and traditional American values. We must analyse the personality and pattern of behaviour of the American President, leader of the strongest country in the world, in order to plan for the future.' Similar considerations also applied during the Second World War when the American Office of Strategic Services commissioned a psycho-analyst, Dr Walter Langer, to undertake a psychological study of Adolf Hitler (which correctly predicted his suicide) that would help in anticipating some of his actions.

I have mentioned above that the interest in the personalities of those who exercise power in the political arena has been a persistent phenomenon throughout history. As a subject of serious study, however, it has had its ups and downs in the changing fashions of academia. After having its heyday in the work of Carlyle, the interest in man as an actor on the political stage steadily waned during the first half of this century as social scientists interpreted events in which the forces of history were examined macroscopically in terms of class, property, religion, nation, and so on. Yet with the emergence of such leaders as Gandhi, Nehru, Hitler, Mussolini, de Gaulle, Mao or even Idi Amin and Lumumba, the nagging doubt persisted whether the personalities of these leaders were really so insignificant for the historical events they initiated and the policies they helped to shape as the academies would have us believe. The problem remains unresolved in the sense that we are still far away from developing a theory of history or a political science which does neither more nor less justice to the individual on the stage of history than his presence demands.

Perhaps one of the chief reasons for the neglect of the leader's personality in the analysis of his actions has been the fact that psychologists have been of little help in this domain. Much of modern, scientific psychology eschews the problem of motives and subjective meaning of action altogether. And simply postulating a power motive of greater and lesser intensity among human beings, as in the work of such psychologists as David McClleland and Henry Murray, only stops the discussion and tells us little about the different ways people acquire and use power. To deal with a leader's personality is essentially to deal with his orientation to power and psychologists have generally shared in the avoidance of this topic that has characterised all intellectuals. The result has been that historians and other social scientists have gone their own way, using home-spun, commonsense psychological interpretations when absolutely unavoidable but mainly concentrating their analyses on social and historical forces with which they are much more comfortable.

The psychologies which focus on human motivation – psycho-analysis and its offshoots – which could make a major contribution to the study of power and personality have still not found widespread favour. This is mainly due to two reasons. The first reason is our tendency to believe that man is divisible into two separate individuals: (i) a rational person who can operate logically, deal with facts and reach purely objective conclusions, and (ii) an emotional person who is irrational and operates according to his biases. All of us prefer to deal with the former 'person' and to exclude the influence of the latter. For an individual, the ability to make this separation, it is assumed, rests in part on his education and intellectual skills but primarily on the exercise of will power and the conscious intention to be rational. This ability is believed to be particularly characteristic of 'the few' whom we elevate to positions of leadership. Yet if we accept the evidence of clinical psychology, we know that emotions will influence thinking, reasoning and decision making whenever they are aroused. We also know that the greater the importance of a problem or issue for the individual, the greater is the likelihood of emotional factors coming into play. Many of these emotional factors lie in the individual's past, particularly in his childhood, have been repressed and now operate unconsciously.

It is to the influence of these latter, unconscious factors that the noted historian Barbara Tuchman referred, when in a speech in February 1973 she remarked: 'Proving his manhood was, I imagine, a factor pushing President Nasser of Egypt into provoking war with Israel in 1967 so that he could not be accused of weakness and appear less militant than the Syrians. One senses it was a factor in the personalities of Johnson and Nixon in regard to withdrawing from Vietnam: there was that horrible doubt, "Shall I look soft?" It was clearly present in Kennedy too: on the other hand it does not seem to have bothered Eisenhower, Truman or FDR.' This example also brings us to the second reason why psychoanalytic approaches to leadership and power have still to find general acceptance. The reason is that the validity of these approaches is yet to be established. For although we know from clinical practice that many men, who have unconscious fears of being emasculated, who have a nagging doubt of not being men enough, act with exaggerated expressions of masculinity, displays of activism, aggressiveness and belligerence, is there comparable evidence in the lives of leaders whom Mrs Tuchman mentions that they shared a similar unconscious anxiety? Students of political science who hold competing theories and intelligent laymen who test theories against commonsense and intuition will demand explanations which are more simple and economical, are capable of being disproved and, above all, explanations which assume rational behaviour on the part of the political actor. The burden of proof squarely lies on those who advance the psychological explanation. But the kind of evidence psychologist can offer is based on empathic intuition and theories which are still widely misunderstood although they might have gained a common intellectual currency. I am of course referring here to Freudian psychoanalysis and some of its offshoots.

Let me illustrate this by considering President Nixon's Christmas bombing of Hanoi in 1973. The rational position would be that the decision to bomb was based on the use of force to shift the stalemate in the Paris negotiations, i.e. it was designed as a tactic in a rational approach to bargaining. One may also argue that the decision was clue to domestic political considerations, as a communication to the right-wing sentiment and as a pre-emptive move to block conservatives who would assert that the USA had sold out South Vietnam. Anyone who would also see the bombing as a part of Nixon's personality pattern, with an unresolved conflict between active masculine and passive feminine wishes arising out of his childhood experiences would naturally challenge the sceptic in all of us. In contrast to the first two approaches, where we might be satisfied with the minimum in the way of evidence the third approach requires a degree and kind of proof which goes far beyond accepted cannons. And it may still leave most people unconvinced – unless, of course, they could directly experience such issues through observation of their own mental life, i.e. through an introspective effort.

Leaving aside the unresolved problem of the validity of psychological explanations of power and leadership, let me turn to the different models which have been so far used in such studies. The first model, which is probably familiar to most of us, is the compensatory model of Alfred Adler who was a disciple of Freud but later broke away from the psycho-analytic movement. Adler's model of man seeking power to compensate for his deficiencies and sense of inferiority has of course been familiar to poets. Consider, for example, the opening scene of Shakespeare's Richard III, where Richard of Gloucester declaims:

But I – that are not shap'd for sportive tricks

Now made to event an amorous looking-glass –

I – that am rudely stamp'd, and want love's majesty

To start before wanton ambling nymph –

I – that am curtail'd of this fair proportion, Cheated of feature by dissembling nature.

Deform'd, unfinished, sent before my time

Into this breathing world, scarce half made up.

And that so lamely and unfashionable

That dogs bark at me as I halt by them –

Why, I, in this weak piping time of peace,

Have no delight to pass away the time.

Unless to see my shadow in the sun

And descant on mine own deformity.

And therefore, since I cannot prove a lover

To entertain these fair well-spoken days,

I am determined to prove a villain....

According to Adler, it is not only the physical but also the psychological deficiencies, arising through neglect or excessive pampering during childhood which the individual tries to compensate for in his acquisition and use of power. In other words, in the unconscious, a grievance once felt remains as a potential claim against others, and conceivably, drives men to seek power and revenge for slights suffered. Un-mastered situations which one passively endured during the early years have to be actively repeated, in forms suitable to adulthood, as individuals seek to master their unresolved tensions and conflicts.

The Adlerian approach found its most brilliant spokesman in Harold Lasswell. In his books *Psychopathology and Politics* and *Power and Personality,* Lasswell presents a number of case histories showing the displacement of an individual's private conflicts onto public affairs. He also set up a typology – agitators, bureaucrats and theorists – according to the kinds of deprivations in different periods of childhood, which lead to one or the other orientation toward power. Perhaps one of the most successful efforts of the compensatory school is the study of Woodrow Wilson by Alexander and Juliette George. Starting from Wilson's need to have one enemy in all the institutions he worked in or later headed, with disastrous consequences for the carrying out of important policies, the Georges trace his desire for power, his need to create and overcome an enemy, and his over-reactions in this process, to his unconscious need to restore self-esteem so strongly damaged in his relationship with his father. This deficiency or 'illness' model has also been applied, with more or less success, to the study of other notable leaders such as Napoleon, Hitler, Mussolini, Stalin and so on.

The sickness model of power, however, does not always seem convincing. Two brilliant studies by Erik Erikson, *Young Man Luther* and *Gandhi's Truth,* have turned this model on its head. Erikson's point of departure is still the individual leader's conflict, rooted in his life history, but the resolution of this conflict is no longer its simple displacement onto the public arena. He does not imply that a leader's actions serve defensive-functions against his inner conflict and reflect his pathological symptoms. In Erikson's model, the conflict serves to create a new reality in the form of some vision if a new order which also meets a pressing psychological need of his potential followers. Pathology, whether in Luther's depressive reactions, sadism and masturbatory guilt or in Gandhi's experiments with sexuality, which might be called a perversion in the clinical context, becomes subordinated to the creation of something new, to the act of genius.

For those without Erikson's sensitive gifts, the risk of applying his model lies in the temptation to detach genius from human experience or idealise it beyond recognition. It is especially seductive in the Indian context where the unconscious need to bestow *mana* on our leaders in order to partake of the *mana* ourselves and thus attempt to restore the perfection of infancy ('You are perfect but I am a part of you'), is particularly strong. Erikson's balance is difficult to achieve for those for whom leaders take on an emotional importance, independent of any realistic evaluation of their performance and their actuality as imperfect human beings.

Both the Lasswellian and Eriksonian models, however, have one serious deficiency. They deal with larger-than-life figures, the tragic heroes, the charismatic leaders or whatever one might choose to call them. The application of their models can give us some insight into the Nehrus and Kennedys but may have little to say about the Shastris and the Nixons. If any question can be raised about the psyches of such leaders it may have to do with their being too normal and well-adjusted, almost to the point of denying conflict. Their credo is getting things done through people and the less introspection there is, the better. Many of them rise to the top by the psychology of deference. They cannot be too humble, too serving, too responsive to the wishes of others. Ask me to open a conference, and I shall be there. Present me with petitions and I am alert and sympathetic. Tell me to appear in a television discussion, and I shall look sincere and compliant. Some of them can be even called the Uriah Heeps of power, 'your humble servant', who ingratiate and even demean themselves while climbing the peaks of power. Having once reached the top however, they can easily shift from deferring to demanding deference. What are the dynamics and structure of their personalities, as compared to the charismatic leaders with whom we are more familiar? In their recent book, *Power and the Corporate Mind*, Zalezmik and Kets de Vries have taken the first steps towards providing an answer. Their typology distinguishes between the personalities and orientation to power of the consensus and charismatic leaders whom they call the 'minimum' and the 'maximum' man respectively.

On a primary emotional level, the minimum man is concerned with the opinion of his peers. He does not lead public opinion, but follows it. He often appears as bland and opaque, functioning like a radar, picking up opinions, ideas, impressions. This scanning approach results in adroit flexibility but seldom in conviction. Intellectually and emotionally, it is like living out of a suitcase, allowing the person to avoid investments and consequently, losses. The minimum man is a survivor, one who clutches power and holds on to it despite major shifts in goals and directions. He keeps his attention fixed on parental authorities toward whom he remains passive, but he actively manipulates his peers over whom he seeks control.

The childhood relationships of minimum man to his parents do not show any evidence of severe trauma. Instead, we find a kind of emotional neutrality on the part of the parents, especially the father, who often appears weak and passive in comparison to the mother. This produces a confusion of internal images – who am I? How due a man behave? – that are so vital later in defining an adult self. Instead of finding strength in his internal self-images, the minimum man as a child seeks it from attachment to prisons and events outside himself. The minimum man has many acquaintances but few friends, many sexual experiences but no deep attachment. In his less successful version, the adaptability which makes him an effective consensus leader can become a weird promiscuity in which friends and lovers, opinions and ideas are adopted and discarded with equal case.

The minimum man devotes his energy to questions of procedure rather than substance. Questions of substance make clear all dimensions of a power struggle, requiring a man to take a firm stand. Procedure, on the other hand, tends to be neutral and to include everybody, so long as people believe the procedure is fair to all and every point of view. In the realm of ethics, the minimum man, constantly scanning with his radar for opinions and sources of power in others, tending by the very structure of his personality not to have an integrated set of commitments, may be led into a decision that is unethical. His consensus style, by its nature, would commit him to the pragmatic, self-serving choice, ethical or not.

We can think of many effective leaders of the minimum man type (Shastri? Harold Wilson? Eisenhower?) and they typically rise to the top when the need of the times is for flexibility and not innovation, stability and not ideology, consensus and not brilliance.

In contrast in the minimum man, people are drawn to the maximum man by the power of his convictions and visions of reality. He is a great innovator, but not always a good leader – he will have little use for subordinates who have different opinions – and his extremely high self-esteem may create problems.

The maximum man is the chosen one in childhood, either because he is the only child, or because he has a special attachment to his parents which is the bedrock for his sense of self-esteem. In the minimum man the images of what is right or desirable are weak and confused; in the maximum man, the images are strong. Their strong presence diminishes his dependence on others, making him self-sufficient. Mania, paranoia, and depression await the maximum man if he loses his balance, as does depersonalization – the feeling of being unreal – await the minimum man if he loses his balance. Short of these severe forms we are certain to find narcissism – the individual's reserving of his most intense love for himself – in every maximum man. With the help of self-love, the maximum man achieves independence from people in the real world. Such narcissistic independence can be very dangerous, as in the case of Hitler, because there is nothing to guarantee a clear view of people and the world. In its benevolent form, as in de Gaulle, narcissism frees the maximum man to lead, rather than follow, the consensus. A love affair with his inner audience, consisting primarily of his parental images, allows him to act according to higher principles, ideologies, and causes.

Maximum men are deeply committed to their internal standards, with all the strength of high self esteem, and they resist adaptation on other people's terms. This strength of conviction and sense of command is the basis of his emotional appeal. It may also be the source of disaster for an organisation or a country when the maximum man refuses to bend or flex, and leads his followers to defy reality.

The maximum man or the charismatic leader may be worshipped by his subordinates, but he is also likely to be mistrusted because he holds firm convictions about right and wrong courses of action while he is inconsistent with people. He may lead his nation to heights of prosperity and power through the strength of his vision and persistence, but he is anathema in consensus situations because he can neither delegate nor be delegated to (except, perhaps by God or 'Motherland'), nor can he wait for initiatives to rise from below.

In summary, Zaleznik maintains, doggedness, narcissism and the sense of being special or displaced – these characterise the maximum man. The scanning of reactions, the desire to fit in, the capacity to adapt oneself to the environment and to live flexibly – these characterise the minimum man, both sets of characteristics can be understood as outgrowths of personality structure erected early in life, and changed only slowly, if at all, during one's lifetime.

The models of personality and power I have described above may be called first approximations to the complexity of leadership. Yet this does not diminish their crucial importance for further studies. For the unresolved conflicts and power orientations of leaders are not played out in relative privacy, affecting only close friends and family members, as is the case with most men, but have a much larger stage for their setting. They have the power to drag whole nations in their wake and to affect, for better or for worse, the lives of millions. For our own protection, with an ever present danger of a critical stance towards leaders being swept away in a flood of archaic feelings, we certainly need all the understanding we can get.

The Prime Performer

Fine performance in a car depends on many factors — power, controls, balance, springing—in fact, the entire conception and construction of the car.

The Ambassador passes this test handsomely. The amazing Over-head Valve Engine gives you 25% more power and 25% more economy The controls are responsive and easy to manipulate. It corners wonderfully, and the springs furnish a smooth ride. In fact, every component and part of the Ambassador is designed to contribute to a superb performance !

HINDUSTHAN **Ambassador**
for top performance

HINDUSTAN MOTORS LIMITED, CALCUTTA.

—— DEALERS ——

Agra; Ambala Cantt; Ajmer; Ahmedabad; Ahmednagar; Allahabad; Baroda; Bangalore; Bhilai; Berhampur; Bombay; Bareilly; Calcutta; Cuttack; Coimbatore; Colombo; Dibrugarh; Dhanbad; Gwalior; Gauhati; Imphal; Indore; Jaipur; Jabalpur; Jodhpur; Jalgaon; Jorhat; Jamshedpur; Jullundur City; Jammu; Kanpur; Kolhapur; Kurnool; Lucknow; Madras; Madurai; Mangalore; Meerut; Nagpur; New Delhi; Nepal; Patna; Poona; Pondicherry; Palayamcottai; Rajkot; Ranchi; Sambalpur; Shillong; Secunderabad; Silchar; Srinagar; Satna; Tezpur; Tiruchirapalli; Trivandrum; Varanasi Cantt; Vijayawada; Vizianagram.

QUEST

Poetry

Agha Shahid Ali

Bones

(Quest 73: November–December 1971)

1

The years are dead. I'm
twenty, a mourner in the Mohorrum
Procession, mixing blood with
mud, memory with memory. I'm

still alone.

2

Death filled the years, there
was no time to mourn. No time to remember
slaughtered martyrs or ancestors
who knew a history of miracles. Grandfather
still mocks me in my dream: did
I light the oil-lamp at his tomb?

In this mosaic-world of silent
graveyards the difference lies between
death and dying. It's

futile to light oil-lamps here
and search for grandfather or
forgotten ancestors. Their

flesh must have turned soft as dust
and how can one complain to bones?

The Walled City—3

(Quest 83: July-August 1973)

1

essential this harshness of language
while explaining to you the predicament
of beggars, their smiles lit with flames of
dust
& you only trying seldom
understanding

the fires of pavements that charred
the meatless bones of children's corpses
undug from the wombs of
tired mothers:

the harvest of peace as someone said!

& what of me? the same old hypocrite
who talked so well of wars & wars
inside the blue walls of a dark room—
reading angry editorials by comfortable men!

Qawwali at Nizamuddin Aulia's Dargah

(Quest 96: July-August 1975)

I

Between two saints, he shares the
earth, Mohommad Shah "Rangeele",
(evoked in Paluskar's khayal)
The beggar-woman kisses the marble
lattice, sobs on Khusro's pillars.
In a corner, Jahanara, garbed in
the fakir's grass, mumbles a Sufi quatrain.

We recline on the grave-stone,
or on the saint's poem, unaware
of the sorrow of the pulverized prayer:

Time has only its vagrant finger:
Knowing no equal, it paused for massacres

II

Suffering still has its familiar patterns:

Darius Cooper

Fraternity Forced on the Under-Privileged

(Quest 101: May-June 1976)

To reassure ourselves, that as teachers
we are human,
we allow the peon
to take the elevator,
while we walk up
the flight of stairs.
We pretend to ignore
the little cup of milk,
he has hidden
for his afternoon cup of tea,
and casually, very casually,
pick out the pebbles
he has not sifted,
from the rationed quantum
of sugar.
We donate five rupees
from our low salary

to his fund,
and sometimes sit on his stool,
watching him comb his hair
with the comb
we have kindly lent him.

Kamala Das

Summer in Calcutta

(Ten Years of Quest, Manaktalas, Bombay 1966,
eds. Abu Sayeed Ayyub and Amlan Datta)

What is this drink but
The April sun, squeezed
Like an orange in
My glass? I sip the
Fire, I drink and drink
Again, I am drunk,
Yes, but on the gold
Of suns. What noble
Venom now flows through
My veins and fills my
Mind with unhurried
Laughter? My worries
Doze. Wee bubbles ring
My glass, like a bride's
Nervous smile, and meet
My lips. Dear, forgive
This moment's lull in
Wanting you, the blur

In memory. How
Brief the term of my
Devotion, how brief
Your reign when I with
Glass in hand, drink, drink,
And drink again this
Juice of April suns.

The Sirens

(Ten Years of Quest, Manaktalas, Bombay 1966,
eds. Abu Sayeed Ayyub and Amlan Datta)

The night, dark-cloaked like a procuress, brought
him to me, willing, light like a shadow,
speaking words of love
in some tender language I do not know.
Aniruddha, dream-lover, hide from him
this kind night's deceit, for I know too well
that he loves me not.

With the crows came the morning, and my limbs,
warm from love, were once again so lonely.
At my door-step I saw a pockmarked face
a friendly smile and
a rolleiflex. We will go for a drive,
he said. Or, go to see the lakes. I have
washed my face with soap and water, brushed
my hair a dozen
times, draped myself in six yards of printed
voile. Ah... does it still show, my night of love?

You look pale, he said. Not pale, not really
pale. It's the lipstick's
anaemia. Out, in the street, we heard
the sirens go, and I paused in talk to
weave its veil with the sound of his mirthless
laughter. He said,
they are testing the sirens today. I am
happy. He really was lavish with words.
So happy, just being with you. But you,
you love another,
I know, he said, perhaps a handsome man,
a young and handsome man. Not young,
not handsome, I thought, just a filthy snob.
It's a onesided love,
I said. What can I do, or you? I smiled.
A smile is such a detached thing, I wear

Gino

(Quest 55: Autumn 1967)

You will perish from his kiss, he said, as one must
Surely die, when bitten by a krait who fills
The bloodstreams with its accursed essence. I was quiet,
For once; my tongue had fainted in my mouth.
It was July, a July full of rain, and darkness
Trapped like smoke in the hollows of the sky, and
That lewd steamy smell of rot, rising out of the earth.
He walked one step ahead of me, the West wind leaking
Through his hair. And, I thought, if I could only want,

Really, really want his love, we shall ride happiness,
Great white steed, trampler of unsacred laws.
If I could only dislodge the inherited
Memory of a touch, I shall serve myself in
Bedroom-mirrors, dark fruit on silver platter,
While he lies watching, fair conqueror of another's
Country. I shall polish the panes of his moody eyes
And in jealous hours, after bitter words and rage,
I shall wail in his nerves, as homeless cats wail
From the rubble of a storm. But one only gets
The life one deserves, and dreams only such dreams as
The old soul can comprehend. I dream of obscene hands
Striding up my limbs and of morgues where the night-lights
Glow on faces shuttered by the soul's exit. And
Of ward-boys, sepulchral, wheeling me through long corridors
To the x-ray room's dark interior.
(Oh, the clatter of the trolleys, with the dead on them,
As loud as untimely laughter) And, of aeroplanes
Bursting red in the sky. . . I should be dreaming his
Peerless dreams, his dreams of sunlit villas and of fat
Half-caste children, lovelier than Gods, and of
Drinking wine in verandahs, he and I, ageing,
And at peace, all disguise gone from us.

*****

But I shall end differently, I know, our bloods'
Tributaries never once merging. It is
A dream-river, keep it so; the children are
Dream-children. Real ones never bear such splendent eyes.
This body that I wear without joy, this body

Burdened with lenience, slender toy, owned
By man of substance, shall perhaps wither, battling with
My darling's impersonal lust. Or, it shall grow gross
And reach large proportions before its end.

* * * * *

I shall be the fat-kneed hag in the long bus queue,
The one from whose shopping bag the mean potato must
Roll out across the road. I shall be the patient
On the hospital bed, lying in drugged slumber
And dreaming of home. I shall be the grandmother
Willing away her belongings, those scraps and trinkets
More lasting than her bones. Perhaps some womb in that
Darker world shall convulse, when I finally enter,
A legitimate entrant, marked by discontent.

Contacts

(Quest 55: Autumn 1967)

When I
Sleep, the outside
World crumbles, all contacts
Broken. So, in that longer sleep
Only
The world
Shall die, and I
Remain, just being,
Also being a remaining...

Gauri Deshpande

For One Who Will Recognize the Poem on Sight: A Cyclical

(Quest 67: October–December 1970)

1

After such want and futile willing
when at last we meet
and want to weave the web
of wishes around each,
find its bright delicacy
broken, bruised again
by the spiny armour we are forced
to wear of straight-spined
staring-ahead pride
and doing-without cheer.
Only as we are parting we see
we haven't got to hammer it on once more
till the next time.

2

Witness my happiness –
it makes me ashamed
that I should smile (and smile)
and forget
last year's anguish
and tearing asunder
and the going and silence.
But this promises to be the year
of the mango.
Witness my foot-high
year-old alphonso
covered with fragrance.

3

We had not thought of it
nor planned;
had been distant and withdrawn
in fact.
Yet it was given
us, a glittering sun –
set in sadness and loss
and we kept it by us
did not speak nor hush
only savoured the bloom
on each other's face
fading with the sun –
set.

4

We had exhausted our glances
in casual encounters
and had refused to meet memories;
fatigued by the necessity
of drawing apart, you flinch
even from my casual touch
upon your fist
for it seems to assume
after so much want
the weight of wanton intimacy.

Nissim Ezekiel

Enterprise

(Ten Years of Quest, Manaktalas, Bombay 1966,
eds. Abu Sayeed Ayyub and Amlan Datta)

It started as a pilgrimage,
Exalting minds and making all
The burdens light. The second stage
Explored but did not test the call.
The sun beat down to match our rage.

We stood it very well, I thought:
Observed, and put down copious notes
On palaces and peasants' lot,
The way of serpents and of goats,
Three cities where a sage had taught.

But when the differences arose
On how to cross a desert patch,
We lost a friend whose stylish prose
Was quite the best of all our batch.
A shadow falls on us—and grows.

Another phase was reached when we
Were twice attacked, and lost our way.
A section claimed its liberty
To leave the group. I tried to pray.
Our leader said he smelt the sea.

We noticed nothing as we went,
A straggling crowd of little hope.
Ignoring what the thunder meant,
Deprived of common needs, like soap.
Some were broken, some merely bent.

When, finally, we reached the place,
We hardly knew why we were there.
The trip had gnawed at every face,
Our deeds were neither great nor rare.
Home is where we have to gather grace.

Poet, Lover, Birdwatcher

(Ten Years of Quest, Manaktalas, Bombay 1966,
eds. Abu Sayeed Ayyub and Amlan Datta)

To force the pace and never to be still
Is not the way of those observing birds
Or women. The best poets wait for words.
The hunt is not an exercise of will
But patient love relaxing on a hill
To note the movement of a timid wing;
Until the one who knows that she is loved
No longer waits but risks surrendering—

In this the poet finds his moral proved,
Who never spoke until his spirit moved.
The slow movement seems, somehow, to say much more.
To watch the rarer birds, you have to go
Along deserted lanes and where the rivers flow
In silence near the source, or by a shore
Remote and thorny, like the heart's dark floor.
And there the women slowly turn around,
Not only flesh and bone but myths of light
With darkness at the core, and sense is found
By poets lost in crooked, restless flight,
The deaf can hear, the blind recover sight.

In The Garden

(Ten Years of Quest, Manaktalas, Bombay 1966,
eds. Abu Sayeed Ayyub and Amlan Datta)

It seemed to me so much like you,
To find the planning of the garden
Faulty, and the birds too few.

Your walk was slow, informal there
Among the trees whose names you knew,
And flowers commonplace or rare.

The elephant of broken stone
Deserved, you said, a closer view

Than animals of flesh and bone.

The spacious lawns with sand defined
Where children shouted, breezes blew,
Or water like a lucid mind

Negotiates obstructive rocks;
And bridges modesty designed;
Were better than the tower of clocks,

And hedges ruining every view—
At which I felt your kindness harden:
It seemed to me so much like you.

Stance

(Quest 81: March-April 1973)

I am not seeking
ideology or sex,
lost identity.

Dreaming of the good
and beautiful
I'm held by sanity.

pull of reason:
ripeness revealed
in the right season.

It's never like that
You cannot choose
to be fat or thin.

you only lose
flesh in excess
or put some on

by various means
construed as art,
to move, not to regress.

Elusive for ever,
the middle road
is never
              strictly

in the middle.

Allen Ginsberg

Allen Ginsberg, *author of HOWL and KADDISH, is now in India, experimenting on the hallucination-inducing properties of certain indigenous drugs. But the poem which appears in this number was written under the influence of a quite different kind of stimulant and in circumstances far different from his Indian journey, though it has been somewhat condensed and reset for* QUEST.

Ginsberg says he has spent longer in Calcutta than in any other city except his native New York and San Fransisco ("and of course Paris") because he finds he has much in common with a group of young Bengali poets who call themselves members of a "Hangry Generation."

This is only apparently surprising. Although the Bengali poets seem to be reacting angrily against India's abysmal poverty and the Beat poets against America's stifling wealth, both share an obsessive craving for an experience which art can hardly give. This experience is supposed to be supersensory, revelatory, mystical. The Beat emphasis on drugs is due to the belief that if poetry fails to give it, maybe narcotics will unlock the gates of vision.

Aether

11.15 p.m. May 27

4 Sniffs & I'm High,
Underwear in bed,
          white cotton in left hand,
     archtype degenerate,
        bloody taste in my mouth

                    of Dentist Chair
              music, Loud Farts of Eternity—
an owl with eyeglasses scribbling in the
              cold darkness—
all the time the sound in my eardrums
                    of trolleycars below
              taxi fender cough —creak of streets —
              Laughter & pistol shots echoing
                    at all walls—
              tic leaks of neon— the voice of Myriad
                    rushers of the Brainpan
all the chirps the crickets have created
ringing against my ears in the
                          instant before unconsciousness
                          before,—
              the teardrop in the eye to come,—
              the Fear of the Unknown—

One does not yet know whether Christ was
                    God or the Devil—
              Buddha is more reassuring.

Yet the experiments must continue!

Every possible combination of Being — all
              the old ones! all the old Hindu
                    Sabahadabadie-pluralic universes
                          ringing in Grandiloquent
                                Bearded Juxtaposition,
              with all their minarets and moonlit
                    towers enlaced with iron
                          or porcelain embroidery,

                              all have existed—
                    and the Sages with
white hair who sat crosslegged on
          a female couch—
    hearkening to whatever music came
          from out the Wood or Street,
whatever bird that whistled in the
                              Marketplace,
                    whatever note the clock struck to say
                    Time—
whatever drug, or aire, they breathed
          to make them think so deep
                    or simply hear what passed,
like a car passing in the 1960 street
          beside the Governmental Palace
                    in Peru, this Lima
          year I write.
                              Kerouac! I salute yr
wordy beard. Sad Prophet!
          Salutations and low bows from
baggy pants and turbaned mind and horned foot
          arched eyebrows & Jewish Smile—
One single specimen of Eternity—each
          of us poets.
Breake the Rhythm! (too much pentameter)
          ...My god what solitude are you in Kerouac
                    now?
          —heard the whoosh of carwheels in the 1950 rain—

And every bell went off on time,
And everything that was created
Rang especially in view of the Creation

For
This is the end of the creation
This is the redemption Spoken of
This is the view of the Created
      by all the Drs, nurses, etc of
           creation;
i.e., —

I just nodded because of the secondary negation

    The unspeakable passed over my head for
        the second time.
           and still can't say it!

i.e. we are the sweepings of the moon
we're what's *left* over from perfection—
The universe is an OLD mistake
I've understood a million times before
and always come back to the same
           scissor brainwave—
The
Sooner or later all Consciousness will
      be eliminated
         because Consciousness is
    a by-product of—
           (Cotton & N_2O)

    Drawing saliva back from the tongue—

Christ! you struggle to understand
                    One consciousness
                    & be confronted with Myriads—
after a billion years
              with the same ringing in the ears
                    and pterodactyl-smile of Oops
                    Creation,
              known it all before.
              A Buddha as of old, with sirens of
whatever machinery making cranging noises in
                    the street
              and pavement light reflected in the façade
                    RR Station window in a
                          dinky port in Backwash
              of the murky old forgotten
                    fabulous whatever
                          Civilization of
                                Eternity,—
with the RR Sta Clock ring midnight,
              as of now,
                    & waiting for the 6th
                          you write your
                                Word,
              and end on the last chime—and remember
This *one* twelve was struck
                          before
              and never again; both.

.... I stood in the balcony
              waiting for an explosion
of Total Consciousness of the All—
                    being Ginsberg sniffing ether in Lima.

The same struggle of Mind, to reach the
　　　　　　　　Thing
　　　that ends its process with an X
　　　　　　comprehending its befores and afters,
unexplainable to each, except in a prophetic
　　　secret recollective hidden
　　　　　　　half-hand unrecorded
　　　　　　　　　way.
As the old sages of Asia, or the white beards of Persia
　　　　　　scribbled on the margins of their scrolls
　　　　　　　　in delicate ink
　　　remembering with tears the ancient clockbells of their
　　　　　　　　　cities
　　　　　　and the cities that had been—
Nasca, Paracas, Chancay & Secrecy of the Priests
　　　　　　buried, Cat Gods
　　　of all colors, a funeral shroud
　　　　　　　　for a museum—
None remember but all return to the same thought
　　　　　　before they die—what sad old
　　　knowledge, we repeat again.
　　　　　　　Only to be lost
in the sands of Paracas, or wrapped in a mystic shroud
　　　　　　of Poesy
　　　and found by some kid in a thousand years
　　　　　　inspire what dreadful thoughts of his own?

It's a horrible, lonely experience. And
　　　Gregory's letter, and Peter's...

　　　　　　　　　　　May 28 – 7:30 pm

　　...In the foul Dregs of Circumstance

Male and Female He created them"
        with mustaches.
There ARE certain REPEATED
(pistol shot) reliable points
of reference which the insane
(pistol shot repeated outside
the window)—madman suddenly
writes— THE PISTOL SHOT
outside—the REPEATED situations
the experience of return to the
same place in Universal Creation
Time—and every time we return
we recognise again that we
HAVE been here & that is the
Key to Creation—the same pistol shot
—DOWN, bending over his book of Un
intelligible marvels with his mustache.

(my) Madness is intelligible reactions to
        Unintelligible phenomena.
                Boy—what a marvellous bottle,
        a clear glass sphere of transparent
                liquid ether—
        (Chloraethyl Merz)

                                        9 PM

I know I am a poet—in this universe—but what good does that do—
when in another, without these mechanical aids, I might be doomed
to be a poor Disneyan Shoe Store Clerk—This consciousness an
accident of one of the Ether-possible worlds, not the Final World

        Wherein we all look Crosseyed
        & triumph in our Virginity
        without wearing Rabbit's-foot

ears or eyes looking sideways
strangely but in Gold

Humbled & more knowledgeable, acknowledge
the Vast mystery of our creation—
without giving any sign that
we have heard from the

GREAT CREATOR

WHOSE NAME I NOW

PRONOUNCE:

GREAT CREATOR OF THE UNIVERSE, IF
THY WISDOM ACCORD IT
AND IF THIS NOT BE TOO
MUCH TO ASK
MAY I PUBLISH YOUR NAME?
I ASK IN THE LIMA
NIGHT
FEARFULLY WAITING
ANSWER.

hearing the buses out on
the street hissing,
Knowing the Terror
of the World Afar—

I have been playing with Jokes
and His is too mighty to hold
in the hand like a Pen

and His is the Pistol Shot Answer
             that brings blood to the brain
And—

             What *can* be possible
                     in a minor universe
                     in which you can see
                     God by sniffing the
                     gas in a cotton?
             The answer to be taken in
                     reverse & Doubled Math
                     ematically *both* ways.

Am I a sinner?
There are hard & easy universes. This
             is neither.

(If I close my eyes will I regain consciousness?)
             That's the Final Question—with
all the old churchbells ringing and
bus pickup snuffles & crack of iron
whips inside cylinders & squeal of brakes
and old crescendos of responsive
demiurgic ecstasy whispering in streets of ear
             —and when was it Not
                     ever answered in the Affir-
                     mative? Saith the Lord?

A Magic Universe

(Quest 36: Winter 1962-1963)

Flies & crickets & the sound of buses & my
        stupid beard.
But what's Magic?
Is there Sorrow in Magic?
Is Magic one of my boyscout creations?
Am I responsible? I with my flop?
Could Threat happen to Magic?
Yes! this the one universe in which
        there *is* threat to magic by
        writing while high.

A Universe in which I am condemned to write statements.

"Ignorant Judgements Create Mistaken Worlds—"
        and this one is joined in
            Indic upion to
            Affirm with laughing
                eyes—
The world is as we see it,
        Male & Female, passing thru the years,
        as has before & will, perhaps
with all its countless pearls & Bloody noses
        and I poor stupid All in G
        am stuck with that old Choice—

Ya, Crap, what Hymn to seek, & in
        what tongue, if this's the most
        I can requite from Consciousness?—
That I can skim? & put in words?

Could skim it faster with more juice—
could skim a crop with Death, perchance
       —yet never know in this old world.
Will know in Death?
       And before?
           Will in
Another know.
      And in another know.
           And
in another know.
      And
       Stop conceiving worlds!
    says Philip Whalen
(My Savior!)   (oh what snobbery!)
    (as if he cd save Anyone) —
    At *least*, he won't understand.
I lift my finger in the air to create
a universe he won't understand, full
    of sadness.

—finally staring straight ahead in surprise
    & recollection into the mirror of
      the Hotel Commercio room.
      Time repeats itself. Including
this consciousness, which has seen
itself before—thus the locust-whistle
of antiquity's nightwatch in my eardrum. . .
I propounded a final question, and
    heard a series of final answers.
What God? for instance, asks the answer?
And whatever else can the replier reply but reply?
Whatever the nature of mind, that

the nature of *both* question and answer,
        & yet one wants to live
in a *single* universe.

             Does one?
Must it be one?
      Why, as with the Jews
      must the God be One?
      O what does
the concept ONE mean?
          IT'S MAD!
        GOD IS ONE!
        IS X
        IS MEANINGLESS—
            ADONOI—
      IS A JOKE—
      THE HEBREWS ARE
      WRONG—(CRIST & BUDDA
         ATTEST, also wrongly!)
      What is One but Formation
           of mind?
      arbitrary madness! 4000 years
Spreading out in all directions simultaneously—

      I forgive both good & ill
& I seek nothing, like a painted savage with
spear crossed by orange black & white bands!
      "I found the Jivaros & was
      entrapped in their universe"
      I'm scribbling nothings.
Page upon page of profoundest nothing,
as scribed the Ancient Hebe, when

he wrote Adonoi Echad or One—
all to amuse, make money, or deceive—

Let Wickedness be Me
and this the worst of all
the universes!
Not the worst! Not Flame!
I can't stand that— (Yes that's
for Somebody Else!
Yet I accept
O Catfaced God, whatever comes! It's me!
I am the Flame, etc.
O Gawd!
Pistol shot! Crack!
Circusmaster's whip—
IMPERFECT!
and a soul is damned to
HELL!
And the churchbell rings!
and there is melancholy, once again, throughout the realm.
and I'm that soul, small as it is.
HAVE FELT SAME BEFORE

The death of consciousness is terrible
and yet! when all is ended
what regret?
'S none left to remember or forget
And's gone into the odd.
The only thing I fear is the Last
Chance. I'll see that last chance too
before I'm done, Old Mind. All them
old Last Chances that you knew before.

—someday thru the dream wall
to nextdoor consciousness
    like thru this blue hotel wall
       —millions of hotel rooms fogging
        the focus of my eyes—
with whatever attitude I hold the cotton
to my nose, it's still a secret joke
    with pinky akimbo, or with effete queer
      eye in mirror at myself,
        or serious-brow mein
          & darkened beard,
I'm still the kid of obscene chance await-
    ing—
      breathing in a chinese Universe
thru the nose like some old Brahamic God.

O BELL TIME RING THY
MIDNIGHT FOR THE BILLIONTH
SOUNDY TIME, I HEAR AGAIN!

I'll go to walk the street,
        who'll find
me in the night, in Lima, in my
33'd year,

On Street (Cont.)

The souls of Peter &
I answer each other.
But—and what's a soul?
To be a poet's a
serious occupation,
condemned to that
in universe—
to walk the city
ascribbling in
a book—just accosted
by a drunk—
in Plaza de Armas
sidestreet under
a foggy sky, and
sometimes with no
moon.

The heavy balcony
hangs over the white
marble of the Bishop's
Palace next the Cathedral—
The fountain plays
in light as e'er—
The buses & the
motorcyclists pass
thru midnight, the
carlights shine
the begger turns
a corner with his
cigarette stub &
cane, the Noisers
leave the tavern

and delay, conversing
in high voice,
Awake,

    Hasta Manana
they all say—
        and somewhere
at the other end of
the line, a telephone
is ringing, once again
with unknown news—
    The night
looms over Lima,
sky black fog—
and I sit helpless
smoking with a
pencil hand—
    The long crack
in the pavement
        or yesterday's
volcano in Chile,
or the day before
the Earthquake
that begat the
world.

    The Plaza pavement
shines in the electric
light. I wait.
    The lonely beard
workman staggers
home to bed from Death.

Yes but I'm
a little tired of
being alone…
Keat's Nightingale—the
instant of realization'
a single consciousness
that hears the chimes
of Time, repeated
endlessly—

What crude Magic
we live in (seeing trolley
like a rude monster
in downtown street
w/electric diamond
wire antennae to sky
pass night café under
white arc-light by
Gran Hotel Bolivar.)

All night, w/Ether, wave
after wave of magic
understanding. A disturbance
of the field of consciousness.
Magic night, magic stars,
magic men, magic music
magic tomorrow, magic death,
magic Magic.

The mad potter of
Mochica made a
Pot w/6 Eyes & 2
Mouths & half a nose
& 5 Cheeks & no Chin
for us to figure out,
serious side-track,
blind alley Kosmos.

(Back in Room)
How strange to remember anything, even a button
much less a universe.
"What creature gives birth to itself?"
The universe is mad, slightly mad.
—and the two sides wriggle away
in opposite directions to die
—lopped off
the blind metallic length curled up
feeby & wiggling its feet
in the grass
the millepede's black head moving inches away

on the staircase at Macchu Picchu
the Creature feels itself
                        destroyed,
        head & tail of the universe
                cut in two
Men with slick mustaches of mystery have
            pimp horrible climaxes & Karmas—
—the mad magician that created Chaos
            in the peaceful void & suave,
with my fucking suave manners & knowitall
            eyes, and mind full of fantasy—
the Me! that horror that keeps me conscious
            in this Hell of Birth & Death.

    34 coming up—I suddenly felt old—
sitting with Walter & Raquel in Chinese
Restaurant—they kissed—I alone—age of
Burroughs when we first met.

Hotel, Commercio
Lima, Peru
May 28, 1960

Adil Jussawala

Love

(Ten Years of Quest, Manaktalas, Bombay 1966,
eds. Abu Sayeed Ayyub and Amlan Datta)

Her eyes were crushed bluebells
Seeking ground, late,
To flourish again or fade
In their spent grooves.
I offered her cracked rock,
Thistles, wildthorn, grit,
A desert without shade
And called it love.

Her eyes blazed to sapphires
To match that hard gift
When, together, we burnt
The lower, matted grove.
The dry rock gushed
Lava, her thighs' cleft
Bred scorpions, but
I called it love.

How explain my death
By voluntary reversions
To a single state,
With her aching to move
Back to parched beds, sand?
We covered the dust, dead scorpions,
Hid the thorns, the grit,
And called it love.

Arun Kolatkar

The Renunciation of the Dog

(Ten Years of Quest, Manaktalas, Bombay 1966,
eds. Abu Sayeed Ayyub and Amlan Datta)

Tell me why the night before we started
      Dogs were vainly
   Barking at the waves;
And while we slept in an unknown temple
      Days and waves away
   A black dog dumbly
From out of nowhere of ourselves yawned and leapt;
      And leaving us naked
   And shame faced,
Tell me why the black dog died
      Intriguingly between
   God and our heads.

Three Cups of Tea

(Quest 74: January-February 1972)

1

i want my pay i said
                to the manager
you'll get paid said
                the manager
but not before the first
                        don't you know the rules?
                coolly i picked up his
                        wrist watch
                that lay on his table
                        wanna bring in the cops
                                i said
'cordin to my rules
                listen baby
                        i get paid when i say so

2

                allow me beautiful
i said to my sister in law
                to step in my brother's booties
                        you had it coming said rehman
                a gun in his hand
                        shoot me punk
kill your brother i said
                        for a bloody cunt

3

   i went to burma
i was arrested and sent back
      to manipur
   no passport
      the police commissioner asked
why did you go to burma?
      prickface i said
what's there in India?

Jayanta Mahapatra

On The Great Temple Road At Puri

(Quest 88: May-June 1974)

A timeless stare
is caught in the sunlight.

The constant stream of ordinary people,
of whom nothing can be said,

what's left
after walking down the rows of wide-eyed ancestors…

But what is choice,
the smoke of ages assembling behind these dead,

the sacred beads, their stubborn stare,
sky and sun living into the human ground.

Puri

(Quest 88: May-June 1974)

Everyone comes to Puri.
The Americans, a German hippie.
A Swiss schoolmaster shuts his eyes:
he has not seen
that much filth on human bodies.
And the energy of their silent sea.

An old pilgrim
walls his guilty look under a tamarind tree.
Weary webs of light
hidden where the centuries go,
regardless of exploding stars.
Miracles of death
for birth to kill the world.

The wall still stands.

Dom Moraes

Cainsmorning

(Ten Years of Quest, Manaktalas, Bombay 1966,
eds. Abu Sayeed Ayyub and Amlan Datta)

Having eliminated his dear brother
He wandered slowly through the springhung street,
Angry with Cain, his heart, and not another.
He sighed. My life runs past on rivered feet.

The wine the Law forbade me I have swallowed.
Still (understand me) I did this for good;
Though I am sorry now that I have hallowed
My thirst for freedom with my brother's blood.

The day grew luminous and cold like starshine.
He looked so odd that people stopped to stare.
Shop windows rich with Cadillacs and Rheinwine
Poised their glazed questions on the lightfilled air.

These things, he thought, do happen; what surprises
At first palls later, hocused by the eye.

The soul and after life are still surmises.
Being for my bettering, let my brother die.
Suburban houses sneered. The stones said, Slayer!
He felt a saraband start in his brain,
And turned his face to heaven, and saw his prayer
Melt in the cold, the grey, the faceless rain.

Tejaswini Niranjana

Dasara

(Quest 97: September-October 1975)

Please come to our house, come look, yes, seven pm'll do, we've got
out the benevolent claygod

        red and gold and
        blue and orange and

there's

        Baby's vinyl slimlegged
        foreign dolls

and the old railway set we'd kept by

        with the real train
        with the brake

and the Channapatna rainbowed wooden villagers and

        the beautiful flour—
        powder rangoli cringing

before the frayed tablecloth covered

paper-carton platform;

the men will eat and argue polities outside in the wind and you can
wear the lovely purplegold sari scented with mothball and talk in a
high voice and coax people who take lessons to sing, and

the children can wipe

their noses on

their petticoats and

plead for more coconutsugar and

pull each other's

prim green-spotted ribbons;

oh, will you be going down *that* road? really, we must write to the
Mayor there's not a single streetlight

have you taken

your rectangles of

kunkum and arashina and

the betel-leaves and

the fruits?

The beggars hunt in packs on nights like these.

R. Padmanabhan

My Oedipus Complex

(Quest 88: May-June 1974)

OH mother
my mother, are you ill?
does your heart crave for explicit love
do tell me.
yes my son, our people are callous; they have no past;
all my work is a waste, all that i did.

our people
they meant a world to me;
all that i did for them...

       oh mother, your people, not our people; i hate to hear of it.
my son, my son, she cried; she stood by my side;

      how i hated it all.
my son, they blame me, they hate me
                she cried for pity.

i had none left, oh my mother, how do i stop her?
my son, my son, they don't like you;
                              she asked for retaliation.

                    i had not the strength for vengeance – morally, physically,
oh mother, leave me alone, i am on my feet
it's a pleasure – they hate me and i don't care a dam.
Comprenez vous?
(Mais je suis tres sûr qu'elle ne comprend pas)
my son, they say you are impious
                              she complained on their behalf
                              her own complaint too.
          impious? je ne sais pas ce que vous dites, ma mère
          but i remained dumb; i can bear no tear.
they say you are imprudent, impudent... do tell me they lie.
          c'est vrai, but i didn't say.
my son, my son, she cried and stood by me.
          i had enough to hate her.
but my son, you are a child, my child – always...
yes mother, yes, i cried
          i love her, my mother.

II

my mother has fallen ill
                    her frail heart too.
she has a heart everywhere
love moist affection
she'd stifle me, my mother,
my mother's ill
          her tender heart too.
she must have a heavy heart

full of warm blood

my mother has a sensitive heart

that turns red with anger.

my son, my son, she'd weep,

my mother

who has a weak heart.

III

my mother recalls the past often

she tells me all that i did

when i was a child

a round-faced little kid

that pissed on bed

felt guilty and

never spoke for the day.

my mother, she knows when i feel guilty

while she calmly removed the sheets

i stood in clumsy reverence

devoid of courage

to look at her face

a black mood on mine

my sight weak and shaky

she smiled not, my mother

(elle était très malin)

lest i should not feel ashamed

lest i should gain any strength

oh my mother, she has lousy morals

(but every mother has)

i never learnt my ethics from her

nor any morals from her parables.

she'd be sad sometimes
with a woebegone face
heaving a sigh often
        lest i should pass unnoticed
        and i like a fool
        would ask her.
she'd say nothing, my child
           thus inviting more enquiries,
         (j'ai dit qu'elle est malin)
on insistence she would yield
as if making an allowance
specially for me.
then comes the whole story
all the past, all the insult
while i listened, she'd lead me
down to the little world
        of her ethics
        of her morals.
while my vengeance gained momentum
she'd pour more down my throat
         till i was fed up
         till i got up
         and left her to her agony.
         (après tout, je m'ai trompé;
         elle n'est plus malin)
but she knows how i'd feel
        i'd feel rotten
        for my mother's in distress
        my mother
         who has a loving heart.

Saleem Peeradina

The Real Thing

(Quest 68: January-February 1971)

Lala says booking-office will open half-an-hour
before the show. Before me in the queue,
inches from my sense of smell, the girl, fresh
from her bath, is letting loose/I am making
f   from/her hair
aaa
nnnnn
ttttttttt
aaaaaaaa
sssssssssss
iiiiiiiiiiiiii
eeeeeeeeee   The failed executive,
sssssssssss   the irritated musician,
              the bored teacher, the boy
     each is paid two hundred rupees, stood
in a row and brought before the nation
sucking cyphoids.

Pran, dressed for the occasion
with blood-shot eye, attempts

as the script directs, to tear

the blouse of the leading lady
leading the ripe life of chastity

and with the right kind of
indignation, the populace straightens

in its seat to keep its spurt
of lust from slipping through its hands

but (help) the country's moral simpleton
is summoned (too soon) to restore

—to the cheers of the populace—
the righteousness of every pinched face

Oh preserve in us, unheroic men and women
the short-lived taste of struggle

* * * * *

When Dharmendra says Truth
                    is greater
than Love
              three-fourths of India nods
its head. Already brimming with love, the rest of India
cannot conceive of anything
                    greater

than Love.

Try intolerance

It is easy to learn
and if developed along the proper lines, incredibly
easy to believe in
whether you are

parent	or	grandparent
elder brother	or	elderly aunt
head of the Dept.	or	assistant clerk
believer	or	priest
violent	or	vegetarian
emancipated	or	stuck
the majority	or	the martyred
law-giver	or	flag holder

you can

project your own style. So order
your action and your life today. Give up
nothing. Least of all your many beliefs

Oh certify our beliefs, fortify our behaviour
Oh Undeceived One, look kindly on our one disability

Asoke Vijay Raha

The Serpent Maiden

(Ten Years of Quest, Manaktalas, Bombay 1966,
eds. Abu Sayeed Ayyub and Amlan Datta)

Two great eyes outlined in black—
A long sleek black body—
Across her bodice a twisted braid winds down.
She bears on her head a basket of snakes.

Two great eyes outlined in black—
Girl, do you make your serpents dance?
Does a snake swing in the braid across your breast?
Does it sway across your body?

A serpent is tattoed on your arm.
Blue glass bracelets are on your wrists.
Does your serpent take blue kisses from your lips?
Will you open the hamper for me?

A cold black snake is on your breast,
A long sleek body—
I see the lifted hoods of serpents dancing in your eyes
And snakes are at play in your heart.

A.K. Ramanujan

Madura: Two Movements

(Ten Years of Quest, Manaktalas, Bombay 1966,
eds. Abu Sayeed Ayyub and Amlan Datta)

In Madura I saw,
enamelled in the corrosive paint
of ailment
the clench of a leper's crab-like claw.

It moved
as nothing in life can move.

But behind him a statuette, a dancer
roused in rock; her lips atremble on the margin
of a smile; the anklet over the lyric foot a virgin
bound in a world of sounds, a question bedded in a well-known
answer.

Unmoving, she moves
as nothing in life can move.

Santan Rodrigues

City Streets

(Quest 78: September-October 1972)

i've lived too long in your arms
to stand the stench
of gutters parading our promenades;
blaring horns—the music you play,
have now deafened my ears.
greasy seas you float in, have changed
their song, its waves the colour
of their foam; and i stand
on a traffic isle death scared
of creeping cars. why do your
unkept walls hang slogans.
your streets opening like mirrored
doors into streets, soon lose their way?
i am tired of those tall shadows
of skyscrapers, trodding my path
and the only greenery i see on your barren roads is dust.
why must my feet walk, where
people too busy to talk have

pawned their tongues? and the rude
nudging of the crowds remain
the only warm things i felt.
shucks i'm thro' with you,
you rotten album of overcrowded
slums; and i am sick of
your tall-talk and
your canvassing smile to be enticed
to stay on
                    like hell!
the city has lost its hold.

Mukul Sharma

Black Bat Night

(Quest 83: July-August 1973)

With the night like a black sheet
shrouding your entrance
as you lock up the day behind you,
you're ready again
to frustrate on your bed
but the walls move in and gag you.

Are these lonely people
who kick stones when they walk?

You could lie on your stomach
with your forehead upon your crossed arms
and try not to remember.
You could lie on your back
and aim little daydreams through smoke rings.
You could sit up with a melodramatic jerk
and smother your cigarette in self pity.

You get scared when you think of tomorrow
because tomorrow is another day
and you're so tired,
you are.
Watch the darkness!
It will stitch a straight jacket for you
made of little night sounds.
Now is the time to think of home
and of this love and that
and the times you were very young
and your philosophy of life
before you furled it
curled it
and stashed it in your ashtray.

Yet tomorrow is an important day;
your schedule floats in your eyes.
You have it memorised.
If you walk all day, you'll be sleepy at night.

Today nothing much happened—
Part of your ambition dropped off
at the no-parking zone,
part of it on the way home
etc.

Then the evening was incomplete.
The sky kept grovelling at your feet
trying to hide its rotten stars
under your bedsheet.

Tonight will lay you on your bed and tuck you in;
then recede to the walls and watch you begin
your pathetic ritual with the pillow.
Later, when you start snatching at the blackness
that hammers on your eyeballs
and the quiet that throbs in your chest
it will come shuffling back to engulf your mind
and slowly start strangling your senses.

Before your very eyes then
the floor will open
and the room will be yawning up at you,
waiting for you to come toppling into
damp dreams that distort the day.

It is October,
the floors are cool.
You could get down on your hands and knees
and crawl under the bulb to pray.
Tell your god to take the night away.
But if he does,
What would you do with the day?

Fiction

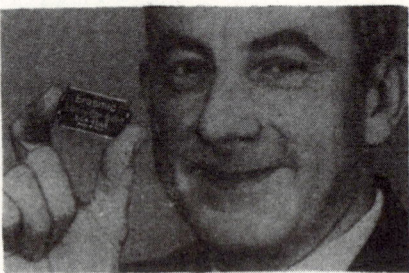

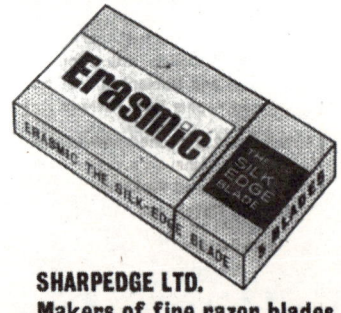

The Departure

Yashwant Chittal

Translated from Kannada by Dilip Chitre

(Quest 61: April-June 1969)

Sometime ago, when it was evening, there was that visitor to see him who had said, 'Tomorrow at dawn, before the cock crows, we start. Be prepared.' And he had left. That was why he had started packing up, soon after finishing his supper. He started packing up in his suitcase the clothes that were untidily lying about in the room for the last four or five days. While rolling up things, he suddenly came upon his shaving set which made him pause. He felt his chin. *Tomorrow morning, when the caller comes again to pick me up, will I be left with enough time to shave? Why not shave now?* As soon as the thought struck him, he got up, as if in panic, to act upon it. Among his friends, he had built up a reputation for being always clean-shaven. Perhaps you have even seen his face in an advertisement of the razor blades manufactured by the company he worked for.

When he stood at the sink in the bathroom, watching his own face in the mirror on the wall and working up the lather of the shaving soap he had rubbed into his beard, brush in hand, a new thought began to bother him, softly; and he stopped, without finishing his shave: *Of all the things, 'before the cock crows' he said, didn't he? Why, it's absurd! How can one hear a cock crow in this modern hotel situated in a central locality in this sprawling city of Calcutta? Gosh! I forgot to ask him! One doesn't even remember what time it is – when a cock is supposed to crow! What a long time it is since I left my village! God alone knows what sort of a village this visitor came from! He asked me to be prepared to start before the cock crows – and left. Anyway, I'd better get up at four o'clock in the morning. That will serve the purpose. But supposing he came earlier? It doesn't matter. He can wait a little.*

His cheeks were now covered by profuse lather. The sharp, new razor blade moved across the skin which barely had any growth of beard. He soaped up his face once again and another disturbing thought struck him. *If I have to leave, early in the morning, I must inform the hotel manager, right now, mustn't I? Oh, I was almost forgetting it!* While the soap was still clinging to his face, he returned to the room and picked up the telephone receiver – 'Reception please!' he said. As soon as he got the right person, he said, 'I am speaking from Room No. 159. I am checking out early in the morning tomorrow. Please arrange to keep my bill ready right now. I have here a voucher from my travel agents. And oh! Could you ring me up so that I get up at 4 o'clock in the morning?' He had hardly finished when a stream of polite words poured in from the other end, 'Excuse me, Sir, but this room has been reserved in your name for ten days....' He was so irritated that he snapped, even before the sentence could be finished, 'Look, I know it was reserved. But due to an unforeseen emergency, I've got to leave. Would it be too much trouble for you if...' The person at the other end broke in, faltering and apologetic. 'Please don't misunderstand, Sir...' But he hardly had the patience to hear the apologetic explanation in full. He hung up and went back to the bathroom. He felt a little elated thinking of his own outburst. The next moment, as the razor resumed its play with his cheeks, he wondered: *What if the fellow who spoke on the telephone were in front of me? Would I have had the guts to scold him? The truth is, I can be harsh to people only when I'm not facing them. Only half an hour ago....*

A little while ago, when it was evening, after the unexpected visitor had called on him, the first thing he did was to ring up the hotel laundry asking them to deliver his clothes immediately to his room. The clothes were due to be delivered the next day. The servant who received his call politely expressed his inability to deliver the clothes earlier. But he flew into a rage and asked to speak to the manager. When the manager was on the telephone he spoke to him in a very grave tone explaining that he had an urgent call from somewhere and he had to leave early in the morning at any cost. Therefore, he had asked the manager to send his clothes that very night in whatever condition they were. Even before the manager could reply he had added, raising the pitch of his voice: If you can't send the clothes, keep them for yourself. I don't need them.' And saying this, he had put the receiver down. To his surprise, a couple of hours later, the manager had personally brought the washed and pressed clothes to his room. He spoke nothing to the manager. He wondered, however, whether the awe and respect he had inspired in him over the telephone had totally evaporated when the manager saw him. The manager left the package on the table without exchanging a single word with him and left the room. Then, a vague dissatisfaction had made his soul recoil.

The shave was over. He collected his shaving set and returned to the room. A fresh doubt plagued him now, suddenly: *Won't they forget to wake me up so early in the morning? It might be a good idea to instruct the bell-boy and also to tip him. Perhaps, I might also order my bed-tea for the morning.* He pressed the bell. The bell-boy entered the room within a few moments. He pressed a five-rupee note into his hand and said: 'Look. I'm leaving exactly at five in the morning. I've asked the people downstairs to wake me up at four. But they may forget to do it. You get me my tea at four o'clock and wake me up. Don't make any mistake about this. Is that all right?' Saluting him gratefully, the bell-boy said, 'Have no worry, Sir! I'll wake you up exactly at four. Good night, Sir!' As he left, he closed the door gently behind himself.

He continued to pack up his; things. But suddenly again, a new problem raised its head and made him shudder: *I say! When that visitor who came some time ago asked me to be ready before the cock crew, I quite forgot to ask him what place we were leaving for – and why – and when exactly! I agreed to go without asking a single question! How did I agree? Did I really agree?* He smiled, and his smile had a touch of regret. *Did he even show the courtesy to wait for my answer?* But this sort of thing was not really new to him.

As a matter of fact, even his present trip to Calcutta had come about much the same way. He was a senior sales representative of his company. But Calcutta fell outside the region he was supposed to cover. Only a few days ago, after travelling continuously for two months – visiting some ten or twelve towns and cities in the region assigned to him – he had returned to Bombay. The very next day, his boss called him to his cabin and said, 'You are going to Calcutta tomorrow.' Not waiting for his answer his boss continued, 'Your passage to Calcutta has been booked on the Calcutta Mail. We have arranged for a room for you in the Grand Hotel. As soon as you reach

Calcutta, get in touch with our branch manager there. He will give you your programme in Calcutta.' Without any protest, he agreed to go to Calcutta. He was surprised that the prospect did not affect him in any way. That was all there was to his reaction. Coming out of his Boss's cabin he came to know the reason for his unexpected journey. His colleague who was to go to Calcutta had got married all of a sudden and was on his honeymoon. The entire staff of the office was discussing the subject of this sudden marriage. As he remembered his romantically-inclined colleague who had bagged a stenographer from the same office for a bride, he could not help chuckling. *If this chap weren't so romantic, I wouldn't be substituting for him in Calcutta now. I am past forty and still alone. I don't have a wife and children. Nor do I have any close relations. Who else is more suited to wandering than me? As for the boss, he's happy he can send me anywhere, any time.* The smile on his face showed a passing shadow of regret.

Except for the suit on a hanger in the wardrobe, all his clothes were now packed in his suitcase. As he was folding his suit, he remembered the last evening, the time he returned to the hotel and stood at the counter when a fair-skinned foreigner was writing details about himself in the hotel register. Coming across the column marked 'Your next destination,' the newcomer expressed surprise and asked the receptionist: 'Now, how is this useful for you to know?' This had reminded him of his own first encounter with the same column in the register. Under the head 'Your next destination' he had simply scribbled 'Not known' and smiled to himself. *The boss who sent me to Calcutta immediately after my return from a weary tour lasting two months may have any kind of whim at any time. Maybe, he'll ask me to go somewhere else even if that means cutting short my stay in Calcutta.*

The recollection of this incident gave rise to another disturbing thought: *I am always cool during travel. Why am I so panicky and so utterly confused this time? Is some occult kind of fear, some strange premonition about tomorrow's journey, disturbing me in the depths of my being? Usually, I am so cool and unperturbed on a journey! And now, while packing up, why are these thoughts coming up to the surface and riddling my mind? My work in Calcutta will easily keep me busy for another five days. What have I done now? I have agreed to go with an anonymous caller without any protest! What if the boss questioned me tomorrow?* The next moment however, he felt a strange kind of satisfaction at the fact that he was defying his boss's orders and leaving his work in Calcutta unfinished, as if the impulse to defy his orders had made him answer the unknown visitor's summons. Still, he felt like conveying his decision to his boss. He picked up the telephone receiver and asked the operator to book a trunk-call at his boss's number in Bombay, adding. 'It's an urgent call, please!' *The boss must be already in bed. He will certainly be in a bad temper when my call disturbs him at this unearthly hour. And when he hears what I have to say, he'll be mad with fury....* Somehow, the very idea gave him deep comfort.

As he lay in bed waiting for the call, he suddenly began to realize that whatever was happening was happening against his own nature: *The journey I am undertaking at dawn tomorrow is a journey that needs no justification. It is not in my nature to protest, to refuse, to transgress, to defy. In my entire life I have neither understood these, words nor felt the need to do so. I accept whatever programmes the boss chalks out for me and I accept them as easily as I accept a friend's suggestion when he says, 'Say, get up! We're going to the pictures now!' It is always someone else who decides for me what I have to do and they always believe it is for my own good. As for me, I always accepted them with a smile meaning I'd never oppose them and disappoint them....*

Suddenly he thought of his father.

His father was a strict disciplinarian. He did not himself remember it, but his uncle had told him about an incident involving him and his father, when he was seven – or perhaps eight – years old. He was sitting with his father in his father's shop when his father went home, asking the son to sit in the shop till he came back. He said he would be back in a short while and that his son should ask visitors to wait till he returned. He warned him against giving away anything to anyone in his absence. Soon after his father left, a school-mate of his – a Christian boy much older than he – had come and given him a guava fruit, taking a rupee from him. At that time, he hardly had any knowledge about the value of coins. The Christian boy had asked only for a copper paisa but he had given him a silver rupee. When his father came to know of it, his uncle had told him, he became as furious as Jamadagni – the mythological rishi who was famous for his violent fits of rage. *Everybody said that Dad was an avatara of Jamadagni.* He dragged him home and tied him to a *Bimbali* tree in the courtyard. He was told that his father had knocked a leaf-nest full of red ants making it fall on his head and that the ants bit him all over and that he screamed and yelled being stung all over. When he had started screaming, his father plucked a twig of the same *Bimbali* tree and started flogging him furiously. He had later heard people say that he had writhed in pain, twisting and turning as much as he could with his hands and feet tied tight to the tree. They said that his father had flogged him more, the more he writhed in agony. It was later remembered by people that in spite of his mother's and his aunt's begging his father to stop, the man would not stop. Then, it was said, the women of the neighbourhood had gathered and upbraided his father who, hysterically, shouted back at them saying that he was beating the son he had fathered and had asked them what right they had to question him.

In the end, he was told, it was his uncle who had caught hold of his father's hand and pushed him aside to rescue his nephew. They said he had been so scared that for the next ten days or so he hardly opened his mouth, speaking to no one. After he grew up, whenever his mother and his aunt referred to his father's cruel treatment of him, he had heard his father say that it was only because of that treatment that the boy was on the right path. Otherwise, his father used to say, he would have gone astray like 'those' boys. *And at that I would just smile. I don't remember whether I loved my father or not. But the reason why I did not disobey my father was not, as my father imagined, that I feared being punished by him for disobedience. It is meaningless to protest or revolt – and that's how I view life. Often, I have really felt satisfied, when I have been able to act according to this philosophy of life. The other day, for instance, when the boss called me and asked me to go to Calcutta, it was clear from his expression that he was expecting some kind of protest from me. But, when I agreed to go, without the slightest hesitation, he was probably a little disappointed himself....*

The telephone rang. He leaped up and lifted the receiver. He tried to recompose mentally the message he wanted to give to his boss. He cleared his throat and his nostrils flared. He held the receiver close to his ears: 'The Bombay line is out of order, Sir. The delay would be indefinite. Should I keep the call pending, Sir?' 'Cancel it!' he said and pulling the receiver down, he burst out into a sudden uncontrollable fit of laughter. *Ho, ho, ho, ho! I've missed my maiden chance of getting angry with my boss!* His laughter would not stop. He lay down in his bed, still trying to laugh it out. Suddenly, he looked at his watch. It was past midnight. *I must go to sleep immediately. Will the room-boy wake me up at the right time? And supposing, I am still asleep when the stranger comes to call me? I shouldn't switch off the lights. With the light on, I can open my eyes any time and check the time.*

Without switching off the lights, he closed his eyes. The entire hotel was quiet. The only noises that came were intermittent, and they came from the street below, the rattle of the last tramcars and the noise made by the last buses. And these noises were a sort of lullaby to his weary mind....

After about an hour or so he woke up suddenly, sitting up on the bed in an instant. Outside, all of a sudden, there was thunder, lightning and rain. The clap of the thunder and the noise made by the rain driving down made his hair stand on its roots. *Where am 1? What place is this? Why am I sitting up like this all of a sudden?* Stunned, he turned his gaze over the room and all the lights burned white. At the foot of his bed lay his suit as it was folded by him, and he caught sight of it. *I am going on a journey. That's it.* He looked at his watch. *It is still at least three hours for the caller to come. May I put this last suit into the suitcase?* He was suddenly very frightened. *Why am I so scared? Why am I so bewildered? I have packed all the clothes in the suitcase, haven't I, without giving a thought to what I should wear when he arrives early in the morning. What clothes shall I put on in the morning? Why not I put on this suit?* With a violent shudder, he remembered something. *The man who came to see me in the evening had no clothes on! Dishevelled hair... broad shoulders... broad chest... sinewy arms... black body... moustaches – thick, long and black... a big black mole on the chest... and a thick black string – a charm – tied around the bare left arm... he came. He knocked. And he entered – opening the unbolted door by himself. He leaned, only the upper part of his body leaning into the room, and said: 'Tomorrow at dawn, before the cock crows, we start. Be prepared.' With this, he had withdrawn his body and gone away, closing the door. I agreed to it as naturally as I agree to my friend's suggestion when he says, 'Get up. We're going to see a movie. Now!' or when my boss says 'Look, tomorrow you are going to Calcutta.' Have I really agreed?*

For the first time ever, he had a doubt. He felt exhausted. As he went towards his bed, he felt confused. He lay down. He closed his eyes. Outside, all of a sudden, the fury of the wind, rain and lightning increased.

He went to sleep, recollecting the night on which his grandfather died. *Will the bearer or someone come from downstairs to wake me up?* And then he fell asleep.

The bell-boy did not wake him up. He forgot all about it until it was already past the time. It was half past five in the morning when, cursing his own lapse and carrying a tray of tea in his hand, the bell-boy reached his room with nervous steps. Thinking that the man must already have left, the boy knocked. There was no response from inside. He turned the handle of the door and pushed. The door opened. It was not locked from inside. The lights in the room still burned. 'He is there,' thought the boy to himself, and went towards the bed falteringly. The man was fast asleep stretched on the bed with his suit and his shoes on. The right hand, which was dangling from the bed, clutched the handle of the suitcase which stood on the floor. The left hand was reaching towards the other edge of the bed. The feet, with shoes on, rested one against the other. The head, with hair neatly combed, lay against the pillow – slightly tilted to the right. The bell-boy placed the tray on the bedside table and said, 'Good Morning Sir!' As there was no reply, he said again, 'Excuse me, Sir, for being late.' Still there was no reply, and the boy said, 'You're getting late, Sir.' Still there was no reply and the boy had a doubt to satisfy, so he went closer and touched his body. He got frightened and ran out of the room. It took another quarter of an hour for the hotel manager to get the news and to bring a doctor to the room. While examining the body, the doctor observed, 'It is at least forty-five minutes since he is "gone."' And looked at his watch. It showed 5.45. The servant, who stood there stiff with fright, broke out, trembling, 'He said, Sir, "Wake me up at four o'clock. I have to leave exactly at five."'

Aunt Matilda is Ninety Years Old

Neela D'Souza

(Quest 60: January-March 1969)

When the phone rang at seven in the morning we both knew who it was. Only Auntie Mary rang up at that hour, often when we were barely awake, rubbing sleep from our eyes, and it was almost a joke now between us.

'It'll get it,' I called out to John. 'Have your tea.'

It was Auntie as we had expected. And she wanted to speak to John. About it being Aunt Matilda's birthday that day, of course, it couldn't be anything else. As if we would forget! July 25 had become a ritual with us. Come home early from office (so that we would avoid the rush hour traffic out of the city), drive the twelve miles or so to the Retreat House where Auntie stayed, pick her up with the assortment of tins and packages that appeared on every birthday in the family, then drive another five miles to the suburb where Aunt Matilda lived. We had done it every year after our marriage, six times in all.

Actually there was another private and more important reason to remember July 25. It was a sort of anniversary for John and me. A secret that we shared and laughed and reminisced over in our quiet, by ourselves moments. John liked to make fun of me by saying that was the day when the great pursuit ended. The day I said yes. Really though, that was the day we had spoken of, decided on, marriage. I can remember the shyness, the wonder, the happiness.... July 25 seems more of an anniversary than the day in October when we were married. Quite early, we had decided to have our own private celebration on July 25 each year rather than on our wedding anniversary which was usually disturbed by telephone calls and visits and telegrams. Routine now, of course, after six years. The stereotyped greeting listed No. 8 on the Greetings Telegrams list – a concessional rate and the Telegraph Office sent it on a hideous coloured sheet and envelope, to give the message a festive air. I loathed those unimaginative messages on the gaudy sheet, never sent them myself and shuddered when I received one. I had noticed a waning of greetings in the last two or three years. To be expected, I suppose. And quite a relief!

But we had never been able to celebrate July 25 after that first time in England. Then we were by ourselves, in our last year at the University, free for any light-heartedness, however inconsequential or trivial. The next year we had returned to India, to Bombay, to be plunged into a vortex of family, relations, birthdays, christenings, Christmas, get-togethers.

John had entirely forgotten then that July 25 was Aunt Matilda's birthday. She is our eldest aunt, John's mother's oldest sister. Then there is Auntie Mary who is on the phone just now. Auntie Mary is ten years younger than Matilda. Aunt Matilda has always been Aunt to John and his sisters. Auntie Mary, on the other hand, because she lived with John's mother, tided them over their lean times, helped John and his sisters through college and generally encouraged them, is called 'Mummie' with as much affection in the term as they use for their mother, who is 'Mamma'. And I, since I am strictly not a niece, call her Auntie.

Auntie Mary, as usual, wanted to remind John that it was Aunt Matilda's birthday, important specially as she was ninety today. 'We must go to see her,' she urged.

'Yes, Mummie,' John replied patiently. 'I'll pick you up about half-past five.'

'Come early.' she said. 'I want to spend some time with *Bai*. Don't forget to bring Sita also.' With that she rang off.

'I mustn't forget to bring you. And we are to go early,' John said, pouring himself a second cup of tea that was lukewarm now. But I knew already exactly what Auntie had said, for this was the invariable formula on birthdays.

I had rather enjoyed birthdays once. And was very puzzled by John's total indifference and even hostility toward them. After we were married, the reason for that was quite apparent. We had a total of thirty-three birthdays in the family. Thirty-three get together days (in addition to Christmas, New Year and Easter) when we had to visit the person concerned and stay on for a birthday dinner, rich and heavy and over-sweet. It became rather tiresome.

Auntie Mary was a sort of Grand Keeper of Birthdays. None of them escaped her; she kept track of every one of ours, remembered those of her thirteen grand-nieces and nephews, and the four great grand-nieces and nephews. She baked a cake for each birthday and a batch of the kind of pastry or sweetmeat the birthday celebrant particularly liked. Dear Auntie Mary, always kind and thoughtful!

Today was a very special day. Aunt Matilda was ninety today. She was a sweet little lady; widowed soon after the birth of her fourth child, she had lived sixty-three – or was it sixty-four? – years in widowhood, gentle, soft-spoken, mild-mannered. Cared for by her eldest son and daughter-in-law, with whom she lived.

I had felt rather hostile toward her after our first meeting, a hostility, however, which quickly melted away, to be replaced by fondness and affection. You couldn't really be hostile to Aunt Matilda, you couldn't be angry with her.

When we returned to Bombay in '56, everyone looked at us critically. At John with open surprise for having deserted his Catholic background and upbringing to marry a Hindu girl. At me with scarcely concealed curiosity – what does *she* have that our girls don't? John's mother had sobbed, embracing her only son, happiness and relief to have him back after five years abroad. Happiness not unmixed, intermingled with resentment that he should have married against her wishes, married a non-Catholic.

Auntie Mary was obsessed with a desire to bring me into the fold. She believed implicitly in the power of prayer, had enlisted the active support of sundry relatives, friends, and fellow workers in the Retreat House to pray for Sita's conversion, that I might see the light. Did she despair sometimes, I wondered, for it was six years now since we were married and still no signs of Sita seeing the light. The last time John had met her she had told him how Father Simon had asked if John's wife had become a Catholic and she had not known what to say and had hung her head in reply. Six years ago that would have irritated me; now I could shrug it off.

And six years ago, at my very first meeting with Aunt Matilda, I found it hard to control the rising resentment and irritation, fed by thoughtless remarks hinting at the difference in our religious backgrounds that would no doubt cause our marriage to fall apart. John had warned me to expect this, it was not that I was caught unawares. But being prepared was not enough to cushion the actual shock and anger that those remarks aroused.

Aunt Matilda had peered at me with the failing eyesight of her eighty-four years. 'So you are the girl John married? Why did he do it?' Was she musing to herself, was she addressing me, was she trying deliberately to hurt me, provoke me? Did she imagine I was a designing vixen who had ensnared her favourite nephew? There were rude things on my lips. But I held them back. Twenty-three approaches eighty-four with caution. Particularly in India where age commands respect in direct proportion to advancing years. Why, this little bent-over lady, her sparse white hair caught back in a small knot, her soft green dress neatly darned and ironed, a rosary of middling sized brown beads dangling from her small hands, this old lady was almost four times as old as me! She was old enough to be my mother's grandmother. I couldn't be rude to her, raise my voice in anger and harshness against her eighty-four years, years that showed plainly in the cobweb of wrinkled lines on her face, the tired droop to the gentle trembling mouth.

So I swallowed my resentment, smiled in a semblance of good humour, and stayed silent. Auntie Mary happened to walk into the room just then and Aunt Matilda drew her aside and spoke to her in Portuguese – an old trick with the older people in my husband's family, when they didn't want the young people to know what they were saying. It was obvious they were talking about me. Auntie Mary listened to what her sister said, replied in Portuguese and after a little while got up from the bed where they had been sitting. All in God's good time,' she said in a tone of resignation. All in God's' good time – what? I wondered.

Aunt Matilda never raised the subject again. She, and all of them, did believe that it would happen in God's good time. Perhaps Auntie had cautioned her against questioning me, making demands. If so, it was odd because Auntie Mary herself kept bringing up the subject from time to time the first three or four years. Gentle persuasion, not so gentle words, all were tried. 'You must see a priest,' she had insisted in the beginning. 'You will break our hearts if you remain a Hindu!'

'Try and read some good books,' she had suggested gently at other times. The 'good books' referred to works on the Catholic church, although our scanty library at home was prudish by all counts, not even extending to Lady Chatterley or Peyton Place, both in a world far removed from Auntie.

Subtler ways were also tried. Any priest from South India who happened to stay in the Retreat House was immediately told the story of her niece; I would be summoned to meet him, with an incentive: 'You can talk to him in your own language.'

It was of no use explaining to Auntie that the South covered many states and many different languages, that a twenty-four hour journey separated Calicut from Madras. We humoured her, the meeting gave her so much pleasure and satisfaction – despite a vague disappointment when it happened, as it often did, that I did not speak his language.

Our visits to the suburb where Aunt Matilda lived were restricted to Christmas and her birthday every year. It was a seventeen mile drive and although we often felt remorse at not being able to see her oftener, the pressures of city life and long hours of work made it impossible. And last Christmas, Ravi had been ill so we had missed seeing her. John and I were the only ones who visited her regularly. Berna, my sister-in-law, with her teaching and family of five noisy children could seldom make it except at Christmas and not always then. She felt bad about it, I suppose, and Aunt Matilda, who was her godmother, often gently remarked that Berna had not been for a long time.

But Aunt Matilda was not one for complaining. Of the three sisters she was the gentlest and most likeable. Perhaps not the most intelligent but that was a mark in her favour for it kept her out of petty family squabbles. She had grown old with grace, though these declining years had sapped her mind as well as her body.

When she heard I was pregnant she busied herself with knitting, and I marvelled at the fine, even work she produced; innumerable little bootees – never worn, of course, in the heat of Bombay – a cape and a pixie cap set. I put them away carefully, in moth balls and plastic wrappers, after thanking her. After that, she made some more pairs of baby socks, odds and ends of wool carefully marched finished with tiny, multi-coloured pompons that gave them a jaunty, festive air. Perhaps Aunt Matilda was pleased that I liked them and expressed my appreciation. I was touched by her kindness and felt rather guilty when I gave several pairs away to friends who had just become mothers.

'Aunt Matilda has always been a sweet person, you know,' John said, putting down his cup. 'Mamma has been inclined to be quarrelsome. Mummie is kind but very domineering, likes to run things and gets offended if we don't listen to her. But Aunt Matilda has always been gentle and good, affectionate and kind, immersed in prayer. The one who has been the least trouble. When Stan, her oldest son, got married she let his wife Juliet run the house completely. Can you imagine Mamma letting you do that?' he teased.

Yes, Aunt Matlida seemed unruffled by what went on around her. She remained calm and unperturbed while the household jostled around her, its affairs and disputes hardly touched her. My mother-in-law was very different; full of complaints and suspicions about the servants, tradesmen, the cook and the gardener – all were actively conspiring to cheat her, do her down.

Auntie Mary was wrapped up in the Retreat House and religious affairs. For her, religion was not a Sunday subject, or even relegated to mass-in-the-mornings, Wednesday worship or a continuing cycle of Novenas. Religion pervaded and infused her entire life and living. Her faith was complete and unquestioning. Some years ago when Rome had made the startling pronouncement that St. Philomena had never really been a person at all, she was quite unshaken. John had pulled her leg a bit, despite my remonstrances. Auntie had been very firm in her reply. 'I don't know about all that. But I believe, and St. Philomena still grants me favours.' What could John do but be silent when faced with faith and belief so complete and unquestioning?

In the moments when I felt harassed at being an 'unbeliever' in the midst of this devoutly Catholic family, rebellious at her desire to have me see the light when I was quite secure and happy where I was and determined to stay there, I reminded myself that Auntie belonged to a very different world. A world that had been badly shaken when John married 'outside'. But also, I often wished that her piety and devotion were accompanied by tolerance in equal measure. And when religion meant so much to her, would the empty form of church going, surface conformity, satisfy her? For, sometimes I felt that the mere act of becoming a Catholic even without *being* one, might appease her. But I was not prepared to do that.

Her generosity, her tremendous capacity and desire to help others, her basic goodness – for Auntie Mary is one of the few people I know who is good through and through in the real meaning of the term

– won you over easily. So even when I bristled over the matter of religion I was drawn to her by genuine fondness and affection. She was demanding, domineering too, as John had said, but you liked her, liked her goodness. Admired, were even in awe of, her deep, unshakable devotion, her dedication to the affairs of the Retreat House which she ran.

Auntie's association with the Retreat House went back to many years ago when she and a group of women workers volunteered their services for this cause. That was when the Retreat movement was first introduced in Bombay, launched on a wave of devotion that had lasted unabated, had grown to encompass Catholic communities around and away from Bombay. The Retreat House had a programme for the five year with special Retreats for girls who were engaged and similarly for young men intending to get married, for newly-wed couples, for school and college students, for people from Bassein which lay across the creek and further, for people who did not understand English – Retreats to look after the spiritual needs of varying groups of people.

Auntie Mary looked after the day-to-day running of the establishment, the buying of provisions, planning of menus, the linen, rooms, the chapel and altar and the stations of the Cross in the large garden. She lived in the Retreat House in a small room upstairs, crowded with mementoes of a full and, in its way, eventful life.

There was a picture on her dresser which I particularly liked. It was of Auntie and Berna taken when they went on a pilgrimage to Rome thirty years ago. Going abroad in those days was an event, to be looked forward to and spoken of with pleasure and excitement for years after. Auntie Mary had worn a *sari* for their audience with the Pope, blessed event in her life. The only time she wore a *sari*, I imagine, for she always wore a dress, long-sleeved, high-necked, right down to her ankles in the prescribed style three decades ago. Berna looked a sort of Indian prototype of the flappers of the thirties, her hair short and sleek, in careful curls around her ears, a long string of beads around her neck, even her *sari* somehow reminiscent of the low-waisted dresses of that period. How that effect was achieved in a sari was something which puzzled me constantly.

For Auntie, the audience with the Pope was the focal point of the pilgrimage and an old, yellowing portrait of His Holiness on the wall still evoked awed memories of that moment. Under her bed Auntie kept a tin of biscuits which she gave to all the children who visited her. Now Ravi no longer waited for her to take it out, he would dive under her bed and pull it out himself.

Auntie disapproved strongly of our child having an Indian name. To her, Indian connoted Hindu, something heathen, alien, undesirable. And although Ravi's middle name was Stephen, after her favourite saint, she was not mollified. She never once called him Ravi, he was always Stephen to her although he himself was hardly aware of having a second name and looked surprised each time she used it.

Once in her room, turning over the pages of an old album, the pages falling apart and held together by a faded blue ribbon, I had stopped at a picture of a bride, a very young girl. The picture was evidently very old, for it had blurred and yellowed but there was enough to indicate a pretty profile. 'Who is that, Auntie,' I asked with interest, 'Such a pretty face!'

'Let me see,' said Auntie, peering at it through her glasses. 'That's *Bai*, my sister, Matilda. She was very pretty as a girl; how beautiful she was on her wedding day!'

I looked at the picture with new interest tried to see the vivacity and radiance of the young bride in the tired, lined, wrinkled features of the Matilda I knew. Only the mouth was the same, the sweetness of youth replaced by the droop of age, but the outline unmistakable.

'Bai is such a good person,' Auntie said. (She and Mamma addressed their sister by this Marathi suffix, a term of respect for older women). 'So good and uncomplaining. She was the best of all of us.' (They had been ten, but only three sisters were alive now.) 'My father was especially fond of her. She looked after all of us when our mother died; you know she is ten years older than me. And so generous, always gives to the poor. She is a saint, God will reward her amply for her deeds.'

Today, on her ninetieth birthday, Berna and her husband, Joe, Auntie Mary, all had special masses, said for her. I had knitted a cardigan for her in soft blue baby wool and though my work was nowhere near as careful or even as hers, I hoped she would like my gift. It wasn't really like taking coal to Newcastle, for Aunt Matilda never knitted anything for herself, she didn't have a knitted cardigan or jersey. In the rainy weather and in Bombay's cold months when the temperature occasionally dropped below 70°F, enough to make old people shiver and bundle themselves in coats and shawls and socks; windows and doors shut tight, Aunt Matilda wore an old, much-darned flannel coat. Now she would have a cardigan to keep her warm....

Auntie was waiting when we got to the Retreat House; waiting with a big square box (cake), two bottles (pickles: tiny mangoes steeped in brine which Aunt Matilda liked), a tall round tin (assorted delicacies, dates and coconut and pastry) and a brown paper parcel (a bedspread, I found later).

'How late you are,' she chided gently. 'I was getting worried so I said a Hail Mary for you. The roads are so full of cars these days, all going fast. I prefer our horse carriages in the old days.'

She spoke of her sister as we drove to Aunt Matilda's, of her goodness and charity. Even now, every year *Bai* made bottles of the mixed spice powder that they used in the Retreat House for their curries; drying the chillies in the sun after having them carefully picked over, sorting out the turmeric, cinnamon, cloves and cardamom, the coriander and cumin seeds that were pounded together in a carefully proportioned recipe to make an aromatic, tasty powder that gave a fine flavour and colour to meat and chicken dishes. The Retreat House used a large quantity of this curry powder every year and Aunt Matilda gave it to them as her contribution. Auntie saved me a small bottle each time which I used often in my own kitchen, delighting in the fragrant dishes it produced.

Aunt Matilda had also been associated with the group of women who managed the Retreat House. But since she had her own family and lived apart, her help consisted mostly of contributions in money with which she was always generous, and, before her eyesight deteriorated, the embroidery and crocheting of lace for innumerable altar cloths that graced the chapel at the Retreat House.

Aunt Matilda was seated on the corner sofa of the living room when we entered. Auntie went in first to greet her sister who had looked up with a 'who is it?' on hearing our footsteps.

'*Bai*, it is Mary. How are you, sister? You are ninety today,' kissing her on both cheeks and with a break in her voice, 'my best wishes. God's blessings.'

'Thank you, thank you,' said Aunt Matilda, almost inaudibly. 'So good of you to come.' All three sisters were formal almost to the point of being stilted, but their affection for each other was deep. In John's family politeness was carried to an extreme. 'Who is with you,' Aunt Matilda asked.

'John,' said Auntie, 'and Sita.'

I went forward and bent to kiss Aunt Matilda's withered cheek. 'Happy birthday,' I whispered.

'Thank you, child. So kind of you to come, dear, Sit down, sit down. Wait, I'll get you something.' But before she could call out, Juliet bustled in with a tray full of glasses of sweet wine which she handed round, went inside and reappeared with cake and sweets.

We drank to Aunt Matilda's health and tried in vain to resist Juliet's hospitality which extended to three and more slices of cake. 'But you must,' she insisted, 'it is Mamma's birthday.'

Auntie opened the parcel she had brought. 'See *Bai*. I brought you a cover for your bed.'

'Thank you, thank you. You are all so kind. I can't see very well but it is nice. So soft too,' she added, fingering the material. 'My eyesight is so poor now, I can't see sometimes. But I mustn't complain. God has been good to me. Now I am just waiting… waiting for Him to call me.'

I broke in, changed the subject. 'I knitted a cardigan for you, Aunt Matilda. Let me put it on you.'

She was pleased as I carefully helped her into the garment. 'How nicely you knit, child,' she said. 'So kind of you, thank you.' She clasped my hand in hers and kissed me. 'I am ninety years old, too old to go on living….'

'Mamma, hush,' said Juliet firmly in her good-natured voice. 'That is no way to talk on your birthday. Auntie Mary, John and Sita have come such a long way to see you and you start talking like this?'

'How is your son?' said Aunt Matilda, dutifully changing the subject. 'His name is Ravi, isn't it?'

'Stephen,' broke in Auntie, but Aunt Matilda did not notice the interruption.

'I forget names, I can't see well, I can't seem to remember anything these days. Why didn't you bring Ravi with you?'

I made some excuse about it being too late to keep out a two-year-old child and asked Aunt Matilda how she had been keeping.

'Pulling on,' she said. 'All right, like that, I can't complain. But ninety is too old. I can't remember anything, I can't see well. Before I used to knit, sew, help Juliet clean the rice. Now I just sit here all day. What am I to do? I feel so useless, just waiting….'

'Pray,' advised Auntie. 'Say the Lord's name. You do say your prayers, don't you?' a tinge of anxiety in her voice.

'Which ones? Yes, I pray, I say Hail Mary, but I can't remember. So old, no? I put my spectacles down here, then I am searching for them there. I leave my rosary under my pillow and then Juliet has to search and find it for me. What is the use of living like this? It is time to go. When will He call me?'

'Mamma has kept quite well,' Juliet came in smoothly and veered the conversation to safer grounds. 'We went to church this morning, you know.'

'Yes,' Aunt Matilda smiled. 'I walked to church. Slowly, slowly, Juliet and Stan holding me, helping me. But when we came back I was so tired. I lay down in bed.'

'You shouldn't go,' John protested. 'Father Basil would have come to the house, given you communion if you had asked him.'

'But John, Mamma wanted to go, wanted very much to go today. And Stan thought it would do her good. She has been feeling cheerless lately,' Juliet dropped her voice.

'Can't remember, can't see. Never mind. You all have come and I am very happy.' Aunt Matilda called to her daughter-in-law, 'Juliet, give them more cake. Have wine, John. That's home-made wine.'

'Made from beetroot, no?' asked Auntie Mary.

'Yes, have some more. Give Sita the recipe, Juliet. You like the wine, don't you? I can't remember how to make it. We used to make wine from plums and raisins before; so much fruit so much sugar… and… yeast? Can't remember, can't remember anything,' she shook her head sorrowfully.

'Do you say your prayers every day,' Auntie asked again.

'Yes, I think so. Which ones?'

'The Office, *Bai*, the Office of the Mystical Rose.'

'Which one is that, Mary?'

'*Bai!* That is our prayer, the prayer of your Retreat House group. You cannot have forgotten.' Auntie was visibly vexed. 'Mary, most holy…?' Auntie paused expectantly.

Aunt Matilda looked blank.

'Try and remember, you have said it all these years. Try,' Auntie pleaded. 'Mary most holy…'

Aunt Matilda searched her mind desperately.

'Say after me, Auntie said compellingly. 'Mary, most holy…'

Aunt Matilda repeated the prayer slowly, falteringly prompted by Auntie. 'Now do you remember *Bai*,' Auntie asked anxiously.

'Something, little, yes. But I forget all the time. So old, no?' She stroked my arm with her light, dry hand. 'So good of you child to knit for me.'

'You must try and say it everyday,' Auntie insisted firmly. 'You mustn't forget, it will give you peace of mind.'

John was ready to leave. I could see the signs: the fidgeting, the easing of the collar, the drumming of fingers on the arm of his chair.

'Come Mummie, we must go. Ravi is alone at home. Goodbye Aunt Matilda, we'll come and see you again. Keep well and look after yourself.'

'Goodbye John, good-bye child. God bless. Thank you, thank you for coming. Goodbye Mary, go safe.'

We drove back in pouring rain, it was the monsoon in earnest. The road was wet, the windshield blurred immediately after each stroke of the wiper. Lightning forked fitfully across the sky. The lights cast long distorted reflections on the road. John drove slowly, peering through the glass to see what was ahead.

Auntie sat quiet, eyes closed, I thought she was sleeping and lowered my voice talking to John. But I saw her fingering her rosary, turning the beads over one by one, slowly, her lips moving in silent prayer. She sighed deeply.

'What time is it? Are we there?'

'Nearly Mummie,' said John. 'It is raining so much I can't see very well. So I have been driving slowly. But don't worry, we are almost there.'

Don't wait,' she said. 'Leave me at the porch downstairs and go back soon. Stephen will be lonely. Don't leave him like that again, Sita,' she reproved. 'Children feel it so much.'

We were at the Retreat House. Charlotte and Alice were waiting, looking out worriedly through the dining-room windows. As we turned in through the gate they smiled in relief and hastened out to the porch with umbrellas.

I helped Auntie out of the car. She was cramped after the drive and nearly stumbled. Alice and I steadied her and walked her up to the steps.

'Go child,' she said. 'Thank you. God bless you. Good night,' and she kissed me.

I paused a minute before going back to the car. Alice was asking after Auntie Matilda as they slowly climbed the steps. 'Is sister well?'

Auntie sighed and shook her head. She cannot remember her prayers. She has forgotten the Office. *Bai* has forgotten our prayer....

They went inside, Alice opening the door for Auntie and closing it behind them. John honked impatiently. I turned and ran back to the car. A few drops of rain splashed on to my hair and *sari*.

Sword and Abyss

Keki N. Daruwalla

(Quest 96: July-August 1975)

The lament came drifting with the wind towards the river. It was routine here, this mourning for the martyrdom of Husain and Hasan. Vespertime was wailing time. The one consuming passion of the village was to foregather in a *Matam Sarai* and listen to the elegies on the *Imams*, and relive the tragedy of Karbala. According to local belief Fatima and Husain were present in spirit as honoured guests at these meetings. The ritual was very dignified. After the storm of weeping, the *Ulema* (divines) gave discourses on the significance of the martyrdom. Even during the peak Moharram days no flagellation was indulged in. The catharsis never touched the physical plane. It was restricted to the spirit.

The village Sarai Pir was a mile from the boat bridge where Irfan sat watching the brown drift of waters beneath his feet. It was early October, the river was full, sweeping past capillariously green landscapes, a hinterland of ravines, each ravine an abyss in its own right with its shell-grit and thorn-scrub and twisted, deformed hillsides that gave no hint whether they led to an exit or a dead-end or wriggled back into the river at the next turn. Ages back the river may have thrashed around in pain, arms akimbo, changing its beds. Otherwise how could one explain the ravines which extended to over two miles to her flanks? The 'majlis' would soon be over, thought Irfan. The muezzin would be summoning the faithful to prayer any moment. Dusk had settled on the ravines and certain tendrillous clouds to the west had shed their amber tint and had turned dull-grey. A woman came down from the left bank and started crossing the boat bridge. 'Who is she?' enquired Irfan of Ajudhi Mallah who manned the ferry. 'Zubeda, a widow of village Mangrol,' he replied. She was firm-breasted and brown and in her twenties, and what intrigued Irfan was that she had not even cared to cover her face with the traditional veil. After all, it was the year 1922 and the countryside here was fanatically orthodox. 'It is not safe to go farther now,' he called out to her. 'You can stay the night at the Chauki (outpost) if you wish.' Mangrol was a good five miles off, and only a week earlier, a woman who was returning after cutting grass in the ravines had been attacked by a pair of hyenas. She was severely mauled and had bled to death.

While Zubeda was taken to the Chauki, Irfan stayed put, watching the grass on the left bank turning into a hedge of black bristles. Line and colour were dissolving into one universal black. Since his discharge from the army three years back, things had not clicked with Irfan. His business ventures flopped. He had stirred out of the village for destinations other than Mecca, had fought a war, had made love to women. His name was anathema to his people. In turn, he considered his village a denial of everything that mattered in life. And now, ironically enough, he held the ferry and the boat-bridge on contract for a year, just a mile from Sarai Pir. Depression weighed on him like a sack of cement as he walked back to the *chauki* and fell into a disturbed, fitful slumber.

Tonight, he thought, he must catch hold of the dream before it drifted back into the bowels of the earth. As a child, an upset stomach had often brought on a nightmare. Since then he could never really get rid of the notion that dreams rose from the intestines. The edges of the dream, ill-defined and numinous, were still imaged before him, an amorphous lump of darkness, palely rimmed with reflected light. Light, that was it! Shreds torn from lunar panels, floating into the room through the window. At times the pockets of light would dwindle in size till he mistook them for animal eyes. At times, they snapped open like animal mouths or rather the primitive masks of animal mouths, the open jaws coated with phosphorescences so that they were visible in even a dimly lighted nocturnal carnival. Then, the lights went off and there were black lumps riding in on a dark wind. Fold on fold of some inner chaos floated on the margins of a fragmentary awareness. And there was something about the wind which made him scratch and blister, a strange subsurface unease.

Irfan got up and instinctively his hand went to his gun. He felt an incredible sense of relief to find that hell had not broken loose around him, that he was not in the midst of an earthquake or a bandit-raid or a flash-flood in the river. A filthy curse for this spell of sleep which had taken away a good slice of the early night with it; a passing thought for the woman sleeping in the room directly beneath his, perhaps waiting for him, perhaps not. And he found his hands and feet suddenly turning cold.

Till dusk he had to keep an eye on his *Munims* who sat near the bridge realising the toll – one rupee on each horse, mule or cattle-head and two rupees for a bullock cart or a camel. But after nightfall during the dark phase of the moon the job got more involved. The police Station was a good thirty mikes away. The responsibilities of a gun license-cum-ferry-contractor were pretty heavy here. It was for him to keep the police informed as to the goings on in the underworld – which dacoit had got hold of a muzzle-loader recently, who had crossed the ferry with a covey of minor girls, and newsy titbits about an army deserter, an illicit still or a blacksmith acquiring a reputation for country-made pistols. And the ferry-contractor had to see that none of the bandit tribesmen from the desert crossed the river to his side. If they did, his connivance was often taken for granted and his people never forgave.

Sarai Pir was a Muslim village, except for the hamlets which were scattered on all sides and inhabited by Lonias, who dug graves and worked salt out of the earth, Manihars, who sold bangles, and the Mallahs, who manned the boats. Across the river was the desert tribe, known in these parts as Pir Pisran ('sons of the Pir') a nomadic tribe which carted its mobile smithies on ponies and retained its passion for blood and lust and loot. They were the original residents of Sarai Pir, who, it is said, were driven across the river two centuries ago. They had been converted to Islam, but even this could not mitigate their intense hatred for the present dwellers of Sarai Pir. Every now and then they would go on a rape-rampage, swooping down on the village and looting it, murdering the men and slashing the breasts of the women. All that the village could do was to secure more firearm licences and arm the Mallahs who manned the *chauki*. An old chief had built an outpost of sorts overlooking the river, a goitered protuberance with thick bulging walls from where his men could keep watch. During the dark fortnights the Mallahs and the ferry contractors were supposed to keep a night long vigil.

Irfan's hand went instinctively to his gun. He found himself in a half-crouch, the head lowered, listening intently for the first snap of sound that would tell him that the raid was on At a distance, a pony whinnied, or so he thought two of his Mallahs were smoking a chillum. He alerted them with a sharp whistle and a gesture. Ten minutes of silence were broken by the cry of a jackal. Then suddenly all hell broke loose. Some tribesmen on pony back made a dash across the boat-bridge. Irfan emptied both the barrels of his greener on them. He could see them all right, for the outpost was located on high ground and the tribesmen as they crossed the bridge were silhouetted against the river water which shimmered faintly in the starlight. A moment after there was a spatter of lead against the outpost walls. Obviously some of the tribesmen had taken up positions before the riders had surged forward. He could hear the Mallahs firing with their muzzle-loaders. Some of the tribesmen were riding towards the village. Later he could never reconstruct the sequence of events. All that stood out in the haze of his memory was the silhouettes riding across the bridge on pony back, bedlam all around and the feel of barrels suddenly turning warm in his left hand as they spat fire.

A half hour or so later, the firing and the babble died down in the village. Irfan heard the raiders retreating but made no attempt to intercept them. With only four Mallahs, it was not a hazard worth taking. Some flame and smoke was visible over the village. A thatch hut or two had been put to the torch, he thought. An hour later he went down and looked around. The Mallahs had dragged two corpses of the raiders from the track. One of these had been found near the boat-bridge. Irfan's greener had done a neat job on him. His Mallahs were fine, except for one of them who had got some pellets in his thigh. Only the woman was crying, breaking out every now and then into a thin tremolo of pure hysteria.

In the morning, he found the villagers ringed around him – the whole scowling lot of them. They had come after the dawn prayer, walking as if in a funeral. Their eyes were the pebble-hard eyes of relatives after a vendetta-murder. For the raid had proved costly in terms of casualties. A farrier had been shot, a weaver speared to death, a twelve-year-old goatherd trampled upon by a horse. Irfan found some of them glowering at him as if in some unaccountable way he was to blame. They hardly paid any attention to the corpses of the raiders. Only the children hummed around them like flies. The elders were concerned with the woman. Who was she? Why and since when was she here? Where did she sleep last night, they asked the Mallahs. No one had mustered up courage to ask Irfan, for they had noticed the smouldering firecoals in his eyes.

Two days later, his half brother had come down to the ferry. He was five years older than Irfan, and after their father's death he was Irfan's only link with the village. 'There is something more to it than mere stupidity,' he said. 'There are times when you seem to lack all feeling. And you give the impression of doing all this out of sheer cussedness. You haven't said a word to the relations of the dead! You weren't even there when they read the *fatiha*. If you come on your condolence rounds after the wailing subsides, where is the point?'

'Do you think the wailing will ever subside here? Isn't it our sole passion?' His brother had given him a dirty look and walked off.

On the first Thursday after the raid, Fakirs were fed in the village by the relatives of the three deceased. And on Friday came the summons from the Village Council. After the noon prayer he faced them – that farrago of nondescript faces, bristling with trimmed beards, the pointed vulpine chin and that uneasy look which comes over men when they sit in judgment over their betters. There was the school master, old and thin and reedy, the farrier who knew more about a horse's feelings than a woman's – he was a bachelor though past fifty, the illiterate but wealthy contractor of the Public Works Department, the only one who was clean-shaven and was wearing a *tahmad* rather than *churidars*. And there were three men from the Ulema, men of unquestioned honour and piety. The Village Council had only one thing in common – all the men were *hajis*, men who had returned from the pilgrimage to Mecca. That way Sarai Pir was a strange village, entirely law-abiding – in twenty years there had been no litigation or crime – and utterly given over to piety. Barring a handful, perhaps every male adult had been to the *naj* and every single individual obeyed the five traditional calls to prayers. No one had ever been known to drink in the village. Even tobacco was frowned upon. No *nautanki* parties or *bhats* or *madarris* were ever allowed inside. Of course, professional mourners were a different thing.

'We hope you are aware that this is the first time in three years that we have had a visit from our brothers,' the *Ulema* opened the attack sarcastically.

'The Pir Pisran have been living for over an year about fifty miles away from the river. This was quite unexpected,' answered Irfan.

'We have paid with three lives for the luxury of being surprised,' said a thin lipped divine with asperity.

'Why exactly were you dismissed from the army?' broke in the contractor.

For a moment Irfan was too aghast to reply. 'I got an honourable discharge. I was never dismissed.'

'But it is generally believed that you were caught sleeping on sentry duty.'

'You are welcome to your own beliefs, but nothing of the kind ever happened. I got a discharge on my own request.'

'When were you married, Irfan Mian?' the farrier took over. He was the most bitter of the lot. His brother had been killed in the raid.

Irfan replied, 'You know very well I am not married.'

'Really!' (much feigned astonishment.) 'But then who was that woman with you that night?'

It was difficult explaining this. Granted she was a widow and had a long way to go and was unescorted. But why was she detained at the *chauki*? Were women who crossed the river at dusk normally asked to stay the night over? Not if they weren't young and good looking and, if one could say so, willing?

Young and good looking yes, but how does a man know at first glance whether a woman is willing or no? She was in her twenties and a widow, that much he knew. He had asked her to stay back and she had stayed back. Her presence had been nagging him beneath the bone. And after the attack she had got the heebie-jeebies. He had sat with his greener across his knees, lost in his own thoughts listening to the babble of her incoherence as one listens to a river. Then a voice had reached Irfan, Ajudhi Mallah's voice — he had been lying in the ferry boat, cowering there till the raiders had left — asking whether Irfan was hurt or no, whether he was alive or no. Yes, he was alive, and after a long time he thought. And then suddenly on impulse he had reached over for her body. He dried her tears and drove the hysterics away. He was overcome by a feeling of overwhelming tenderness as he found her quivering body turning quiet against his. A little while after they had made love, she opened up the abysses of her soul to him, her innermost thoughts, her griefs, the loneliness of her unloved body, and the sweeping terror of the raid. Two hours later when he got up he thought he had been among the very sediments of her being.

They all said their piece – the woman Zubeda, the Mallah at the ferry, the Mallah at the Outpost. There were also those who suspected that in some mysterious way Zubeda was related to the bandit tribesmen and was a plant.

Two days before the verdict, a silence descended on the village. Five miles away, a cattle fair was being held but no one went from Sarai Pir. There was less talk in the bazar and no wailing at the Matamsarai.

Villagers led three hesitant horses across the boat-bridge. After having crossed the bridge, three men mounted them and rode out, with flies buzzing around the manes of the horses and the children laughing and hollering behind. They had gone to meet the contacts of the tribesmen.

Irfan never heard the verdict. All that concerned him was that a dozen men came before dawn and took him across the river to the ravines on the other side. They went down a deep, uneven ravine and then climbed up the slope to where a dead, branchless tree stood like an amputated limb. They asked him to have his fill of water. Suffering from thirst was unthinkable. No one wanted the sin of Karbala on his soul! In fact for fifty miles around all the *piaoos*, places where drinking water was distributed free, were manned by men from Sarai Pir. They tied Irfan's hands in front of him and lashed his body firmly to the tree. As they left, all except the school master who was to give him water at intervals, the farrier said, 'You shouldn't be worrying. They will come for you soon.' The villagers took it for granted that the tribesmen would come and take him away and treat him as one of them! After all, the Council had said so!

At two o'clock, the sun hit him. Till then he had remained in the shadow, but now the sun was pouring smelted iron into the ravine-mouth. The rope which tied him became a coil of fire. Only a few minutes ago he had been given water, but already his throat was parched. An entire cataract could disappear into his belly with no harm to him. The sands were a white fire, each granule an ember in its own right. It was all too fitful – flashes of delirium, followed by periods of complete blankness and then spasmodic returns to a searing consciousness. He tried to focus his eyes on the minaret of the village mosque. But retina and pupil let him down. Slowly the evening inclined towards dusk. Yes, and here they were, the hooded horsemen riding out of the dusk. Now he could see them, now he could not – he just heard the pounding of hooves. As they entered the ravine they were a single file. Then they fanned out and converged on him from all sides. To Irfan they looked like his own past years riding towards him. That boy who was finding trouble retaining his saddle on this uneven ground, that must have been him when he was ten-years-old. And that youth whose chin was sprouting with the first shoots of a beard, that was him again, trying to blood his knife for the first time. And that greybeard trying to prove that he could still curse loudly and brandish a weapon and cling to a saddle despite his dentures, that would be him thirty years later. A strange sort of a peace descended on Irfan. For once, he felt no enmity towards the raiders as the fresh-bearded boy severed his head with one neat stroke of his sword. It was so deftly done, he involuntarily found himself applauding the neatness, the finesse of it all.

Like the proverbial rats, his hallucinations left him. He was face to face with himself. At last, things became clear to him as a landscape does after rain. His village was a denial of life. Laughter, dreams flowering with the marrow, the pulse turning into a hammer at the mention of a woman – all this had to die here ritually. For fifty generations, his people had only wept. Perhaps, and he shuddered at the thought, he had greater affinity with the Pir Pisran!

It was still half an hour to dusk. The school master gave him a drink. He drank the entire urn empty. His mind cleared. 'Look,' he told the school master, 'this is crazy! They'll never come for me. And if they do, it will be to finish me off not to carry me away with them. I won't survive the night, I tell you.' But the school master knew what was coming – a plea for being untied. He slipped away.

Next morning they found only his head and his torso. His face had turned into a mask of naked terror. The rest had been eaten away. That pair of hyenas was getting bolder. They had started devouring him while he was still alive.

In the *matamsarai*, there was a storm of weeping. A stranger passing through the village asked what it was all about. A divine rose up, still swaying to the rhythm of the lament, his face giving the appearance of being semi-drugged. 'There has never been weeping such as this since the first lament for Karbala. This is *Khumar*. This is ecstasy!'

Kalyani

Kamala Das
Translated by R. Nandakumar

(Quest 100: March-April 1976)

She was driving home after dropping her husband at his office. She brought the car to a stop at the bridge seeing five men standing in a line blocking her way. She could understand that they were policemen.

One of them moved closer and asked, 'Is this the way to drive?'

She was too stupefied to utter anything. He looked very rude. She replied in a very low voice, 'I had been driving very slow.'

'Not that,' said the policeman.

'What harm have I done?' she asked.

Making a gesture to the others he got in and seated himself on her left. And the others on the back seat.

'Well, drive now,' said the man beside her.

'Drive as I direct. We just have got to go to the police station.'

'The police station! What have I done for that? Nothing, I suppose. Why do you take me there?'

Her voice had a sob in it. The policemen kept silent. At last they asked her to stop the car before a two-storeyed red building.

All of them got down with her.

'Come on,' said one of them. 'You can submit all your complaints to the person inside.'

When she was about to turn back he clutched her hand. She felt her fingers cracking within his clasp.

She did not see any other policemen anywhere around. They walked to the foot of a staircase. There were marks of dried betel spittle on the corner. On the wall to the left of the stairs was written something in Bengali. The policeman did not loosen his grip even when she was going up the stairs. Tears trickled down from her eyes.

'Do you weep after committing the crime?' he asked.

'What crime have I committed?' she asked. 'On what charge are you dragging me in here?'

'Are you going to argue with me?' he asked with a nasty chuckle. Those walking behind also laughed. They paused on entering a large hall. There were windows with dark blue curtains. There was not a single table or chair or anything of the sort in that room. A colour picture of a lovely woman alone was hung on the wall.

'He will be coming soon,' the policeman told her.

'Who?'

They did not answer. One fellow drew out a pair of handcuffs and fastened them on her hands.

'Please ring my husband up,' she said. 'Let him come over.'

'Why should he? It is not your husband who has committed the crime, after all. Is it not you?'

'What crime?'

'Just think.'

Leaving her in the middle of the room they made their exit. She tried to console herself. This is all a dream. What crime have I committed? Nothing. So all this might be an evil dream…. But her arms were aching. She began weeping again.

'Oh, you have come. I have been waiting for you,' said a middle-aged man walking in. He was short and fatty.

'Who are you?' she asked embittered.

'You ask who I am? Ha, ha! Don't you hear her asking?' he said, looking back. The policemen appeared suddenly at the door. One of them said:

'He is our master.'

'The inspector?' she asked. They nodded. The man called master wore white pants and a blue shirt with no buttons at the top. His teeth were dark and clumsy, stained with betel juice. She moved back and leaned on the wall with revulsion.

He said, 'So you have admitted the charge, haven't you?'

'What charge? I was driving. These policemen stood in my way and made me stop the car. And brought me here without giving any reason for doing so. If my husband comes to know this…..'

'Husband! Have you too a husband, Kalyani?' he asked.

'I am not Kalyani,' she replied.

'Did you think that I won't recognize you?' he asked.

'You are mistaken, somehow,' she said. 'Better let me go.'

'Three months' rigorous imprisonment for her,' he ordered.

The policemen came forward and dragged her along a verandah into another room. That was a dark little room. She discovered that it had no windows.

'Give me your clothes,' said a policeman.

'Why?' she enquired.

'The uniform will be issued here. That will be your dress from now on.'

She began to cry. 'I cannot,' she said.

'When did you begin to blush, Kalyani?' asked one fellow.

'I am not Kalyani,' she answered sobbing. 'I am called Ammini. I am the wife of Mr Menon.'

'Wife!' he cried scornfully. Unlocking the handcuffs he let her free. They collected her clothes in a roll and went out, closing the door. She could not see anything afterwards. That was very much a dungeon. She groped around and felt the wall. She sat down on the floor, leaning back on the wall.

Still she muttered, all this is not real, this is only an evil dream. Why did the policemen seize me? When I wake up the next morning, I'll tell my husband about this. And then…..

The door was opened abruptly. A policeman came up to her with a torch.

'Drink this and go to sleep. We'll bring the uniform,' he said, taking out a bottle from his pocket.

'I don't want anything,' she said, trying to cover her body with her arms.

'Drink it,' he said. She did not hesitate. Taking the bottle, she gulped down all the bitter drink in it.

The policeman left the place. She lay there motionless for a long time. She felt as if floating in that darkness, flinging out her body like a veil.

She sat up hearing the door open. Suddenly the room was flooded with electric light. She closed her eyes out of shame.

'Ammini, I never thought that you would do this,' said her husband. Opening her eyes she saw him and said in excitement of jubilation. 'You have come! Please take me from here immediately.'

He said nothing. His eyes were turned to another side of the room. She glanced aside. There was a man sleeping on a cot.

'I didn't believe it even when I got the letter,' said her husband. 'Even now when I had a call on the phone I thought that somebody was trying a trick. I never thought you were a harlot....'

'What are you speaking about?' she asked. 'What do you say I have done? The policemen brought me here.'

Saying nothing, he stepped out of the room hurriedly.

'Don't leave. Please listen to me,' she called out.

Her shame prevented her from running after him. She began to sob aloud hiding herself behind a pillar on the verandah.

'Why are you so worried?'

Hearing that familiar voice, she looked back. What she saw was the man called master coming toward her with a smile. Again she began to weep.

'Why do you weep, Kalyani?' he asked. 'Is it because that man called your husband has gone? Am I not here for you? How old a relation is ours! Why should you worry as long as that is there?'

'I don't know what you are saying,' she said.

'I am not Kalyani at all. I am Ammini.'

'You are Kalyani,' he said, laughing. 'You are ever, ever my Kalyani.'

She looked at that hairless face with eyes drooping in fatigue.

'Am I Kalyani?' asked she.

'Yes, you are Kalyani.'

She collapsed unconscious.

The Accompanist

Anita Desai

(Quest 97: September–October 1975)

It was only on the night of the concert, when we assembled on stage
behind the drawn curtains, that he gave me the notes to be played. I
always hoped he would bring himself to do this earlier and I hovered
around him all evening, tuning his sitar and preparing his betel leaves,
but he would not speak to me at all. There were always many others
around him – his hosts and the organisers of the concert, his friends
and well-wishers and disciples – and he spoke and laughed with all
of them, but always turned his head away when I came near. I was
not hurt: this was his way with me, I was used to it. Only I wished
he would tell me what he planned to play before the concert began so
that I could prepare myself. I found it difficult to plunge immediately,
like lightning, without pause or preparation, into the music, as he did.
But I had to learn how to make myself do this, and did. In everything,
he led me, I followed.

For fifteen years now, this has been our way of life. It began the
day when I was fifteen-years-old and took a new *tanpura*, made by
my father who was a maker of musical instruments and also played
several of them with talent and distinction, to a concert hall where
Ustad Rahim Khan was to play that night. He had ordered a new
tanpura from my father who was known to all musicians for the fine
quality of the instruments he made for them, with love as well as a
deep knowledge of music. When I arrived at the hall, I looked around

for someone to give the *tanpura* to but the hall was in darkness as the management would not allow the musicians to use the lights before the show and only on the stage was a single bulb lit, lighting up the little knot of musicians and surrounding them with elongated, restless and, somehow, ominous shadows. The Ustad was tuning his *sitar*, pausing to laugh and talk to his companions every now and then. They were all talking and no one saw me. I stood for a long time in the doorway, gazing at the famous Ustad of whom my father had spoken with reverence. 'Do not mention the matter of payment,' he had warned me. 'He is doing us an honour by ordering a *tanpura* from us.' This had impressed me and, as I gazed at him, I knew my father had been truthful about him. He was only tuning his *sitar*, casually and haphazardly, but his fingers were the fingers of a god, absolutely in control of his instrument and I knew nothing but perfection could come of such a relationship between a musician and his instrument.

So I slowly walked up the aisle, bearing the new *tanpura* in my arms and all the time gazing at the man in the centre of that restless, chattering group, himself absolutely in repose, controlled and purposeful. As I came closer to the stage, I could see his face, beneath the long locks of hair and the face, too, was that of a god: it was large, perhaps heavy about the jaws, but balanced by a wide forehead and with blazing black eyes that were widely spaced. His nostrils and his mouth, too, were large, royal, but intelligent, controlled. And as I looked into his face, telling myself of all the impressive points it contained, he looked down at me. I do not know what he saw, what he could see in the darkness and shadows of the unlit hall, but he smiled with sweet gentleness and beckoned to me. 'What do you have there?' he called.

Then I had the courage to run up the steps at the side of the stage and straight to him. I did not look at anyone else. I did not even notice the others or care for their reaction to me. I went straight to him who was the centre of this gathering, of the stage and thereafter of my entire life, and presented the *tanpura* to him.

'Ah, the new *tanpura*. From Mishra-*ji* in the music lane? You have come from Mishra-*ji*?'

'He is my father,' I whispered, kneeling before him and still looking into his face, unable to look away from it, it drew me so to him, close to him.

'Mishra-*ji*'s son?' he said, with a deep, friendly laugh. After running his fingers over the *tanpura* strings, he put it down on the carpet and suddenly stretched out his hand so that the fine white muslin sleeve of his *kurta* fell back and bared his arm, strong and muscular as an athlete's, with veins finely marked upon the taut skin, and fondled my chin. 'Do you play?' he asked. 'My *tanpura* player has not arrived. Where is he?' he called over his shoulder. 'Why isn't he here?'

All his friends and followers began to babble. Some said he was ill, in the hotel, some that he had met friends and gone with them. No one really knew. The Ustad shook his head thoughtfully, then said, 'He is probably in his cups again, the old drunkard. I won't have him play for me any more. Let the child play,' and immediately he picked up his *sitar* and began to play, bowing his face over the instrument, a kind of veil of thoughtfulness and concentration falling across it so that I knew I could not interrupt with the questions I wished to ask. He glanced at me once, briefly, and beckoned to me to pick up the *tanpura* and play. 'Raga Dipak' he said, and told me the notes to be played in such a quick undertone that I would not have heard had I not been so acutely attentive to him. And I sat down behind him, on the bare floor, picked up the new *tanpura* my father had made, and began to play the notes, the three notes he gave me – the central one, its octave and quintet – over and over again, creating the discreet background web of sound upon which he improvised and embroidered his *raga*.

And so I became the *tanpura* player for Ustad Rahim Khan's group. I have played for him since then, for no one else. I have done nothing else. It is my entire life. I am thirty years old now and my Ustad has begun to turn grey, and often he interrupts a concert with that hacking cough that troubles him, and he takes more opium than he should to quieten it – I give it to him myself for he always asks me to prepare it. We have travelled all over India and played in every city, at every season. It is his life, and mine. We share this life, this music, this following. What else can there possibly be for me in this world? Some have tried to tempt me from his side, but I have stayed with him, not wishing for anything else, anything more.

Ours is a world formed and defined and enclosed not so much by music, however, as by a human relationship on solid ground level – the relationship of love. Not an abstract quality, like music, or an intellectual one, like art, but a common human quality lived on an everyday level of reality – the quality of love. So I believe. What else is it that weaves us together as we play, so that I know every movement he will make before he himself does, and he can count on me to be always where he wants me? We never diverge: we leave and we arrive together. Is this not love? No marriage was closer.

When I was a boy many other things existed on earth for me. Of course music was always important, the chief household deity of a family musical by tradition. The central hall of our house was given over to the making of those instruments for which my father, and his father before him, were famous. From it rose sounds not only of the craft involved – the knocking, tapping, planning and tuning – but also of music. Music vibrated there constantly, sometimes harmoniously and sometimes discordantly, a quality of the very air of our house: dense, shaped by infinite variation, and never still. I was only a child, perhaps four-years-old, when my father began waking me at four o'clock every morning to go down to the hall with him and take lessons from him on the *tanpura*, the harmonium, the *sitar* and even the *tabla*. He could play them all and wished to see for which I had an aptitude. Music being literally the air we breathed in that tall, narrow house in the lane that had belonged for generations to the makers of musical instruments in that city, that I would display an aptitude was never in question. I sat crosslegged on the mat before him and played, gradually stirring to life as I did so, and finally sleep would lift from me like a covering a smothering that belonged to the night, till the inner core of my being stood forth and my father could see it clearly – I was a musician, not a maker, but a performer, of music, that is what he saw. He taught me all the *ragas,* the *raginis,* and tested my knowledge with rapid, persistent questioning in his unmusical, grating voice. He was unlike my Ustad in every way, for he spat betel juice all down his ragged white beard, he seemed to be aware of everything I did and frequently his hand shot out to grab my ears and pull till I yelped. From such lessons I had a need to escape and, being a small, wily fellow, managed this several times a day, slipping through my elders' fingers and hurtling down the steep stairs into the lane where I played *gulli-danda* and marbles and *kho* with the luckier, more idle and less supervised boys of the *mohalla*.

There was a time when I cared more passionately for marbles than for music, particularly a dark crimson, almost black one in which white lines writhed like weeds, or roots, that helped me to win every match I played till the pockets of my *kurta* bulged and tore with the weight of the marbles I won.

How I loved my mother's sweetmeats, too – rather more, I'm sure, than I did the nondescript, mumbling, bald woman who made them. She never came to life for me, she lived some obscure indoor life, unhealthy and curtained, undemanding and uninviting. But what *halwa* she made, what *jalebis*. I ate them so hot that I burnt the skin off my tongue. I stole my brothers' and sisters' share and was beaten and cursed by the whole family.

Then, when I was older, there was a time when only the cinema mattered. I saw four, five, as many as six cinema shows a week, creeping out of my room at night, barefoot, for silence, with money stolen from my father, or mother, or anyone, clutched in my hand, then racing through the night-wild bazaar in time for the last show. Nargis and Meena Kumari were to me the queens of heaven, I put myself in the place of their screen lovers and felt myself grow great, hirsute, active and aggressive as I sat on the straw-stuffed seat, my feet tucked up under me, a cone of salted gram in my hand, uneaten, as I stared at these glistening, sequined queens with my mouth open. Because of their attractions, their graces which filled up the empty spaces of my life and swelled and rolled there, moaning, I became aware of the women of our *mohalla* as women: ripe matrons who stood in their doorways, hands on hips, in that hour of the afternoon when life paused and presented possibilities before evening duties choked them off, and the younger girls, never still, always moving, eluding touch, like reeds in dirty water for their clothes, however grimy, did not quite lack the enticement of gold braid and lace. Some answered the look in my eyes, promised me what I wanted, later perhaps, after the late show, not now.

But all fell away from me, all disappeared in the shadows, on the side, when I met my Ustad and began to play for him. He took the place of my mother's sweet *halwa*, the cinema heroines, the street beauties, marbles and stolen money, all the pleasures and riches I had so far contrived to delve and extract from the hard stones of existence in my father's house in the music lane. I did not need such sweets any more, such toys and dreams. I had found my purpose in life and, by following it without hesitation and without holding back any part of myself, I found such satisfaction that I no longer wished for anything else.

It is true I made a little money on these concert tours of ours, enough to take care of my father during his last years and his illness. I even married. That is, my mother managed to marry me off to some neighbour's daughter of whom she was fond. The girl lived with her. I seldom visited her. I can barely remember her name, her face. She is safe with my mother and does not bother me. I remain free to follow my Ustad and play for him.

I believe he has the same attitude to his family and the rest of the world. At all events I have not seen him show the faintest interest in anything but our music, our concerts. Perhaps he is married. I have heard something of the sort but not seen his wife or known him to visit her. Perhaps he has children and one day a son will appear on stage and be taught to accompany his father. So far it has not happened. It is true that in between tours we do occasionally go home for a few days' rest. Inevitably the Ustad and I both cut short these 'holidays' and return to his house in the city for practice. When I return; he does not question me, or even talk to me. But when he hears my step, he recognises it, I know, for he smiles a half-smile, as if mocking himself and me, then he rolls back his muslin sleeve, lifts his *sitar* and nods in my direction. 'The *Raga Desh*,' he may announce, or '*Malhar*,' or '*Megh*,' and I sit down behind him, on the bare floor, and play for him the notes he needs for the construction of the *raga*.

You may think I exaggerate our relationship, his need of me, his reliance on my *tanpura*. You may point out that there are other members of his band who play more important roles. And I will confess you may be right, but only in a very superficial way. It is quite obvious that the *tabla* player who accompanies him plays an 'important' role – a very loud and aggressive, at times thunderous one. But what is this 'importance' of his? It is not indispensable. As even the foremost critics agree, my Ustad is at his best when he is playing the introductory passage, the unaccompanied *alap*. This he plays slowly, thoughtfully, with such purity and sensibility that I can never hear it without tears coming to my eyes. But once Ram Nath has joined in with a tap and a run of his fingers on the *tablas*, the music becomes quick, bold, competitive and, not only in my opinion but also in that of many critics, of diminished value. The audience certainly enjoys the *gat* more than the quiet *alap*, and it pays more attention to Ram Nath than to me. At times, he even draws applause for his performance, during a particularly brilliant passage when he manages to match or even outshine my Ustad. Then my Ustad will turn to him and smile, faintly, in approval, or even nod, silently, for he is so great-hearted and generous, my Ustad. He never does this to me. I sit at the back, almost concealed behind my master and his accompanist. I have no solo passage to play. I neither follow my Ustad's raga nor enter into any kind of competition. Throughout the playing of the raga I run my fingers over the three strings of my *tanpura*, again and again, merely producing a kind of drone to fill up any interval in sound, to form a kind of road, or track, for my Ustad to keep to so that he may not stray from the basic notes of the *raga* by which I hold him. Since I never compete, never ask for attention to be diverted from him to me, never try to rival him in his play, I maintain I am his truer accompanist, certainly his truer friend. He may never smile and nod in approval of me. But he cannot do without me. This is all the reward I need to keep me with him like a shadow. It does not bother me at all when Ram Nath, who is coarse and hairy and scratches his big stomach under his shirt and wears gold rings in his ears like a washerman, puts out his foot and trips me as I am getting onto the stage, or whom I see him helping himself to all the *pilaf* on the table and leaves me only some cold, unleavened bread. I know his true worth, or lack of it, and merely give him a look that will convey this to him.

Only once was I shaken out of my contentment, my complacency. I am ashamed to reveal it to you, it was so foolish of me. It only lasted a very little while but I still feel embarrassed and stupid when I think of it. It was of course those empty-headed, marble-playing friends of my childhood who led me into it. Once I had put them behind me, I should never have looked back. But they came up to me, after a rehearsal in our home city, a few hours before the concert. They had stolen into the dark hall and sat in the back row, smoking and cracking jokes and laughing in a secret, muffled way which nevertheless drifted up to the stage, annoying those who were not sufficiently immersed in the music to be unaware of the outside world. Of course, the Ustad and I never heard them till we had stopped playing. Our ability to simply shut out all distraction from our minds when we play is a similarity between us of which I am very proud.

I noticed them only as I was leaving the hall and met them in the doorway, a jumbled stack of coloured shirts and oiled locks and garish shoes. They clustered around me and it was only because of the things they said, referring to our boyhood games in the alley, that I recognised them. In every other matter they differed totally from me, it was plain to see we had travelled in opposite directions. The colours of their cheap bush-shirts and their loud voices immediately gave me a headache and I found it hard to keep smiling although I knew I ought to be modest and affectionate to them as my art and my position called for such behaviour from me. I let them take me to the tea-shop adjoining the concert hall and order tea for me. For a while we spoke of home, of games, of our families and friends.

Then one of them – Ajit, I think – said, '*Bhai*, you used to play so well. Your father was so proud of you, he thought you would be a great Ustad. He used to tell us what a great musician you would be one day. What are you doing, sitting at the back of the stage and playing the *tanpura* for Rahim Khan?'

No one had ever spoken to me in this manner, in this voice, since my father died. I spilt tea down my lap. My head gave an uncontrolled jerk, I was so shocked. I half-stood up and thought I would catch him by his throat and press till all those ugly words and ugly thoughts of his were choked, bled, white and incapable of moving again. Only I am not that sort of a man. I know myself to be weak, very weak. I only brushed the tea from my clothes and stood there, staring at my feet. I stared at my broken old sandals, streaked with tea, at my loose clothes of white homespun. I told myself I lived so differently from them, my aim and purpose in life were so different from anything these gaudy street vagabonds could comprehend, that I should not be surprised or take it ill if there were such a lack of understanding between us.

'What sort of instrument is the *tanpura?*' Ajit was saying, still loudly. 'Not even an accompaniment. It is nothing. Anyone could play it. Just three notes, over and over again. Even I could play it,' he ended with a shout, making the others clap his back and lean forward in laughter at his wit.

Then Bhola leaned towards me. He was the quietest of them, although he wore a shirt of purple and white flowers and had dyed his moustache ginger. I knew he had been to jail twice already for housebreaking and theft. Yet he dared to lean close to me, almost touching me, and to say: '*Bhai*, go back to the *sitar*. You even know how to play the *sarod*, the *vina*. You could be a great Ustad yourself, with some practice. We are telling you this for your own good. When you become famous and go to America, you will thank us for this advice. Why do you spend your life sitting at the back of the stage and playing that idiot *tanpura* while someone else takes all the money and fame from you?'

It was as if they had decided to assault me. I felt as if they were climbing to top of me, choking me, grabbing me by my hair and dragging me down. Their words were blows, the idea they were throwing at me an assault. I felt beaten, destroyed, and with my last bit of strength, shook them off, threw them off and, pushing aside the table and cups and plates, ran out of the tea-shop. I think they followed me because I could hear voices calling me as I went running down the street, pushing against people and only just escaping from under the rickshaws, tongas and buses. It was afternoon, there were crowds on the street, dust and smoke blotted out the natural light of the day, I saw everything as vile, as debased, as something amoral and ugly, and pushed it aside, pushed through as I ran.

And all the time I thought, are they right? Could I have played the *sitar* myself? Or the *sarod*, or the *vina?* And become an Ustad myself? This had never before occurred to me. My father had taught me to play all these instruments and disciplined me severely, but he had never praised me or suggested I could become a front-rank musician. I had learnt to play these instruments as the son of a carpenter would naturally have learnt to make beds and tables and shelves, or the son of a shopkeeper learnt to weigh grain and sell and make money. But I had practised on these instruments and played the *ragas* he taught me to play without thinking of it as an art or of myself as an artist. Perhaps I was a stupid, backward boy. My father always said so. Now these boys who had heard me play in the dark hall of our house in the music lane told me I could have been an Ustad myself, sat in the centre of the stage, played for great audiences and been applauded for my performance. Were they right? Was this true? Had I wasted my life?

As I ran and pushed, half-crying, I thought these things for the first time in my life, and they were frightening thoughts, large, heavy dark ones that threatened to crush and destroy me. I found myself pushed up against an iron railing. Holding onto its bars, looking through tears at the beds of flowering cannas and rows of imperial palms of a dusty city park. I hung against those railings, sobbing, till I heard someone address me – possibly a policeman, or a beggar, or perhaps just a kindly passer-by. 'In trouble?' he asked me. 'Got into trouble, boy?' I did not want to speak to anyone and shook him off without looking at him and found the gate and went into the park, trying to control myself and order my thoughts.

I found a path between some tall bushes, and walked up and down here, alone, trying to think. Having cried, I felt calmer now. I had a bad headache but I was calmer. I talked to myself.

When I first met my Ustad I was a boy of fifteen – a stupid, backward boy as my father had often told me I was. When I walked up to the stage to give him the *tanpura* he had ordered from my father, I saw greatness in his face, the calm and wisdom and kindness of a true leader. Immediately I wished to deliver not only my *tanpura* but my whole life into his hands. Take me, I wanted to say, take me and lead me. Show me how to live. Let me live with you, by you, and help me, be kind to me. Of course, I did not say these words. He took the *tanpura* from me and asked me to play it for him. This was his answer to the words I had not spoken but which he had nevertheless heard. 'Play for me' – and with these words he created me, created my life, gave it form and distinction and purpose. It was the moment of my birth and he was both my father and my mother to me. He gave birth to me – Bhaiyya, the *tanpura* player.

Before that, I had no life. I was nothing: a dirty, hungry street urchin, knocking about in the lane with other idlers and vagrants. I had played music only because my father made me, teaching me by striking me across the knuckles and pulling my ears for every mistake I made. I had stolen money and sweets from my mother. I was nothing. And no one cared that I was nothing. It was Ustad Rahim Khan who saw me, hiding awkwardly in the shadows of an empty hall with a *tanpura* in my hands, and called me to come to him and showed me what to do with my life. I owe everything to him, my very life to him.

Yes, it was my destiny to play the *tanpura* for a great Ustad, to sit behind him where he cannot even see me, and play the notes he needs so that he may not stray from the bounds of his composition when gripped by inspiration. I give him, quietly and unobtrusively, the materials upon which he works, with which he constructs the great music for which the whole world loves him. Yes, anyone could play the *tanpura* for him, do what I do. But he did not take anyone else, he chose *me*. He gave me my destiny, my life. Could I have refused him? Does a mortal refuse God?

It made me smile to think anyone could be such a fool. Even I, a backward, feckless boy from the streets, had recognised his god when he met him. Even I, Bhaiyya, had known when the hour of my destiny struck. I could not have refused. I took up the *tanpura* and played for my Ustad, and I have played for him since. I could not have wished for a finer destiny.

Leaving the park, I hailed a tonga and ordered the driver to take me to my Ustad. Never in my life had I spoken as loudly, as surely as I did then. You should have heard me. I wish my Ustad had heard me.

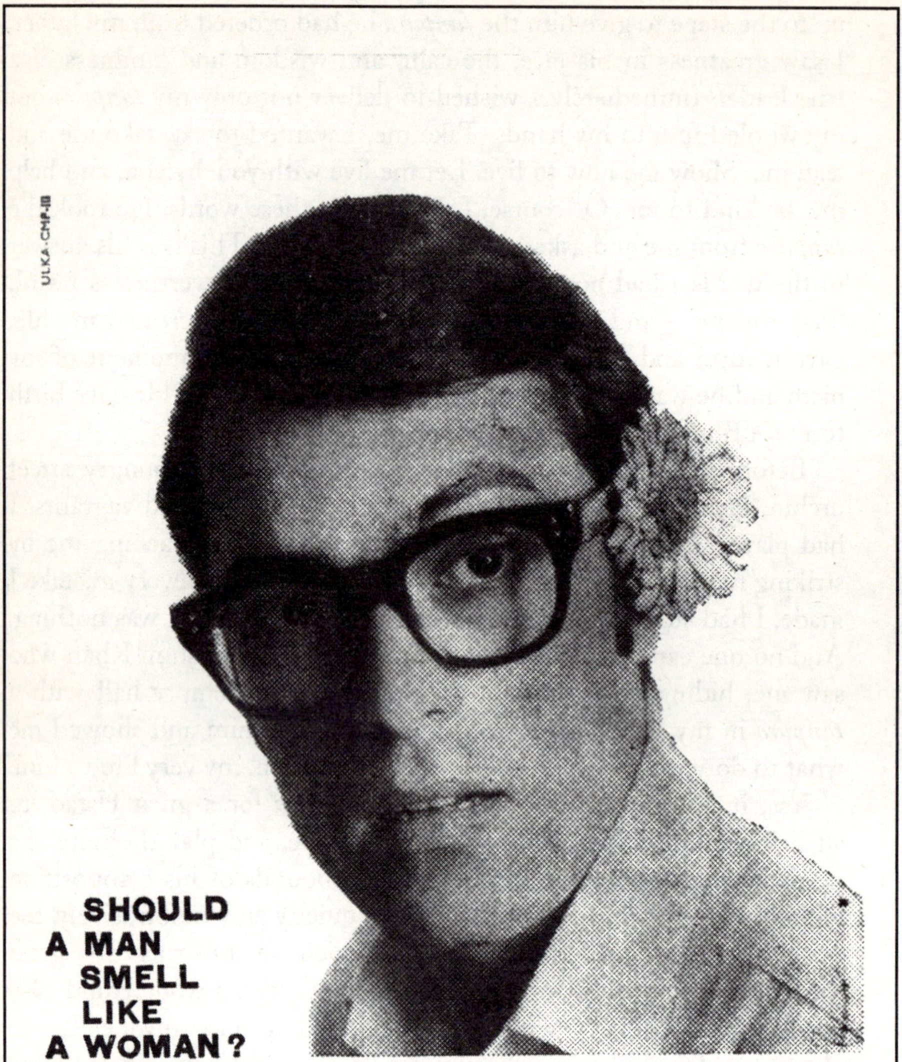
SHOULD
A MAN
SMELL
LIKE
A WOMAN?
For years you have used sweet, flowery, all-purpose talcs. Smelt exactly like your wife and baby. Now CIBA puts things into proper place with Binaca men's talc. That smells, looks, is a talc for a man.
Binaca
talc for men
Everything about Binaca men's talc is different. The decidedly masculine perfume, to please the most particular man. The five-cornered pack, designed to fit a man's grip. Puffer pack for convenience, to shower on after a bath. Makes it a willing traveller too.
Binaca men's talc contains nearly as much as the standard size tins. And costs less than you think.
In a man's world—
It's Binaca men's talc
CIBA
QUEST

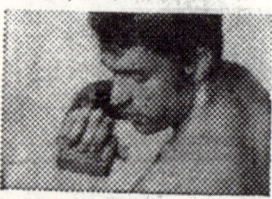

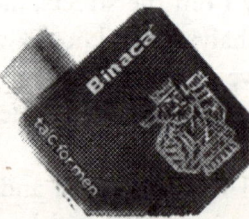

Tangents

Abraham Eraly

(Quest 55: Autumn 1967)

From the road below you could see them, the two women, one in a red sari, carelessly worn, and the other, the plump one, prim in white, trudging up the hill along the rough, winding track. They were alone. The midday sun shone cruelly on them, and on the rain-eroded, leprous hill, and on the cluster of women down at the quarry; and the air was still, without a breath. They now turned the curve of the hill, and were out of sight from the road and the railway-track, and of the women at the quarry.

'How far is it?' one of them asked.

'Close, Malu,' Leela said, waving her arms, 'quite close.'

Malathi said nothing. She was quiet now, subdued, but still angry, angrier, if anything, because she was now thinking about Ganesh and had reasons for worry. He had phoned her in the morning, asking whether she could kindly have dinner with him that evening: he had something important to discuss. And there was something in his voice, a tremor of anxiety, which set her aflutter with the thought that this might well be the day she had been waiting and praying for, for so long. And remembering this now again, anxiously, Malathi was afraid that Leela would ruin for her this evening of all evenings.

'Look!' Leela said. 'See there: that is the shrine. The place is close by it.'

'On the other side?' Malathi asked.

'Yes, but quite close,' Leela said.

Distance was elastic with Leela, and so were time and love and all relationships, everything stretching or shrinking and meaning different things with every change of her mood. And Malathi no longer believed her. The only reality now was the worry that was balling in the pit of her stomach. And the reality of the sweat that was collecting inside her *choli*. And of the cruel sun. And of the spreading wet patches in the *choli* under the armpits.

Malathi pulled the sari around her shoulder, covering the wet patches. Of late she had become exceedingly self-conscious about her appearance. Any small thing, like a displaced tress or a stain in the sari, was enough to drive her to distraction. Everyday she spent hours before the mirror, arranging and rearranging her appearance precisely so, knowing fully well that a chance gust of wind, or the hand of a passer-by in the bus or on the pavement, or some such small thing, was enough to reduce her to ruin. And yet, despite the knowledge, she was incapable of tearing herself away from the obsessive morning ritual before the mirror, or from returning in the evening to the mirror to carefully examine the day's ruin, putting away the mirror in disgust only to take it up again to repeat the scrutiny, over and over, to hope and despair again and again, and day by day to age inexorably, and to watch the terrible process of ageing. And to spend the nights sleepless and tossing, and to spend the days unfresh and tense, not daring to live! And yet to appear to be like other women, to behave casually, to smile, to speak politely, without bitterness, and to take care that the hand which lifted the tea cup to the mouth did not shiver and spill the tea, and to take care that no one noticed her taking care! But was it all really necessary? Probably not. Most probably not. If one could see oneself through the eyes of other people, then probably one wouldn't be so anxious about oneself, seeing that others do not quite see so much; and yet other people torment us by their very presence, and like mirrors placed around us, they compel us to see ourselves, judge ourselves. And yet, truly, the terror is in one's own senses, when they are turned inward, sensing oneself, acutely.

But there was a time when her eyes were turned outward, her adolescence, the college years, when every season had its lusty joys and she was part of it. But Malathi now found it difficult to believe that once she was so carefree and happy. In her childhood – or even afterwards, for that matter – she had not received much love from her parents, for they were hoping for a son when she was born, and she was not pretty either, nor obedient, and anyway there was always her elder sister, Rani, so fragile and coyly pretty, with everybody doting on her. But these were things which Malathi realized only when she looked back to her youth from her middle age; when she was young she was not conscious of such things, whether she was loved or not, for she was brimming with the zest for life, and life was all wonder and joy, and love was not necessary, and if occasionally there was a little bit of pain too, that never took root, for life was all movement, and she shed things and assumed things with the seasons, a child of nature, and she was happy, and time was a continuous ascension. And then, suddenly, time stood still, when she crested her youth and stood quivering on the verge of middle age, and she was a little frightened, but not much; and then again time raced on, and now time was all terror, for now it was not time with her, but against her, and it was a battle, and she was alone, and she needed love to find harmony with time again, love to grow old gracefully and to die in peace. But love eluded her. She tried to meet the situation in other ways. She gave up wearing a watch. She banished time. She read philosophy and took up painting. She cultivated culture, became a bit of a bore. But here there was another problem; she found that she was not entirely free to change her way of life; people expected her to be exuberant. And so, though it was a great strain, she continued the farce, and her companions, now with husband and children and the many fanciful worries which lazy housewives invent to spice their lives, said: 'You are just the same, Malu. You haven't changed a bit!' They meant it to be a compliment, and only she heard the ringing irony of those words. And then, exhausted, she gave up the pretence, and her companions said: 'Malu has changed, such a sudden change! Poor Malu!' And in the YWCA, the younger residents called her 'aunt,' and not always without malice.

And then at the age of thirty-five she found love. With another woman. And love was now fully requited. It was a love that was realized in many subtle ways, by a tender look, a glance exchanged, almost without intent, not a knowing glance, nor of emotion, but beneath the plane of thought and feeling a stirring and coalescing of essential being; a contemplative love, secret and mysterious, and never reduced to the banality of stated love. It often verged on the carnal in many unconscious ways, but it was never consummated in the carnal act, was never even considered in terms of such an act, which is an act of finality, a binding act, after which everything changes, for the better or the worse. And because it was not carnally realized or considered, it was a love that was intricate and entwining and yet free and guiltless. A love that was like a *leela*, a play. A play of wind upon wind.

Yet they were unlike persons. Malathi was stolid, responsible, retiring, with a preference for white saries, the headmistress of a small but exclusive girls' school; while Leela was very much younger, sparkling, open, and irrepressible, with lively bright eyes, and a tiny teasing flesh growth at the edge of her nose. She was the lost and found youth of Malathi, her lost innocence, and through her Malathi rediscovered the miracle of laughter, the luxury and joy of not caring. They shared a double room in the YWCA, the headmistress and the college girl, and they were innocently happy together. And then one day Leela was gone, gone as she had come, without ceremony, and in the evening when Malathi returned from school, she found Leela's mattress rolled up and her things all gone, a faint mustiness in the room, and a letter from her on the table. And seeing that Leela was gone, Malathi slowly sat on her bed, with the letter in her lap, unopened, staring at the blank wall opposite, and she heard the twang of racquets in the tennis court, and in the next room a glass bangle falling and breaking, sudden loud laughter in the common room, and beyond that the clang of traffic, and suddenly a crow on the tree by the window – hearing everything very distinctly, listening with rapt attention, and telling herself, now that is the electric-train, and this the double-decker bus, followed by a Herald car, and now the crow on the neem tree, and so on. And then, slowly and laboriously, she pulled her mind back to herself, and she thought of the day that was now ending, a very ordinary day, without any premonition of calamity, and she remembered that she and Leela had planned to see a film that evening. *The Householder*, starring Leela Naidu, and many a time through the humdrum routine of the school that day she had yearned for the evening to come, to go with Leela to the cinema and afterwards to the restaurant; and now Leela was gone, and the evening stretched empty before her, and suddenly she was very weary. Slowly she got up. She put the letter aside, still unread. Then, not quite knowing what to do, not quite knowing what she was doing, pulled only by the strings of unconscious habit, she went to the bathroom and washed her face, peering in the dim mirror above the washbasin, and then at the mess-hall, among the milling college girls, she sipped a cup of tepid tea, and then returning to her room, she once again sat on her bed, with the letter again in her lap, and she thought of her childhood and youth, all now gone away, for ever, and she thought of what was happening to her, and slowly tears welled in her eyes.

Next morning she read Leela's letter. Gone with Sreeni. Eloped. And Malu, forgive me for going like this, without goodbye, but you know how Sreeni is, so impulsive, and this is the way he wanted it, and he said you would understand, and I am sure you would, but forgive me all the same, and you know how fond of you I am really, and how I would miss you; goodbye. Yes, gone with Sreeni. And now, after three years, Leela was back again, taking the guestroom in the YWCA, coming into her life again without warning, mysteriously, giving no reason for this coming, ebullient as ever, unchanged, except that her breasts were now fuller and her tender body had matured, not grown coarse, but simply matured, with the skin still soft and sheen, perhaps not so bright as in her maidenhood, but mellow and warm. But this time she evoked no flutter in Malathi, who seemed to have gone behind an opaque curtain, and her voice grown distant and muffled. Leela was immediately conscious of this change in her friend, but she mistook the hardness for the hardness of a just-healed wound, and she wanted to apologise for the hurt caused.

'Hope you have forgiven me, no?' she said.

'Yes,' Malathi said, meaning not that she had forgiven, but that she had forgotten, or more accurately, that she had been unable to remember, a stage into which she had entered soon after Leela's elopement, entered not with any great effort, but naturally, so that afterwards there was only a vague and nameless ache and emptiness in her, and that too only for some time – a quickness of forgetting hurt which, if she were more sensitive, she should have recognized as the most cruel sign of ageing, of the springs of feeling and passion drying up in her, making her sapless and friable like a dead twig.

'You know, Sreeni is joining an advertising firm here?' Leela said. 'Yes. He is arriving tomorrow. And he said he's going to do penance at your feet – oh, he is so fond of you, so fond!'

'Yes,' Malathi said, Sreeni? Who is Sreeni? The youth whom she had once loved – desired? – now gone away, become stranger? 'Yes,' Malathi said again, recollecting with effort, like the plot of a story read long ago. It was at an art exhibition that she first met him. There was a painting there which intrigued her. A yellow painting, with perhaps touches of brown, a little of green here and there, but mainly yellow, a dull yellow. Yes. A sick yellow. Painting of a garden with three nude persons. For some reason Leela was not with her there. She was wearing a pink sari that day, Malathi remembered, because pink was so gay, and Leela had said it suited her well, and she had a matching handbag, and indeed she felt gay. Yes, it was the painting of a garden. At the centre of it – a tree, a fruit tree, and a woman against it, a plump woman, yet curiously weightless, not leaning against the tree, but floating, by some miraculous suspension of gravity. A fruit among fruits. Almost as large as the tree itself, but not quite. Merging with the tree. Tapering limbs almost tendrils. Her two arms resting on, curling around her belly big with seed; her eyes lowered, contented. At her feet cactuses, a skull, a squirrel. Above and to the left of the woman, a girl. Tender. Virginal. Growing. Her belly softly pulsing like a tissue membrane, flat, and yet ready and eager to swell. And imminent over her, a man. A thinking, doubting man, faintly satanic. An interloper. The picture puzzled and fascinated Malathi, and she wished that Leela were with her to share the experience. And suddenly beside her a voice spoke, addressing her: 'You don't like it?' The surprise, the fluster. 'Oh,' she said, meaning nothing in particular. And turning her head she found herself peering into two close-set intense eyes which, the moment they met her eyes, wrinkled softly with laughter. 'I hate it,' he said. And because she was gay, and because she was lately feeling young again, she smiled back, and asked: 'Why?' Because I painted it, and it is a lie, he said. 'I never met an artist before,' she said. I am sorry the first one is such a sorry specimen, he said. And she said, 'I am proud to meet you, really,' and he said would she please join him for a cup of tea, perhaps they could talk, and Malathi demurred, considered, doubted, and then said yes, and they walked over to the restaurant.

'Tell me about the painting,' she said, sipping iced tea; 'what does it mean?' Must we talk about it, he asked. 'Yes, please, very much interested,' she said. I was born a Christian, he said; the painting is my repudiation of it. I even changed my name. 'Oh really? How interesting,' she said; 'I am also a Christian.' I am sorry for you; he said. 'Tell me about the painting,' she said. I told you, he said. The Mephistopheles in it is me. An intruder in the garden. The garden is life, see. I am an intruder in it because you see I embody reason and will. Cogito ergo sum and all that. I am self-consciousness. But the woman is not. No ego in her. She is part of the garden. An integral part. Do you see? 'Yes,' Malathi said. It is like this, he said; see: in the

Hindu there is no opposition between man and nature. You are just part of nature, birth and procreation, and sickness and death and all. It is like the seasons; they come and go and come again. 'I understand,' she said, thinking how disturbing his eyes were, and how queer he looked, his face absurdly young, almost childish, except for the eyes, and his hands nervous and knobby, and yet strong, with tufts of hair growing on them, everything so strangely mixed-up and contrary in him. So nothing in particular has any particular significance, he said. And everything is equally significant and holy, everything. There is no evil, no sin. And really there is no death, because you see the cycle goes on. Do you see? Do you see? He asked, gripping her hands and shaking them, seeing that she was not now really listening but only watching. 'Yes,' she said; 'yes'. I wish I could really tell you what I mean, he said wearily. It is all in the picture. The woman – she accepts life. Life in its totality. Everything, There is no tension in her. You see she is like the tree. That is what I mean: a state of grace, I mean, to be a Hindu. Why, that is heaven! Only no one sings alleluia. There is no need... 'But you said it is a lie,' she said. The painting? Yes, he said. Maybe. A personal hallucination. I believe it of course. It's my truth. But so pretentious, I mean, to state it so forcefully, and so it must be a lie, no? And I am not even sure whether this is what I want. To be in this sort of heaven. Or in any heaven. 'What do you want then?' she asked, teasing him. I? he asked. I only want to die, he said, laughing. 'Don't mean it, do you?' she said. Of course not, he said. I only want to live.

And finding conversation easy with her, and comforting, unlike with other persons, he talked on, not always making sense, but just talking, and Malathi said, 'You must meet Leela. She is part of nature, like you say,' and he said, it's just a knack. We all have it when we are young. But we lose the knack, some sooner than others, and she said again, 'Leela is a Hindu, as you say,' and she brought him to the YWCA and introduced them, proud to share her discovery with Leela, and soon they became close friends, the three of them. Quickly. Without apparent straining or effort. But strain there must have been, even from the beginning. The two women couldn't admit him entirely to their intimacies, at least Malathi couldn't, because he was a man, and men dazzled and frightened her at the same time, and he was unpredictable, moody sometimes, and when gay, hysterically gay, and though lovable inspite of the unpredictability or because of it, still a man, hairy and muscle-bound, sometimes harsh in his ways and capable of causing hurt. And sometimes when he and Leela bantered one another, Malathi, pulsing a different and slower rhythm, would suddenly become conscious of the great difference in their age, conscious that the playfulness was natural to them and not to her, and she would then feel vaguely estranged from them. And this made her feel a certain resentment, which she couldn't focus on either of them, or rather, sometimes she resented him and sometimes her, and because she couldn't clearly focus the resentment, she blamed herself for it, felt guilty, and slowly the old uneasiness of her lonely years began to show its head again. Moreover, Malathi couldn't trust him, not entirely, or trust herself with him, because he was impulsive and wayward in his ways, and after all she was middle-aged and a virgin, her maidenhead her one prized possession, which she couldn't now offer freely for fear of it being taken lightly, for if that were now gone cheaply, there would be nothing else for her to hold on to or cherish, to fall back on, nothing else to sacrifice if occasion for such a sacrifice came. Once she nearly lost it. He had persuaded her to sit for a portrait, and no sooner had she stepped into the room than he began teasing and pawing her, saying, 'You are pure Khajuraho, dear; pure Khajuraho!' and she said, 'Keep your hands off me,' and he said, 'How can an artist paint unless he has a feel of the subject,' and he went on pawing her; all in. fun of course, but all the same it roused passions, and he kissed her on the mouth, without really meaning to, perhaps, and his hands wandered, and she pulled his head down to her breasts, and he nestled against them, and her breasts felt curiously heavy and burdened, and tense and aching with the burden, and she lifted his head and kissed him again and again with the surge of passion; and yet she could go no further, some nameless terror constricting the final generosity, the homage to love and good companionship, to him as well as to herself, to life, really, and she came away with tears in her eyes, not even quite knowing why or for what she was weeping. And she was ashamed of it afterwards, not because she went that far with him, but that she did not and could not go further, and was petty and cowardly and ungenerous, because after all that holding back indicated a certain lack of trust, and so it was in a way a point of turning away in their relationship, for they both now knew that they were, and would for ever remain, strangers to each other in some ways, where it mattered. It was then that Sreeni definitely veered close to Leela. Or perhaps those two were always really close, because of the closeness of their age, and it might be just that Malathi now became conscious that she did not quite belong to their world. But whether it was always there, or whether it was a new thing, it was doubly her loss, and she was the one to suffer. Yet, inspite of everything, and the difference in age and temperament, the three of them were gay together. And then suddenly two of them were gone. And Malathi once again retreated into the shadow. And once again she was face to face with time. And time now revealed a new quality to her, the quality of discontinuity, of the units of time stretching and breaking from one another, and then falling one by one, slowly, heavily, as in a nightmare, and indeed life was a nightmare.

And now Malathi conducted her life with the utmost circumspection. She plotted her life. Perhaps she would now never know happiness. But she would learn to get along without happiness. But security she should have. And security she would have. Yes. Perhaps security is happiness. And Ganesh would certainly give her security. She could trust him, trust his accountant's precise ways and 'middle-class stolidity. She had once doubted him, not doubting his goodness and dependability, but fearing them, fearing that being married to him would probably be very dull, everything so clean and hygienic and dead; but she put away that childishness, realizing that at her age she should think only of organizing her life and not living it, for life was really past her, and there was nothing to be done about it. And she went for him carefully and methodically, and now at last the day for which she had been waiting for long had come. But she was afraid that everything would now be ruined because of Leela. And she thought, surely, if she missed this chance, then it was goodbye, adieu, unless of course she went in for some lecherous old man with decaying teeth, and that would be a fine ending, indeed!

Now they crested the hill. Before them the hill suddenly banked and dipped and then ran level for about twenty yards to the edge of an abandoned shallow quarry, the whole of that area covered by the shadow of a huge banian tree. 'Here we are,' Leela said, a little dramatically, not quite sure of herself, finding Malathi distant and unresponsive; and because she was not quite sure of herself, and felt somewhat foolish in speaking so dramatically, she said it again: 'Here we are!' 'Yes,' Malathi said, glad to be out of the sun. She sat on a humped root of the tree, arranging herself carefully, rather formally, waiting for Leela to begin. Leela continued to stand, eagerly, looking about, recalling with pleasure, her concern for Malathi momentarily gone. Remember, that day we had planned to see a film, she asked. Remember? Well, right after you left for the school Sreeni came, drawing pads and all. Wanted me to go with him to make some sketches of this shrine. And I said, No, I have been cutting too many classes. But he said, Damn the classes, come. And with us in the train there was a blind couple, foreigners, Germans, I think, and Sreeni got all excited about it. You know how he is sometimes! So earnest! 'Yes,' Malathi said. Oh, you have no idea, Malu, what it has been to be married to this man, Leela said; his moods so quick and changing, like that, and so many. It's like being loved by a hundred persons. 'Yes,' Malathi said. He is wonderful, Leela said; oh, wonderful. 'Yes,' Malathi said. Well, as I was saying, he got all excited about blindness, Leela said. Don't remember all he said – that all misunderstandings arise from the senses, I think, particularly seeing and hearing, he said. Oh, I don't know. Something like that. And I wasn't even sure he was really serious. Difficult to tell with him. 'Yes,' Malathi said, and she was thinking that if Ganesh saw her messed up, like she was then, he certainly wouldn't like it, because unlike his cousin Sreeni he was so fastidious, and he had good reasons to be fastidious, for it wouldn't suit him to have a slovenly spouse, it wouldn't suit his business: but she would look after him well, Malathi resolved; yes, she would resign her job and look after him well, and bear him his children, and she would be a good wife and a good mother, and would be firm with the servants, and she would greet him from the office with a cup of hot tea, and there would be soft music and rose curtains, and she would keep the ashtrays clean, and she would be the gentle hostess to his friends, friendly but not familiar, so that he would be good to her and be proud of her, and that would be worth any sacrifice, to have somebody to be proud of you. 'Shall we go?' she asked. But I haven't told you, Malu, Leela said. 'Alright,' Malathi said. I tell you it's funny, Leela said. Well, he made a couple of sketches, soon as we got here, but he said it was no good, wasn't in the mood, and he took out some sandwiches from the basket, and he started jabbering about the senses once again, but now more in fun than seriously, and he climbed up the tree, this tree here, and got on that branch there, and he stretched up his hands to the skies and said, O Lord God of Hosts, strike me blind, this moment, and you know, Malu, the funniest thing happened, you see, he had a sandwich in his hand, holding it up, and a crow dived and tore it from his hand, and believe me, Malu, I think he thought it was his Lord God of Hosts striking him, and he screamed and came tumbling down the tree, and I was rolling with laughter on the ground. And he came over to me. And I couldn't stop laughing, and I was lying on my stomach and laughing, and he stretched on the ground beside me, and as I turned I saw him laughing beside me, and this set me off again, and he gathered me in his arms, and oh he kissed me, laughing, and..... Well, you see how it happened. It just happened. And he asked would I marry him, and I said yes I would, and, I don't know why, I laughed again, and he kissed me again and he said I am the spark of life, the original spark, that's what he said, and he kissed me again, and we were coming down the hill, and he said we should elope, rightaway, and how could I say no to him, Malu! So you see how it happened, don't you, Leela asked.

'Yes, I see,' Malathi said, without enthusiasm, her thoughts far away, in the world of soft music and rose curtains. 'You are strange today, Malu,' Leela said. 'I have a headache. I am sorry,' Malathi said. 'It is not that,' Leela said, seating herself before Malathi. It was something else, she knew; it was not the unforgiven hurt caused by her elopement either, she knew; it was something else, some all pervading anxiety, which Malathi would share with her, and which, if Malathi refused to share it with her, would divide them, and then there would be no sharing of anything else between them, and their friendship, or love, could not be redeemed, ever. And sensing this, Leela felt helpless, and a little angry, affronted, for she had come early, a day ahead of Sreeni, particularly for this, to gather and weave again the threads of their intimacy, and she had persuaded Malathi to go with her to the shrine on the hill, not so much to explain her running away as to share a very personal experience with her, so that some sort of tenuous link between them could be formed, bridging over the years of separation arid divergent experiences. And Leela knew that Malathi needed her, and she wanted to give herself generously to her, and being not allowed to give herself so was painful, like the ache in the full breasts of a mother wanting but forbidden to suckle her crying baby. It was necessary somehow to get at Malathi, move her, somehow. Gradually, as Leela sat there on the ground, plucking the weeds moodily an idea began to take form in her subconscious mind, not so much conceptive idea, expressible in words, as a slow pivoting of her whole being to face Malathi differently, a pivoting which, however unconscious, nevertheless had behind it, in however unformulated a fashion, the idea that perhaps she would be able to find her friend again only by hurting her, for Malathi had built walls all around her, making herself impregnable, and to reach her it was necessary to breach the walls somewhere, cause a small opening, through which she could penetrate her friend, or through which her friend could be brought out, and this had to be done, for her own sake as well for Malu's, for inside those walls there could be only putrefaction and death for life is a coming out and not a going in. 'My! It is hot,' Leela said, and she took a kerchief from her handbag and wiped her face, and then shaking off the sari from her shoulder, she opened her choli and wiped her chest, and then her breasts, pushing the kerchief inside the brassiere, and then, more tenderly, she wiped her belly, and then, putting the kerchief aside, she ran her fingers softly over her belly, relishing it, and she looked at Malathi, and smiling sweetly she said: 'It doesn't show yet.'

It was said with such apparent innocence that it took Malathi a moment to grasp the meaning and the witchery of those words, and then slowly realization came to her that Leela was saying that just then, and had brought her all the way to say it, only to hurt her, and this surprised Malathi, for she had not suspected such viciousness in her. When Leela first spoke of the trip, Malathi had believed that its purpose was to explain to her their elopement, and this Malathi could appreciate and condone, for in a way she held herself responsible for causing the need for self-expiation in Leela, by being unresponsive towards her and thus giving the impression of unforgiveness. Hers was not, of course, a studied coldness. Certainly she did not mean to hurt Leela. In fact, there was no feeling at all towards Leela, either way. However, she knew that this lack of feeling, and the consequent coldness, was not right, for after all they were once such close friends, and so Leela deserved, and had reason to expect, warmth and friendliness from Malathi and knowing this, that what she was doing was not right, Malathi wanted to do something to redeem the situation, make a gesture at least, and that was why she agreed, though without enthusiasm, to go with Leela to the shrine on the hill. But that was before Ganesh had phoned her. Afterwards she tried to put off Leela, but without success, and she could not bring herself to explain about Ganesh to her, and so there was nothing to do but to go along. But it had now turned out that Leela's purpose was not to seek reconciliation, but rather to hurt her again, to force her to remember things she had forgotten and was grateful to forget, to make her aware of her lost womanhood and to regret it: to make her feel the need for Leela and to bring her again under her vicious power. But Malathi would not concede this now, to be a slave of memories, for she had now dreams to live by, of which Leela knew nothing. And so she would not yield to Leela, nor would she fight her, for to fight her would be to concede her power; she would merely suffer her. Above all she would remain calm, for in it was the whole of safety. And it was not now difficult for her to remain calm, for she considered that there was nothing for her to be jealous about in this fulfillment of Leela's womanhood, for she herself would now have the assuaging of the demon in her loins, and she herself would bear children; and what was more, these things were not so very important for her now, for the demon had been quiescent for sometime now, and the ache of emptiness was not great in her womb, and marriage was important only as a social fulfillment, a necessary social status, and that status she would now have, for Ganesh would give it to her abundantly. And so she merely smiled and said nothing. 'It's only two months now,' Leela said, buttoning up her choli. 'I am glad,' Malathi said. And Leela asked: 'Are you, really? Are you?' 'Yes. Why?' Malathi asked. 'Don't you want to be a mother yourself? Don't you?' Leela asked. 'It's alright,' Malathi said. 'You are still a virgin, aren't you?' Leela asked. 'This is a wretched life, yours, isn't it? A wretched life?' she asked. And Malathi suggested, politely, that they need not go into her affairs, and if Leela had finished her story they could go back. 'And you are unnatural in your desires, unnatural,' Leela said. 'Yes, I know. Haven't I seen you ravishing me with your eyes, haven't I? And just now, when I opened my choli.....' 'No! That is not true,' Malathi said. 'I had not desired you that way. I had only loved you.'

But now there was no holding Leela back. She set on Malathi blindly and viciously, groping for vulnerable points and hammering at them. The very calm of Malathi seemed to infuriate her. And Malathi sat rigidly upright, her hands crossed in her lap, primly, and she rested her eyes on Leela, smiling calmly, keeping her distance. Yet undeniably she was hurt by all that was true; and perhaps it was even true that she had desired Leela that way; and anyway, even if she had only loved her and not desired her, that too was unnatural, to love without desire, and in a way this dichotomy between body and mind adumbrated the whole tragedy of her life. Thus had she become desiccated, her life withering inside her. And she had desiccated not because she had given liberally of herself, but because she had not given herself at all, because she, frightened woman, had kept her thighs locked tightly, and hugged her heart close to herself tightly, for fear of – of what she knew not, perhaps for fear that what she had to offer was not worth offering and would bring only rejection and ridicule. Ultimately it was because of her lack of confidence in her own body. So ultimately it was her self-consciousness, her mind, ultimately yes it was her intelligence penetrating matter and destroying its spontaneity; and so ultimately it was the original sin, of *ahankara*. And therefore it was that she still a virgin, had really fallen, lost her innocence, while Leela, though easy in her morals, retained her innocence, for innocence is spontaneity, and Malathi had lost her spontaneity. And now it was too late to retrieve the lost innocence, for that required the repudiation of her upbringing and religion, and of the values and culture which had become ingrained in her; in fact it couldn't be redeemed without repudiating her whole life, and this she could not do, for she had not the energy or the time to repudiate her life, was too old and weary. And since she could not change it, her way of life, it was necessary to justify it, for to justify it was to justify her continued living to make such continued living possible, and so it was imperative for her to maintain that there was more to life than merely living it, and this she calmly maintained with Leela. But Leela was convinced, and indeed, Malathi was not talking to convince Leela but only to convince herself; and finally wishing not to talk any more, regretting that she had talked at all, Malathi said: 'You have learned something from Sreeni.' 'Yes,' Leela said; 'and I have taught him something too: I taught him to live his philosophy.' 'Good,' Malathi said.

Above them now, suddenly, the tree whispered, at the first touch of the sea breeze. The evening had come. 'Let's go,' Malathi said, getting up in a flurry and smoothing her sari, suddenly remembering about Ganesh again. 'Go?' Leela asked, 'why, what's the hurry? No one waiting for you, you know!' 'I am not quite so finished yet,' Malathi said, 'not as you think.' And then softly, as though telling herself, persuading herself, she added: 'I shall be happy, yet.' But the moment she said it she realised it was a mistake to say it, but since it was anyway said, it was necessary to explain it, and so she added: 'I am getting married, if you want to know. Soon.' 'Married?' Leela asked; 'married? Who is going to marry you!' 'A gentleman,' Malathi said, 'a gentleman.' 'A gentleman? Hurrah!' Leela said; 'the lady is going to marry a gentleman! Hurrah! Hurrah!' 'Yes, a gentleman. Somebody with a position,' Malathi said. 'There is no one,' Leela said; 'you are just making it up.' 'Ganesh, if you want to know,' Malathi said; 'Ganesh, that's who.' 'Ganesh? Sreeni's cousin?' Leela asked, and when

Malathi nodded her head to mean yes, Leela burst out laughing. But she quickly checked herself, and her face took on a shrewd look, and with all the facile witchery of her young years, she said: 'Oh, Malu, Malu! Now I am truly sorry for you, truly sorry! Ganesh is marrying someone else. Wait, what's her name? He told me. At the station. He was there to receive me. Oh god, god!' From the way Malathi's face paled, Leela knew that the blow had at last been struck, that the walls of defence had finally crumbled, that she had found her friend again; and so the lie and the hurt were justified, for now, after the rage and the tears, there could be reconciliation and love, and later on they might even joke about the incident; and so the lie and the hurt did not matter.

'You lie, lie!' Malathi cried. But the words came out only as a meaningless gurgle in which echoed all the nameless terrors of her life, for she knew deep within herself that what Leela said was true. It had to be true. It fitted well with the pattern of her life. With the raw childhood. The frenzied youth. The years of drought. The coming of locusts. And now the long farewell. As for Ganesh, a thousand times she had told herself: you are being silly, woman; he means nothing, will turn away from you soon; who will ever want you, you powdered old hag! Better not dream, she told herself, better not. But she dreamed on, wanting to go on living. She dreamed of getting married and setting up a home of her own, she dreamed of children, of music in the evenings and peaceful sleep in the nights – a tranquil resolving of her life. But now clearly her life had to be resolved in another way.

Malathi looked about her with teary, distraught eyes. Before her the shallow quarry seemed to darken and deepen enticingly. With a stifled sob she covered her eyes and stumbled forward. And Leela, now full of tenderness for her, rushed to her and held her in her arms, soothing her, and then no longer soothing her, but caressing her, betraying at last the nature of her passion towards Malathi, the reason for her wrath and viciousness. 'I love you, love you,' she whispered hoarsely. For a moment Malathi stood still, allowing herself to be caressed. Then with a parched moan she came alive again. 'You lie, lie!' she cried, and fought free from Leela and ran towards the quarry. But just at the edge of the pit she stopped short, as though halted by an invisible leash, and making a half turn she looked over her shoulder towards Leela, but not at Leela or at anything else, for she was glancing back not at the space behind her but at time past, her now ending life. To Leela, who watched her helplessly, herself petrified with fright, it seemed that Malathi then smiled sadly, tiredly, as though forgiving everything and everybody, forgiving herself, for ever. For a moment Malathi stood free at the edge of the quarry, against the vast blue of the horizon, the breeze billowing her sari, and then she turned her face away from the breeze, and she turned herself towards the evening sun, so that her shadow now lay behind her, and she closed her eyes – and when she opened her eyes again, she was lying in bed, swathed in bandages, and Ganesh was sitting beside her. Presently Leela came in, her eyes anxious. 'You fell,' she said. 'Yes,' Malathi said, and she closed her eyes again.

The Gherao

Arun Joshi

(Quest 65: April-June 1970)

Let me tell yon about this *gherao* that happened at our college. I say happened because there is no other word for it. It was perhaps the heat, or the mood of violence in the city, or, maybe, the simple act of a capricious fate that dogs us through life.

The occasion was small. A blackboard stands next to our administration office. It is an old weathered object that cracks with the first onslaught of heat and swells up in the rains. It is meant for official announcements; and until that afternoon it had never been suspected that it could be the cause of such strange events.

On this particular afternoon, as the Principal and I returned from lunch, we noticed that the board was covered with blue and green writing of a sort that looked anything but official. It was the end of April. The sun was already without mercy. I wanted to hurry along but the Principal paused before the board blinking his short-sighted eyes with dull curiosity. Sweat poured down my back. A hot wind, carrying the first dust of summer, soughed in the neem trees. A knot of boys in narrow trousers and pointed shoes watched us from a distance trying to snigger away the tension that had begun to smoulder.

The Principal stood in silence as if struck. Then he said,

'Do you see this, Chatterjee?'

'Yes, sir,' I said curtly.

I was getting quite annoyed, to tell you the truth. I knew he could not read a thing without his glasses. What then was he doing, standing there like a marionette, exposing us to the heat and the ridicule of the steadily swelling crowd of boys? 'Have you seen this?' the Principal asked again. He was quite old and frequently forgot what he had said earlier.

'Yes,' I said.

'Read it out to me.'

This only shows how lazy he was. He had his glasses right there in his shirt pocket but it was apparently too much trouble for him to pull them out. Anyway, I read the demands out.

By and large they were ridiculous, ridiculous or threatening, and all of them were badly spelt. As I recited them one by one I noticed that the Principal had begun to gently rub himself in the middle of the chest. I had seen him do this before, in staff meetings or at the visit of VIPs, usually under circumstances of stress. I came to the end of my list and hesitated. I did not want to read out the last demand.

'Is that all?' he said.

'There is one last one.'

'Read it out.'

'You may not like it.'

'As if I like the rest? Read it out.'

'It says we do not want an old owl for a Principal.'

I had hardly finished when he cried, 'Wipe them off, Chatterjee, wipe them off.'

Still rubbing his chest he stomped towards his room. I followed him in.

I had to see him urgently in connection with our Annual Sports Day which I was meant to organise and which, as things stood, promised to be a disaster. He had told me to catch him right after lunch. It was funny how he told people – frequently several people at the same time – to catch him at this time or that as if he were not a Principal of flesh and blood but some kind of a shadow or a mirage, that one might miss unless one were there to grab at the right moment.

'Abominable,' he muttered as he sank into his chair. That was a favourite word with him even though very few people understood what he meant by it.

He was surprised to see me come in.

'Have you done it?' he asked.

'Done what?'

'The blackboard. Didn't I tell yon to wipe it off?'

'What is the point? It will only create more trouble. We have only a week before vacations. Let it fizzle out.'

'That is not the point,' the Principal said. 'If you don't want to do it, I'll go myself.'

'What if there is trouble?'

'I'll see to that.'

As I went out, hating the heat, I wondered what the point was. I could have refused, but I did not have the heart to refuse the old man who, I must admit, I liked in an odd, good-humoured way.

As I picked up the duster the Union President – a dwarfish boy by the funny name of Chiru Pandey – materialized from behind the yellow columns.

'Leave those things there, sir,' Chiru said in his hoarse cackling voice.

'Go to hell,' I said starting to erase.

Now you must understand that I am very young – only twenty-three – and rather strongly built. I have been teaching English for the past two years. As a rule, I fool around quite a bit with the boys and, by and large, they like me. At this moment, however, the heat and the worry of the annual sports were getting the better of me.

'Leave our sacred demands,' Chiru cried incoherently. He had trouble speaking English even though he insisted on addressing every faculty member in that difficult language.

'I am only following orders,' I said continuing to erase.

'Whose orders?'

'The Principal's.'

'Ha,' Chiru said making me fear for a moment that he was going to spit on me. 'Ha, who cares for the Principal?'

'He is my boss even if you don't consider him yours,' I said.

'There will be trouble,' Chiru said.

'The Principal says he will see to that.'

Pandey now stepped forward and tried to snatch the duster away from my hand.

'If you do that again, Pandey,' I said, 'I will break your head.'

He looked at me in amazement. I finished dusting and returned to the Principal's room adding over my shoulder 'If you want to mess around with demands, Chiru, you might at least spell them properly.'

The Principal, I was surprised to see, was dozing. He was quite old really – sixty-five, seventy, maybe more. He had done his M.A. in geography, or some such thing, way back in the twenties, right after the war, as he put it. I did not know anything specific about the forty-odd intervening years except that in some way he had always been connected with 'educating the young,' another one of his pet phrases. Well, if he had there was nothing very much to show for it the two years that I had known him. I certainly had failed to discover any spark of brilliance in him. As I have said earlier, however, we all had a certain fondness for him, as one might have, for instance, for one's grandfather who has quite forgotten his own name.

There he sat now, his grey head lolling on one of his shoulders. His hair was cotton white and thin so that you could see the chocolate scalp. His eyelids were heavily wrinkled and wafer thin containing in them a hint of long lashes and sparkling retinas that the years had inevitably destroyed. His dentures, even in his sleep, gave his jaw a structural rigidity so that it seemed that they were composed with pieces of girder and angle irons and not with the bone and muscle of other men. His hands were resting in his lap and between the tightly compressed lips a thin line of dried spit had formed just as it forms on the lips of a sleeping child.

I did not wake him immediately because I wanted to recover my own cool. I opened the top button of my shirt and let the fan-air breeze through it. Finally, when I was ready, I coughed several times.

The Principal opened his eyes and sat up very straight in his chair.

'Yes, Chatterjee. What is it?' He seemed to resent my intrusion. 'We have to decide a few things about the Annual Sports Day.'

'Yes?'

I started giving him the details. The grounds had to be cleared and marked; seats for the guests and the students had to be arranged; buntings and flags had to be put up, etc. All this required manpower but I was getting virtually no cooperation from Administration who commanded all the peons. The Principal yawned at this point putting me off momentarily. Above all, I went on, there was just no money to do anything decently, even half-decently. The visitors could either have a marquee above their heads or refreshments for their gullet. They couldn't have both as things stood just then. The athletes were clamouring for free sweat-shirts and shoes. They might even insist on underwears, I added for his amusement. But his mind was working in a totally different direction.

'Who is coming to inaugurate?' he interrupted suddenly.

I must confess I was completely put off. Here I was trying to save the damn thing from a total disaster and the only thing that worried him was who was coming to inaugurate. This shows you how his mind worked.

'Who is coming to inaugurate?' he asked again.

'I don't know,' I said sulkily. 'Chairman of the Governing Body should do.'

'Why not the Prime Minister?'

I was quite taken aback, to say the least.

'I doubt if she would want to come,' I said.

'Why not?'

'I imagine she has more pressing things on her hands.'

'You leave that to me,' he said raising his voice. 'I have known her since she was a little girl. I knew her father and her grandfather. I was teaching at Allahabad at the time. I met them everyday. You know that – everyday. They spent the whole night talking with me. Once Panditji put his arm around my shoulder and do you know what he said?'

I shook my head wondering what on earth had got into him. 'He said, "Ravi Babu, if we only had a thousand teachers like you, we could change the face of this country." That is what he said.'

He was leaning forward on his table and his eyes were bright with excitement.

'What do you say to that?'

'I am sure he meant it,' I said evasively.

We stared at each other in silence. He had obviously not heard me. 'To come back to this matter of the sports budget, I was wondering…'

'Those were great days,' he said. 'You were probably too young at the time. (I was sure I wasn't even born.) All of us were young then. We would meet in the maidan or on the banks of the river and the great leaders would all be there. And when they took us to prison we would sing through the night. And there wasn't a policeman who dared to…' He stopped abruptly. In the sudden silence that now descended on the little room I became aware of the soft hubbub outside. The Principal had snapped on his spectacles and was staring straight through the open window that faced him.

'I think they are disfiguring the board again. Pigs. Dogs.' I could hear the sudden crunch of his dentures as he ground his teeth.

I turned to follow his gaze. He was right. There was Chiru Pandey printing away in his best hand, copying from a scrap of paper, probably to ensure his spellings. A crowd of students surrounded him, giggling, laughing, goading him on, glancing every now and then in our direction as if their caustic gaze could pierce the thick walls and witness our humiliation.

'Aren't they, Chatterjee?'

'What, sir?'

'Aren't they writing those abominable demands again?'

'It does look like that.'

'It is like that. Now go and get the blackboard. Bring it here. I'll keep it in my room.'

'Let them write,' I said in exasperation. 'Where is the harm?'

'It is a matter of principle,' he said. 'Now go and get it. Or, I'll go myself.'

I wish now I hadn't obeyed him. But at that moment with the hot air churning around me I wanted to quickly get over my Sports Day problems and I knew that I would not be able to do so as long as this juvenile horseplay went on.

A lightning shaft of summer sun hit me in the eye as soon as I stepped out into the verandah. I stood still for a moment adjusting my vision to the blinding glare. Then I strode towards Chiru Pandey. I ploughed through the crowd of onlookers whose faces were now all turned towards me, and lifted the board off its stand, right from under Pandey's nose.

'I am sorry,' I said. 'But these are the Principal's orders. I think he is wrong but if you try to stop me I will have no choice but to break your head.'

I grinned at Chiru but his reaction was unexpected. He clenched his fist and shook it under my eyes, long enough for me to notice the livid, narrow scar that ran diagonally across the back of his hand.

'You will regret this,' he cried hysterically.

I returned with the board and dumped it in the Principal's room. I noticed that I was breathless which is quite unusual for me. I went out and brought in a glass of water draining most of it at one gulp. The Principal was much quieter when I came back. I was determined not to let him get on his hobby horse again. Before I had even sat down I said, 'And one more thing; there is no money, absolutely none, for the prizes in case you want to give any.'

I never did find the answer to that question for immediately after the *gherao* began.

The first sign of it was a slogan, shouted at the top of somebody's voice that, translated, meant, 'Death to the Principal.' This was followed by two others 'Death to Chatterjee' and 'Death to Principal and Chatterjee.'

I burst out laughing, considerably surprised at the prominence I was receiving. But the Principal had visibly paled and I pulled myself up.

'What is this?' he asked weakly.

'I'll find out,' I said, getting up.

But when I tried to step out of the room four boys faced me. 'Get back in, sir,' one of them, a tall boy in imitation American jeans and an ugly hairlip, replied. 'What on earth do you think you are doing?'

'It is a *gherao*.'

'Whatever for?'

'For the blackboard. We won't let you come out until you return us the blackboard.'

I looked at them in silence, quite at a loss.

'Where is Chiru?' I asked.

'Over there.'

He was there all right, standing on a peon's wooden stool under the meagre shade of a neem tree. A crowd of boys, about fifty strong, surrounded him. It seemed he was addressing them but half the time his face was turned in our direction, as if he was not so concerned with the speech itself as he was with its effect on us. I had half a mind to fist my way through the foursome and get hold of Pandey but something told me that wouldn't be the right thing just then. I returned to the Principal who had slumped back in his chair.

'It is a *gherao*, they say,' I reported briefly.

'I know. I heard the boys. It is abominable.'

'I think it is,' I said, feeling all of a sudden quite depressed.

It was three in the afternoon. The slogans now came in quick succession, like bids in an auction. From the volume of response the crowd besieging us appeared to be growing. Now and then there was a break in the shouting and someone made a speech the content of which, because of the distance, eluded us. At other times they burst into a spontaneous, weird chanting that, had it been night, would have convinced us that we were being carried to the grave. I had shifted my position so that I now faced the large window. I kept the other eye on the Principal. He had fallen strangely silent.

Suddenly, he said, 'We must call the police.'

I started at his suggestion. It was perhaps the mention of the word police that made me react so. I had had a happy childhood and a happier youth and I had the instinctive recoil at the word of all happy people.

'It may not be such a nice idea just yet,' I said.

'These hoodlums have to be taught a lesson.'

'I know, but calling the police may not be the right way of doing so.'

'I have never seen such ingratitude.'

I had nothing to say to that so I kept quiet.

'I work day and night for this college and this is what I get for my labours. I did not know I would live to see such a day. Abominable, abominable.'

'I am going to speak to them,' he added abruptly.

He extricated himself from his chair with some difficulty and proceeded towards the door. I followed him. The guards, who had now doubled their number, stopped us.

'Let me pass,' the Principal said.

'Not possible,' replied the tall boy smiling crookedly through his hairlip.

'Don't give me that nonsense. Move out of my way or I'll…'

'Yes,' the boy said cockily.

'Or I'll throw you out.'

'You will, eh, no doubt you will,' the boy jeered. 'Why don't you just try that, old owl?'

The Principal trembled with rage and humiliation. I wanted to pull him back into the room but he was already shouting inducing his voice to carry his indignation as far as his weak lungs would allow.

'You are my children,' he shouted, 'but I am ashamed of you.' The crowd, nearly two hundred strong now, jeered. I could feel the Principal physically cringe before this sea of derision.

'If you don't behave,' he shouted trying hopelessly to make himself heard above the din, 'if you don't I will call the police.'

'Old owl, old owl, old owl, old owl,' the crowd chanted.

He turned around abruptly and staggered back to his chair. I stood for a moment longer watching, in a befuddled, perplexed manner, this vision of jeering, gesticulating India, feeling within me a growing revulsion of all youth, there or anywhere else.

I had barely resumed my seat when shattering glass broke such equanimity as we still possessed. The Principal was leaning way forward in his chair, shrieking hoarsely, beating the table top with his clenched fists. I went behind his chair and picked up the stone. It was really a pebble, quite harmless. I was even surprised that it had shattered a window-pane.

'This must stop,' the Principal was shouting, his face utterly red. 'Call the police. I am ordering you.'

I did not quite know who was to be contacted. I picked up the phone and dialled a number that I had seen advertised in movie-theatres and which, I believed, put one in touch with the police.

A man with a squeaky voice picked up the phone almost before it had rung. I gave him the address.

'We will be over right away,' he said.

'Thanks,' I said.

'Will you tell us if any explosives are involved?'

'Explosives? No. Anyway, I don't think so.'

'Wood or petrol? Anything highly inflammable.'

'No, no, nothing of the sort.'

'You do have a fire, don't you?' the man asked doubtfully.

'Fire? Oh no. Not yet anyway. We have something… something like a *gherao*.'

'Well, we only fight fires. We have nothing to do with *gheraos*. You had better call the police.'

He hung up. I looked up the directory this time and dialled the headquarters. They gave me the number of the local station house. The Station House Officer himself picked up the phone. I told him what had happened.

'It is a *gherao*,' I concluded, hoping that the magic of the word would work. But it seemed to leave the SHO unmoved.

'You say these are students?'

'Well, yes.'

'We may not be able to do much if it is students that are involved,' he said sceptically. 'But I'll come over if you so wish.'

The phrasing of his last sentence surprised me, but I told him that was my wish and I should be grateful if he came over.

The time by my watch was twenty past five. The crowd which, during the afternoon, had had its peaks and troughs like the fluctuations of a business graph, seemed to be in a trough right now. But there was no knowing when the upswing might start. Chiru sat cross-legged, a little away from the main body of boys, holding a bottle of lemonade. An older boy, probably from a neighbouring college, had commandeered the peon's stool. It was remarkable that they had still not managed to procure a loudspeaker. The absence of this simple tool of revolutions had a bizarre effect on the proceedings giving the impression not of adversaries of substance but of kafkaesque figures, as one meets in the twilight of a nightmare, figures that only gesture and judge giving their victims a chance of neither defence nor survival. For the moment, the fifty yards that separated us represented all the agony and the hopelessness that divide one generation from another.

It was past six – the shadows in the quadrangle had begun to lengthen – when the SHO arrived. The Principal who had been silent all this while, except for the sporadic mutterings which were addressed only to himself, sat up at the entry of the SHO.

He was a thin little man with long hair and vacant, tired eyes. He was young but already he seemed to have given up life as a hopeless proposition. I was touched by the gratitude with which the Principal greeted him; I had not informed him of our conversation over the phone.

The SHO sat impassively while the Principal explained to him the situation, garnishing it here and there with his 'philosophy of life' as he called it. He explained to the SHO what was wrong with the youth of today and the country in general. According to him, all this fracas was due to a few ring leaders who were more like hoodlums than students.

'I am glad you have come,' he concluded. 'Now let us go and get hold of the ring leaders.'

He got up with a spring that I did not think he still possessed. The SHO continued to sit.

'As I explained over the phone we may not be able to do much in a case like this.'

'What do you mean, not being able to do much?' the Principal said.

'We have orders, you see, not to interfere in the internal disturbances of colleges. You are a college, aren't you?'

'You mean they could kill us and you will merely look on.'

'I didn't mean that.'

'What did you mean, then?'

'I mean we can't break them up unless they do something violent or threaten the peace of the locality.'

'Well, they threw this.'

He pushed the pebble angrily towards the officer.

The SHO hesitated.

'Well, this is rather a small stone.'

'For god's sake, officer, how big a stone do you want?' I broke in, not because I shared the Principal's fears but because I was astounded at the policeman's logic. I don't suppose he liked this intervention from a man as young and inconsequential as myself. He wrinkled his brow and turned sulky straightaway.

'Well, I'll see that they don't throw any more stones,' he said getting up.

'Thanks,' I said without bothering to hide my opinion of him.

'You will have to do something more than that,' the Principal said. 'We can't sit here all night.'

'I am afraid I can't do much else.'

'Why not?'

'I just told you.'

'That is not a good enough reason.'

Suddenly the SHO was very angry.

'I'll give you a good enough reason. The good enough reason is that if I raise my little finger against this rabble half a dozen politicians will crack down on me and have me transferred to some god-forsaken village. There is a good enough reason for you, I hope.'

He turned and disappeared. Once again we were left alone with the shadows, the terror and the hot air that the fan overhead continued to churn up quite oblivious of the drama that was being played below.

A howl went up from the boys as the SHO went out of the college gates to wait there in the growing dusk. The howl was followed by a steady spell of the weird chanting which seemed the more weird because of our awareness that we had played our last card and failed. I can't say I was much worried about myself. For one thing, I knew their anger was not directed against me. For another, I was confident I could always smash my way through their cordon leaving a score of bloody noses behind. That would be some *gherao*! I chuckled silently at the gory vision.

What was worrying me, of course, was the Principal. I found his silences puzzling. I had a feeling he was undergoing great mental and physical strain. I did not like the way he had slumped in his chair since the departure of the SHO nor the way he spasmodically rubbed his chest as if he were in pain or something. I knew he was old, but in the half-light of that April evening he seemed almost on the verge of collapse. The young perhaps have an exaggerated idea of the frailty of old people, but I certainly did not like the looks of this one.

As if to prove my doubts the Principal suddenly said, 'I want some water, Chatterjee.'

'Certainly,' I said making, out of habit, a move towards the verandah. The guard of boys stopped me.

'I need some water for the Principal.' I said.

'Not possible.'

'He is not feeling well.'

'We can't help it. He has brought it on himself.'

For a moment, I forgot myself. I raised my fist having decided to silence physically the speaker's tongue, with all its venom and cleverness. In time, however, I realized that once I did that I would be inviting them to assault us which was quite all right for me but would most likely spell something terrible for the Principal. I also remembered the tumbler that I had brought in with me a few hours earlier. As I had expected, it had some water left which I gave to the Principal.

'Some more, Chatterjee,' he gasped draining the glass, 'I am very thirsty.'

I went back to the boys. They were all looking towards the quadrangle where the tall boy could be seen in earnest discussion with Chiru Pandey. Presently, he returned rushing towards us at a trot.

'The Principal needs some water,' I said, quite determined now to get it even if it meant killing some of them. Their answer surprised me.

'He can have water,' the tall boy said. 'But Chiru will himself bring it in.'

I was silent for a minute wondering if there was a trap in it somewhere. Events of the day had certainly made me a suspicious person, which I had never been. But what trap could there be? 'All right,' I said.

A little later, Chiru walked in carrying a glass of water for the Principal and, quite unexpectedly, a lemonade for me.

He sat down across from the Principal, his head cocked arrogantly to one side. We watched the Principal empty his glass. 'What do you want?' he said weakly, addressing Chiru Pandey.

'You have seen our demands. But right now we want the blackboard back.'

'You can't have it,' the Principal said, a little fire entering his voice.

'I'll go then,' Chiru said, getting up.

'Don't be silly, Chiru,' I broke in. 'Sit down.' I took him by his wrist and forced him into the chair. My mind raced feverishly to find a solution to the tangle, but before I could propose anything I was startled by a funny noise that came from the direction of the Principal. It was like that of a small boy sniffing in the dark. I thought he wanted to say something and I waited.

'Have you no shame, Chiru?' he said shortly. 'Have you no shame?' He fell silent except for the sniffling sound that seemed to be a part of his breathing. Chiru crossed and uncrossed his diminutive legs. 'I am an old man, Chiru, a very old man. I am older than your father, perhaps even your grandfather. And you imprison me here like a common thief. You deny me even a glass of water. When we were your age we did many things but we did not deny an old man a glass of water. We learnt many things but we did not learn to rub our father's grey head into dirt.' 'I did not…' Chiru started to speak but the Principal silenced him with his hand.

Even though it was light outside, the room had considerably darkened so that each of us appeared only as a vague silhouette against the grey walls. It was as if we were strangers met in somebody's funeral, not knowing what to do with ourselves even though the funeral was over. The Principal was silent, gathering breath as it were. He had surprised me by his eloquence even though his speech was not as coherent as it may appear here.

'I am a very old man, Chiru,' he said again. 'I have a weak heart and six months in the year I have asthma so that I cannot sleep at night. If I sleep I have nightmares. My wife is dead. When she was alive she rubbed my chest at night with warm oil so I could breathe. Now she is dead and I do it by myself – as best as I can. You wouldn't know what that means, Chiru. What do you know about sleepless nights? But some day you will. Don't forget, we all grow old, Chiru. Sooner or later we all grow old.'

After a brief pause in which he sniffled some more, the Principal continued, 'I have a son but he does not answer my letters. My daughter-in-law says she does not ever want to see my face again. And all because I did not give them the ten thousand rupees which is all that I have. But they think I have a lot more stashed up somewhere. They think I lie. Some nights I wake up and I wonder what I am living for. At times I wish I were dead and done with. Through all these years I kept going because I believed I was of use in this college. I thought I was respected. Maybe it was all an illusion. But please don't take away my illusion.'

He was crying now: freely and silently. In the grey darkness I saw him take out his handkerchief – a piece of torn cloth – and dab at his tears. But the torrent seemed much too copious for the little piece of cloth and he soon gave up.

Chiru and I looked at each other. The boy was obviously embarrassed even though the glint of arrogance had not left his eyes. We looked at each other mutely considering our next move. The problem that confronted us was very different from the one that we had gathered to resolve. As if to escape his responsibility, Chiru got up to go. The Principal waved him back into his seat. He had obviously not finished. What he wanted to say, however, appeared to have got lost somewhere in the labyrinths of his enfeebled brain. It was as if an old railway engine were stuck on an incline, puffing vainly to gather steam to move ahead.

'Please don't destroy my world,' he sobbed, losing once again the thread of his thoughts. A few more minutes passed.

'When I was your age, they locked me up for five years just because I asked for freedom, not merely for myself but for you and your father and the rest of us. When I came out I had asthma and for two years I lived on gram and water because I had no money. I am not saying this to impress you or to seek your pity. I say this only to tell you who I am and where I come from. Millions like me toiled to create a world where children like you could grow in freedom. Please don't destroy that world, Chiru. Please.' Sobs choked him.

Chiru got up hurriedly and moved towards the door. Then he retraced his steps, quietly picked up the controversial blackboard and dissolved into the engulfing darkness. Wild cries of jubilation greeted him as he emerged from the room. The *gherao* was over.

I waited until the Principal had quietened down. Then I escorted him out of the room. He stopped briefly in the verandah staring vacantly at the deserted quadrangle. We moved on. At the first crossing I hailed a taxi and dropped him at his house, seeing him safely in bed.

The next day he was absent from the college. The Chairman of the Governing Body had apparently been very upset at the events of the previous day. He had advised the Principal to take leave for the week before the commencement of summer vacation. There was a strong rumour that we would have a new Principal when the college opened after the holidays.

All this is not, however, why I sat down to tell his story. I decided to do this because of a letter that I received yesterday from a complete stranger, one Dr Sharma of Mussoorie. He wrote to say that he was a neighbour of Principal Ravi Mathur who had gone up to Mussoorie to spend his summer holidays. Two days ago, while climbing the stairs to his first floor flat the Principal had collapsed because of a heart attack. He lived alone and it was some time before the people downstairs discovered him. Dr Sharma was called in but there was not much he could do. The Principal passed away half an hour later. In a brief moment of consciousness – he had been unconscious most of the time – he told the good doctor my name and requested him to write to me.

From where I sit I can see the city slumbering restlessly under a carapace of moonlight. There is a hot wind blowing in from the river carrying with it the dust of our civilization. I must admit I have found it difficult to sleep tonight. When I could not bear it any longer I decided to write all this down, hoping thereby to ease my own oppression. But the night seems endless and, I am afraid, I do not feel that young any more.

The World of the Dead

Kamleshwar

Translated from Hindi by Jai Ratan

(Quest 67: October–December 1970)

Summer had set in. A public *piau* had been set up by the well, opposite the bus stand, to serve water to the thirsty. Narain Pandit had placed four large, wide-mouthed earthen pitchers by his side. He would pour water into a pipe made from a bamboo stem. The passers-by bending under the pipe would drink from cupped hands and go their way. Most of the time one saw three or four buses standing under the nearby tamarind tree, one of them always under repair.

It was known as the Itah-Kurwali bus-stand, conspicuous for its adjoining stone masons' shops where they chiselled away at red stone slabs shaping them into millstones, pestles and mortars and the like. When off-duty, the drivers and cleaners would sleep on bus cushions under the shade of the tamarind tree or play cards.

With the departure of the last bus the bus stand had become quiet. Narain Pandit yawned uttering a 'Hey Ram!' which was distorted into 'haram'. Nisar wearing a knitted *bunian* and sitting erect on his haunches on a wooden plank was feeding beans to his goat. He suddenly stopped as Narain Pandit's 'haram' fell on his ears. 'Maharaj! Let me taste your tobacco,' he said. 'I'm told it's excellent. Give me some lime paste too if you haven't licked your box clean!'

'Keep to your own manure-like stuff,' Narain Pandit snapped. 'My tobacco is too good for your gaping mouth. Its taste will be lost on your tongue like a tiny grain between a camel's jaw!'

'What a niggard you're, Maharaj!' Nisar said. 'Your heart is no bigger than a thimble that you can't even part with a pinch of tobacco.' He hitched up his *tehmet* and started feeding his goat.

He saw the Contractor hurrying down the paved road.

'Nisar Mian, when is the bus from Kurwali due to arrive?' he asked.

Nisar cast a perfunctory glance at the Contractor and plucked a handful of beans from the dry stalk he was holding. The stalk jingled like ankle bells.

'Are you listening?' the Contractor repeated. 'When will the bus from Kurwali arrive?'

'That's the way to speak,' Nisar eyed the Contractor. 'There's no need to add Mian to my name.' Then he rolled his head as if saying to himself, how the fellow bleated all the time. 'Well, it'll be here in half an hour. It may even take an hour. Are you expecting someone?'

'Yes.' The Contractor proceeded towards the *piau*.

Nisar rubbed the goat's sides, pressed its hind legs, and making a clucking sound, thumped its thighs.

Nisar was very fond of the animal. Nur – that was the name he had given it. It walked with mincing steps, throwing its full weight on its black hoofs, like the strong-limbed Chinese women of old walking on their small, bound feet.

Conscious of its master's admiring look, Nur craned its neck with the imperious dignity of a lion. Nisar picked it up in his arms. 'Live long, my cub, my brave one!' he said in a cloying, throaty voice.

The card players under the tamarind tree had started quarrelling. It had started with Raja Ram. Driver Nathu Singh tried to collar him. 'You're a cheat!' he cried. 'On top of that you call me names. I'll suck your blood!'

'Be fair!' Raja Ram cried, taking shelter behind a hefty driver. 'I never abused you. You punched me first!'

'Don't bleat like a woman,' Nisar shouted from where he was standing. 'Be a man. Face him, if he has called you a cheat. Don't hide like a woman!'

Nisar's admonition worked. Other players intervened and they stopped quarrelling. And then they saw a bus hurtling down the road in blazing heat, leaving a cloud of dust behind.

There was a flurry of activity at the bus stand. The ice vendors hurriedly lined up their hand-carts along the road. They sprinkled water over aerated water bottles, struck chisels over slabs of ice, and wiped them clean of saw dust with ragged cloth dusters. The bus stand had come alive.

Covered with dust, the bus came lurching and stopped with a growl.

Brushing off dust from their coarse vests and holding oil-fed *lathis* at the ends of which hung small bundles of food, the villagers climbed down the bus. She was the last to get down.

'This way, Savitri!' The Contractor guided his daughter through the crowd. 'Lallua has not come with you?'

Nisar's eyes travelled to Savitri and remained fixed on her face. Buxom, tall, upturned nose, hair tightly swept back, lines of red *missi* showing between her teeth, coloured glass bangles on her flashy wrists and strong, hard hands. The cleaners whispered among themselves and gave leering looks. As she passed by, the ice-vendors shouted: 'Soda, lemonade, lime juice, iced water!'

Admiration peeped from Nisar's eyes. He took out his embroidered *kurta* from his tool box and putting it on, rolled up its sleeves. The Contractor picked up Savitri's tin box.

'You've been walking in the sun all day, Contractor Saheb,' Nisar said. 'Have some rest. Let the afternoon cool down a bit.'

Savitri looked at Nisar as she passed by him. She had a manly walk as if the loose pebbles on the road would sink into it under her firm, steady steps. Nisar smacked his lips.

The noise at the bus stand gradually died. The bus started and leaving a trail of smoke behind, stopped under the tamarind tree. Another bus took its place. Passengers started getting in. Between the honking of the horn one could hear Nisar's voice. 'Itah-Kurwali! Hurry up! Itah-Kurwali!' His throat dried up. Kicking away the mud-smeared pariah dogs, he lowered his head under the *piau*.

'Perhaps this woman is the Contractor's daughter,' Narain Pandit said, as if recalling something, while pouring water in Nisar's cupped hands. 'She was widowed three years ago. Her in-laws live in a village four miles from here.'

Nisar perked up his ears. 'She had a hand in her husband's murder,' Pandit continued in a reminiscent vein. 'But she got away scot free. This woman has guts!'

* * *

In the evening, while going to his hut with Nur, Nisar stopped short in front of the Contractor's house. A she-goat was tied under his shed. Savitri who was carrying an armful of peepul leaves to the shed stopped on seeing Nisar.

'When did the Contractor buy this goat?' Nisar asked, quailing under her gaze.

Her stance suddenly changed and a scowl appeared on her face. 'Doesn't look older than one year,' she tossed the information at him as if his question had no importance for her.

Holding the goat's jaws she pressed open her mouth to look at her teeth. Then she turned the animal's head towards Nisar. 'Yes, couldn't be more than one year, what do you think?'

Seizing the cue with alacrity, Nisar stepped forward and looked at the animal's teeth with the air of a connoisseur.

'A he-goat?' Savitri asked pointing towards Nur. 'What good is a he-goat? A butcher may give you fifty rupees for it. At the most sixty. A she-goat is preferable any time. She gives milk. If you had kept a she-goat your body would have glistened with fat.'

'A lone bird like me has no time to bother about a she-goat,' Nisar said. 'I haven't kept Nur to sell. It's a male. Keeps company with me the whole day.'

In the meanwhile, the Contractor came and they gossiped for a while. When Nisar returned to his hut, Savitri was no longer a stranger to him. 'She's one in a thousand!' Nisar said to himself. 'How freely she talks! And how she moves about! With not a care in the world.'

* * *

After putting the passengers in the bus for which he was working and receiving his commission from the bus owner, Nisar would repair to Savitri's house. Savitri was generally alone in the house, though at times he found other people too with whom she had picked up acquaintance. Tongues had started wagging about Savitri and Nisar. That afternoon Nisar was alone with Savitri. The thatched door had been drawn against the shed to keep the loo out. Wearing a thin, old dhoti, Savitri was sitting by his side stitching buttons on her vest. Nisar's eyes gleamed as they roved over her body. Then unable to hold himself any longer he put his hands over her arm. His fingers went round her arm, his two thumbs standing out like horns over her flesh. He pressed her elbow down on the ground. 'Look at your arm,' he said. It's not half as thick as

I thought. Do you call this flesh or flour dough? See how flabby it is!'

'What have you got to do with my arm?' Savitri said incensed. 'Whether it's iron or flour how does it concern you?' Then she started laughing. Nisar's eyebrows went up.

Gorakh came in, pushing aside the door. He hesitated and looked at them, embarrassed. Then he rolled his eyes and gave Nisar a mocking smile. 'Is the Contractor not at home?' he asked.

Nisar had removed his hands from Savitri's arm but his fingers were still tingling. Savitri shifted her leg. 'Nisar, give a pull to my foot,' she said, wiggling her toes. 'I seem to have pulled a muscle.' Then she jerked her foot and sat up straight.

'*Arre* Mian, that Bachchan was looking for you at the bus stand,' Gorakh said in a mocking tone. 'You give money for wrestling, don't you? He's your protégé. Well, he must pay you back in kind if not...'

Without completing his sentence he looked at Savitri from the corner of his eye and then watched the changing expression on Nisar's face. Savitri looked uneasily at Gorakh.

Nisar brushed down his *tehmet* and got up, peeved.

'What rubbish are you talking?' he barked at Gorakh. 'Bachchan is a gem of a man though he doesn't have money. A wrestler requires a lot of money to keep himself in trim. Can you show me another wrestler for miles around who is a match to him?'

'Huh!' Gorakh gave a derisive laugh. Savitri suddenly turned grave. Nisar proceeded to untie Nur.

'Now that it has been here for a week let it stay in the shed,' Savitri said. 'It'll be safe from the heat.'

While going Nisar forgot to pick up his bunian. Savitri pushed it away to one side.

'Savitri! Have you no compunction?' Gorakh said. 'How dare you touch the cast off clothes of a polluted man? Who doesn't know Nisar and his notorious cronies? He's a tout and gets a commission on the passengers he brings round to the bus. Is it an honourable job? He's a brawler and spends all his money on those boys in the wrestling pit.'

'What's that to me?' Savitri said nonchalantly. 'It doesn't affect me one way or the other how he makes his living. He comes here just to kill time. That's all there's to it.'

Gorakh could see that she was trying to cover up her discomfiture by providing him with a plausible alibi.

'Just watch and wait,' he said. There was an edge in his voice. 'Nisar won't be able to sow his wild oats for long. I'm told from next month this bus route will be taken over by the government. Private buses will go off the road. It's only a matter of one more week. Then I'll see how Nisar feeds his goat on *arhar*. He won't even have a bunian on his back.'

Savitri had other ideas about Nisar. He had been coming to her for the past many days. But he had never taken any liberties with her. Yes, he had held her arm the other day. But that was just to demonstrate his strength. He ran Nur four miles every morning. After that when he came to her panting, he said that if he didn't have sufficient exercise his body would become flabby. 'Fatness and strength are not the same thing, Savitri.' He was right, of course.

Sitting at the bus stand, Nisar was lost in his own thoughts. He went to Savitri just to while away the time. She was clever, vivacious, and he liked to look at her firm body. What good were those wretched drivers and cleaners? He didn't like their company. They drank and took opium to stimulate strength. Their strength drained away as the effect of the intoxicant wore off. It was like a stream overflowing its banks in the rainy season and then drying up when the rains were gone. After he had been to the wrestling pit and finished with the bus, he had the whole day to himself. What was wrong about spending the rest of the day with Savitri? What a large hearted woman she was! That was one reason why so many people gathered in her shed. Then he remembered Nur and thought that he would bring it back from Savitri's shed. It must be missing him.

Suddenly he heard a noise in the distance. The tyres hissed over the stones on the road and a cloud of dust blinded his eyes. A bus sped past him etching the pattern of the tyres on the road. The bus stopped and out came Makhan Lal, the bus owner. People gathered round him. They learned that in spite of his ceaseless efforts the government had not agreed to leave that route to the private operators. From the first of the next month government buses would ply on that route. He was in a hurry to get a private carrier's permit from the Transport Department at Lucknow. He may be able to engage one or two drivers. The rest would have to fend for themselves.

Gloomy news, Nisar's last hope was also gone. Pulling out a bus cushion from a cabin he stretched himself on it, feeling distraught and listless. He had a slight head-ache. His thoughts turned to

Savitri. No, he was alone in the world and would have to plough a lonely furrow in future too. And as for Gorakh – he had always seen him hob-nobbing with Savitri. How he put on airs! As if he had a hold over her. For all he knew, she might even be submitting to his carnal desires. What else could you expect from a woman? A woman was a woman even if she had a man's strength.

He fell asleep. When he woke up the sun had gone down and the bus stop was steeped in silence. A lantern hung on a pole and under its dim light the knots of the pole shone like the skin of a python. Some cleaners had spread their beddings on the roofs of the buses and were preparing to sleep.

* * *

Nisar proceeded towards Savitri's house to take away Nur with him. When he came near the shed he was confronted with a strange sight. A couple of policemen were carrying out a search in Savitri's house. Things lay about in confusion. The Contractor, his hand resting against his waist, was leaning against a pillar with bowed head, while Savitri was standing by, her alert eyes darting all over the room. 'Go ahead, search every nook and corner,' she said again and again. 'But mind you, my things should not be damaged. Be careful, Havaldar Saheb, that box contains my glass bangles!'

People had collected outside the house, excitedly watching the goings-on. At last, the policemen took away the Contractor to the police station. Nisar quietly un-tethered Nur from the shed, thinking that in the morning he would find from Savitri herself the cause of this rumpus.

He tied Nur to the leg of his cot and tried to sleep. Then he realised that the month would be over in another five days. What would he do after that? What would he live on? How would he feed Nur? There was no hope of getting any sort of work in that town. As he lay on his cot, he turned Nur's head towards him and rubbing its mouth against his cheek held it against his neck. He fell asleep after some time.

* * *

The morning had far advanced. Putting his things in a small bundle and holding Nur by the rope he proceeded towards Savitri's house.

'Didn't you take out Nur for its morning run?' Savitri asked. 'Or are you thinking of fattening it up? It'll fetch a better price.'

Nisar was cut to the quick. But he controlled himself.

'I'm going to Karimganj by the first bus,' he said. 'The chances of finding work here are very slender. My uncle lives in Karimganj. He may be able to find some work for me. I'll return in two or three days. Look after Nur in my absence.' He tied Nur to the thatched door.

'Still there's a lot of time for the bus,' Savitri gave him a perfunctory look. 'Where is the hurry?'

'No, the bus leaves quite early,' Nisar said. 'If I miss it my whole day will be spoiled.' Taking big strides he turned towards the *pucca* road. Craning its neck, Nur was watching him innocently.

Nisar was gone for ten days. From Karimganj he went to a neighbouring village, famous for its *tazias*. The *tazias* were in great demand from far and near and work went on round the year. Nisar hoped to find some work there.

On his way back, the ramshackle *ekka* gave him so many jolts that every joint of his body seemed to have come loose. He was taken aback as he got down from the *ekka* at the bus stand. He knew what was coming but he was not prepared for what he saw. The whole scene had changed. Shining government buses were lined up at the bus stand and the drivers and the cleaners were strutting about, wearing khaki uniforms and boat-shaped caps. A sherbet shop run by the refugees had come up alongside the *piau*. Colourful festoons hung across a tin shed with a few more blue coloured buses standing under its roof. On one side lay a table and chair. A new era seemed to have begun.

Nisar was shocked. Where were they all gone? Those familiar, smiling faces which used to raise such glorious squabbles at the bus stand? And those card players under the tamarind tree? Also gone were the buses which used to growl and howl before they decided to move. The new buses were no doubt beautiful and sleek to look at. But they had deprived Nisar of his bread. His lips curled up with contempt. No, he would have nothing to do with these buses, much less travel in them. Hoping that Savitri's congenial company may give him some relief, he decided to go to her house.

He stopped in his tracks and looked up again. Yes, the house was locked. He stood stock-still for a moment and then turned to the nearby shop. 'Sonu, do you know anything about Savitri?' he asked the shopkeeper.

'Savitri?' Sonu gave Nisar a quizzical look. 'I wish I knew. She was a clever woman. She has brought a bad name to the whole place. Did you ever hear of opium being pedalled in this part of the country?'

'Opium?' Nisar looked at him confused. 'Tell me what happened. Don't talk in riddles.'

'Yes, she used to sell opium,' the shopkeeper said. 'The police were trying to unearth the racket. They got a clue ten days ago and searched her house. But nothing incriminating was found. The police warned the Contractor and let him go. Day before yesterday they again raided her house. This time they were able to lay their hands on a quarter seer of opium. Gorakh used to bring the opium while Savitri sold it. The poor Contractor is now in the police lockup. But Savitri slipped away with Gorakh.'

Nisar's strength suddenly away from his body. Spreading out his legs he sat down on the edge of the well.

'Do you know anything about my goat?' he asked getting over the initial shock. 'Has she taken it away with her or left it with someone?'

'Oh, no, she sold away the goat. She sold it to Zahid, the butcher, at a throw away price. She was in such desperate hurry, you know. Zahid was the only customer. She must have been badly in need of money.'

Nasir's blood became thin like water. His teeth were clenched, his nostrils flared. His hand went under the fold of his *tehmet* and came out with a wad of dog-eared notes. He counted the notes. Fifty.

Bewildered, he went to Zahid butcher's shop. Pushing aside the reed curtain he glared at Zahid.

'For how much has she sold you my Nur?' he asked.

'Twenty-five! But Nisar bhai, I bought it only after she had assured me that you had sold it to her. Allah is my witness. I'm telling you the truth.'

'Stop blabbing!' Nisar cried. 'Give me my goat. I must have it at once.' Nisar looked hard at Zahid. The butcher wilted under his gaze.

'But...' he said in a cringing voice. 'But I killed the goat this morning. What more can I say? It's hanging there.' He suddenly fell silent.

Molten lead seemed to be coursing through Nisar's vein. His hand slipped down the reed curtain. Nur, his companion of day and night, was helplessly hanging upside down from an iron hook.

His strength was gone. With great difficulty he walked up to the bus stand. The engines of the new buses were purring gently. They seemed to lack power of the engines of the old private buses. The drivers and cleaners seemed to be dragging their feet like lifeless men.

He wondered if he had left all the gaiety and excitement of life behind and was now stepping into the world of the dead.

Should he go back to Karimganj and make *tazias*? *Tazias* in front of which walked a procession of mourners, beating their breasts and singing elegies, and ending up in front of the graveyard.

His heart was filled with contempt. No, not for him the world of the dead. He must have the thrills and excitement of the living and rub shoulders with the crowd.

Kicking up dust with his feet he made for the village.

The Discovery of Telenapota

Premendra Mitra
Translated from Bengali by Kironmoy Raha

(Ten Years of Quest, Manaktalas, Bombay 1966,
eds. Abu Sayeed Ayyub and Amlan Datta)

When Saturn and Mars come together, you too, may discover Telenapota. That is, when you, an indifferent angler – never had a catch larger than a "punti" – find, after weeks of slogging, a couple of days' leisure; and someone comes and tempts you, saying that somewhere there is a magical pool in which the world's most simple-minded fish are anxiously waiting to swallow any bait – well, you are already on your way to discover Telenapota.

Discovering Telenapota, however, is not as easy as all that. Late in the afternoon you will have to board a bus packed to its roof with men and things. Once inside, you will be pushed about by fellow passengers, get drenched in sweat and coated with dust. After two hours of such clammy misery you will be suddenly dropped, without any warning.

Before you collect your wits and look around, you will find that the bus is disappearing over a bridge across the low swampy puddle in front. The thick jungle around is dark, as if night was already there, though the sun has still not set. The air is damp and stifling, and the place is eerily quiet. There is not a soul in sight. Even the birds have left the place, as if in fright. Your mind will be filled with strange fancies and you will imagine that from out of the marshy morass below some sinister curse is slowly rearing its ugly head.

Leaving the main road and getting to the side of the swamp, you will find that someone has cut a narrow muddy path into the jungle. But even that unformed path gets lost amongst the thick groves of bamboo and big, leafy trees.

To discover Telenapota you should have a couple of friends with you. You, yourself, will be going there for fishing, but what induced your two friends to go, you will not be able to tell.

Your most immediate problem will be mosquitoes. They will come in hordes and you will try to drive them away by stamping your feet on the ground. Not quite knowing what to do next, the three of you will stand there and look enquiringly at one another's faces. Soon it will grow quite dark, and you will not be able to see clearly the faces of your companions. The buzz of the mosquitoes will become louder and louder and their attacks more insistent. You will start wondering whether you should not try to get to the main road and catch a bus back.

Just then, a weird noise will startle you. It will seem to originate at the point where the mud track gets lost in the jungle. To your startled nerves, it will appear to be an inhuman cry forced out by someone wringing the dumb wood around. You will become tense, with expectation and waiting. Mercifully, you will not have to wait for long. Presently, you will see, through the darkness, the gentle swaying of a faint light and a bullock cart will come out of the wood with a slow, rocking gait.

It is a tiny cart and the bullocks are no bigger. You will wonder whether they did not come out of Lilliput. However, you will not wonder for long and the three of you will get inside the covered awning. The space available is small, and you will have some difficulty in accommodating three pairs of arms and legs where there is room for only one; but you will manage it.

The cart will return along the path it had come. The wall of darkness in front of you will appear impenetrable. But, much to your surprise, the thick dark jungle will yield a narrow tunnel-like passage, a little at a time, for the cart to pass. The bullocks will go unhurriedly forward, as if creating with each step the path they slowly thread.

For a while, you will be acutely bothered by having to sit anyhow in the narrow space available. Gradually, however, your limbs will get benumbed. A feeling of being drowned in the deep darkness around will fill you. You will feel that you have left the world you knew far behind and have entered another that was full of mists and empty of all feeling. Time will appear to have stopped.

You will have no idea how long you have had this feeling. Suddenly a racket of beating drums will jerk you into a wide wakefulness. You will find that the driver of the cart is furiously beating an empty can. You will also see that the stars have come out.

You will ask what the matter was. The driver will reply, most casually, "Oh, just to drive those damned tigers away." You will be about to ask how it is possible to drive tigers away by just raising a racket, when he will add reassuringly, "No, not real tigers. Only panthers. Ah, yes. Unless they are really hungry, a can and a stick are all you need to keep them at a safe distance."

Tigers! Within thirty miles of the big city! Before you have had time to wonder about it, the cart will have crossed a wide moor. The late moon will have, meanwhile, arisen. By its pale light you will see that you were passing through an area full of ruins of deserted palaces and mansions. A solitary column here, a broken arch there, a wall of a courtyard and a portion of a temple further on – there they will stand like litigants, waiting in futile hope, for the recording of some evidence in the court of Time.

You will try to sit up and a tingling sensation will go all over your body. Once again, you will be overwhelmed with your former feeling of having left the world of the living behind and of having entered a misty world peopled only by memories.

You will have no idea how far gone the night was then. Indeed, it will seem to you that night never ends here and everything lies submerged in a stillness that has no beginning and no end. The whole thing will remind you of those specimens of extinct animals they keep, immersed in acid bottles, in museums.

After a few turns the cart will stop. You will collect your benumbed limbs and get down, one by one – stiff, like wooden dolls. The first thing you will notice is the strong rancid smell. You will guess – rightly – that the stink is of rotting leaves in the pond right in front of you. By its side, stand the ruined remains of a big mansion. With its caved in roofs, fallen sides and frameless windows, it stands there like the battlements of a fort, in guard against the moon.

You will learn that you will have to spend the night in this house. You will find for yourself a habitable room – comparatively speaking, that is. From somewhere the cart driver will fetch a broken lantern and a jug of water. It will seem to you that ages must have passed since a pair of human feet stepped into the room. Someone had tried to clear the room and rid it of the accumulated dust and dirt, but not very successfully. The musty stench will show that it was done long ago and was even then not welcomed by whatever spirit it was that lived there. On the slightest movement, little bits of plaster and mortar will fall on you from the walls and the roof, like curses from the angry spirit. A few bats will be all the time shrilly questioning your right to be there for the night.

Of your two companions one is a toper and the other would have slept through a storm. You will have hardly spread your bed when the latter will fall upon his and start snoring, and the other begin to seek the consolation of the bottle.

The night will wear on. Soot will slowly accumulate on the glass of the broken lantern and soon it will shut the light out wholly. As if in response to some mysterious broadcast, all the adult and able-bodied mosquitoes of the region will come out to greet you. If you are a knowledgeable person, you will know from the distinctive manner in which they sit on the walls and on you that they belong to the blue-blooded aristocracy of mosquitoes – the anopheles variety, the carrier of malaria. By then, both your companions will have become oblivious, for different reasons, of their surroundings.

It will be oppressively hot. Taking the electric torch with you, you will try to escape from it into the terrace. At each step, the danger of a brick of the stairs giving way will try to dissuade you from climbing further. But something will draw you on irresistibly. Ignoring the danger of falling down, you will keep on and finally get to the top.

On arrival, you will find that at most of the places the parapet has come off in bits. Into every crack and hole in the walls and the roof, small trees have taken firm root. It will seem as though they were fifth columnists, already there, making things easy for the inexorably advancing jungle.

And yet, by the pale light of the declining moon everything will appear transformed and beautiful. You will fancy that if only you looked long enough, you could find in which of the secret chambers of this sleep-drenched palace, the captive princess has been sleeping through the ages with the golden and the silver wands beside her.

Even as you will be wondering about this, you will notice a faint light in one of the windows of what you had taken to be a totally ruined house, across the street. After a while a mysterious shadow of a figure will come and stand by the window blocking the light. Who could she be? Why should she be awake when everyone else was asleep? Try as you may, you will not be able to know the answers. Looking after a brief moment, you will see that the figure was no longer there and the faint light had also gone out. Was it real, or did you fancy the whole thing? It will seem to you that from the bottomless depth of this world of sleep, a dream bubble had floated silently up for a moment into the world of the living and had as silently melted away.

After a while, you will come down the stairs carefully and fall asleep by the side of your companions.

Getting up, you will be surprised to find morning there already and the place full of the chatter of birds.

You will not forget what you had primarily come here for. Before long you will complete your preparations and find yourself a seat on one of the broken moss-covered steps by the pond. You will throw your line into its greenish waters and wait patiently.

The day will wear on. A kingfisher from the bent branch of the tree across the tank will swoop down, now and again, in a flash of colour. Each time it will return to its perch with the successful catch and, as if to ridicule you, will burst into a frenzy of babble: giving you quite a turn, a fat and long snake will come out of some crack in the steps and get unhurriedly into the water: it will swim across and get out on the other side: two grasshoppers, their glass-like wings fluttering, will go on trying to land on the float of your line: a dove will call intermittently: its lazy notes will fill you with lassitude and your mind will wander.

You will be startled out of your mood of reverie by the sudden sound of ripples. The still water is no longer still and you will find your float gently rocking. Looking sideways, you will find a woman pushing away the floating weeds and filling up her shiny brass pitcher. There is curiosity in her eyes and her movements are easy and free from any awkwardness. She will look straight at you and at your line. She will then pick up her pitcher and turn away.

You will not be able to guess her age. Looking at her face – calm, reserved and sad, you will think that she had already traversed the pitiless road of life; but if you looked at the thin unnourished lines of her body, you will think that she had never grown out of her girlhood.

Even as she is going away, she will turn and say, somewhat suddenly, "What are you waiting for? Pull hard." Her voice is so mellow and sweet that you will not think it odd that she – a stranger – should have spoken unbidden to you like that. Only the suddenness of it will make you flustered and when, eventually you get the hook out, you will see that the bait is no longer there. You will feel a bit of a fool and will not be able to help looking at her. She will also look at you and then turn and go away with slow, unhurried steps. As she is going, you will think that you saw the suggestion of a bright smile light up her sad and peaceful face.

After this, nothing will disturb the loneliness of the place. The kingfisher, perhaps realizing the uselessness of trying to shame you, will have flown away. Even the fish will ignore you, apparently in contempt for your angling skill. Once again, you will have a feeling that the happening of a moment ago was not real at all. How could there ever be a woman like that in this land of sleep?

After sometime, disappointed, you will collect your tackle and start back. On returning, you will find that news of your fishing skill has reached the ears of your friends. Slightly peeved at their cracks, you will ask how they came to know about it.

'Know about it?' the toper will reply. 'Why, Jamini saw it just now with her own eyes.' Feeling curious you will ask who Jamini was. You will learn that she was the person you had seen at the pond and that she was distantly related to him. You will also learn that you were having your lunch at her place.

Looking at the falling ruins across the street – wherein the shadowy figure had caused you such wonderment the night before – its wretched condition will give you something of a shock. You could not have imagined that the veil of night, now stripped rudely by the harsh light of day, could have concealed a nakedness so ugly. You will be surprised to learn that that was where Jamini lived.

It will be to one of the rooms in that house that you will go for your lunch. It will be a simple meal and Jamini herself will serve it. As you had noticed before, there was nothing awkward or ungainly about her demeanour. Looking at her now at such close quarters, you will also be struck by the sad immobility of her face. It was as though all the mute agony of this forgotten and deserted place had cast its shadows across her face. Her eyes will seem to be submerged in a sea of infinite tiredness. It will seem to you that one of these days she herself will dissolve slowly, very slowly, into these ruins.

You will notice that even while she was serving, Jamini seemed to have something on her mind. Maybe, you will also hear an occasional faint voice calling from a room upstairs. Every now and then Jamini will leave the room rather hurriedly. Each time she returned, the shadow of suffering in her face will appear to have deepened and her eyes will betray a helpless anxiety.

After finishing your meal, you will sit down to rest awhile. Jamini will hesitate a few times, and then call out, in desperation from the other side of the door, "Manida, could you please come over here once?" Manida is the toper. He will go to the door, and the conversation that will follow, will be loud enough for you to overhear.

Jamini's voice is greatly troubled. "Mother is being troublesome again. Ever since she learnt that you were coming with your friends, she has become quite unmanageable."

Mani will reply somewhat irritably, "Bother! I suppose it is that old notion of hers? She believes Niranjan is here?"

"Yes. She goes on repeating – 'I know he is here. He hasn't come up to see me only because he is embarrassed. Go, fetch him. Why are you keeping things from me?' – Manida, I really don't know what to do. Ever since she became blind she has become so irritable. She won't listen to anything. Flies off the handle all the time. I am sometimes frightened that she will die in one of her fits."

"What a mess! If only she had her eyes, I could have shown her that Niranjan was not here with me now."

The shout of the shrill, angry ghost of a voice from upstairs will be clearly audible this time. Jamini will say in a pleading voice, "Do please come with me once, Manida – see if you can make her understand."

"All right. You get along. I'll be there."

Mani will get back to the room muttering to himself. "Why in heaven's name doesn't this old crackpot die? She can't see, she can't use her limbs, and yet she is determined not to die."

You will ask him what the matter was. Mani will reply in an annoyed tone, "Matter? Oh, nothing very much. Years ago, she had fixed Jamini's marriage with Niranjan – the son of a distant cousin of hers. The last time the chap was here, was about four years ago. He told her then that as soon as he returned from abroad he would come and marry Jamini. And ever since she has been waiting."

"Hasn't Niranjan returned?" You will ask.

"Why, of course not. How should he return when he never went at all? Of course, he was lying. He had to, seeing that the old ruin wouldn't let him go. And why should he bother to marry this rag-picker's daughter. Oh, yes! He is married all right and rearing a family. But who's to tell her all this? She won't believe you, and if she did she will straightaway die of shock. Who's going to take that risk anyway?"

"Does Jamini know about Niranjan?"

"Oh, yes. But she can't speak about it to her. Well, let me go and get it over." Mani will turn to go.

Almost without being conscious of it, you will also get up at the same moment and say, "Just a second. I'll come with you."

"You? With me?" Mani will wheel round, plainly surprised.

"Yes. Do you mind?"

"No, of course not," Mani will reply, a trifle taken aback, and proceed to show you the way.

After you had ascended the dark and broken stairs, you will get into a room that looked more like an underground tunnel than a room above. There was only one window and that too was shut. Coming from outside, at first everything will look blurred to you. After a while you will see that in a large, decrepit wooden cot a shrivelled up woman, wrapped in a torn rag, lay still. By the side of the cot Jamini stood motionless like a statue.

At the sound of your footsteps, the bag of bones will show signs of animation. "Niranjan? My child! So you are here at last! Could spare a thought at last for your poor wreck of an aunt! You know, I have been keeping death at bay, hoping that you'll be here some day. You won't slip away again like last time?"

Mani will be on the point of saying something but, interrupting him, you will suddenly blurt out, "No, Auntie, I promise you I won't."

You will not look up, but you will feel the bewilderment of Mani and the stunned surprise that will break out in Jamini's immobile face. You could not have looked up even if you wanted to. Your eyes will be riveted to the sockets of the old woman's sightless eyes. It will seem to you that two tongues of darkness issued from those empty sockets and licked every inch of your body -- to test, to know. You will feel that those few still moments were dropping like dewdrops into the ocean of time.

You will hear the old woman saying, "My son, I knew you would come. That is why I am still living in this house of death – counting the days." The effort of speaking so many words will leave her panting. You will look up at Jamini. You will fancy that somewhere, behind the steely mask of her face, something was slowly melting away, and it will not be long before the foundation of a vow – a vow made up of boundless despair, a vow taken against life and fate – will give way.

The old woman will speak again. "I am sure Jamini will make you happy, my son. She surely will. There's none like her, even though

I, her mother, say it. I am old and ill and out of my senses most of the time. I try her beyond endurance. But does she snap back? No, not once. This graveyard of a place – you search ten houses and you won't find a man – it's only the likes of me, more dead than alive, that you'll find here – and here, Jamini, a slip of a girl, carries on and manages everything."

Even though you will want to, you will dare not lift your eyes lest someone might discover the tears that have been welling there. Sighing, the old woman will say, "Promise me you will marry Jamini. If I do not have your promise I will know no peace even in death."

Your voice will have become nearly choked. You will be able merely to say, "I promise you. I will not fail you."

Soon it will be afternoon. The bullock cart will appear once again to take you back. One by one, the three of you will get inside. As it leaves, Jamini will look at you with those sad eyes of hers and merely remark, "You are forgetting your fishing tackle." You will smile and reply, "Never mind! Let them be. I missed the fish this time but they won't escape me the next."

Jamini will not turn her gaze away. Her eyes, you will see, were lit up with a smile that was full of gratitude and tenderness. Like the white clouds, of autumn, it will float across your mind and suffuse it with an ineffable gladness.

The cart will rattle along. The lack of space will not bother you this time; nor will the monotonous creak of the moving wheels sound harsh. Your friends will, perhaps, discuss how a hundred years ago, malaria, like a relentless flood, carried off Telenapota and left it here, in this forgotten borderland of the world of the living. You will not be listening, for your mind will be elsewhere. You will have ears only for your own heartbeats and hear in them the same words, echoed over and over again – "I will come back, I will come back."

Even after you reach the city – with its hurrying crowds and harsh lights – the memory of Telenapota will be bright in your mind like a shining star – distant yet intimate. A few days will pass with their petty vexations and troubles. If, in your mind, a slight mist had begun to form, you will not be aware of it. Then, just when you have overcome the obstacles and start preparing to return to Telenapota, you will, suddenly, feel the shivering touch of the oncoming fever. Soon the headache and the fever will be on you and you will lie down with a lot of blankets. The thermometer will register 105°F and the last thing you will hear, before falling unconscious, will be the doctor saying, "Well, well! Where did we pick up this malaria?"

It will be days before, weak and exhausted, you will be able to come out of the house and sit in the sun. Meanwhile, unknown to yourself, your mind will have undergone many changes. Telenapota will have become an indistinct dream, like the memory of a star that has set. Was there ever such a place as Telenapota? You will not seem to know. The face that was hard and serene, and the eyes that were far away and sad – were they real? Or, were they, like the shadows of Telenapota's ruins, creatures of the misty realm of your imagination?

Telenapota, discovered for one brief moment, will be lost again in the timeless immensity of night.

The Moon Had to be Mended

Kiran Nagarkar

(Quest 62: July-September 1969)

She died this morning. Six o'clock and she had rolled up her mattress. It was chill. She tightened her dirty purple sari around her. Not much help that. She missed wearing a blouse at such times. Eighteen years since he died and they stripped the blouse off her. It had felt funny then. Almost naked. All the more so because the hair had been completely shaved from her head. It was as if her body played bo-beep with her. She would tug at her sari constantly, pull it into odd places. That only made things worse. But not any longer. By the time the habit had taken effect she didn't feel exposed. Unless in winters and that was physically. Besides her hair had grown again, long enough for her to tie a tiny bun just above the nape of her neck. It was against the custom but she hated to give her head to the hands and raw blade of a barber.

She took the brass pot of water and went out of the house to rinse her mouth. No teeth. Hardened gums and caving cheeks. If she lived another year they would lie against each other. She swallowed the last mouthful and came inside. She would have to sit on her haunches if she wanted to tie the bamboos. That was going to be painful. But it had to be done and this was the last time she would have to bend. She placed the palms of her hands on her knees, brought her body forward slightly and dropped herself on to the ground as she released her breath. She kept the two, long bamboos a foot and a half from each other. That would be enough to fit her in comfortably. With strings of coir she fastened the four smaller sticks at right angles to the other two. The coir burnt into her fingers as she strained to make the joints firm. They would have to bear the brunt of the burden and however miniature she was, still, a dead woman must weigh a lot. She looked around after she had made sure that they would hold under pressure. There wasn't anything else to be done. Holding her bier by the two inner horizontal bars she hefted it up and out of the door. Then beyond the porch into the open and down on the yellow-brown earth. A cut sun lay on the horizon. He was edging up rapidly. She didn't have much time. There were the ear-rings to be dug out of the floor yet. She went back into the hut, picked up the shovel and broke down the earthen stove in the corner of the rear wall. Three strokes below the earth and she had the pierced nuggets on the flat of the shovel. She had worn them since she was twelve. When she was married. They had come as part of her dowry. Heavy and deformed, she had loved them. They had tugged at her ears till their lobes had descended to her neck. Her husband had died and she was made to part with all her jewellery. She didn't mind the rest of it being taken away from her to be burnt on her husband's pyre. The ear-rings she had quietly stowed into the fat cylindrical fold of her sari at her stomach. Then after everyone had left she buried them into a hollow under the stove.

She came out of the hut and placed the ear-rings next to the stretcher. They would pay for the wood which was to burn her. The sun was fully out now. She had a quick look at the potter's wheel and the forge. They looked lost without work. To die without the moon, she thought. In darkness there is no forgiveness. Then she came back and closing her eyes lay down on her bier.

Rangappa shifted the stick from his left hand to the right behind his back and then continued a thin gritty scratch on the dry earth. He stopped abruptly and held on to his breath when he saw something unfamiliar in front of the old woman's house. It didn't move. He shu-shu-ed it. It didn't move. He went nearer, the stick no longer trailing on the ground. He got within two yards of her and stood still. Holding the stick under his armpit he watched her intently out of the corner of his eye. He wasn't sure that she wasn't watching him back in spite of her closed eyes. He knew she couldn't lie down for long without changing her side. Who could sleep so soundly on one's back on a bare bamboo scaffolding? Then he got bored, took two steps forward, thought about it for a moment and prodded the stick lightly into the side of her left foot. He recoiled instead of her. She hadn't moved. The depressed sole filled back into the momentary hollow.

He wasn't going to move. He was certain. He lifted up the end of his dirty shirt and started walking. Slowly a trickle of piss came forth. He had bordered her with an unsteady wet line from the right hand to the left thigh when it stopped. He would have to wait for an hour at least to join up the two ends. He decided to stick around. He sat on her left provoking dust from the hardened ground with the end of his stick.

He was still at it when his father came over. He looked at the old woman on the stretcher and turned to his son. 'What are you doing here?'

'Nothing.'

'Get back home, son.'

Rangappa took the dirty end of his shirt and began to chew it.

'You heard me, didn't you?' He placed his foot below Rangappa's seat and lifted him slightly off the ground.

'I want to wait.'

'For what?'

Rangappa picked up his stick and walked away. His father reluctantly brought his eyes to look at her. She was dead, wasn't she? There was no doubt about it. It was high time she died. Eighty-three years and eighteen after your husband's death is a long time to live. He settled down on the ground where his son had squatted. He would have to wait for the others to come.

The moon broke last night. A slight ping. She had been sleeping. A sped cobweb coursing through it. The thin disk of diaphanous mica cracking like badly baked old china. Something had gone wrong with the temperature. Not enough heat most probably. A shivered moon holding on to its wholeness for a moment. Then the gauze in the moon disintegrated and the pieces began to huskily descend down. Snowfall of moon. She went dumb with the ache of a breaking moon. She knew that she alone was witness to it. She would have to get up. There would be millions of bits, scattered God knows where. She was so old now and she couldn't see properly. A rain of silvery husk still poured from the sky. The pot was fast diminishing along with its contents. How much of it there was to the moon. Alone, standing palely incandescent and now to disappear. A forsaken night caught in the malt of tar. On feet of sleep, stalking noiseless. The blind man who gouges eyes walks here. She felt the tinkle of crystal dread spread with her. A smudged cry rose in her pit but shied of coming forth. At least she had her wheel. She must light the forge early tomorrow and soften the adhesive clay. She would have to be sparse with it. There was very little left with her. It was going to be difficult. She had always been such a stickler for perfection. She wouldn't want a single crack to be visible. But her fingers didn't bend too well these days. And you needed delicate fingers. But that was irrelevant. She must get up now. To be alone in a task was a mission.

They were coming single file. Eight of them. The shot streaks from the gold earrings on the ground turned the middle two brass-yellow from where he saw them. He got up when the oldest man from the village approached him.

'You were here when it happened?'

'No.'

'How did you find out?'

'I came looking for my son.'

'Who told him about it?'

'Nobody. He wandered here dragging his stick.'

'Did he touch her?'

'No.'

'How do you know?'

'I asked him.'

'Does he bear a true tongue?'

'Yes.'

'How long have you been waiting?'

'Since the sun shone on my scrotum.'

'Two hours is a heavy time to be alone with a dead woman.' He walked to the head of the old woman, brushed the absent dust on the ground with his bare feet and turned to the others.

'An old woman, four score and three years old. Nine years my senior. She died between when last seen alive by somebody and this morning when Rangappa, this man's son, saw her dead. She outlived her husband eighteen years. Eighteen summers she ran his potter's circle without him. A barren woman, eighteen winters to each new pot she gave the hollow of her palm while all his life she froze the seed within him. Eighteen monsoons she blew her narrow breath into the forge for the flame to lash and lick the jug and the saucer into shape when all his life he rained upon her but never did she put a period to her cycle to receive him.'

He stopped and scanned them individually. Ebony and teak faces. His eyes and theirs. They had nothing to say to each other. They watched their feet in silence. The old man lifted his unwashed, yellowing *lungi* above his knees and tucked the lowered of it at his waist. Leaning heavily on his staff he lowered himself to the ground. A yard and a half between him and the old woman dead on the bamboo. His tired eyes stared patiently at her. The other men sat around and behind him in an uneven semi-circle. It must have been past two o'clock. The sun had set up a blur above her. The men felt it shimmering on their backs while their heads dropped in tepid sleep from their necks.

Rangappa's father saw them first when he lifted his hand to let it hang down his side. They had risen from silence. All eleven of them. Like omens they perched dumb on the tree next to the potter's wheel, diffusing their presence and an aura of expectation. The men waited in silent premonition for the vultures to take over. The old woman's toes wilted in the heat. The birds stood motionless in their places. The sky had emptied itself of all subtleties. The dead woman kept roasting, an unforgiving blue above and the earth erupting into heat.

Five minutes before the sun plunged below the horizon the men relaxed. The birds had decided to come down. They must have had a leader. The rest followed him. He landed gently away from the old woman's breast, on her right. The others stood in a line parallel to her, extending down her legs. For a moment or two in that hour of darkness, she turned visible as darkness. Where the body had scooped out a hollow, a continuum of dark presented itself. The men and the birds were sucked into a hush. A precipitate doubt blinked on them. The first of the vultures took a step forward. Lifted his head and sent his eyes searching the black. She was there. He felt shaken and turned back.

Night, eleven birds with food on their minds, the old woman, a group of men and now the first sour odour of a body rotting. It grew colder and colder. The old woman tautened and the stink congealed around her. It whipped up the appetite of the birds. The men bore it patiently. At midnight they turned Rangappa's father out of the village. He was asked to take his family with him. They were forbidden to return.

Next morning it was again day. The old woman had distorted during the night. Her left leg had warped and was fretting to get out of the stretcher. A vehement sun was out in the sky. She visibly stiffened under it. Each joint and limb protested viciously as the sun came to focus itself directly above it. The heat hissed everywhere and the putrid stench issuing from the old woman grew unbearable. It was becoming difficult to breathe. One of the birds, the third from the leader, grew faint and dropped in a thud to the ground. His throat worked up and down nervously. Gradually his entire body picked up the rhythm. His feet twitched awkwardly and gaped at the sky. With a convulsive spasm he drew into himself. The tremor lasted for five minutes. He seemed to have lost all volition over himself. When the fit released him he was flung forward violently. His head dashed very near the old woman's right foot. He lay panting heavily for some time, his eyes a glassy stare. When the focus returned to them, they fixed themselves on the soft of the arch in her right foot. Painfully, without moving his eyes he sat up once again. He rocked unsteadily in the heat and the hunger. Then suddenly, without warning and unknown to himself, he lunged at the old woman. But not fast enough. The others had anticipated him. Within a few moments he was in shreds. The leader caught him by the neck in his beak and dropped him far away on the mud road. Soon, the birds resumed their original positions. The men had watched, dazed. The birds maintained their silence, still distant, still wailing.

Towards evening the weather turned dirty. The sky was clogged with dark clouds. They had jostled the sun out. An impending sky hung over the land. The air had nowhere to escape. The men and the birds turned a sick green breathing the poison from the old woman.

And all night long it rained. The men went under the roof of the verandah. The birds waited in the open. For hours the parched earth refused to let in the water. Then with a sibilant rush the water found its way into the innards of the earth. The ear-rings stubbornly held on to the ground. They disappeared from time to time in the muck but the rain would nose them out and in the dimness of the night a tarnished glow would accrue to them. The old woman soaked and swelled throughout the night. By the time it stopped pouring, the stink from her had disappeared.

On the morning of the third day she was wedged between the end bamboos of the stretcher. Only the tip of her head and her heels pressed on the bamboo frame. The dead woman kept raising herself in the stomach, the arch getting rigidly angular. The men were out again. The birds and the men stared at each other in rising animosity from under the triangle that she formed with the ground. As the sun rose up, her tumescence gradually vanished with the heat.

She was tired of waiting. Her bones creaked harshly and she flopped down. She turned on her left and got up. The moon had to be mended.

Bullock-Race Ramanathan

P.S. Sundaram

(Quest 92: November–December 1974)

When I learnt from my sister in the village that Bullock-race Ramanathan was no more I felt inexpressibly sad; and when she told me the cause of his death I was bewildered.

'He died of small-pox,' she said.

'But how could that be?,' I asked her. 'He had had a severe attack of small-pox when he was young and bore the marks all his life.'

'I don't know. That is what they all said,' said my sister in a tone of finality. It was no use pursuing the argument, asking her who the 'they' might be. I knew when my sister was in a mood to carry on a conversation, and when she was not.

Bullock-race Ramanathan was my mother's paternal aunt's son. He acquired the epithet fairly early in his life on account of his favourite pastime of taking part in every race where bullocks were involved. His exploits by all accounts were so heroic that he had as good a title to the clinging epithet as fleet-footed Achilles or laughter-loving Aphrodite.

It was not that he raced the bullocks, though I have no doubt that if he had made up his mind to do so he would have beaten them at least half the time. In the spacious cattle shed at the back of his house there were not merely cows and buffaloes for the daily milk and curds, but also at least one pair of fierce-looking bullocks which he sometimes yoked either singly or together, to his vehicles. When he got into these vehicles and cracked his whip, the entire village stood back with feelings compounded in equal measure of fear and admiration.

The only time I actually saw Ramanathan in action was on one of my rare visits to the village. The five miles by *tonga* from the railway station to the township had been negotiated, but the mile and a quarter from the township to my village had still to be covered. No bullock cart being available that particular day, I was forced to walk the distance with my uncle who accompanied me. Halfway through, my uncle shrieked to me to get out of the way: Ramanathan was flashing towards us in his *ekka* drawn by two bullocks. In a matter of seconds he had gone.

Ramanathan was a good twenty years older than myself, and my father must have been twenty years older than he. But it was part of his charm that he was never aware of any generation gap. Whenever I went to my village he would entertain me with endless anecdotes and the very best coffee in a place famous for its coffee. Not having had much schooling himself, his regard for me could sometimes be embarrassing; that did not mean that he did not value at their true worth his own numerous accomplishments.

He was a brilliant chess player and this must have been the bond between him and my father. This and the coffee. Whenever my father went to the village he went straight to Ramanathan's, had his steaming cup of coffee, and they sat down to a game of chess.

Village chess is something that must be seen to be believed. If there were sixteen men on the board on each side when the game began, there was almost the same number of young men and old on either side behind the pieces. Every move was made after consultation and debate, and the noise was deafening when a piece was captured or a check announced. In such an atmosphere Bobby Fischer would not have survived for more than a few seconds.

But when Ramanathan played with my father, if anybody wanted to look on he was welcome but no one was allowed to make the slightest noise and there was no consultation. I wondered whether this could be because of the respect Ramanathan had for age. But during the daily bouts with my father's cousin in the same village there was no such consideration though my father's cousin was older than my father.

It should not at this stage be necessary to describe Ramanathan as a colourful personality. He was that without a doubt. I am not sure at this distance of time whether it was he or his son who always affected a red *dhoti* instead of the usual white. In my younger days these *dhotis* were worn by youngsters because being coloured they did not show dirt. Ramanathan hardly ever wore a shirt: but when he drove his *ekka* like Jehu he sported a coloured turban.

My mother must have been fond of Ramanathan but was not particularly anxious that we should cultivate him. His exploits with bulls and bullocks frightened her; and that he was a drop-out from his school was something she could not get over. When his son Balu did equally badly at school and failing in his Fifth Form ran away to join a dramatic troupe, my mother did not fail to point out how much more example counted than precept.

Father and son did not get on too well: and joining a dramatic troupe was something that Ramanathan could never forgive. Four or five years later, when the prodigal returned, there was no fatted calf for him. Ramanathan himself had fallen on evil days. His cattle had all been sold except one lean cow, and his only hobby now was chess.

I spent an evening with Balu on the sands of the river. He did not have much to say, continuously drawing triangles in the wet sand and bisecting them. Freudians might have an explanation for this.

Ramanathan had a daughter, a pretty girl, whose husband died when she was hardly eighteen. It was a hard life for her in the village, everyone crowding round and insisting that she should shave her head and put away all vanity. Poor girl! What possible vanity had the village to offer? I was horrified to hear that once her father had lost his temper so much as to thrash her with a log of firewood. Soon after that she disappeared, and there were whispers that she had gone to the bad. I don't blame her.

For some unknown reason Ramanathan's wife had the sobriquet 'pepper'. She might have been peppery to others, but I should like to see the man or woman who could have been peppery to Ramanathan and got away with it. I remember her referring to my mother once in terms of the utmost reverence. 'Ah, those were the days,' she said, 'when all eight Lakshmis ran after her!' My mother was a pious woman and, if she had heard her, would have been shocked at the sacrilege of the suggestion that the Goddess of Bounty in her manifold aspects would pay court to any mere mortal.

On the last two occasions when I visited the village, Ramanathan's wife was dead and his fortunes had shrunk to nothing. But he was never one to whine. By now I had graduated to the level of asking him whether he would care to have a game with me. He brought out his old set, a bishop and a rook missing, their places taken respectively by a pebble and a piece of chalk. We played quietly, most of the old gang having either died or migrated to sons and daughters in distant towns. Ramanathan played with his usual *éclat*.

'There is not much life in the village now,' he said. 'Not as in the old days when your father used to come and have a tumbler of coffee with me. Even the coffee we get nowadays is poor stuff. They say the best seeds are exported. You should know?'

'Very true, Ramanathan,' I said.

'Some day I may have to come to you,' said Ramanathan. 'But not yet. After all, if I go to you saying '*dehi*,' you are not the one who will turn me away with a '*nasti*'.

Ramanathan liked to air his Sanskrit now and then. His father was a learned man in his time, a Shastri who could not only expound the *Mahabharata* to the village women and children but also knew portions of the Rigveda by heart and could chant them in the correct pitch.

Besides, Ramanathan must have felt that even begging and denial put on nobility when translated into the language of the gods.

'You are always welcome, Ramanathan,' I said. 'You don't have to say "*dehi*".'

And on the next occasion when I visited the village he was no more. Small-pox? I have a feeling that it was a case of death by starvation.

SECTION VI

Endnotes

Looking Back

The role of journals, both serious and of lighter intellectual baggage, in the making of public opinion is well known and often commented upon. Along with newspapers and weeklies they have remained indispensible in the creation, guidance and direction of public opinion.

This has been attested in the modern histories of England, France and other countries. The eighteenth century was the age of weeklies and many of them have been associated with some of the most illustrious figures of English literature, Addison, Steele, Defoe, Dr. Johnson. However, by the nineteenth century they were to occupy a stellar place. It is well known that the *Edinburgh Review* not only initiated a new era in literary criticism, but also in the creation, dissemination and the propagation of ideas generally championing the Whig cause. In opposition to this was the *Quarterly Review,* which was conservative and therefore, could be savage and biting. "Who killed John Keats? 'I' said the *Quarterly."* Jeremy Bentham saw the need for a journal to popularise his philosophy of liberalism and he started the *Westminster Review* with which James Mill and John Stuart Mill were closely linked. Later dawned the *Fortnightly Review* and *Macmillan's Magazine;* John Morley had close connections with both these and edited the first. Some of our then-young congress were familiar with the *Fortnightly Review* and *Nineteenth Century* and they went to political school through its pages. Students of literature are familiar with the American *DIAL,* the literary organ of the Transcendentalists mainly because the names of Emerson and Thoreau are linked to it. *The North American Review* too was not unfamiliar to the earlier contemporaries of Ranade – and Lord Acton occasionally wrote in its pages.

In our country the *Quarterly Journal of the Poona Sarvajanik Sabha* and the *Madras Review* in the South, each in its distinctive way, carried discussions of social and political issues. The *Madras Review* was more academic while the *Quarterly Journal* touched upon more immediate social issues. Another important journal was the *Madras Christian College Magazine* which had no equals in its day and which moulded learned opinion in the Madras Presidency. Some of the contributions to this magazine, later collected in books, were to become important intellectually and partially gave rise to the Dravidian Renaissance.

While these magazines were addressed to an elite audience, three journals were to be deeply pervasive in their lifetime through the first half of the twentieth century – *The Indian Review,* the *Modern Review* and the *Hindustan Review.* Each had the distinct stamp of its editors. G.A. Natesan, the liberal who edited the *Indian Review* was Catholic to give publicity to Mahatma Gandhi and his work. The *Modern Review* was as much political as it was cultural and sociological and its editor Ramananda Chatterjee opened up new aesthetic, literary and political vistas for an all-India public – who, through it, received exposure to fine arts, history and literature. It popularised Tagore by publishing his works, had reproductions of Indian paintings, was fiercely nationalist and conducted political debates and contemporary happenings in its "notes". The *Hindustan Review* had a narrower ambit and was more political though not exclusively so. It too had pages for many other things besides. Between them they covered a very wide canvas indeed.

However, nationalism and the struggle for freedom dominated the pages of these journals and other issues were subordinated. With the dawn of freedom and the setting of an Indian political system they lost their primary thrust. With the spread of higher education and the awakening of new sensibilities, a different mood dawned over our land.

India with its linguistic diversity naturally found its intellectual moorings with language journals and almost every language had its own characteristic journal. Some of the most eminent figures started, nurtured and contributed to these. A few of the names are *Prabhakar* (Marathi), *Samvad Koumadi* (Bengali), *Swadesamitran*

(Tamil), *Vivekavardhani* (Telugu), *Prabhudha Karnataka* (Kannada), *Desabhimani* (Malayalam), among many more. What was mentioned of the British periodicals is equally true of these and there was no figure of eminence who did not write therein. Mention has to be made of *Kesari* in Marathi which was a lonely star in the national firmament.

Compared to these *Quest* had a modest presence and remained a dim star but had its own place among the discriminating intellectuals. Like Stendhal's works, it was addressed to the happy few and commanded fierce loyalties; its contributors remained the very select of the Indian intellectual world.

New challenges began to emerge and the old verities that freedom would usher in the millennium were now questioned. Many among the educated were attracted by the siren voices of communist utopia. Ideology, particularly of the leftist variety, was to be seen as having great potential. Even earlier to Independence, socialism had its own votaries and some members of the Indian National Congress were equally committed to ushering in the new utopia. The realities of Soviet communism were not widely known and the 1930s was not a decade of widespread understanding of "a new civilisation." With the winning of Independence and the drafting of a Constitution, the attractions of a planned society and of Soviet-type planning became fashionable and popular. *Freedom First* was started mainly to expose the perils of these popular nostrums and the Democratic Research Service did an excellent job of exposing them when there was no institution in India to warn Cassandra-like of the dangers that lurked beneath the benign phrases.

However, the thrust of *Freedom First* was political and one needed a magazine of ideas to boldly experiment new ideas, to explore alternatives and to examine the social and intellectual varieties of developing an open society. It is this task that *Quest* engaged itself in. There was no journal similar to it, and its exploratory curiosity of different points of view within the ambit of an open society indeed remained without parallel. It was to be an exercise in the adventure of ideas. Literature, cultural and philosophical explorations, social science enquiries, serious discussion of books, elucidation and critical appraisal of literature in Indian languages were all grist to its mill. It tried to encompass all these as well as explore ideas and ideologies both seriously and systematically. It tried to do many of the things that the journals referred to in an earlier paragraph had done in a different cultural milieu. However, what was needed in a country of the vast geographical dimensions, cultural varieties and temporal differences that our country encompassed was a variety of journals which would discuss, disagree and express difference as well as consensus. Unfortunately, there were not many journals similar or dissimilar that *Quest* could debate and discuss alongside with. To that extent, our country was poorer. However in the regional languages – particularly in Marathi and Bengali – the situation has remained very different; in fact, vibrant and creative.

An anthology of writings that appeared during the first ten years of *Quest* was edited by A.B. Shah – *Ten Years of Quest*. It proved to be, indeed, quite unique. The present collection will hopefully bring to a new generation of readers some knowledge of the superlatively good things contained in its pages, and will doubtless introduce them to an intellectual climate that has passed us by.

(R. Srinivasan is a former professor of political science, University of Mumbai)

From Quest to New Quest

Dilip Chitre

The year 1972 was a turning point in independent India's history. It was the year in which Indira Gandhi found her formula for success and popularity. India had just humiliated Pakistan in a large-scale war and helped the people of East Pakistan to carve out their own nation-state – Bangladesh. In her own strident style, India's first female prime minister brought under her own control all intelligence agencies: the RAW, the CBI, the IB, even revenue intelligence. This was a step towards autocratic rule though hardly anybody saw in it the seed of the forthcoming national emergency in 1975 – after the Allahabad High Court nullified her own election and her opposition demanded her resignation in vociferous chorus.

It was during the Emergency that Minoo Masani insisted that the publication of *Quest* be suspended in protest of the censorship laws imposed by Mrs. Gandhi. A.B. Shah's response was exactly the opposite. He wanted to defy censorship by publishing the magazine without submitting its contents to government censors. When there was a deadlock on the use of the name *Quest*, Shah opted to launch *New Quest*.

It was both a personality clash between Masani and Shah and a difference in their political response to dictatorial rule. To get to the beginning of the end of *Quest* requires a flashback to ten years before the Emergency. Shah's style was closer to that of Jayaprakash Narayan's. It was Gandhian in a way. *New Quest* was to be a voice of protest, freedom, and democracy as well as of faith, in the use of the intellect as a weapon to preserve its own liberty.

Minoo and J.P. were close friends and comrades since they were both in the socialist wing of the pre-Independence Indian National Congress. But they had drifted away from each other in their political views since Minoo was for a liberal, capitalist political-economy and J.P. was still a socialist and more Gandhian than ever before. J.P. courted imprisonment by confronting Mrs. Gandhi. Masani distanced himself from what became the biggest political upheaval since India became an independent nation state.

Quest was a periodical launched during the Cold War; unknown to its management or the Indian Committee for Cultural Freedom, some of its financial support came through conduits set up by the CIA. *Quest* was modelled on *Encounter* – a magazine that was also financed by the same secret sources. The Indian Committee for Cultural Freedom was rocked when its alleged CIA connection was exposed.

Stephen Spender, the editor of *Encounter* and a leading British poet, resigned to distance himself from the scandal. Communists the world over took the opportunity to sling mud at liberal intellectuals associated with the Congress for Cultural Freedom. The Cold War had peaked during the Cuban missile crisis. John Kennedy was assassinated. Chinese troops had crossed the McMohan line into Indian territory. Jawaharlal Nehru had died.

During this turbulent period of transition, I became a member of the executive committee of the Indian Committee of Cultural Freedom at the instance of Professor A.B. Shah, who was the new director of programmes in India of the Congress for Cultural Freedom, now openly financed by a time-bound grant from the Ford Foundation – capitalist yes, but State Department controlled, positively no. I joined Shah as his assistant, looking after cultural programmes and publications.

Two stalwarts of the freedom struggle era, Minoo Masani and Jayaprakash Narayan, lent their prestige to the Indian Committee for Cultural Freedom. The image of *Quest* remained untarnished in the community of liberal Indian intellectuals. Ably edited by A.S. Ayub and Amlan Datta, *Quest* was the only magazine of its kind in India with wide and varied contents.

Laeeq Futtehally was its literary and reviews editor and V.V. John and G.D. Parikh were the new editorial duo when I started writing regularly for *Quest*. Antoinette Diniz (who later married the physician, poet, and painter Gieve Patel) also worked in the same office, as did Sheila Singh whom Minoo Masani married after a long courtship.

Our office was in the colonial-style Army and Navy Building at Kala Ghoda, right across the street from the Jehangir Art Gallery. V. K. Sinha had been right there long before me and his friend, S.V. Raju, who worked in Minoo Masani's personnel and productivity consultancy next door on the same floor, also functioned as secretary of the Swatantra Party of India founded by C. Rajagopalachari and Minoo Masani.

Sinha and I were given a lift every evening by Raju in his car. We discussed politics all the way. Masani was not only Raju's employer but also his mentor and along with Rajaji, a father figure to him. Raju had exceptional organisational skills, a ground-level understanding of how politics works, and an ability to relate to people of all kinds. He was a key figure in the Swatantra Party, though he remained behind the scenes. Sinha and he had been fellow students. Sinha was a political scientist by training and taught political science in reputed colleges in Mumbai. He and I were hand-picked by Shah when he resigned as a college principal to join the Indian Committee for Cultural Freedom as its full-time secretary.

A clash between Masani and Shah was inevitable. Both were liberal in ideology but autocratic in behaviour.

Masani's illustrious career awed us. After being educated at the London School of Economics and being called at Lincoln's Bar, he briefly practised law in Mumbai before joining the freedom movement as a member of the Congress Socialist Party along with Jayaprakash Narayan, Achyut Patwardhan, Yusuf Meherally, and Ram Manohar Lohia. During the movement for Independence he was imprisoned in 1932 and 1933. He was only thirty-eight when he was elected mayor of Bombay in 1933.

When Gandhiji launched the Quit India movement in 1942, Masani resigned his jobs in the Tata organisation to become a satyagrahi and spent two years in the Nashik jail. Once out of jail, Masani entered legislative politics and was a member of the Indian Legislative Assembly that later became the Constituent Assembly. There, he was a member of the Fundamental Rights Sub-committee and the Union-Powers Sub-committee. The Government of India nominated Masani as its representative on the United Nations

Sub-Commission on Minorities. Later, he was India's ambassador in Brazil.

In his student days in London in the 1920s, Masani became an ardent admirer of the Soviet Union, which he visited twice. However, Stalin's excesses made him recoil and revise his views. Eventually this disillusionment drove him towards a more open, liberal ideology and its free-market corollary. He was co-founder of the Indian Committee for Cultural Freedom along with Jayaprakash Narayan, Asoka Mehta, and A. D. Gorwala; they were affiliated to the Congress for Cultural Freedom in Paris. *Quest* was a periodical brought out by the committee during the peak of the Cold War.

Minoo Masani was about twenty years older than A.B. Shah and came from an entirely different background. He was from a Gujarati Jain family near Surat, but came to Pune for his higher education and settled there, becoming a part of Maharashtrian society. Shah studied and later taught higher mathematics in colleges in Pune and Bombay. He had a deep interest in the history and the philosophy of science and believed that a renaissance could be brought about in Indian society only through the spread of scientific culture and rationalism. He was a staunch secularist and critic of obscurantism in all forms.

Shah was a follower of M.N. Roy and the Royists were neither with the Congress Party nor with the Communists. Roy himself was a prominent member of Communist International and had once rubbed shoulders with the likes of Lenin, Trotsky, and Stalin, before differences with Stalin made him turn away from Soviet communism. On his return to India he founded his own Radical Democratic Party, which had a minuscule following; later, he disbanded the party, advising his colleagues to get into the core of Indian culture to promote his idea of a cultural renaissance. Roy's followers Lakshmanshastri Joshi, V. B. Karnik, and G. D. Parikh were members of the Indian Committee for Cultural Freedom.

Both Masani and Shah opposed Indira Gandhi's Emergency rule and the suspension of fundamental rights during that time. Masani was already seventy years old in 1975 and he was withdrawing from active politics. His old comrade Jayaprakash Narayan – though suffering from an irreversible kidney ailment – found the strength to not only oppose Indira Gandhi but to also lead a mass movement to demand the dissolution of her government. Shah was close to J.P., and when Masani refused to continue publishing *Quest*, Shah showed his dissent by launching *New Quest*.

In September 1975, I joined the International Writing Program of the University of Iowa and stayed on in the United States till the Emergency was lifted. Mrs. Gandhi was decisively humiliated by a nation-wide mandate. *New Quest* was launched when I was away from India but I remained its columnist and contributor during that period, and on my return, Shah made V. K. Sinha and me its joint editors.

(Dilip Chitre is a writer, critic and editor of New Quest*)*

Registered with the Registrar of Newspapers for India Under: No. R. N. 1909/57

FOR TODAY'S FASHION SWINGERS...
SHOES THAT ARE STRICTLY NOW!

Bata GOGO

These are the shoes that are strictly NOW! Young ... dashing ... hip. Styles that move in a new kind of groove, for dressing up or going casual. They're your kind of shoes if you're a today's fashion swinger. See the full Go-Go range. Today.

Style 23
Rs 29.95

Style 90
Rs 29.95

Right : Style 66 Rs 26.95

SECTION VII

Postscript

I was "D"

Dilip Chitre

During my college days, I grew a beard. Being short, skinny and completely undistinguished, I thought my beard would make me stand out among the clean-shaven and well-groomed. An extraordinarily clairvoyant person I once came across said to me, "Shave that beard off and let there be light on your face. The day you shave it off, you'll receive a letter of appointment from a foreign country." For four years, I kept that beard on my face. The day I shaved it off, the strange prophesy came true. I received a registered letter from the (then) Imperial Ethiopian Ministry of Education informing me that they had selected me as a high school teacher of English.

Pseudonyms are like beards. They conceal one's real face. In popular Hindi movies of the 1950s and the 1960s, the hero wore a fake beard to get into the heroine's proximity. I distinctly remember Dev Anand and Shammi Kapoor doing that.

I was a serious creative writer and literary critic. I used my real name for all my serious writing, including journalistic writing. However, I am not quite as serious as I am reputed to be. There is a comedian inside me who is restless to burst into the open. I love to mark the absurdity underlying most seriously regarded things; I love to expose the pretense and vanity of celebrities. I also love to take the comic as seriously as it deserves to be taken.

Quest was so far above popular culture and so disdainful in its indifference to the strange and bizarre events of everyday India that it needed at least one regular column that did some lampooning. I worked as A.B. Shah's assistant and helped him copy edit or rewrite the kind of atrocious prose only the most learned can write – and many of our contributors were, to say the least, most learned.

Of course, among the editors of *Quest* there were some excellent writers of English prose too: Nissim Ezekiel, Amlan Datta, A.S. Ayub, A. B. Shah, G. D. Parekh, V. V. John and M. P. Rege are some examples. The wittiest among them was V. V. John. He had an impish sense of humour and could make devastating understatements. But an editorial chair is like a chair in the judiciary. *Quest* published some fine creative writing, but generally, it ignored laughing matter.

When Shah suggested to me that I write a regular column, he added – in his own *bania* style – that I would be paid extra for it. That was a double inducement and incentive. I asked him if I would have the freedom to write on any topic I chose. He reminded me that we were all equally committed to cultural freedom. Since I already wrote book reviews and occasional articles for *Quest*, I asked him if I could use an acronym of my first name as a pseudonym. He said it was up to me. I asked him if he would keep it a secret, and he nodded with tiredness.

The secret was very well guarded. Initially, only Shah, V.K. Sinha and S.V. Raju knew who "D" was. Later, Antoinette Diniz, who worked in the same office and became a friend, came to know. As time went by, my column created its own cult following among the readers of *Quest*. Shah and V.V. John were among my avid fans. V.K. Sinha and S.V. Raju were my regular companions and I would often bounce topics and themes off them, during the ride Raju gave us in his car every evening. I used the column to write on popular and art-house cinema, painting and artists, populist movements and politics, upcoming gurus and godmen, theatre, music, and the variously hued moral police who sought censorship of art.

Now the column is dead and my pseudonym will hardly ring a bell. Few readers of the current age will care to dig through the archived coffins in the expired journal's graveyard to find "D". But I know it's me – of another time and season – grinning back at my present self, an older, wiser and infinitely more boring self.

Acknowledgements

The editors are grateful to:

S.V. Raju and Sheela Masani from the Indian Committee for Cultural Freedom, Mumbai, for making this project possible by readily allowing copyright permission, for being early and enthusiastic supporters of this book, and for providing perspective and help throughout the process,

Ford Foundation, Delhi, for supporting travel and research in the making of this book,

A.R. Nizamuddin and Zafar Futehally for loaning us their collection of *Quest* magazines and books,

Subbarao and Chitti Prabhala for keeping their archive of *Quest* magazine intact,

Dilip Chitre (1938-2009) for being there, always, and

Ramachandra Guha, for wanting this to happen.